JEWS AND JUDAISM IN A MIDWESTERN COMMUNITY:

COLUMBUS, OHIO, 1840-1975

Marc Lee Raphael

Ohio Historical Society
Columbus, Ohio
1979

ISBN 0-87758-013-8

LC 79-87559

Printed in the United States of America.

For Linda

CONTENTS

Columbus Jewish History Project Advisory Board

Chairman: Robert Glick

REPRESENTING THE COLUMBUS JEWISH FEDERATION:

Ben Mandelkorn, Executive Vice President
Phyllis Greene
Norman L. Meizlish
Edward Schlezinger

REPRESENTING THE OHIO HISTORICAL SOCIETY:

Dennis East, Ph.D., Chief, Archives-Manuscripts Division
Edward R. Lentz, Chief, Audio-Visual Department, Archives-Manuscripts Division
Linda E. Kalette, Archivist, Archivist-Manuscripts Division

REPRESENTING THE OHIO STATE UNIVERSITY:

Warren Van Tine, Ph.D., Associate Professor, Department of History
Robert Chazan, Ph.D., Professor, Department of History
Simon Dinitz, Ph.D., Professor, Department of Sociology

Throughout the Columbus Jewish History Project which began in 1973, Advisory Board members have generously given their enthusiasm, time, and expertise to the endeavor. Although diversity sometimes creates weakness, in this case the board's tri-partite sponsorship has been a strengthening factor. This is reflected in Marc Lee Raphael's history of the Jewish community as well as in the variety of Columbus Jewish history materials now held by the society. I sincerely appreciate the board's unstinting determination to reach what at times appeared to be a very distant goal.

Patricia B. Gatherum
Development/Membership Officer
Ohio Historical Society
CJHP Director
April 1979

PREFACE

Early in 1974 the Advisory Board of the Columbus Jewish History Project invited me to write a history of the Columbus Jewish community. The board proposed that I should devote 1974 and 1975 to research, 1976 to writing, and submit the completed manuscript to them early in 1977. I submitted a six-hundred-page manuscript to the board and made some changes in the manuscript during the summer of 1977 in response to many helpful comments offered by the board members after they completed reading the typescript. The result is now before you.

The Advisory Board provided me with generous assistance during the project. The Ohio Historical Society collected personal papers as well as organizational and institutional records of all kinds, and carefully inventoried, processed, catalogued, and indexed them for my use. The Columbus Jewish Federation helped me establish contacts in the community, arranged for me to attend meetings, and sensitized Columbus Jewry to the project. Two of the board members from The Ohio State University, Robert Chazan and Warren Van Tine, read the manuscript part by part during 1976 and provided exceptionally useful criticism. Robert Glick, chairman of the Advisory Board, coordinated much of this support, and endeavored in every way possible, to guarantee my "absolute scholarly independence."

The list of my obligations is long and would be longer if it could include everyone who contributed to the making of this book during the three-and-one-half years of this project: David Larson first suggested a liaison between an academic community, a religio-ethnic community, and a historical society; Linda Elise Kalette helped with research and oral interviews; several talented OSU and OHS typists provided outstanding typing and interview transcription; Thomas Smith, OHS Director, and Patricia B. Gatherum, OHS Development/Membership Officer, who provided continuous encouragement and assistance; and dozens of persons at the OHS and in the Jewish community volunteered their time during phases of research. Of special note were my first editor, Nelson Lichtenstein, who offered many suggestions; my second editor, Clare Wulker, who not only provided me with patient and helpful criticism but worked tirelessly to bring the book to birth; Clara Goldslager, who gave me unfailing cooperation and the very best librarian assistance; Mildred Tarshish, a treasure house of Columbus Jewish memorabilia; and my graduate students, who listened endlessly to my ideas about Columbus Jewry.

I am also deeply appreciative of the help provided by a large number of my friends: Arthur Adams, Michael Austin, Stanley Chyet, Ilse Ebstein, Peter Glick, Uri Herscher, Steven Hertzberg, Harold Himmelfarb, Michael Meyer, Jacob Neusner, Lawrence Raphael, Moses Rischin, Linda Schulman, and Bernard Wax. They helped in making the writing of this book a gratifying experience.

Marc Lee Raphael
April 1979

INTRODUCTION

In the past few years American urban historians have criticized what they termed the "elitist" study of the past and have offered in its place history from the "bottom up." Their argument against the former approach generally involves a two-fold indictment: First, an excessive concentration on the most articulate members of the community by reliance upon institutional records, biographies, autobiographies, and newspapers; second, the failure to utilize those available, albeit less accessible, sources which touch upon the inarticulate majority of urban people. Such records — whether federal, state, county, municipal, or organizational — abound virtually everywhere.

Notwithstanding the abundance of these sources, studies of nineteenth- and twentieth-century American Jewish communities represent an overemphasis on elites and elite sources. For example, almost all utilize the local English and/or Anglo-Jewish press as the major source. This results in the impression, if not the explicit assumption, that the secular and religious experience of the anonymous community is identical with the activities of the visible elite, and that the utilization of traditional written records is sufficient to explain the texture of American Jewish life.

Such assumptions remain untested. My study of the *Columbus Jewish Chronicle*, during 1918 — its first full year of publication — revealed that the newspaper recorded the activities of 9 percent of the approximately nine thousand Columbus Jews, and that the *Chronicle* ignored more than 95 percent of the Russian Jewish immigrants. B'nai B'rith Lodge and synagogue board minutes, city and county histories, and the general as well as Anglo-Jewish press, simply have not recorded the activities of the majority of the city's Jews in the past. For an understanding of the totality of an American Jewish community, it is necessary to both exhaust the traditional and explore the previously ignored sources. Only in this way will the activities of all count and be counted.

Among the most accessible and useful records for writing urban history are federal, state, county, municipal, and organizational sources. The federal records include population schedules of the census which are available through 1900, passenger ship manifests, declarations of intention to naturalize, and naturalization records. The most useful state records include the incorporation dockets of organizations, precinct and ward voting records, divorce registers, personal property tax returns, and vital statistics documents.

County sources include tax duplicates, voter registration records, assignee and trustee dockets, records of civil cases, birth and death registers, declarations of intention to naturalize, naturalization records, wills, inheritance tax records, inventories, appraisement records, marriage records, ministers' licenses, deeds, mortgages, and juvenile arrest records.

The best municipal sources for the historian are birth and death records, student transcripts, fire reports and alarms, sanitation reports, arrest records, and city directories. Organizational records include minutes, dues, membership lists, cemetery plot purchases, school yearbooks, cancelled checks, budgets, and correspondence. In addition, two invaluable tools are available to urban historians. First, tape recorders have simplified oral history interviews and made permanent records available. Second, newly-developed surveying techniques enable historians to speak accurately about larger units of people than ever before.

Jews and Judaism in a Midwestern Community incorporates all of these sources and tools in recording the lives of the elite and the less articulate segments of society. Part I surveys the early years of the Columbus Jewish community when German Jewish immigrants rapidly ascended the socioeconomic ladder to form a largely merchant society. They created a religious institution, B'nai Israel, as well as a variety of Jewish philanthropic, fraternal, and social organizations, reflecting their sense of economic security and commitment to American values.

Part II describes the east European Jewish immigrants who created an ethnic neighborhood containing Jewish butchers and markets, Orthodox synagogues within walking distance, Jewish neighbors nearby, and a network of recreation centers, social clubs, organizations and associations that solidified a separate sense of identity within the new American environment. At the same time, the established middle-class, Americanized German Jews, continued to shape their communal life in response to their environment.

Part III portrays the attempt by Columbus Jewry — second generation children of east Europeans and more economically secure descendants of the earlier immigration wave — to clearly define itself. At the end of transit lines were new homes in less congested neighborhoods where Columbus Jews maintained primary group contacts, ethnic identification, and a sense of community inextricably woven into a fabric of activity dictated by the American environment. Synagogues reflected their sense of American as well as Jewish identity; a centralized, sectarian, philanthropic organization synthesized Jewish and American charitable traditions. Jewish organizations, social groups, and recreational activities provided a sense of ethnic identity permitting them to blend securely into the Columbus scene.

Part IV describes a thoroughly acculturated, Americanized community which has, nevertheless, preserved a strong sense of community and ethnic identity. A demographic profile of Columbus Jewry in 1975 delineates this concomitant sense of being an American and a Jew — comfortably — while the chapters on selected aspects of post-World War II Columbus Jewry highlight areas of emerging interest among American Jewish scholars. Other than briefly sketching the accomplishments of communal agencies, organizations, and religious institutions, I have left the description of the part played in Columbus Jewish life by men and women with whom I work and live to future distantly-objective historians.

About 80 percent of America's approximately six million Jews reside in ten large cities, but there are numerous medium-sized Jewish communities of ten to twenty thousand in the United States similar to Columbus. These communities are just beginning to find their historians and to uncover their fabric. Thus far, their sagas reveal the same themes that engaged the larger Jewish communities of the east coast.

As in the larger centers, German Jewish life was characterized by remarkable opportunities for economic enrichment, religious self-expression, and organizational experimentation. East European Jews in Columbus, as elsewhere, faced the problem of finding homes, jobs, and economic security; establishing close contacts with fellow Jews; sustaining their religious practices; and adjusting rapidly to their new language and environment. They accomplished all of these, with much success, through means identical to those of other American Jews.

In the decades after the First World War, the children and grandchildren of these immigrants reveal a familiar pattern of willingness and resourcefulness as well. They won a major degree of security for themselves by obtaining college educations, entering white collar professions and independent business careers, and — unlike some other cities — gained social acceptance. Adjustment to America was rarely exacerbated by anti-Semitism or discrimination, and Communism seems to have won none of its widespread Jewish following in Columbus. Most of all, like Jews everywhere in America, Columbus Jewry revealed a passion for entering American middle-class life — the "middle" of the middle-class — created and joined attractive looking synagogues, and enjoyed abundant amounts of leisure time, travel, and family activity, as well as club and organizational membership. Columbus Jews have fully completed the process of embourgeoisement in America.

Jews and Judaism in a Midwestern Community demonstrates, especially in the post-World War II section, that recent developments within the field of American Jewish history offer a wealth of material of relevance and importance to sociologists. With the blurring of interdisciplinary lines between sociology and history in the sixties and seventies, historians have adopted sociological concepts, theories, and data sources to explore selected areas of the past. I am in debt to both traditions.

PART I

THE EARLY YEARS

1840-1880

One of the founding families of Columbus Jewry was the Gundersheimer family. Nathan Gundersheimer arrived before 1840; his brothers Joseph, Isaac, and Abraham soon followed. After peddling Yankee notions, each Gundersheimer eventually became a proprietor of a small clothing store such as that pictured at the left of this early South High Street photograph.

With gravel streets, plank sidewalks, and a population of 6,048, the capital of Ohio seemed little more than a village in 1840. Although state legislators had established Columbus as the seat of Ohio government, the city itself had not been incorporated until 1834. The old Statehouse, "a common, plain brick building," inornate county offices, and a courthouse comprised the buildings of the capital's "Public Square" in 1840.[1] Tanneries, blacksmiths, and taverns typified the small businesses that lined Broad and High streets. Much of the city remained undeveloped, however, due to large tracts of swampy land. Yet Columbus was ready for a spectacular era of economic growth that would make it hospitable to a generation of immigrants from the villages and cities of Germany. An excellent weekly German newspaper, *Der Westbote*, and several *Vereine* or societies, enabled Columbus' Bavarians and other German Jews to remain in touch with the literature, drama, music, and politics of their homeland while being introduced gently to life in an American community. On the eve of the Civil War, Germans composed almost 30 percent of Columbus' population; this community grew as immigrants were attracted to a place with familiar faces and familiar names and idioms.

In addition to Columbus' cultural security, signs of potential growth were everywhere. As the capital city, Columbus became the center for internal improvements; the National Road entered Columbus on Friend Street — now Main Street — placing the city in a direct line of march for overland travelers heading west. In addition to being in the projected path of the railroad running from Cincinnati to Cleveland, Columbus was accessible by water in 1840. The 309-mile-long Ohio Canal from Cleveland to Portsmouth which passed through Lockbourne was connected to the Scioto River and downtown by an eleven-mile "Columbus Feeder." By 1861 five railroads served the city: the Columbus and Xenia together with the Little Miami linking Columbus to Cincinnati, the Columbus and Cleveland Railroad linking Cleveland with the capital, and the Central Ohio Railroad connecting Columbus to Wheeling and providing easy access to Pittsburgh.[2] In 1863 a street railway company fitted Columbus' main commercial artery, High Street, with tracks the entire length of its business district and ran a car every six minutes during the first summer. Thereafter street railroads began to link the residential districts with the merchants of High Street. This principal business artery was 100 feet wide, surpassed in width only by 120-foot-wide Broad Street.[3]

Located on the banks of the upper Scioto River, Columbus' immediate surroundings ranked among the most agriculturally productive in the state. In addition to a growing state government establishment, Columbus presented an equally advantageous economic picture. In 1850 Columbus' 17,900 residents owned more than $5 million in real estate, while personal property exceeded $1.5 million. Merchandising offered attractive opportunities as well, for only 434 grocers, clerks, and proprietors served 1,914 mechanics (carpenters, smiths, etc.), 1,706 laborers, 1,485 industrial workers, and their families. Although the population growth leveled off at a 3.8 percent increase in the decade immediately before the Civil War, that conflict provided a major catalyst for expansion. Thousands of troops were quartered in the city and many small manufacturing enterprises were established. As one chronicler noted, "Improvement [during the war] was in most respects rapid, and large acquisitions in wealth and population were made."[4] By 1870 the population was 31,300 and by 1880 more than 51,600; of these 17 percent were foreign born, chiefly German, and 6 percent were Negroes.

All available evidence suggests that Columbus Jews initiated a positive process of socioeconomic advancement prior to 1880. In terms of property acquisition, occupational security, and religious activity, they began to take advantage of opportunities in Columbus and to create a rich ethnic subcultural complex.

After reviewing the causes of German Jewish emigration, we will take a kaleidoscopic look at Columbus Jewry in 1880, and then proceed to examine more closely its economic, religious, and social life during the three decades prior to 1880.

1. FAMILIAR FACES AND FAMILIAR NAMES: GERMAN JEWISH EMIGRATION

Much more complex than the attractions of Ohio's capital city loom the conditions which propelled Jews out of the Germanies in the middle of the nineteenth century.[1] Some historians agreed with Solomon Grayzel who explained that "in 1848 and thereafter political persecution and reactions induced many [central European Jewish emigrants] of high culture, and frequently of means, to migrate to this land of freedom." Still others noted that the "discovery of gold in California tempted the more venturesome European Jews," while several scholars agreed with the view that

> America also lured the European Jew with its promise of political and social equality, the lack of which most others did not sense quite as keenly. The opportunities he looked for, moreover, expressly included the intellectual, since intellectualism had been an important value in Jewish life.[2]

But neither the abortive 1848 revolutions, the economic lures of America, the egalitarian society of the new land, nor all of these together, sufficiently explain the German Jewish migration of the nineteenth century. For example, while it is true that German emigration became quite heavy in the early 1850s, a significant causal relationship to the 1848 revolutions is most unlikely. A few thousand intellectuals, radicals, and politicians came to the United States as a result of the 1848 failures, but many more came who were only indirectly concerned with politics and its ramifications. The same insecurity which sent Bavarians here in the late 1830s and 1840s continued to propel them out of Europe in the early 1850s, and Jews were no exception. Jews accounted for perhaps 1 percent of the politically discontented German emigrants after 1848; most left Germany for the same reasons their friends and relatives had given earlier.

More than 1.2 million Germans came to America from 1820 to 1855; 2 or 3 percent of these were Jews. To understand this immigration, the social and economic background in central Europe, the image of America, and varying local conditions should be considered. These areas do not exhaust the "causes" of emigration — for nationalism, emancipation, liberalism, romanticism, republicanism, and radicalism all caught the Jews in their vortex — but simply delineate the general contours of the movement.

At the end of the Napoleonic wars, Jewish emigration became a mass movement for the first time; and its sweep and its depth, although dependent upon local conditions, derive from sources general to the whole European emigration. The population of Europe grew extraordinarily in the nineteenth century. In the century after 1750, Europe almost doubled its population to 266 million; the Jewish population increased even more rapidly from 2.73 million in 1825 to 6.77 million in 1880. Western European Jews surged from 458,000 in 1825 to 1.3 million in 1900. Marcus Fechheimer was a typical west European Jew. Born in 1818 in Mitwitz, Bavaria, he "felt too cramped in the parental house where he was the eldest of fourteen children," and emigrated to New York City in 1837.

During this period of rapid population growth, the Industrial Revolution displaced millions of artisans throughout western Europe. These craftsmen were set loose when large-scale factory enterprises destroyed the traditional handicraft industries. Village shopkeepers and small town craftsmen — a high proportion of whom were Jews — were squeezed out by interacting social and economic forces, for they had little income and were losing the small financial reserves they still possessed.

Southwestern Germans in particular lived on agricultural lands fragmented into a multitude of tiny holdings where they eked out a marginal existence. Population growth increased economic pressure on peasant families that had little surplus to exchange for goods from city dwelling — often Jewish — artisans. With the "trades becoming so easily overcrowded in hamlets and villages," too little agricultural productivity, and expanding factory competition from English goods, a contemporary noted that "the emigration fever has steadily increased among the Israelites."

Shopkeepers and artisans who failed and remained in Germany emerged in the towns and villages as a propertyless class — a proletariat. They could not escape — emigration was not for the very poor who could not obtain the necessary funds; but the sight of the impoverished drove others to leave before impoverishment happened to them. As the weekly periodical *Allgemeine Zeitung des Judentums* explained, emigration was to "escape becoming lost in great numbers in the European proletariat."

In the 1830s and 1840s private correspondence was more important than any other agent in creating the second stimulus for emigration — a favorable image of America. Emigration soared to record levels, as the emigrants wrote home and later sent newspapers, photographs, and maps, many of which were reprinted in the Jewish press. The *Allgemeine Zeitung des Judentums,* for example, began regular reports about Jewish emigrants who had settled in America. Of course, a few returned home to personally tell those who remained behind about the new country. One returnee, Julius Weis' cousin, "created quite a stir" when he returned home to provide "an account" of the south. So much so that Weis emigrated from the Rhenish Palatinate in 1837 and became a successful businessman in Fayette, Natchez, and then New Orleans.

Some American Christians expressed enthusiasm over prospective Jewish immigration. W. D. Robinson issued a pamphlet in 1819 emphasizing religious tolerance, equality under the law, and the abundance of land available in America. Robinson concluded his invitation with a vision of "Jewish agriculture spreading through the American forests; Jewish towns and villages adorning the banks of the Mississippi and Missouri."

By and large, personal reports were overwhelmingly favorable. Bitter disappointment was rarely recorded, so eager were the newcomers to prove to themselves and their friends that they made the right choice. For example, Ernst Troy, who came to Columbus in 1856 from Bavaria, recalled a letter from his brother who settled in Iowa, which noted that "it was believed that all 'Americans' were rich. From those who led a toilsome life in America, however, one rarely heard anything." A Jewish tailor of Bavarian origin wrote home in 1835 that

> all craftsmen whose trade is not in competition with factory production were very well off and every one can live well and still lay aside a nice sum of money. No craftsmen who is ready to work will have anything to regret if he comes to America.[3]

As more and more friends and relatives of German Jews became established in America, communication increased rapidly. Some spoke of "God's free air," others of "the land of the brave and the free" and the "garden of the Lord," but most wrote home of their prosperity in the new land: "Prosperity is growing day by day; those who had immigrated as beggars are rich after six to ten years," and "very many of these beggarly-poor emigrants are nowadays at the head of business concerns that own enormous property, command unlimited credit and amass every single year

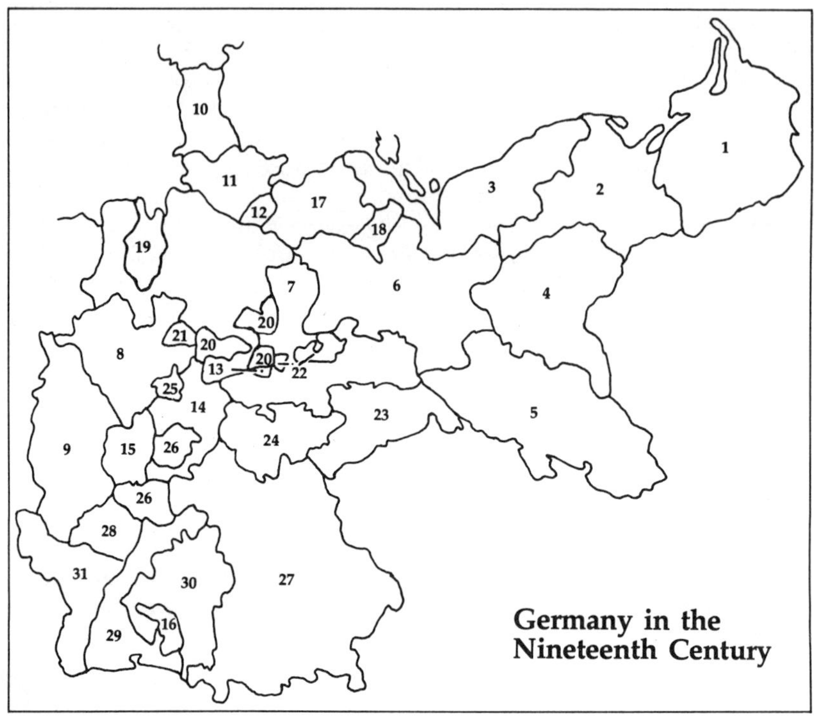

Prussian Provinces until 1865:

1 East Prussia	4 Posen	7 Saxony
2 West Prussia	5 Silesia	8 Westphalia
3 Pomerania	6 Brandenburg	9 Rhineland

10 Schleswig* (until 1865 to Denmark)
11 Holstein*
12 Lauenburg (Since 1866 Prussian Province, 1876 to Schleswig Holstein)
13 Hanover (Since 1866 Prussian Province)
14 Hesse (Electorate)**
15 Nassau**
16 Hohenzollern (Since 1849 Prussian Province)

17 Mecklenburg-Schwerin	22 Anhalt	27 Bavaria
18 Mecklenburg-Strelitz	23 Saxony (Kingdom)	28 Palatinate (to Bavaria)
19 Oldenburg	24 Thuringian States	29 Baden
20 Brunswick	25 Waldeck	30 Württemberg
21 Lippe	26 Hesse (Grand Duchy)	31 Alsace-Lorraine (1871—1918 to the German Reich)

*Since 1866 Prussian Province Schleswig Holstein
**Since 1866 Prussian Province Hessen

an independent fortune in pure profit." Charles Lucius Mailert, a Jewish teacher in Kessel, wrote to his brother August, who emigrated to the United States in the 1830s, that "there is only one land of liberty which is ruled according to natural, reasonable laws, and that is the Union."

Still other appeals were aimed at attracting young Jewesses: "German girls . . . are very popular. They find situations easily. They are also taken in marriage in preference to American girls. Anyone can marry at will." Whatever the exaggeration, scores of sources attest to the pervasive influence of these letters; "as often . . . as good letters come in from the emigrants, more people make up their minds anew to take up the wanderer's staff." Rebecca Gratz, writing to a Mrs. Hoffman shortly after the Napoleonic wars, best summed up the American Jewish bewilderment over European Jewish existence: "I wonder they do not come to America."

Legal restrictions imposed by southwestern German governments constituted the third stimulus to emigration. The political or legal complaints of the German Jews were personal and substantive; they cannot be totally ignored. Two restrictions were especially troublesome: *Familiantgesetze* (Familiants Laws) and denial of letters of protection.

Governments in nineteenth-century Germany, sensitive to the socioeconomic upheavals, tried to limit population growth through Familiants Laws or marriage restrictions designed to prevent the establishment of households without a secure economic basis. Württemberg's marriage legislation of 1828 and 1833 required proof of "ability" and "honesty" and, in 1852, of "substance." Bavaria issued similar decrees in 1813, 1818, and 1834, and many other states followed with legislation either regulating the number of Jews entitled to found families or the number of Jewish families permitted to reside in a certain locality.

The *Matrikelbesitzer (Matrikel)* helps explain the high rate of Jewish, both male and female, emigration. This register gave settlement rights to only one son — usually the eldest — as the heir of his father, while a daughter could acquire the right to settle only by marriage and a heavy tax. Thus, only holders of a *Matrikel* number gained recognition as legal inhabitants of the community; others had to wait for a number to become available in order to establish a lawful residence. "The register," the *Allgemeine Zeitung des Judentums* reported in 1839, "makes it little short of impossible for young Israelites to set up housekeeping in Bavaria; often their head is adorned with gray hair before they receive the permission to set up house and can, therefore, think of marriage."

The German states also fixed the legal status of the Jews by a maze of ordinances and regulations. Swabian Jewish "artisans in various trades . . . encountered such obstacles in obtaining the right of permanent residence," the *Israelitisch Annalen* noted in 1839, "that they have decided rather to emigrate." More often than not the states deprived them "of their natural and civil rights because they cling to the faith of their fathers." Jews in Bavaria, for example, could be farmers, tailors, weavers, butchers, or manufacturers, but in order to engage in business or in a profession, a license was necessary; and the state severely limited the number of such licenses issued in any community of Jews. The *Allgemeine Zeitung des Judentums* complained in an 1837 report from Bavaria:

> We have young men who have completed their apprenticeship and journeymen's years of travel just as precisely as any one of another faith, who can legally prove possession of no inconsiderate fortune, who meet all the requirements that may be made of them, and yet cannot obtain letters of protection and domicile on account of their faith.[4]

Württemberg followed Bavaria's example in 1828 by prohibiting Jews from exchanging or selling property unless it had been occupied or farmed by the owner for at least three years. Baden-Baden (as well as other towns in Baden) refused to grant civil rights to Jews throughout the decades of mass emigration. While all of these restrictions may not have altered significantly the general flow of emigrants, the constant correlation between areas of high emigration and oppressive disabilities suggests the importance of these political complaints. Opportunities came about so infrequently that their paucity is a constant theme in emigrant reflections.

The Jewish emigrants to America between 1820 and 1870 came from the same regions as the mainstream emigrants, the villages and small towns of Saxony, Swabia, Hesse-Darmstadt, Baden, Württemberg, and especially Bavaria. In 1816 the seven largest cities in Germany held only 7 percent of the Jewish population. Of the 12,356 Jews in Württemberg in 1846, 10,030 lived in villages and only 2,326 in towns. Of the first twenty-seven Jewish families to settle in Columbus, Ohio, between 1838 and 1860, twenty-five came from these small communities of south and southwestern Germany.

These predominantly lower middle class emigrants engaged in productive occupations as horse and cattle dealers — Bavarian Jews took a particularly active interest in the livestock trade — storekeepers, manual laborers, artisans and craftsmen of every kind, and traders in agricultural produce. Typical were: Seligman Harth, born in 1815 in Lauterbach, Bavaria, in the Rhenish

Palatinate, where his parents had a small store; Moses Henochsberg, born in the same year in the small town of Fuerth in Bavaria and educated in his youth for the "petty" merchant class; and William Frank of Burgpreppach Township, Hopheim, a journeyman shoemaker and weaver before emigrating in 1840.

The high price of land in much of Europe enabled many Germans to finance their families' passage to America by selling their farmsteads, while the Jewish artisan or journeyman could rarely save enough money to pay the emigration expense of more than one child in any given year. The fact that German non-Jews tended to migrate as families, rather than individually, is borne out by sources which note as many females as males and usually more children than adults. The proportion of single emigrants became larger in the mid-1840s and continued so through most of the 1850s, but even so this meant only that 30 percent instead of 20 percent of southwestern German emigration consisted of individuals.

Both before and after 1848, in contrast, single emigrants predominate in the Jewish sources. The mean rate of emigration from eighteen communities in Kissingen between 1830 and 1854 was 1.17 persons per family. Historian Jacob Toury explains this quite cogently, noting that once in possession of a *Matrikel* number it was easier to remain at home. The *Allgemeine Zeitung des Judentums* accurately noted this contrast in 1839: "When comparing the gentile with the Jewish emigrants one finds that the former have more family groups than single persons, the latter by far more single persons than families."

Jewish emigrants left with small amounts of money, usually just enough to cover travel expenses to America. Young Jewesses emigrated almost exclusively to marry, for the unmarried women who remained behind had only a small chance of finding a husband with a free *Matrikel* number. But whether male or female, the emancipated child usually proved an economic blessing for the Jewish families. And while the family at home became a bit more secure, the emigrant attained greater mobility in the new land. The success stories of so many Jewish emigrants of the mid-nineteenth century were helped no small amount by their single status. Few immigrants in American history have been as geographically mobile as the German Jews.

Nevertheless, the popular imagination, working backwards from the end result, dwells upon the "Great German Jewish Families." In actuality the "pulling-after" of brothers, sisters, parents, and other relatives, usually by the oldest son settled in Columbus, became a common feature of Jewish emigration from Germany. The *Archives Israélites* noted in 1853 that Central Franconia, Swabia, and Lower Franconia

> which a few years ago were inhabited by thousands of Jewish families, are reduced to a few old folks, while the younger generation has settled in the Free States of America. Generally the oldest son departs first, he is provided with recommendations to relatives or friends established in America; shortly afterwards the rest of the family comes to join him.

Jesse Seligman of Baiersdorf, who left about $30 million when he died, recalled that his seven brothers emigrated individually to the United States during the 1830s and 1840s as each succeeding one convinced the next eldest of the opportunities in America. A family chronicle perhaps, but an individualistic emigration story.

Mittelsinn

From the small Bavarian Jewish community of Mittelsinn, which sent Columbus its first two Jewish families (Gundersheimer and Nusbaum), there remains a tantalizing booklet preserved in Jerusalem at the Central Archives for the History of the Jewish People.[1] *For a period of more than fifty years, the Jüdische Gemeinde of Mittelsinn recorded and preserved all of its births between 1810 and 1875, marriages between 1821 and 1875, and deaths between 1821 and 1875. These entries offer a variety of demographic facts about the community; there were a large number of single men and women living in the community, most couples married relatively late and had large families, and the most common occupations consisted of storekeeping and trading. More significant, however, for the study of a nineteenth century Jewish community in America, was the information revealed about Gundersheimers and Nusbaums.*

The Gundersheimers and Nusbaums were two of the three families which dominate the extant vital statistics of Mittelsinn Jewry. The registrar recorded more births and deaths for each of these families than for any other, and it is clear that many more members of each family lived and died in Mittelsinn than emigrated anywhere within or outside of Bavaria. Further, we traced more than half of the German-born Gundersheimers recorded in federal manuscript census schedules in Columbus in the birth and marriage records of Mittelsinn. Thus we resolved contradictory information from consecutive census schedules and gravestones, and discovered additional biographical facts. A full exploration of the relationship between an American Jewish community and its German "cousins" remains a desideratum.

[1]*Jüdische Gemeinde in Mittelsinn,* Mittelsinn/Unterfranken (G5/2083).

TABLE 1
BIRTHPLACES OF EARLY COLUMBUS JEWISH IMMIGRANTS

*Bavaria**	
Adolph Aaron	
Johanna Adler	
Rachel Amburgh	
Samuel Amburgh	
Caroline Goodman	
Fanny Goodman	
Joseph Goodman	
Selkan Goodman	
Mary Gumble	
Max Gumble	
Abraham Gundersheimer	
Esther Gundersheimer	
Isaac Gundersheimer	
Joseph Gundersheimer	
Louisa Gundersheimer	
Nathan Gundersheimer	
Henry Harmon	
Josephine Hart	
Meyer Hecht	
Samuel Hecht	
Celia Kahn	
Clara Kleeman	
Louis Kleeman	
Fannie Mayer	
Hannah Nusbaum	
Judah Nusbaum	
Otto Nusbaum	
Barbara Pfifferling	
Israel Schlesinger	
Jacob Schoenberg	
Regina Strauss	
Louis Trautman	
Sophia Weil	
Fanny Weis	
Aaron Wise	

Baden
Isaac Hoffman
Leo Pfifferling
Barbara Straus
Leo Straus
Henry Strauss
Hesse-Darmstadt
Morris Mayer
Prussia
Amelia Lazarus
Simon Lazarus
Saxony
Jacob Goodman
Joseph Goodman
Württemberg
Julius Adler
Rebecca Goodman
Emanuel Weis

*Almost every Bavarian Jewish family was from Mittelsinn, a tiny village on the Sinn River about eight kilometers north of Burgsinn at latitude 50° 12′N and longitude 9° 37′E.

SOURCE: Population Schedules of the Seventh, Eighth, Ninth, and Tenth Censuses of the United States, 1850, 1860, 1870, and 1880, and cemetery records.

TABLE 2
JEWS IN COLUMBUS IN 1850

Name	Age	Occupation	Birthplace
Nusbaum, James	36	Grocer	Germany
Nusbaum, Joana	23		Germany
Mack, Simon	23	Merchant	Germany
Mack, Anadora	25		Germany
Mack, Isaac	4		Ohio
Mack, Henry	1		Ohio
Nusbaum, Samuel	48		Germany
Nusbaum, Regina	35		Germany
Nusbaum, Otto	11		Germany
Nusbaum, Isadora	7		Ohio
Nusbaum, Rosetta	2		Ohio
Nusbaum, Carolina	1/2		Ohio
Gundersheimer, Peter	62	Laborer	Germany
Gundersheimer, Joseph	30	Laborer	Germany
Gundersheimer, Esther	29		Germany
Gundersheimer, Jane	15		Germany
Gundersheimer, Samuel	49	Laborer	Germany
Gundersheimer, Samuel J.	10		Germany
Gundersheimer, Caroline	20		Germany
Gundersheimer, Nathan	35	Merchant	Germany
Gundersheimer, Phoebe	39		Germany

SOURCE: Population Schedules of the Seventh Census of the United States, 1850.

NOTES FOR PART I

1. Alfred E. Lee, *History of the City of Columbus.* (New York and Chicago, 1892) Volume 1, p. 254.

2. Walter R. Marvin, "Columbus and the Railroads of Central Ohio Before the Civil War." Ph.D. dissertation, The Ohio State University, 1953, pp. 118a, 167a, 229a.

3. Jacob H. Studer, *Columbus, Ohio: Its History, Resources and Progress* (n.p., 1873), pp. 559-61; Osman C. Hooper, *History of the City of Columbus* [1797-1920], (Columbus and Cleveland, n.d.), p. 230; *Tenth Census of the United States, 1880, Report on the Social Statistics of Cities, Part II, Southern and Western States* (Washington, D.C., 1887), p. 391; George W. Hawes, *Ohio State Gazetteer and Business Directory for 1859 and 1860* (Cincinnati, 1859).

4. Hooper, op. cit., pp. 53 and 229; Lee, *History,* Volume I, pp. 320-29 and Volume II, p. 221; Hawes, loc. cit. At least two Columbus Jews experienced the war directly; Moses Adler, who served in Company A, 4th

Regiment, Ohio Valley Infantry (1861-62) and William Hart, who served in Company B, 128th Regiment, Ohio Valley Infantry (1861-65); see Ohio, Division of Soldiers' Claims, Grave Registration Cards, OHS. Hart's discharge papers are in the possession of Edwin Levin of Newark, Ohio.

CHAPTER 1

1. This chapter is drawn from three types of printed materials:

BOOKS

William J. Bromwell, *History of Immigration to the United States* (New York, 1856, 1970); Joseph L. Blau and Salo Baron, *The Jew of the United States, 1790-1840: A Documentary History,* 3 volumes (New York, 1963); Ismar Elbogen, *A Century of Jewish Life* (Philadelphia, 1944); Herman Eliassof, *German-American Jews* (Chicago, 1915); Rudolph Glanz, *The German Jew in America* (Cincinnati, 1969); Marcus Lee Hansen, *The Atlantic Migration 1607-1860* (Cambridge, 1940); idem, *The Immigrant in American History* (New York, 1940); Eric Hirshler, ed., *Jews from Germany in the United States* (New York, 1955); Guido Kisch, *In Search of Freedom: A History of American Jews from Czechoslovakia* (London, 1949); Adolf Kober, *Cologne* (Philadelphia, 1940); Paul Masserman and Max Baker, *The Jews Come to America* (New York, 1932); W. D. Robinson, *Memoir Addressed to Persons of the Jewish Religion in Europe, On the Subject of Emigration to, and Settlement in, One of the Most Eligible Parts of the United States of North America* (London, 1819); Stefan Schwarz, *Die Juden in Bayern im Wandel der Zeiten* (Muenchen and Wien, 1963); George von Skal, *History of German Immigration in the United States* (New York, 1908); A. Taenzer, *Die Geschichte der Juden in Jebenhausen und Göppingen* (Berlin, 1927); idem, *Die Geschichte der Juden in Württemburg* (Frankfort am Main, 1937); Donald R. Taft, *Human Migration* (New York, 1936); Mack Walker, *Germany and the Emigration, 1816-1855* (Cambridge, 1964); Isaac Mayer Wise, *Reminiscences* (Cincinnati, 1901); Harry Simonoff, *Jewish Notables in America, 1776-1865; Links of an Endless Chain* (New York, 1956).

ARTICLES

F. Burgdorfer, "Migrations across the Frontiers of Germany," in Walter Willcox, ed., *International Migrations,* Volume II (New York, 1931), pp. 313-89; Ludwig Elster, "Bevölkerungslehre und Bevölkerungspolitik," in *Handwörterbuch der Staatswissenschaftern,* 4th ed., Volume II (Jena, 1924), pp. 735-812; Albert M. Friedenberg, "An Austro-Hungarian Movement to Encourage the Migration of Jews to America, 1848," in *Publications of the American Jewish Historical Society (PAJHS)* No. 23 (1915): 187-89; Rudolph Glanz, "Source Materials on the History of Jewish Immigration to the United States, 1800-1880," in Yidisher Visnshaftlekher Institut *(YIVO) Annual* VI (1951): 73-156; idem, "The German Jewish Mass Emigration, 1820-1880," in *American Jewish Archives (AJA)* 22:1 (April, 1970): 49-66;

idem, "The Immigration of German Jews up to 1880," in *YIVO Annual* II/III (1947/48): 81-99; Geoffrey T. Hellman, "Sorting out the Seligmans," in *The New Yorker* (October 30, 1954): 34ff; Leo Goldhammer, "Jewish Emigration from Austria-Hungary in 1848-49," in *YIVO Annual* IX (1954): 322-62; Guido Kisch, "The Revolution of 1848 and the Jewish 'On to America' Movement," in *PAJHS* 38 (1949): 185-234; Adolph Kober, "Jewish Communities in Germany from the Age of Enlightenment to Their Destruction by the Nazis," in *Jewish Social Studies* 9 (1947): 195-238; idem, "Jewish Emigration from Württemburg to the United States of America, 1848-1855," in *PAJHS* 41 (1951/52): 225-73; Max J. Kohler, "The German Jewish Migration to America," in *PAJHS* 9 (1901): 87-105; Bertram W. Korn, "Jewish Forty-Eighters in America," in *Eventful Years and Experiences* (Cincinnati, 1954), pp. 1-26; Jakob Lestchinsky, "Das jüdisch Volk im Wandel der letzten hundert Jahre" (Yiddish), in Jakob Lestchinsky, ed., *Schriften für Wirtschaft und Statistik,* Volume I (Berlin, 1928); Hanns G. Reissner, "The German American Jews (1800-1850)," in *Leo Baeck Institute Year Book (LBIYB)* (1965): 57-116; Selma Stern-Taeubler, "The Motivation of the German Jewish Emigration to America in the Post-Mendelssohnian Era," in *Essays in American Jewish History* (Cincinnati, 1958), pp. 247-61; Herb Strauss, "Immigration and Acculturation of the German Jew in the United States of America," in *LBIYB* (1971): 63-94; Jacob Toury, "Jewish Manual Labor and Emigration Records from Some Bavarian Districts (1830-1857)," in *LBIYB* (1971): 45-62.

MEMOIRS AND BIOGRAPHIES

Gotthard Deutsch, "Dr. Abraham Bettman: A Pioneer Physician of Cincinnati," in *PAJHS* 23 (1915): 105-16; Ferdinand Doubrava, "Experiences of a Bohemian Emigrant Family," in *Wisconsin Magazine of History* VIII (1924): 393-406; Frank William, "Pilgrim Father of Pittsburgh Jewry," in Jacob Marcus, ed., *Memoirs of American Jews, 1775-1865,* Volume I (Philadelphia, 1955), pp. 302-08; Abram Vossen Goodman, "A Jewish Peddler's Diary, 1842-43," in *AJA* 3:3 (June, 1951): 81-111; Isaac A. Meyer, "Bad Luck Incarnate," in Jacob Marcus, op. cit. Volume II (Philadelphia, 1955), pp. 330-50; Philip Sartorius, "Small-Town Southern Merchant," in Jacob Marcus, op. cit., pp. 21-46; Alfred and Emily Seasongood, "Jewish Family Life in the Queen City of the West," in Jacob Marcus, op. cit. Volume III (Philadelphia, 1955), pp. 50-72; Henry Seesel, "Typical German Jewish Immigrant," in Jacob Marcus, op. cit. Volume I, pp. 353-67; Jesse Seligman, "The Making of a Financier," in Marcus, Volume I, pp. 343-52; Louis Stix, "Honesty Is the Best Policy," in Marcus, Volume I, pp. 309-42; Ernst Troy, "My Biography," Private translation in possession of author, courtesy Ronald Robins of Columbus, Ohio; Julius Weis, "Peddler in the Deep South," in Marcus, Volume II. pp. 47-57.

2. Solomon Grayzel, "[Review of] *The Uprooted,*" *PAJHS* 42 (1952): 208.

3. Alfred and Emily Seasongood, "Jewish Family Life in the Queen City of the West," in Jacob Marcus, ed., *Memoirs of American Jews 1775-1865,* Volume III, p. 53.

4. *Allgemeine Zeitung des Judentums,* September 9, 1837.

Columbus' Major German Language Newspaper, *Der Westbote*

The first issue of the *Westbote* — one of more than thirty-five German newspapers in Columbus' history — appeared on Monday, October 2, 1843, and the second issue four days later. On August 3, 1903, the *Westbote* merged with its rivals, the daily *Express* and the *Express'* Sunday edition, *Der Ohio Sonntagsgast;* the combined publication survived until World War I when it went out of business, like dozens of other German language publications.

A well-edited newspaper published in remarkably literate German by Friedrich Fieser and Jacob Reinhard, the *Westbote* appeared semi-weekly and occasionally weekly for its first four decades. Fiercely Democratic until the Civil War, *Der Westbote* adopted a Republican position in 1860 which was maintained for twenty years. By 1874, when fifty-eight German daily newspapers existed in the United States, the culturally sophisticated *Westbote* reported a circulation of 1,200 for the semi-weekly and 7,000 for its weekly (Thursday) edition. This compared with a circulation of 3,600, 5,040, and 5,676 for the weekly editions of the *Ohio Statesman, Ohio State Journal,* and *Columbus Evening Dispatch.*[1]

1. Karl J. R. Arndt and May E. Olson, *German-American Newspapers and Periodicals 1732-1955* (Heidelberg, 1961); Carl Wittke, *The German Language Press in America* (Lexington, Kentucky, 1957); George Rowell and Company, *American Newspaper Directory* (New York, 1876); [S. M.] Pettengill's *Newspaper Directory and Advertiser's Handbook for 1877* (New York, 1877). On Fieser and Reinhard, and the *Westbote,* see LaVern J. Rippley, "The Columbus Germans," in *The Report: A Journal of German-American History* 33 (1968): 5-9.

TABLE 3
JEWISH WEDDINGS IN COLUMBUS BETWEEN 1848 AND 1888*

Date	Groom	Bride	Officiant
7- 7-48	Joseph Gundersheimer	Esther Greenenbaum	(none recorded)
1- 3-54	Isaac Gundersheimer	Louisa Hacker	Josef Goodman
1- 3-54	Isaac Hoffman	Caroline Gundersheimer	Josef Goodman
5-16-54	Jacob Goodman	Regina Gundersheimer	Josef Goodman
8-12-56	Louis Kahn	Amelia Hecht	Solomon Weil
4-15-58	Samuel Hoffman	Caroline Goodman	Josef Goodman
12-21-58	Moses Kleeman	Jenette Hecht	Josef Goodman
6-12-59	Samuel Adler	Cecilly Fleishhauser	Josef Goodman
1-11-60	William J. Goodman	Rebecca Straus	(none recorded)
8- 1-60	Morris Mayer	Fannie Wise	Lippman Liebman
2-28-61	Elias Lehman	Helena Meyer	Lippman Liebman
5- 7-61	Abraham Goldsmith	Mina Gumble	(none recorded)
1-26-62	Abraham Klein	Regina Hoffman	Lippman Liebman
9- 6-63	Max Leaser	Fanny Kahn	Meyer Wetterhahn
2-28-64	Hersch Straus	Regina Slessinger	Meyer Wetterhahn
9-20-64	Meyer Childs	Lenora Childs	Meyer Wetterhahn
9-29-64	L. Rosenberg	Therese Amburgh	Justice of the Peace
12-28-64	Arnold Steinhauser	Sallie Wechsler	Meyer Wetterhahn
8-25-65	Myer Hecht	Rosetta Nusbaum	Meyer Wetterhahn
9- 6-65	Otto Nusbaum	Bertha Weil	Meyer Wetterhahn
4- 3-67	Joseph S. Lazarus	C. Sigmon	Jacob Schoenberg
6- 2-68	Leopold Gumble	Caroline Goodman	Jacob Schoenberg
7-17-68	Joseph Goodman	Fannie Oberdorfer	Jacob Schoenberg
5- 5-72	Levy Mendel	Elise Levy	Judah Wechsler
8-20-72	Moses Adler	Sarah Landauer	Judah Wechsler
9-25-72	David Pimentel	Louisa Perles	Judah Wechsler
5-15-73	Isaac B. Jashenosky	Mary Frank	Samuel Weil
8-17-73	Aaron Summerfield	Rebecca Hymes	Samuel Weil
12-23-74	Louis N. Baer	Rebeccah Horkheimer	Samuel Weil
11-25-75	Louis B. Stern	Matilda Lazarus	Samuel Weil
1- 2-76	Samuel Weill	Fannie Wechsler	Samuel Weil
2- 9-76	Samuel H. Smit	Flora Frankel	Samuel Weil
2-23-76	Joseph Maier	Rosa Horkheimer	Samuel Weil
3-19-76	Herman Dombrower	Rosalie Weis	Samuel Weil
5- 1-77	Abraham Cohen	Rosalie Lazarus	Emmanuel Hess
1-20-78	Marx Hirsch	Amelia Schonfield	Benjamin Bonnheim
1-22-78	Isaac Frankel	Hannah Jashenosky	Benjamin Bonnheim
2-17-78	Henry Stern	Bertha Lazarus	Benjamin Bonnheim
5-15-78	Joseph G. Goodman	Bertha Amburgh	Benjamin Bonnheim
11-27-78	Max Ambach	Addie Gundersheimer	Benjamin Bonnheim
10-22-79	Simon Blumenthal	Minnie Harmon	Benjamin Bonnheim
11-16-79	Levi Rosenbusch	Emelia Schoenfield	Benjamin Bonnheim
7- 2-80**	Germain Joseph	Emma Weil	?
3- 2-81	David Turkenopf	Celia Gundersheimer	Benjamin Bonnheim
11-20-81	David Haase	Bertha Pfifferling	Benjamin Bonnheim
9-21-82	Samuel Leveen	Therese Kahn	Benjamin Bonnheim
10- 1-82	Jacob Mayer	Babbette Adler	Benjamin Bonnheim
10-24-83	Benjamin Harmon	Selma Liebenthal	Felix Jesselson

COLUMBUS JEWISH WEDDINGS — CONTINUED

Date	Groom	Bride	Officiant
1- 9-84	Robert Eisner	Flora Cahen	Felix Jesselson
3- 9-84	Myron Rindskop	Sarah Philipson	Felix Jesselson
9-24-84	Sidney Brown	Florence Rhoades	Felix Jesselson
10- 5-84	Isaac M. Mayer	Henrietta Frankel	Felix Jesselson
10-29-84	Max Mohr	Addie Gundersheimer	Felix Jesselson
11-23-84	Abraham Ramsfelder	Tillie Kleeman	Felix Jesselson
11-27-84	Aaron Harmon	Eliza Gumble	Felix Jesselson
12-21-84	Moritz Schwartz	Carrie Frank	Felix Jesselson
12-28-84	Samuel Strauss	Minnie Lehman	Felix Jesselson
1-11-85	David Goodman	Sarah Schwarz	Felix Jesselson
1-11-85	Morris Perles	Maggie Schwarz	Felix Jesselson
1-25-85	Solomon Childs	Bertha Kahn	Felix Jesselson
3- 8-85	Philip Office	Hannah Sabledosky	Felix Jesselson
9-24-85	Michael Harmon	Mina Leah Kuhn	Felix Jesselson
9-27-85	Sam Gundersheimer	Rosa Lehman	Felix Jesselson
7-21-86	Reuben Goldberg	Rose Lazarus	Felix Jesselson
10-15-86***	Nathan Gundersheimer	Frederica Leopold	Felix Jesselson
10- 5-87	Max Gundersheimer	Amelia Gumble	Felix Jesselson
11-17-87	Joseph Loeb	Amelia Steinfeld	Felix Jesselson
11-11-88	Charles Margulis	Dora Rosenthal	Felix Jesselson
2-26-88	Joseph Kleeman	Louise Gumble	Felix Jesselson
3-15-88	Isaac Kleeman	Fannie Cahen	Felix Jesselson

*This list does not include, with one exception, ceremonies performed by an officiant other than a Jewish clergyman.

****American Israelite**

******Ohio State Journal***

SOURCES: Columbus Marriage Licenses, Probate Court, Franklin County, Ohio.

Columbus, Ohio, Ward Lines as Established March 1, 1880, by Ordinance of City Council

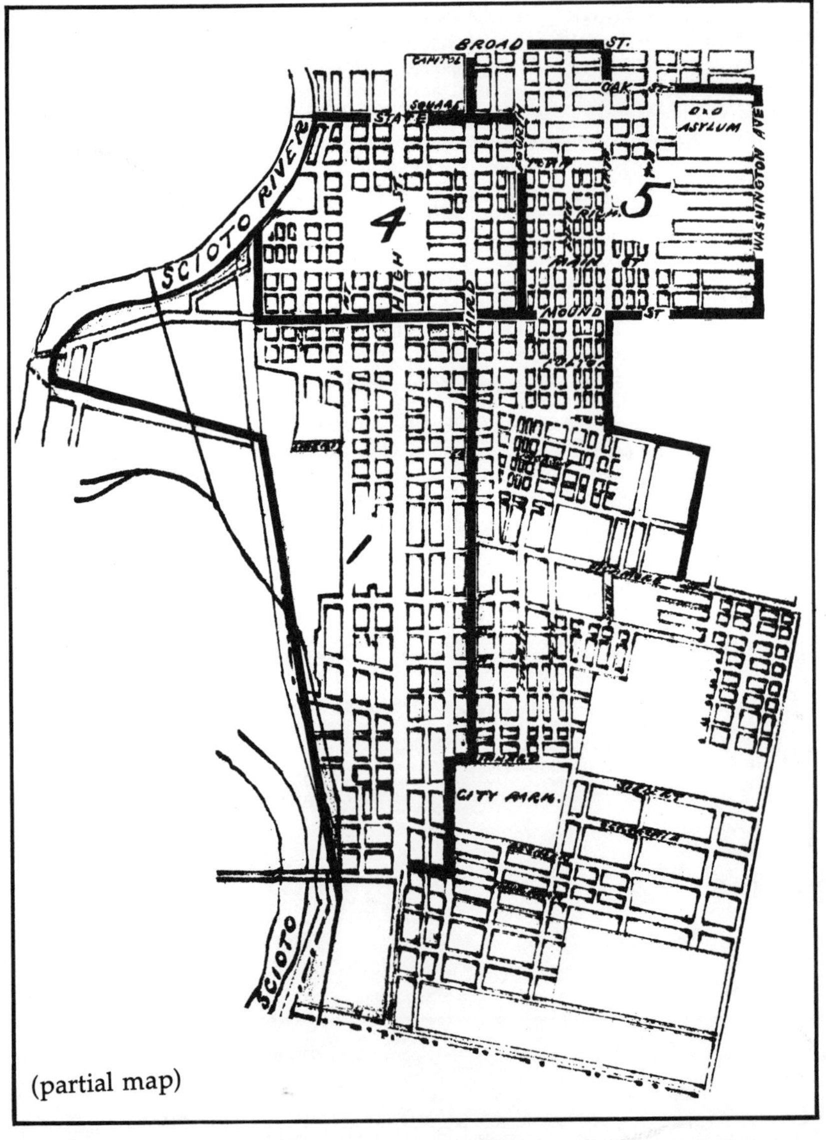

SOURCE: Ward Map, Columbus, 1880, Ohio Historical Society

2. COLUMBUS' GERMAN JEWISH NEIGHBORHOOD IN 1880

During the summer months of 1880, while federal census takers made their rounds of Columbus, central Ohioans witnessed a dramatic increase in political activity. During the Republican presidential convention in late June, the Ohio press enthusiastically championed its native son, James A. Garfield. The Democratic convention, which nominated colorless Winfield Scott Hancock, also met in June and generated considerable interest in Columbus. One month later, at the Columbus City Hall, the Ohio Greenback Labor Party, despite being labeled "communists" in the local press, nominated its delegates and espoused woman's suffrage. The Greenbacks (described in the *Ohio State Journal* as "claptrap and humbug"), together with the Republicans and Democrats, dominated the summer news in Columbus.[1]

Census takers found Columbus to be a rapidly growing medium-sized city in 1880. Tinware and copperware, tobacco, boots and shoes, together with blacksmithing, dominated the manufactures, while three daily newspapers in English and one in German kept the city informed. There is no evidence available to contradict the view of a perceptive contemporary that Columbus deserved its reputation as "one of the most conservative cities in the land."[2]

By following the census taker on his rounds, albeit from a distance of one hundred years, we reconstructed in detail the wards and predominantly Jewish neighborhoods of 1880: the largest, Ward 1, lay south of downtown and held the bulk of Columbus' Germans.[3] Ward 4 formed a square surrounding downtown, and Ward 5, situated directly east of the commercial center, was the city's most populous ward. Sixty-seven out of eighty-six Jewish households identified by the census taker were in these three wards: twenty-one in Ward 1, twenty-one in Ward 4, and twenty-five in Ward 5.[4] Incidentally, the census taker found no more than 80 percent of the Jewish households our research discovered! Our attention will focus on Ward 4, since more complete information is available for its Jewish residents than for those of the other two wards.

The Bureau of the Census divided Ward 4 into two enumeration districts; in the northern half of the ward, 672 persons of all ages worked at more than 100 different jobs. In Table 4, those occupations are arranged by broad categories, excluding only those jobs held by two or less persons (circus performer, straw bleacher, sailor, cattle dealer, missionary, auctioneer, soldier, etc.). The occupations of Columbus Jewry contrast quite strikingly with the general population's work profile: One third of the general population in Ward 4 — which was typical of other wards — labored in unskilled and semi-skilled occupations; only 28 percent were in the proprietor and clerical categories. Virtually absent from those first two groupings, a majority of Jews in Columbus fell into the latter two classifications. While the general population consisted of a large number of skilled workers, hardly any Jews worked with their hands. In short, Ward 4 contained primarily unskilled, semi-skilled, and skilled workers; the Jews of Columbus (and even more so the Jews of Ward 4) consisted almost exclusively of merchants and clerks.

TABLE 4
OCCUPATIONS OF COLUMBUS' WARD 4 RESIDENTS IN 1880*

Category	Percentage	Occupation
Unskilled	13%	44 laborers, etc.
Semi-skilled	20	46 dressmakers, etc.
Proprietor	14	21 merchants, etc.
Skilled	31	26 carpenters, etc.
Clerical	14	44 clerks, etc.
Semi-professional	2	5 dentists, etc.
Professional	6	12 attorneys, etc.

*N = 582

SOURCE: Population Schedules of the Tenth Census . . . 1880 . . . Ward 4, district 25.

This occupational profile is illustrated in a microcosm of the community: one block of Rich Street. According to the federal census and city and county records in 1880 these nine households existed on Rich Street, in the first block east of High Street:

27 Rich
Mrs. Mary Hubbard (48); children: Herman M. (22, bookkeeper at

Three of the residents at 45 Rich Street were Simon Lazarus' widow, Amelia (1822-1899), and her two sons, Fred and Ralph (seated).

Deshler Bank), Fred W. (18, student), Ralph N. (11); boarders: Mary and Jane Jenkins (servants).

35 Rich
Charles Patterson (66, retired clerk, formerly at O'Hara and Sims, boots and shoes) and Jane Patterson, (65, clerk); children: Mary (30, clerk at O'Hara and Sims), Eliza (28), Margaret Maynard (26); boarders: H. J. Maynard (30, son-in-law, Maynard Bros. grocers), Alex (38, dentist) and Kate Cotton, Mary Saunders (57), Joseph King (45, state house clerk), B. D. Sinclair (attorney, Van Fleet and Sinclair) and 2 servants.

45 Rich
Amelia Lazarus (58, Prussia); children: Fred (30, Prussia, F. & R. Lazarus & Co. and S. Lazarus Sons & Co.), Ralph (28, Ibid.), Sallie Cohen (26), Rose (14, school); boarders: Abe B. Cohen (32, son-in-law, Prussia, S. Lazarus Sons & Co.) and 1 servant.*

49 Rich
Zachary Heed (41, agent, unemployed 3 months during previous year) and Addie Heed (38); children: Burt (22, agent, unemployed 3 months), Bront (20, restauranteur), Bell (School); boarders: Elizabeth Heist (58, mother-in-law).

*Only foreign places-of-birth are listed here although all birthplaces are included in the census.

51 Rich
Samuel P. Elliot (54, S. P. Elliot & Sons, bakers and confectioners) and Margaret Elliot (54); boarders: Mrs. Mary West (89, mother-in-law), Edward Taunchass (20, teamster), Carrie Blaze (19, domestic).

55 Rich
Elizabeth Schroll (50, Hesse-Darmstadt); children: Amelia (20), Emma (18), William (17), Otto (14).

61 Rich
Emma Lathrop (31, dressmaker); child: Earl (12); boarders: Eliza McCrener (56, mother).

65 Rich
Henry Harmon (50, Bavaria, produce) and Nettie (31, Prussia); children: Aaron (27, clerk at S. Lazarus & Sons & Co.), Harry (25, trunk maker), Michael (24, clerk), Minnie Blumenthal (22), Benjamin (18, buggy shop), William (15, clerk), Mary (13, school), Max (6), Jesse (3); boarders: Samuel Blumenthal (25, son-in-law, cigar store).

67 Rich
Philip Haldy (54, Alsace, machinist) and Kate Haldy (53, Bavaria); children: Kate (18, clerk in dry goods store), Lena (16, Bavaria), Louise (14), Lizzie (11); boarder: Fred Schmidt (12, nephew).

Property acquisition records in the Franklin County Recorder's office give specific insights into the people on this block. During the 1870s only three Rich Street residents — excluding the Harmons and Lazaruses — purchased property: Herman Hubbard made acquisitions of $2,000 and $1,700; Charles Patterson had purchases of $500 and $2,400; and Elizabeth Schroll bought property on three different occasions during the decade, spending $295, $2,250, and $2,800.[5] Veteran dealers in real estate, the Harmon and Lazarus families were by no means the most substantial property owners in the Jewish community in 1880, although they even prospered during the depression of the mid-1870s.

After leaving Bavaria with his brother Moses, Henry Harmon settled in Pendleton County, Kentucky, prior to 1850. His first "live-birth" son, Aaron, was born to his wife Bertha in 1853; by the time their second child was born in 1855 the Harmons had moved to Ohio. In Columbus he and Bertha had a total of seven children by the time of her death in 1873. Henry and his second wife Nettie had several more children, making his family the largest in Columbus' Jewish community. In addition to being a successful grocer, Henry Harmon held elected offices in both Congregation B'nai Israel and Zion Lodge No. 62. Harmon purchased considerable property throughout the 1860s and 1870s, both to move and expand his grocery as well as to find larger accommodations for his family. His five purchases in the 1860s totalled $18,200, while in the 1870s his many property sales included a home for $8,000 and a store for $6,000.[6]

The Harmon family, like almost any other Columbus Jewish family of the period, had marriage ties with many other Jewish families in the city. By the 1880s, for instance, a Harmon had married a Gumble; a Gumble, a Gundersheimer; a Gundersheimer, a Goodman; a Goodman, a Straus. Without continuing any further we have enumerated the majority of the officers of the B'nai Israel in the period under discussion. Accurate indeed was this 1884 comment in Cincinnati's *American Israelite* about the capital city's Jews: "A friend from Columbus, Ohio, assures us that one-half of the young people of that city are engaged to the other half."[7]

Henry Harmon's grocery was at most a five-minute walk from his home; Fred and Ralph Lazarus lived equally close to work. Most Columbus Jews lived within a short walk of their places of business. The non-Jewish residents on Rich Street hardly resided further away: bookkeeper Herman Hubbard, clerk Charles Patterson, grocer H. J. Maynard, and baker Samuel Elliot had but short walks to work. Although street railroads existed in 1880, there is little evidence that Columbus Jews used them to get to and

Amelia Gumble and Max Gundersheimer were married in Columbus on October 5, 1887.

from work. On the other hand, the track linkage to some of the residential areas of the city proved a boon to the Jewish merchants of High Street, who were anxious to serve that part of the community which was not within walking distance of their stores.

Down the street from the Harmons, Fred and Ralph Lazarus continued to live in their mother's home after Simon died in 1877, more out of concern for her loneliness than because of need. The sons sustained Simon's reputation as "one of the substantial businessmen of Columbus"; their property acquisitions are too numerous to list. Even before his death, advertisements for Simon Lazarus' clothing stores dominated the local newspapers; as early as the 1870s he claimed $8,000 in personal property. While the economic success of the Harmon and Lazarus families could be repeated and even surpassed in other parts of Ward 4, it is representative of the majority of Columbus Jewry in 1880.[8]

At 174 Rich, a few doors east of the Harmon and Lazarus families and across the street, lived the Gumbles. Max and Mary had nine children in 1880, many of whom helped their parents in Max's saloon after school. Max had prospered in Columbus, for by 1869 he was able to purchase an $8,500 home.[9]

One of Max's sons, Henry, graduated from Columbus' only high school in 1880 and subsequently earned a Bachelor of Law degree at age twenty. After serving as secretary to five-term Congressman Joseph H. Outhwaite (1841-1907), Gumble ran unsuccessfully for Columbus City Council as the Democratic candidate of Ward 4. Later as a partner in a prominent Columbus law firm — Gumble & Gumble — Henry provided generous personal and financial support to B'nai Israel, and served as the president of the first civil service commission in Columbus.

Henry Gumble was not only the first Jewish student to complete high school in Columbus, but the sole Jewish student in a class of seventy-two persons. In his first year of high school Henry studied: algebra, English, Latin, and physiology; in his second year: geometry, history, Latin, and Greek; and in his third year he chose trigonometry, chemistry, Greek, Latin, and botany — all of these in addition to music, drawing, and rhetoric. The following final examination questions tested the knowledge of all seniors at Columbus High School in 1880:

> Livy: explain mode and tense of *retulisset, manserit, ignoraretis* and decline in full *civis, iter, fides, mihi*
>
> English literature: finish the quotation beginning "Tomorrow and tomorrow and tomorrow . . ."
>
> Political economy: may railroads be profitable to the country at large, while unprofitable to the stockholders? How?

Astronomy: what would be the width of each zone if the earth's axis run inclined 15 degrees from a perpendicular to plain of orbit?

Music: from a fork giving the pitch C, how would one find the pitch of A, F sharp, E flat, D flat, A flat, respectively?

Physics: the radius of a curved mirror is 20 inches; locate the image when an object is placed 15 inches from the mirror.[10]

SOURCE: Examination questions, High School 1880, Columbus Board of Education

The size of the Gumble family was typical of most Jewish families; more often than not, immigrant families had at least six children.[11] The usual pattern — and its consistency is quite remarkable — was for the wife (who never worked unless widowed) to bear a child every other year as demonstrated in Table 5. Indeed, there is much to suggest that only age or exhaustion put an end to childbearing; several women bore children well into their forties and a number of Columbus Jewesses died shortly after childbirth.

Extremely large Columbus Jewish families cannot be explained by the fact that these Jews were immigrants from Germany where large families appeared commonplace. First, there is evidence to suggest that German Jewish families may not have been as large in the Old World as the stereotypes portray. Further, according to a demographic study of four pre-Civil War Jewish communities in America, the average family size ranged only from 3.0 members in Boston to 4.1 members in Charleston in 1850, and from 3.7 in Charleston to 3.9 in Philadelphia in 1860. Tradition has it that even this number decreased in subsequent decades, as the immigrants "Americanized" and had fewer children. While Columbus may be unusual, perhaps its middle-class character enabled parents to give adequately to many children rather than to give generously to a few.[12]

TABLE 5
COLUMBUS JEWISH FAMILIES IN 1880[13]

Parents	Children	
	Number	Birthyears
Henry and (Bertha and) Nettie Harmon (31*)	10	1853-55-56-58-62-64-66-73-75-77
Max and Marianne Gumble (48)	9	1860-62-63-66-67-69-71-73-78
Lewis and Hanna Shonfield (34)	9	1861-63-65-69-71-73-77-78-79
Lewis and Iline Jacobs (36)	9	1866-68-70-72-74-75-76-77-80
Lewis and Mary Goldstandt (40)	8	1859-61-63-65-67-69-73-79
William and Bertha Goodman (40)	8	1860-66(2)-67-69-73-76-78
Alex and Rosa Shonfield (30)	8	1865-67(2)-69-74-76-78-80
Jacob and (Regina and) Caroline Goodman (42)	7	1855-57-60-67-69-71-73
Aaron and Bertha Margolinsky (55)	7	1849-51-54-59-61-63-68
Henry and Regina Straus (39)	7	1865-67-69-71-73-75-77
Leo and Sarah Straus (53)	7	1855-59-61-63-65-67-71
Morris and Fannie Mayer (43)	7	1860-62-64-66-68-72-76
Joseph and Eliza Philipson (40)	6	1862-66-68-69-74-76
Max and Johanne Cahen (32)	6	1862-64-66-68-74-76
Abraham and Regina Gundersheimer (52)	6	1856-58-60-62(2)-64
Joseph and Fannie Goodman (32)	6	1869-71-73-75-77-79
(Simon and) Amelia Lazarus (58)	6	1850-52-54-56-58-66
Michael and Caroline Steinfeld (38)	6	1865-67-69-70-72-74
Samuel and Cecilia Adler (43)	6	1860-62-64-68-70-73
Joseph and Esther Gundersheimer (54)	6	1851-53-55-57-60-64
Moses and Jennie Kleeman (41)	5	1860-62-64-66-68
Augustus and Lena Basch (48)	5	1857-61-63-65-67
Israel and Eva Schlesinger (48)	5	1861-63-65-67-68
Rudolph and Rosa Hirshberg (26)	5	1870-71-73-77-79
Adolph and Sarah Aaron (32)	5	1868-70-73-75-79
Moses and Amelia Friedenberg (28)	5	1868-70-73-75-77
(Joseph and) Celia Kahn (53)	5	1859-60-62(2)-65
Louis and Regina Trautman (44)	4	1861-63-67-70
Israel and Rosa Jashenosky (25)	4	1872-74-76-79
Moses and Mary Hyneman (34)	3	1865-67-71
Jacob and Emma Shonfield (25)	3	1874-75-77
Getz and Maggie Frankel (28)	3	1873-75-77
Isadore and Hannah Nusbaum (28)	3	1875-77-80
Casper and Leah Lowenstein (36)	3	1872-74-75
Joseph and Catherine Trautman (27)	2	1877-79
Otto and Bertha Nusbaum (32)	2	1868-70
Solomon and Lena Rothschild (26)	2	1877-80

*Mother's age in 1880.

SOURCES: Jewish section of Greenlawn Cemetery and the Jewish Cemetery on Mt. Calvary Avenue; The Seventh, Eighth, Ninth and Tenth United States Censuses; Franklin County Probate Court [Birth Records] 1867-99; I. M. Schlesinger, *Circumcision Record Book* 1873-1904.

NOTES FOR CHAPTER 2

TABLE 6
COLUMBUS POPULATION IN 1880

Wards	Population
1	4,510
2	4,471
3	2,619
4	3,894
5	5,645
6	2,200
7	2,897
8	3,819
9	4,753
10	3,960
11	2,052
12	5,440
13	2,671
14	2,716

SOURCE: *Annual Report of the Secretary of State . . . 1881* (Columbus, 1882), pp. 512-13.

1. *Ohio State Journal,* June 2-9, June 22-25, July 29, 1880; Leonard Dinnerstein, "Election of 1880," in *History of American Presidential Elections 1789-1968,* Volume II, Arthur M. Schlesinger, Jr., ed., (New York, 1971), p. 1491.

2. "Columbus, Franklin County, Ohio," in *Report on the Social Statistics of Cities, Part II, Southern and Western States* (Washington, D.C., 1887), pp. 389-93; *Annual Report of the Board of Education of the Columbus Public Schools for the School Year Ending August 31, 1879* (Columbus, 1879), pp. 19-20 ("Loving school is occupied exclusively by colored pupils"); Deshler Welch, "The City of Columbus, Ohio," in *Harper's Weekly* 76 (1887): 715-26; Alfred E. Lee, *History,* Volume I, pp. 565-77.

3. A random sample of Ward 1 heads of household — the first family on each of the ninety-two pages of the federal manuscript census of 1880 — revealed 65 percent (60/92) to be natives of Germany.

4. For a careful study of the accuracy of census enumeration in the nineteenth century, see Michael B. Katz, "The People of a Canadian City: 1851-52," in *Canadian Historical Review* 52 (1972): 402-26. Our own research, concerned with the relationship between the city directory and the federal manuscript census, revealed that the directories included far more Columbus Jews than did the census schedules. While the directories may have been less inclusive of those lower on the socioeconomic scale, from a methodological viewpoint we proceeded from the directory to the census, and not vice-versa, in order to move from the more to the less complete. For a contrasting view, see Peter R. Knights, "City Directories as

Aids to Ante-Bellum Urban Studies: A Research Note," in *Historical Methods Newsletter* II:4 (September, 1969): 10, and for evocative reflections on the entire subject, see Theodore Hershberg, et al., "Record Linkage," in *HMN* IX:2-3 (March-June, 1976): 137-63.

5. Franklin County Recorder, Deeds, 100:335, 112:95; 110:96, 114:271; 69:635, 82:549, 85:57.

6. *Columbus City Directories;* Franklin County Recorder, Deeds, 76:106, 78:138, 83:242, 88:93, 92:129 (Grantee), and 105:280, 129:1 (Grantor).

7. Franklin County, Ohio, Probate Court, Marriage Records [1803-1865]; *AI*, October 27, 1884, p. 7.

8. Franklin County Recorder, Deeds, 126:462; Population Schedules . . . 1870, p. 52 (Ward 7); Lazarus Family Scrapbook 1915, Box 1, Lazarus Family Papers.

9. Population Schedules . . . 1870, p. 8 (Ward 4); Franklin County Recorder, *Deeds*, 99:253; Morton Gumble to Marc Lee Raphael, April 30, 1974, telephone conversation.

10. *History – Columbus High School 1847-1910. Alumni Association of the Columbus High School* [*1847-1893*] *and Central High School* [*1893 on*], *Inc.* (Columbus, 1925), p. 17. Hattie Levy (1882) and Clara Goodman (1885) were the second and third Jewish high school graduates; ibid., pp. 90, 92. David Philipson noted that as late as 1875 "no Jewish lad in Columbus . . . had attended the high school"; *My Life as an American Jew* (Cincinnati, 1941), p. 2. William Alexander Taylor, *Centennial History of Columbus and Franklin County, Ohio,* Volume II (Chicago and Columbus, 1909), pp. 579-80; *Annual Report of the Board of Education . . . for the School Year Ending August 31, 1880* (Columbus, 1880), Part I, p. 74 and Part II, p. 45; *CP,* April 4, 1892, p. 4; University of Cincinnati Law College, Records of Graduation.

11. National Archives, *1850 Census Population Free Schedules, Kentucky,* microcopy number M-432, roll number 216, District No. 2, Pendleton County, p. 700. Population Schedules . . . 1870, p. 3 (Ward 4); Population Schedules . . . 1880, 12-5-26. The number of children in each family is calculated from the federal manuscript census and Franklin County, Ohio, Probate Court, Birth Records, 1867-1899.

12. Kenneth Roseman, "The Jewish Population of America, 1850-1860: A Demographic Study of Four Cities," Ph.D. dissertation, Hebrew Union College, 1972.

13. These children were not all born in Columbus, but their parents were residing in the city in 1880. An occasional date may be plus or minus one year, for the federal manuscript census provides only the age, not the month or year of birth. Those children born during the summer, when the census taker made his rounds, are particularly difficult to date precisely, for their ages usually increased by either nine or eleven years every "decade." It should also be kept in mind that half of the families listed had additional children after 1880.

3. FROM MODEST BEGINNINGS: ECONOMIC LIFE

Any student of nineteenth century American Jewish history can list a handful of Jewish immigrants whose economic successes rivaled those almost legendary fortunes of non-Jewish Americans. But economic portraits of entire Jewish communities, not merely the most prominent Jews, have been ignored by historians. The prevailing "rags-to-riches" ideology is well known; Calvin Colton noted in 1844 that

> this is a country of self-made men . . . a man has only to work on, and wait patiently, and with industry and enterprise, he is sure to get both [money and property]. The wheel of American fortune is perpetually and steadily turning, and those at the bottom today will be moving up tomorrow, and will ere long be at the top.[1]

To what extent was the "success cult" characteristic of the Jews that settled in antebellum Columbus, Ohio?

Although in 1840 only the Nusbaum and Gundersheimer families were permanent residents of Columbus,[2] by 1851 enough families inhabited the community to establish the first Jewish congregation.[3] Every Jewish head of household included in the 1850 federal manuscript census came from Bavaria.[4] It is commonplace to point out that Bavarian Jewish immigrants became peddlers upon arrival in America; if successful, they eventually traded their packs for stores in stable communities.[5]

Accounts indicate that an individual needed little or no capital to embark upon peddling. Since most German Jewish immigrants arrived poor, a majority of them drifted into the only occupation in which one could get a start with virtually no means. Isaac W. Bernheim was outfitted, at no cost to him, by an agent in Wilkes-Barre, Pennsylvania, in 1847; in exchange the agent retained seven out of every ten cents Isaac earned. In the same year in Philadelphia another agent supplied Simon and Meyer

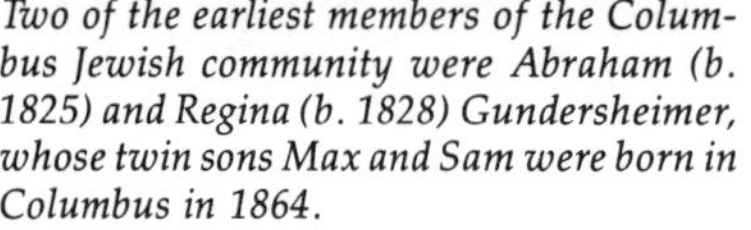

Two of the earliest members of the Columbus Jewish community were Abraham (b. 1825) and Regina (b. 1828) Gundersheimer, whose twin sons Max and Sam were born in Columbus in 1864.

One of the two founding families of the Columbus Jewish community was that of Samuel Nusbaum. He and his wife Rachael came from Mittelsinn. Of their several children, Otto became the most active in the community.

Guggenheim with packs at no cost for the first week. The Kuhn family in Cincinnati regularly "recruited" young Bavarian Jews, usually males aged fifteen through twenty, and financed them as outreach peddlers for their shirt business. Most familiar of all emerges the immigrant peddler whose landsleit or relatives furnished the initial merchandise; Levi Strauss is only the most famous of the dozens who left records of such familial generosity.

Columbus Jews followed this same pattern, with financing by agents (particularly eastern) and already established brothers most common. While no one could guarantee that the pack would turn into a counter in Columbus or elsewhere, the initial break came with little difficulty.[6] All of the Gundersheimer brothers peddled from farm to farm throughout Franklin County in the 1840s. By 1845 Nathan (1814-79) and Joseph (1821-1903) had opened stores, while their brother Isaac (1821-92) continued peddling. In the mid-1850s when Nathan and Isaac established themselves as independent merchants, Joseph and Abraham (1825-75) became partners in a retail store. Well before the first shot exploded at Fort Sumter all four brothers owned their own clothing stores on High Street.[7]

Other peddlers soon joined the Gundersheimer brothers on High Street: Samuel Amburgh, a peddler in the late 1840s, opened Amburgh & Company, a clothing store, at 143 South High in the early 1850s. Simon Mack opened Mack & Brothers, another clothing store, on the same street at just about the same time. Samuel and Judah Nusbaum peddled in the early 1840s until Judah opened a clothing store in the middle of the decade at 378 South High. Samuel peddled for another ten years, and then opened a store on South High Street. Poor immigrants had few surer ways to self-support, and Columbus Jewish peddlers, as a whole, enjoyed considerable success.[8]

Working as both tailors and merchants some of these clothiers made, sold, and repaired shirts, pants, vests, coats, and collars in the same store. In the 1840s it was common to sell at retail what they made in the rear, where they were also cutting, fitting, and sewing for the custom trade. Despite the growth of ready-made Yankee clothing, merchant tailoring continued into the subsequent decades. Part of the Gundersheimer's success resulted from merchant tailoring — employing craftsmen to make clothing for

[*Advertisement*] *Glorious News*
30,000 Men on the Battlefield!

and just arrived in the store of J. Nusbaum and Gundersheimer the most beautiful and most reasonable selection of fall and winter goods that have ever been brought to Columbus. Our stock consists partly of: a large selection of woolen cloths, cassinettes, tweeds, Kentucky jeans, flannel, fabrics for vests in all colors, bed linens and shirt fabrics; also, a large selection of goods for ladies, such as cashmeres, alpacas, ginghams, scarves, handkerchiefs, ladies' and men's hats; also, a large selection of ready-made clothing, trousers, jackets, vests, ties (or neckties), shirts; also tea, coffee and sugar, in short – we have everything you might wish to find in a store.

German Landsmen! Try us before you buy somewhere else, and if we can't convince you that we are selling our merchandise cheaper than anywhere else, then we will pay you for the time you lost. Our motto is: Small profit and quick turnover is better than big profit and no customers.

[*J*] *Nusbaum and* [*N*] *Gundersheimer*
No. 170 High Street, between the Franklin House and National Street

SOURCE: *Der Westbote*, December 11, 1846 (Author's translation)

their ready-made stock, catering to the jobbing trade, and financing both local and eastern manufacturing. Thus they not only absorbed — but used profitably — friends, relatives, sons, and daughters in the family stores.[9]

Although off to a much later start than the Gundersheimers, Simon Lazarus (1808-77) soon caught up. In 1864 he expanded his twenty-by-thirty-foot men's clothing store on South High Street, three doors from the southwest corner of High and Town streets, by purchasing an adjacent shoe store for $2,100 and an adjacent lot for $7,800 in 1876. Simon was described in 1877 as "one of the substantial businessmen of Columbus." Indeed, by the middle of the 1880s the spring and summer business hours often ended at 10:00 p.m. causing the clerks of the Lazarus and Gundersheimer stores to petition their employers for shorter hours: "8:00 p.m. when busy, 6:00 p.m. when dull." Simon himself, at age sixty, claimed $2,000 in real estate and $8,000 in personal property. Possessing $11,000 in investments and a net worth estimated at $40,000 at the time of his death, he left his wife Amelia (1822-99) in a position to bequeath $15,000 to one daughter, $10,000 to each of three daughters, and $5,000 to her son David (by a previous marriage) upon her death in 1899.[10]

Simon Lazarus typified many of the Jewish merchants in

After arriving in Columbus in 1851, Simon Lazarus opened his store; the same year he conducted High Holiday services for the new Jewish congregation, Bene Jeshuren. Described as "one of the substantial businessmen of Columbus," Simon Lazarus left his store to sons Fred and Ralph, who changed the name to the F. & R. Lazarus & Company.

Columbus during the Civil War. As a result of the government's demand for military uniforms, the stimulus to large-scale production of ready-made clothing, and the invention and perfection of the sewing machine, he employed seven salesmen after the war in contrast to one in 1860. Intuiting that the newly discharged veteran would want to shed his uniform as quickly as possible for ready-made clothing, Lazarus aggressively sent out salesmen to attract this patronage. With the growth of the street railway he was able to attract customers from previously remote areas. Finally, Lazarus initiated, albeit one per day, home delivery service by wagon.[11]

During an interview at the dedication of the new five-story F. & R. Lazarus & Co. building in 1908, Fred Lazarus recalled the influence of the Civil War upon the clothing business:

> They were buying clothes and doing away with their army blue and the clothing business was good. The soldiers had money and were willing to spend it. Soldiers would go into the basement of the store and change their army togs for the store clothes . . .

In the spring of 1879 Fred and Ralph Lazarus opened S. Lazarus' Sons & Co. at 6 South High Street with their brother-in-law, A. B. Cohen. Never as successful as the parent store, this clothing store enjoyed considerable respect for many years.

> The proprietors slept in the backs of the stores in most cases and would get up at any time of the night, thinking that the soldiers were coming.[12]

An extant *Day-Book*, preserved by the Lazarus family and dating from December 1877, reveals that Simon left a business with $15,260 in merchandise, a total of $33,528.60 in assets, and only $1,346.88 in liabilities for his wife and two sons, Fred (1850-1917) and Ralph (1852-1903). Weekly summaries of merchandise sales and profits reveal the sons' successes; profits generally hovered above 15 percent of total sales and grew steadily throughout the century.[13]

A complete description of a men's clothing store of the 1860s or 1870s is not available, but an 1886 inventory and appraisement of Joseph Goodman's clothing store, located on the southwest corner of Broad and High streets, has survived. The entire collection of men's and boys' clothing was appraised at $5,067.16. This included 216 men's suits ($3-$8.50), 401 pairs of men's pants ($1.25-$3), 150 overcoats ($2-$7.50), 230 boys' suits ($1.50-$5.25), 101 vests ($.20-$.60 each), 2,100 paper collars, and $20 worth of furnishing goods in the window on High Street.[14]

While the pattern of German Jewish movement into retail trade appears common throughout America, the extent to which the Jews of antebellum Columbus established clothing stores is quite unusual. With only one exception, every Jewish family entered the clothing business, and each located on the main shopping avenue of South High Street. This pattern of concentration, and heavy financial commitments to the clothing industry, continued for some time and became even more pronounced, for these Jews eventually dominated the Columbus retail clothing scene.

This domination had not gone unnoticed. As early as 1867 a Columbus newspaper featured this joke obviously offensive to Jews:

> Dat Ish Me
>
> We have among our inhabitants a good share of Hebrews. They are first-rate, quiet citizens, all businessmen, but keeners on a trade. Sharper than chain lightning, there is nothing allowed to stand between them and a trade. They seem to take as naturally to the clothing business as a duck does to water. Not long ago a gentleman wishing to purchase a fine blue cloth indigo dyed coat, called upon a Hebrew friend of ours, "in whom there is no guile," and, looking over his stock, found that which appeared to suit him. The purchaser was very particular to impress upon the seller that he wanted an indigo, not logwood dyed cloth, the smell of the latter being

offensive to him. The coat was selected and tried on, when our Hebrew friend commenced his encomiums: "Now, yust look at dat! It vas feet you like de baber on de vall. Dat ish yust vat you vant!"

"Yes," said the customer, "but this is not what I want. This is a logwood dyed coat. I don't like the smell."

"My frient," says our dealer, "dat coat is yust vat you want. Dat is not dat coat vat smells dat vay; no sir, dat ish me!"

It is needless to say that the gentleman did not purchase.

Three Columbus Jews responded to this tale in the form of a bitter letter to the editor.[15]

By 1872 *every* retail clothing establishment listed in the Columbus "yellow pages" belonged to a German Jew:[16]

TABLE 7
COLUMBUS CLOTHING STORES IN 1872

7 S. High	Henry Harmon	213 S. High	B & W Frankel
39 S. High	Joseph Goodman	227 S. High	Samuel Amburgh
81-83 S. High	Joseph Gundersheimer	243 S. High	Samuel Adler & Bro.
100-102 S. High	Louis Kahn	348 S. High	Judah Nusbaum
101 S. High	H & N Gundersheimer	359 S. High	Raphael Vogel
139 S. High	Simon Lazarus	174 N. High	Isaac Hoffman
159 S. High	Abe Gundersheimer	12 W. Livingston	Leo Straus
183 S. High	Arnold Steinhauser	2 Neil House Block	Adolph Aaron
204 S. High	J & H Margolinsky	172 E. Friend	Elias Lehman

SOURCE: *Bailey's Columbus Directory 1872-73* (Columbus, Ohio, 1872).

Although most Columbus Jewish men engaged in the retail clothing trade, success in business was by no means limited to retail clothiers; Max Gumble, a twenty-eight-year-old saloon keeper from Bavaria with only $400 in personal property in 1860, claimed $12,500 in real and $1,300 in personal property by 1870. Similarly Louis Kleeman, a forty-year-old jeweler, possessed $5,000 in real estate and $3,000 in personal property in 1870.[17]

It would appear that the preceding description concentrates on the most successful Jewish merchants in Columbus and ignores the others. While there were others, to be sure, rarely was a family without some real or personal property, or without employment suggesting relative economic security. In 1870 the average real and personal property per family for the entire Jewish community reached substantial amounts in every ward, with the exception of Ward 6 ($2,833 per family). But Ward 6 housed people like Henry Strauss, thirty-one, just beginning a clothing store business which quickly enjoyed success; Israel Marcus Schlesinger, thirty-six, soon to emerge as a prosperous merchant; Joseph Philipson who had just come to Columbus (his son David was to become a prominent rabbi); and Solomon Weil, a seventy-year-old retired grocer (and former local "rabbi"), whose eighteen-year-old son Samuel was already an independent businessman. Its residents as well as those in other wards stood in secure positions for the coming decade.[18]

TABLE 8
PROPERTY OWNED BY COLUMBUS JEWISH FAMILIES IN 1870

Wards	Total Families	Real Property Total	Real Property Per Family	Personal Property Total	Personal Property Per Family	Total Property Per Family
3	5	$17,000	$3,400	$10,800	$2,160	$ 5,560
4	10	44,000	4,400	15,300	1,530	5,930
5*	12	72,900	6,075	38,800	4,233	10,308
6	9	13,500	1,500	1,200	1,333	2,833
7	7	24,500	3,500	31,400	4,485	7,985

*Includes Joseph Gundersheimer's $88,000 in real and personal property.

SOURCE: Population Schedules of the Ninth Census of the United States, 1870 (Washington, 1965), Microcopy No. M-593, Roll 1201 (Ohio).

The concentration of Jewish merchants in the clothing trade, of course, emphasizes numbers rather than their degree of success. Were these merchants all small proprietors who owned less than a total of $1,500 in real and $1,500 in personal property, or large proprietors who owned more than $1,500 in real and $1,500 in personal property?[19] An examination of federal manuscript censuses leaves no doubt; every one of the merchant families recorded in 1850 prospered. The Gundersheimer brothers, who bought and sold real estate for over four decades, achieved the most success. Abraham, at age thirty-five in 1860, claimed $1,200 and $1,000 in real and personal property while Nathan, forty-six years old in 1860, claimed $3,000 in real and $3,000 in personal property. They prospered even more under the stimulus to the economy provided by the Civil War, and by 1870 attained major proprietor status. Abraham, then forty-five, possessed $8,000 and $3,200 ("solvent and safe" noted the credit report); Nathan, fifty-six, had $18,000 and $15,000; while Joseph, forty-nine, owned $60,000 and $28,000 in real and personal property respectively ("a man of wealth" the credit reporter observed).[20]

Further evidence of the tremendous economic progress of the Gundersheimers, as well as most of Columbus Jewry reporting taxable income, is provided in a published list of Franklin County

Printed and for sale by] WARRANTY DEED. [Randall & Aston.

Know all Men by these Presents, That we Nathan Gundersheimer and Babet Gundersheimer his wife of the County of Franklin and State of Ohio in consideration of the sum of Five Thousand Dollars, to them in hand paid by Penelope Hancock, wife of Elijah S. Hancock of the State of Ohio and County of Franklin have BARGAINED AND SOLD, and do hereby GRANT, BARGAIN, SELL AND CONVEY, unto the said Penelope Hancock and unto her heirs and assigns, FOREVER, the following Real Estate, situate in the County of Franklin State of Ohio and in the City of Columbus and described as follows, to-wit: Part of In Lot Number Twenty Seven (27) of the subdivision of the Central Reserve, as the same is known and designated on the Recorded plat of said subdivision, Said premises lying on the Southwestern Corner of said Lot No 27, measuring Thirty feet six inches on State Street, and running back, of that width One hundred feet.

TO HAVE AND TO HOLD said premises, with their Appurtenances, unto the said Penelope Hancock her Heirs and Assigns, FOREVER. And the said Nathan Gundersheimer for himself and heirs, doth hereby covenant with the said Penelope Hancock, her Heirs and Assigns, that he is seized of the Premises aforesaid, and that the Premises are FREE AND CLEAR from all incumbrances whatever; and that he will forever WARRANT AND DEFEND the same, with the Appurtenances, unto the said Penelope Hancock and unto her Heirs and Assigns, against the lawful claims of all persons whomsoever. And the said Babet Gundersheimer doth hereby release and convey to said Penelope Hancock her Heirs and Assigns, forever, her right of Dower and Dower Estate in said Premises.

In Testimony Whereof, The said Nathan Gundersheimer and Babet Gundersheimer, his wife have hereunto set their hands and seals, this Thirtieth day of March A.D. 1867.

Signed, Sealed, and Acknowledged in Presence of

Geo. W. Meeker

O. P. Hines

Nathan Gundersheimer [SEAL]

Babet her X mark Gundersheimer [SEAL]

The State of Ohio, Franklin **County, ss.**

BEFORE ME, George W. Meeker Justice of the Peace in and for said County, personally appeared the above named Nathan Gundersheimer and Babet Gundersheimer, his wife and acknowledged the signing and sealing of the above conveyance to be their voluntary act and deed; and the said Babet Gundersheimer being at the same time examined by me, separate and apart from her said husband, and the contents of said instrument made known to her by me, she then declared that she did voluntarily sign, seal and acknowledge the same, and that she is still satisfied therewith; this 30th day of March A.D. 1867.

Geo. W. Meeker
Justice of the Peace

A warranty deed conveying Lot 27 on State Street from Nathan and Babet Gundersheimer to Penelope Hancock on March 30, 1867.

"Income Tax Payers" for 1864. More than half the Columbus Jews on the tax lists had more than $1,000 in taxable income, in contrast to only 28 percent of all Columbus taxpayers.

Not only early arrivals, but even those German Jews who came to Columbus after 1855 and owned their own clothing stores by the early 1870s unanimously attained large proprietor status. For example, Henry Harmon claimed $15,000 in real estate and $3,000 in personal property; Raphael Vogel acquired $10,000 in real

TABLE 9
COLUMBUS JEWS' INCOMES DURING 1864*

Childs, M.	$24,050	Kahn, L.	$1,349
Gundersheimer, Jos.	7,426	Gundersheimer, I.	898
Gundersheimer, N.	5,254	Goodman, Jos.	834
Lehman, A.	4,133	Lehman, I.	731
Gundersheimer, A.	2,378	Childs, Wm.	600
Kraft, M.	2,208	Hoffman, I.	574
Kleeman, L.	1,994	Freeman, B.	447
Kleeman, M.	1,994	Wise, A.	337
Aaron, Ch.	1,850	Nusbaum, J.	296
Steinhauser, A.	1,510	Holderman, B.	235
Harmon, H.	1,487	Gumble, M.	195

*"A [partial] list of Income Tax Payers in Franklin County . . . with the taxable income of each annexed, as returned to the Collector of this District. 5% tax on incomes of $4,400 and less, 10% of excess."

SOURCE: *Ohio State Journal*, September 18, 1865.

TABLE 10
INCOME LEVELS OF ALL COLUMBUS TAXPAYERS IN 1864*

Incomes	Taxpayers	Incomes	Taxpayers
$ 1- 99	242 (12%)	$ 6,000- 6,999	19 (1%)
100- 499	775 (40%)	7,000- 7,999	3 (–1%)
500- 999	397 (20%)	8,000- 8,999	9 (–1%)
1,000-1,999	238 (12%)	9,000- 9,999	12 (1%)
2,000-2,999	86 (4%)	10,000-19,999	26 (1%)
3,000-3,999	60 (3%)	20,000-29,999	13 (1%)
4,000-4,999	34 (2%)	30,000-39,999	4 (–1%)
5,000-5,999	21 (1%)	40,000+	3 (–1%)

*N = 1,942

SOURCE: Calculated from *Ohio State Journal*, September 18, 1865.

and $500 in personal property; Leo Straus owned $4,600 in real estate and $900 in personal property; while Adolph Aaron possessed $4,000 in personal property in 1870.[21]

The occupational distribution of the early Columbus Jewish community during these two decades provides another method of determining the success of these immigrants. While nineteenth century occupations, in and of themselves, may not easily be ranked in terms of prestige a century ago, they nevertheless provide, together with indicators of property acquisition and real and personal property possessions, a reasonably reliable index of economic well-being.[22]

Our exhaustive reconstruction of the 1880 Columbus Jewish community, based on a variety of sources,[23] revealed a minimum of 440 Jews identifiable by name: 124 men, 103 women, 77 teenagers and 136 children.[24] Considerably more than half of the Jewish community were school children and housewives, and of the remainder we tallied the occupations of 135 employed persons:

TABLE 11
OCCUPATIONS OF COLUMBUS JEWS IN 1880

39	Clerks
34	Merchants
6 each	Peddlers and salesmen
4 each	Dressmakers, saloon keepers and agents
3 each	Boardinghouse keepers and manufacturers
2 each	Postmen, laborers, cigar makers, publishers, bartenders, dry goods sellers, physicians, grocers, tinners
1 each	Railroad worker, butcher, watch maker, waiter, barber, shoe maker, clergyman, trunk maker, tailor, gambler, lawyer, house painter, broker, bookkeeper

SOURCE: Population Schedules of the Tenth Census of the United States, 1880 (Washington, 1965), microcopy No. T-9, roll No. 1016 (Columbus, Ohio).

The occupational scheme in Table 12 divides the Jewish community into seven main groupings. The most striking observation is the concentration of the Jews in small proprietor, proprietor, and clerical positions: 92 percent of those employed in 1860, 97 percent in 1870, and 79 percent in 1880! No Jews in 1860 or 1870 and only two in 1880 held unskilled positions. This was not the case for Columbus generally. More than 25 percent of Columbus workers in all three census years, as well as a sizeable number of the employed in other nineteenth century American cities, were unskilled, while less than 10 percent of Columbus working men occupied clerical or sales positions.[25]

TABLE 12
COLUMBUS JEWS' OCCUPATIONAL GROUPS

	Percentage in		
	1860	1870	1880
Unskilled and menial			2%
Semi-skilled and service			5
Small proprietors, managers, officials	50%	26%	42
Skilled		2	10
Clerical and sales		15	37
Semi-professional and professional	8	1	4
Proprietors, managers, officials	42	55	*
N	12	47	135

*The 1880 Census does not permit us to distinguish small proprietors from proprietors.

SOURCE: Calculated form the Population Schedules of the Tenth Census of the United States, 1880 (Washington, 1965), microcopy No. T-9, roll No. 1016 (Columbus, Ohio).

TABLE 13
COLUMBUS WORKERS' OCCUPATIONAL GROUPS, 1880

	Persons	Percent
Unskilled and menial	4,497	26%
Semi-skilled and service	1,163	7
Proprietors, managers, officials	3,565	21
Skilled	5,696	33
Clerical and sales	1,364	8
Semi-professional and professional	763	5
N	17,048	

SOURCE: Calculated from *Statistics of the Population of the United States at the Tenth Census (June 1, 1880)*, Washington, 1883, p. 873.

Not discernible from Table 13, but of much importance, is the large extent to which the sons of Columbus Jewish merchants continued in their fathers' businesses. In 1870 only Henry (age eighteen) and Nathan (sixteen) Gundersheimer (sons of Joseph), Fred (twenty) and Ralph (eighteen) Lazarus (sons of Simon), Otto (thirty) and Isadore (twenty-five) Nusbaum (sons of Samuel), and Marcus (seventeen) Harmon (son of Henry), were old enough to work, and every one accepted employment in his father's clothing store. Rabbi Louis Weiss of B'nai Israel took note of this pattern in a sermon preached to his congregation: ". . . parents would do wisely if they saw to it that their children acquire an education of mechanical order instead of forcing them behind the counter as clerks as soon as they can."[26]

One Columbus native recalled hearing her father's stories about the role of sons in securing business for their father's stores:

> High Street merchants carefully ascertained the dates, times, and places for payday [of "freespending" railroad men]. Their sons set out in rented carriages, with the fastest horses obtainable, in a competitive race. Their object was to entice the railroaders, by descriptions of merchandise and offers of free rides, to downtown Columbus, where the fathers were waiting to sell them clothing.[27]

In 1880 eighteen of the nineteen Columbus males between age sixteen and twenty-seven were employed in clerical capacities in their fathers' stores. Only Benjamin Harmon, eventually to become Deputy County Auditor and Assistant Postmaster, demonstrated unusual daring and found employment outside of the family business. For many of these sons, apprenticeships in their fathers' stores either enabled them to continue successful businesses or launch businesses of their own. Henry and Nate Gundersheimer, who left for Baltimore in 1892 after "accumulating considerable

Columbus Dispatch

HENRY GUNDERSHEIMER. NATHAN GUNDERSHEIMER, JR.

SPRING. 1880. SUMMER.

HEADQUARTERS

—FOR—

BOYS' AND CHILDREN'S CLOTHING.

BOYS' SUITS FROM $2.25 TO $15.00

CALL AND SEE OUR LARGE STOCK BEFORE YOU PURCHASE.

H. & N. GUNDERSHEIMER,

LEADING CLOTHIERS,

mar22eod3m 101 SOUTH HIGH STREET.

property" and feeling they had "reached the limit here," explained their "prosperous career" as a result of "a strict maintenance of business principles and honest methods of conducting their affairs" learned from "working in dad's clothing business."[28]

Yet another indication of the success of the early Jewish families is suggested by the abundance of live-in servants employed by the Jews of Columbus. In 1870 six families maintained at least one servant; in 1880 Henry Strauss, Leo Straus, Saul Herman, Aaron Harmon, Moses Kleeman, Jacob Shonenberg, Amelia Lazarus, Aaron Margolinsky, Rev. B. A. Bonnheim (rabbi), and Solomon Loeb each had one servant while Jacob Goodman, Joseph Gundersheimer, and lawyer Caspar Lowenstein each employed two servants.[29]

Unusually high residential persistence shown in Table 14 helped to explain and reinforce the economic success of the early Jewish families in Columbus. It was almost literally true that only death eliminated a head of household present in Columbus in 1870, from a subsequent city directory. Without correcting for death, 61 percent of the Jewish heads of household of 1860 were still present in Columbus two decades later. When Louis and Clara Kleeman moved to Cincinnati in 1878 they became the first Jewish family, traceable in the sources after 1860, to leave the community. Their departure from Columbus appeared such an unusual event that it occasioned a proclamation in the local fraternal organization records.[30]

TABLE 14
COLUMBUS JEWISH HOUSEHOLD HEADS' RESIDENTIAL PERSISTENCE

	Percent of N Present				
Year (N)	1860	1866	1869	1872	1880
1860 (33)	100%				
1866 (16)	96	100.0%			
1869 (6)	93	93.7	100%	100%	
1872 (9)	85	93.7	100	100	
1875	82	93.7	100	100	
1880 (116)	61	87.5	100	100	100%
1890					65

SOURCE: *Columbus City Directories.*

Despite the persistency of the Jewish community within the city of Columbus, these immigrants actively moved from one residence to another. Computing mobility ratios for the entire group, the thirty-three families of 1860 averaged two moves every five years, the sixteen families that arrived after 1860 averaged almost one every two years, and the additional nine families residing in Columbus in 1872 averaged almost one move every three years during the 1870s. This, of course, is an absolute minimum, for the directories could only reveal one move per year. Nevertheless, the Jews of Columbus in the 1860s and 1870s were at least twice as mobile, and perhaps even more, as their descendants a century later.[31]

Not one of the early Jews of Columbus has left a written record of either the factors bringing him to Columbus or those accounting for his economic success. We do possess, however, a memoir by William G. Dunn, a successful dry goods merchant in Columbus in the 1870s and 1880s. Some of his reflections are illuminating:

> . . . I looked for a location further west, and finally decided upon Columbus, Ohio where I opened business . . . in April, 1869. I chose Columbus because it was pleasantly and centrally situated with a good prospect for enlargement; also because the dry goods business there did not seem to be overdone, and was conducted upon the old time plans, trade being held to each store mainly by the influence of the salesman and credit, as it still is in many country stores. . . . The retail business was at that time all done south of Broad Street, and mostly on High Street.
>
> I opened at the appointed time, and was successful from the start. The people seemed pleased with a one price store and good merchandise. Our sales the first year amounted to $170,000. My trade has embraced not only a large number of Columbus families, but also many from neighboring cities.[32]

No doubt the Gundersheimers, Lazaruses, Goodmans et al. shared Dunn's dream of economic success; there is absolutely no doubt that the drama must have been heightened by the actual success of so many of the early Jews of Columbus. While rarely going from peddling to riches, theirs is certainly a story of solid entry into the middle class.

NOTES FOR CHAPTER 3

TABLE 15
POPULATION GROWTH IN COLUMBUS

Census Year	Population	Percent of Population Increase Over Previous Decade	Over 1840
1840	6,000	148.3%	-
1850	17,900	195.6	298%
1860	18,600	3.8	310
1870	31,300	68.5	520
1880	51,600	65.1	860

SOURCES: *Columbus City Directories*, 1840, 1850, 1860, 1870, 1880.

1. *Junius Tracts* (New York, 1844), pp. 6 and 15, quoted in Stuart Blumin, "Mobility and Change in Ante-Bellum Philadelphia," *Nineteenth Century Cities: Essays in the New Urban History*, Stephan Thernstrom and Richard Sennett, editors (New Haven, 1969), p. 165.

2. On the Nusbaums, see *Der Westbote*, April 30, 1891; and *OSJ*, April 30, 1891, and November 12, 1928, ("Otto, born in Bavaria in 1840, arrived in Columbus with his parents at the age of eight months"). On the Gundersheimers, see *Westbote*, December 21, 1879 ("Nathan Gundersheimer resided in Columbus more than forty years") and *OSJ*, December 22, 1879. This conclusion, however, is not supported by I. J. Benjamin, a visitor to Columbus in 1862; he noted that the first Jews arrived in Columbus in 1842. See *Three Years in America 1859-1862*, Volume II (Philadelphia, 1956), pp. 280-81.

3. The Jews in Columbus as of 1850 included: Peter, Nathan and Phoebe, Joseph and Esther, Abraham, Isaac, Samuel, Samuel J., Jane, and Caroline Gundersheimer; Judah and Joana, Samuel and Regina, Otto, Isadore, Rosetta and Carolina Nusbaum; Simon and Anadora, Isaac, and Henry Mack; Samuel and Regina, and Terressa Amburgh; Moses Kleeman; R. Aronson; and Jacob Goodman. In addition to the federal manuscript census of 1850, see *OSJ*, November 19, 1900, *Westbote*, May 4, 1849, and *Tägliche Columbus Express*, October 31, 1898.

4. This conclusion is drawn from federal manuscript censuses and cemetery records.

5. Columbus' non-Jewish peddlers provide a striking contrast. The 1845-46 *Columbus Directory* lists eleven such individuals; not a single one of them still lived in the city five years later.

6. Bernheim, pp. 36-39; Atherton, pp. 53ff.; Lomask, *Seed Money: The Guggenheim Story* (New York, 1964), p. 15; Dr. Kenneth Roseman to Marc Lee Raphael, correspondence, March 5, 1974; R. G. Dun and Company 63:104, 152, 437; 65:516; 66:707 and 826.

7. Joseph, Nathan, Abraham, and Isaac owned stores at 75, 115, 129,

and 177 South High Street respectively. The occupational information is derived from the *Columbus Directories* from 1843 through 1867, and the R. G. Dun and Company credit reports (Baker Library, Harvard University), Volume 63, pages 92, 113, 133, 165, 202, and 258. On peddling, see Isaac W. Bernheim, *The Story of the Bernheim Family* (Louisville, 1910); Thomas Clark, *Pills, Petticoats and Plows* (New York, 1944); Richardson Wright, *Hawkers and Walkers in Early America* (Philadelphia, 1927); Lewis Atherton, "Itinerant Merchandising in the Ante-Bellum South," *Bulletin of the Business Historical Society* 19:2 (April, 1945); and A. V. Goodman, "A Jewish Peddler's Diary, 1842-43," *American Jewish Archives* (June, 1951).

8. R. G. Dun and Company 63:58, 89, 134, 138, and 196.

9. *CPP,* December 20, 1908; R. G. Dun and Company 63:113, 133, 165, 202, 258; 65:315, 397, 455, 516; 66:707 and 826. By 1870 Nathan and Joseph Gundersheimer, "merchant-tailor manufacturers," each employed ten adult workers to produce men's and boys' clothing; Joseph's capital investment in his store exceeded $20,000. Moreover, Joseph opened a branch of his store in Chicago (1871), stocked it with $8,000 in merchandise, and placed a son in charge. United States, Census Schedules, 1870, Franklin County, Ohio. Products of Industry-Schedule 4, Role 46, Microfilm Publication T 1159, p. 7, and R. G. Dun and Company (Chicago): 13:16.

10. William Diehl, Jr., "Lazarus," *Cincinnati* I:3 (December 1967): 32; Tom Mahoney, *The Great Merchants* (New York, 1947), pp. 103-5; Franklin County Recorder, Deeds, 79:343 and 126:462; R. G. Dun and Company 63:111; *OSJ,* December 6, 1877, and April 2, 1886; Population Schedules . . . 1870, p. 52 (Ward 7); "Deceased Tax List of S. Lazarus" in [Ledger of Annual Statements, Tax Records, and Finances of Individual Family Members 1877-1920], p. 211, Lazarus Papers, Box 6, OHS; Franklin County Probate Court, Wills, T 367 (1899).

Simon seems to have chosen to settle in Columbus because he had a step-brother named Lazarus Aronson who preceded him and opened a small store (Aronson & Brother) with the financial support of a brother in Philadelphia. Simon quickly invested whatever money he possessed in Aronson & Brother, and by the late 1850s became the sole owner of a men's clothing store at 153 South High, between Town and Rich streets. See R. G. Dun and Company 63:77, 80, and 154P; 66:765; 67:961, 1015, 1138 and 1159 (which includes rich sources of information on both S. Lazarus Sons & Co. and F. & R. Lazarus & Co.).

11. Diehl, op. cit., p. 32; Fred Lazarus, "The Development of the Delivery System," *Enthusiast* (November, 1915); *CC,* November 5, 1939; R. G. Dun and Company 63:111, 161; 65:315.

12. *CCP,* December 20, 1908.

13. *F. & R. Lazarus & Co., Day-Book No. 1* (Charles Lazarus, Chairman of the Lazarus Stores, graciously showed this to me.) R. G. Dun and Company 66:765; 67:961, 1015, 1113, 1138, 1159.

14. "Inventory and Appraisement, Assignment of Joseph Goodman, Schedule E, Personal Goods and Chattels." In Franklin County Probate Court, Administration Records. Inventory and Sale Bills, Volume 32, pp. 60-65. See also R. G. Dun and Company 63:44.

15. *Ohio Statesman,* November 13 and 16, 1867.

16. Actually this pattern was far from unique to Columbus, for German

TABLE 16
F. & R. LAZARUS & COMPANY, 1878

Week Ending	Merchandise Sales	Profit
September		
2	$1,256	$228
9	1,694	311
16	1,887	348
23	1,754	312
December		
2	2,797	478
9	2,723	489
16	2,377	377
23	3,673	573
30	3,270	557

SOURCE: *Day-Book No. 1 F. & R. Lazarus & Co.* (Courtesy Charles Lazarus)

immigrants across the United States "were the traders and dealers in 1880. The commodities in which they traded most prominently were, for males, clothing and men's furnishings . . ." E. P. Hutchinson, *Immigrants and Their Children, 1850-1950* (New York, 1956), p. 109.

17. Population Schedules . . . 1860, p. 204, and Population Schedules . . . 1870, p. 8 (Ward 4), p. 13 (Ward 3).

18. Population Schedules . . . 1870, passim.

19. This figure of $3,000 is far from arbitrary. It is higher than that utilized in a slightly different context by Peter Knights in *The Plain People of Boston, 1830-1860* (Oxford, 1971), and was selected as the dividing line after careful study of the 1850, 1860, and 1870 federal manuscript censuses.

20. National Archives Microfilm Publication, Population Schedules of the Seventh Census of the United States, 1850 (Washington, 1965), microcopy number 432, roll number 679 (Columbus, Ohio), pp. 622 and 624; idem, Population Schedules of the Eighth Census of the United States, 1860 (Washington, 1965), microcopy number 653, roll number 964 (Columbus, Ohio), pp. 167 and 594; idem, Population Schedules of the Ninth Census of the United States, 1870 (Washington, 1965), microcopy number M-593, roll number 1201 (Columbus, Ohio), p. 8 (Ward 4), p. 65 (Ward 7), and p. 75 (Ward 5); R. G. Dun and Company 63:202, 258, and 65:315. Joseph Gundersheimer's net worth was consistently estimated at $75,000 during the early 1870s.

21. Population Schedules . . . 1870, p. 3 (Ward 4), p. 2 (Ward 6), p. 86 (Ward 5), p. 86 (Ward 4).

22. Twentieth-century images of nineteenth-century occupations are often misleading: Joseph Kahn, a perpetual peddler, had $9,000 in real and $2,000 in personal property by 1870. He was only one of Columbus Jewry's successful "peddlers." On the other hand, Abram Polasky, an optician from Hungary, claimed no real or personal property in 1870. With respect to real estate, 38 percent (17/45) of the Jewish heads of households

TABLE 17
SELECTED GUNDERSHEIMER PROPERTY TRANSACTIONS, 1850-90

ACQUISTIONS

Joseph Gundersheimer

1850	from Wm. Mixon for	$ 1,600 cash
1853	from John Rice for	800
1854	from Miller for	3,400
1864	from Joyce & Miller leased store on High St. for	1,500/year through 1869
	from Crum for	3,500
1865	from Wm. Gill for	4,000
	from Wm. Gill for	2,000
1867	from John Gill for	3,800
1868	from Lorenzo English for	12,500
1869	from Rosina Hecht for	4,000
1870	from John McCoy for	19,950
1873	from Anson Govton for	15,000
1884	from Leopold Gumble for	3,000

Nathan Gundersheimer

1850	from James Bryden for	2,000
1852	from Andrew Backus for	2,100
1855	from Jos. Gundersheimer for	4,000
1862	from Weaver for	800/year through 1867
1865	from John Coulter for	2,900
1866	from Owen Huff for	7,900
1867	from Brooks for	5,800
1871	from Robt. Shusling for	3,500
1875	from Schneider for	1,900
1876	from Jos. Gundersheimer for	8,000
1884	from State of Ohio for	2,975
1888	from John Cashatt for	2,250
1889	from Jones for	2,700
1890	from Haydn for	3,000

Abraham Gundersheimer

1854	from Jos. Gundersheimer for	1,100
1868	from Rickley for	8,000

Isaac Gundersheimer

1854	from Jos. Gundersheimer for	900
1866	from Phillip Constons for	1,250

Gundersheimer Transactions — Continued

SALES

	Joseph Gundersheimer		
1853	from A. Gundersheimer for	$ 1,100	
	to I. Gundersheimer for	900	
	to N. Gundersheimer for	4,000	
	to N. Sawhill for	2,500	
1870	to J. T. Harris for	1,650	(with Nathan)
	to J. T. Harris for	1,650	(with Nathan)
1873	to Laura Williams for	—	
	to Laura Williams for	1,500	
1874	to Laura Williams for	1,400	
1875	to S. H. Rosencrans	12,500	
	to L. Olney for	1,600	
	to Sam Brooks for	3,500	
	to M. Skillen for	1,500	
1876	to N. Gundersheimer for	8,000	
1879	to Jas. Williams	—	
1881	to Henry Stern for	8,000	
	to C. H. Frisbie for	37,000	
1883	to David Hudson for	3,500	
	to Caroline Gumble for	8,000	
1884	to John Stone for	600	
1886	to Peters & Firestone for	—	
	to S. J. Gundersheimer	500	
	Nathan Gundersheimer		
1849	to James Bryden for	1,200	
	to V. J. Williams for	2,400	
1853	to J. W. Ream for	2,500	
1867	to Penelope Hancock for	5,000	
1870	to J. T. Harris for	1,650	(with Joseph)
	to J. T. Harris for	1,650	(with Joseph)
1875	to Amelia Kahn for	—	
1884	to C. D. Firestone for	12,500	(with Regina)
	Abraham Gundersheimer		
1868	to J.J. and S.S. Rickly for	2,500	
	Isaac Gundersheimer		
1872	to S. Black for	1,300	

SOURCES: Franklin County Recorder, Grantee Index No. 1, Grantee Index No. 2, and Deeds; Grantor Index No. 1, and Deeds.

in 1870 owned their own homes. On property ownership in nineteenth century cities, see Theodore Hershberg et al., "Occupation and Ethnicity in Five Nineteenth Century Cities: A Collaborative Inquiry," *Historical Methods Newsletter* 7:3 (June, 1974): 192.

23. We reconstructed the Columbus Jewish community of 1880 as follows. First, we constructed detailed membership lists from B'nai Israel and Zion Lodge records of the 1870s and 1880s. To these we added Jews listed in the *American Israelite* during the same decades, as well as all persons buried in Columbus Jewish cemeteries between 1880 and 1950. We discovered additional names by searching every marriage license signed by a "rabbi" or "Jewish Reverend" between 1850 and 1890, and by studying the birth and school records from 1860 to 1879 using every Jewish name already identified. Finally, we obtained names from the naturalization lists available from the nineteenth century. We then checked all of the above in the 1880 federal manuscript census and the 1879, 1880, and 1881 *Columbus City Directories* in order to establish their Columbus residency in 1880.

24. This represents a bare minimum, as many Jews, identified in the 1879, 1880, and 1881 *Columbus City Directories,* were not included in the 1880 federal manuscript census. As a result, no possibility existed for accurately including their spouses and children.

25. For occupation distribution in other mid-nineteenth century cities, see the essays in Part One of *Nineteenth Century Cities: Essays in the New Urban History,* Stephan Thernstrom and Richard Sennett, editors.

26. Population Schedules . . . 1870, passim, and the appropriate city directories; Louis Weiss, "Which Is the Best Education," in *Sermons and Essays.* Box 2395a, American Jewish Archives.

27. Bernice Nusbaum Bernstein to Marc Lee Raphael, correspondence, April 22, 1974.

28. Population Schedules of the Tenth Census . . . 1880, microcopy number T-9, roll No. 1016 (Columbus, Ohio) and the appropriate city directories. On Ben Harmon, see "Columbus 1812-1912," *The CSD, Centennial Library Edition,* p. 9. On the Gundersheimers, see *OSJ,* April 3, 1892, p. 3.

29. Population Schedules . . . 1870, and Population Schedules . . . 1880, passim.

TABLE 18
PERSISTENCE OF JEWISH MALES OVER EIGHTEEN IN 1880

In Columbus	Number	Percent
Present in 1880	116	100
Died 1881-90	6	
Moved 1881-90	35	
Present in 1890	75	65

30. B'nai B'rith Minutes, September 15, 1878. Although precise comparisons are difficult, these persistency rates are much higher than those of Atlanta, a relatively stable city close in size to Columbus. See Richard J. Hopkins, "Patterns of Persistence and Occupational Mobility in

a Southern City: Atlanta, 1870-1920," unpublished Ph.D. dissertation, Emory University, 1972, p. 54; and Charles Stephenson, "Determinants of American Migration: Methods and Models in Mobility Research," *Journal of American Studies* 9:2 (1968): 189-97.

31. Contrast this with Albert Mayor's conclusion ("no trend towards mobility either inside or outside the Columbus area exists") after discovering that 85 percent of Columbus Jewry sampled in 1968 had no plans to move. *Columbus Jewish Population Study: 1969* (Columbus, 1969), p. 31.

32. Lee, op. cit., Volume I, p. 394.

TABLE 19
MOBILITY RATIOS FOR HOUSEHOLD HEADS FROM 1860 THROUGH 1880

	N	Ratios	Standard deviation
1860 through 1866	33	0.407	0.200
1867 through 1872	16	.473	.240
1873 through 1880	9	.300	.200

SOURCE: *Columbus City Directories.*

4. WHAT WILL THE NON-JEWS SAY?: SYNAGOGUE LIFE

Seventeen years after constituting the first *minyan* in Columbus, German Jews moved away from familiar Orthodox Judaism to embrace Reform Judaism. By the 1880s their Reform service resembled many Protestant services, thus eliminating a part of their lives which made them foreign or different and speeding assimilation into the mainstream of Columbus middle class life. During this process they evinced a continuous concern about, "What will the non-Jews say?"

By the fall of 1851, in time for the holidays of Rosh Hashanah and Yom Kippur, the Jews of Columbus were numerous enough to constitute a *minyan* (ten adult males) and to organize an Orthodox congregation: Bene Jeshuren.[1] On the Day of Atonement, after a "general closing of their shops," the members immediately began to make plans to purchase ground for a Jewish cemetery, obtain Scrolls of the Law, rent rooms for a temporary synagogue, and secure the services of a Jewish minister.[2]

The acquisition of a cemetery has long been the first activity of an organized Jewish community. Thus it did not take long for the congregation to obtain a burial ground; as one Columbusite reminisced:

> Some twenty years ago [1852], the few Israelites then in the city, who were organized as a congregation for public worship, purchased a half-acre lot, to be used as a cemetery, in the eastern part of the city. It is still in use as a cemetery . . .[3]

This earliest Jewish cemetery in Columbus lay in the East Grave Yard at Meadow Lane and Livingston Avenue, one and one-half miles from the center of downtown.

Along with a cemetery, the Bene Jeshuren congregation immediately rented facilities for worship and obtained Torah scrolls for scriptural readings. They held worship services at various "halls" during the 1850s and 1860s — all located in the heart of the downtown business district and a short walk from every residence. The congregation conducted its initial services, and perhaps those of the entire 1850s, in Siebert's Building on South High Street between Rich and Friend streets; subsequent worship took place in nearby buildings. When Rabbi Isaac Mayer Wise visited Columbus in 1858, he worshipped in Siebert's Building, and reported that the congregation possessed two Scrolls of the Law, which had been obtained in 1852-53. According to Rabbi Wise, the embroidery on the cover of the Ark which housed the scrolls read, "this was donated by the Ladies Hebrew Benevolent Society of Columbus in the year A.M. 5613 . . ."[4]

Although some years would pass before Columbus Jewry could obtain the services of an ordained rabbi, Bene Jeshuren always had the services of a minister. The first was Simon Lazarus, who volunteered his services as "reader" in the fall of 1851, the year of his arrival in Columbus. In his "low, touching, and solemn voice," he chanted the Kol Nidre prayer as late as Yom Kippur of 1855 and caused "many a heart and many a soul . . . to soar aloft on the wings of devotion to their God." His successor, Joseph Goodman (1832-1904), became the first salaried minister; Goodman's responsibilities probably included leading the worship services, teaching the children, officiating at weddings and funerals, and ritually slaughtering the cattle and poultry for the members of this Orthodox congregation.[5]

Joseph Goodman seems to have served the congregation intermittently (1853?-55, 1856-60, 1863-64), perhaps offering his services when no other candidates appeared. A successful clothier and restauranteur, Goodman belonged to a well-known Columbus Jewish family. His brother Jacob (1826-98), who came to Columbus in 1846, was "one of the best-known jewelers in Columbus," president of Congregation B'nai Israel for two years, and "one of the best-known and most public-spirited men in the city." Selkan Goodman (1795-1886), his father, laid claim to the title of "the most learned Jewish layman" in nineteenth-century Columbus.[6]

Joseph Goodman's ministerial services to Bene Jeshuren were interrupted twice; once by Solomon Weil, whose German Yom Kippur discourse of 1855 may stand as the "first lecture ever delivered" in Columbus,[7] and subsequently for three years beginning in 1860 by Lippman Liebman. Both ministers performed all the duties required while holding other jobs.[8] When Goodman's services to the congregation ended in 1864, Meyer Wetterhahn succeeded him. Wetterhahn served previously at the

Joseph Goodman

Euclid Avenue Temple in Cleveland and, immediately prior to Bene Jeshuren, at Beth Israel in Jackson, Michigan. According to the financial records of Beth Israel, Wetterhahn received $300 annually for the same functions he performed in Columbus as a "reader, teacher, and *shochet*" (ritual slaughterer). He earned another $90 each year for teaching children, and received five cents and three cents for slaughtering large and small poultry respectively.[9] Such a salary, in Jackson or Columbus, would have necessitated an additional occupation. Following the services of Joseph Schoenberg from 1866 to 1867 and Joseph Rosenthal from 1868 to 1870, Columbus Jews were prepared not only to hire a full-time ordained rabbi, but to provide a reasonable remuneration.[10]

Rabbi Judah Wechsler was not hired by the Orthodox congregation, Bene Jeshuren, but by the new congregation, B'nai Israel. In August 1868, the majority of the members of Bene Jeshuren created B'nai Israel after finding it too difficult or impossible to establish Reform worship services in the old synagogue.

The first recorded efforts to build a Jewish house of worship date from that summer. Twenty-two of thirty-five B'nai Israel members contributed $5,100 to purchase a lot for $5,200 on the northwest corner of Friend and Third streets. By November of the following year, with $3,200 already pledged, the new congregation signed an $8,800 contract for the erection of a building, while planning an exhaustive out-of-town fund-raising campaign.[11]

This fund-raising effort received its greatest impetus from Nathan and Joseph Gundersheimer, first president and treasurer of B'nai Israel respectively. They left their busy clothing and tailoring stores in the care of family members, and spent several weeks during the spring of 1870 soliciting contributions in Cleveland, Baltimore, Philadelphia, and New York. More than forty-five out-of-town firms and individuals were recorded in a "Subscription List," including the following entries from Cleveland:

$25 Harris and Shrier [wholesale hats, caps, furs]
20 Mann S and Son [wholesale clothing]
10 Halle J and Co [retail clothing]
10 Mr. Halle
5 Mr. Halle
5 Nausbaum and Straus [retail clothing]
10 Hays Bros. [wholesale notions and fancy goods]
25 Koch, Goldsmith and Company [wholesale clothing]

Through the efforts of the Gundersheimers and other solicitors, more than $5,000 was raised from out-of-town sources. As a result of the Gundersheimers' generous contributions of time and money — Nathan donated $1,000 and Joseph $600 — the congregation ordered their pictures hung in the vestry room of the new temple.[12]

In the spring of 1870, ground was broken and the cornerstone of the new temple laid with grand ceremonies conducted by the Masons, Odd Fellows, Maennerchor, and B'nai B'rith, and featuring an oration by Rabbi Wise of Cincinnati. After a procession from the old "synagogue" on Town Street, the new temple was dedicated on September 16, 1870, again with Rabbi Wise as the principal orator.[13]

Built of brick with limestone trim, in the popular "Franco-Italian" or "Italian Villa" style of the day, the structure had a mansard roof, twin towers with minareted corners, and a "plain, substantial manner." The lower floor of the temple was used for Sunday school classes, and the upper floor for worship. The sanctuary contained permanent pews for three hundred persons with additional space for another one hundred persons. The woodwork consisted of plain ash; large windows with "figured" glass provided abundant light and ventilation; gaslights illuminated the room at night. The wall to the left of the Ark declared "Progress is our Motto," while that to the right proclaimed "Peace and Unity our Watchword"; above the scarlet velvet and gold Ark hung the Tablet of the Ten Commandments in Hebrew.[14]

The new congregation resolved to introduce instrumental music and a choir, to engage a rabbi and cantor, to use Rabbi Wise's Reform *Minhag America* prayerbook (an abbreviation, alteration, and simplification of the traditional liturgy) together with English hymns and prayers instead of Hebrew, to insist upon equal rights for women by having family pews rather than segregated seating, to establish a dignified service, and to have sermons in both English and German.[15] The inability to accomplish these goals at Bene Jeshuren left unpleasant memories:

> Bene Jeshuren was in existence for the last nineteen years [1851-1870] and did not enjoy a very enviable reputation of usefulness . . . and it deserved every reproach. A congregation which cares only for the stomach, or in plainer words, for a *Shochet* only, and neglects everything else . . . is a dead branch of the living tree of Judaism.[16]

The innovations proved enormously successful, and Reform respectability seemed solidly established in the congregation's new temple:

> We have now a well regulated Reform worship . . . order and decorum in the temple, regular Friday evening service at 7:00 p.m.,

The cornerstone for B'nai Israel was laid on May 15, 1870. This temple served the Reform congregation until 1904.

> sermons delivered alternatively in the English and German languages every Friday and Sabbath morning.
>
> Reform was not known here, but not all admit its wholesome influence.
>
> While it was not possible to interest an audience before with the many long prayers, which no one understood . . . Reform alone can gain the masses.
>
> The temple on each and every occasion, when English sermons are to be delivered, is crowded to its utmost capacity by Christians.[17]

Bene Jeshuren seems to have dissolved within two or three years after B'nai Israel's emergence. Although "I. B. Jashenof" (probably Isaac Baer Jashenosky) officiated at Orthodox services on Rosh Hashanah 1870, the remaining members of the old congregation affiliated with Congregation B'nai Israel, and initiated plans to sell the property belonging to Bene Jeshuren and give the proceeds to B'nai Israel.[18]

B'nai Israel, like Bene Jeshuren, enrolled an overwhelmingly German-born congregation. Of the nine Bene Jeshuren founders the six survivors became charter members of B'nai Israel; all had emigrated from Bavaria. The congregation's minutes exist only in German through 1878; vernacular prayers were said in German more often than English, and even during the 1870s rabbis preached more often in German than in English. The movement toward more and more English generally paralleled the growth of Reform. An increasingly Americanized generation of German Jews moved from a form of Judaism congenial to recent immigrants to a mode appealing to an Americanized generation of Jews and non-Jews. Reform thus expressed itself in nineteenth century America primarily as an attempt to improve the decorum and dignity of Jewish worship; to create a more appealing, intelligible liturgy using the vernacular and musical instruments and by eliminating traditional prayers for the return to Zion, the advent of the Messiah, and the restoration of the sacrifices.[19]

B'nai Israel's new rabbi, short and stocky Judah Wechsler (1833-1905), appeared a perfect choice for an incipient Reform congregation. Born in Bavaria and educated at the University of Wuerzburg and the Wuerzburg Talmudic Academy, he received a rabbinic diploma from the progressive Seligman Baer Bamberger (1807-78). Wechsler served congregations in Cumberland, Maryland, and Indianapolis, Indiana, from the early 1850s through 1867. Hired as lecturer by Beth Ahabah in Richmond, Virginia, in August 1867 he was to steer the congregation in the direction of Reform through lectures, choir, and melodeon. He remained there until January 1869 when the congregation, unqualifiedly Reform, sought an English-speaking lecturer.[20] Immediately prior to coming to Columbus Wechsler served in Nashville, Tennessee.

In the summer of 1870 B'nai Israel advertised for a *hazzan* (cantor) and teacher, offering $800 to $1,000 as well as a free apartment in the temple. Wechsler arrived as B'nai Israel's second choice, for J. S. Goldammer of Cincinnati *schaendlich betrogen* (disgracefully betrayed) the congregation by refusing to come to Columbus after agreeing to a five-year contract, resigning from his congregation, and preaching a farewell sermon. But the congregation was not disappointed; Wechsler became exceedingly well liked and moved the congregation and its Protestant-like Reform services steadily toward Reform.

The German Jews of Columbus, as elsewhere, responded to the prevailing Protestantism of the new environment by adapting their outer religious forms to the Protestant model. The essence of the Reform movement became its adoption of Protestant style. By March 1871, as the temple became more widely known in the community, Wechsler could already state: "I believe there would be not one single member of this Congregation who would vote for Orthodoxy . . . for our Temple is frequented by the most intelligent Christians." Nearly two years later Wechsler still remained convinced of Reform's permanency, and again primarily because of its appeal to Christians:

> [There] is an overwhelming majority in favor of our present mode — those who have predicted that a Reform congregation could not be maintained for any length of time . . . have not been good prophets — as our temple is yet visited week after week by the most intelligent Christians . . . and favorably spoken of by the different clergymen of the city.[21]

Several additional events indicate the congregation's move away from Orthodoxy. A choir, organized for the temple dedication and composed of non-Jews as well as Jews, gained fame within the city. The trustees, and then the congregation, voted to observe only one day, not two, of Rosh Hashanah. After rejecting a motion that all men should pray with uncovered heads, the trustees agreed that those who wished to pray without hats should be permitted to do so. The move to Reform culminated in November 1873, when B'nai Israel officially joined the Union of American Hebrew Congregations (the national organization of Reform congregations). The credit for this decision went primarily to Rabbi Wechsler for initiating and sustaining the Reform services.[22]

Interfaith activities comprised an important part of Rabbi Wechsler's ministry; indeed, he seems to be the first in a line of B'nai Israel rabbis who, like their colleagues in other "German" congregations in America and abroad, were becoming Jewish versions of Protestant ministers. He spoke in Columbus churches, invited Christian clergymen to speak at the temple, encouraged Christians to attend worship services, opened legislature sessions with prayers, participated in civic ceremonies as unofficial ambassador of the Jews to the general community, and seems to have gained a favorable reputation in the Christian community. Even the annual confirmation exercises (public examinations in which sixty to seventy questions were asked of the students in rotation followed by worship services) took place in the presence of Christian clergymen — one or two of whom regularly gave addresses at the services.[23]

B'nai Israel held its first Hebrew Fair during Rabbi Wechsler's ministry to raise funds to liquidate the congregation's debt. Staged at the new Columbus City Hall from November 25 to December 2, 1872, the fair drew the enthusiastic support of Columbus citizens — especially churches and societies — whose support evinced a "catholic spirit." The fair offered not only abundant Christmas presents, raffles, and featured entertainers, but a contest to determine the most popular minister and butcher. The congregation's motto, "Love to all without distinction of creed and nationality, and hatred toward none," was prominently displayed at the fair.[24]

When he resigned in the spring of 1873 to accept a position in New Haven, Connecticut, Rabbi Wechsler recommended Samuel Weil (1830-1901) of Alleghany City, Pennsylvania, as his successor. In April the congregation elected Weil as minister and teacher for $1,000 annually with the stipulation that he preach two Friday nights a month in German and one Friday night a month in English (one wonders in what language he preached on the fourth Friday each month).[25] During his ministry, Weil prepared Columbus' David Philipson for his bar mitzvah in 1875 and entrance examination to Hebrew Union College. Philipson became the distinguished rabbi of Cincinnati's Congregation B'nai Israel from 1888 to 1949. Concomitantly with hiring Weil, the congregation employed David Green as the new *shamash* (sexton) and *shochet* (slaughterer). Green received an annual salary of $150 as a *shochet* and $100 as a *shamash,* and was permitted, when slaughtering "big animals," to charge $.75 for the first piece but only $.25 for the rest.[26]

In 1874 the Jewish community purchased a cemetery site adjacent to Mt. Calvary Catholic Cemetery for $1,000, having rejected use of a tract of land in Greenlawn Cemetery after lengthy negotiations. During the winter of 1874-75, Congregation B'nai Israel held several meetings to lay out the new cemetery in twelve-by-sixteen foot plots, to establish the price of $15 (with $5 down) for members, to determine that non-members' fees would

Emanuel Hess

Samuel Weil

be set by the board of directors, and to set policy, i.e., no burials within forty-eight hours of death except for special cases. The plots went on sale at a special congregational meeting on January 3, 1875, and twenty-three members made down payments of $5 each to reserve graves. When the city passed an ordinance prohibiting internment within the city limits by 1881, the Jews of Columbus were forced to remove one hundred graves from East Grave Yard to their Mt. Calvary Avenue cemetery.[27] (A chart of the earliest burials in this cemetery is included in the notes at the end of this chapter.)

When Rabbi Samuel Weil left Columbus for Denver early in 1876, the congregation offered a $1,000 salary and a free apartment in the temple to his successor. Emanuel Hess of Kansas City applied for the position, requested a three-year contract at $1,350 annually, refused to compromise, and won the position in March of 1876. Born in Meerholz, Kurhessen, and educated at the Gymnasium of Hanau, at Marburg and Frankfort am Main, Hess had studied under both a leading Orthodox (Samson Raphael Hirsch) and a Reform rabbi (Leopold Stern).

Before accepting a position in Columbus Hess served at B'nai Jehudah in Kansas City for four years. A contemporary there described his English sermons as "correct, fluent, chaste and full of poetry," and those in German as "among the best." During his first year in Kansas City, Hess had replaced the *Minhag America* prayerbook with the radically Reform *Olat Tamid* of David Einhorn which contained Hebrew, German, and English prayers. When B'nai Jehudah faced financial problems and cut the rabbi's salary, Hess made plans to leave B'nai Jehudah and serve B'nai Israel.[28]

Armed with the longest and largest contract B'nai Israel had yet awarded a rabbi, Hess gave the congregation its money's worth immediately by articulating the essence of Reform Judaism in a forty-minute inaugural sermon, "What is Judaism?" In this address Hess argued that the goal of religion is human happiness; that Judaism, as a reasonable (e.g., without superstition) and wise religion, attains that goal but is no better than any other religion; and that Mosaic Law, which for Hess consisted of only the Decalogue, is the essence of Judaism.[29]

During Hess's brief tenure, the financial picture of B'nai Israel appeared bleak. In November 1876 the annual report noted that there had been "hard times this year"; that although the annual dues were $60, that only eighteen of the forty-seven members could pay the required fee; that Israel M. Schlesinger had served as secretary for three years without pay; and that disbursements of $3,019 exceeded receipts by $37. One year after Rabbi Hess accepted the position, B'nai Israel had no money in the treasury to pay him. This situation alone, however, did not force Hess' resignation in the summer of 1877. The rabbi violated Article 12 of the congregation's constitution by officiating at the wedding of a non-member without permission, and generally had not "fulfilled his duties" as preacher and teacher. Perhaps because of the financial plight and the president's censure, Hess' year or so in Columbus left a strong negative impression. Years later, when he provided his vita to a national publication, Hess omitted Columbus from the list of cities in which he served.[30]

The successor to Rabbi Hess was Benjamin Aaron Bonnheim (1845-1909), elected in July 1877 and reelected for four consecutive years.[31] Born in Gemuenuden, Hessen-Nassau, he studied under the supervision of the Isralitisches Vorsteheramt in Marburg (Hesse) before arriving in the United States in October of 1866. In 1869 after serving congregations in Baltimore, Maryland, and Columbus, Georgia, Bonnheim became the principal of the English-German Academy in Atlanta; from 1870 to 1873 he served the Hebrew Benevolent Congregation there, preaching exclusively in German. Bonnheim returned to B'nai Israel in Columbus, Georgia, where he preached in German and English for the next three years. During his tenure in Columbus, Ohio, Bonnheim earned a medical degree from Columbus Medical College in February of 1882 after entering the college in the fall of 1879.[32]

Despite his medical studies, Bonnheim felt that education was his specialty and his accomplishments gained communitywide recognition.[33] By scheduling classes before and after 10:00 a.m. worship services, he was able to teach all the children in the Sabbath school. Bonnheim took special pride in preparing his charges for confirmations that were regularly witnessed by "very large crowds of Jews and gentiles." The highly secular confirmation ceremony at B'nai Israel during Bonnheim's ministry had two parts: a performance by the distinguished choir led by a graduate of the Leipzig Conservatory, and an examination and exhibition of the students' and teacher's accomplishments. In the spring of 1880 all sixty youngsters paraded "their skill and display of knowledge in answering intricate and pointed questions" which demonstrated the most "thorough and systematic teaching" and "reflected great credit on the reverend gentleman." The examination was typical of Bonnheim's confirmation exhibitions: biblical questions, Hebrew readings, Palestinian geography, theology, and festivals taking precedence.[34]

Bonnheim influenced several areas of congregational religious life. On the High Holidays he preached regularly in German in the evenings and English in the morning; during these sermons the ushers were required to lock the doors so that no worshippers could leave the temple until the conclusion. Bonnheim also officiated at "grand weddings" not only in Columbus but in

Benjamin Aaron Bonnheim

Zanesville, Circleville, Chillicothe, and Newark, Ohio. He received a percentage of the annual Hebrew Fair receipts as a reward for his efforts on the project. On two separate occasions in 1882 he joined the trustees in rejecting an appeal from the national Board of Delegates "to appoint a committee to devise means of raising funds to be kept here to be enabled of assisting the Russian refugees which may come to [Columbus] . . . until they find work to support themselves." Later the trustees rejected an appeal from the Union of American Hebrew Congregations that each member donate one dollar to purchase farm implements for Russian refugees.[35]

The financial difficulties which plagued the congregation earlier continued to dominate Bonnheim's ministry. Late in 1879 the secretary reported that only one new member joined B'nai Israel during the preceding year and the "congregation had not been very prosperous." Possibly this is the reason the trustees voted not to spend more than $15 on *matzot* (unleavened bread) for poor immigrant Jews. During 1880 almost half of all the members in the highest dues category ($60) petitioned for a reduction; more than half of the other members of the congregation did the same. The secretary reported that "the prospects looked dark and gloomy"; and that B'nai Israel borrowed $400 from the Hebrew Benevolent Society.[36]

At the end of Bonnheim's tenure the situation had not improved: the secretary complained that the temple could not "make ends meet," that the treasury possessed only $1.34, and in a typical understatement, that the "finances [were] not in good condition." Indeed, some members now began to urge that the dues of other members be raised; yet the congregation defeated Henry Gundersheimer's motion to raise Judah Nusbaum's dues from $30 to $40.[37]

Bonnheim's unique accomplishment of completing medical school during his ministry in Columbus not only provided him rich fulfillment but became the cause of his departure from B'nai Israel. At the congregation's annual meeting in April 1883, his contract was not renewed after "heated electioneering and a nineteen to twenty-three vote against him." Bonnheim's opponents offered two unsubstantiated arguments against him, theorizing that: First, Bonnheim, "having finished his course of study as a physician, intends to leave the ministry and devote himself entirely to his new profession," and second, by the very act of receiving his medical degree, Bonnheim could not have put sufficient time and effort into his rabbinical duties.[38]

The *real* controversy was more interesting still: Bonnheim came to Columbus as a licensed *mohel* (circumciser), and even worse for him, became a licensed physician. Before his arrival, a very prominent congregant who had been the secretary for many years had monopolized circumcisions — a ritual that provided from $5 to $25 per circumcision. Bonnheim became the community *mohel* for two years when this congregant moved to Richmond, Virginia. When the latter returned to Columbus, he demanded that Bonnheim confirm his monopoly again; but Bonnheim responded that he would circumcise if requested to do so, and would permit the congregant to do the same. The congregant did not approve of this arrangement. Bonnheim then proposed a fifty-fifty split, and this too was rejected. The ensuing struggle between the prerogatives of congregant and rabbi — to be repeated many times in Columbus — brought on a bitter feud and culminated in a virtual defamation of Bonnheim's character. This inflammatory situation was frequently headlined by the local press as "Gehanna in Israel," "Revenge on a Rabbi," "Charges of Heartless Cruelty," and "Rabbinical Difficulties." Unlike many of his Columbus successors, Bonnheim refused to "say anything negative about the congregation" and remained "certain he always acted justly." After departing Columbus in 1883 he served as both superintendent and resident physician of the Baltimore Hebrew Hospital and Asylum.[39]

Bonnheim's successor was Felix W. Jesselson (1839-1920) of Titusville, Pennsylvania. A native of Renau, Baden, he studied at Karlsruhe and Heidelberg and came to the United States at the age of twenty-one. Defeating several other candidates by an overwhelming vote, Jesselson was elected to the position in July 1883, and remained the minister until 1890 when he resigned to accept a position in Parks, Illinois.[40]

During the first few years of Jesselson's Columbus ministry reports on the financial and religious affairs of the congregation were discouraging. In 1885 B'nai Israel reported debts of $1,265 ($765 to Capitol Lodge 150, $400 to the Ladies Benevolent Association, and $100 to Capitol Lodge Workingmen), in part the result of "the members who are most able to pay up are general in arrears, and your secretary [I. M. Schlesinger] has to call every month few times and then get no money." The following year receipts added up to $1,900 and expenses to $2,200, causing the congregation to be described as "barely solvent" in their annual report. Not until 1888 could Aaron Wise claim to be "the first president since this congregation was organized that has seen the congregation out of debt." Indeed, when the treasurer discovered a $400 surplus later in the year, the board of directors expressed such surprise that they could not decide quickly what to do with the funds.[41]

Apathy and indifference exclusively characterize descriptions of religious life during the 1880s. A report during 1885 stated:

TABLE 20
B'NAI ISRAEL DUES 1871-93

Year	Total Budget	Members and the Amounts They Pledged									
		-$20	$20	$25	$30	$35	$40	$45	$50	$60	$75
1871	$1,715	—	—	5	—	—	18	—	—	12	—
1873	1,720	—	1	10	—	—	12	—	5	12	—
1874	1,715	—	2	9	—	—	12	—	5	12	—
1876	2,030	—	2	14	—	—	9	—	4	18	—
1877	1,870	—	2	14	1	—	10	—	3	15	—
1878	1,750	—	2	12	2	—	10	—	3	13	—
1881	1,360	—	3	13	1	3	8	—	2	7	—
1882	1,385	1	5	15	2	1	7	—	2	7	—
1883	1,455	1	7	16	2	5	4	—	4	5	—
1884	1,717	2	6	21	3	2	8	—	4	6	—
1885	1,706	4	6	20	4	1	9	—	3	6	—
1886	1,950	3	9	23	5	2	9	—	3	7	—
1887	2,040	2	12	19	9	1	9	—	3	8	—
1888	2,058	2	15	16	8	3	9	—	4	7	—
1889	2,028	2	12	16	—	3	9	—	4	7	—
1890	2,249	2	13	15	7	3	9	—	4	7	—
1891	2,775	2	6	21	4	16	9	—	16	11	1
1892	2,775	13	4	27	4	9	6	—	9	10	1
1893	2,697	13	5	25	3	8	6	1	9	10	1

> there is nothing going on. The apathy in religious matters is appalling. People never go to temple. Sometimes as many as ten people [attend] divine services, but seldom as many as that. Our Jewish men are so engrossed with business matters that they have no time to devote to the church.

A communication the following year echoed the same theme:

> A great many of our young married men and single men never visit our temple; they are indifferent to religion . . . their parents never go to Temple . . . if they can walk in the street with a *shikse* [non-Jewish girl] that is more to them than a temple.

The situation remained unchanged in 1887 and 1888: "indifference is the watchword," often "not more than two or three members are present at divine services," there are "nothing but empty benches," and "few attend on Friday evening and fewer on Saturday morning."[42]

Perhaps Jesselson prompted the indifference. His sermons — lengthy, repetitive, and fairly dull whether in English or German — droned on so long that the doors often had to be locked to prevent a mass exodus. Typically, in his memorial eulogy for English Jewish philanthropist Moses Montefiore at special services

Felix W. Jesselson

I. M. Schlesinger

in 1885, he sermonized for seventy minutes! This might help explain a decline in financial, moral, and participatory support, despite a small growth in membership: fifty-two members in 1884, sixty-one in 1886, and sixty-four in 1888.[43]

Several important developments in temple life occurred during Jesselson's years of service to the congregation: The board of directors required worshippers to remove their hats at the door and worship without head covering; a step which, although not in direct violation of Jewish law, overturned a custom which had long distinguished Jewish from Christian worship and announced a desire to worship in a form which corresponded to the American pattern. High Holiday pew rentals and the annual fair continued to provide an important source of congregational revenue; and there emerged an awareness that the present temple was inadequate for the holidays and that a new temple would soon be needed. Additionally, public conversion ceremonies highlighted many Sabbath worship services; the gentile choir gained city-wide fame; post-confirmands were organized into a class for study with Jesselson; and the city of Columbus demanded the removal of the hitching post in front of the temple.[44]

During postwar economic prosperity, B'nai Israel's struggle for survival and then middle-class respectability, as well as the rapid spread of Reform Judaism, made it a typical congregation of its day:[45] B'nai Israel's rabbis possessed sufficient secular education from European universities to represent the Jews before the Christian community, and to seem as closely aligned in form and articulation to Protestantism as to any form of traditional Judaism. Temple reforms, regarding the wearing of hats, separate seating of women, use of an organ, and the adoption of a prayerbook, marked turning points in the congregation's history. Proper religious education of children loomed as a serious problem because of an absence of teachers, texts, and curriculum; and the worship services became things of great solemnity. B'nai Israel, a close-knit German-Jewish congregation as the 1880s drew to a close, subsequently found rabbis who would bring dignity and prestige to the pulpit.

TABLE 21
PERSONS BURIED IN THE JEWISH CEMETERY ON MT. CALVARY AVENUE

55 A	56	57	58	59	60
54 A	53	52 A	51	50 A	49
43	44	45 A	46 A	47 A B	48 A B
42 A B	41 A	40 A B	39	38	37
31 A B	32 A B	33 A	34 A	35	36
30	29	28 A	27 A B C	26 A B	25 A
19	20	21	22 A B	23	24
18 A B C	17 A B	16 A B C D	15 A B	14 A	13 A
7 A	8 A B	9 A	10	11	12
6 A B	5 A	4	3 A B C	2	1

(Rubbings made by students from Temple Israel in 1975 and 1976, and Beth Tikvah in 1976 and 1977, greatly aided my reconstruction.)

NOTES FOR CHAPTER 4

Jewish Cemetery on Mt. Calvary Avenue*

Today some of the tombstones at the Jewish Cemetery are in their original places; the devastating flood of 1913 washed others away; and some, despite patient efforts at restoration, are not only illegible but perhaps marking different graves. Further complicating any attempt to inventory and mark the graves is the knowledge that most of the original purchasers of plots are not buried in those spots. While European Jews usually buried persons in the order of death, the Jews of Columbus quickly adopted the American system of family plots. Such practices make missing graves more striking, as one expects to find entire families together. Therefore, Table 21, compiled after several visits, is an uncertain attempt to describe the earliest burials in the oldest extant Jewish cemetery in Columbus.

3A Amie Goldstein, died December 6, 18?9, age one year, nine months, twenty days
3B Goldstein
3C Ida Goldstein, daughter of B. and R. Goldstein, died March 7, 1868, at age two
5A Caroline Hoffman, wife of I. Hoffman, died June 5, 1884, at age fifty-eight
6A Jennie Nusbaum, daughter of I. and H. Nusbaum, died April 17, 1876, at age one
6B Samuel Nusbaum, son of I. and H. Nusbaum, born February 14, 1873, and died October 11, 1879
7A Mariana Bonnheim
8A Agnes Bonnheim, died October 16, 1879, at age two
8B Theodore Bonnheim, died April 16, 1878, at age eight
9A Leopold Rosenberg, born in Osterode, Prussia, December 4, 1843, and died in Chicago, March 15, 1890

13A Abraham Adler, born March 31, 1861, and died May 1, 1864
14A Joseph Kleeman
15A
15B Hannah Gumble, born in Hoffenheim, Baden, and died January 15, 1891, at eighty-four years
16A Regina Amburgh, wife of Samuel, born in Gerstfeld, Bavaria, died January 28, 1861, at age thirty-eight
16B Hattie Amburgh, born February 15, 1855, and died April 5, 1869
16C Samuel Amburgh, born October 3, 1814, and died April 13, 1876, at age sixty-one

---

*For a detailed description of the flood, see the *OSJ,* March 26 through March 30, 1913; for a more imaginative, but useful, account, see James Thurber, "The Day the Dam Broke," in *My Life and Hard Times* (New York, 1933). On the cemetery, see B'nai Israel's Cemetery and Pew Record Book [1875] at Temple Israel.

16D Henry Amburgh, son of Samuel and Regina Amburgh, died February 14, 1880, at age twenty

17A Lewis Goldman, born in Bavaria

17B Mathilde Vogel, wife of Raphael, died July 30, 1878, at age fifty-three

18A

18B Bertha Harmon, wife of Henry, died October 3, 1873, at age forty-nine

18C Moses Harmon, died October 17, 1860, at age one

22A Moses Mayer, son of Morris and Fannie Mayer, born June 1876, and died March 1880, at age three

22B Norene Mayer, born December 10, 1887, and died August 30, 1888, at age eight

25A Julia, wife of David Cohen, died January 6, 1877, at age sixty-two

26A Zebora Kahn, died November 22, 1869, at age seventy-three

26B Aaron Kahn, died in London, Ohio, April 11, 1859, at age sixty-eight

27A I. M. Schlesinger, born April 21, 1834, and died March 26, 1905, ("one of nature's noblemen")

27B Eva Schlesinger, wife of I. M. Schlesinger, born April 7, 1832, and died March 6, 1899

27C Yetta, wife of Sol. Frank, died November 17, 1882, at age forty-one

28A Louis Margulis, died December 30, 1888, at age forty-five

31A Isaac Gundersheimer, born September 27, 1821, and died September 27, 1892, at age seventy-one

31B Louise Gundersheimer, wife of Isaac, born July 2, 1831, and died August 15, 1892, at age sixty-one

32A Samuel Gundersheimer, died February 8, 1888, at age twenty-four

32B Babette Gundersheimer, wife of Nathan, died July 2, 1876, at age sixty-eight

33A Nathan Gundersheimer, born in Mittelsinn, Bavaria, December 21, 1814, and died December 21, 1879

34A Marcus Frankel, born May 1825, and died May 4, 1872

40A Regina Strauss, wife of Henry, born in Mittelsinn, September 8, 1839, and died August 5, 1888

40B Mathilde Strauss, daughter of H. and R. Strauss, born July 16, 1875, and died June 23, 1876

41A Lewis Shrier, born in Bavaria, died at Columbus, November 29, 1852, at age twenty-nine

42A Hannah Leveen, died January 6, 1889, at age seventy

42B Hannah Nathan, died March 11, ?

45A Hattie Aaron, died September 22, 1877

46A J. A. Goodman, native of Hungary, died October 22, 1876, at age fifty-nine

47A Moritz Bresslau, died October 26, 1879, at age forty-two

47B Deborah Rosenthal, died in 1862

48A Caroline, daughter of Samuel Weil, died May 18, 18?3, at age ten months, nineteen days

48B Minnie, daughter of Isaac Loeb, born May 4, 18?8, and died October 22, 18?1

50A Solomon Frank, died February 10, 1876, at age thirty-eight
52A died on July 11, 1863, at nine months of age
54A Henry, son of R. and C. Reiceiman, died August 5, 1854, at age six months, eleven days
55A Rosa, wife of D. Frebourg, died October 11, 1864

1. In addition to Isaac Leeser's report on his November 16, 1851, visit to Columbus ("30 Jews have formed a congregation and adopted the German *minhag.*") in *The Occident and American Jewish Advocate* X:1 (April, 1852), the 1851 date is recorded in I. J. Benjamin, *Three Years in America, 1859-1862,* Volume II (Philadelphia, 1956), p. 281 (Benjamin visited Columbus in January, 1862); *Ohio Statesman,* September 17, 1870; *AI,* September 23, 1870, ("Bene Jeshuren . . . was organized in the fall of 1851 with twelve members.") and October 28, 1870, ("Bene Jeshuren was in existence for the last nineteen years" — Rabbi Judah Wechsler); *OSJ,* September 17, 1870; *CED,* July 19, 1903; *Cornerstone Laying of Temple B'nai Israel Programme* (Columbus, Ohio, July 19, 1903); *OSJ,* October 6, 1924, ("73 years ago . . ."); Mrs. Felix (Celia Schanfarber) Levy (Chicago) *Reform Advocate,* November 14, 1908, ("Bene Jeshuren was formed by six families in 1851.")

Two county histories erroneously list 1852 as the founding of Bene Jeshuren; these are William T. Martin, *History of Franklin County: A Collection of Reminiscences of the Early Settlement of the County* (Columbus, 1858), p. 388, and William A. Taylor, *Centennial History of Columbus and Franklin County, Ohio,* Volume I (Chicago and Columbus, 1909), p. 210.

The first president of the congregation, Joseph Gundersheimer (1851-53), was succeeded by Judah Nusbaum (1853-55); *AI,* September 28, 1855, and *CDT,* July 11, 1886.

2. *OSJ,* October 7, November 24, 1851; *AI,* August 13, 1858.

3. Jacob H. Studer, *Columbus, Ohio: Its History, Resources and Progress* (n.p. 1873), p. 223.

4. Martin, op. cit., p. 388; Benjamin loc. cit.; *Williams' Columbus Directory . . . Mirror,* Vol. 2, 1858-59 (Columbus, 1858), p. 22; *Lathrop's Columbus Directory, 1860-62* (Columbus, n.d.), p. 53 (251 South High Street); *Poland's Columbus Directory . . . for 1864* (Columbus, 1864), p. 29 (253 South High Street); *OSJ,* August 19, 1865, (Walcutt's Hall, 18 East Town Street); *Williams' Columbus Directory for 1866-67* (Columbus, 1866), p. 34 (253 South High Street); *Williams' Columbus Directory for 1867-68* (Columbus, 1867), p. 36 (16 East Town Street); *AI,* September 28, 1855 ("the chandeliers shed their brilliant gas-light all around . . . in the halls of the synagogue on High Street") and August 13, 1858.

5. *Der Westbote,* December 24, 1879; *The Occident and American Jewish Advocate,* loc. cit.; *OSJ,* December 6, 1877; Fred Lazarus, Jr., *Autobiography,* pamphlet, p. 16; *AI* September 28, 1855; Benjamin, loc. cit.; Studer, op. cit., p. 216; *History of Franklin and Pickaway Counties* (Columbus, 1880), p. 527.

6. These dates of ministerial service are calculated from signatures on

marriage licenses in Franklin County Probate Court during the 1850s and 1860s, the appropriate city directories, and newspaper references. The obituaries of Jacob and Selkan Goodman are in the *OSJ*, October 30, 1898, and August 11, 1886, respectively.

7. *AI*, September 28, 1855. Solomon Weil (1800-82) is recorded in the 1850 federal manuscript census as a Cincinnati resident (teacher) with a two-year-old daughter born in Maryland, and in the 1870 (with an eighteen-year-old son born in Ohio) and 1880 federal manuscript censuses as a Columbus resident. He died in Columbus; see *Der Westbote*, March 25, 1882.

8. On Liebman, see *Die Deborah* VI (May 31, 1861), p. 192 and X (August 1, 1862); *The Occident* XVII (1859), p. 216 ("teacher in Madison, Indiana"); Franklin County marriage licenses (1860-63); Benjamin, loc. cit.; *Williams' Columbus Directory 1860-62* (Columbus, 1862). Liebman came from Cincinnati to Columbus, and then served in Youngstown, Ohio. He was the grandfather of Rabbi Joshua Loth Liebman; see *AI*, April 27, 1860, and Dora Brown, "History of the Jews of Youngstown," in "History of the Jews of Canton and Alliance" in the *Reform Advocate* (Chicago, n.d.). Liebman officiated at the first recorded confirmation in Columbus and introduced Rabbi Isaac Mayer Wise's *Minhag America* prayerbook; see *Die Deborah* VI (May 31, 1861), p. 192 and *AI*, April 27, 1860. A description of Columbus Jewry, based on a visit by Rabbi Wise during Liebman's first months of service, is in *AI*, July 13, 1860.

Weil worked as a grocer, and Liebman directed a German and English Select School almost adjacent to the rented hall used as a synagogue.

9. Irving Katz, "History of Temple Beth Israel" (Jackson, Michigan, n.d.), typescript; *Williams' Columbus Directory for 1866-67* (Columbus, 1866), p. 34; Franklin County marriage licenses (1866). Bene Jeshuren advertised in the *AI*, as early as 1864, for a *hazzan, shochet,* and teacher; *AI*, July 22, 1864. See also Arthur Lelyveld, "Economic Life of American Jewry 1860-1875," Prize Essay, Hebrew Union College (Cincinnati), 1934, p. 159.

10. On Schoenberg, see *Die Deborah* X (April 20, 1866), p. 167 and XI (December 7, 1866), p. 88; *Williams' Columbus Directory for 1867-68* (Columbus, 1867), p. 36; Franklin County marriage licenses (1866). On Rosenthal, see *Grier & Co's Columbus Directory for 1869-70* (Columbus, 1869), p. 25.

11. *AI*, August 28, 1868; T. I. Minute Books, August 15, September 1, 1868; Franklin County Recorder, Deeds 95:543; T. I. Minute Books, November 7, 1869.

12. T. I. Minute Books, May 15, 1870; B'nai Israel Miscellaneous Book, 1868- , pp. 60-63; *W. S. Robins & Co.'s Cleveland Directory 1871-72* (Cleveland, 1871); T. I. Minute Books, November 16, 1870. B'nai Israel itself would receive frequent invitations from out-of-state congregations, such as Rodef Sholem of Pittsburgh, which requested funds for a new building; T. I. Minute Books, July 4, 1875. Honoring the Gundersheimers for their financial contributions was not unusual; at B'nai Israel, as elsewhere in the land, money and not scholarship was becoming the crucial factor in the selection of synagogue leadership.

13. *CDT*, July 11, 1886. As befitted the symbolism of their name, it was

common to lay the cornerstones of synagogues with Masonic ritual. Moreover, many Columbus Jews were buried with Masonic rites.

14. T. I. Minute Books, May 15, 1870; *OSJ*, May 14, 1870; *Ohio Statesman*, May 16, 1870; *AI*, May 20, 1870 ("6,000-7,000 persons were present"!); *OSJ*, September 17,1870; *Ohio Statesman*, September 17, 1870; *AI*, September 23, 1870; *Archives Israélites*, Vol. 31 (1870), p. 447; *Der Westbote*, September 22, 1870. For examples of Italian Villa architecture approximating B'nai Israel (well-defined rectilinear blocks and round headed windows), see Marcus Whiffen, *American Architecture Since 1780: A Guide to the Styles* (Cambridge, Massachusetts, 1969), p. 69.

15. T. I. Minute Books, August 15, 1868 and passim. Rabbi Wise's *Minhag America*, a curtailment (with modifications) of the traditional Hebrew ritual, was published in 1857; see *Minhag America. A form of worship for American Israelites in Hebrew. Also issued together with the following English and German versions* (Cincinnati, 1857).

16. *AI*, October 28, 1870. For further examples of Wechsler's attitude toward traditional Judaism, see W. Gunther Plaut, *The Jews in Minnesota: The First Seventy-Five Years* (New York, 1959), p. 76.

17. *AI*, October 28, 1870.

18. *OSJ*, September 17, 1870; interview with Jerome Bornheim; *Bailey's Columbus Directory 1871-72* (Columbus, 1871), p. 148; T. I. Minute Books, June 26, 1870.

19. T. I. Minute Books, passim; "Jews of Columbus: Brief History of Their Coming and Progress," undated Columbus newspaper clipping [1897 or 1898]; federal manuscript censuses 1850, 1860, 1870. For a discussion of nationwide synagogue reforms about this time, see Leon A. Jick, *The Americanization of the Synagogue, 1820-1870* (Hanover, New Hampshire, 1976), pp. 174-94.

20. *American Jewish Year Book* 5664 (1903-04), p. 104; *The Occident* XII (1854), p. 117, XVII (1859), pp. 162, 211-12, 217-18, XXV (1867), p. 413; Plaut, op. cit., pp. 75-77; Herbert T. Ezekiel and Gaston Lichtenstein, *The History of the Jews of Richmond from 1769-1917* (Richmond, Virginia, 1917), pp. 197, 263, 268; W. Gunther Plaut, *Mount Zion 1856-1956* (St. Paul, [1956]), pp. 48, 52; CCAR *Yearbook* V (1895), p. 149, XVIII (1908), p. 26. On Wechsler's subsequent career, see the two volumes by Plaut, and A. A. Chiel, *The Jews in Manitoba* (Toronto, 1961), p. 77.

21. The advertisements for the position appear in the *AI*, June 17-August 26, 1870. See also *AI*, July 29, 1870; March 17, 1871, October 25, November 8, 1872; T. I. Minute Books, July 16, August 3, 1870.

22. T. I. Minute Books, August 7 and September 3, 1871, October 27, 1872, November 2, 1873, May 7, July 2, 1876; *AI*, October 25, 1872, May 4 and November 7, 1873.

23. *AI*, December 29, 1871; T. I. Minute Books, May 4, 1873; *SMN*, June 9, 1872, April 6, 1873; *OSJ*, May 27, 1871.

24. *OSJ*, November 21, 23, 25-28, and 30, December 2, 1872; *AI*, December 20, 1872; *Der Westbote*, November 23 and 30, 1872.

25. *SMN*, April 6, 1873; David Philipson, *My Life As An American Jew* (Cincinnati, 1941), pp. 1-2. Weil, a *hazzan* in Washington, D.C. in 1863, served Congregation Beth Israel in Jackson, Michigan, as *hazzan* and teacher in the mid-1860s; see *The Occident* XXI (1863), pp. 275, 285, 383;

Hillel Marans, *Jews in Greater Washington: A Panoramic History of Washington Jewry for the Years 1795-1960* (Washington, D.C., 1960), p. 64; Irving Katz, op. cit., p. 13.

26. T. I. Minute Books, April 26, 1874; *The Hebrew Union College Monthly* (April, 1946), pp. 24-25; *Wiggins and M'Killop's Directory of the City of Columbus for 1875-76* (Columbus, 1875), p. 139.

27. William T. Martin, op. cit., p. 392; *Bailey's Columbus Directory 1872-73* (Columbus, Ohio, 1872), p. 38 (the grass in front of Columbus Children's Hospital presently occupies the area of the East Grave Yard); T. I. Minute Books, July 7 and August 18, 1872, August 30, 1873, July 5 and 12, November 1, 8, and 29, December 13, 1874, January 3 and 10, March 7 and 21, 1875, March 28, 1880, June 5, 1881, April 9, 1882. Columbus City Ordinance No. 91 (September 5, 1881) stated "To provide for the removal of the dead and the monuments and tombstones in the East Grave-yard, and for the establishment in the place of such grave-yard of the South Park, in the city of Columbus, Ohio"; *General Ordinances of the City of Columbus, Ohio In Force January 1st, 1882 . . .,* collated by H. E. Bryan, City Clerk (Columbus, 1882).

Among the remains moved were those of Lewis Shrier, whose gravestone is the earliest extant marker in a local Jewish cemetery. Shrier, perhaps one of three brothers living in Columbus, died at the age of twenty-nine on November 29, 1852, during Columbus' second cholera epidemic, a scourge which accounted for 225 deaths during the summer of 1850 alone and which struck hardest in the German wards of the city; see Alfred E. Lee, *History,* Volume II, p. 714; Jonathan Forman, "Ohio Medical History — Pre-Civil War Period — The First Year of the Second Epidemic of Asiatic Cholera in Columbus, Ohio — 1849," *Ohio State Archaeological and Historical Quarterly* (October-December, 1944): 303-12; Charles E. Rosenberg, *The Cholera Years: The United States in 1832, 1849, and 1866.* (Chicago, 1962).

28. T. I. Minute Books, March 19, 1876; *AJYB* 5664 (1903-04), p. 63; Frank Adler, *Roots in a Moving Stream: The Centennial History of Congregation B'nai Jehudah of Kansas City 1870-1970* (Kansas City, Missouri, 1972), pp. 24, 26, 28, 31, 39, 333; *AI,* January 17, 1907, p. 3.

29. *AI,* June 9, 1876; *OSJ,* May 6, 1876.

30. T. I. Minute Books, November 5, 1876, April 15, May 6 and 27, 1877; *AJYB,* loc. cit.

31. Bonnheim defeated both S. M. Fleischman of Akron, Ohio, ("the best English speaker who had ever preached in the Temple") and Jacob Voorsanger of Washington, D.C. On the former, see *SMN,* July 15, 1883, and on the latter, Marc Lee Raphael, "Jacob Voorsanger of San Francisco on Jews and Judaism: The Implications of the Pittsburgh Platform," in *American Jewish Historical Quarterly* 63:2 (December, 1973): 185-203.

32. *AJYB* 5665 (1904-05), p. 46; Brant and Fuller, *History of the Upper Ohio Valley* (Madison, Wisconsin, 1890), pp. 225-26; Janice O. Rothschild, *As But A Day: The First Hundred Years 1867-1967* (Atlanta, 1967), pp. 5-18, 120; CCAR *Yearbook* XX (1910), pp. 117-18; Ohio State University Medical School Records.

33. An exception to this acclaim was Caspar Lowenstein, a prominent attorney, who resigned from B'nai Israel in 1882 because "for nearly three

years I have sent one of my children to the . . . School, whenever one was kept, and the result is, she knows as much now as she did before attending same"; see T. I. Minute Books, June 4, 1882. Despite impressive confirmations, Jewish education in nineteenth century Columbus was minimal at best.

34. T. I. Minute Books, January 4, 1880; *OSJ*, March 23 and 24, 1880, June 6, 1881; *AI*, June 20, 1879, December 10, 1880, May 6, 1881. The Sabbath School of B'nai Israel was so intimately tied to the rabbi in the nineteenth century that, when a rabbi quit during the 1891-92 school year, the board dismissed the Sabbath School. T. I. Minute Books, February 14, 1892.

TABLE 22
B'NAI ISRAEL CONFIRMATION PROGRAM

Part I	Prayers, Songs, Readings, Examinations
Part II	Declamations: Miss Ida Meyer: "Good Night" Miss Fannie Hirschberg: "The Rainy Day" Misses Fannie Lehman, Sarah Hart, Tillie Steinhauser: "What I Love to See" Miss Jennie Mendel: "Rules of School" Miss Hannchen Bonnheim: "Was Ich Habe" Master Marcus Schonfeld: "Till Eulenspiegel" Master George Goodman: "Der Pfau und der Kranich" Master Moses Goodman: "Die beiden Hunde" Miss Rosa Freiberg: "Work and Play" Master Herman Hirschberg: "Kaiser Karl" Miss Rebecca Schonfeld: "Guilty or not Guilty" Master Abraham Rodelsheimer: "Die schlaue Zahnharst" Miss Clara Goodman: "Der Mensch und die Welt" Master Leo Phillipson: "Moses und der Todte" Miss Bertha Strauss: "Das eitle harterzige Fraeuline"
Part III	Dialogues: "The Irishman from Cork" — Masters Margolinsky, Solomons, Schonfeld, Kleeman, and Strauss "David and Goliath" — Masters Phillipson and Schonfeld "The Irish Servant" — Masters Basch and Gumble
Part IV	A Song by the Scholars Distribution of Prizes

SOURCE: *Ohio State Journal*, March 23, 1880.

35. *AI*, December 10, 1880; T. I. Minute Books, September 26, 1880, April 17, 1881, March 5, September 3 and October 1, 1882.

36. T. I. Minute Books, October 5, 1879, March 28, May 2, 1880, April 17, 1881.

37. Ibid., April 29, 1883.

38. Ibid., October 15, 1882, April 29, 1883.

39. *SMN,* May 5 [sic; 6th], and 13, 1883; *OSJ,* May 7, 1883; *CED,* May 7, 1883.

40. CCAR *Yearbook* V (1895) p. 146, and XXXI (1921), p. 149; T. I. Minute Books, June 3, July 22, 1883. On his resignation, see *OSJ,* May 27, August 31, 1890; *AI,* June 5, September 18, 1890; *CED,* May 28, 1890.

41. T. I. Minute Books, April 5, September 27, 1885, April 4 and 25, 1886, April 8, July 1, 1888. Mr. Schlesinger's efforts to collect the dues were spurred by his 5 percent commission on the monies collected; see ibid., October 13, 1889.

42. *AI,* April 3, 1885, October 22, 1886, August 5, 1887; T. I. Minute Books, April 10, 1887, April 8, 1888. Even the trustees of the congregation were accused of apathy for "keeping their places of business open on Yom Kippur"; see ibid., September 27, 1885.

43. *AI,* April 13, 1884, October 16, 1885, April 25, 1886, April 8, September 28, 1888; T. I. Minute Books, September 24, 1883, October 5, 1885; *CDT,* October 5, 1885.

44. T. I. Minute Books, October 21, 1883, December 7, 1884, May 8, 1887, September 2, 1888; *AI,* April 15, 1887, June 1, October 12, December 28, 1888; *CDT* July 11, 1886.

The board asked Jesselson to move out of the temple in 1888, and the following month the congregation seriously considered buying a church at Rich and Third streets for $15,000; see T. I. Minute Books, December 2, 1888, January 27, 1889.

One public conversion was described in some detail; Mina Kuhn, "suddenly after services last Friday, renounced her faith, and after answering Felix Jesselson's questions in a clear and distinct voice, converted by kissing the Torah"; *AI,* August 14, 1885, and see ibid., November 9, 1877.

45. On the battles for liberalization of ritual in the American Jewish community, see Allan Tarshish, "The Rise of American Judaism," Ph.D. dissertation, Hebrew Union College, pp. 185-95.

5. SECURITY THROUGH BELONGING: ORGANIZATIONAL LIFE

The highly organized Columbus Jewish community of the 1970s has its roots in the nineteenth century, for both the men and women in that early community initiated, generously supported, and built the Jewish part of their lives around societies. These organizations contributed to the development of a middle class and Americanized Jewish community in Columbus, for together with the intensive network of business affiliations, social ties cemented and reinforced through lodges, clubs, and synagogues, provided the economic opportunities for Columbus Jewry. Social and economic mobility cannot be understood apart from the matrix of ethnically-exclusive voluntary associations.

The inception and growth of social organizations occurred at a time when Columbus Jews hungered for leisure time activities; during decades when few other activities offered any serious competition for the few social hours of hard-working immigrants. The women organized first, perhaps by 1852-53, as the Ladies Hebrew Benevolent Society. Upon discovering the society, Isaac Mayer Wise noted that "charity finds its way to all places where Israel's daughters flourish." While accounts indicate that this group donated a Torah scroll to Bene Jeshuren, nothing else is known of their activities or philanthropy. At about the same time, the men organized the First Hebrew Society of Columbus, incorporating on December 3, 1852, with a meeting at the home of their president Judah Nusbaum. Later that decade they formed the short-lived Young Men's Hebrew Association primarily for social activities.[1]

The most signficant men's society throughout much of Columbus Jewish history, Zion Lodge No. 62 of the Independent Order of B'nai B'rith was incorporated by the authority of District Grand Lodge No. 2, on August 20, 1865, with seventeen charter members, including all of the most prominent Columbus Jews.[2]

German Jews organized the national B'nai B'rith, a fraternal organization, in 1843. In a short time it lost its German caste and became the major middle-class men's organization in the Jewish community. Out of its ranks came outstanding Jewish community leaders and under its sponsorship emerged significant communal organizations. In addition to hosting regional conventions and supplying officers to the midwestern district, Lodge No. 62 dominated Jewish community life for at least seventy-five years.

Zion Lodge No. 62 has carefully preserved minutes dating back to its inception. Membership lists reveal that the lodge, like most nineteenth-century societies, included clerks and petty merchants alongside the most prominent members of the Jewish community. All sought a sense of security through "belonging," and few drew apart to join or form exclusive private clubs. A secret organization which initiated members "into the mysteries of the order," B'nai B'rith maintained its secrecy for more than two decades.

While the Cleveland Jewish Orphans Asylum became a special philanthropic project of District Grand Lodge No. 2, "benevolence" or mutual assistance quickly became the goal of the local organization. Zion Lodge No. 62 developed a full program of support activities to accomplish this goal. By the early 1870s a mutual endowment or insurance fund provided generous grants upon the death of a member and smaller amounts upon the death of a member's wife. The lodge attained these revenues through fund-raising events as well as dues contributions from each member. Indeed, the first recorded activity of Zion Lodge was a ball, which raised $140 for the Widows' and Orphans' Fund. Lodge No. 62 also established "sick benefits" and provided members' survivors with funeral funds through a regular assessment. Mutual assistance was encouraged by imposing fines; members not attending the funeral of a brother member paid a one dollar fine or two dollars if they missed the roll call held before such processions.[3]

Sick members received benefits of four or five dollars each week throughout the 1880s. Such sick benefits attracted members, but also created contention for Zion Lodge. Two of the by-laws suggest the difficulties involved in awarding these benefits:

> Article 14, Section 1 — Any member of this lodge who through sickness is inabled from following his usual vocation provided such sickness has not been caused by his own immoral conduct, who has been a member for one year and is clear in the books shall be entitled to benefits.
> Article 9, Section 2 — A member of this Lodge residing in this city who being sick for five days and failing to report to the Lodge shall not be entitled to benefits prior to being reported.[4]

A brother who took sick while out of town had to submit a doctor's certificate of illness "sworn to" by a notary public that "he is unable yet to follow his vocation," while a brother ill in Columbus had to be checked by the lodge's "visitation" committee. That committee often reported unfavorably: "Brother ———, who was reported sick on August 4 was not entitled to benefits and the Committee does not think him sick enough to prevent him from following his usual vocation." In such cases the "president would send a Physician to examine" the brother; if the doctor sustained the committee's report, the sick brother could — and often did — appeal to the entire lodge membership and, if unsuccessful, to the District Grand Lodge. Such appeals occurred frequently, with the lodge's secretary recording the details.[5]

Concomitant with the transition at B'nai Israel, Zion Lodge began to move from German to English during the 1870s. In 1875 members agreed that lodge work would be carried out in English but that debates must remain in German. By 1877, however, the by-laws read the "Workings of the Lodge shall be in the English language."[6]

The Free and Accepted Masons, a society distinguished by its secret, quasi-religious ritual and benevolence, nearly matched B'nai B'rith in popularity. Columbus Jews, particularly the future leaders of Zion Lodge, emerged as active Masons several years before the Civil War. The Gundersheimers, for example, joined early; by 1850 and 1852 Nathan and Joseph Gundersheimer, respectively, became Master Masons in Columbus Lodge No. 30. Freemasonry was a growing order in Columbus during the 1850s and 1860s, and despite the existence of three lodges, twenty-three men, including the Gundersheimers, Jacob Goodman, Henry Harmon, and Louis Kahn, petitioned the Grand Lodge in September 1873 for yet another lodge. The new Humboldt Lodge No. 476 consisted of "stalwart and outstanding German citizens"; sixteen of the twenty-three Master Masons were born in Germany and seven were sons of German emigrants. Through 1890 the German language was used to confer various degrees and to conduct Masonic business. When its growth came to a virtual halt, the lodge changed to English and again grew rapidly, so that by 1923 it had developed into the largest lodge in Ohio with 2,150 members.[7]

By the early 1880s the number of social, fraternal, and cultural organizations serving Columbus Jewry had increased considerably; unfortunately none of their minutes has survived. Early in 1875 Rosalie Lazarus led twenty-four unmarried women in forming the Young Ladies Hebrew Association for benevolence, mutual improvement, and amusement. Capitol Lodge No. 150 of Kesher shel Barzel (Chain of Iron) had about twenty-seven male members

Brought to Columbus during the first year of his life, Otto Nusbaum was the first Jewish child raised here. Otto married Bertha Weil in 1865 (left); by the time they had celebrated their golden wedding anniversary in 1915 (right), Otto had not only devoted many years to Jewish communal life, but had served five terms on the Columbus City Council and had been instrumental in developing a municipal street lighting system.

in 1880; its president, Otto Nusbaum, was a member and two-time former president of Zion Lodge. Lodge No. 150's special philanthropic project was Cleveland's Montefiore Home for Aged and Infirm Israelites. In 1880 the Standard Club, composed of thirty young Jewish men, elected twenty-year-old Willie Kleeman as president; the club modeled itself upon similar Standard Clubs in other cities which had been organized for social functions. Another try at a Young Men's Hebrew Association occurred in 1883, with seventeen charter members age thirteen to sixteen; like so many other young people's groups of the time it aborted.[8]

Throughout the 1880s additional societies emerged amidst Columbus Jewry: Various groups of Jews formed the Harmony Singing Club, composed of young Jewish men under the direction of a professor of music. The Ladies Coffee Klatch met monthly and raised funds for the poor. A variety of new social clubs was formed — including the Phoenix Club, a prestigious social group founded in 1890. A drama club, Hebrew Ladies Sewing Circle, and a Young People's Literary Association also began. The latter, started in 1886, sponsored musical evenings, dramatic readings, instrumental and vocal solos, and literary entertainments, some of which Columbusites patronized quite regularly.

In the mid-nineteenth century the organizations of Columbus Jewry served a regular diet of secular nourishment, occasionally uniting an activity with a Jewish festival. Unable or uninterested in finding social fulfillment elsewhere, German Jews formed exclusive clubs and fraternal lodges as they developed their social structure.[9] B'nai B'rith and the Order of Kesher shel Barzel utilized social occasions — Purim balls, picnics, concerts, and hops —

throughout the 1870s and 1880s to raise funds for their philanthropic projects in Cleveland and Columbus. Interest in these lodges declined with the new century, partially due to a lack of excitement over elaborate ritual, but largely because prominent Jews had no need for mutual aid features and left the lodges for the popular social clubs of the late Gilded Age.

As Columbus' German Jews entered the last two decades of the nineteenth century, they had become acculturated socially and religiously; economically they had adjusted quite comfortably to America. They had become, in short, a bourgeois and Americanized Jewish community.

NOTES FOR CHAPTER 5

TABLE 23
B'NAI B'RITH ZION LODGE NO. 62 PRESIDENTS

1865	Louis Kleeman
1866	Joseph Gundersheimer and Otto Nusbaum
1867	Leo Straus and William J. Goodman
1868	Louis Kahn and Henry Harmon
1869	Isaac Hoffman and Julius Adler
1870	Arnold Steinhauser and Isaac M. Schlesinger
1871	Simon Lazarus and Moses Kleeman
1872	Joseph Goodman and Leo Pfifferling
1873	Moses Adler and Isaac Roedelsheimer
1874	Joseph Philipson and Samuel Adler
1875	Otto Nusbaum and Myer Hecht
1876	Solomon Loeb and Abraham Strauss
1877	Bernhardt Holderman and Morris Mayer
1878	Louis Kleeman and Isaac Jashenosky
1879	Max Gumble and Aaron Wise
1880	August Fribourg and Charles Liebenthal

1. *Die Deborah* I, September 21, 1855; *AI*, September 21, 1855, August 13, October 29, 1858.

2. B'nai B'rith (B. B.) Minutes, August 20, 1865, at the Columbus Jewish Center. By this time there were about seventy-five lodges and seven thousand B'nai B'rith members throughout America. See Allan Tarshish, "The Rise of American Judaism," p. 202.

3. *Die Deborah* X, November 17, 1865; B. B. Minutes, October 16, 1865, June 12 and 26, 1887, December 9, 1888, March 16, 1890, November 29, 1898. The dues were $8 per year in 1866, $7 per year in 1873, and $25 annually in 1889.

4. B. B. Minutes, October 26, 1890.

5. B. B. Minutes, October 23, December 9, 1888, April 10, 1892. See especially the appeals of Bernhardt Holderman, August 17, October 26, November 9, 1890.

6. "The Work of this Lodge shall be carried on in the English language, but in debate those not well acquainted with this may use the German tongue"; B. B. Minutes, January 31, 1875.

7. *Masonic Directory* (Columbus, Ohio, 1875), [p. 4]; Harry Meyer, compiler and editor, *History of Humboldt Lodge, No. 476, F. & A. M. of Columbus, Ohio* [1873-1948], [Columbus, 1948]. German Jews also became active in the Odd Fellows, and several funerals were conducted under their auspices; see *OSJ*, February 2, 1880 (Emanuel Weis), and May 3, 1894 (Isaac Hoffman).

8. *AI*, March 12, 1875, December 10, 1880, November 2, 1883. Kesher shel Barzel, founded in 1860, held meetings rich in ceremony and biblical imagery; its last national convention occurred in 1890. B'nai Israel members, in 1892, reorganized the YMHA, together with a Ladies' Auxiliary, and had a very active schedule of parties, balls, and suppers during the early months of that year. It claimed to be "one of the largest associations of Hebrew young men in the history of Columbus"; *OSJ*, January 10, March 13 and 27, April 3, May 1, 1892.

9. *OSJ*, December 23, 1886, February 25, 1887; *AI*, January 28, March 4, 1887, December 19, 1889, February 20, March 13, April 17, 1890; B. B. Minutes, December 2, 1888. On the Phoenix Club during the 1890s, see *AI*, January 29, 1891, May 11, 1893, January 28, February 18, and November 4, 1897, as well as *OSJ*, May 1, 1892.

PART II

YEARS OF GROWTH

1881-1925

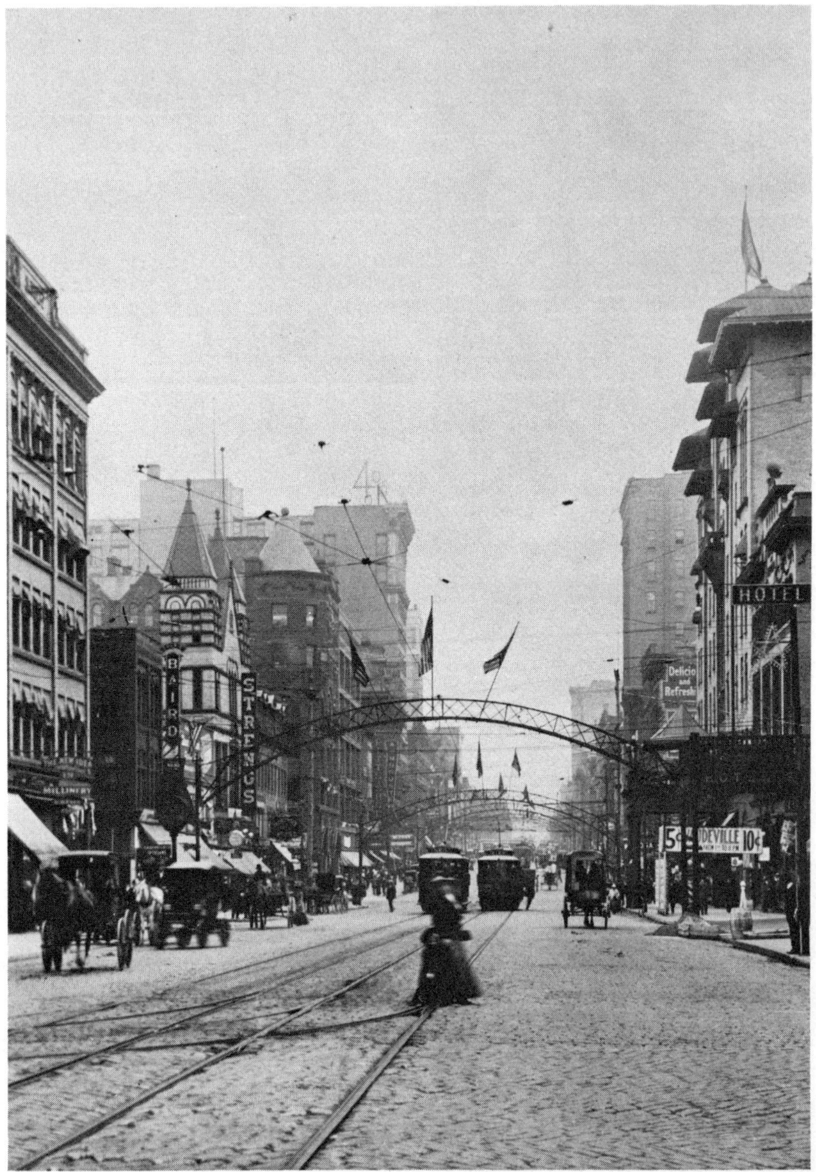

The center of the Columbus business community was on South High Street, where arches spanned an exceptionally wide thoroughfare in the early twentieth century.

Just after the turn of the century, a quarter would buy seven train rides on any of the nine interurban railways which entered Columbus daily, and a nickel would buy either a loaf of bread or a ride to almost any part of the city which was crisscrossed by 124 miles of street railway tracks. By 1910 the capital city's population was three times greater than it had been in 1880, when roughly fifty-one thousand people lived in Columbus. By 1925 the population was estimated to be over two hundred and fifty thousand.

Each sector of society expanded to meet the needs of a burgeoning populace. Within the slightly over twenty-square-mile city limits, forty-seven hotels, twenty-five banks, twelve hospitals, two universities, one medical college and four daily newspapers were established by 1912. Each day 163 passenger trains entered Columbus as well as 408 interurban, or electric, trains. As Ohio's canal system had at last abdicated in favor of the railroads, Columbus' manufacturing sector became increasingly dependent on them; by 1925 twenty-one railroads served the capital.

Before the turn of the century one of Columbus' chief industries was buggy making; more than twenty companies produced over twenty thousand buggies for a worldwide market in 1880. The buggy makers' prosperity declined as the auto industry developed; in 1900 the Columbus Motor Vehicle Company built the area's first experimental horseless carriage. Throughout the city over one thousand companies were manufacturing foundry and machine shop products, boots and shoes, carriages and wagons, malt liquors, cars, or medical compounds in 1912. Columbus' varied products found both national and international markets.

In 1880 General William T. Sherman proclaimed to the crowd assembled in Franklin Park that "war is hell." Columbus entrepreneurs, however, found that the military encampments resulting from war stimulated business. In September of 1888 Columbus hosted the mammoth National Encampment of the Grand Army of the Republic. Ten years later Camp Bushnell was established for Spanish-American War soldiers; this camp was a five-hundred-acre mobilization and training center at East Broad Street and Drexel Avenue in Bexley. Because of its central location, Columbus again became a mobilization and training center for the army during World War I when the state fairgrounds were commandeered and troops processed at Fort Hayes.

Before the turn of the century, arches were a familiar symbol in Columbus; in 1888 wooden gas lamps arched over High Street, illuminating it from sidewalk to sidewalk. Columbus was officially named the Arch City twenty-one years later. The long-familiar arch of Union Station appeared on High Street in 1898; the railroad station was built at a cost of $750,000. Columbus' civic resource development program was both interrupted and stimulated by the 1913 flood. Although the inundation caused $5.6 million damage, totally or partially destroyed over forty-four hundred buildings, and drowned over ninety persons, it led to a long-needed flood-control program.

The changes within the Jewish community were almost as great as in the city of Columbus. By 1912, the exclusively German Jewish community of 1880 found itself considerably outnumbered by newcomers. More than nineteen hundred east European Jews resided in Columbus; of these only one owned a city telephone, two had automobiles, and one had become famous: Hymie Levy undoubtedly thrilled his father Jacob and the entire immigrant community when he scored a touchdown in South High's fourteen to seven upset victory over North High in November. On the other side of the coin, eleven Jews occupied cells in the Franklin County Jail; thirty-five Italians, twenty-four Irish, and eighteen Germans shared the same quarters.[1]

A stable community in its early years, Columbus Jewry changed radically during the thirty-five years prior to World War I. By the 1920s, the future Jewish community of Columbus rested on very firm foundations, for the Jews of Columbus became an independent ethnic group with a distinct cultural and religious ambiance; they developed an identifiable social system, occupational structure, and Jewish neighborhood. Mass immigration had an impact on their organizations and synagogues, as did the movements and events engulfing Jews everywhere. We will look at each facet of immigrant life beginning with the causes of east European Jewish migration.

6. CHEAP TICKET, SAFE VOYAGE: EAST EUROPEAN JEWISH EMIGRATION [1]

The American press labeled September 9, 1881, when the first group of eighteen pogrom refugees arrived in New York, as the precise date when the mass migration of east European Jews began. Since the beginning of the twentieth century, scholars and lay people alike have almost universally recognized the sharp distinction between this east European period and the previous German period of American Jewish immigration. The two migrations, Jewish historians have agreed, differed from each other just as much in their motivation as in their composition. Scholars view the immigration from Germany as largely spontaneous and self-directed, while the east European movement was involuntary and the result of political and religious persecution.

The geographic origins of those immigrating to America shifted in the late nineteenth century. The five million immigrants who composed the pre-Civil War wave, and the ten million who arrived between 1860 and 1890, came predominately from the British Isles, Germany, Scandinavia, and western Europe. Between 1890 and 1924 fifteen million emigrated largely from Austria-Hungary, Italy, Russia, Greece, Rumania, and Turkey. More specifically, of the approximately six hundred and fifty thousand Europeans who arrived in the United States in the year after July 1, 1881, more than 80 percent emigrated from Germany, the British Isles, and Scandinavia; of the 1.2 million European immigrants of 1906-07, more than 80 percent came from southeastern and eastern Europe. Only scattered east European Jews arrived with the German Jewish immigrants, and only 1 percent of the "east European" immigrants consisted of German Jews. By 1906, when Jewish immigration to America peaked at more than one hundred and forty thousand, German Jews numbered less than 1 percent of the newcomers.

The east European Jews came from Russia, Poland, Lithuania, Rumania, Hungary, Galicia, and adjacent areas. Regardless of their homelands, the newcomers were collectively labeled "Russians" by Jews who had immigrated earlier; nevertheless, these new Jews felt a keen sense of pride about their unique origins. The city, country, or province where they had lived usually served as an organizing principle for their religious, social, and cultural lives; they stereotyped each other upon this basis. A Voliner *landsmanschaft* (a social, philanthropic organization) existed in Columbus early in the twentieth century; its members even looked down upon Jews from the same Russian province. Food preferences were clear indicators of places of origin: *borscht* for Russian Jews, *goulash* for Jews from Hungary, *ziys* (sweetened fish) for Polish Jews, and either *karnetzlach* (fried sausages) or *mameliga* (cornmeal bread) for Jews from Rumania.

Historically speaking, these distinctions were not quite so great as they appeared to individual immigrants. The enormous population explosion, the changing national boundaries of eastern Europe, the intermarriages, and the continual external migrations, all combined to so thoroughly mix these Jews that precise national origins are almost indistinguishable. As Salo Baron has repeatedly pointed out, although almost every Jewish immigrant after 1881 had pre-partition Poland ancestry only a century earlier, this common background did not stop these immigrants from asserting superiority over fellow Jewish immigrants from the same area.

Early in the 1880s the east European Jewish migration inundated approximately two hundred eighty thousand Jews already in the United States. By the outbreak of World War I, more than two million had found their way to America's shores. Early studies of this migration, heavily influenced by the Anglo-Jewish press and its descriptions of czarist horrors, attributed the exodus of Jews almost solely to political persecution. A United States government publication also echoed this theme, claiming that "in Galicia and Rumania, as in the case of Russia, an impelling force was persecution."

Marcus Lee Hansen noted that of all the historical interpretations, the political is the simplest; yet this explanation errs by both failing to differentiate Galician, Rumanian, and Russian contexts and by ignoring the larger historical environment of immigration. The new Jewish migration did not result solely from pogroms, although such atrocities accelerated the movement and frequently provided the last necessary prod toward emigration. Rather, the context of mass emigration from east Europe differs little from that of the earlier west European migration, and it too consists of diverse threads. The revolution in transportation, the constantly increasing population which could not be absorbed into productive sectors of the society, the economic aspirations of persons whose occupational advancement was limited, the search for political freedom or the desire to escape from persecution, and America's favorable image all provide the background of east European Jewish immigration to America.

The transition from sail to steam made mass migration to America possible. A safe, although still uncomfortable, journey could be virtually guaranteed; rare, indeed, were reports like that of Marah Boroitz who, upon arriving in Columbus, informed her husband that four of their five children died from diptheria and typhoid during the voyage from Poland.[2] Passage could be obtained quite easily from any place in Europe; the length of the journey was measured in days rather than months. In 1846 Rabbi Isaac Mayer Wise sailed from Bremen to New York in sixty-three days and Abraham Kohn, four years earlier, in sixty days; Jacob Davisky made the same trip, fifty years later, in nine days on a steamship. The European Jewish press proclaimed this transportation revolution with Yiddish advertisements like the following from *HaZefirah:*

North German Lloyd

Cheap, Rapid and Comfortable Steamship Accommodations

From Bremen to America

Steamships made possible an inexpensive, prepaid passage system, and hardly any Jewish settlement in America lacked an agent who would book passage for relatives and friends. The Hamburg-Amerika line alone had thirty-two hundred American agencies, and advertised in the Anglo-Jewish press from San Francisco to Philadelphia. The United States Immigration Commission noted that between 1908 and 1910, 58 percent of the "Hebrew" immigrants had prepaid tickets from relatives in the United States;[3] this compared with 30 percent of all immigrants. Abe Yenkin of Columbus remembers that "my mother's brother came here two years earlier than we did; he was a single person. He sent for my mother and father, my brother Ben, and myself; I mean he sent tickets so we could come over."[4]

Sara Reznikoff recalls that her neighbor in Elizavetgrad "was going to America. Her husband had been there nine months and sent her steamship tickets and money for herself and the children." On June 23, 1892, Coleman Tokerman (later Tuckerman) paid $75 in Columbus to transport his family from Europe to America. In his discerning autobiography, Marcus Ravage recalls "lengthy, affectionate communications to beloved uncles and very dear

This slip must be kept by the purchaser.

STEERAGE PREPAID RECEIPT.

N 58301

PURCHASER'S RECEIPT.

AMERICAN LINE.

PHILADELPHIA AND LIVERPOOL.

PETER WRIGHT & SONS, General Agents,
PHILADELPHIA—NEW YORK.

Agency .... 23 June 1892

Received of C. Tokerman

$75.00 ———— *for* **STEERAGE** *Passage*

of Rosa Tokerman & family

subject to the rules, regulations and conditions of the carriers over whose lines the passengers are forwarded,

from Hamburg to Philadelphia

A. C. I.

equal to 2, 2, — *Ocean Fares to Philadelphia,*

——— *Emigrant R. R. Fares to* ....

and $ ———— *cash to be paid passenger.*

The American Railroad portion of the passage is only good for ——— months.

ENGLISH.

It is expressly agreed by the purchaser that if upon arrival at the forwarding station it is found that the children are older than represented on the certificate, or should the passengers require more tickets than have been paid for, the passengers must pay for the additional tickets; if they cannot pay, and have neither means to enable them to wait for money nor return to their old home, the American Line is empowered to pay the passengers a sufficient amount to carry them back to their starting point, and deduct it from the amount paid for the ticket, which will then be considered cancelled.

Passengers should not leave home without sufficient money to pay board and lodging, baggage charges or other incidental expenses, if they should become necessary, and thus avoid trouble and delays, and the danger of being forced to return home.

The passage money, less the usual deduction, will be refunded *only upon return* of this receipt, the "Notice to Passengers," and all other papers connected with the passage, and after the passage has been stopped in Europe.

cousins and most precious nephews" from Rumanian Jews in the town of Vaslui. These letters urged those in America to "send us a ticket and a few dollars for our Yankel or Moishe, who is now a fine boy, and you ought to see him."

With the development of new transportation facilities and the simultaneous disappearance of official restraint, emigration to the United States was frequently stimulated by local conditions. The economic and social dislocations generated by the industrial revolution had the same expulsive effect, as they spread southward and eastward in the last decades of the nineteenth century, as in western Europe. The 1869 famine in the Suwalk area provided the initial catalyst for east European Jewish emigration, an exodus dominated by Lithuanian Jews. Nearly forty thousand Russian Jews arrived in America between 1871 and 1880; by 1881 Ukrainian and other Jews from the interior far outnumbered the impoverished Lithuanian emigrants.

The enormous growth of the Jewish population in modern times peaked during the years of east European mass immigration. Despite the movement of more than two million Jews from eastern Europe to America between 1881 and 1914 — and more than three hundred thousand others to additional lands — the Jewish populations actually increased in Austria-Hungary, Rumania, and Russia. In Moldovia, a northern province of Rumania, the Jewish population grew from twelve thousand in 1800 to two hundred thousand in the 1890s. In Russia the average annual rate of natural increase rose from 8.1 per thousand between 1841 and 1860 to 14.2 per thousand between 1871 and 1890. When the emigration wave crested between 1881 and 1897, the net population increase among Russian Jews totalled 22 percent. Overall, with a birth rate alone of 2 percent annually, the Jewish population of Russia tripled after 1847, swelling to over 5.2 million in 1897.

This population growth made absorption difficult. In some Galician districts, contemporaries reported, there was "one merchant to every eight or ten families, while in many villages of less than one hundred peasants there were generally six or seven Jewish traders trying to scratch a living out of the air." Census reports from the 1890s appraised the stock of the average Jewish shop in Galicia at about twenty dollars. In addition, nearly 80 percent of all the agricultural properties in the country included less than twelve and one-half acres and nearly half consisted of less than five acres.

Reflecting upon this situation, Galician immigrants noted that "emigration somewhere was almost inevitable," for little hope existed of earning a livelihood from debt-ridden and dislocated peasants. Looking back to better times, a Galician Jew named Furman remembered:

> My mother came from Galicia . . . where they had farmlands . . . one of the handful of Jewish farmers in Austria. They had lived there three or four hundred years and used to hire for the harvest; they'd hire people in to help with the harvesting, and the milking, and the storing up for the winter, and the picking of nuts.[5]

The desire to improve one's economic position was intimately connected with the growing overpopulation. The 1882 "Temporary Orders Concerning the Jews" (more popularly, the "May Laws") forced Russian Jews to move out of the villages of the Pale of Settlement and huddle even more closely together in incorporated cities and towns. By the late nineteenth century the Pale included Lithuania, White Russia, New Russia, and certain cities of the Ukraine — the fifteen western gubernias of European Russia and the ten gubernias of Congress Poland. From 1890 to 1892 tens of thousands of "privileged" Jews were forced into the overcrowded Pale by the czarist government which expelled them from the great cities of the Russian interior. A foreign correspondent claimed that as many as twenty thousand Jews poured into Berdichev, the chief town of the province of Kiev, during 1891-92, and despaired of finding shelter. Other cities were no better: Lodz had eleven Jews in 1793 and only 2,775 in 1856, but there were 98,677 in 1897 and 166,628 in 1910. Warsaw, with 3,532 Jews in 1781, grew to 127,917 in 1882 and 219,141 in 1897. The number of city dwellers in the empire nearly doubled between 1863 and 1897; the Jews, 4 to 5 percent of the total population of the empire, represented almost 60 percent of the urban population in Vilna, Kovno, Vitebsk, Grodno, and Minsk, the northwest provinces of the Pale. By 1897, 4.9 million or 95 percent of all Jews in the Russian Empire lived in a *gorod* (city) or *mestechko* (town) of the Pale; in these densely populated communities the competition, the overcrowding and squalor, and the absence of ways and means to earn a livelihood prodded many to migrate.

The "swarming throngs of unwashed, unkempt wretches packed into the narrow thoroughfares on the look-out for food" appear far more frequently in immigrant memoirs than do memories of pogroms and pillaging. One Russian Jewish immigrant to Columbus explained that

> my father didn't leave Russia like, you know, running away from the military, which was usual, or getting involved in some kind of trouble, or what have you. It was another reason. Not for any political reasons . . . it was economic and it was the trend of the time. The Jewish people were just going away to America . . .[6]

The press echoed these words of Harry Schwartz:

Eastern Europe in the Late Nineteenth Century

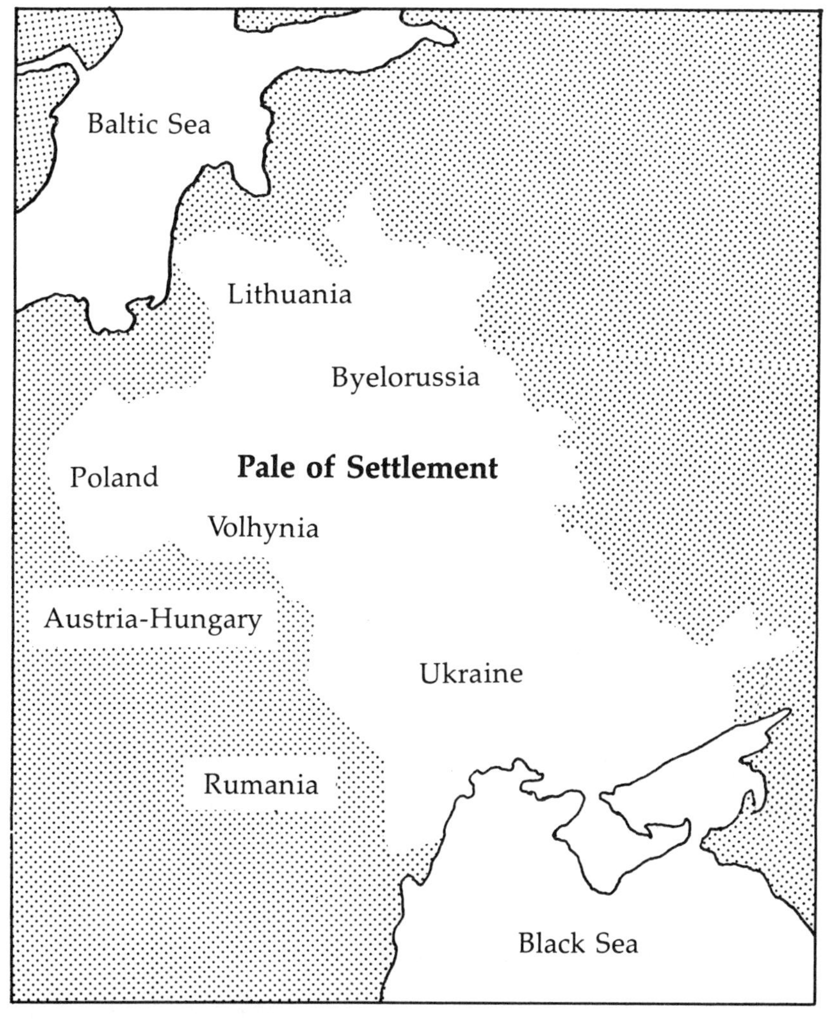

> from our entire region of Bychow, Minsk, a great emigration again commenced. Old and young, healthy and weak, all going to New York, to Galveston, etc., and here only depleted towns remain.
>
> The causes of this emigration are almost entirely economic. Before shoemakers made a good living. Today, the shoe machine occupies his place, and the shoemaker is forced to leave here. Before tailors are working and the competition is forcing out, understandably, the Jewish tailor. The same is the case with the small trader . . . as a result of this exodus our dark, muddy region is becoming poorer and poorer.[7]

Immigrants also recalled many academic and occupational restrictions upon their lives in the Pale. The czars prohibited Jews from engaging in a long list of trades and professions — exclusion from government service was particularly onerous — while the virtual impossibility of buying or renting farms or living in villages almost completely closed agriculture to Jews. When the liquor traffic in Russia became a government monopoly in 1897, thousands of Jewish innkeepers and restauranteurs lost their jobs as well. Additionally, the czars established quotas for students: no more than 10 percent of the total student body in high schools and universities within the Pale, 5 percent outside the Pale, and 3 percent in the technical and professional schools of Moscow and St. Petersburg. In 1881, in contrast, before these *numerus clausus* took effect, and at a time when the great mass of Jews did not yet speak Russian, eighty-two hundred Jewish boys accounted for 12 percent of all the students in the gymnasiums and progymnasiums. One immigrant, denied entrance to high school for three consecutive years, recalled his thoughts after the final rejection: "There must be some place where there are no quotas. There must be some place where I can be accepted as a man, without questions about religion being spit into my face." And for him such a place existed: "there was America."

Whether in Russia or Galicia, Rumanian or Polish territory, poverty characterized most east European Jewish communities and almost all Jewish emigrants. Although it is surely an exaggeration to claim that Russian Jewry underwent, after 1881, the "most rapid process of proletarization . . . ever known in the history of the modern world," this community was certainly in economic straits. Despite the census label "skilled labor," petty handicraft and petty commerce remained the primary occupational choices open to the Jews. In Odessa at the end of the nineteenth century, community charity supported 48,500 of 150,000 Jews and paid for 63 percent of the pauper burials. The Palen Commission, established by the czarist government to examine the legislation governing Jewish life, reported in 1888 that "about 90 percent of the whole Jewish population . . . came near being a proletariat." Pauperization, estimated by the number of families that sought public assistance at Passover, increased rapidly; by the late 1890s about 20 percent of the Jewish population in twelve hundred localities were paupers. Economic strangulation led to desperate measures; emigration on a grand scale became a permanent feature of life.

Galician poverty was even worse. Only a fraction of Galician Jews had any economic security; the rest lived as *luftmenschen* or on petty trade, pawnbroking, "casual" occupations, and primitive crafts. A growing nationalism, following in the wake of Galicia's administration becoming wholly Polish after 1866, eliminated Jews from their jobs and produced a boycott against Jewish merchants. Jewish traders, already living at the expense of a people nearly as poor as themselves, competed with cheap factory products which flooded the eastern provinces of the empire; the completion of a vast net of railways destroyed Jewish teamsters and truckers; Christians replaced Jewish restaurant keepers and salt and tobacco merchants in the Galician provinces, and the state eliminated Jewish purveying of beverages, a function landowners had granted to the Jews. While comprising only 11 percent of the population, Jews accounted for 52 percent of the "independents of no vocation" in the 1897 census. As one reporter from Taronbrzeg, a judiciary district of Galicia, described in *Die Welt:*

> Industries and factories are not to be found in the district . . . Jews suffer boundless misery. Chicory with milk for breakfast; potato soup for dinner; potatoes and buttermilk for supper . . . no Jewish worker eats meat during the working days of the week . . . average income is one florin per week . . . the children walk about barefooted and almost naked, and in the muddy streets. Absolute beggary is constant here. Every Friday some eighty families beg for the means to fix a Sabbath meal . . . no surprise that there is a strong emigration movement of Taronbrzeg Jews to America. Almost every Jewish family in Taronbrzeg had a relative in America, and the majority of the emigrated support those of their family who stay at home.[8]

The intensity of the economic crisis, especially in Galicia, is underscored by the fact that from 1890 to 1914 over three hundred thousand Jews came to the United States from Austria-Hungary, although there were no pogroms and an abundance of civil and religious freedom. As petty merchants par excellence, Jews reacted especially sensitively and swiftly to economic developments; many non-Jews too felt the same pressures and left. The ratio of Jewish immigration to general immigration from eastern Europe fell during this period.

The search for political freedom was usually linked with the drive for economic mobility. The urge to throw off political restraints and to escape discrimination was widespread; at times it was prompted by the desire to escape from something, while at other times by a wish to reach a land of freedom. The great immigration historian, Marcus Lee Hansen, once warned against assuming that the reason an immigrant gave for leaving home upon arrival in America was the real incentive for leaving. Too often the immigrant merely glorified American democracy more for his listeners' benefit than as a conscious reason for emigration; it was more pleasant to tell and more pleasant to hear about political freedom than the difficulties of supporting a family in Europe. Also, economic complaints might cause immigrant agents to question the newcomer's fitness.

Nevertheless, almost every immigrant source preserved a memory of political and religious discrimination. Many recalled the expulsions from Moscow, St. Petersburg, and Kiev in 1891-92, the onerous May Laws of 1882, and other instances of persecution throughout east European lands. But most vivid memories of all are of the government supported pogroms. These beatings, lootings, burnings, and mutilations of Russian Jews reached their peak in 1881-82, 1891, 1899, 1903 (Kishinev), and 1905. One contemporary described a pogrom in Libedski graphically:

> Feathers and leaves of books filled the air; porches and balconies fell with explosive roaring; on every side were mangled babes, mutilated old Jewish women, aged Jews with crushed limbs and fractured skulls, lacerated girls fighting for their honor. Here and there fashionably dressed Christian women bent down to pick up a piece of precious jewelry or a trinket which the rioters had dropped in their wild excitement . . . I muttered to myself as the violators began to tear the scrolls of the *Torah* in strips and trample the parchment under foot.[9]

The pogromists attacked in more than two hundred places in 1881; damage to twenty thousand Jewish homes and stores reached $80 million while the attackers impaired the livelihoods of perhaps one hundred thousand Jews. The Kishinev pogroms resulted in 447 persons killed or injured and property damage of 2.5 million rubles. As a result of such final catalysts, many Jews consciously chose America. Elizabeth Hasanovitz succinctly noted: "I am tired of being condemned to eternal violence. I want to be free. I shall go to America."

And yet, notwithstanding the pogroms, potential immigrants often took the time to make inquiries of Jewish institutions and individuals in America before final departure. In 1905 I. Papish of Loobetoff, Minsk, wrote to the Industrial Removal Office (IRO) in New York inquiring about the employment situation in America. He explained that he was "an authorized religious functionary from the greatest geniuses; a splendid ritual slaughterer, a wonderful circumciser, and a magnetic and great preacher." In addition, Papish could "do everything" and "loved the big city," while being especially fond of the "small town." More realistic and common than Papish's correspondence was the letter Moshe Tzelnick sent to the IRO in 1913. As a liquor distiller faced with poor business in Russia, Moshe was contemplating emigration. In order to determine whether or not he could pursue his profession in the United States, he wanted to know: 1) do Americans drink much liquor; 2) are there many liquor distillers in America; 3) how much are licenses; 4) does one need to advertise for such a position?[10]

Pogroms alone, however, appear to have driven few away. Galician Jewry, emancipated in 1867 and unaffected by pogroms or the Pale of Settlement, provided a higher proportion of immigrants to America than any other Jewish group in Europe. Twice as many Jews left Galicia in the 1890s as in the late 1880s, although measurable anti-Semitism grew no more intense. The May Laws and the pogroms unquestionably aggravated Russian Jewry's economic and social situation, and induced a substantial number of more well-to-do Jews to leave that country. If extant letters, interviews, and memoirs are studied, however, these factors were not the chief stimuli.

Rumanian Jewish memoirs, no less than Galician and Russian, reflect a combination of factors propelling emigration. Despite the guarantees of the Paris Convention of 1856 and the Berlin Treaty of 1878, between 1878 and 1903 Rumania granted citizenship to only 200 Jews. While the government treated Jews as "foreigners" in terms of rights, Jews were considered "natives" in terms of duties such as serving in the military and paying taxes. Neither a successful military career nor a father born in Rumania would win citizenship for a Jew. Later a series of regulations against foreigners stripped Jews of the few rights they had.

The economic conditions under which Rumanian Jews eked out their livelihoods also proved restrictive: the government prohibited foreigners from selling liquor in 1873, excluded Jews from the tobacco trade in 1872 and 1879, prohibited foreigners from acting as money brokers or commission merchants in 1881, forbid itinerant trading and hawking in urban districts in 1884, proclaimed in 1887 that "in five years' time from the opening of a factory, two-thirds of the employees must be Rumanians," and forbid foreigners from entering the professions of advocate, physician, chemist, and pharmacist in 1893. The Artisans Bill of 1902 sealed the fate of the Jewish artisan class by making the practice of a trade dependent upon proving that in the respective "countries of foreigners" reciprocal rights were accorded to

Rumanians. These decrees fell especially harshly upon the Jews, since Rumania exempted only 1.6 percent of the 266,000 Jews in the 1899 census from the category of "foreigners," and Jews possessed no country of their own. Excluded from more than two hundred occupations, the government placed severe economic pressure upon the Jews of Rumania.

Pogroms were also a constant feature of Jewish life in Rumania: in 1866 immediately after the accession of Prince Charles of Hohenzollern at Bucharest, in 1867 at Jassy and Galatz where eighteen Jews were drowned in the Danube, in 1869 at Botoshian, in 1872 at Ismail, and continuously through the century, the populace attacked and pillaged Jewish homes, stores, and synagogues. In 1897 police protection accompanied a large pogrom in Bucharest, while in 1899 a pogrom originated in Jassy under the direction of the Anti-Semitic Alliance and spread throughout much of the two provinces.

Rumanian Jewish immigrants to the United States tend to recall both economic limitations and physical attacks. Nevertheless, there is no attempt here to exhaust "causes" by isolating a number of external factors; the conscious motives of individuals may be very different from observed and measurable causation within a society. From the vantage point of the country of origin, the pressures of deprivation appear to be the most potent expulsive force accounting for mass population movements; while from the vantage point of the host country, the pressures of opportunity appear to be potent, attractive forces that account for mass population movements. The images in their minds and the persons with whom they peopled their worlds appear often more real and more crucial than the view which any statistical analysis can provide: "They wanted to come to the golden land. You know, they thought they could take money from the trees." So the image of America strongly influenced the image of eastern Europe; the "motives" of the immigrants came from the interaction of both images.

Such a reciprocal influence is abundantly illustrated in emigrant letters, published regularly in such places as the Hebrew journal *Hamagid.* As the earliest members of the mass emigration settled in America, letters from them began to pour into Europe with favorable, usually exaggerated, accounts of life in the New World: "all talked of it, but scarcely anybody knew one true fact about this magic land." Mary Antin reminisced about her youth in Polotsk, Russia, "America was in everybody's mouth." Another immigrant Jewess noted that "not even the Marco Polos with all their great wealth on their return from China . . . could cause the sensation that a 'letter from America' did." One Columbus Jewish immigrant from Russia recalls his father receiving letters which "told him this is a wonderful country . . . you can work on the outside, you can become a food peddler and you'll be in the outdoors all the time."[11] Emigrants who returned to their old homes occasioned ever more excitement, particularly when they kept their visit short. As Marcus Ravage's father described the return of a cousin to Vaslui in Rumania:

> I never saw so many trunks and bags in all my life as they unloaded for him. And jewelry! He had diamonds in his cravat and brilliants on his fingers . . . and a great locket stuck full of more diamonds. He is a millionaire, if ever there was one in America.[12]

Along with the letters came equally exaggerated promotional pamphlets; the Hebrew press in eastern Europe widely publicized both. One journal printed a promise from a Jewish publishing company in San Francisco that "east European Jews who come to California as workers in the forests are offered the best of everything materially and even the opportunity of building a new temple like that which Solomon built in Jerusalem." Another report in the same Hebrew newspaper, *HaYom*, told of a New York conference of Jews from all over America which considered building a "Hebrew University in America dedicated to Jewish culture." Some American Jewish agencies were particularly active in recruiting European Jews. The Anglo-Jewish press took pride in describing the "success" of "energetic agents" of the Jewish Colonization Association in their imaginative "promise of America" broadsides. One such pamphlet, distributed widely in Rumania in 1907, promised "free education, the separation of church and state, democratic elections, Jewish politicians and a haven from persecution."

An immigrant journalist, Peter Wiernik, wrote home of a "fine group of people, sometimes a hundred in number, who meet in Chicago regularly every Sunday to read Hebrew books and to discuss Jewish literature and problems," while Joseph Morrison wrote from New York's Lower East Side of "stores which bear signs of merchandise in Jewish letters and many book shops; in general the life is carried on here as in the cities of Lithuania and Poland." A study of two Russian-Hebrew periodicals for the years 1883 and 1884 found, on the one hand, no incidents of anti-Semitism reported from America, and, on the other, numerous articles describing American politicians' support for American and world Jewry. Potential immigrants found little in any written sources to deter them from crossing the sea, but much information available about their country of destination.

The pressure of mounting population and contracting opportunities as the economy failed to keep pace with the five-fold increase of east European Jewry in the nineteenth century, repressive legislation and physical attacks, and fully developed modes of transport provide the primary context for this Jewish emigration wave. But no less important was the reciprocal development of passive east European governmental responses to the emigration and open entry at Ellis Island upon arrival in the United States. European governments rarely attempted to prevent the emigration and the United States government permitted virtually unrestricted immigration. The federal government barred convicts, lunatics, and idiots in 1882 and contract laborers as well in 1885; but not until 1917 did Congress require immigrants over sixteen years of age to read a paragraph in the language of their choice. This legislation affected Jews little, as overwhelming numbers were literate, and by this time the mass migration had begun to abate. When Congress virtually stopped immigration in 1920, 1924 and 1927 with the Johnson Act, the Jewish wave had long since crested.

This east European Jewish immigration to America had a number of significant features during the fifteen years before the First World War:[13] More than ninety thousand Jews entered the United States annually. The Jews constituted 9.5 percent of the United States immigrants, an increase of 5.5 percent from 1881 to 1890. Only 1.5 percent of the Jews returned home; for while 30 percent of the total immigration to the United States in these years returned to their country of origin, 95 percent of the Jewish immigrants stayed. Between 1908 and 1914 when 44 percent of the southern Italian, 58 percent of the Hungarian, and even 29 percent of the Polish entrants returned to Europe, only 7 percent or 53,150 Jews left the United States. Few places seemed as attractive, no matter one's circumstances, as America.

Even though Jews constituted a small percentage of the total immigrants to America, federal immigration authorities turned away tens of thousands. Jews who landed in ports other than New York stood a better chance of passing the authorities; Galveston was reputed to be the easiest port to enter. Occasionally those turned away at New York were rejected because of criminal convictions or "immoral purposes" while authorities rejected 20 to 25 percent because of diseases, and 75 to 80 percent because of the likelihood that they would become dependent on the government. In one case on June 28, 1909, the Immigration Board excluded seventeen able-bodied Jewish men, ages eighteen to fifty, because of "insufficient money." Despite the appearance of relatives brought by the Ellis Island Commission of the Hebrew Sheltering and Immigrant Aid Society, and the guarantee of support, the United States government deported all seventeen because they might become public charges.

Between 1899 and 1914 two of every three of the Jewish immigrants to America possessed manufacturing or mechanical skills, a figure three times that for all other immigrants. This was certainly not the case during the 1880s and 1890s, but eastern Europe had become widely industrialized by the beginning of the twentieth century. Sixty percent of these skilled workers, or 40 percent of all Jews with occupations, labored as dressmakers, seamstresses, tailors, furriers, hatmakers and shoemakers; their value for the United States' economy and the source of their expected incomes consisted of these skills and their ability to employ them gainfully. Jews provided the bulk of the immigrants occupied in the paper trades, graphic arts industries, jewelry, and building trades as well, while they were almost nonexistent in general labor, domestic service, and agriculture. The 1897 Russian census confirms what the immigration authorities on American soil recorded: 75 percent of all artisans in the Pale were Jews and the manufacturing or "commerce" sector included 70 percent of all Jews, compared with 10 percent of all Russians. Agriculture, the most common Russian occupation, accounted for only 3 percent of these Jews.

Within the east European Jewish family, the husband usually emigrated first. Parents or matchmakers, especially in Poland and Russia, arranged marriages for young adults at an early age. After arrival in America, the young husband found a job, saved money to pay back what he had borrowed for passage, and then sent a ticket home for his wife, or for a girl selected for him by someone in his former home. Scores of Jewish immigrants to Columbus followed this pattern; they included Simon Josephson, who brought his family to join him three years after his arrival in Columbus in 1885; Nathan Kohn, who arrived here in 1902 and sent for his family in 1905; Abraham Mellman, who preceded his family's arrival in 1910 by three years; and Samuel Pass, who peddled from 1907 to 1913 in Columbus before he could send for his family.[14] The years east European men spent in America without their wives and children acquainted them with Columbus life, and prepared them to introduce their dependents to the ways of the city and the language of the land.

NOTES FOR PART II

1. Department of Commerce, Bureau of the Census. *13th Census of the United States Taken in the Year 1910*. Volume I. Population 1910 (Washington, 1913), p. 854; *Annual Statistical Report of the Secretary of State to the Governor . . . For the Year Ending November 15, 1912* (Springfield, Ohio, 1913), p. 168; *Columbus City Directory* 1912-13 lists residential and business telephones, while the *Columbus Sunday Dispatch, Centennial Library Edition,* August 26, 1912, pp. 115 ff. lists all automobile owners in the city; *Ohio State Journal,* November 3, 1912, and South High School, Roll 40, Graduates and Non-graduates 1900-1925, Abbott-Slavin (microfilm, Board of Education, Pupil Personnel).

CHAPTER 6

1. This chapter is based upon the following types of sources:

BOOKS

Patrick Alston, *Education and the State in Tsarist Russia* (Stanford, 1969); Mary Antin, *The Promised Land* (Boston, 1911, 1969); Sholem Asch, *The Mother* (New York, 1937); Emily Balch, *Our Slavic Fellow Citizens* (New York, 1910; Salo Baron, *The Russian Jew Under Tsars and Soviets* (New York, 1964); Michael Davitt, *Within the Pale: The True Story of Anti-Semitic Persecution in Russia* (Philadelphia, 1903); Michael Florinsky, *Russia: A Short History,* 2nd edition (London, 1969); Harold Frederick, *The New Exodus: A Study of Israel in Russia* (New York, 1892); Moritz Friedlander, *Funf Wochen in Brody: Ein Beitrag zur Geshichte der russischen Judenverfolgung* (Vienna, 1882); Irving Fineman, *Hear Ye Sons* (New York, 1933, 1939); Louis Greenberg, *The Jews in Russia,* Volume I (New Haven, 1944), Volume II (1951); Israel Friedlander, *Jews of Russia and Poland* (New York, 1920); Oscar Handlin, *Adventure in Freedom: 300 Years of Jewish Life in America* (New York, 1954); idem, *A Century of Jewish Immigration to the United States* (New York, 1949); Marcus Hansen, *The Immigrant in American History* (New York, 1940, 1964); Sidney Harcave, *Russia: A History,* 6th edition (New York, 1968); Edmund James, ed., *The Immigrant Jew in America* (New York, 1907); Joseph Kissman, *Studies in the History of Rumanian Jews in the Nineteenth and Early Twentieth Centuries* (Yiddish, New York, 1944); Bernard Lazare, *Les Juifs en Roumanie* (Paris, 190?); Jean Lahovary, *The Jewish Question in Roumania* (London, n.d.); A[rthur] Ruppin, *The Jews of Today* (New York, 1913); Solomon Schwarz, *The Jews in the Soviet Union* (Syracuse, 1951); C. B. Sherman, *Jews and Other Ethnic Groups in the United States* (Yiddish, New York, 1948); Edward Steiner, *The Immigrant Tide: Its Ebb and Flow* (New York, 1909); Henry Tobias, *The Jewish Bund in Russia* (Palo Alto, 1972); Michael Traub, *Judische Wanderbewegungen vor und nach dem Weltkriege* (Berlin, 1930); Mark Wischnitzer, *To Dwell in Safety: the Story of Jewish Migrations since 1800*

(Philadelphia, 1948); *Recueil de Materinaux sur la Situation Economique des Israélites de Russie* (Paris, 1904-1906).

ARTICLES

Salo Baron, "United States, 1880-1914" in *Steeled by Adversity: Essays and Addresses on American Jewish Life* (Philadelphia, 1971), pp. 269-414; R. A. Easterlin, "Influences in European Overseas Emigration Before World War I" in *Economic Development and Cultural Change* (April 1961): 331-51; Marc Fried, "Deprivation and Migration: Dilemmas of Causal Interpretation" in Daniel Moynihan, ed., *On Understanding Poverty* (New York, 1968), pp. 111-59; Moses Gaster, "The Jews in Roumania" in *North America Review* 175 (1902): 664-75; Joel Geffen, "America in the First European Hebrew Daily Newspaper: *HaYom* (1886-1888)" in *American Jewish Historical Quarterly* LI:3 (March 1962): 154-74; Liebmann Hirsch, "International Migrations of the Jews" in Walter Willcox, ed., *International Migrations,* Volume II (New York, 1931), pp. 471-520; Samuel Joseph, "Jewish Immigration to the United States, 1881-1910" in *Studies in History, Economics and Public Law* LIX:4 (Columbia University, 1914), pp. 417-625; Joseph Kissman, "Jewish Emigration from Rumania up to World War I" (Yiddish) in *YIVO Bleter* XIX:2 (March-April 1942): 157-91; Raphael Mahler, "Jewish Emigration from Galicia and Its Causes" (Yiddish) in E. Tcherikower, ed., *History of the Jewish Labor Movement in the United States,* Volume I, (Yiddish) (New York, 1943), pp. 113-27; Jacob Lestchinsky, "The Jews in the Polish Cities, 1921-1931" (Yiddish) *YIVO Bleter* XXI:I (January-June): 20-46; George Price, "The Russian Jew in America" in *PAJHS* 48 (1958): 78-133; Sanford Ragins, "The Image of America in Two East European Hebrew Periodicals" in *American Jewish Archives (AJA)* XVII:2 (November 1965): 143-61; E. Schwarzfeld, "The Situation of the Jews in Roumania Since the Treaty of Berlin (1878)" in *AJYB* 5662 (1901-1902), pp. 63-86; E. Schwarzfeld, "The Jews of Roumania: From the Earliest Times to the Present Day" in *AJYB* 5662 (1901-1902), pp. 25-62; Zosa Szajkowski, "How the Mass Migration to America Began" in *Jewish Social Studies* IV (1942): 291-310; idem, "Jewish Emigration Policy in the Period of the Rumanian 'Exodus,' 1899-1903" in *JSS* XIII (1951): 47-70; Bernard Weinryb, "Eastern European Immigration to the United States" in *Jewish Quarterly Review* XLV:4 (April 1955): 497-528; Jeffrey G. Williamson, "Migration to the New World: Long Term Influences and Impact" in *Explorations in Economic History,* 2nd series, Volume II (Summer 1974): 357-89; "From Kishineff to Bialystok" in *AJYB* 5667 (1906-1907), Philadelphia, 1906, pp. 34-89.

MEMOIRS

Mary Antin, *From Polotzk to Boston* (Boston, 1899); Boris Bogen, *Born a Jew* (New York, 1930); Ezra Brundno, *The Fugitive: Being Memoirs of a Wanderer in Search of a Home* (New York, 1904); Samuel Chotzinoff, *A Lost Paradise: Early Reminiscences* (New York, 1955); Morris Cohen, *A Dreamer's Journey* (Boston, 1949); Rose Cohen, *Out of the Shadow* (New York, 1918); S.

Cohen, *Transplanted* (New York, 1937); Philip Cowen, *Memories of an American Jew* (New York, 1932); Melech Epstein, *Pages From a Colorful Life* (Miami Beach, 1971); Joseph Gollomb, *Unquiet* (New York, 1935); Elizabeth Hasanovitz, *One of Them: Chapters from a Passionate Autobiography* (Boston, 1918); Bernard Horwich, *My First Eighty Years* (Chicago, 1939); Rebekah Kohut, *My Portion: An Autobiography* (New York, 1927); Benjamin Laikin, *Memoirs of a Practical Dreamer: From a Russian Shtetl to an American Suburb* (translated from the Yiddish, New York, 1971); H. Masliansky, *Fertig Yor Lebn un Kempfn* (Yiddish) (New York, 1924); Sidney Meller, *Roots in the Sky* (New York, 1958); M[arcus] Ravage, *An American in the Making: The Life Story of an Immigrant* (New York, 1917, 1971); Nathan Reznikoff, "Early History of a Sewing-Machine Operator" in Charles Reznikoff, *Family Chronicle* (New York, 1936), pp. 101-98; Sarah Reznikoff, "Early History of a Seamstress" in ibid., pp. 7-99; Bella Rosenbaum,,"In My Lifetime" in *AJA* XIX:1 (April 1967): 3-33; Nathan Platnick, "From Kielem to Bluefield" in *AJA* XXI:1 (April 1969): 48-56; Louis Singer, "Now an American: The Autobiography of Louis Singer" in *AJA* XXII:1 (April, 1970): 3-14; Goldie Stone, *My Caravan of Years: An Autobiography* (New York, 1946); [Sarah Thal], "Early Days: The Story of Sarah Thal, Wife of a Pioneer Farmer of Nelson County, North Dakota" in *AJA* XXIII:1 (April 1971): 46-62; Max Vanger, "Memoirs of a Russian Immigrant," in *AJHQ* 63:1 (September 1973): 57-88; Isaac Mayer Wise, *Reminiscences* Cincinnati, 1901; Miriam Zunser, *Yesterday* (New York, 1939).

2. *OSJ*, November 9, 1903.

3. Reports of the Immigration Commission, III, Statistical Review of Immigration 1820-1910, Distribution of Immigrants 1850-1960, 61st Congress, 3rd Session, Senate Document No. 756, Washington, D.C. (1911), Table 39.

4. Interview with Abe Yenkin.

5. On the role of agriculture in the lives of several Columbus Jewish families while in the old country, see interviews with Abe Yenkin, Edward Schlezinger, Jacob Pass, Eleanor Yenkin, and Sylvia Schecter.

6. Interview with Harry Schwartz.

7. *Der Yiddisher Emigrant*, IV:5 (1910), pp. 11-12.

8. "Zur Lage der Jude in Galizien," in *Die Welt*, January 1900, pp. 3-4.

9. Ezra Brundo, *The Fugitive* (New York, 1904), p. 254.

10. The excerpts from the letters come from Letters of Personal Request from Immigrants 1906-1922, located in the Papers of the Industrial Removal Office, Box 105, American Jewish Historical Society, Waltham, Massachusetts.

11. Interview with Harry Schwartz.

12. M. Ravage, op. cit., p. 9.

13. To be precise, the data available for the years 1899-1914 are for all Jewish immigrants. As immigration historians have done for two generations, these data are being used to represent the immigration of Jews from czarist Russia.

14. Interviews with Bertha Josephson Seff, A. S. Kohn, Robert Mellman, and Jacob Pass.

7. COLUMBUS' EAST EUROPEAN JEWISH NEIGHBORHOOD IN 1912

"Stores and shops bear signs in Yiddish and all sorts of goods are being offered for sale, from prayer books to suits." This was the way the *Columbus Citizen* described the Jewish neighborhood as early as September 1904. By 1910 Columbus Jews lived in a highly visible neighborhood, but this territory was far from the more homogeneous ghettos that housed immigrant Jews in New York, Philadelphia, and Chicago. Even on the most Jewish streets in the heart of their neighborhood, Jews were often a small minority among other ethnic minorities.

Columbus' population reached 181,511 by 1910, a staggering 46 percent increase over 1900. The total foreign-born white population was 16,285, or 9 percent of the city. This proportion of foreign-born residents was only one-half that of 1880, despite the enormous east and southeast European immigration to the United States in the intervening years. Thus Columbus had a much larger proportion of native-born residents than most United States cities of 100,000. German immigrants continued to be predominant, but almost 10 percent of the immigrants in Columbus consisted of Russians (i.e., Jews), while there were almost one thousand Hungarians and, perhaps, as many "poles." The east European Jewish population consisted of almost two thousand persons in 1910, little more than 1 percent of the city's population.[1]

Such raw 1910 census data and similar information for 1920 reveal these facts about the residential patterns of Columbus immigrants:

First, the number of foreign-born remained small throughout the decade; the percentage of those born outside of the United States did not exceed 10 percent in either 1910 or 1920.

Second, the total number of east European Jews remained small; as late as 1920, Russian, Polish, Lithuanian, and

TABLE 24
COLUMBUS' MOST NUMEROUS
NATIONALITIES IN 1910

Nationality	Persons	Approximate percentage of foreign-born population
German	5,722*	35%
Irish	1,809	11
Italian	1,619	10
Russian	1,528*	9
English	1,127	7
Hungarian	970	6
Austrian	818*	5
Canadian	696	4
Welsh	534	3
Swiss	339	2

*These groupings include "Poles."

SOURCE: Department of Commerce, Bureau of the Census. *Thirteenth Census of the United States taken in the year 1910. Population* I, p. 854.

Rumanian-born Jews numbered less than twenty five hundred, just over 1 percent of the Columbus population.

Third, many nationalities were residentially segregated from each other. In 1920 the three most populous Italian wards housed 1,118 Italian-born persons and 69 Russians, while in the two most populous Russian wards, 1,197 Russians lived with only 68 Italians.

Fourth, the degree of residential segregation per se measured very low for all the immigrants. While Wards 3 and 4 had the largest concentrations of Russian immigrants in 1920, these numbers (640 and 557 respectively) constituted less than 5 percent of each ward's population. Like most other cities, only a handful of Columbus streets had a 50 percent or higher concentration of Italian or Jewish immigrants. The population density of Jews and Italians in the immigrant sections of Columbus fell well below 40 percent.

Finally, while "new" immigrants often lived isolated from each other, and no single nationality delineated a ward, Jews, Italians, Germans, and Hungarians clustered relatively tightly. In 1920, 65 percent of the Russians in Columbus lived in two wards; more than a third of the Italians dwelt in Wards 12 and 13; while more than half the Hungarians resided in Ward 1. Although there were no Jewish or Italian wards, clearly defined ethnic and nationality subregions of the community may be easily noted.[2]

While residential patterns both maximized and minimized

TABLE 25
RESIDENTS ON ONE BLOCK OF SOUTH WASHINGTON AVENUE IN 1912

492	A. F. Scholl	518	H. Izenmann*
496	Wolf Cohen*	520	Joseph Wasserman*
500	Simon Silverman*	522	Louis Lakin*
502	Harold E. Wolf*	524	Samuel Brody*
508	Israel Levy*	528	H. J. Lichtner
510	C. L. Baker	532	August Keichley
512	Morris Bloom*	540	Jacob Bernstein*
514	Solomon Uretzky*	542	C. M. Rosenthal*
516	Simon Holland*		

*Jewish residents

SOURCE: *Columbus City Directory*, 1912.

contacts among many groups, Columbus' Italian, Jewish, and Hungarian neighborhoods were clearly visible. Although they represented only minor portions of their respective wards, ethnic neighborhoods were easily identifiable and therefore labeled because more persons of one group resided there than did anyone else except native whites. Indeed, some streets became virtual enclaves of one ethnic group, as demonstrated by Tables 25 and 26.

Despite such ethnic districts, and the distance between ethnic minorities, groups could not avoid contact with each other. The 557 Russians of Ward 3, almost a third of Columbus' Russians, shared an area of only about two square miles with 103 Swiss, 112 Austrians, 1,147 Germans, 696 Negroes, and 13,475 native-born whites. Negroes and east European Jews were especially mixed residentially. The north side of Donaldson Street in 1912, for example, had twenty-nine households between Seventh Street and Washington Avenue: five were Negro; eighteen Jewish; and six white non-Jewish. On Washington Avenue, between Engler Street and Donaldson Street in the same year, five Negro, six Jewish, and two white non-Jewish households existed. Italians were just as unlikely to form a ghetto community: Ward 9 was occupied by 131 Greeks, 110 Austrians, 100 Hungarians, 2,675 Negroes, and 6,275 native whites in addition to 283 Italians. This blending of races and nationalities, in wards only one and one half to two square miles in size, guaranteed a certain amount of ethnic interaction.[3]

In the decade following 1910, Flytown developed into a clearly delineated Italian district. This twenty-five block residential section on Columbus' near north side was bounded by Goodale Street on the north, Dennison Avenue on the east, Spruce Street on the south, and Harrison on the west.

TABLE 26
EAST STAURING STREET RESIDENTIAL PATTERNS

	1912	1916	1920
438	Solomon Cross, shoemaker	Joseph Finestein, tailor	Joseph Finestein, tailor
440	Jacob Sherman, blacksmith	Alex Moskowitz, meatcutter	Louis Udian, shoemaker
442	Isaac Goodman, watchmaker David Goodman Bessie Goodman, tailoress	Morris Briar, peddler	Joseph Oxenhandle, cooper
444	Harry Cabakoff, cabinetmaker	Harry Cabakoff, cabinetmaker	Minnie Goldberg
446	Samuel Miller, painter	Samuel Miller, painter	David Gessells, marketman
455			David Felger, tailor
456	Herman Sonkin, junk Bessie Rosin, clerk	Morris Hurwitz, painter	Sarah Kominsky
457			Morris Gordon, furrier
458	Mizel Greenblatt, fruits	Louis Eisman, blacksmith	Harry Tammadge, machinist
459			Louis Eisenman, machinist
461			Isadore Levin, car repair
463			Dry Cleaning Company
471	Max Cohen, tailor	Max Cohen, tailor	Max Cohen, tailor
475	Morris Cohen, tailor Harry Cohen, motorman William Cohen, blacksmith	William Cohen, blacksmith	William Cohen, president of Reliable Wet Wash Laundry
476	Joseph Bale, tailor	Jacob Charmi, peddler	Jacob Charmi, junk
477	Isidore Swartz, car repair	Mrs. Mary Cohen	
478	Nathan Cohen, peddler	Samuel Cohen, carpenter	M. L. Johnson
480	David Rosin, tailor		Benjamin Howell, insurance
483	Max Cohen, blacksmith	David Zisenwein, presser	Geroge Jacobs, driver
484	Harry Fine, tailor Samuel Fine, presser	Harry Fine, tailor	Minnie Jacobs
485	Harry Goldberg, tailor	Harry Goldberg, tailor	Harry Goldberg, shoemaker David Goldberg, machinist
486	John Polzer	Jacob Cohen, real estate	Frank Horvath, dry cleaner
487	Jacob Piatigorsky, tailor	Max Eisman, blacksmith	Anna Berliner

SOURCES: *Columbus City Directories*, 1912, 1916, 1920.

Subdivided into city lots in 1865 and dotted with brick and frame houses during the subsequent years, Flytown did not attract industry until the 1880s when annexation by Columbus provided the area's water, power, and light. In the late nineteenth century hundreds of unskilled Flytown immigrants were employed by U.S. Pipe and Foundry Company; Columbus Forge and Iron Company; The Commercial Paste Company; Franklin Lumber and Furniture Company; The Columbus, Piqua, and Indianapolis Railroad, and other companies. When Eugene, Eli, and Louis Rosenthal's factory, Rosenthal Brothers wool pullers, was moved to Spruce and Henry streets in 1904 or 1905, the lack of sufficient housing for their employees caused a building marathon. By the early twentieth century Italians began to replace Negroes and Irish in this growing immigrant "port of entry," and "cheap two and three-story brick and frame tenements were built throughout the district."[4]

Flytown, upon assuming its Italian character, became a tough and colorful area where gypsies roamed in the late spring and newcomers established themselves by fighting, for "you either fought or you didn't stay." Most of all, Flytown became a place remembered romantically:

> Flytown was a wonderful place because of its togetherness. I don't remember ever anyone using the term color or creed except in the studying of history. My father used to say that if we got into a fight with the neighborhood children he would whip us, never taking our part against the others. There will never be another place like it because there will never be another group of people produced like the Flytowners . . .[5]

By 1912 Flytown's northern and eastern sides bordered prosperous middle-class districts. On its southern and western edges lay a tangle of railroad tracks, yards, foundries, and small machine shops. Names like Adorno, Albanese, Boggioni, Botti, Capretta, Cennamo, Cherubini, Cincione, Cordesco, Gaetano, Missanilli, Morette, Nofrio, Piarulli, Salvatore, Sigari, Sinibaldi, and Zigarelli could be found in the heart of the community, on Goodale between Harrison Avenue and Henry Street. Like most of their fellow countrymen, these men engaged primarily in unskilled work as laborers at the nearby stone quarries and on the railroads. Some were fruit vendors, with backyard sheds serving as their stables, while others owned "small groceries and shops patronized only by the Italian and the colored." Few enjoyed Joseph Adorno's success; located in a big brick building on the northwest corner of Goodale and Delaware avenues, Adorno had a steamship agency, a bank of foreign exchange, an import grocery, and owned the Savoia Theater.[6]

While some immigrant groups, like the Jews and Italians, were residentially segregated, daily business contacts offered unlimited possibilities for social and cultural interaction. On West Goodale, between Delaware Avenue and Harrison Avenue, flourished the "shops of butchers and grocers, barbers' establishments, dingy and gorgeous saloons, all crowded in between uninviting dwellings more or less adorned by board and lodging signs." In 1912 and for many more years, Jewish merchants alternated here with Italian merchants: Max Wise & Son ran a saloon, Max Cohen owned a clothing store, and Nathan Cohen owned a dry goods store. (Cohen's multilingual abilities remain legendary; his command of Gaelic and Italian earned him the honor of reading aloud hundreds of letters to illiterate newcomers.) "Some families," one old

Flytown resident once recalled, "lived above or to the rear of their stores"; Louis Levinson, whose clothing store and home were at the same West Goodale address, was the fourth Jewish merchant on the block.[7]

TABLE 27
WEST GOODALE AVENUE RESIDENTIAL PATTERNS

	1912	1920
390	Joseph Adorno, grocer	Joseph Adorno
393	Alphonse Raymond, laborer	Jacob Benjamin's Clothing
394	Frank Boggioni, laborer	Sereno Rossi
	David Nofrio	Acello Chicco
395	Louis Levinson's Clothing	Louis Levinson's Clothing
399	Joseph Adorno's Grocery	Francesco Nigro
400	Union Mission	Macedonia Baptist Church
401	Joseph Ward, barber	Gus Pantreutakis, restaurant and home
404	Donatilla Salvatore	Joseph Fisher, laborer
	Samuel Salvatore	Michele Prezioso's Confectionary
	Umberto Salvatore, shoemaker	
407	Isabel Kneeland, widow	Isabelle Kneeland, widow
408	Goodale Street Theater	Mack Curcio's Billiards
		Jacob Benjamin
409	Tony German's Grocery and home	Samuel Benson's Tailor Shop
410	Nathan Cohen's Dry Goods	Joseph Steinberg's Men's Clothing
411		Nathan Cohen's General Store
411½		Nathan Cohen, merchant
414	Dominico Capretta, grocer	Dominico Capretta's Soft Drinks
414½		Philip Lord, grocer
415		Guiseppi Pardi, soft drinks
415½	Vincenzo Salvatore, shoemaker	
416	Nathan Cohen, merchant	Dominico Capretta, soft drinks
418	Angelomarino Cordesco, laborer	Vincenzo Salvatore's Shoe Repair and home
419	Antonio Zentena's Grocery	Hugh Bracaloni, laborer
		Geno Bracaloni, tailor
420	Peter Gasbarro, laborer	Peter Gasbarro, laborer
421	John Rotondo, boilermaker	Mary Rotondo, widow
423	Max Cohen's Clothing	Morris Gertner's Tailor Shop
424	C. A. Williams' Saloon	David Pettiford, barber
425	Max Wise & Son, Saloon	Abraham Schneider's Soft Drinks

SOURCE: *Columbus City Directories,* 1912 and 1920.

Flytown, like other immigrant areas of Columbus, served also as a focal point of Americanization activity. This effort centered in the Godman Guild House, where "hyphenated citizenship was being eradicated naturally and scientifically" through organized classes in "language, citizenship, and ideals." Italians constituted the bulk of Flytown residents "who wished to become more like the people of the land of their adoption."[8]

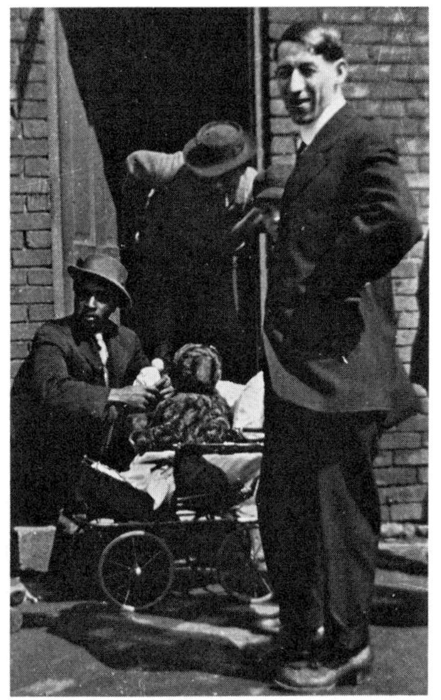

Scenes from Flytown in the early twentieth century.

The Neighborhood in 1912

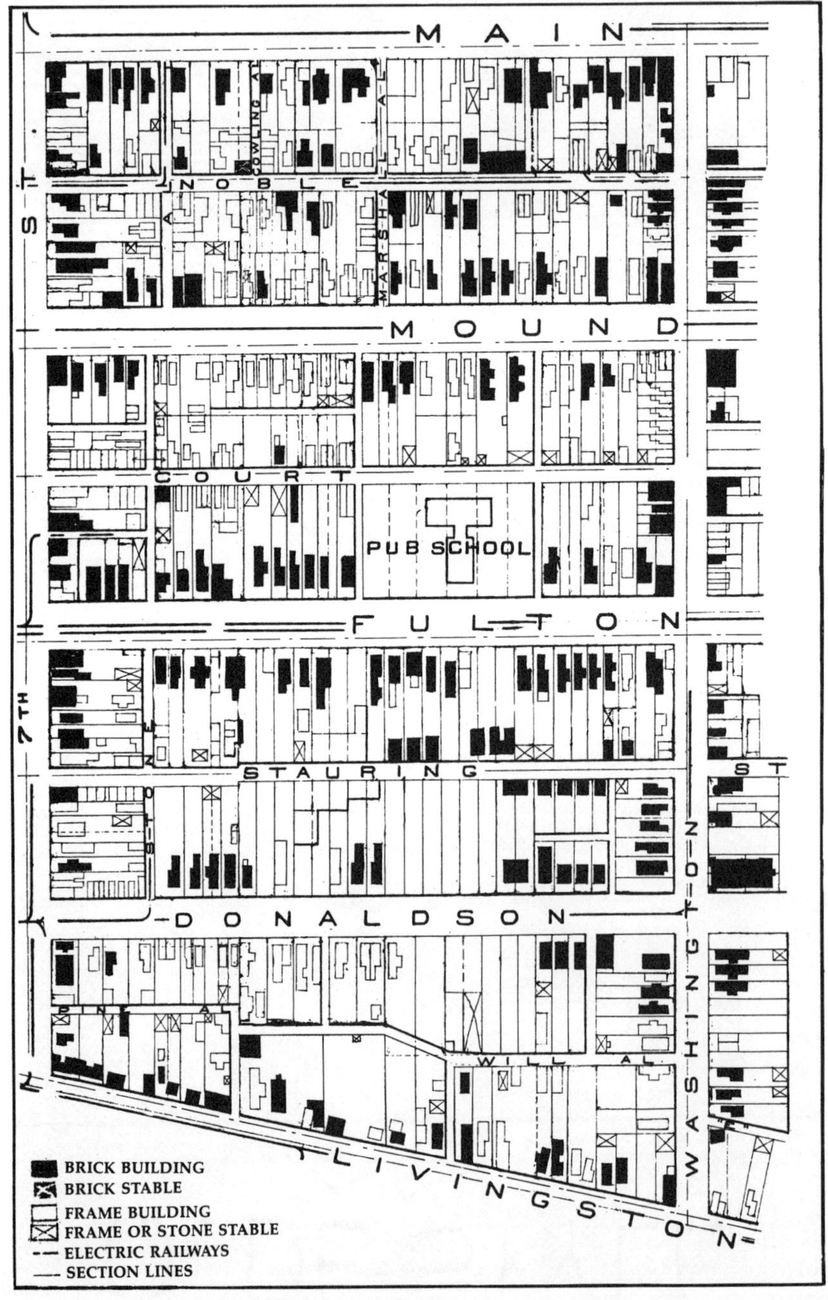

A Jewish section, composed almost exclusively of immigrants who had recently arrived from Russia and Poland, coalesced on the near east side of Columbus. Its heart consisted of Precincts 42A, 43B, and 44C of Ward 2 in the 1910 United States Federal Census; its borders were formed by Main Street on the north, Washington Avenue on the east, Livingston Avenue on the south, and Seventh Street on the west. This entire section lay within one mile of the heart of downtown; inside its less than one-and-a-quarter mile perimeter resided almost thirty-five hundred persons in seven hundred households. While some streets formed virtual Jewish enclaves, in reconstructing the entire neighborhood it seems safe to conclude that, at most, Jews made up 25 to 30 percent of the households. In a neighborhood owned largely by absentee landlords, there emerged very little resistance to the invasion of a people with a lower standard of living and an alien culture.

Unlike Flytown's recently-constructed areas, both brick structures built before 1900 and more recent frame houses were found in the Jewish section. For example, thirty-nine of the forty-four structures on Fulton Street were brick, while other streets contained almost all frame buildings. This was especially true of narrow streets such as Court, where twenty-three of the twenty-six buildings were of frame construction. A sizeable number of the older homes had deteriorated considerably by 1912, but the continuing influx of immigrants kept the rents rising. On the other hand, many new dwellings filled the area in the early years of the century; several former residents recall large numbers of brick duplexes where only two (usually large) families shared the dwelling, each in its own unit; the streets were wide and uncluttered, complemented by a virtual absence of industry and manufacturing within or near the section. Indeed, while there was a scarcity of parks, comfortable streets comprised the Jewish section. Front footage, at least fifty feet almost everywhere, and plenty of empty space dotted the neighborhood.[9]

Despite the absence of tenements, the neighborhood hardly qualified as attractive. Sewers could not be found; every other east-west "street" was merely an alley or byway dignified by another name. As late as 1925 a survey of 101 homes in the neighborhood found that 48 had no running water, and 84 lacked toilets in the house. Privy vaults or "outhouses" in the yards made the area undesirable to anyone other than impoverished Negroes or immigrants.[10]

Signs of ethnicity appeared everywhere; these included businesses, organizations, and synagogues. The "Jewish Branch" of the Socialist Party met biweekly above Rubin's Liquors at Washington and Livingston. Seventh Street housed Benjamin's secondhand goods, Lena Wolf's grocery, Finkelstein's secondhand goods, Max Bloom the tailor, Rosenthal's grocery, Einhorn and Cowan Kosher Meats, Kaufman's secondhand goods, Harry Schleng's grocery, Jacob Ziskind's junk, and Shlansky's confectionary. Another street, Donaldson, served as the location for meetings of socialists, Zionists, and Voliners, and contained a Settlement House and Benjamin Shapiro's Bathhouse as well. In the heart of this area stood three Orthodox synagogues — two adjacent to each other and the third so close that it was not only possible but commonplace to shout from it to the others and be heard.[11]

An essential psychological element in the success of many of the newcomers lay in the fact that their real world, the one where they felt both the security and identity which flow from a structured system of values and relationships, emerged from the private sphere of the family, the organization, and the synagogue. This is where the immigrant belonged, surrounded by men and women who noted with pride the individual's every success.

More often than not an individual Jew, not an organization, provided assistance to fellow Jews of the neighborhood. All the immigrant reminiscences recall this, although the kinds of

Seventh Street merchant Nathan Finkelstein and his wife Jennie came to Columbus from Russia with Herman (standing center) and Bess (second from left). Rose (second from right), Carl (seated on left) and Dorothy (seated on right) were born in Columbus, c. 1910.

assistance rendered vary considerably. Most commonly offered was food, around which east European Jews built much of their life:

> One thing about the Jews, which you must know, is that . . . they are one bunch. For instance, if someone did not have enough for the *Shabbos* [Friday evening and Saturday], they didn't have enough in their homes that they could eat there properly, Reb Moishe would always single me out that I should accompany him, and we'd go around from house to house and he would ask if they could spare a little bread, an orange, apples. So he used to carry a big basket and sacks, and he knew who didn't have anything. So he would place some stuff in each sack, and I would accompany him, and we would go to a house and he would say "Avramala, you place this sack on the steps, knock on the door, and run." He didn't want anyone to know who had brought the stuff, so that's what I did. Each week I accompanied him; he looked after everyone. So that's the way the Jews lived then. No one went hungry. No one had anything, but no one went hungry because there were contributions.[12]

Like most neighborhoods during the early years of the century, the Jewish neighborhood encompassed a wide variety of life-styles. Rabbis and petty criminals, peddlers and teachers, religious functionaries and craftsmen practiced their trades on the front steps; even residents of "Jewish houses of ill fame" lived and worked within its bounds. Meat markets, synagogues, a bathhouse, and stores of all kinds ringed its edges. The Jewish Sabbath, former residents concur, revealed the diversity of the area: morning found large numbers of immigrants praying in the synagogues, while the afternoon served as the section's main marketing day. David Schwartz became only one of a large number of Orthodox men and women who spent his Sabbath day worshipping and merchandising. Surprisingly, the Sabbath did not become a day of complete cessation from work until the immigrants' children and grandchildren made it so.[13]

The strong relationship between propinquity and marriage selection emerged as another feature of the neighborhood. Most immigrant weddings in the early part of the century involved families from the neighborhood. Occasionally, one of these weddings received unusual notoriety, inside as well as outside the neighborhood. Clothier Wolf Zeitsman's eighteen-year-old daughter, Kate, eloped with Jacob Goldsmith, a twenty-two-year-old pawnbroker, in 1905. This otherwise common event received much attention in the press because not only was Goldsmith already engaged (against his wishes) to Ida Rosenfield, but invitations had been sent out for the Rosenfield-Goldsmith wedding, and the groom had borrowed $500 from Ida for the ceremony! Jacob Goldsmith's subsequent explanation that he married for love, not money, did little to subdue Ida's outraged parents who had arranged the match. They urged the police to close his store and issue a warrant for his arrest.[14]

The tenuous economic situations facing many of the neighborhood's young immigrant couples often drove them to save as much on rent as possible. Many newlyweds, such as Rose Bendersky and Samuel Fleischmann, lived for a time in the bride's parents' home. Frequently this was a temporary expedient, but when lengthened by necessity, desertion and divorce became common alternatives. Kittie and Morris Finkelstein were one of many couples whose marriages collapsed partially because of living arrangements.[15]

Burnet Horkin, a nineteen-year-old immigrant, kept a diary which provides a glimpse of daily neighborhood life in 1910. Although preoccupied with thoughts about his girlfriend Iva in Delaware (which was twenty-five miles north of Columbus), and the meaning of his own existence, Burnet describes in abundant detail how he spent his leisure time, his employment experiences, and his participation in Jewish communal and religious life.

While continually complaining about his small amount of free time, Burnet made maximum use of what he had. He "read a bit in nearly everything I could find," completing more than twelve books in 1910.[16] Burnet also enjoyed cards, dancing, fishing, hiking, and going to movies with his friends; he took piano lessons regularly, studied French often, saw opera whenever possible, and spent much of his time "copying poetry into my book." Always happier reading and thinking than working, Burnet even managed to find time for many of his leisure-time interests during free minutes provided workers throughout the day.

Burnet worked at more than a dozen jobs during 1910 alone, but most of his time was spent making and selling cigars. Burnet's father, Samuel, who had brought the family from Russia to Columbus in 1900, worked and lived at 621 Wager Street in 1910, and encouraged his four children to assist him whenever they could. Burnet hated the work:

> I sold [cigars] this [morning] making me one dollar and a quarter this certainly is tough (February 21).
>
> I sold a few hundred cigars this morning making a few cents (February 28).
>
> Oh what misery. I advice no one to work for his father, feels so bad, I cried in shop (March 2).

The only joy in the job was the opportunity to "talk about life and its ways" while selling cigars, but sales were erratic and when necessary Burnet sought other work. He "hauled and trucked potatoes and onions" in January, worked in a box factory in August (where he earned as much as $1.50 one day), sold life insurance in September and the *Family Home Journal* in October, asked Emil Kohn for work as a bartender in November, and began a shorthand course to prepare for office work in December.

There is no evidence that Burnet found any more of a sense of order in Jewish communal life than he found elsewhere. He regularly attended meetings of the Herzl Club, a group of young Zionists whose companionship he enjoyed immensely, but when placed on the club program for December this aspiring actor noted that "I hope I'm not in town." Although not especially observant of Jewish ritual and ceremony, for he worked on the Sabbath, Burnet attended "Dr. Wernikosky's church" (i.e., Agudas Achim) briefly on Jewish holidays. During services he was usually immersed in thoughts about Iva, employment, and whether or not human existence had any purpose. Never really at home in the Columbus of 1910, Burnet eventually went to New York City to pursue an acting career and died there before the age of thirty.[17]

The continued presence of Jews in this near East Side neighborhood has led many local residents to imagine that immigrant Jews and their children remained in the same houses for much of their lives. Decidedly this was not the case; the city's neighborhoods experienced rapid population turnovers and immigrant Jews, too, were immensely mobile. Stauring Street, like every other street in the heart of the Jewish residential area, lost almost every one of its residents between 1912 and 1920. Indeed the only street in the district on which fewer than 90 percent of the 1912 residents had moved to new addresses eight years later, was from 438 to 487 East Stauring, as illustrated by Table 26. Thus the area contained a sizeable Jewish element over the decade, but individual residents moved in and out frequently.

In the towns, villages, and even some of the cities of Poland and Russia where Columbus Jews began life, persons often were born and died in the same home. In Columbus, however, they moved frequently, especially during their early years of settlement. Quite often after achieving some financial success they sought better housing and living conditions outside of the initial area of settlement. Isaac Goodman, a watchmaker who resided at 442 Stauring in 1912, occupied ten different residences during this sixteen-year period:

1912-15	442 Stauring	1923-24	500 Fulton
1916-17	502 Fulton	1925	711 Wager
1918-19	516 Washington	1926	826 Livingston
1920-21	498 Seventh	1927	809 Wager
1922	575 Engler	1928	711 Wager

More often than not, the Jewish residents changed addresses at least every other year between 1912 and 1928.

By 1930 many immigrant Jews had moved to streets directly east and southeast of the initial area of settlement. The Jewish section of 1912, part of Tract 2B, deteriorated to such a degree that by 1930 it was the most dense east side tract with 30.8 persons per acre. Here many times more families lived in multiple-family dwellings (31.5 percent of the total families) than in the adjacent tracts (8.2 percent in 8B and 4.6 percent in 9B). Monthly rents were higher in Tract 2B, averaging $35.17 per month; the area consisted of primarily rented, rather than owned, homes (80 percent in 8B and 40 percent in 9B), and included a population more than a quarter Negro. While this area remained filled with as many Jews as any other census tract, primarily because all three Orthodox synagogues still remained there, the two adjacent tracts contained equal numbers of Polish and Russian Jews. Additionally, directly east of these on the edge of the city's eastern limits, Tracts 12B and 13B had begun their inexorable build-up of Jewish immigrants, as the threat of commercial expansion encouraged families, whose income and working hours permitted a longer journey, to abandon the central residential areas.[18]

Many former residents agree that the synagogues — the central institutions of the community — prevented a mass exodus from the old Jewish district. As the community moved eastward, stores, restaurants, and small businesses moved; but synagogues remained in the neighborhood for many years because of the cost of relocation. By 1928, seventy members of Beth Jacob Synagogue already lived in the suburban tracts 8B and 13B while only fifty-eight lived in tracts 2B and 3B. This proportion became even more lopsided in the 1920s. By World War II the initial area of settlement, despite its three synagogues, had almost completely emptied of Jews.[19]

Before turning to the role of politics in the east European Jewish neighborhood, it should be noted that residential segregation between the east European and B'nai Israel Jews measured greater than that between the immigrants and Negroes. Far more Negroes lived within the heaviest concentrations of immigrant Jews than did B'nai Israel members.[20] In direct contrast to the German Jews, the east European immigrants changed addresses quite frequently within the neighborhood,[21] welcomed boarders who could share the rent,[22] encouraged their wives and daughters to work part time,[23] and lived in some of the most run-down housing available in Columbus.[24] The 199 Jews from B'nai Israel lived largely north and east of the newly arrived Jews, in newer homes which they generally owned and remained in for several years, with wives who were not employed, and in a neighborhood described, a few years later, by an urban sociologist in this manner:

> The so-called "reformed" Jews, which include, as a rule, the Jews of German nationality, are dispersed along the eastern section of the city in the better residential district between Broad Street and Bryden Road.[25]

Very little can be said about the Jewish vote, and little more about the political issues which excited the Jewish community. Whether Orthodox or Reform, Russian or German, it did not matter; apathy prevailed. Neither levies which angered large

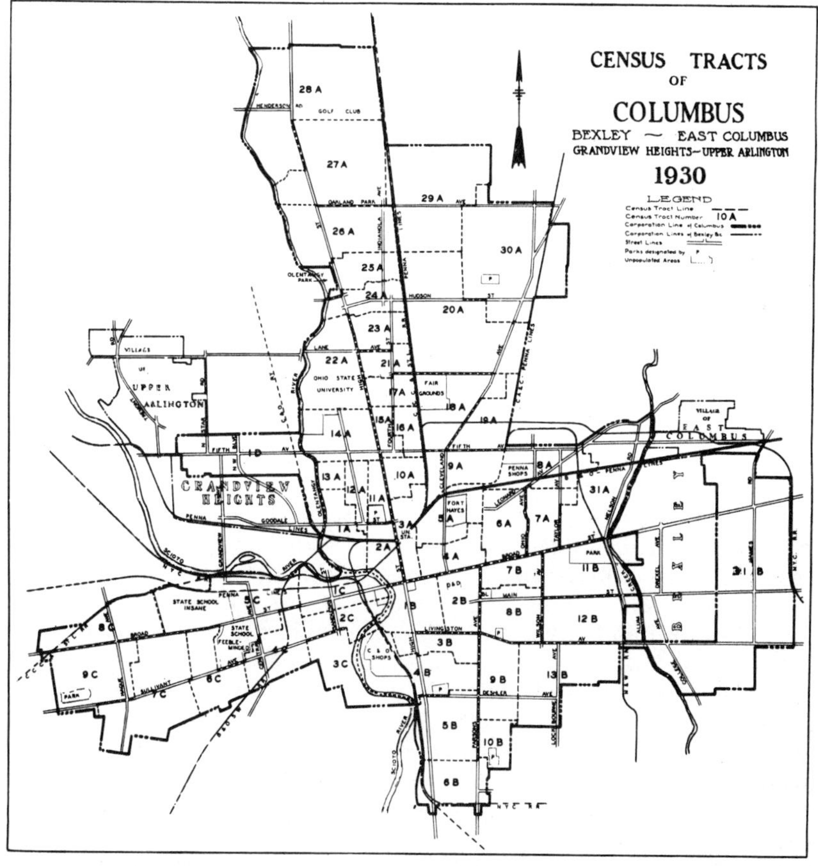

SOURCE: *Population Characteristics by Census Tracts, 1930*
Bureau of Research, College of Commerce and Administration, The Ohio State University, Columbus, Ohio, 1933

segments of the electorate like the proposed Third Street Viaduct levy, nor even the presence of both east European and Reform Jewish candidates for county offices, attracted Jewish voters.[26] Before examining the possible reasons for Jewish political passivity, let us look at one of the most colorful presidential contests in our history.

By the end of May 1912, Columbus citizens had recovered from the back-alley fight which had characterized the Roosevelt, Taft, and LaFolette campaigns for the Republican vote in the Ohio primary. During one frantic week Teddy Roosevelt traveled eighteen hundred miles within Ohio for ninety scheduled speeches, and Taft covered even more territory and spoke more often. Roosevelt's address at Memorial Hall in Columbus on May 17 drew more than ten thousand persons while Taft's Columbus campaign was no less enthusiastically received. Columbus also celebrated its centennial during the week of August 26, 1912 — a week that began with thundershowers and ended with blistering humidity — and President Taft made a midweek appearance at the Ohio State Fair to participate in the "jollities."[27]

Americans in 1912 enjoyed a period of relative international calm for noises from revolutionary Mexico were more irritating than menacing. Notwithstanding some industrial violence and racial tension, this was a period of domestic prosperity: agricultural prices were rising, unemployment remained low, the stock market looked buoyant, and Wilson's huge electoral triumph (435 votes to Roosevelt's eighty-eight and Taft's eight) hid the fact that Roosevelt and Taft garnered more combined popular votes than Woodrow Wilson and that Socialist Eugene V. Debs received a surprising 900,000 votes.[28]

Despite his electoral triumph, Wilson was unable to secure a majority of votes in any state outside the old Confederacy; but thanks to the Republican split, Wilson won Ohio's twenty-four electoral votes. Much more unusual was the fact that Debs polled more votes in Ohio than in any other state. Ohio was one of the few states to prefer the conservative Taft over the progressive Roosevelt. In Columbus, the candidates generally duplicated their statewide showing, with Wilson's 16,333 votes overshadowing Taft's 10,470 and Roosevelt's 9,702; while Debs received 4,439.[29]

Singling out the Jewish vote within Columbus, or any other medium-sized or small Jewish community, has not been possible, but there is much indirect evidence available about the political behavior of Columbus Jews. The east European-born Jewish population was quite small, probably two thousand persons at the very most.[30] This makes the precinct singled out for close observation all the more striking. Ward 3, Precinct A (labeled such by the Columbus Board of Elections in 1912), or Ward 2, Precinct

44C (as numbered in the 1910 Federal Census), contained a sizeable number of east European Jewish immigrants.[31] The 1910 census taker enumerated 303 families consisting of 1,279 persons in this precinct; after reconstructing the entire neighborhood, we identified at least one-third of the households as immigrant Jewish families of east European background.[32]

Extant voting registration records for the 1912 elections in Columbus provide the name of each registered voter, street, and house number, by precinct and ward. Of the 273 men who registered to vote in 3A, at least 43 men, or 16 percent, were immigrant (naturalized) Jews. Representing the largest proportion of registered Jews of any precinct — including those areas in which the children of the Jews here in 1880 resided — this precinct provides a glimpse into Jewish voting patterns.

In addition to 3A, several other precincts contained concentrations of east European Jewish immigrants: Ward 8, Precincts C, D, and E (directly north of 3A) and Ward 4, Precinct N (east of and adjacent to Ward 3A). Of the four precincts named above, 4N had the largest number of Jewish voters registered (13 percent of the precinct), and none of the registrants in any of the four — highlighting the residential segregation of Orthodox and Reform — affiliated with the old and prestigious Reform Congregation B'nai Israel.

Four precincts included voters who were exclusively members of B'nai Israel: Ward 4, Precincts B, C, F, and H (north and east of the immigrant wards). The percentage of Jewish voters here was much smaller than in the east European wards; in part because the latter probably outnumbered the Reform Jews by a two-to-one margin by 1912, and in part because more than half of the 199 B'nai Israel members did not register to vote in November of 1912. Finally, there was precinct 0 of Ward 4, which spanned the Reform and the east European areas, and appears roughly half and half in composition.[33]

In Columbus the 1912 election came at a time when the Socialist Party seemed to be making its most promising bid for power. Following a paralyzing and violent three-month streetcar workers' strike in 1910 which kept the Ohio National Guard in Columbus for two months, the party amassed 12,000 votes in the municipal election of that year, twelve times their 1908 total and almost one third of the 40,000 votes cast, by pledging municipal ownership of public utilities. The next year the Socialist candidate for mayor came within 2,000 votes of the incumbent Democrat. In 1912 the party's influence peaked; it published a weekly newspaper, *The Socialist*, and swung the Columbus City Council toward some of the party's more moderate programs.[34]

We know two things about the Jewish vote in the tumultuous

1912 election. Although Jews may have been as stirred by the rise of the Socialists or by Roosevelt's vigorous rhetoric as other Columbus citizens, remarkably few actually voted in the November elections. In nine of the most heavily Jewish precincts of the city only about 150 were registered, in part because such registration required American citizenship, which many immigrant Jews had not yet acquired, or because the city itself imposed a lengthy residency requirement. More importantly, perhaps, political issues did not excite Columbus Jews in these years. More than half of the B'nai Israel members failed to register, although most of these longtime German-Jewish residents of Columbus were probably eligible. The Hebrew Political Club, composed of east European immigrants, could not muster support for Jewish candidates.[35] It is probable that the Italians and Welsh voted far more often than did the Jews.[36]

The second thing we know about the Jewish vote is that it divided among economic and class lines, like that of most other Columbus groups. Socialist candidate Eugene V. Debs received his largest vote in those wards which encompassed the heart of the east European Jewish community. In two of these wards Debs won two-thirds and three-quarters of the total vote Roosevelt received. And in Ward 8E Debs lost to Roosevelt by only three votes, his best performance against the progressive candidate within the city.[37] On the other hand, Debs did not receive a single vote in Ward 4B where the highest concentration of B'nai Israel members were registered. They included the large proprietors and professionals: Dr. Louis Kahn, president of the Board of Health; Frank Basch, proprietor of Basch Brothers Junk; and Erwin Rosenthal of Rosenthal Brothers wool pullers.[38]

As a group, Jews were politically passive or apathetic, but some individuals achieved citywide recognition. The first recorded effort of a Columbus Jew to enter city politics ended successfully. Clothing merchant Marcus Frankel (1825-1872), a Prussian immigrant who arrived in Columbus in 1861, was elected by the heavily German Ward 6 to the city council in 1868. Upon receiving word of Frankel's election, Isaac Mayer Wise of Cincinnati, editor of the *American Israelite*, noted that "the Democrats must consider Marcus quite a wise man. He will make a good city daddy." A Mason and member of B'nai B'rith and several other societies, Democrat Frankel was reelected in 1870 and 1872 despite heavy Republican victories in the city. His sudden death in May 1872 ended what might have been a long political career.[39]

Two other Columbus Jews served on the city council in the nineteenth century: Henry Harmon (1829-1901), a Democrat elected by Ward 4 in 1892, and Otto Nusbaum (1840-1928), a Democrat elected to city council by Ward 1 in 1888 and reelected in 1890 and

1892 by the same ward. In 1894 and 1896 Ward 2 sent Nusbaum to city council, and he handily defeated his Republican opponent each time. Vice-president of the council for many years, Nusbaum gained wide recognition for his role in developing a municipal street lighting system in the city and for helping steer Columbus through a period of rapid urbanization and municipal socialism.[40]

Anti-Semitism infrequently became a factor in the political arena. In 1887 Republican Dr. H. L. Shepard ran against Democratic Representative Joseph H. Outhwaite for a congressional seat; the *Columbus Times* carried part of a Shepard supporter's campaign speech in Somerset, Ohio, where he referred to "Outhwaite's . . . web-footed Jewish relations, who . . . are common enemies of mankind." The following day a strong defense of "my people" came from *eine vone unsere leute* (one of our people), B'nai Israel member Solomon Loeb, together with a statement from Shepard disavowing any support for such a declaration.[41]

The most controversial Jewish politican in Columbus' political annals was Melville D. Frank (1900-70). A former rabbinic student at the Hebrew Union College and an insurance dealer whose many activities in the Jewish community included serving as superintendent of the Schonthal Center Sunday School, Frank was elected to city council in 1929 on a platform of "Progress, Prosperity, and Payrolls." During his eight years on city council, this fiercely independent Republican fought hard for a "bigger, better and more industrial Columbus" as a response to the Great Depression. He introduced and steered through council a $.50 an hour minimum wage law on city contracts, successfully battled to prevent the sale of seventeen acres in Sunshine Park to the Columbus Red Birds baseball team, initiated Columbus' first work relief program early in 1930, repeatedly opposed rising gas and electric rates, demanding that the city establish a municipal light plant to compete with private utilities, and led the way for council to pay city employees with cash rather than redeemable tickets during the depression.

Frank's relationship to the Republican organization remained unstable at best. Elected in 1929 without Republican organizational support, he served as the lone Republican on council. By late 1932 the Republican leaders turned against him, both because of his challenging the "regular" Republican candidate for mayor in 1931, thus "giving city hall to the Democrats," and because of his "merciless attacks upon the Republican organization." The party hoped he "will get it in the neck at the coming municipal election," and explained Frank's success as a result of people thinking he was Charles Frank, a popular South Sider. While party leaders had vowed to have the "knives of the organization stalwarts whetted for 'Mellie,'" by the fall of 1933 they endorsed his reelection, as he generated the most popular support of any council member. Having led the city council ticket, far ahead of the other candidates, Frank launched an intensive campaign for mayor in 1935. Running as an "Independent Republican" against Henry Worley, the incumbent Republican mayor, Frank sought to defeat Worley in the Republican primary. During the summer campaign the Republican organization bitterly attacked the challenger. According to Frank, former Franklin County Republican Chairman H. C. Arnold had circulated pamphlets and leaflets asking "Do you want a Jewish mayor?" and pointing to Frank's personal "poverty." This resulted in a $150,000 lawsuit filed by Frank in common pleas court for "false, malicious and defamatory" accusations.

Frank also found opposition within the "establishment" of the Jewish community. Preferring a "low profile and non-visibility," many prominent Columbus Jews, including E. J. Schanfarber, shuddered at the thought of a Jewish mayor at a time of heightened anti-Semitism in America. Frank, nonetheless, campaigned intensively on his city council record and received the endorsement of the *Ohio State Journal.* Although retaining his seat on council, he lost his bid for mayor, and, at the end of his term, retired from politics at thirty-seven. Frank subsequently devoted substantial amounts of time and energy to Jewish organizations; with the completion of the new Jewish Center in 1950 he became the first membership chairman, and from 1956 to 1958 served as president of the Jewish Community Council.[42] "Mellie" remained the only Columbus Jew active in community politics through the first six decades of this century.

While Columbus' Jewish community appeared disinterested in local, state, and national politics, when the need arose the community proved it could utilize the same methods usually employed by political strategists. Columbus Jews contacted the newspapers, lectured to civic organizations, held mass meetings, and won the support of the City Council of Columbus. The reason was the Kishinev (Ukraine) massacres in April 1903, when pogromists killed about fifty Jews, seriously wounded eighty-six, hurt hundreds and plundered or destroyed perhaps five hundred to one thousand shops. The news of the Kishinev pogroms spread quickly not only through Russia but through Europe and America as well, and Columbus Jewry rallied financial and moral support for Russian Jews. The horror of the attacks not only appeared prominently in the local press, but in letters which local Jews received from families still in Russia. Beryl Pass wrote to his son Aryeh, "I can hardly imagine that the Inquisition in Spain would be more terrible."[43]

Many responses emanated from the local Jewish community.

Mrs. Sam Friedlander, who had recently returned to Columbus from a visit to Russia, addressed local organizations and wrote letters to Columbus newspapers ("Russian Jews are peaceable and peace loving; very few are socialists . . ."). Others, like Mrs. Sam Levy, told of personally visiting Kishinev and learning how Christian anti-Semitism caused the pogroms.[44]

Almost every local Jewish organization, and many non-Jewish as well, devoted several programs or special meetings to Kishinev. Rev. Saul Silber lectured to the men's club of the First Congregational Church about Russian persecution of Jews; Madame Bronislawa Pevsner, a "Semitic champion" and thirty-one-year-old Russian physician, lectured in German to a large audience in hopes of "arousing interest in the cause of the Russian Jews"; while Joseph Lipman addressed both the Hebrew Alliance and the Jewish Ladies Helping Hand Association.[45]

More potent than individual meetings were mass gatherings, largely attended by immigrant Jews and seeking both to draw the attention of the Christian community to the plight of the Russian Jews and to raise money for relief. The first such rally, jointly sponsored by more than a half dozen groups, occurred in June of 1903, and others followed periodically. One result of the first meeting was a pledge by the community, under the leadership of Rabbi David Klein, to "adopt" twenty to forty families fleeing from Russia.[46] Another result of the rally took the form of the following resolutions adopted by the Columbus City Council on June 8, 1903:

> WHEREAS, The story of the recent outrageous massacre of the Jews at Kishineff furnishes unquestionable evidence of the inhuman policy of the Russian people if not the government, toward the Jewish people who are among the most industrious, capable, thrifty and law-abiding of the citizens of that vast empire toward which our own government sustains most friendly relations, and
>
> WHEREAS, This great cruelty is but another proof of the unfriendly policy of that government which has been for twenty years growing up in its laws and regulations respecting the civil and religious rights of the Jews, and
>
> WHEREAS, These savage abuses of an inoffensive but most energetic and intelligent people seem to be based on no other reason or excuse, upon the part of the people of that government, than a sullen and revengeful hatred of religious and economic liberty arising out of wicked bigotry in matters of church and state, which in that nation are inseparably bound together, and
>
> WHEREAS, This barbarous procedure upon part of the Russians has the inevitable effect of driving these terror-stricken people in great numbers to foreign countries and especially the United States for refuge, and

WHEREAS, The disabled and pitiable industrial, financial and social conditions of these helpless refugees, when arriving at our shores, brought about by a continual experience of unjust and extreme suffering at the hands of their oppressors in their own country, renders them unable to comprehend and assimilate the spirit of our laws and institutions and become independent and useful citizens of our republic as readily as they would otherwise do, and

WHEREAS, The policy of the abuse tolerated if not encouraged by the Russian Government is a gross violation of all of the principles and rules of political, religious and social justice, as between even despotic rulers and their subjects, recognized throughout the world, which policy has in the past and must in the future result in great loss and discouragement to all of the interests of enlightened government and life, and

WHEREAS, This exhibition of tyranny at the hands of the Russian people is most revolting to the people of this country who enjoy untrammeled political, religious and industrial liberty and are interested in promulgating and establishing the same privileges throughout the world, and

WHEREAS, All over our country there is a feeling of profound sympathy with the Jews of Russia, and their countrymen among us, in this great racial calamity which to be effective should have definite, forcible and official expression, therefore be it

Resolved, That the people of the city of Columbus, Ohio, through and by its Common Council, do hereby protest against this cruel and unreasonable policy and conduct toward the Jews at the hands of the Russians and by the tolerance of the government of that country, and do hereby extend our sincere sympathy to that suffering and oppressed people in this time of distress.

Resolved, That we believe the friendly offices of this and all other liberty and justice loving nations of the world should be exerted in behalf of the Jews in Russia to the end that justice shall be done them, and that a duly certified copy of this minute and resolutions be forwarded by the clerk of this Council to Honorable John Hay, Secretary of State of the United States, to be used or communicated by him as the justice and dignity of the situation may suggest to him to be proper.[47]

Many other responses resulted from mass meetings of the community. B'nai Israel adopted a resolution denouncing Russian brutalities against Jews and requesting President Roosevelt to intervene; Washington Gladden, Columbus' most distinguished Protestant clergyman, preached several sermons on behalf of the Jews of Russia and urged his followers to generously aid those victimized by czarist terror; and the children of the Hebrew Free School, "emptying their penny savings banks," contributed three dollars to the relief efforts.[48]

The Jews of Columbus may not have taken advantage of the

vote, but the same could not be said of education: every available source reveals a strong commitment to learning by both German and east European Jews. Despite numerous obstacles, the educational achievements of the "new" immigrants rank alongside the mercantile successes of the "old" in any story of Columbus Jewry.

Located at the very center of the immigrant Jewish community of 1912, the Fulton Street School enrolled students in grades one through seven. There were less than fifteen east European Jewish children in the entire school in 1900, but a decade later considerably more than 50 percent of the student body consisted of Jewish pupils, almost all of them immigrants from Russia; this influx of so many new pupils in a comparatively short time found the school system unprepared.[49] Thus, most classes were extraordinarily large, as demonstrated in Table 28.

TABLE 28
FULTON STREET SCHOOL: 1911-12

Grade	Teacher	Russian Jews	All Jews	All Students
1 A-B	Emily L. Beck	23	45	71
1 A-B	Ella Howe	12	27	59
1-2	Cora Metzger	32	55	90
2 A-B	Olga Zapp	31	61	98
3	Matilda Koch	33	53	91
3	Florence Callis	30	46	96
4 B	Kate Jewett	56	?	85
4	Mary Evans	55	?	87
5	Esther Freahey	55	?	89
6	Mary Will	52	?	84
6-7	Pauline Kaefer	39	?	74
7	Katharine Kaefer	34	?	59

SOURCE: *Columbus School Register and Record. Fulton Street,* 1911-12.

In addition, at least half of the class consisted of new arrivals who spoke little English; hence the large number of immigrant children, five to twelve years of age, in Emily Beck's first grade class. New arrivals had some unusual encounters, such as that described by one former Fulton Street first grader:

> . . . that September when school opened, I registered at Fulton Street School . . . They put me in the first grade, got me a bridge table and a chair and I was sitting with those little kids in the first grade with six year-olds and within two or three weeks they discovered that I belonged some place else. And the way they discovered it was that

TABLE 29
FULTON STREET SCHOOL FIRST GRADE STUDENTS IN 1911-12

Jewish Students	Age	Birthplace	Parent	Home	Parent's Occupation
Abe Goer	7	Russia	Fishel	427 Engler	peddler
Louis Nachmanovitz	5	England	Joseph	491 Noble	peddler
Jerome Office	6	Columbus	Ben	561 Main	merchant
Milton Rabinowitz	6	Columbus	Samuel	534 Donaldson	peddler
Isadore Rosenbloom	6	Russia	Harry	470 11th	tailor
Harry Raffeld	8	Russia	Nathan	389 Cherry	laborer
Sam Raffeld	9	Russia	Nathan	389 Cherry	laborer
Abe Wolman	10	Russia	Robert	512 Elmwood	peddler
Jacob Wolman	5	Russia	Robert	512 Elmwood	peddler
Robert Weshnesky	6	Russia	David	425 Engler	tailor
Sam Goldstein	5	Columbus	Jacob	513 Parsons	tailor
Carl Lieberman	6	Columbus	Isaac	478 11th	peddler
Myer Marcus	8	Russia	M.	438 Parsons	peddler
Louis Raffeld	5	Russia	Nathan	389 Cherry	laborer
Isadore Roberts	5	Columbus	Harry	378 Washington	tailor
Harry Cherry	5	New York	I. Novak	423 Cherry	tailor
Leah Bale	5	England	Joseph	476 Stauring	tailor
Esther Feinstein	8	Russia	Morris	398 Cherry	tailor
Sadie Feinstein	6	Russia	Jacob	462 Noble	tailor
Annie Goodman	6	Russia	Abe	533 Elmwood	rag picker
Ida Greenberg	5	Columbus	Emil	529 Engler	tailor
Bessie Goldberg	6	Columbus	Max	466 Noble	tailor
Rebecca Kabelcov	7	Russia	Harry	617 Cherry	mechanic
Millie Louis	8	Russia	Esther	537 Parsons	merchant
Mollie Luper	6	Russia	Morris	486 Mound	merchant
Fanny Nusbaum	9	Russia	Meyer	468 11th	mechanic
Jenny Nusbaum	8	Russia	Meyer	468 11th	mechanic
Jeanette Papier	5	Columbus	Leo	396 Donaldson	peddler
Pearl Plotnick	6	Russia	David	516 Pine Alley	mechanic
Mary Topolosky	6	Columbus	Isaac	551 Main	peddler
Beatrice White	5	Columbus	Max	503 Washington	tailor
Eva Wolman	8	Russia	Herman	512 Elmwood	peddler
Kate Mellman	12	Russia	David	567 Mound	teacher
Rose Mellman	11	Russia	David	567 Mound	teacher
Hattie Shusterman	6	Ohio	Isaac	439 Parsons	huckster
Helen Cohen	5	Columbus	Max	471 Stauring	tailor
Anna Einhorn	6	Columbus	Rabbi H.	471 Washington	meat market
Freda Levy	5	Columbus	Israel	508 Washington	merchant
Anna Mellman	7	Russia	David	567 Mound	teacher
Sarah Minitzky	5	Columbus	Nathan	425 Mound	merchant
Toubie Rosenthal	5	Columbus	David	333 Washington	Hebrew teacher
Pearl Silverman	6	New Jersey	Simon	500 Washington	reverend
Jennie Gerwich	10	Russia	Abe	391 Engler	tailor
Hermine Brender	6	Columbus	Max	426 Main	merchant
Gertrude Reed	5	Columbus	Anna	384 Donaldson	mechanic

TABLE 29 — CONTINUED

Non-Jewish Students	Age	Birthplace	Parent	Home	Parent's Occupation
Harold Althauser	6	Columbus	William	580 Fulton	clerk
Chester Decker	6	Ohio	Jacob	611 Cherry	laborer
Edward Detrick	8	Ohio	Walter	569 Cherry	laborer
Theodore Fields	6	Ohio	James	379 Washington	chef
Harry Keefer	6	Ohio	William	598 Mound	laborer
Miles Maupin	6	Ohio	George	547 Cherry	packer
Edward Parks	7	West Virginia	Howard	477 Cherry	laborer
James Polzer	7	Columbus	John	486 Stauring	laborer
Carl Schumacher	6	Columbus	Emil	605 Cherry	teamster
James Yates	6	Columbus	Nathan	601 Engler	laborer
William Zurflich	6	Columbus	William	579 Fulton	merchant
Frank Shuflin	5	Columbus	Frank	456 Main	mechanic
Charlie France	9	Ohio	William	456 Parsons	laborer
Sam Brandt	5	Ohio	David	529 Elmwood	laborer
Rudolph Gess	5	Ohio	Estella	397 Cherry	cook
Thora Bussard	6	Columbus	Homer	413 Fulton	mechanic
Daisy Butler	6	Ohio	George	431 Noble	laborer
Thirza Butler		Columbus	Robert	385 Washington	laborer
Edith Gary	6	Columbus	John	482 Mound	oil prospector
Clarice Streets	7	Columbus	Ernst	583 Donaldson	laborer
Katie Taylor	6	Columbus	William	592 Fulton	chauffeur
Goldie Stout	7	Ohio	Edwin	370 Washington	saloon kpr.
Helen Pyles	6	Columbus	Charles	591 Fulton	painter
Minnie Garland	6	Columbus	Harry	632 Noble	laborer
Gertrude Beck	5	Columbus	John	471 Will Alley	blacksmith
Bessie Sheridan	6	Columbus	Eva	417 Fulton	

(Also preserved is first grade teacher Emily Beck's grade book for reading, writing, arithmetic, language, drawing and music.)

> they were beginning to teach the kids two and two equals four, you know, stuff like that, on the blackboard so the teacher put down several figures and I went over to the blackboard and added it up in Yiddish and I might have put down the total on the bottom and she was shocked that I knew that much coming out of the wilds of Russia. She then went ahead and put on a larger problem and I added that up in my mind in Yiddish to myself and put it down. And she gave me an exam right there in front of the class for addition and subtraction. By that time she went to the office and called in the principal who stood there with her hands folded up watching me do my math on the blackboard. I was already at division and doing it all in Yiddish and they didn't know it. And so I went to the fifth grade right there.[50]

During the fall of 1906, the Columbus Board of Education discussed at some length the problems created by having so many immigrant "Hebrew" children enrolled in one school. The most viable alternative to "so many children [who] could not speak

English" appeared to be to set aside some rooms at Fourth and Fulton, or elsewhere, exclusively for "Hebrew refugees." After some "parental persuasion," this idea was discarded when the board determined that the vast majority of the children seemed "bright and energetic" and not in need of separate facilities. Instead, a special teacher was assigned to Fulton Street School for the forty students in need of language instruction. The board assured the community that "the American flag will be hoisted and they will be taught patriotism for their adopted country."[51]

American Jewish immigrants heartily accepted the public schools as vehicles for the assimilation of their children and as a means of upward economic and social mobility. They were unconcerned that the Fulton School teachers knew little of the historical and cultural backgrounds of the Russian Jewish children in their classes. Instead, immigrant parents wanted their children to learn to read and speak quickly and to complete as many years of public school as possible. When necessary they used the synagogues and Hebrew schools to supply Jewish culture and values. Between 1910 and 1920 Jewish high school attendance rates increased steadily.

One indication of Jewish support for public schools in Columbus was the absence of any form of Jewish parochial school education until well after World War II. The Talmud Torah remained an afternoon and Sunday appendage to the public schools, generating only limited support within the immigrant community (its only supporters) for many decades. Although the Talmud Torah's emphasis on rote learning and drills may have served as a helpful model and practicum for public school achievement, few if any Jewish parents suggested that it replace the public schools as a vehicle for the education of their children.[52]

Two other factors helping to account for or reinforce the great attachment Jewish parents felt for the public schools were their own occupational histories and the hope that education would lead to economic mobility. Between 1899 and 1910 almost two-thirds of the Jewish immigrants reporting Old World occupations identified themselves as skilled workers. By way of contrast only 15 percent of the immigrants from southern Italy reported having skilled occupations, while 77 percent were classified as laborers.[53] Not surprisingly, therefore, Italian children left Columbus public schools as soon as possible to enter the labor force and supplement the family income, while Jewish offspring were kept in the classroom in the hope that they might complete high school or actually go on to college. Unlike Italian students in Flytown, the Fulton Street first-graders of 1912 entered the occupational structure at rather high levels after attending high school: only one entered as an unskilled or general laborer, more than half became proprietors, and the large majority of women married either professionals or independent businessmen.[54]

Table 30 brings together five separate occupational enumerations from the Jewish "neighborhood" of 1912 as well as

TABLE 30
SELECTED OCCUPATIONAL GROUPINGS IN COLUMBUS IN 1912

Employed Jews in Ward 3A (Ward 2, Precinct 44c).

19 peddlers	3 blacksmiths
18 tailors/tailoresses	2 cigarmakers
8 clerks	2 cabinetmakers
6 grocers	2 shoemakers
6 proprietors (clothing, soda water, junk, coats, meat, confectionary)	2 painters
	2 car repairers
	2 secondhand goods
4 fruit vendors	2 tinners
	16 miscellaneous jobs
	N = 94

Occupations of All Heads of Households of Jewish Students' Families in Grades 1, 2, 3, 1911-12.

36 tailors (25%)	3 teachers (-4%)
25 merchants (18%)	3 shoemakers (-4%)
23 peddlers (16%)	2 rabbis (-4%)
18 unclassified (13%)	2 cabinetmakers (-4%)
10 laborers (7%)	1 each: butcher, baker, tinner, saloon keeper, upholsterer, blacksmith, painter, policeman (-4%)
7 mechanics (5%)	
5 clerks (-4%)	
	N = 142

Employed Negro Men in Ward 3A (Ward 2, Precinct 44c).

11 laborers	3 misc. jobs
2 domestics	N = 16

Parental Occupations of Jewish Children in Emily Beck's First Grade Class.

13 tailors	3 mechanics
11 peddlers	2 laborers
6 merchants	1 rabbi
3 teachers	N = 39

The Italians of Flytown: All the Employed Italians on West Goodale Street.

20 laborers	2 musicians
4 shoemakers	2 barbers
4 grocers	6 misc.
	N = 38

Flytown. A consistent occupational pattern exists on almost every Jewish immigrant block: peddling and tailoring overwhelmingly dominate, while "merchants" with a fruit stand, open air stall or junk wagon, a grocery or meat market, are close behind.[55] While far removed from the Jews of German ancestry in either security or status,[56] these Jews certainly emerged better prepared for their own, and their children's, upward economic mobility than either neighboring blacks or Italians.[57] Their urban ancestry and long experience in the local commercial life of eastern Europe enabled many of them to make their adjustment to Columbus long before arriving in America.[58] Shifting to small-scale trade and independent mercantile positions, pursuing familiar skilled occupations, and maintaining home-centered activities enabled large numbers to keep their families intact, to send their sons and daughters to college, and to purchase homes in the more comfortable residential areas of Columbus. By starting with certain skill advantages, Russian Jews were able to quickly translate these into higher occupational roles and family incomes than Italians achieved. So ethnic differences in school performance and attendance may well have been due, in part, to economic differences.

The extent of acculturation and upward mobility that characterized the immigrant Jewish community becomes apparent by following the life histories of the forty-five Jewish first graders who sat in Emily Beck's Fulton Street classroom.

Over the next half century or more, seven changed their names: Nachmanovitz to Nachman, Rabinowitz to Robins, Rosenbloom to Rosen, Marcus to Marks, Weshnesky to West, Topolosky to Topy, Minitzky to Monett. An extraordinary proportion — 62 percent — remained lifelong residents of Columbus. Sixty-five years later ten of sixteen boys and eighteen of twenty-nine girls either still lived in Columbus or had died there. Such residential continuity had important implications for the social, psychological, political, economic, and religious behavior of Columbus Jewry during the post-World War II years.[59]

The Jewish children in Emily Beck's classroom achieved economic and social security in their own generation. Although more than half were Russian-born, they did not have to await vicarious socioeconomic success through their children. The majority of the women married either professionals or independent businessmen, and the men soon entered Columbus' growing middle class. In the 1950s and 1960s the children of these immigrants gravitated to the professions of law, dentistry, or medicine, or became self-employed managers in the wholesale or retail trade.[60]

While few of Emily Beck's first graders graduated from college, most secured some higher education and many retained life-long interest in learning and personal improvement. Although most of these students possessed minimal formal Jewish educations, many of them made public and private libraries a second home. This largely immigrant group born in the first decade of the twentieth century was quite well educated in secular terms.

Finally, mothers and fathers of our first graders not only emphasized education, but secured jobs which offered avenues to upward mobility, and enjoyed the material advantages of the American middle class as quickly as possible. By the end of World War I almost all of these families had automobiles, by the 1920s more than 70 percent owned homes, and perhaps most telling of all, the Great Depression seriously hurt very few. Rare was the father whose job was lost or changed during this critical period, for most of the men worked in sectors of the economy either lightly hit or shorn up by the New Deal, and the abundance of family-owned or family-run businesses became a great asset as well. By the 1920s, then, the fathers and mothers attained fairly permanent economic security; in 1968 their children and grandchildren made up part of a Jewish community whose median income, one sociologist noted, figured as "the highest of any Jewish community yet studied."[61]

During the early decades of the twentieth century the east European Jewish neighborhood developed in the midst of other minorities and then declined into an overcrowded area — a good place to start, but a bad place to remain. Most of its residents were involved in a day-to-day struggle for existence; they had no time and little desire to vote, but enough time to attend Americanization classes so that they could vote. For most east Europeans, education and hard work eventually provided paths to better lives in another neighborhood.

NOTES FOR CHAPTER 7

TABLE 31
ESTIMATED JEWISH POPULATION IN COLUMBUS

Year	Population	Source
1877	420	*American Jewish Year Book,* Vol. [16]
1878	165	*Encyclopaedia Judaica,* Vol. 5 (Berlin, 1930), p. 633
1880	420	*Statistics of the Jews of the United States* (UAHC, 1880), p. 31
c. 1900	1,500-1,800	*The Jewish Encyclopaedia,* Vol. IX (New York, 1901), p. 390
1905	1,500	*AJYB,* Vol. [16]
1907	4,000	Ibid. and *AJYB,* Vol. [9]
1912	6,000	*AJYB,* Vol. [16]
1918-20	9,000	*AJYB,* Vols. [20] and [21]
1927-29	8,500	*EJ,* p. 633 and *AJYB,* Vol. 30
1938	8,500	*AJYB,* Vol. 40
1939	6,250	*AJYB,* Vol. 50
1940	9,250	*AJYB,* Vol. 42
1940	6,500	*Universal Jewish Encyclopaedia,* Vol. 3 (New York, 1941), p. 311
1941	9,250	*AJYB,* Vol. 43
1948	7,200	*AJYB,* Vol. 50
1956	9,000	*Columbus Jewish Center Self Study 1956.* Prepared by the Department of Community Surveys and Studies of the National Jewish Welfare Board.
1957	7,200	*AJYB,* Vol. 58
1964	10,000	*The Standard Jewish Encyclopaedia,* (New York, 1966), p. 464
1966	10,000	*AJYB,* Vol. 68
1968	13,000	*The Jewish Community of Columbus,* p. 3
1971	13,000	*AJYB,* Vol. 74

1. Department of Commerce, Bureau of the Census. *13th Census of the United States Taken in the Year 1910. Population* (Washington, 1913), I, pp. 94, 158, 208, 550. Thirteen hundred and thirty-four persons listed Yiddish-Hebrew as their "linguistic group" or mother tongue. For a useful attempt at reconstruction similar to that of this chapter, see Frederick A. Bushee, "Ethniç Factors of the Population of Boston," *Publications of the American Economic Association,* Third Series, Volume IV, Number 2 (May, 1903): 299-477.

2. Department of Commerce, Bureau of the Census. *14th Census of the United States Taken in the Year 1920. Population 1920* (Washington, 1922), II, passim.; *14th Census of the United States. State Compendium. Ohio* (Washington, 1924), pp. 29-30, 69-70; *Columbus City Directory 1912;* Sue Snorf, "A Sociological Study of the Hungarian Settlement in Columbus,"

M.A. thesis, The Ohio State University, 1925. Stanley Lieberson, using unweighted mean indexes of residential segregation, has noted that Columbus "Russians" were more segregated from native whites than from Negroes in both 1910 and 1920; *Ethnic Patterns in American Cities* (New York, 1963), pp. 121, 122, 127-28, 130.

3. Ibid.

4. *CC*, August 17, 1959, January 1, 1974; "After Sixty-Five Years 1898-1963," Godman Guild House, 321 West Second Avenue; Jon Alvah Peterson, "The Godman Guild," M.A. thesis, The Ohio State University, 1959; "Flytown," Historical Marker at Goodale Street and Harrison Avenue, erected by The Franklin County Historical Society, June 18, 1961; Jon A. Peterson, "From Social Settlement to Social Agency: Settlement Work in Columbus, Ohio 1898-1958," *The Social Science Review* 39:2 (June 1965): 191-208. Of the structures existing in Flytown in 1940, 67.9 percent went up between 1900 and 1919, and only 0.5 percent thereafter. See John C. Alston, "Cost of a Slum Area" (Wilberforce, Office of School Administration, 1948).

Many Italians, of course, came to Flytown even earlier than 1900. Elia Francisco arrived in 1888, and, after walking about the streets ringing a bell, sharpening scissors and knives with the grindstone strapped to his back, opened a saloon; Nicholas Casbarro worked on the Pennsylvania Railroad upon his arrival in 1884. As late as 1900, however, only 349 Italian-born persons resided in all of Columbus. See *CC*, May 25, August 18, 1959.

5. Doris Friend Boyer to Ben Hayes, correspondence, November 30, 1961. In possession of Ben Hayes.

6. *Columbus City Directory*, 1912; *CCJ*, September 20, 1969; Leonore Pitts, "The Italians of Columbus — A Study in Population," in *Annals of the American Academy of Political Science* (January 1902): 154-59.

7. Florence Louise Bell, "The Social Settlement Columbus, Ohio," *Annals of the American Academy of Political and Social Science* (May 1902): 176; Jarvis MacIlvane to Ben Hayes, Ben Hayes' column in *CC*, July 31, 1956. This was no less the pattern in other parts of town. At the turn of the century the Schottensteins, with small shops on East Long Street, "built a long room so that people had their little businesses in the front part, and they partitioned off two or three rooms to live in; as the family grew they put in another partition and made a smaller room." (Interview with Sadie Schottenstein)

8. *OSJ*, November 14, 1915.

9. *G. W. Baist's Property Atlas of the City of Columbus* (Philadelphia, 1899), Plate 6; *G. W. Baist's . . . Columbus* (Philadelphia, 1910), Plates 5 and 6. The influx of east European Jews to Columbus, and the neighborhood, was so sudden that a decade prior to 1912 almost all the signs of Jewish ethnicity were absent.

10. Mary Louise Mark, *Negroes in Columbus* (Columbus, 1928).

11. *Columbus City Directory, 1912;* interview with Jack Greenwald; *The Socialist*, December 23 and 29, 1911, January 27, February 3, March 23, July 13, August 24, and November 16, 1912.

12. Interview with A. S. Kohn.

13. Interview with Jenny Goldberg Brief; B'nai B'rith Minutes, March 14,

1910; David Schwartz, *My Townlet-Fachenbrod* (Israel, 1956). The Committee on Legal Aid, early in 1910, asked Columbus City Council for more time to "eliminate Jewish houses of ill fame"; *OSJ*, March 14, 1910.

14. *OSJ*, October 25 and 26, November 24, 1905; Flo Gurwin to Marc Lee Raphael, August 25, 1976, telephone conversation.

15. *OSJ*, November 2, December 11, 1901, November 25, 1907.

16. These included *The Fortune Hunter* by David Phillips, *The Calling of Dan Matthews* by Harold Wight, and especially the Hebrew Scriptures. For an announcement of Burnet and Iva's "betrothal party," see *Delaware Journal-Herald*, July 5, 1911.

17. Burnet Horkin, Diary, [January 1-December 31, 1910]; telephone conversation with Marvin Horkin, October 12, 1975.

18. *Population Characteristics by Census Tracts* (Columbus, 1930), passim.

19. "Membership Names" [1929], Beth Jacob.

20. A sociologist noted this a few years later when he wrote: "Columbus had one large Jewish colony, lying a few blocks east of the southern end of the main business section of the city. The population is a mixture of colored and Jewish people." See Roderick Duncan McKenzie, *The Neighborhood: A Study of Local Life in the City of Columbus, Ohio* (Chicago, 1923), p. 155.

21. As we have indicated, we noted who occupied a certain address at various intervals. More than half the residents of every ward block in 1912 lived at different addresses by 1916, while more than three-fourths had moved by 1920. Yet another indication of immigrant mobility is found in the voter registration records; only eleven of the forty-three Jewish voters in Ward 3A in 1912 registered to vote in the same ward four years later. Nevertheless, the neighborhood continued to reflect a visible ethnic identity.

22. Interview with Earl Sonenstein. Feeding, clothing, and balancing the budget of large families on a few dollars per week required enormous inner resources, and it was not made easier by the presence of boarders. Everyone had boarders, for they provided a sizeable slice of the monthly rent. Overwhelmingly single, male, and distantly related, they interfered in domestic affairs, told the wife how to do things correctly, and made lasting impressions on the immigrant children. See also Michael Zedek, "The Stones are *Tref:* An Oral History of Jewish Immigration to the United States," rabbinic thesis, Hebrew Union College, 1974; and John Modell and Tamara Hareven, "Urbanization and the Malleable Household: An Examination of Boarding and Lodging in American Families," in *Journal of Marriage and the Family* 35 (August 1973): 467-79.

23. Since the *Columbus City Directories* seem to list employed boarders, wives, and children about as accurately as heads of household are listed, it is possible to enumerate these persons. In contrast to the immigrant Jews, rare was the B'nai Israel member with a working wife.

24. This conclusion is based on the oral histories in the Columbus Jewish History Project, and the rental advertisements in the 1912 Columbus newspapers.

25. See Roderick Duncan McKenzie, op. cit., p. 156.

26. The business community and numerous civic groups, through costly circular handouts and advertising campaigns, enthusiastically supported

the levy for the Third Street Viaduct (adjacent to High Street), *OSJ*, May 8-15, 1912; when the community became aware that the $425,000 figure consisted of only the initial — and partial — expenditure, strong opposition overwhelmed the business community and the levy. (*OSJ*, May 16-19, 1912).

27. *CSD*, Centennial Library Edition, August 26, 1912, p. 33; Andrea Lentz, "The Question of Community: The 1910 Street Car Strike of Columbus, Ohio," M.A. thesis, The Ohio State University, 1970, p. 7; George S. Mowry, *Theodore Roosevelt and the Progressive Movement* (New York, 1946), p. 234; *OSJ*, May 6, 8, 9, 10, 17, 18, 20, 1912; Osman C. Hooper, *History of the City of Columbus, Ohio* [1797-1920] (Columbus and Cleveland, n.d.), pp. 62 and 86.

28. Arthur S. Link, *Woodrow Wilson and the Progressive Era 1910-1917* (New York, 1954); George S. Mowry, *The Era of Theodore Roosevelt* (New York, 1958); Eric Goldman, *Rendezvous with Destiny* (New York, 1952).

29. In the presidential vote of 1912, 423,152 Ohioans voted for Wilson, 277,066 for Taft, 229,327 for Roosevelt, and 89,930 for Debs; *Annual Statistical Report . . . For the Year Ending November 15, 1913* (Springfield, 1913), p. 263; Board of Deputy State Supervisors and Inspectors of Elections, Franklin County, Ohio, List of Electors Registered in the City of Columbus, Ohio . . . 1912, p. 14.

TABLE 32
PARTIAL RESULTS OF THE 1912 ELECTIONS

Ward	Presidential Electors[1]				Bond Issues $80,000[2]		Bond Issues $30,000[2]		$425,000 Third St. Viaduct[2]	
	Dem	Rep	Soc	Prog	Yes	No	Yes	No	Yes	No
3A	78	75	28	35	94	61	80	57	18	32
4A	62	89	9	43	105	76	101	74	55	64
B	57	66	0	26	81	58	73	54	31	70
C	109	49	17	30	95	84	89	78	38	87
D	79	127	3	75	137	125	133	122	43	129
E	68	88	6	49	113	78	102	81	35	106
F	66	72	8	47	100	81	99	78	37	89
G	106	59	12	54	96	114	91	108	33	107
H	142	44	10	40	106	105	102	99	45	112
I	108	50	19	47	94	105	91	105	37	95
K	100	34	14	67	97	95	100	90	37	89
L	27	53	6	17	35	23	27	23	15	21
M	81	47	16	39	81	70	70	65	19	58
N	46	77	14	21	49	50	41	54	26	28
O	87	48	16	30	90	62	88	63	21	47
Total	1,138	903	150	585	1,279	1,126	1,207	1,094	472	1,102
8C	78	59	25	47	94	68	88	67	46	73
D	52	73	7	17	71	35	55	32	35	33
E	33	60	17	19	52	30	47	32	28	20
Total City	16,333	10,470	4,439	9,702	19,146	15,180	18,029	13,499		

1. SOURCE: *Abstract of Votes. Presidential Electors. Franklin County, 1912.*
2. SOURCE: *Abstract of Votes. Judicial and Bond Issue. Franklin County, 1912.*

30. Department of Commerce, Bureau of the Census, op. cit., pp. 801, 854, 1007-15. The Bureau of the Census itself equated Russians with Russian Jews; see Department of Commerce, Bureau of the Census, op. cit., Volume II, p. 1006, and Erich Rosenthal, "The Equivalence of United States Census Data for Persons of Russian Stock or Descent with American Jews: An Evaluation," *Demography* 12:2 (May 1975): 275-90. "Poles" were included under the heading Germans in the 1910 census.

31. The published census volumes of the Bureau of the Census provide only gross ward information; it is necessary to purchase detailed precinct boundaries and statistics, available for most cities for every federal census, from the National Archives. Federal ward and precinct boundaries do not usually (do not ever in Columbus) correspond in any coherent fashion to local election board precinct and ward boundaries.

32. National Archives, Bureau of the Census, "Descriptions of the Enumeration Districts of the 11th Supervisor's Districts of Ohio." The reconstruction of a neighborhood is done with the *Columbus City Directories* and the Franklin County Auditor, Tax Duplicates, for the years after 1880 when no federal manuscript censuses are available; thus one may enumerate both the people that live there as well as the business, social, and religious institutions of the area. To identify Jews specifically, we utilized membership lists of religious and social institutions, Franklin County Probate Court marriage records and birth records, cemetery records, Columbus Board of Education records, and the memories of dozens of former neighborhood residents.

33. Board of Deputy State Supervisors . . . op. cit., passim; Annual Report of Congregation B'nai Israel, 1912 (this lists all 199 members);

TABLE 33
ETHNIC SETTLEMENTS IN COLUMBUS, 1920

Wards	Blacks	Italians	Russians and Poles
1	762	161	29
2	106	41	42
3	696	35	631
4	1,425	33	705
5	408	10	110
6	4,045	229	52
7	3,642	81	36
8	1,407	50	226
9	2,675	283	80
10	441	128	20
11	1,142	84	56
12	2,502	406	91
13	1,796	403	20
14	782	309	16
15	87	13	6
16	265	24	15

SOURCE: U. S. Bureau of the Census, *Fourteenth Census, 1920, Population*, II, pp. 803-04.

Board of Elections, Columbus, Ohio, Ward Boundaries, January 1911 (1 inch = 2,640 feet).

34. Andrea Lentz, op. cit., p. 9; *CD*, November 7, 1912, p. 1; *The Socialist*, Volume II, March-May, 1912, passim.

35. Among the easily identifiable Jewish candidates for county delegate and committeeman positions on the Democratic General Ticket were Harry Bornstein and Simon Josephson (Ward 4), Henry Rosenbaum (Ward 3 — Rosenbaum received more votes in every Ward 3 precinct without Jewish voters, save one, than in 3A), Moses Adler, Arthur Aaron, and Jacob Schlesinger (Ward 8); see Abstract of Votes. Primary Election, May 21, [1912] and *OSJ*, May 23, 1912.

The Schlesinger family became especially active in Democratic politics. Hugo ran unsuccessfully for prosecuting attorney in 1918, while Mose went down to defeat in his try at county recorder in 1924. As early as 1904 Mose, identified as a "well-known local Democratic politician," managed the county campaign, and was indicted for tampering with juries (*OSJ*, October 9, 10, and 11, 1904; *CJC*, September 6, 1918; *OJC*, August 8, 1924).

36. This is a tentative conclusion based on cursory surveys of Columbus ethnic voting in 1912. Contrast this with a conclusion about Jewish immigrants in New York City: "The [Lower] East Side Jews registered and voted in greater proportion than any other immigrant group, except perhaps the Irish, and they treated the franchise with greater seriousness than any other group, especially the Irish"; see Lucy S. Dawidowicz, "From Past to Past: Jewish East Europe to Jewish East Side," *Conservative Judaism* 22:2 (Winter 1968): 20-21. On voting patterns in general, see Roderick Duncan McKenzie, op. cit.; on the Welsh, see Daniel J. Williams, *The Welsh of Columbus, Ohio: A Study in Adaptation and Assimilation* (Oshkosh, Wisconsin, 1913).

37. Abstract of Votes. Presidential Electors. Franklin County, 1912. Perhaps it is significant that the "Jewish Branch" of the Socialist party met weekly at Rubins Hall, located at the intersection of Wards 4N and 3A (see *The Socialist*, January 27 and November 16, 1912), and that much of the New York Yiddish press supported Debs.

38. Abstract of Votes. Presidential Electors. Franklin County, 1912; *Columbus City Directory* 1912-13.

39. *OSJ*, April 7, 1868, April 5, 1870, April 1, 2, May 6, 1872; *AI*, May 15, 1868; *Columbus City Directory* 1870-71, p. 330; *Columbus City Directory* 1872, p. 320. The support given the Democrats by Columbus Jews during the years of Lincoln's successors is in contrast to the conclusion of Lawrence Fuchs: "Everywhere Jews were enlisting in the new Republican Party," and "the vast majority of Jewish voters supported the emergent Republican Party." *The Political Behavior of American Jews* (Glencoe, 1956), pp. 35, 42.

40. *CP*, April 4 and 5, 1892; *OSJ*, April 3, 1888; *CDT*, April 3, 1888; *Der Westbote*, April 3, 1888; *CDP*, April 8, 1890; *CDPP*, April 2 and 3, 1894; *CEP*, April 6 and 7, 1896; *Der Tag Westbote*, April 7, 1896; Mrs. Joseph Nusbaum Bernstein to Mildred Tarshish, September 30, October 29, November 12, 1973, correspondence. On City Council's efforts to illuminate Columbus, see Michael S. Speer, "Urbanization and Reform: Columbus, Ohio, 1870-1900," Ph.D. dissertation, The Ohio State University, 1972, pp. 218-31. Among those running unsuccessfully for City Council in 1900 was

Nathan Gumble (Democrat), a candidate from Ward 6.

41. *CT,* October 29, 1886; *OSJ,* October 30, 1886; *CD,* October 29, 1886. Other examples of such defenses against printed slurs can be found in the *OSJ* of November 15 and 18, 1906.

42. *CC,* October 9, 1931; *Sunday Star,* December 4, 1932; *OSJ,* July 15, October 13 and 27, November 4, 1931, January 7, 1932, April 20, August 9, November 9, 1933, April 5, August 6 and 28, September 10-16, November 21, 1935, December 20, 1937; *OJC,* November 10, 1933, February 25, 1938; Melville D. Frank, Scrapbook; L. W. Wilson to Melville D. Frank, correspondence, August 14, 1931; "A Message to the Intelligent Voter,"1935.

43. *OSJ,* May 23, 1903.

44. *OSJ,* November 18 and 20, 1903.

45. *OSJ,* May 7 and 25, 1903, December 5 and 13, 1906.

46. *OSJ,* June 1, 3 and 15, 1903, November 13, 18 and 22, 1905.

47. *Journal of Council Proceedings – Book No. 42,* June 8, 1903, p. 164.

48. *OSJ,* November 14, 17 and 18, 1905; Washington Gladden,"The Enemies of Israel," Sermon No. 1060, Roll No. 37, Washington Gladden Collection, OHS.

49. Fulton Street School's boundaries are in the *39th Annual Report of the Public Schools of Columbus, Ohio for the School Year Ending August 31, 1912,* p. 18. For the composition of the student body, see Columbus School Register and Records, Fulton Street School. 1900-01, 1910-11, and 1911-12.

50. Interview with Harry Schwartz. Immigrant "children" were usually older than their classmates. Bert Wolman, for example, a bright Russian-born boy, was twenty-three when he graduated from South High. See Columbus School Register and Records, South High School. 1911-12.

51. Record No. 15. Board of Education, Columbus, Ohio, Clerk-Treasurer's Office, September 10, 1906, to August 31, 1908 — see especially November 5 and 19, 1906, and *OSJ,* November 13, 1906.

52. Interview with B. W. Abramson. See also Mark Zborowski, "The Place of Book Learning in Traditional Jewish Culture," in Margaret Mead and Martha Wolfenstein, editors, *Childhood in Contemporary Cultures* (Chicago, 1955), p. 139.

53. Samuel Joseph, *Jewish Immigration to the United States from 1881 to 1910* (New York, 1914) pp. 556-61; *Reports of the Immigration Commission* (1911), Volume I, p. 766 (U.S. Congress, 61st Congress, 3d session, Senate Document No. 747).

54. These conclusions are based upon the *14th Census of the United States. Population, 1920;* an analysis of the Fulton Street School (Jewish), Park Street School (Italian) and First Avenue School (Italian) records; and the *Columbus City Directories.* Ten years earlier (1902), an observer of education in Flytown noted:

> A public school stands to the southwest, and another a half-dozen squares to the north, but [neither] exert the influence needed on the children of the neighborhood. Two years ago a truant officer could spend all his time looking after 500 children of the district. But one girl attended school in the district, while boys were not expected to attend. (Florence Louise Bell, "The Social Settlement, Columbus, Ohio," *Annals of the American Academy of Political and Social Science* (May 1902): 176.)

Additionally, the total number of Italian-born students in Columbus public schools was extremely small in the first decade of this century. Italian boys and girls combined numbered only twenty-seven in 1904-05, thirty-nine in 1905-06, fifty-two in 1907-08 and forty-six in 1910-11, with 1907-08 the peak during the first decade. See *Annual Report of the Board of Education of the City of Columbus for the Year[s] Ending August 31, [1905, 1906, 1908, 1911]*. More specifically, we discovered only eight Italian-born students at Park Street elementary school in 1911-12, although this served dozens of Italian families by encompassing almost all of Flytown. First Avenue School served the area it missed, and it numbered only two Italian-born students in 1911-12. See Columbus School Register and Record, Park Street, 1911-12, and First Avenue, 1911-12. For similar conclusions, see Moses Rischin, *The Promised City: New York's Jews, 1870-1914* (Cambridge, 1962, 1977), p. 200 and Selma Berrol, "School Days on the Old East Side: The Italian and Jewish Experience," *New York History* 57:2 (April 1976): 201-13.

55. Although the Russian Jews had travelled halfway around the world, their occupational patterns in Columbus hardly differed from those in Russia. Seventy percent of all Jews (vs. 10 percent of all Russians), according to the 1897 Russian census, worked in manufacturing or "commerce." See Isaac M. Rubinow, "Economic Conditions of the Jews in Russia," *Bulletin of the Bureau of Labor,* No. 72 (Washington, 1907): 500, 554. Additionally, the occupational pattern in Columbus of these Jews from eastern Europe was quite representative of their occupational distribution in the United States: "They [Russian Jews] were very highly concentrated in two occupational categories, as tailors and as hucksters and peddlers." *Reports of the Immigration Commission* (1911), Volume I, pp. 821-29 (U.S. Congress, 61st Congress, 3d session, Senate Document No. 747).

56. We identified with certainty eighty-one of the one hundred ninety-nine B'nai Israel members as proprietors or co-proprietors, and more than ten others as managers.

57. Identification of Ward 3A Negroes was made possible because the 1912 *Columbus City Directory* identified them with the designation (c); we enumerated Italians in the heart of Flytown by identifying common Italian names and confirming their places of birth in school, parish, marriage, or death records.

58. On the relationship between the urban background and upward mobility of Jews in America, see David Ward, *Cities and Immigrants: A Geography of Change in Nineteenth Century America* (New York, 1971), p. 110; Caroline Golab, "The Immigrant and the City: Poles, Italians, and Jews in Philadelphia, 1870-1920," *The Peoples of Philadelphia,* Allen F. Davis and Mark H. Haller, editors (Philadelphia, 1973), pp. 220f.; Bernard Rosen, "Race, Ethnicity and Achievement Syndrome," *American Sociological Review* 24 (October 1959): 46-60.

59. In contrast, more than half of all the Italian adult males in Flytown in 1912 were not in the *Columbus City Directory* in 1916.

60. This pattern of occupational distribution among Russian Jews and their children in Columbus between 1910 and 1975 characterized Jews in other cities as well. See E. P. Hutchinson, *Immigrants and Their Children 1850-1950* (New York, 1956).

61. Albert Mayor, *Columbus Jewish Population Study: 1969* (Columbus, 1969), 32.

8. I NEVER PROMISED YOU A ROSE GARDEN: THE INDUSTRIAL REMOVAL OFFICE[1]

Conjecturing precisely what attracted several thousand east European Jews specifically to Columbus at the turn of the century is difficult. Some came because Columbus was Ohio's capital, another group because of Columbus' steady economic growth, while an earlier arriving friend or relative provided the decisive ingredient for others. One group, however, did not choose the city to which they migrated — the decision was made by an organization.

For a decade and a half the Jewish Agricultural and Industrial Aid Society had been active in resettling immigrant Jews on farms. On January 24, 1901, the executive committee of this international organization created the Industrial Removal Office (IRO). This office was to remove east European Jews from the large, congested east coast cities — especially New York — and relocate them in American communities where both Jewish communities and jobs existed. In its annual reports, the IRO claimed to have enjoyed great success — at least in quantitative terms — during its brief existence from 1901 to 1922. In the first five years alone, the IRO removed twenty-two thousand, five-hundred persons; in the second five-year period the agency resettled another twenty-seven thousand persons, and by the end of World War I the IRO had sent more than seventy-five thousand Jews to over seventeen hundred cities.[2] The IRO's response to the social and economic problems which came in the wake of the ghetto congestion was dispersal and deflection of the immigrants to the interior of the country.

But such nationwide gross figures for removals, or even small totals from Ohio,[3] camouflage a direct appreciation of the headaches, and failures, involved in this operation within each community. Case studies of local branches of the national organization provide us with opportunities to flesh out the bare skeleton of large numbers and national directives.

Following the pattern established by the Industrial Removal Office, Federated Jewish Charities of Columbus selected an agent or representative of the IRO whose salary was paid by the national organization.[4] In this way the IRO freed local communities from financial responsibilities and, by so doing, gained their cooperation more readily.

Once or twice a month the Columbus agent requested applicants in particular trades:[5]

> I have need for a good repairer on second hand shoes. If you have a man on hand that can fill this place, send him at once, as the position is a good, steady place to make a fine living.[6]

> If you have at hand a few good tailors, who have worked at custom work, please send me them at once. If they are good tailors they will get a very good salary.[7]

> If you will have a good upholsterer between now and the 15th of this month, please send him here. I have a good place for the right man. Surely to make from two to three dollars a day.[8]

> [I need] a first class shoe maker for repairing work. Must be sober, steady, and willing to work.[9]

In addition to writing to the IRO himself, the local agent would encourage companies to send requests like these directly to the New York office: A Columbus tailor, Herman Radzek, needed "two custom man's tailors." Star Loan Bank asked the IRO to send a "presser for 2nd hand work" for which they would pay twelve to fifteen dollars per week with a maximum of ten hours' work each day.

Resettlement was not always handled smoothly. When Peer Brothers Shoe Repairs requested two shoemakers, IRO sent four, causing the firm regretfully to return two of them to New York. The IRO did not, however, automatically send an immigrant in response to each request; frequently the agent or company had to provide more specific information; sometimes requests were rejected. When David Sachs, the "Shoe Man," bombarded the IRO with requests for a shoemaker, the IRO informed him that he was considered a poor employer, because cobblers sent to him quickly quit. In response to another demand by Sachs, the office responded, "we have a shoemaker for you but since he cannot use a jack and you will only thus pay $7 we will not send him. This is not a man's wage."[10]

The IRO did not always wait for requests from Columbus; frequently it advertised its wares:

> Louis Berg, electrician, at his trade eighteen years, shows a very good reference from his former employers where he was employed as

electrician and wireman for a year, and wishes to leave his family here. He is in good health; may we send him to your city.[11]

The IRO never promised that an applicant would find a particular job at a certain salary in any of the more than seventeen hundred communities to which it sent men. Armed with a small subsidy, and at times some tools, each man was sent to an agent in a specific city who assured him that an effort would be made to find work either in the man's trade or in something else. Nevertheless, misunderstandings, complaints, and accusations abounded. One man complained that he lost his job after three days because the Columbus agent placed him in the wrong craft, and in "dingy" lodgings which were filled with "foul air" and lacked a stove. The agent informed the IRO that the man refused to work at the place assigned to him and hence could not be guaranteed permanent work and that

> we paid for his board and lodging for two weeks and give him $50 [sic] for shaving and car faar. I told him we will make it good, we have never yet allowed a man to hunger. As to his lodging place, we placed him in the same house where mostly of the people sent by you to us are placed . . . the house is a seven room house . . . all well ventilated, all bed rooms are provided with stoves for natural gas. I visit twice every week and see that the men should get what we pay for.[12]

Along with incessant complaints from the men assisted by the IRO, the agents, as well as the sponsoring agency in the community, registered regular protests over IRO actions. They complained most about the quality of men sent by the IRO:

> We are sending back to New York No. 35685 who is at least a mental incompetent if not a moral one. We have found him five jobs of all varying kinds of work but the man absolutely refuses to do anything except file brass . . . He is a mental incompetent . . . and the person would have to be blind who could not see it by looking at or talking to this man for two minutes.[13]

The response of the IRO arrived quickly: "No. 35685 was sent as a brass worker and turner and the fact that he does not wish other work doesn't demonstrate mental incompetence."[14]

The IRO paid the local agent to undertake a wide range of tasks: locating jobs; arranging lodging, board, transportation, and other necessities of daily living; providing "friendly suggestions and counsel" (particularly financial); and "getting the confidence of the men that are sent to your city." A typical request from the IRO to its Columbus agent involved tasks such as the following:

> Monia Mandel has applied to us for transportation to your city. He claims that his uncle P. Margulies . . . will assist him and his sister whenever the necessity arises. Will you please advise us whether we shall comply with his request or not. If your investigation proves favorable will you inform us how much P.M. will contribute toward their transportation.[15]

A variety of responses to the IRO characterized agents' letters when they were attempting to answer the queries. Sometimes relatives could provide transportation costs: ". . . hes brother in law gave two dollars toward hes transportation. at es very difficult, too secure money, as all clame the have not." At other times the agents totally rejected such requests: "S. never heard of his 'cousin' and will send no money"; or, "Send H. Gurevitz as he is a good tailor and here is an opening for a good tailors even though his cousin will not send money." When a relative could not afford to send money, help might be offered instead: "Mr. R. earns only $10 week and supports a family so cannot send money but will receive his brother in law and assist him when he arrives."[16] Despite the efforts of several dedicated agents, they were damned by both the immigrants sent to them and local zealous and/or jealous persons.

East European immigrant Herschel Gurevitz, a tailor, was sent to Columbus by the Industrial Removal Office. In this photo from the early 1900s Herschel and Rina Gurevitz are surrounded by their children and grandchildren. Next to Rina is her son David holding Bernard. Behind David is his wife Dora Marion and beside him is his sister Bessie, holding Simon who is next to William. Behind his wife Bessie, Israel Kahn holds Ben. The unmarried Gurevitz children are Max and Dora (third row) and Sam (front). Next to Herschel is son Meyer holding Martha. Behind Meyer is his wife Libbie Lurie holding S. Myron. Beside Meyer is his sister Helen with husband Nathan Zuckerman and Robert and Aaron (extreme right).

Saul Silber (1881-1946)[17] was the IRO agent in Columbus from 1905 to 1908. He met with vehement denunciations from the Columbus Hebrew Educational and Benevolent Society after almost two years of work for the IRO. They accused him of "not caring for an emigrant at all, but for himself," not "spending one hour a day for those emigrants," not "speaking English well," and "dumping them in Panhandle shops, steel plants for night work and for seven days a week, where even Italians and Negroes refuse to work." The society had a suggestion for the IRO, which probably revealed its motivations in criticizing Silber: ". . . pay us the $50 each month and we will handle up to 20 per month and make mechanics, tradesmen, etc. of them. We offer you a one month 'free trial.'"[18]

Several members of the local advisory committee defended Silber. They praised him for "perseverance, integrity, and indomitable will," and urged the IRO to raise his salary from $50 to $75 per month because he worked at his job "day and nite." Taken together, their support of Silber and the IRO's response provide much information about IRO operations in Columbus.[19]

IRO activities had begun in Columbus at the end of 1904; by late summer 1906, the local community incorrectly claimed that thirty-two IRO "removals" were employed in Columbus, nine of whom had already sent for their families.[20] Not impressed with these figures, the IRO noted that Silber was required to place only twenty-nine men in 1905 (a minimum of three per month) and forty-five through August 1906 (a minimum of four per month), a task which should have left him abundant time for other work. Furthermore, in 1905 alone, agents in St. Louis, Cincinnati, Pittsburgh, and Buffalo placed 393, 318, 196, and 111 men respectively. These agents were paid only $75 per month. Thus the IRO denied Silber's salary raise, although it did agree to consider a small increment if Silber would place more men each month. Silber's defenders angrily claimed that he could easily place more men each month but the IRO refused to send any more.[21]

The issue was finally resolved by forces outside the control of either the IRO or Silber. Following the financial panic of 1907 and the industrial depression into which it flowed, like so many cities in the country, Columbus faced severe unemployment. "To my sorrow," wrote Silber,

> we are not able to place any man no difference what trade and what mechanic he is. There is more than thirty men of the IRO with work, and it is estimated that eight thousand men were discharged from work within the last three months . . . Pan Handle Railroad Shop layed off 800 men, Ralston Steel Car Co. 800 men, Columbus Buggy Co. 100 men, Columbus Iron and Steel 1,500 men . . . We had a good number of Jews in the above mentioned plants. Many are thrown out from them. The City Council granted some work in the Water Dept. to the unemployed men

After serving as the IRO's local agent, Saul Silber (left) moved from Columbus and subsequently became president of the Hebrew Theological College in Chicago. During 1912 Sam Edelman served as the local agent; he later became one of the most well-known physicians in Columbus.

> for ten cents an hour, and we got fifteen men work. We are trying everything to prevent starvation for these people.[22]

By the end of 1908 Silber had moved to Youngstown, Ohio, to become principal of the Hebrew school. IRO work in Columbus, as in dozens of cities, came to a virtual halt. The winters of 1908-09 and 1909-10 saw little or no improvement, although by January 1910 Rabbi Joseph Kornfeld noted that although "industrial conditions [are] terrible," we "hope for an agency here again by April."[23]

As economic conditions slowly improved throughout 1910-11, and much of 1912, the IRO operated minimally in Columbus; by the fall of 1912 the German Jewish leadership of Federated Jewish Charities had formed a Columbus Committee of the IRO. The committee agreed to supervise an agent, accept at least eight men per month, and provide a monthly allowance of $8 to individual removals. Because two of the eight removals were to be family men, the committee also agreed to a family allowance of $16 per month.[24]

All of the problems which arose during the Silber years reappeared between 1912 and 1916, the final period of IRO activity in Columbus: IRO complaints about agents as well as the committee, criticisms of the IRO from Columbus, and difficulties in placing the men sent to the city. For example, the committee worked hard to make things run smoothly, insisting that its first agent, Sam Edelman (1891-1977), carefully and continuously describe Columbus industries to the IRO. This seemed to be precisely what the IRO desired; its general manager noted that "the Removal Office must always be kept informed of the actual industrial conditions in all parts of the country, in order that an intelligent distribution may be made." Edelman sent lists of Columbus companies to the IRO: "our main industries are buggy and auto factories; machine factories; shoe, couch, mattress, cash register, and piano factories; foundries, and steel industries." The office, however, considered these too vague, refused to send men without notice of specific job opportunities, and demanded "more exhaustive efforts." Meanwhile, Edelman and the committee complained that they were receiving no men, and the exchange of letters often became bitter.[25]

The most common complaint expressed by local agents continued to concern the quality of men sent to Columbus. "I'd write for a shoemaker and they'd send me a blacksmith," Edelman recalled.[26] Arthur Ginzler (1868-1947), Edelman's successor, scorned the IRO for sending a Turkish and an Arab Jew, "both of whom are dishonest and should never have been sent." Paul Karger, a subsequent agent, informed the IRO that Mr. S. "is an absolutely worthless cuss, and has been a charge upon the charities practically the entire time that he was in Columbus."[27] Karger again notified the IRO that

> we received in the last several weeks five tailors from your office. For your information I want to state that we are not able to use more tailors at present. It is the slowest time of the year in the tailor trade and more than half of our local tailors are without work.

While successful placements occasioned no written communications, it is clear from IRO correspondence that Columbus had little hesitancy in making its complaints fully known to the national office.[28]

Most Jews who left the eastern metropolitan ghettos were not assisted by the IRO, but left for inland communities such as Columbus on their own. Some heard rumors of good job opportunities, others stopped on their way west and stayed permanently, while still more joined relatives or landsleit already in Columbus. While comparisons between immigrants who came to Columbus independently and those sent by the IRO are difficult, little evidence suggests that the latter had any significant advantage. Not only was the adjustment of "removals" to the new city often painful, but a striking number failed to become permanent residents of the community. Despite the enormous relief efforts, both nationally and locally by IRO personnel, their contribution to Jewish life in Columbus seems minimal.

Immigrants with craft skills and help from the IRO, whether successful in their relocation or not, constituted only a part of the Jewish migration. Those with no craft skills often turned to peddling, which still offered an opportunity to rise and perhaps even the chance to become "store princes" like the German Jews.

NOTES FOR CHAPTER 8

1. Historical studies of American Jewish institutions and organizations have overwhelmingly concentrated on the national headquarters of such groups, and generally ignored personalities and activities on the local level. A look from the "bottom-up" clarifies the effect of national decisions on local branches, the pressures local groups exerted upon national organizations, and the values and concerns otherwise anonymous members of a local group bring to their activities.

2. On the IRO, see Samuel Joseph, *Jewish Immigration to the United States* (New York, 1914); Boris D. Bogen, *Jewish Philanthropy* (New York, 1917); Samuel Joseph, *History of the Baron de Hirsch Fund* (Philadelphia, 1935); Rose Margolis, "History of the IRO," M.A. thesis, Graduate School for Jewish Social Work, New York, 1935. For the total removals, see the *Annual Reports of the Industrial Removal Office,* located in The Papers of the IRO, American Jewish Historical Society, Waltham, Massachusetts (hereafter cited as *Annual Report of the IRO*).

3. From 1901-13 there were 8,773 removals to Ohio, ranging from 152 in 1901 to 1,207 in 1913; *Thirteenth Annual Report of the IRO,* 1913, January 1, 1914.

4. Where no federation of Jewish philanthropies existed, groups such as B'nai B'rith would direct the removal efforts.

5. At the same time that the IRO requested this of its agents, IRO protested that it "must not be regarded as an employment agency whose province it is to cater to the demands of employers"; David M. Bressler, "What is the Removal Office?" *National Conference of Jewish Charities* (May 27, 1904), p. 2.

6. Saul Silber to IRO, August 27, 1906, The Papers of the IRO, American Jewish Historical Society (hereafter cited as IRO Papers).

7. Silber to IRO, October 15, 1906, ibid.

8. Silber to IRO, August 1, 1907, ibid.

9. Silber to IRO, April 28, 1908, ibid.

10. Herman Radzek to IRO, August 31, 1910; Star Loan Bank to IRO, May 9, 1912; Peer Brothers Shoe Repairs to IRO, December 1, 1917; IRO to Peer Brothers, December 13, 1917; Peer Brothers to IRO, December 26, 1917; David Sachs to IRO, September 9, September 20, October 13, October 26, December 28, 1909; IRO to David Sachs, January 5, 1910; David Sachs to IRO, February 13, March 28, April 12, 1910; IRO to Sachs, November 9, 1910; ibid.

11. IRO to Arthur Ginzler, March 16, 1913, ibid.

12. IRO to Ginzler, April 16, 1913; IRO to Silber, January 30, 1907; Silber to IRO, February 1, 1907; ibid.

13. Fred Lazarus to IRO, March 20, 1913, ibid.

14. IRO to Lazarus, March 24, 1913, ibid.

15. IRO to Ginzler, December 9, 1912; IRO to M. Pollatsek, January 12, 1905, ibid.

16. Pollatsek to IRO, n.d.; Silber to IRO, March 3, December 14, 1905, March 1, 1906; ibid.

17. Saul Silber, born and educated in Russia, arrived in the United States in 1900 and worked in various capacities in Columbus from 1904 to 1908. His work included preaching in Agudas Achim synagogue and teaching in the Hebrew Free School. Residing in Chicago from 1910 until his death, he served as spiritual leader of Anshe Sholom congregation and president of the Hebrew Theological College. See Fred Lazarus et al. to IRO, August 17, 1906, ibid.; *Columbus City Directories* 1905, 1906, 1907; *OSJ* September 9, 1904; Alex J. Goldman, *Giants of Faith: Great American Rabbis* (New York, 1964), pp. 207-15; *WWAJ*, Volume 3 (New York, 1938), p. 988; interview with Marvin Fox.

18. Dr. Joseph Lipman to IRO, July 23, 1906, IRO Papers.

19. Fred Lazarus et al. to IRO, August 17, 1906, ibid.

20. These local figures supplied to the IRO appear to be greatly exaggerated. Of the twenty-nine men sent to Columbus in 1905, only four tailors and one cutter appear in a *City Directory* in any year between 1905 and 1910. Even granting the possibility that many roomed with friends or relatives during these years and hence were not heads of households, it is doubtful that the directory canvass, which attempted to tally all adults at an address, would have continuously missed these removals. Either Saul Silber's placement efforts or the newcomers' employment records were less than admirable. This conclusion places in question the annual IRO summary of removals, which regularly claimed that at least 75 percent — and in 1912 as many as 94 percent — of the removals found their new surroundings attractive and decided to remain; see *Twelfth Annual Report of the Industrial Removal Office*, 1912, p. 16.

Most removals came alone to Columbus, saved some money from their salaries, and, when married, brought their families. Morris Berliner, for example, who arrived in 1905, earned enough money as a ladies' tailor to bring his family to Columbus in 1907. (A conversation with Morris' son, A. H. Berliner of Columbus, May 1, 1975) and IRO to Silber, April 25, 1905, IRO Papers.

21. Lazarus et al. to IRO, August 17, 1906; IRO to Lazarus, August 28, September 7, 1906, October 11, 1907; IRO to Lazarus, October 14, 1907; ibid.

22. Silber to IRO, January 8, 1908, ibid.; see also Jewish Charities of Columbus, Ohio, to IRO, December 11, 1907, January 1, February 5, 1908, ibid.

23. Silber to IRO, October 4, 1908; Jewish Charities of Columbus, Ohio, to IRO, November 6, 1907; Joseph Kornfeld to IRO, January 20, 1910; ibid.

24. Simon Lazarus to IRO, July 26, 1911; Fred Lazarus to IRO, September 9, 1912; ibid.

25. Samuel Edelman to IRO, September 23, 1912; IRO to Fred Lazarus, February 17, 1913; ibid., Bressler, op. cit., p. 2, Edelman to IRO, October 20, 1912; IRO to Fred Lazarus, November 13, 1912; IRO Papers.

26. Interview with Samuel Edelman.

27. Paul Karger, one of the most active Columbus Jews in providing support for Russian immigrants, headed the Relief Committee of the B'nai B'rith Lodge No. 62 for many years. As early as January 1901, Karger tried unsuccessfully to convince the lodge to send for and support fifteen Rumanian refugees. See B'nai B'rith Minutes, January 13, 1901.

28. Lazarus to IRO, November 27, 1912; Karger to IRO, January 4, February 16, 1914; IRO Papers.

After immigrating from eastern Europe many Jewish peddlers "stood on market" at the Central Market on Fourth Street between Town and Rich streets. These pictures were taken from Rich Street looking north, and show only a small section of the large market center. The top photograph was taken during the 1880s and the bottom one after 1910.

9. MOVING IN AND MOVING UP: ECONOMIC LIFE

From the 1880s through World War I, significant numbers of immigrant Jews settled in Columbus; their major occupation was street peddling. Few of Columbus' east European Jews labored in the capital city's leading manufacturing companies, in the stone quarries, or on the railroads.[1] A Jew at work at the Jeffrey Manufacturing Company or Kilbourne & Jacobs Manufacturing Company was a rarity.[2] Most sought to be "their own bosses"; thus the abundance of tailors, merchants, and peddlers. Since the immigrants' most pressing problem upon arrival became finding work, those who "had no trade in their hands," little or no capital, and a desire to control the hours and days that they worked, turned to peddling or "independent merchandising." Some, despite the expanding network of retail trade and mail order companies, found the rural areas once crisscrossed by the German Jews still profitable. S. J. Wasserstrom (1855-1922) "used to go out for a week at a time to sell and would talk about the different little towns around that he would go to and it would take a whole week to go and come back with his horse and wagon."[3] I. H. Schlezinger (1878-1940), who peddled through several Ohio counties at the turn of the century,

> would trade with them and they would trade back to him if they had some old scrap iron, or something like that, that he could get a value out of when he would bring it back to Columbus. Many a time he would stay at their farmhouse . . . a farm-wife would give him an order; please, can he find this for her, find a hat for her or find something else, maybe a wash basin or an ironing board, or something. He would make up these lists and go out and trade in the country.[4]

Another immigrant recalls accompanying his father on his rural route:

Our first summer in Columbus my father took us to the country for the entire week while he was peddling for junk and trading for housewares we took along with us. We slept in farmhouses that were offered to us by most kind farmers. Some farmers were extremely kind. They invited us to dinner at their table, prepared a nice clean sleeping room, and in the morning they prepared a big breakfast for us and sent us off with baskets of fruits and vegetables.[5]

Most Columbus Jewish peddlers, however, preferred hawking notions, dry goods, fruit, junk, and rags on the streets. Eventually municipal ordinances required that each street peddler buy a peddler's license; in 1886 the police arrested Robert Gordon, a "Hebrew peddler," for neglecting to do so.[6] Solomon Kramer, who peddled for years,

had a cart, and he sold small stuff; odds and ends, scubadids, a steel pan in which you fry, and he sold stuff like that. His house was the dirtiest house you ever saw in your life. One time he asked me in there to help him, and he had some bread lying there which was moldy; bugs were crawling through it. He was eating it, bugs and all.[7]

One immigrant recalls that his father

would go in the alleys and holler, "Rags . . . old iron." Years ago a lot of our Jewish, old early people, use to do that. People would come out, young kids, "Here mister, I've got rags and iron." So little by little he use to load up his wagon . . . on Donaldson he use to have a pushcart. He didn't have the money to buy a horse and wagon.[8]

While some hawked their merchandise from a pushcart, others made their rounds with a horse and wagon. Stables dotted the Jewish section in the early years of the century; in 1899 there were seven horse stables on Noble Street between Seventh and Washington.[9] The peddler's wagon varied depending on the type of merchandise he sold and the success of his trade. The best had

what they called glass wagons, wagons especially built with glass windowpanes and bins, you could go into the wagon and shop. They were pulled by horses and later on they had trucks, these fellows.[10]

Some peddlers owned their own barns close to or at their homes, and had no need for the communal stables:

They lived on Mound Street . . . and they'd rent a big barn with a haymow on top to feed the horse. They kept the horse right there behind their home. When we moved on Gilbert Street we built our own barn; it was a big one, had stalls for two horses, and the wagons we kept in the yard outside.[11]

The routes varied, but in the days before refrigerators the community depended extensively upon the peddler:

> They would possibly buy like twice a week in those days. They'd go north twice a week, then go west twice a week, know what I mean? They kind of established a route. Sometimes there would be two or three different peddlers in that same area, but they would buy from one man one day and the other fella the next day because they couldn't hold perishables too long in those days, they didn't have refrigeration. They used to have ice, ice boxes, but that was limited. Winter time there was no problem; people would store potatoes, onions, cabbage, apples. Everybody would have a storage area in their basements and they would buy enough to last them nearly right straight through the winter.[12]

With modest success, enterprising hucksters could divide their time between stationary and mobile commerce:

> . . . on the days when the North Market was open, which I think was Monday, Wednesday, Friday, and Saturday, he worked at the market, you know, tending the stand. On the odd days, Tuesday and Thursday, he peddled; he had a horse and wagon.[13]

Friends and relatives bankrolled most of the peddlers. For example, William Callif's relatives outfitted him with the supplies necessary for peddling fruits and vegetables. Not all, however, were so fortunate:

> We had rich people that support these peddlers. They would lend him a hundred dollars, take off the first twenty dollars first of all and the eighty dollars they paid out in ten weeks. So you can imagine the interest. One of them went to jail on account of it because he had accumulated over $80,000 just from usury alone.[14]

While peddling offered independence, and unlimited opportunities for advancing to stationary merchandising positions, the road to success was arduous:

> A lot of them got out of it completely, didn't like it, it was long hours and hard work, then you were out in the elements; in the winter you'd freeze to death, and in the summer you'd burn up. A lot of them got into other trades, but this was a good sounding board for a person who had come over from the old country. They got a lot of basic business training as far as dealing with people and everything is concerned; they couldn't have asked for a better learning ground.[15]

Indeed the "learning ground" served as a useful path; almost every east European Jew who arrived in Columbus during the 1880s, like the German Jews fifty years earlier, began his occupational career as a peddler. The vast majority continued in a derivative occupation during the subsequent two decades.

Some peddlers, although certainly not the majority, became quite successful:

> Mr. [Abe] Goldberg arrived in Columbus from New York by horse and wagon peddling junk in the countryside. The horse died, so he remained in Columbus peddling junk with a pushcart because he did not have enough money to buy another horse. Every night he parked the pushcart on a vacant lot with only a broken shed on it. When he accumulated a little money, he bought the lot, stopped peddling and started buying junk from other peddlers and stored it in the street and then resold it to a junk dealer. In time he saved enough money to bring his family from Europe. By the time his family arrived, he had already outfitted a nice big house on Donaldson Street directly across the street from the junk shop.[16]

TABLE 34
OCCUPATIONS OF THE EARLIEST EAST EUROPEAN JEWISH IMMIGRANTS IN COLUMBUS

Name	U. S. Arrival	Earliest listing	1897 listing	1907 listing
Benjamin Wise	—	1882 watchman	—	junk
Kalmon London	—	1883 peddler	—	—
Benjamin Skuller	8- 1-1881	1883 peddler	—	—
Benjamin Margolis	—	1884 fruit	—	—
Louis Margulis	9-1881	1884 peddler	—	peddler
Samuel Isaac Gilberg	7-1882	1884 peddler	secondhand goods	clothing
Solomon Kramer	—	1884 peddler	peddler	peddler
Moses Freidenberg	—	1885 peddler	notions	—
Isaac Minitsky	6-1881	1885 notions	secondhand goods	clothing
Nathan Skuller	9-1881	1885 peddler	clothing	clothing
Philip Office	11-15-1881	1885 peddler	fruit	fruit
Jacob Sabledosky	7-1882	1885 peddler	huckster	—
Charles Margulis	9-1881	1885 clerk	pawnbroker	—
Jacob Margulis	—	1885 peddler	—	—
Simon Josephson	11- 1-1882	1885 peddler	—	fruit
August Margulis	—	1886 peddler	—	—
Simon Margulis	—	1886 peddler	—	—
S. Kohn	—	1886 renovator	—	—
Max Glick	7- 4-1883	1887 fruit	peddler	—
Abraham Goldberg	—	1887 peddler	junk	junk
Mayer Margulis	—	1888 peddler	peddler	—
William Margulis	—	1888 peddler	—	—
Louis Gilberg	7-1887	1888 peddler	—	clothing
Isaiah Waks	11-1888	1888 fruit	—	—
Isaac Finkelstein	—	1889 rags	dairyman	—

SOURCES: *Columbus City Directories.* General Index to Naturalization Declarations. A to Z 1859-1905.

Another success story was that of Jacob Schottenstein (1869-1947),[17] a Lithuanian immigrant who peddled in Columbus for more than a decade after his arrival in 1888 and then moved from secondhand clothing to pawnbroking to establishing the Columbus Cycle and Sporting Goods Company. His peddling and pawning became so profitable that even before the first decade of this century ended, Schottenstein had purchased in nine separate transactions $28,105 in commercial and residential property. No less prosperous were the Martlin brothers, Abraham (1869-1965)[18] and Isaac (1878-1950),[19] Russian immigrants who peddled secondhand clothing and later established a tailoring shop. The success of these endeavors enabled them to purchase $36,350 in property between 1900 and 1910. Such accumulations of property, during or shortly following years of peddling, were not uncommon in the immigrant community. Nevertheless, the overwhelming majority of east European immigrants, peddlers or otherwise, owned no property.

A large number of Jewish peddlers — well over the majority — seem to have been "on market." This was the expression used to describe one who either rented a permanent stall, or set up occasionally ("stood"), at Central Market on Town and Fourth streets. Erected in July of 1850, Central Market expanded as the lines of secondary commerce gently pushed eastward from High Street. Because Central Market House served as Columbus' first City Hall until 1872, the market's upper floor had elegant rooms for the mayor and other city officials. In 1875 the City Council passed an ordinance designating spaces for hucksters, flower stalls, and fish vendors, and putting all fresh meats at interior stands. By 1946 Central Market reportedly served 50,000 patrons and did $2 million worth of business. Market days — especially Saturdays — became times of fantastic activity, beginning with the pre-dawn clop-clop of horses as farmers drove in to "stand on market," and ending with streams of carriages with filled market baskets heading up Fourth Street.[20]

Jewish peddlers rented many of the permanent stalls in the market; they also comprised the bulk of the city peddlers who "stood on market," waiting for central Ohioans to come to them several days each week. They stood amidst color, shouts, odors, and dirt; the mingled aromas of garlic, cheeses, and onions, and the shouts of buyers and sellers. For more than one hundred and ten years, Central Market acted as a springboard for many successful peddlers who moved on to wholesaling, jobbing, manufacturing, and retailing.

While the sons of German Jewish merchants were expanding their fathers' stores, a number of east European Jewish men were establishing their own businesses between 1890 and 1925. Although the German Jews continued to dominate the clothing field, men with east European roots like Harry Gilbert, Robert Schiff, and Alfred Kobacker began to respond to Columbus' growth and venture into other areas of commercial activity.

Harry Gilbert (1893-1974) was one of eleven children born in Columbus to immigrants Samuel Isaac (1859-1913) and Sarah Schaeffer (1864-1931) Gilbert. Samuel Gilbert, present in Columbus by 1884, peddled through the countryside and city for more than twenty years. When Harry was thirteen, his father gave him seventy dollars; Harry bought forty pairs of shoes to stock a tiny fourteen-by-twenty-eight-foot cobbler and shoe store at 210 East Town in the heart of the old Central Market district. He worked there after school hours until graduation, then on a permanent full-time basis. From the beginning he bought factory closeouts, imperfect and bankrupt stocks, and store cancellations at large discounts and sold them cheaply. Harry Gilbert's second store — on Fourth Street — eventually became the largest and most widely known discount shoe outlet in central Ohio. Each subsequent outlet operated as a subsidiary corporation, with administration, buying, merchandising, and warehousing handled through central offices in Columbus. By the time Harry Gilbert celebrated his seventieth birthday, Gilbert Shoes operated leased discount shoe departments in six states, owned thirty stores with annual sales of over $3.3 million, and had placed its first stock issue of 30,000 shares and debentures worth $300,000 on the market. After 1940, Harry Gilbert succeeded Abe Goldberg as the leading philanthropist in the Orthodox community. In addition to generous financial contributions, he served as the first president of the Columbus Torah Academy, the first president of the Jewish Community Council, and a founder of the Agudas Achim Pre-School.[21]

Another success story is that of Robert W. Schiff (1886-1971). Born in Lithuania to Chaim Hirsh and Ethel Schleszinger Schiff, he studied at the famous Telsa Yeshiva from 1902 to 1905, and entered the shoe business as a clerk six years after his arrival in America in 1905. When he and his brother Albert organized the Schiff Shoe Corporation headquartered in Columbus in 1920, Schiff had already sold his interest in a chain of twelve stores he founded with another partner. The 1920s were years of rapid growth for the Schiffs: they added thirty-two stores in 1928 alone. Gross sales that year for ninety-one stores were $5.4 million — a 40 percent increase over 1927 and a 228 percent increase over 1924 — and net profits totaled almost $300,000. By 1940 Schiffs was America's third largest shoe chain; in 1946 Schiffs became Shoe Corporation of America. Operating 332 stores under various names in thirty-two

Many immigrant Jews from eastern Europe rose from street peddling to retailing and manufacturing. Examples were Jacob M. Schottenstein, who was the proprietor of the Ohio Soda Water Company at 448 East Livingston Avenue by 1909, and Mendal Trope, who owned a saloon (or grocery) on High Street in 1897.

states by 1950, SCOA grew within five years to 550 retail outlets and six manufacturing plants with total sales of $73 million. Known as SCOA Industries after 1969, the firm's net sales for fiscal 1972 reached $310.8 million.

Robert Schiff served as president of the company from 1920 through 1965; he received national recognition for his unique marketing concept: centralizing the buying and formulation of basic policies while individualizing store operation to fit local needs. An active Zionist and generous philanthropist, Robert Schiff served on the National Cabinet of the United Jewish Appeal, the Board of Directors of the Joint Distribution Committee, and as campaign chairman of the United Jewish Fund from 1940 to 1944.[22]

The Kobacker family were Lithuanian Jews who also did well in Columbus retail trade. With his sons Alfred (1886-1945) and Jerome, Hirsh Kobacker (1859-1930) opened a small dry goods store in Mt. Pleasant, Pennsylvania, in 1903; then a cloak and millinery shop in Connellsville two years later. By 1919 Alfred and Jerome had purchased the Boston Store in Columbus and after a $7 million merger in 1928, operated two department store chains in Ohio and New York. Like his father, Alfred was active in Columbus' civic and communal life. He served as director of the Ohio Chamber of Commerce, treasurer of the Columbus War Services Board, and director of the Retail Merchants Association. He was a member of the Board of Directors of Temple Israel and the first Board of Directors of the United Jewish Fund. At the time of his death the Kobacker stores had annual sales of more than $15 million.[23]

First and second generation Central European Jews also established numerous businesses in Columbus between 1890 and 1925. Saul M. Levy (1863-1965), a young Chicago merchant of German parentage, visited Columbus in the spring of 1894 and stayed long enough to found The Union Company, a clothing store for men and boys at High and Long streets. As a result of a 1903 fire he built a new two-story store on the site in 1904 and expanded it upward in 1910 to accommodate women's clothing. By 1923 he completed a six-floor addition, doubling the size of the store, and in subsequent years this family-owned and operated store added branch stores throughout the city.[24]

The United Woolen Company, a large clothing manufacturing plant located at 74-82 East Spring Street for many years, was founded by William A. Hersch (1867-1950). Born in Hungary and apprenticed to a soapmaker at the age of eleven, Hersch came to the United States at thirteen and began his own tailoring firm in Beaver Falls, Pennsylvania. Later moving to Parkersburg, West Virginia, he was doing $1.5 million worth of business annually by 1920. Hersch came to Columbus in the early 1920s and produced all the made-to-order clothing sold in his retail stores. Almost

Union Company founder Saul M. Levy with his wife, Hattie K.

thirty years later the Columbus plant employed three hundred persons and United Woolen Company's fifteen stores in three states sold forty to fifty thousand suits annually. A pioneer in employer-employee relationships, Hersch signed a collective bargaining contract with the A.F.L. Garment Workers Union shortly after World War I and initiated the five-day work week in his factory.[25]

At the end of the Civil War, German merchant Isaac Adolph Feibel (1839-1891) came to America. Within a few years he opened a dry goods store in Hillsboro, Ohio; later his sons opened another store in Blanchester, Ohio. By 1903 Jacob, Michael, Louis, and Julius owned Feibel Brothers Department Store at High and Russell streets in Columbus as well. Adorned with "35 arc lights and 40 Welsbach cluster lights for nite shopping," the store expanded rapidly to 32,400 square feet by 1908. Feibel Brothers Department Store sold all of its merchandise to Kobacker's Boston Store and Lazarus' basement in the early 1920s when the Feibel brothers closed the store to enter the real estate field. Julius, president of the Columbus Retail Merchants' Association from 1915 to 1916 and the leader of North Side merchant activities, typified dozens of Columbus Jews who traveled a similar route — Europe to a small Ohio town to Columbus.[26]

In addition to selling shoes and clothes, Jews were the pawnbrokers of Columbus. After peddling around Columbus for a few years, Morris Levison (1879-1941) opened Star-Loan Bank, a pawn shop, in 1896 in an area to be dominated by Jewish pawnbrokers for years. Indeed, the Levison brothers, Russian immigrants from Kovno, had three pawnshops on the same block: Morris was at 50, Dave at 56, and Isaac at 58 East Long Street. Other Russian Jewish pawnbrokers operated on the same street as well, for Jews overwhelmingly dominated this field throughout the twentieth century: Morris Freedman at 47, Max Greenstein at 52, Saul Ruben at 68, and Louis Rapenport at 80 East Long Street.[27]

While their husbands were employed as merchants, tailors, and pawnbrokers, a significant number of women became some of the most interesting and successful merchants in immigrant neighborhoods. This continued a pattern of the Russian Pale, for many immigrant Jewish women in Columbus had shared the burden of supporting families in the old country, usually by either selling goods and produce, or working in a factory. In the new land, most single women began working to support themselves or to help pay family expenses. After marriage, they worked to supplement husbands' earnings, to utilize their entrepreneurial talents, or simply to "get ahead." And, of course, widowed or deserted Jewesses had to support their families.

Anna Levin peddled fish in Russia for a short period before emigrating to Columbus in 1914 with her husband Isidore. While her husband worked as a carpenter, Anna began to sell fish in a garage on West Alley. On *erev shabbat* (Friday) she would peddle the leftovers through the neighborhood. From the small garage she moved her fish store to a garage at 424 Washington Avenue (near Fulton) in 1912, and expanded to include poultry. Outgrowing this location, she obtained a store at 402 Washington, and in 1925 her husband left carpentry to join her. Selling fish, poultry, fruits, and vegetables, the Levins became successful enough to raise seven children with Anna working full time.[28]

Minnie Gurevitz sealed matchboxes in a Minsk factory before coming to Columbus at the age of seventeen when she worked for a short time as a seamstress. Married at eighteen, she was a twenty-four-year-old mother of three when her husband William died in 1920. Never remarrying, she raised her family while "on market." For about the next thirty-five years she "stood on market," hawking fruit and vegetables obtained from a friend at the commission house. Her outdoor stall was open on Tuesday and Thursday while the kids were in school, as well as Saturday when the kids tossed apples around her.[29]

Goldie Godofsky arrived in Columbus from the Pale in 1906. At first she sewed in her Parsons Avenue rooming house for a dollar a week, but eventually she worked for Ohio Coatmakers as one of many Jewish tailoresses. She married her cousin, a meatcutter named Hyman Godofsky in 1915; soon after the young couple opened a small butcher and grocery shop at 705 Parsons below their second-floor rooms. Within seven years the Godofskys moved their store and home to larger quarters at 686 and 690½ Parsons, where they remained for two decades before finding larger store space. Until her first child arrived, Mrs. Godofsky worked as many hours in the store as did her husband; she felt she "built the business."[30]

Chava Goldfarb detrained in Columbus with her husband Sam just before World War I. While Sam peddled she began to sell chickens in the garage behind their Noble Avenue rooms. Within a year or two Sam joined her business, and by 1916 they operated out of a larger garage behind their residence at 330 South Washington Avenue. Each week Sam traveled to farms around Mt. Sterling, Ohio, to purchase the chickens which were slaughtered by the *shochet* who came regularly on Thursday mornings. For the next twenty-four hours Chava sold the farm chickens and eggs stored in her basement. The Goldfarbs raised their family on South Washington Avenue; well into the 1950s Mt. Sterling Poultry remained in Goldfarb hands at the same address.[31]

It was also not uncommon for Jewish women immigrants to work beside their husbands in small towns throughout southeastern Ohio. Pauline Luckoff, whose husband owned a general store in Nelsonville when they married in 1917, spent the next decade and a half opening and "breaking in" Luckoff's stores in Athens, Chauncey, Gloucester, Logan, and Lancaster. The Luckoffs settled permanently in Columbus in the 1930s after opening their first store in the city.[32]

In 1908 Lena Furman followed her brother from Poland to Savoy and then Gloucester, Ohio. A maid in Gloucester, and then a seamstress in Columbus, Lena married peddler Harry Margulies in 1912. Lena began selling Harry's extra merchandise in her living room at 247 East Livingston Avenue. Bit by bit Lena's business grew: she made and sold aprons and dresses, expanded her "store" to another room, acquired adjacent property, increased her stock, and built Margulies & Son on the same street. While Harry delivered merchandise and collected payments, Lena, the mother of four children, managed the store for nearly twenty years.[33]

These women of energy and talent obviously do not fit the kitchen-bound Jewish mother stereotype which persists whenever turn-of-the-century immigrant women are discussed. While these women contributed to many areas of the neighborhood's economy they virtually monopolized the fish, herring, and poultry businesses — playing their most active roles on "chicken day" (Thursday), when the Jews would purchase their supplies for the Sabbath meal.

Thus the years between 1880 and 1925 were a replay of an

earlier period of Jewish immigrant history. Previously the success stories belonged to the Lazaruses and Gundersheimers; after Columbus' second wave of immigration, these stories belonged to new names like Gilbert, Schottenstein, and Kobacker. While the names changed, the same process was repeated in each man's or woman's desire for independence and success. This desire propelled peddlers into the middle class and a few into the upper stratum of Jewish society.

NOTES FOR CHAPTER 9

1. A 1907 industrial survey revealed twenty factories made and sold over $8 million worth of machine shop products in 1906, eight shoe companies produced $6 million in shoes, while carriages and wagons ($5 million), malt liquors ($4 million), lumber and planing ($4 million) and medical compounds ($3 million) also constituted sizeable industries. Herbert Brooks, "The Financial Interests of Columbus," *The Ohio Magazine* 3:6 (December 1907): 462.

2. Not only did Jews shun industrial employment, but Columbus workers generally were nonindustrial. In 1905 wage earners in the manufacturing industries constituted only 10 percent of the city's population, while in Toledo, Dayton, and Cleveland the percentages were 17, 17, and 18 respectively. See Robert L. Tavenner et al., *Columbus Manufactures: A Statistical Paper on the City of Columbus, Ohio* (The Ohio State University, 1906-07), p. 5.

3. Interview with Etta Brandt.

4. Interview with Edward Schlezinger.

5. "Autobiography of Herman Perlman," typescript.

6. *OSJ*, September 25, 1886.

7. Interview with A. S. Kohn.

8. Interview with Jacob Pass; see also interview with Ben Yenkin.

9. *G. W. Baist's Property Atlas of the City of Columbus* (Philadelphia, 1899), Plate 6.

10. Interview with Paul Callif.

11. Ibid.

12. Ibid.

13. Interview with Harry Schwartz.

14. Interview with B. W. Abramson.

15. Interview with Paul Callif. Peddlers plied their wares in Columbus' Jewish sections for years after automobiles were commonplace. In 1927 one peddler, Harry Greenstein, parked his horse and wagon, laden with $155 of fruit, in front of a grocery; his entire "store" was stolen; *OSJ*, November 8, 1927.

16. "Autobiography of Herman Perlman," typescript.

17. *OJC*, September 12, 1947.

TABLE 35
MARTLIN AND SCHOTTENSTEIN PROPERTY ACQUISITIONS

Year	Person	Amount
1900	Isaac Martlin	$4,500
1902	Jacob Schottenstein	4,500
1903	Isaac Martlin	1,500
1903	Jacob Schottenstein	1,025
1903	Jacob Schottenstein	650
1906	Jacob Schottenstein	1,200
1906	Jacob Schottenstein	8,930
1907	Abe Martlin	4,650
1907	Isaac Martlin	4,200
1907	Jacob Schottenstein	2,600
1907	Jacob Schottenstein	3,000
1907	Jacob Schottenstein	3,700
1908	Abe Martlin	8,500
1908	Isaac Martlin	6,000
1908	Jacob Schottenstein	2,500
1910	Isaac Martlin	7,000

SOURCE: Franklin County Recorder, Grantee Index No. 2 and Deeds.

TABLE 36
CENTRAL MARKET MERCHANTS, 1947*

Stall	Merchant	Stall	Merchant
10	Morris Thall (fruit)	20	Charles Shenker (produce)
11	Jacob Sussman (produce)	21	Leo Federer (groceries)
13	David Rich (produce)	22	Harry Kauffman (produce)
16	Charles Gallione (produce)	23	Anna Clebone (produce)
17	Isaac Kauffman (produce)	24	Phillip Flichia (groceries)
18	Toby Berlin (fruit)	26	Piedro Lusianola (produce)
19	Toby Berlin (fruit)	27	Morris Brodsky (produce)

*partial list

SOURCE: *Columbus City Directory*, 1947.

18. *OJC*, July 30, 1948; Mrs. Dewey (Martha) Rosenfield to Marc Lee Raphael, telephone conversation, September 6, 1976.
19. *OJC*, March 31, 1950.
20. *CC*, July 17, 1950, November 15, 1955; *CD*, March 19 and May 14, 1950, March 12 and 21, 1961, June 21, 1966.
21. Conversations with Jacob Gilbert and Marion Gilbert; *OJC*, February 6, 1931; Harry Gilbert Scrapbook; *CCJ*, March 16, 1962; *CC*, March 5, 1951; *OSJ*, March 6, 1951.
22. M. M. Chanis, *Robert W. Schiff: A Talmudic Scholar in American Business. A Biographical Portrait and Tribute* (July 4, 1966); *WWAJ*, 1938-39, Volume 3, p. 936; *Who Was Who in America*, Volume V, p. 640; *OSJ*, March

6, 1929, May 17, 1940; *CC,* June 16, 1950; *CD,* June 12, 1955; *OSJ,* July 6, 1955; SCOA Industries, Inc. Annual Report, 1972; *Chain Stores in America,* p. 382. The only United States manufacturing company among the 500 largest industrial corporations (ranked by sales volume) claiming Columbus as home in 1954 was SCOA; *Fortune,* July 1955.

23. A. Kobacker Scrapbook (n.p., n.d.), courtesy of Arthur J. Kobacker of Brilliant, Ohio; *CD,* June 3, 1936; Regina Kobacker Fadiman to Marc Lee Raphael, correspondence, August 6, 1974; *OSJ,* January 11, 1928; *CD,* April 14, 1942; *OJC,* November 3, 1922, March 7, 1924, January 13, 1928, September 13, 1929, September 12, 1930, and February 2, 1945.

24. *CD,* April 14, 1950, October 6, 1952; *OSJ,* January 1, 1953, *CC,* November 9, 1956.

25. *CC,* October 14, 1950; January 19, 1951; *OSJ,* October 16, 1950; *OJC,* October 20, 1950; *CD,* December 16, 1951; Arthur J. Hersch to Marc Lee Raphael, telephone conversation, March 16, 1975.

26. *WWAJ,* Volume 3, p. 256; "Feibel Family" — an unpublished typescript; *CS,* April 24, 1902; *CC,* April 24, 1902; *OSJ,* December 12, 1903, July 2, 1910; *CD,* December 6, 1908, June 28, 1909, July 1, 1910; *OJC,* April 23, 1954. Another successful merchant to repeat this pattern was Frank Glick (1876-1931), who opened the Climax Clothing Store and then Glick's Furniture Company in Columbus after he and his father bought and sold stores in Richwood, LaRue, North Lewisburg, and Fort Recovery, Ohio; *OJC,* June 12, 1931, and *CD,* September 29, 1954.

27. Dave Levison to Marc Lee Raphael, telephone conversation, July 1975, and various *Columbus City Directories.*

Other early east European businesses included the Silberstein (Harry and Max) Brothers' Columbus Pipe and Equipment Company, a major seller and fabricator of structural steel (*CC,* December 31, 1957); Schottenstein's, a department store chain founded by Ephraim Louis Schottenstein (1893-1955) in 1917 in a small one-floor building on Parsons Avenue which at the time of his death had grown to a three-story structure covering half a city block (*CD,* July 13, 1952, May 27, 1961; *OJC,* August 5, 1955); Topper (Isaac and Max) Brothers Iron and Metal Dealers, begun in 1902 by two peddlers from Bialystock (*OJC,* March 1, 1934, February 8, 1946; *Columbus City Directory* 1902-03; *Eminent Jews of America,* pp. 304-05; telephone conversation with Reva Goldberg Shaman, September 12, 1975.)

28. Lee Levin Goodman to Marc Lee Raphael, telephone conversation, February 9, 1977. Additional information was obtained about Anna, as well as the subsequent women, from a variety of public records.

29. Minnie Goldberg to Marc Lee Raphael, telephone conversation, February 10, 1977.

30. Goldie Godofsky to Marc Lee Raphael, telephone conversation, February 10, 1977, and *Food Store Review* 5:8 (September 1946).

31. Lou Goldfarb, telephone conversation to Marc Lee Raphael, February 11, 1977.

32. Pauline Luckoff, telephone conversation to Marc Lee Raphael, February 10, 1977.

33. Conversation between Lena Margulies and Linda Elise Kalette, February 23, 1977.

10. THE OLD AND FAMILIAR: SYNAGOGUE LIFE

Between 1880 and 1925 Columbus' Jewish community founded one Reform and five Orthodox synagogues — one of which joined the Conservative movement. While the Reform Jews intensified their efforts to become adherents of the Protestant ethos, Russian and Hungarian Jews desired to remain separate and retain their ethnic values, and for a while, their Orthodox beliefs.

Orthodoxy completely enveloped the lives and guided much of the behavior of a sizable number of Russian-Jewish immigrants. Membership in a Reform temple like the German Jews' B'nai Israel was unimaginable; for to the Orthodox, Reform Judaism was little more attractive than Christianity. The precise origins of the earliest synagogue established by the east European Jews of Columbus are obscure, however. Five men, including Abraham Milder, S. Kohn, Isaac Minitsky, and Moses Freidenberg, incorporated Agudas Achim on May 24, 1889, but there is little question that the congregation began several years earlier.[1] A September 1885 item in Congregation B'nai Israel's Minute Book stated:

> The renting of pews did not realize very much this year and for various reasons, the most of which is first: The Orthodox Congregation begging away from us some young men who every year took seats during the holidays . . .[2]

At the dedication of Agudas Achim's second synagogue on December 29, 1907, a local reporter commented that the ten men who founded Agudas Achim "twenty-five years ago" on South Fourth near Town Street all appeared at the dedication.[3] The presence of nine of these ten "founders" in 1882 cannot be confirmed; much evidence indicates they could not have been in Columbus.[4] Therefore, Agudas Achim apparently was organized sometime prior to the High Holidays of 1885.[5]

For the most part, synagogue members were poor and their treasury inadequate. Every one of the identifiable men who signed the incorporation document in 1889 was a peddler; not one owned any property in Columbus prior to 1900. Additionally, as late as 1907-08 the 165 members (another source claims 280 members) provided an annual income — excluding the building fund — of only $2,500 for Agudas Achim.[6]

The congregation dedicated its first synagogue on October 26, 1896, at South Fifth Street, very close to Central Market Hall where services had been conducted previously. On that Sunday, Reverend Solomon Lurie chanted psalms, Rabbi Weiss of B'nai Israel delivered the dedicatory address, and I. B. Jashenosky, the president of the congregation, also spoke. He told the assembled members, guests, and "prominent citizens" that in addition to the Torah scrolls which members of the congregation had copied on parchment, the American flag represented their "most sacred religious possession."[7] "A plain but substantial structure," the Fifth Street synagogue was described as a "bit of the far east set down in Columbus" — the result of seeing "gloomy faced men" on the main floor and women seated separately in the balcony above. As Table 37 indicates, a large number of non-ordained men officiated as sextons, cantors, preachers, ritual slaughterers, and prayer readers before the arrival of the congregation's first rabbi in 1908. However, with the hiring of Rabbi Isaac Wiernikowsky (1876-1940) a continuous line of ordained men served Agudas Achim.

TABLE 37
AGUDAS ACHIM CLERGYMEN

188?-1896	Kalmon London[8]	1907-1909	Henry Schneider[15]
1889-1894	Mordechai I. Altfeld[9]	1908-1911	Isaac Wiernikowsky[16]
1894-1897	Solomon Lurie[10]	1910-1913	Solomon Don[17]
1896-1899	Joseph Rapenport[11]	1911-1934	Simon Silverman[18]
1899-1900	Abraham Wohlkin[12]	1912-1918	Morris Taxon
1900-1907	Nathan Silverman[13]	1917-1920	Solomon Neches
1904-1908	Saul Silber[14]	1921-1933	Isaac Werne

The dedication of a new imposing synagogue at Donaldson Street and Washington Avenue began a period of sustained growth for this congregation.[19] Little more than eleven years after the opening of the first temple, more than twelve hundred assembled on December 30, 1907, for the elaborate dedication of the new synagogue. This $42,000 building served the congregation for more than forty years. Even at this auspicious occasion the shadow of the German Jewish community loomed large, as the guest speaker,

Rabbi Rudolph Coffee of Pittsburgh, berated the leaders of Agudas Achim:

> You Hebrews of Columbus pride yourself on your Orthodoxy . . . and on your spirit of religious tolerance . . . but it is a burning disgrace that you have not a school in which your children are taught in the English language the principles of the Hebrew faith.

Coffee urged the Orthodox congregation to model itself on Congregation B'nai Israel, where more than one hundred children received instruction in English rather than Hebrew, for the "true principles of Judaism are found in the English language."[20]

The "burning disgrace" to which Rabbi Coffee pointed was Columbus' Hebrew Free School or Talmud Torah. A fledgling

Prior to the 1920s, only two synagogues provided religious instruction through confirmation – B'nai Israel and Agudas Achim. Rabbi Taxon confirmed this Agudas Achim class of 1915. In the front row, from the left: Goldie Bonowitz, Esther Levy, Fanny Goldberg, Fanny Luper, Rose Finkelstein, Betty Solomon, Anna Rosenthal, Sarah Godofsky, unknown, Sarah Rabinowitz, Sarah Bonowitz. Second row: Sam Silverman, Jack Erlen, Earl Reed, Abe Rubin, Anna Wohlstein, Fannie Horkin, unknown, Louis Bornstein, Aaron Sachs, Sam Wolman. Third row: Alta Gilberg, Gertrude Nachmanovitz, Tillie Topper, Bertha Wolman, Edith Schottenstein. Back row: Synagogue President Nathan Finkelstein, unknown, Harry Lebeson, unknown, teacher Bert Wolman, Rabbi Morris Taxon, Louis Josephson, Morris Levison, ? Kadeshevitz.

attempt at communal Hebrew education, the Talmud Torah was organized about 1896 and incorporated on September 29, 1900, to provide "instruction to Jewish children" and aid "their moral and physical development." With more hope than money, its first president, B. Silverman, announced that teachers would be paid $20 per week; by the time Rabbi Coffee denigrated the Talmud Torah in his 1907 address, Abraham Goldberg was presiding over a small school housed at 337 East Livingston Avenue with a meager $1,100 income. Significant growth of the Talmud Torah still loomed some decades in the future.[21]

During the first twenty-five years following the dedication of the new synagogue, three rabbis directed the religious life of the congregation. Rabbi Morris Nathan Taxon (1890-1940) came to Agudas Achim in 1912 after spending two years at his first rabbinate in White Plains, New York. By signing a two-year contract, at $1,200 per year, this twenty-two-year-old agreed to "perform all duties required of an Orthodox rabbi." These included visiting the homes of the members and advising them about their domestic ritual and business problems; preaching on Friday nights, Saturday mornings, and holidays; and conducting Sabbath and Hebrew schools.

Born in Yavadna (Edwabna), near Lomza in Polish Russia, to Abraham Solomon and Gruna Taxon, Morris received ordination in New York at the Isaac Elchanan Seminary in 1910. Reputedly the first Orthodox rabbi in America to have dared to preach in English on the High Holidays, Taxon's extant writings reveal a fluency in both the English language and contemporary philosophy — a rarity among Orthodox rabbis of his time. His sermons reveal that he was a theist sustained by a belief in a creating, revealing, redeeming, miracle-working, loving, and judging God, and that he was an adamant champion of Orthodoxy:

> Orthodox Judaism is an unbroken chain of Jewish tradition connecting the days of Moses with our own. Never in the whole course of Jewish law has any change been made that was not written in the law. All new ordinances represented but application of precedent to new conditions. Orthodox designates the genuine Jew, the man or woman who lives in accordance with traditional Jewish law.

On July 4, 1917, Taxon married Edythe Irene Schottenstein, the daughter of Sarah and Jacob Schottenstein, who was the president of Agudas Achim. Rabbi Taxon's troubles with the congregation seem to have begun with his marriage, for some of the leadership accused him of making a "political *shiddach*" (match) for security. Those dissatisfied with either Schottenstein's leadership or the rabbi lined up against Taxon; by 1918 they were numerous enough to virtually force him to resign.[22]

Rabbi Solomon M. Neches (1891-1957) succeeded Taxon. A Palestinian-born descendant of Poland's Elijah Vilna Gaon (1720-1797), Neches was educated at the Etz Chaim Yeshiva in Jerusalem and ordained in Palestine in 1909 and in America three years later. After serving Pittsburgh's B'nai Israel congregation from 1913 to 1918, Neches led Agudas Achim from 1918 to 1921 before beginning a long career in Los Angeles. The author of several collections of Hebrew and English stories and sermons, as well as the compiler of numerous volumes of commentaries to biblical and medieval literature, Rabbi Neches gained recognition for his work as "dean" of the Western Jewish Institute, a program of evening classes and lectures in Los Angeles.

Neches' most enduring contribution to Agudas Achim and Columbus Jewry was his Zionist activity. As president of the Columbus Zionist District from 1918 to 1920, he brought to Agudas Achim several well-known religious Zionist speakers. In addition he organized Pirchei Zion, a group of Agudas Achim students that met on the first Sunday of each month to discuss Palestine; he began a Hebrew Club for young men who listened to his lectures in Sephardic Hebrew two nights a week; and he convinced four young men to join the Jewish Legion (the Palestine Unit of the British Army). Neches also initiated a communitywide course on Zionism under the direction of Henry Feinberg, a brilliant graduate student at The Ohio State University.[23]

Isaac Werne (née Wiernikowsky), probably the most distinguished intellectual to serve Columbus Jewry prior to the Second World War, followed Neches. Born in Slonim, Russia, in 1876, Werne studied at *yeshivot* in Slonim, Vilna, and Warsaw before his 1897 ordination. After secular studies at Heidelberg and Marburg, Werne received his doctorate in 1902 from Koenigsberg for his German dissertation on "The Book of Job as Interpreted in the Rabbinical Literature of the First Five Centuries A.D."

Werne served in New York City's Emunat Israel in 1904, and then moved to Massachusetts where he led Holyoke's B'nai Zion in 1905, and Worcester's Sha'are Torah in 1906. He remained at Agudas Achim synagogue from 1908 to 1910. Fluent in several languages, already publishing Hebrew articles and editing the Hebrew monthly *Ha'am* from 1907 to 1908, Werne must certainly have felt himself a "light in the wilderness," as one long-time resident put it. It seems unlikely that Werne found much, if any, intellectual stimulation during these years. According to one of his loyal followers, "he nearly starved to death"; another remembers:

> Poor Rabbi Werne was actually starving with his family because his salary was about five to eight dollars a week. The Ezras Noshim

> Society would collect food and money and on Friday there sure was a big basket of food for the family. He was so poor that — he had the most beautiful Hebrew library at that time and he sold it piece by piece in order to maintain his family.

By 1910 Werne had left Columbus, and served in Chicago at Ohev Zedek until 1914; he stayed at Los Angeles' Beth Israel for six years, and served in Dallas at She'arith Israel for one year. Returning to Columbus in 1921 for more than a decade of service, Werne left to accept a congregational position as well as the presidency of the Los Angeles United Orthodox Rabbinate where he served until 1940.[24]

During his second term at Agudas Achim, Dr. Werne brought dignity and distinction to Orthodox Judaism in Columbus. His most popular undertaking was the Agudas Achim "Open Forum," a late Friday evening program of brief prayers, reading, and singing, featuring a lecture and discussion. Its purpose, Werne explained, consisted in "the instruction and enlightenment of Jews in the basic principles of Judaism and the problems of the Modern Jew." An active participant in the Open Forum recalled:

> It was an attempt to familiarize the members and families with the more modern day questions, as well as to answer questions which the rabbi didn't always answer. The rabbi was always on the pulpit during these forums, and the members of the audience would question him and all sorts of questions were shot at him and he was very frank in trying to answer them.

Sometimes Werne would review popular motion pictures like *The King of Kings, The Ten Commandments,* and *Ben Hur,* or books like *American Tragedy* or *Future of an Illusion.* On other occasions he would deliver lectures about "Anthropomorphisms in the Bible," "Higher Criticism of the Bible," or "The Humanistic Appeal of Judaism"; frequently members of the local Jewish community would lecture or participate in symposia and/or debates. Dr. Werne's forums were the most popular programs of their kind in the Columbus Jewish community during the 1920s. The non-Jewish press regularly discussed the Open Forums and the Orthodox community generously attended them. Indeed, one of Werne's colleagues remembered that although "he would speak in English with a terrible accent, he drew a thousand people on a Friday night to listen to his lectures."[25]

Like several of Columbus' Reform rabbis, Werne lectured frequently during the week. Unlike Rabbi Tarshish of Temple Israel, who spoke primarily to non-Jewish audiences, Werne brought his message to his coreligionists. For many years he lectured to the older students in the religious school on Sunday, to the confirmands on Mondays, to the adults on Tuesday, to the teachers on Thursday, at the Open Forum on Friday evening, and to the congregation on Saturday morning. In addition, he conducted a daily Talmud session in the late afternoon, a Talmud Study Circle on Saturday afternoon *(Chevrah Shass),* and a daily *Mishnah* session following 6:00 a.m. services *(Chevrah Mishnayoth).* At the Talmud Study Circle according to one student, he "propounded tractates [Talmud pages] not in a fashion to which Orthodox Jewry was accustomed during which he injected legal and critical observations." Extant notes leave no doubt that Werne was an Orthodox rabbi deeply grounded in traditional Jewish learning, as well as a modern scholar widely read in contemporary philosophy, theology, literature, biblical criticism, and popular culture, who felt equally at home with questions on ritual impurities or best-selling novels.

Zionist activities, initiated under Rabbi Neches, continued to distinguish both Agudas Achim and Beth Jacob from the city's other congregations. With the support of the Columbus Zionist District, Werne led annual memorial services for Zionist leaders such as Theodor Herzl and Max Nordau. In addition Werne spoke frequently — and occasionally in Hebrew — at the Open Forum and elsewhere about Palestine and conducted appeals for the Jewish National Fund on Tisha B'Av and other holidays. He initiated a conversational Hebrew group, vociferously supported political Zionism, and organized youth clubs dominated by Zionist groups (Young Israel, Blossoms of Israel, Zionites). Public lectures at the synagogue frequently featured out-of-town Zionist leaders like Jacob de Haas, Golda Meir (née Myerson), Louis Lipsky, Abba Hillel Silver, and Maurice Samuel. Werne's influence, decades later, still echoes in the Orthodox community.[26]

The lay person most prominently associated with Agudas Achim during these years was Abraham Goldberg (1858-1940). Born in Russia, the son of Rabbi Isaac Goldberg, Abe and his future wife Toba became engaged as children. Their daughter recalled:

> She was engaged when she was nine years old, for the rabbi says, "As soon as she gets old enough, get her engaged, and then she'll be okay." She was nine years old and she was engaged to my father and he was in another city and every year they use to visit and see how my mother was getting along — because she was a little, teeny, dried-up thing. [Then] she was engaged six years to my father, and they never saw each other. He said he never saw the bride until he lifted the veil to give her a drink of wine, and he said he nearly died — her face was so green, and so thin and puny. And that's the first time he ever saw his bride.

Abraham and Toba Goldberg provided leadership for almost every organization in the Orthodox community. Toba was one of the founders and president for forty years of Ezras Noshim, an Orthodox women's charitable organization. Abe was president of Agudas Achim for twenty-five years.

Married in 1878, Goldberg came to the United States seven years later without his family. Unable to adjust to farming a 160-acre government allotment in Wichita, Kansas, he decided to travel east. According to several independent accounts, his horse died when he reached Ohio's capital. Goldberg is first listed in the 1887 *Columbus City Directory* as a peddler boarding at 410 East Cherry. Within two or three years he saved enough money to bring his family over from Russia. Before long he owned the Goldberg Iron & Steel Company, and later emerged — together with Toba — as the most dedicated philanthropist in the Orthodox community. He served Agudas Achim as president for a quarter century, was elected and reelected president of the Talmud Torah continuously from its inception, and devoted much time to personally raising funds for both institutions.[27]

Orthodox Columbus Jews had founded three other synagogues by the time Agudas Achim dedicated its new sanctuary in 1907, and one other was founded shortly thereafter. Congregation Etz Hayim (Tree of Life) has left few traces other than the fact that it shared Agudas Achim's first synagogue at 646 South Fifth Street from 1897 to 1905. During the first year of its brief existence, Rabbi

This Beth Jacob Synagogue on East Donaldson served the congregation for more than four decades.

David Falk served; he was followed by Abraham Wohlkin from 1898 to 1900, and Nathan Silverman from 1900 to 1905. Little more is known of the congregation which apparently ceased organized existence about 1905.[28]

More successful was Beth Jacob, which began in 1898 with eleven Orthodox men who sought to serve God, study Torah, and worship in the Sephardic (Spanish-Portuguese) rather than the Ashkenazic (German-Polish) mode of ritual. Of the original members these five were united not only by their perseverance but by their poverty: peddlers David Factorow, Louis Duscoff, Louis Lieberman, and David Bonowitz who all lived on the same block of Livingston Avenue, and tailor Max Keretsy who lived on a street adjacent to his friends. They conducted meetings in Yiddish and held their worship services in various homes on the Sabbath, while celebrating holidays in public buildings such as Schenck's Hall on South High Street and Reeb's on East Mound Street.

By 1909 the original pioneers, little more than a *minyan,* had grown to more than one hundred members (two contemporary sources say two hundred). On Sunday, August 23, despite the tremendous financial sacrifice, the cornerstone of a forty-six by

TABLE 38
CONSTITUTION AND BYLAWS OF BETH JACOB CONGREGATION

Article I	
Section II	*The Purpose* *The purpose of the congregation is to serve God, study Torah in the old traditional manner according to the* minhag S'fard.
Section III	*Existence* *The congregation cannot be disbanded as long as a third of the membership in good standing will support it.*
Section IV	*The Language* *The language in which the business and the protocol (minutes) shall be conducted shall be Yiddish. However, when one wishes he can express himself at a meeting in English.*
Section V	*Ownership of the congregation can never be given away to someone.*
Article II	
Section IV	*The paid religious officers of the congregation shall be the following: a qualified rabbi, well-known and in strict accordance with the orthodox belief, a cantor, a* ba'al Koreh, *a* shamash.
Article V	
Section X	*Every member of the Board of Trustees shall, whenever possible, be at every worship service and see to it that there should be order and conduct in shul.*
Section XIII	*The Board can fine, suspend, or expel a member of the congregation for unbecoming conduct at meetings or at a shul during services . . . and for conduct which is against the moral Jewish and ethical principles.*
Article VI	
Section I	*The President . . . shall, on the Sabbath and on the holidays, be in shul during services and take care that the best decorum is in order.*
Article VII	
Section I	*The paid officers must give of their entire energy that there shall be peace between the members in particular, and between all Jewish people in general.*
Article XII	
Section XI	*No member has a right to walk around in the synagogue or to make disturbance when the* Chazan, *or the* Ba'al Tiphila *davens, when the president speaks or the rabbi is giving a sermon or when the reader of the Torah reads.*

sixty-foot house of worship was laid at 446 East Donaldson. The ceremonies, held in a tent before six hundred persons, included brief remarks by Governor Judson Harmon, former governor James Campbell (who spoke about religious freedom), an address in Yiddish by Reverend Benjamin Gittelson of Cleveland, and a message from the distinguished New York City Superior Court Judge Leon Sanders. This modern brick building had two large cathedral windows flanking the entrance, with a small circular leaded glass window centering the gable, and a *bimah* (pulpit) in the center of the sanctuary.[29]

Notwithstanding the great commitment displayed by its membership in erecting their new synagogue, Beth Jacob was without an ordained rabbi for almost fifteen years. During this time other signs of synagogue life were visible: the Ladies Auxiliary was formed in 1909; one or two years later Beth Jacob's first clergyman, Rev. Simon Holland (b. 1874), began four years of service; and by 1919 a *Va'ad Hakashrut* (Dietary Council) existed.

Finally in 1922, in partnership with Congregation Ahavas Sholom, Beth Jacob extended an offer to Ephraim Pelkovitz (1885-1966), a "learned and famous and totally observant" rabbi who had served the Orthodox Jewish community of Canton, Ohio, since 1914. Born in Lomza, Poland, and trained in the Lomza, Roden, and Slabotke *yeshivot,* Pelkovitz was ordained by the Grand Rabbi of Slutzk, and occupied a pulpit in Russia at the age of nineteen. Rabbi Pelkovitz came to America in 1914 and served briefly in Roxbury, Massachusetts, before moving to Canton.[30]

Rabbi Pelkovitz's primary responsibilities centered around Beth Jacob, although on the second day of major holidays he would preach at Ahavas Sholom. Undoubtedly, his most lasting contribution was the leadership he provided the Columbus Hebrew School. The rabbi taught Talmud to the senior class and, together with the officers of the school, examined the students in *siddur* (prayer book) reading, vocabulary, sentence construction, and grammar.[31] But as Nathan Pelkovitz recalls, much else kept him busy:

> . . . the pride we took in our [Pelkovitz] home on Mound Street with its side porch, grape arbor, tomato and corn, fruit trees and delapidated rear barn. The house was used as more than a parsonage. It was a wailing wall, a refuge for the disturbed, a hostel for visiting mendicants and collectors for *yeshivot.* But more important, the rabbi was busy in *kashruth* [dietary laws] — examining the entrails of chickens surrounded by the *shulchan aruch* [a sixteenth-century legal compendium] code to see if he couldn't tease out a verdict of "kosher" while the poor housewife stood apprehensive that the fowl was flawed; in marital affairs, ranging from counselor to president of a Jewish divorce court; in business affairs, since it was still not

uncommon for civil disputes about money matters to be taken to the rabbi as arbiter in a *din torah* [court].

In the twenties the most intriguing time around the house and in *shul* was the week before Passover. Congregants would troop in on a dual mission — to sell their *chometz* [leavened food] and chat about communal affairs and to purchase the jug of sacramental concord grape wine (sometimes also muscatel and for favored folk my mother would make a gift of her homemade honey-based mead). This was Prohibition time and in Ohio the rabbi became the wine merchant at *Pesach* [Passover] time and a most welcome source of income it was for the clergyman who lived on the edge.[32]

Pelkovitz, "a deeply learned rabbi of the old school," became an active Zionist as a member of the national executive committee of the Mizrachi Organization, and a member of the executive committee of the midwest region of *Agudath Harabanim*. Eventually, during his more than thirty years of service as rabbi of the *Kehilla* of five synagogues in Bridgeport, Connecticut, he became a distinguished *halachist* and a national vice-president of the *Agudath Harabanim*.[33]

Rabbi Pelkovitz's influence upon his congregants during his three-year tenure at Beth Jacob is still traceable. Placing the Columbus Hebrew School before his own synagogue's needs, Pelkovitz insisted that one hundred dollars raised by the Beth Jacob Ladies Auxiliary in 1922 be donated to the Talmud Torah building fund. He also increased the utilization of Beth Jacob's facilities by making room for more than two hundred Talmud Torah students when larger facilities could not be obtained, and allowing Beth Jacob to be used as a polling place. Two of his congregants, N. Danziger and C. H. Furman, were persuaded by Pelkovitz to run as delegates to the recently-formed American Jewish Congress. Rabbi Pelkovitz never missed an opportunity to plead for funds for worthy causes. Sam Solove's bar mitzvah at the Talmud Torah in December of 1923 featured three sermons; Sam delivered one in Yiddish and another in Hebrew, while Rabbi Pelkovitz's Yiddish address urged the guests to empty their pockets for the Talmud Torah. The rabbi must have been convincing, for Mr. and Mrs. Joseph Solove delivered $590 courtesy of their guests.[34]

The fourth Orthodox congregation founded in Columbus was Tifereth Israel; there is a widespread consensus in the Columbus Jewish community that its origins date from the *brit* (circumcision) of J. Nathan Polster, the son of Louis R. Polster, early in October of 1901. A group of Hungarian Jews who attended that ceremony decided late in 1901 to organize what became known for a decade as the First Hungarian Hebrew Church.[35] Meeting initially at 392

East Livingston, the congregation moved to its own building at 330 South Parsons in 1909 and dedicated a new building at the Parsons Avenue address in September of 1915. The Hungarian congregation grew slowly for many years; in 1912 there were only thirty-three members.[36]

Although these Hungarian Jews, like Jews from adjacent lands to the east, were often labeled "Russians" by German Jews already here, these new immigrants felt a keen sense of pride about their origins. The city, province, or country of their birth frequently served as the organizing principle for religious and social life, as seen in the Voliner Society. Thus the origin of the Hungarian *shul*, as explained by Rabbi Nathan Zelizer, may be more truthful than apocryphal:

> According to the information that I received from all of the old timers . . . the congregation was founded following a Jewish service on Yom Kippur at the old Agudas Achim . . . sometime in 1901 . . . when a number of Hungarian Jews were congregated on the steps of the synagogue while services were going on. One of the officials of the congregation came out and began to chastise them for congregating, and talking, and making noise, and he used the phrase, "You hunkies, will you either get out, leave the premises of the synagogue, or come in and sit like men should." Now this, of course, antagonized the Hungarian Jews . . .
>
> So a number of these Hungarian Jews . . . decided not to associate themselves in religious activities with the Polish and Russian Jews of the Agudas Achim Congregation and they founded the Tifereth Israel Congregation (or, as it was called then), the First Hungarian Hebrew Church . . .[37]

Seven Hungarians signed the congregation's incorporation papers on December 4, 1901: two saloon owners, a bartender, two "traveling agents," a peddler, and a furniture dealer. Occupationally and residentially these founders differed from Beth Jacob's founders who lived close together and from the early members of Agudas Achim who were almost exclusively peddlers. The Hungarians' occupational diversity matched their residential dispersion: Emil Kohn, the congregation's first president and a prosperous saloon keeper, lived in an Italian and Irish immigrant neighborhood outside of the concentration of synagogues, while several of the others lived on the periphery of the near east side, in neighborhoods with large numbers of blacks and few Jews. Thus their common origin, not propinquity, brought them together for worship.[38]

Not only were all the incorporators Hungarians, but several were from adjacent villages and related to each other. The Polsters, Schlezingers, and Wasserstroms knew each other well in

This Tifereth Israel Synagogue on South Parsons Avenue was dedicated in September of 1915 and served the congregation until 1923.

northeastern Hungary. Marriages among the families had already occurred in Europe, including that of Herman Wasserstrom and Miriam Schlezinger. Other families like the Meltons, née Mendlowitz, and Gutters, came from these same villages and towns a few years later and joined their former "neighbors" in worship at Tifereth Israel.[39]

The early clergymen of the Hungarian congregation, usually Hungarians themselves, performed many functions. Tifereth Israel engaged Henry Einhorn, who came to Columbus from Beth Abraham synagogue in Zanesville, Ohio, primarily as a prayer reader and ritual slaughterer. As a *shochet* Einhorn "went to . . . houses to kill fowels"; he sometimes "killed free for members, and if he go to kill for any butcher in this city that money belong to him he had to collect them for himself," while other times he collected fees from members for "killing geese, chickens and fowels." After a series of unreasonable demands for slaughtering one year, the congregation agreed to support his request that he "cannot be compelled to go to the members on Saturday evening to kill fowl." Rev. Einhorn also conducted services which, combined with his work as a slaughterer, earned him $350 in the twelve months following June 1908. Einhorn was held in such high esteem that in 1915 the congregation asked him to come back to Columbus from Bridgeport, Connecticut, with assurances a butcher would be found with whom he could work.[40]

When they had enough money, the congregation sought rabbis to serve the membership. In 1907 Rabbi Schoenbrun of Cleveland received an offer of $250 for preaching on the High Holidays if he would supply "250 advertising bills printed by a Jewish printer; there should be on the bills . . . also Rev. Einhorn's name as *ba'al shacharit*" (morning service leader). Two years later the Hungarian congregation "decided about getting a modern rabbi . . . for $900" and, after considering Agudas Achim's Isaac Wiernikowsky, sought an out-of-town man.[41]

TABLE 39
TIFERETH ISRAEL CLERGYMEN

1901-10	Leopold Dumb[42]	1915-18	Solomon Don[46]
1904-12	Henry Einhorn	1918-21	Jacob Klein[47]
1910-11	Morris Lichtenstein[43]	1921-22	Morris Schussheim[48]
1911-13	Arthur Ginzler[44]	1923-25	Benjamin Werne[49]
1915-18	David Shohet[45]	1925-26	Jacob Klein

On several occasions, despite the possible emnity between the Russian and Hungarian Jews, Agudas Achim and Tifereth Israel seriously contemplated a merger. On March 1, 1908, a delegation from Agudas Achim "presented a plea for merger" to the Tifereth Israel trustees; the latter agreed to poll the members during the month and report the results to Agudas Achim in April. At the meeting on April 5, the trustees instructed the secretary to "write to the Agudas Achim Congregation [that] their request is not accepted."[50]

In 1915 Tifereth Israel hired David Shohet (1888-1961), a graduate of the Jewish Theological Seminary, America's only institution for training Conservative rabbis. A Lithuanian Jew who had been ordained that same year, Shohet spent three years with the congregation, and introduced non-sectarian American holiday services. He gained lasting fame for his subsequent scholarship — particularly for *The Jewish Court in the Middle Ages: Studies in Jewish Jurisprudence* which was published in 1931.[51]

Shohet's successor, Jacob Klein (1870-1948), a Hungarian-born and educated rabbi, served congregations in Chicago; Sumter, South Carolina; Peoria; and Cleveland before coming to Columbus in 1918. Described by one colleague as "a pleasant and corpulent gentleman," and by a contemporary as "an able English preacher and modern man," Klein was a strict rationalist who denied that anything in Judaism need be accepted without "reasonable proof," and that any conflict existed between Judaism and science.[52]

Tifereth Israel formally declared itself a Conservative congregation in 1922 under the direction of Morris Schussheim. During his second period of tenure at Tifereth Israel, however, Klein discovered that there still existed a large number of congregants who wished to remain Orthodox. In several sermons, the rabbi argued that the "old rigid Orthodox faith" now appeared "unreasonable and impracticable" as well as "not compatible with the spirit of our age." Since the majority of the congregation could "not join in sympathy with Orthodox Judaism" and found Reform unappealing, "it was the middle ground which they chose."[53]

Tifereth Israel had been a nominally Orthodox synagogue for about a quarter century, although rejecting certain traditional practices such as daily *minyan* (worship) and separate seating for men and women. In proposing the construction of the new temple at 1354 East Broad Street in 1924, the trustees determined to make it "modern Orthodox [i.e., Conservative], not like the other Orthodox places." The trustees announced the first change shortly before the laying of the cornerstone on August 15, 1926: "Special attention will be given to improving the decorum during prayer." More substantial changes followed; and the new building housed a congregation staunchly affiliated with the Conservative movement.[54] The congregation prided itself on its educational program, particularly the Hebrew classes which met for two hours after school, Monday through Thursday. This began what became a well-developed and independent Hebrew program exclusively for members of the congregation.[55]

A fifth Orthodox synagogue emerged during this period, as a result of a dispute within Agudas Achim over some of the typical concerns debated by Orthodox Jews all over the country: the rabbi, the ritual, the home town, and the synagogue leadership. Three Columbusites have described the origins of Ahavas Sholom:

> Ahavas Sholom broke off from Agudas Achim. You remember hundreds of Ahavas Sholom were originally members of Agudas Achim and as I recall it, since you mentioned it, I think that there was a dispute developed with reference to Werne . . . it evolved around Werne and, I think, that was when Werne went to Ahavas Sholom.[56]
>
> I'll tell you how it started: my dad use to go to the Agudas Achim. Them days, you know, there was three or four old people they didn't like the rabbi. So they said, "Let's go get together and we'll open up another *shul.*"[57]
>
> They were called the *obgerisener,* that is they "pulled themselves away" from Agudas Achim . . . they decided because they wanted to *daven* [pray] Sephard, use of *nusach* [style] Sephard, mostly Voliners from Volin, and believing that this *nusach* should be the *nusach* of the *shul,* but in the Agudas Achim they just couldn't budge the management. Schottensteins were very strong there, and they would not budge to change from Ashkenaz to Sephard.
>
> They decided they had better form their own *shul.* Why the Ahavas Sholom people did not join the Beth Jacob people in those days was a matter of politics. An old man, Bendersky . . . was one of the originators of the Ahavas Sholom *shul,* and he would not budge or go

> together with the Goodmans, a force in the Beth Jacob in those days. Also a question of *nusach tefillah* [prayer style]; even in Sephard you have many *nusachim*. There's one, let's say, who will say a *Kaddish* [mourner's prayer] here but not there, the other one will not say it here, but there.[58]

Founded during 1913, the congregation turned a stable at 460 South Washington into Ahavas Sholom Synagogue which remained in use for more than twenty years. Although the congregation broke off from Agudas Achim, the worshippers did not hesitate to pray at both their own and their former synagogue:

> They could not possibly afford to have a rabbi because it was a small congregation . . . and then they didn't have the need, they *davened* [prayed], and just next door was the Agudas Achim. The Agudas Achim had a rabbi, Rabbi Werne was an exceptionally good speaker, and they used to finish up the *daven* very fast, in order to go in to listen to Rabbi Werne's *d'rashah* [sermon] which he spoke every Shabbos.[59]

As the Orthodox synagogues proliferated B'nai Israel's Reform congregation enjoyed, and worried over, its own growth. Alexander Geismar (1868-1939), the first American-born rabbi to serve B'nai Israel, followed Rabbi Jesselson in 1890. Although he subsequently became a New York City magistrate, Geismar's only recorded achievement before leaving Columbus in 1892 for Beth Elohim in Brooklyn was to supervise the erecting of a screen around B'nai Israel's outhouse.[60]

New sources of revenue increased the congregational income considerably, including regular contributions from the Ladies Koffee Klatch and generous annual gifts ($400 in 1891, $600 in 1894) from the Hebrew Ladies Auxiliary. This improved financial situation allowed B'nai Israel to establish a new Hebrew Relief Association to provide food and lodging for persecuted immigrants who stopped "briefly" on their way west. Six years later the Jewish Alliance was organized to extend relief and assistance to Jewish immigrants. When the Associated Charities of Columbus, Ohio, formed on February 1, 1900, the Hebrew Relief Association became the only Jewish philanthropy to join the association. Providing transportation, meals, lodging, and even some funds for the "transient poor," the association acted in concert with the United Hebrew Charities. This New York-based organization agreed not to forward more immigrants than Columbus Jewry could care for, in order to prevent the established Jews of Columbus from depending upon non-Jewish charities to care for poor Jews. A Ladies Hebrew Relief Association, also directed by B'nai Israel leadership, "worked in harmony" with the Hebrew

Although confirmation ceremonies to culminate religious school studies began in the 1860s at B'nai Israel, the earliest extant class photo dates from 1887. From left to right: Abe Goldsmith, Lena Frank Nelson, Mollie Rieser, Rabbi Felix W. Jesselson, Clara Goodman, and an unidentified student.

Relief Association to care for both transient and resident poor.[61]

Rabbi Geismar's successor, Maurice Eisenberg, was born in Poland in 1862; at nineteen he succeeded his father as Rabbi of Canterbury before emigrating to America. His one-year tenure at B'nai Israel was marked by controversy, even though upon his arrival in Columbus from Birmingham, Alabama, the initial reaction appeared extremely favorable: "His address was remarkable for its strength and beauty, and by many is believed to have been the strongest ever delivered over this pulpit." Another report exuded equal enthusiasm: "Thirty years old, slight of stature, lithe, with easy, graceful gestures, a voice well modulated, clear, distinct and capable of moving an audience at the will of the speaker."[62]

The honeymoon soon ended and Eisenberg clashed repeatedly with leaders of the congregation. For example, he fought with the trustees because they refused to pay his family's travel expenses from Birmingham despite a verbal commitment. The wife of the previous congregational president, Rosalie Lazarus Cohen, resigned in 1893 because of Eisenberg's "indifference to, and the poor condition of, the Sabbath School." The congregation did not renew his contract in December 1892 but then renewed it a month later. By the summer of 1893 Eisenberg departed for Peoria, Illinois, where he launched a successful literary career.[63]

Louis Weiss was born in 1848 in Hungary and educated there; he came to B'nai Israel in 1893 from Columbus, Georgia, and found the congregation demoralized:

> . . . there is a deplorable lack of interest on the part of the members . . . there is poor attendance . . . there is often not even a *minyan* . . . the bad condition of the cemetery . . . disorganization of the religious school.

Rabbi Weiss expended much energy revamping congregational programs: he improved the Sabbath school, moved it to Sunday afternoon, welcomed non-members, and included Hebrew in the curriculum.[64] His most significant and controversial change was his decision to invest enormous amounts of time in ecumenical activities. Lecturing and preaching in churches as often as possible, Weiss encouraged Protestant ministers to preach at B'nai Israel for:

> There are two religions, Judaism and Christianity, which above all others in the world should look each other in the face as kindred. They have the same origins, the same sacred books, the same prophets, the same God.[65]

During his three-year tenure at B'nai Israel, Weiss wrote out in careful longhand his sermons, eulogies, and lectures in the style of the day. Dozens of these manuscripts dating from 1893 to 1896, as well as hundreds from other years, are extant and provide an insight into the thought of a Columbus rabbi in the middle 1890s.[66]

Ceremonies and rituals, the mainstay of traditional Judaism and a favorite subject of Rabbi Weiss during his B'nai Israel years appeared of "no vital importance" and "not essential." While they "are supposed to help us in obtaining future bliss," ceremonies were merely "the barnacles and excrescenses grown out as the result of superstitions." The Mosaic Laws, however, provided a source of pride for Weiss for they were "the prime foundation of Judaism," but he never associated them with ceremony; they were laws of "morality, humanity, and of all that perfects man internally in his heart and conscience."[67] Indeed there is "more real religion in good life than in all ceremonies, functions, and worships."

Weiss turned Jewish history on its head and saw in cultural assimilation an end to anti-Semitism: while in many cities of Europe non-Jews treated Jews well, "those who were treated better were the ones who had laid aside a great many rituals." Rabbi Weiss' interpretation of world history was equally tenuous: "All who were progressists are known in history, those who stood still are unknown — unknown to Judaism and the world."[68]

Salvation, a word used often by Weiss, depended not on "ordinances and rituals" but "upon the performance of human duty." And Judaism, "founded on principles more sublime than any other religion . . . the parent of enlightened religions," stands as the greatest salvific religion. It combined a faith of "ethics, laws of virtue, efficacy, and usefulness," he wrote, with "good homes, virtuous people, desirable citizens and neighbors." As such, it should be the religion of all "intelligent humanity"; for it is "simple, reasonable, exact and convincing." Judaism, in fact, had no bounds: "It smiles benignantly upon its constituents, sweetly commending virtue, morality, and every human trait that lifts man and woman up to a higher integrity, to a more perfect condition, and builds character and principle."[69]

Weiss' enormous optimism concerning Judaism's possibilities appeared no less fervent when it came to reflections on his own age. Progress was real, and evolution provided cosmic sanction for trust in the ultimate triumph of good:

> Progress is the twin sister of evolution . . . Forces moved the wheel of progress . . . to a state of higher perfection. Each age kindled a new light, each generation formed a new belief, though it was built on the old; everything moves the pinions of advancement, culminating now in the establishment of the . . . brightest period, the loftiest epoch.[70]

Joining not only his own rabbinical colleagues but Protestant clergymen as well, Rabbi Weiss reflected the mood of his America as he noted progress everywhere:[71]

> Science has risen luminously to lead us up to the skies; everywhere God's glory is manifest, and the higher human intelligence rises, the more perceptive the human mind grows, the clearer becomes the conception of God's omnipresence . . . this is an age of luminous reason, when culture and civilization have touched the human mind; there are very few of the more intelligent Jews who are not in the movement of reform . . . and we're far enough advanced to know exactly what is right and wrong and what is proper and improper.[72]

Only one mode of Jewish expression, Reform Judaism, had grasped these "forces of progress and world spirit." It "stands today preeminently the advocate of the purest reason and sublimest truth," for, Weiss argued, it had improved traditional Judaism intellectually and morally. Judaism once "dozed in the obscure valley of blind belief and frivolous superstition," offering up "muttered prayers amidst sighs and lamentations in Russia and Roumania," but "as the clouds began to recede and Jews began to have a little light," they "removed the fences that surround our religion, leaving it visibly beautiful and sublime." Every "onward march in Judaism," Weiss assured his listeners, "disregarded old meaningless customs not understood but blindly followed." Accommodating liberal religion to the leading scientific philosophy of the nineteenth century, the theory of evolution, emphasizing the moral aspects of Judaism and linking moral and religious improvement to the current optimistic belief in progress, Weiss emphasized repeatedly that Reform Judaism joined "perpetual progress with a religion of "understanding and reason."[73]

But this progress, Weiss regularly warned, remained incomplete, for the culminating event had not yet occurred. The task of Reform Judaism must be to unite Christians and Jews: to tear down "barriers separating man from man, Jews from Christians . . . and have man and man stand side by side marching on the road of human progress." Or again, the "mission of Judaism" was "to bring the time when there is no *Jewish* virtue or morality, no *Christian* virtue and morality, but merely enlightened virtue and morality." To realize this goal, the rabbis of America must "teach all men," for Christians "today are our friends, our neighbors, our brothers."[74]

Weiss often denied both the importance of, and his interest in, theology:

> Theology — the less we apply it, the purer, the better, the sublimer religion remains. Religion is not a theology by which we have to seek interpretations to find God; nor is it a knowledge that has to be studied with persistent care and close application of mind and thought. It is simple, so reasonable, so exact and convincing that it needs but a sound, reasonable mind to grasp it, a perceptive and receptive heart and will to acknowledge when convinced.[75]

Whether or not Weiss' theology was "simple" or "convincing" is debatable; that he preached frequently on theological matters is certain. On theodicy, or the explanation of evil, Weiss denied that God, "a loving Father, was responsible for sickness, destruction, or death." All of these derived in the "course of nature, from natural causes," for God's work was exclusively "good and positive." Judaism was a "divine religion," for "its fundamental is the belief in God — the One and indivisible and unchangeable God, who is Good." On revelation, and even divine inspiration, Weiss spoke negatively: "in vain it may be claimed that the Bible was written by inspiration." He doubted the divine origin of the Decalogue, and even felt no serious loss to the "sublimeness of Judaism" if miracles, Moses, and even the prophets disappeared. On only one occasion, in more than two hundred extant sermons, did Rabbi Weiss acknowledge the existence of "inspiration." "All good men and women," he explained, "are inspired. Every good idea is inspired . . . and so far is the Bible inspired."[76]

In speaking about one of his favorite themes, the Jewish woman, Weiss agreed with the position of traditional Judaism and with contemporary nineteenth-century views as well. The Jewish woman was superior to the Jewish man, argued the rabbi in "moral virtues, in religious propensities, as a model for children, and as an exemplar, a criterion of humanity." And since, furthermore, "the woman makes the home, she should always be at home" where she "is in purer spheres and is, therefore, morally and virtually better." Not only is she superior to her male counterpart, but to non-Jewish women as well: "there are no women in this world sweeter in disposition, lovelier in appearance, and more sensible in mind."[77]

By the spring of 1896 the congregation had had enough of Weiss. Culminating months of controversy and dissent, a majority of the membership agreed not to renew his contract for a variety of reasons: a few objected to Rabbi Weiss' constant preaching at churches; some became upset by a continuous stream of Protestant ministers in B'nai Israel's pulpit; others felt uncomfortable worshipping with all the "poor" that Weiss brought to the temple as a result of his nonsectarian church work. Still others objected to his efforts to attract large numbers of outsiders by announcing sermon titles in the local press. In sum, his "broad policy" led to his undoing.[78]

This did not end the tension between Weiss and B'nai Israel; encouraged by the president, Simon Burgunder, who stated that the rabbi would always be welcome in the pulpit, Weiss offered himself as a candidate for reelection in June of 1896. When the congregation unanimously elected David Klein rabbi of B'nai Israel, Weiss attacked the election procedure in a letter from St. Louis, necessitating a strong — and final — response from the trustees.[79]

In August of 1896 Rabbi David Klein (1868-1925) succeeded Louis Weiss. Klein was the son of a distinguished rabbinic family in Hungary, the last European-born and educated rabbi to serve B'nai Israel. He emigrated to America at the age of twenty and served congregations in Reading, Pennsylvania, from 1890 to 1892, and Akron, Ohio, from 1893 to 1896 before coming to Columbus to serve B'nai Israel for a ten-year stint.[80]

Much continuity, as well as innovation, characterized Klein's work at B'nai Israel. He initiated the custom of preaching in German once on Rosh Hashanah and once on Yom Kippur. The congregation continued to remain completely closed during the rabbi's three-month summer vacation. Like many of his predecessors, Klein maintained an active speaking schedule in the community: during one week in the spring of 1903 he read "The Influence of Spinoza on Modern Thought" before the Emerson Club, a literary society of the First Universalist Church; on Tuesday he addressed the Men's Social Club of the First Methodist Episcopal Church on "Friendly Relations" and on Thursday he presented "Shylock or Nathan Wise: A Study in Comparison" before the Magazine Club, a group of the "most prominent men in the professional and business world in the city."[81]

Klein also ventured into some new areas: he filled the High Holiday services with secular music from German composers; brought a national Zionist figure, Jacob de Haas, to the temple to speak about "Zionist Propaganda"; and, almost singlehandedly, negotiated the $12,000 sale of the B'nai Israel Temple to the Knights of Pythias in 1902. For his efforts as an agent the trustees gave Klein a 2 percent "commission."[82]

The financial condition of the congregation during Klein's ministry remained unstable. The trustees borrowed money from local organizations and banks; in 1899 the congregation owed $1,600 to Zion Lodge No. 62 and $400 to the Ladies Benevolent Society, while in 1902 the trustees needed to borrow $700 from the sisterhood treasury. One attempt to solve this problem seems to have met with success. The trustees amended the bylaws to deny burial in the cemetery, or the use of the rabbi's services to those Columbusites deemed able but unwilling to join the congregation. This accounts, in part, for the growth in membership from 82 in 1892 to a substantial 166 in 1907.[83]

More likely, however, the new temple on Bryden Road, which was completed in 1904, explains the growth of the congregation. Even though the congregation found balancing its budget difficult, the building fund for the new temple on tree-lined "suburban" Bryden Road progressed rather steadily. Having raised more than $10,000 by the end of 1901, the congregation successfully solicited substantial contributions in the next few years. The Ohio Grand Lodge of Free & Accepted Masons laid the cornerstone on July 20, 1903, before more than one thousand persons. Rabbi Klein, who spoke after featured guest Rabbi Tobias Schanfarber (1863-1942) of Chicago, articulated the hope of the builders:

> The religion of the temple is creedless. This temple has over its entrance the lettered inscription spelling out the prophet's glowing invitation: "For my house is a house of prayer unto all nations."[84]

After auctioning off the new pews to complete financing of the building, the congregation occupied the $40,000 structure in June of 1904. Then three days of ceremonies and celebrations culminated the dedicatory activities: On Friday evening, June 4, "hundreds of glowing incandescents garnished the archives of the dome, with its art glass windows lighted reflectively"; more than a dozen Christian clergymen addressed "hundreds" at the "good-will" ceremonies on Sunday. Echoing his remarks of the previous year Rabbi Klein proclaimed: "The character of the Hebrew Temple is that it is open to all peoples of all creeds . . . we extend a warm welcome to all children of God to regard the new temple as a home."[85]

Even before the completion of the new temple, which would serve the congregation more than fifty years, the members hinted to Rabbi Klein that his stay at B'nai Israel was tenuous at best. Although he was reelected for two years in 1902, the membership denied Klein a $200 increase in his salary; his reelection in 1904 seemed mostly good fortune, for the vote was forty to forty with one person abstaining. Only subsequently did someone discover that abstentions counted in the affirmative. By the end of 1905 an

A wide tree-lined fashionable residential street in the early decades of the twentieth century, Bryden Road was the site of the new synagogue and the homes of many of its members.

enormous rift developed in the congregation; threats and accusations were common. When the trustees declared the rabbinate vacant Klein refused to leave, and both rabbi and trustees utilized the pulpit to accuse each other of wrongdoing. After his successor was elected, Klein refused to relinquish the confirmation certificates for the president's signature.[86]

David Klein responded to what he considered a breach of contract by establishing a new synagogue, Congregation Beth El, in time for the High Holidays in 1906. By October when the members chose officers of the congregation, Beth El described itself as "blessed with a large membership" and "in a prosperous condition."[87]

Meeting in the Universalist Church at State and Sixth streets on the edge of downtown Columbus, the new congregation does indeed seem to have gotten off to an enthusiastic start: In October

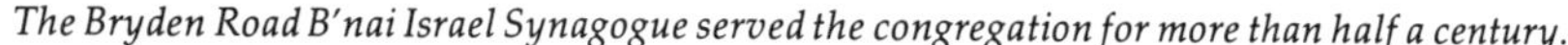

The Bryden Road B'nai Israel Synagogue served the congregation for more than half a century.

the women organized the Beth El Sisterhood and opened the Sunday School; in November Rabbi Klein organized a Jewish Sabbath School in the Deaf and Dumb Institute of Columbus and arranged for the youngsters to attend Sabbath services at Beth El. By December the sisterhood and Young People's Society arranged to host a dinner for three hundred, while the congregation sought permission to bury its members in B'nai Israel's cemetery. Beth El could boast of eighty-five member families as well as six classes, five teachers, and seventy-eight pupils in the Sunday School by the end of the year. Before long Rabbi Klein demonstrated his ecumenical penchant; when Rev. E. L. Rexford delivered the principal address at the Beth El Purim celebration in 1907, Rabbi Klein proclaimed it "the first time that a Christian minister had taken so prominent a part in one of the strictly Jewish feasts." A local reporter noted that Klein preached "time after time in gentile churches of Columbus," and that "he has invited gentiles to his pulpit and has preached in return."[88]

Despite the enthusiasm and promise of the early months, there exists no evidence that Beth El endured past the spring of 1907. By the High Holidays of that year David Klein, despite a five-year contract at Beth El, had accepted the rabbinate at the Progressive Synagogue of Brooklyn, and the congregation probably disappeared. In any event, soon all of the officers rejoined B'nai Israel.[89]

Joseph Kornfeld (1876-1943), a Hungarian-born rabbi educated in Cincinnati and ordained at Hebrew Union College in 1899, succeeded David Klein at B'nai Israel. Kornfeld served congregations in Pine Bluff, Arkansas, and Montreal, Quebec, before his election to B'nai Israel in 1906 at a salary of $2,400. Elected to the position despite his refusal to give the customary trial sermon, Kornfeld argued that "it was hardly the measure of a person's capabilities to be judged on one sermon alone," and invited the search committee to investigate him in person. They didn't, but their choice proved a good one, for Kornfeld served B'nai Israel from 1906 to 1921.[90]

Kornfeld demonstrated widespread interest in Columbus' municipal organizations, "enrolling himself in a great many worthy projects outside of the church and people." The mayor appointed him to the Commission of the Department of Public Recreation and Social Education in 1911 and to the Columbus City Charter Commission in 1913, while the community elected and reelected him to the Columbus Board of Education from 1915 to 1919. Acknowledging that the "public school is the greatest social force in American life . . . where children are fused . . . as in a melting pot," the board elevated Kornfeld to the presidency in January 1918. The congregation seemed thrilled by this attention;

the president noted that "the rabbi was looked upon by the best citizens of this city as a man of power, sincerity, and intelligence."[91]

Rabbi Kornfeld's enormous popularity at B'nai Israel was reflected by the generous salary increases the congregation gave him each time he was reelected: $2,400 in 1906, $3,000 in 1910, $3,600 in 1911, $4,000 in 1912, $5,000 in 1916. His most celebrated innovation, the introduction of Sunday morning "nondenominational" services for "Jews and Gentiles," became a popular though controversial development in many midwestern Reform congregations and a logical development at B'nai Israel. Sunday services offered maximum exposure to non-Jews, and a response to the problem of poor Sabbath worship attendance. Kornfeld recommended Sunday morning worship services as early as 1907, but not until the winter of 1911-12 did the congregation approve, by a sixty to seventeen margin, Sunday services in addition to those of the Jewish Sabbath. By 1915 the president could declare that "this innovation is filling a long felt want, both among the members and others in this community, who, knowing of Dr. Kornfeld's work for Civic Righteousness, have been very eager to hear him."[92]

Several developments of importance occurred in the congregation's educational program during the Kornfeld years: religious school enrollment grew steadily from 110 in 1908 to 227 in 1915; for the first time teachers were paid, but only $5 per month; the beloved Carrie Loeb (1852-1935) celebrated her twenty-fifth year of Sunday school teaching in 1913; and following a report that more than one hundred children in the school had parents who were not affiliated, the temple board voted to forbid children of non-members from attending the overcrowded school. Finally, the congregation changed their name from Church B'nai Israel to Temple Israel.[93]

Kornfeld's ministry at Temple Israel ended in 1921 when President Warren Harding, whose campaign the rabbi had energetically supported, nominated Kornfeld as minister to Persia. Before completing a three-year term, Rabbi Kornfeld won the gratitude of Persian Jews for intervening in their behalf during anti-Semitic disorders in 1922. Kornfeld left Persia in 1924 to continue his rabbinical career in Toledo.[94]

A parade of rabbis and other functionaries served Columbus Jews during the thirty-five years detailed above. Serving a largely impoverished immigrant population, Orthodox synagogues found scholarly men steeped in Old World learning, piety, and a strong sense of religious and ethical self-consciousness. Only Tifereth Israel took major steps away from Orthodoxy and joined the rapidly emerging Conservative movement. In contrast, the Reform congregations chose messengers of good will who not only offered modern-rationalist forms of belief to affluent members of the Jewish community, but took an active role in Columbus' civic life and got on splendidly with their Christian counterparts. Although the names and events would change in the next quarter century, the pattern of synagogue leadership remained the same.

NOTES FOR CHAPTER 10

1. Secretary of State, Ohio. Articles of Incorporation. Article V.49, p. 125. The 1889 founding date is also given in the *AJYB* 5668 (1907-08), p. 359.

2. Temple Israel Minute Books, September 27, 1885.

3. *OSJ*, December 20, 1907. The reporter listed the following ten men: I. B. Jashenosky, J. W. Sabledosky, N. Minitsky, A. Goldberg, B. Weis, J. Schottenstein, P. Wolman, S. Kramer, P. Office, and S. Thall.

4. Only one of the ten is in a *City Directory* prior to 1883; only one other is in a *City Directory* before 1886; Abraham Goldberg, one of the "founders," declared on his "Intention to Naturalize" application that he arrived in the United States in October 1885 and his son Isaac was born in Russia that same year; Philip Wolman, another "founder," was in Russia as late as 1890 for his daughter Ella was born there in 1891; and Amon Thall, son of Samuel Thall, was born in Russia in 1891. See General Index to Declarations. A to Z. 1859-1905. I. Volume 4, p. 28, and Fulton Street School Attendance Records 1900-11.

5. There is one piece of evidence to support an 1881 origin; *OSJ*, November 30, 1908. A 1939 survey of the congregation, however, determined that the date of origin was 1884; Works Progress Administration. Survey of State and Local Historical Records: 1936. October 3, 1939.

6. *AJYB* 5668 (1907-08), p. 359; *OSJ*, April 29, 1907. Of all the east European Jews that arrived in Columbus after 1880, only the Office brothers, Philip and Benjamin, owned any property prior to 1895; Franklin County Recorder, Deeds, 211:352 and 260:129 (a $3,000 and a $1,800 purchase in 1889 and 1894 respectively).

7. *CEP*, October 24 and 26, 1896; WPA Survey . . . lists the places of worship as Market House on South Fourth (1884-89) and 337 Donaldson (1889-95). See *OSJ*, October 26, 1896, November 30, 1908. I. B. Jashenosky (president), Jacob Schottenstein (vice-president), Nathan Skuller (secretary), Isaac Martlin (treasurer), Henry Stone, Solomon Kramer, B[?] Golden, and Coleman Tuckerman (trustees) served as the officers in 1896. "I. B." is either Israel B. (1853-1928) or Isaac B. (1851-1930) Jashenosky, two brothers whose families are both listed in the 1880 federal manuscript

census of Columbus.

8. Kalmon London, the first clergyman of Agudas Achim, appears in the *Columbus City Directories* from 1883 to 1887 as a peddler, and from 1888 to 1896 as a reverend. The brother of Rabbi Meyer London, who founded a kosher matzo factory and became wealthy, Kalmon apparently came to Columbus to serve the Orthodox Jewish community as a *shochet* and *hazzan;* see Benzion Eisenstadt, *LeToldath Israel Be'America,* Volume I (New York, 1917), p. 27; interviews with Samuel Rubenstein and Abe Yenkin; Jacob Gilbert to Marc Lee Raphael, telephone conversation, August 1974; interview with Eleanor Yenkin. (Eleanor Yenkin's mother, Sara London Weiner, was Kalmon's daughter.)

9. See the *Columbus City Directories* from 1890 to 1894, and Records of Ministers Licenses, Franklin County Probate Court, 2, p. 39 (November 8, 1889).

10. See the *Columbus City Directories* from 1895 to 1897, and Records of Ministers Licenses, p. 51 (April 30, 1894).

11. See the *Columbus City Directories* from 1896 to 1900; Records of Ministers Licenses (1895); *OSJ,* September 5, 1898.

12. See the *AJYB* 5661 (1900-01), p. 413; Records of Ministers Licenses, p. 67 (April 26, 1899); *OSJ,* September 3 and 14, 1899.

13. See the *Columbus City Directories* from 1900 to 1905; Records of Ministers Licenses, p. 69 (May 15, 1900); *OSJ,* September 16, 1900, December 9, 1901; *CC,* September 24, 1900. Rev. Silverman preached his Rosh Hashanah sermon of 1900 in Hebrew.

14. See the *Columbus City Directories* from 1905 to 1907; *OSJ,* September 9, 1904, December 30, 1907; Saul Silber, *Selected Essays of Rabbi Saul Silber* (Chicago, 1950).

15. See the *Columbus City Directories* from 1908 to 1910; *OSJ,* December 29 and 30, 1907.

16. See the *Columbus City Directories* from 1909 to 1911; Records of Ministers Licenses (December 1, 1908); *OSJ,* September 14, 1909.

17. See the *Columbus City Directories* from 1910 to 1913; Records of Ministers Licenses (May 25, 1910).

18. See the *OJC,* October 12, November 2, 1934. Simon Silverman, a *hazzan, mohel,* and *shochet* at Agudas Achim for twenty-three years, was born in Slonim, Russia, and came to the United States in 1882 at the age of thirteen. Simon's son Morris, educated at Columbus public schools and The Ohio State University, became a distinguished Conservative rabbi. More than two thousand persons attended Simon's funeral in 1934. See *Biographical Encyclopedia of American Jews* (New York, 1935), p. 507.

19. *OSJ,* September 14, 1899; interview with Jennie Goldberg Brief. Congregation Beth Jacob turned down an earlier opportunity to build on this site; see *OSJ,* November 21, 1904.

20. *OSJ,* December 29 and 30, 1907; *CED,* December 30, 1907; *CPP,* October 30, 1907. At the cornerstone-laying ceremony in April 1907, "selling bricks" raised $2,500; *OSJ,* April 29, 1907.

21. *OSJ,* September 29, October 15, 1900, November 3, 1904. The incorporators consisted of C. Tuckerman, C. Skilken, A. Milder, F. Silberstein, P. Wolman, and A. Martlin. For a description of a Hanukkah program presented by the children of the Hebrew Free School, see *OSJ,*

December 9, 1901.

22. *WWAJ*, 1926, Volume 1 (New York, 1927), p. 616; "Articles of Agreement" Contract. Columbus, Ohio 5672 (July 3, 1912); Jordan Taxon to Marc Lee Raphael, correspondence, May 16, 1974; "God," "Existence of God," "Judaism I," "Divine Authority," "Orthodox Judaism," "Religion in a Scrutinizing Age," are manuscript sermons in the possession of Rabbi Jordan Taxon. Rabbi Morris Taxon's subsequent career took him to the United Jewish Congregations in Omaha (1918-22), She'areth Israel in Dallas (1922-26), where he succeeded Rabbi Isaac Werne, Agudas Achim North Shore in Chicago (1926-31), and Baron Hirsch in Memphis (1931-40).

23. *WWAJ*, 1928, 2nd edition (New York, 1928), p. 510; *WWAJ*, 1938-39, Volume 3, (New York, 1938), p. 773; Max Vorspan and Lloyd Gartner, *History of the Jews of Los Angeles* (Philadelphia, 1970), pp. 221, 338; *CJC*, December 20 and December 27, 1918; *Agudas Achim Sunday School Bulletin*, S. M. Neches, editor, Volume I, Nos. 1-6 (April-September, 1918) in New York Public Library.

24. *WWAJ*, 1926. Volume 1, p. 644 (mostly erroneous); *WWAJ*, 1938-39. Volume 3, p. 1133; *WWAJ*, 1928. 2nd edition, p. 743; Vorspan and Gartner, op. cit., pp. 140, 161, and 211 ("he returned to Los Angeles in 1930 after a nine-year sojourn in Columbus" is inaccurate); *Universal Jewish Encyclopedia*, Volume 10, p. 503; Benjamin Werne to Marc Lee Raphael, correspondence, April 1, 1975; hand-written four-page vita in Hebrew in possession of Benjamin Werne (Jamaica, New York); interviews with Bertha Josephson Seff and B. W. Abramson; *NYT*, March 12, 1940. Installed on November 29, 1908, and already the author of several hundred encyclopedia articles, Werne delivered his initial talk in Hebrew; *OSJ*, November 20 and November 30, 1908. Werne resigned from Agudas Achim in November of 1931, ostensibly "because of the strenuous work in the congregation and of the work necessary to the compilation of his new book" (*OSJ*, December 9, 1931). He finished his rabbinate in Columbus at Agudas Achim's neighbor — Ahavas Sholom.

25. Interviews with Robert Mellman and Julius Baker; *OSJ*, November 5, December 10, 1927, March 3 and 10, October 13, December 22 and 29, 1928, January 5 and 12, 1929; March 17, 1929; *OJC*, February 23, March 2, 9, 16 and 23, 1923, September 5, 1924, November 11 and 25, 1925, December 3 and 10, 1926, December 6, 1927, January 20, 1928.

26. *OJC*, November 24, December 8, 1922, January 26, February 16 and 23, 1923, August 15, 1924, February 20, July 17, October 16, December 11, 1925, November 25, 1927, May 10, 1929, January 24, February 14, December 12, 1930, December 23, 1932; *OSJ*, January 26, 1930. Werne published books in German (*Das Buch Hiob*, Breslau, 1902), Yiddish (*The Rambam: His Philosophical and Theological Views on Jewish Thought and Creed*, Los Angeles, 1936), and Hebrew (*Meditations of Isaac: A Collection of Responsa and Other Materials*, Columbus, n.d.), and completed several unpublished manuscripts of sermons and commentaries.

27. *Eminent Jews of America* (Toledo, 1918), p. 101; *OSJ*, June 18, 1940; interview with Jenny Goldberg Brief; *WWAJ*, 1928. 2nd edition, p. 230; General Index to Declarations of Naturalization, A to Z. 1859-1905. I; *OJC*, October 12, November 23, 1923, October 16, November 27, 1925, October

7, 1927, January 11, 1935, March 20, June 12, 1936. Goldberg's obituary, as well as a biographical entry in *Eminent Jews of America,* place him in America ten years before the date of entry recorded on his naturalization certificate.

28. See the *Columbus City Directories* 1898 through 1907.

29. Secretary of State. Articles of Incorporation . . . November 16, 1898 to November 15, 1899, p. 451; Works Progress Administration. Survey of State and Local Historical Records: 1936. Beth Jacob Congregation, March 22, 1939; The Constitution and By-Laws of the Congregation Beth Jacob in Columbus, Ohio (Yiddish), Article 1; *Columbus City Directory* 1899-1900; *OSJ,* August 23, 1909; *AI,* August 26, 1909; interview with Jacob Pass; *Cleveland City Directory* 1907 (Cleveland, 1907).

30. *OJC,* May 26, September 29, 1922, June 16, 1969; *Columbus City Directories* 1912, 1913, 1914, 1915; *WWAJ,* 1926. Volume 1, p. 471; *OSJ,* October 8, 1905. Several "reverends" served the synagogue during these years, including Osher Yablok and Benjamin Liss, as *shochet* and *hazzan;* in addition, laymen frequently led the High Holiday services (i.e., David Bonowitz and Max Glick in 1905).

31. *OJC,* May 26, 1922, September 10 and 21, 1923, April 18, September 5, 1924; Nathan A. Pelkovitz to Marc Lee Raphael, correspondence, September 29, 1974.

32. Nathan A. Pelkovitz to Marc Lee Raphael.

33. *OJC,* May 23,1924; Samuel Mellitz, Connecticut State Referee to Marc Lee Raphael, correspondence, June 20, 1974; Nathan A. Pelkovitz to Marc Lee Raphael, correspondence September 29, 1974; Ralph Pelkovitz to Marc Lee Raphael, correspondence, May 16, 1974.

34. *OJC,* August 11, September 18, 1922, May 4, June 22, October 19, December 7, 1923.

35. As late as World War II, the congregation was still widely viewed as Hungarian; Moshe V. Goldblum to Marc Lee Raphael, correspondence, August 7, 1974, and Hyman Chanover to Marc Lee Raphael, correspondence, August 28, 1974.

36. Interviews with Nathan Zelizer and Tobias Polster; *AJYB* 5668 (1907-08), p. 359; *Columbus City Directories* 1910-11ff; *OSJ,* October 3, 1902, September 9 and 19, 1904; September 19, 1906, September 14, 1909, September 30, 1914, September 8, 1915; *CED,* September 30, 1914. High Holiday services took place in rented halls for several years (Marquette, Germania, I.O.O.F. Temple, Masonic Cathedral, etc.); the change of name to Congregation Tifereth Israel won the approval of the trustees in March 1912; and for $5,500 the trustees purchased the Parsons Avenue property, which consisted of two buildings: a five-room brick single facing Parsons and a five-room frame double on McAllister (see the Tifereth Israel Congregation Minute Book, April 7, 1907-January 2, 1916, at Tifereth Israel, and *OSJ,* September 5, 1915).

37. *CT,* October 29, 1886; *OSJ,* October 30, 1886; *CD,* October 29, 1886. Other examples of such defenses against printed slurs can be found in the *OSJ* of November 15 and 18, 1906.

38. The charter members consisted of Max L. Bayer (253 North 19th), Emil Kohn (43 East Russell), Louis R. Polster (545 Chamberlain), Morris Polster (519 East Elmwood), Isaac Harry Schlezinger (239 South

Washington), Jacob H. Stern (239½ Main), Samuel J. Wasserstrom (699 McAllister). Their addresses and occupations came from the *City Directory*, while we determined the country of origin from cemetery inscriptions and/or conversations with their descendants.

39. Interviews with Samuel Melton, Edward Schlezinger, and Etta Brandt.

40. Interview with Nathan Zelizer; *Zanesville City Directory* 1903 (Zanesville, Ohio, 1903); Muskingum County Probate Court, Marriage License Certificates, December 18, 1903; Tifereth Israel Minute Book, July 7, 1907, April 5, 1908, June 5, 1910, June 4, 1911, April 4, 1915; *Columbus City Directories* 1905 through 1911. Rev. Einhorn was born in 1879; see B'nai B'rith Minutes, November 8, 1909.

41. Tifereth Israel Minute Book, July 21, 1907 (the congregational income was $1,200 during the year of 1907), October 24, 1909, April 10, 1910 (systematic dues collections were instituted on the latter date to enable the congregation to hire a rabbi).

42. See the *Zanesville City Directory*, 1894 (Zanesville, 1894); Muskingum County Probate Court, Marriage License Certificates, June 21, 1893; *Columbus City Directories* 1902 through 1910.

43. See *Columbus City Directory* 1911; Records of Ministers Licenses, June 1, 1911; Tifereth Israel Minute Book, September 11 and 26, 1910, July 1, August 6 and 20, 1911; *NYT*, November 7 and 9, 1938; *WWAJ*, 1926. Volume 1, p. 387; *WWAJ*, 1938-39. Volume 3, p. 659; *Universal Jewish Encyclopedia*, Volume 7, pp. 48-49; *OSJ*, November 4, 1910, May 26, 1914. Rabbi Lichtenstein (1889-1938), a student of a Lithuanian *yeshiva* (1903), came to the United States in 1907 and spent one year as a student at The Ohio State University and "rabbi" of Tifereth Israel (1910-11) before entering the combined rabbinic-undergraduate programs at the Hebrew Union College and the University of Cincinnati. The founder of the Jewish Science Movement (a theology rooted in the affirmation that one's "God consciousness" is inside one's body and expresses itself in health, calmness, peace and happiness) and the author of many books, Lichtenstein's thought is best summed up in an early work, *Jewish Science and Health* (New York, 1925).

44. See *OJC*, February 23, 1923, January 9, 1948; Records of Ministers Licenses, May 31, 1912; Gladys Ginzler Gassman to Marc Lee Raphael, correspondence, October 5, 1974; interview with Rabbi Nathan Zelizer. Arthur Ginzler (1868-1947), born in Erdobenya, Hungary, studied at several Hungarian *yeshivot*. Receiving a B.A. (1900, City College of New York) and ordination (1906, Jewish Theological Seminary) after his arrival in the United States in 1893, Ginzler served as rabbi, cantor, and teacher in more than a dozen congregations east of the Mississippi before his retirement in 1930. He is buried in Columbus, Ohio.

45. See *WWAJ*, 1926. Volume 1, p. 564; *WWAJ*, 1938-39. Volume 3, p. 980.

46. Records of Ministers Licenses, May 25, 1910; *Columbus City Directories* 1916 and 1917. Rev. Don was born in 1878; see B'nai B'rith Minutes, October 24, 1910.

47. See below, note 52.

48. *OJC*, June 6, 1922.

49. Benjamin Werne, the son of Isaac Werne, was a practicing attorney

in the field of government regulation and labor law as of 1975, and the author of several volumes in his field; Benjamin Werne to Marc Lee Raphael, correspondence, April 1, 1975. See also *OJC*, August 28 and September 11, 1925.

50. Tifereth Israel Minute Book, March 1 and April 5, 1908.

51. *WWAJ*, 1926. Volume 1, p. 564; *WWAJ*, 1938-39. Volume 3, p. 980; *OSJ*, November 28, 1915. Shohet's attitude toward revelation is revealed in a statement he made at "Patriotic Services" in 1918: "Next to the Bible, the Declaration of Independence was the greatest document written by men who were inspired by God"; *CJC*, July 12, 1918.

52. *OJC*, September 3, 1926; William S. Gibberman to Marc Lee Raphael, correspondence, June 13, 1974; Judah Rubinstein to Marc Lee Raphael, correspondence, July 5, 9, and 12, 1974; Rudolph M. Rosenthal to Marc Lee Raphael, correspondence, July 17, 1974; *AJYB* 5664 (1903-04), p. 69, 5665 (1904-05), p. 219; "The Religion of Reason, Reverence, and Righteousness" in *OJC*, June 4, 1926.

53. *OJC*, June 6, 1922; "The Need of a Conservative Jewish Congregation in Columbus" June 25, 1926; "Israel's True Mission" March 12, 1926.

54. *OJC*, November 24, 1922, July 18, 1924, July 30, 1926; *OSJ*, August 16, 1926. The ground breaking ceremony — which opened with "America" and closed with the "Star Spangled Banner" — took place on October 5, 1924; *OSJ*, October 6, 1924.

55. *CJC*, May 24, October 11, 1918; *OJC*, June 29, 1923.

56. Interview with Robert Mellman.

57. Interview with Harry Bender.

58. Interview with Julius Baker.

59. Interview with Julius Baker. The 1913 origins are based on Robert Mellman's bar mitzvah in the synagogue in 1913 and a statement in the *OJC*, November 18, 1929 ("Ahavas Sholom is sixteen years old"). In 1913 no buildings stood between Ahavas Sholom (460) and Agudas Achim (484 South Washington); *Baist's Real Estate Atlas of Surveys of Columbus, Ohio, 1910* (Philadelphia, 1910) and *Columbus City Directory* 1913.

60. Temple Israel (T. I.) Minute Books, January 4, February 1, April 5, June 6, December 20, 1891, March 1, 1894; *AI*, January 7, 1892. On Geismar, see CCAR *Yearbook* 1 (1890-91): p. 21, 3 (1893): p. 48, 5 (1895): p. 145; *AJYB* 5681 (1920-21): p. 124, 5683 (1922-23): p. 144; *OSJ*, September 15, 1890; *NYT*, May 21, 1921, December 31, 1922, November 3, 1926. Geismar served as a justice on the New York City Court from 1927 to 1939, for two terms as city magistrate, and chief assistant district attorney for four years.

61. *AI*, March 26, 1886; *OSJ*, March 22, 1886, February 23, 1892; Associated Charities of Columbus. *First Annual Report*. February 1, 1900-November 1, 1900, p. 20; *OSJ*, March 16, 1900; Associated Charities of Columbus. *Third Annual Report*. November 1901-November 1902, p. 22.

62. *OSJ*, March 25 and 27, April 9, 1892. On Eisenberg, see *WWAJ*, 1926. Volume 1, p. 136; Mark Elovitz, *A Century of Jewish Life in Dixie: The Birmingham Experience* (University, Alabama, 1974), pp. 14, 15, 17, 104. Eisenberg coauthored several well-known novels; his *Doctor Cavallo* is among the earliest examples of American Jewish fiction.

63. T. I. Minute Books, June 26, September 4, December 11, 1892; January 1, February 5, April 9, 1893; *AI*, December 22, 1892, January 5, 1893.

64. T. I. Minute Books, October 1, 1893. On Weiss, see *AI*, July 2, 1896; *AJYB* 5665 (1904-05), p. 225; CCAR *Yearbook* 3 (1892-93), pp. 17, 38.

65. T. I. Minute Books, January 7, 1894; February 3, November 28, December 12, 1895; January 23, February 27, April 23, 1896. Rabbi Weiss exchanged pulpits most frequently with Rev. Everett Rexford (1842-1923), minister of the Universalist Church.

66. Weiss was a prolific writer; more than twenty books and unpublished manuscripts of his survive, as well as lengthy plays, musicals, novels, and hundreds of Torah commentaries, essays, and sermons. Some of his novels were serialized in newspapers; see weekly *Southwestern Jewish Settlement* (Texas), March 21 to November 28, 1902.

67. Weiss' approach to the Talmud paralleled his handling of the Pentateuch. The former "urged, above all, neighborliness, tolerance, charitableness, morality and humanity, though all around were immoral and inhuman." Even more he argued: "Whenever Jews made the Talmud secondary and the Bible primary, their treatment became very favorable"; for the Talmud was a "Cain mark upon the Jew." See "Periods of Progress in Judaism-7," and "The Written and Unwritten Law," in Rabbi Louis Weiss, Sermons and Essays, Box 2395a, American Jewish Archives (all subsequent sermons are in Box 2395a).

68. *More Light: A Rational Treatise on Biblical Subjects* (Cincinnati, 1892), p. 6; "Periods of Progress in Judaism-12," "The Written and Unwritten Law," "Progress of Judaism," "The Differences Between Orthodox and Reform Judaism," "Functions in the House of God," "Should Religion Progress?" *More Light* was translated into Marahti in 1895 at the request of India's Jews; *AI*, October 10, 1895.

69. *More Light*, p. 40; "Periods of Progress in Judaism-12"; Some Burning Questions: An Exegetical Treatise on Christianizing of Judaism (Columbus, 1893), p. 7; "Why We Are Jews-II"; "Theology and Religion"; "Functions in the House of God."

70. "Periods of Progress in Judaism-2," "Periods of Progress in Judaism-1," "Hasty Conclusions," "Periods of Progress in Judaism-4."

71. Marc Lee Raphael, "Rabbi Jacob Voorsanger of San Francisco on Jews and Judaism: The Implications of the Pittsburgh Platform," *American Jewish Historical Quarterly* 63:2 (December 1973): 185-203, and especially note 12.

72. "God's Omnipotence," "The Drift of Ages," "Visions," "Periods of Progress in Judaism-10."

73. "Periods of Progress in Judaism-12," "Should Religion Progress?," "Differences Between Orthodox and Reform Judaism," "In What Measure to Progress," "The Drift of Ages."

74. "Retrospection, Perception, and Prospection" (a lengthy, abstract sermon delivered at B'nai Israel on the eve of Rosh Hashanah and typical in its complete lack of stories, anecdotes, quotes or illustrations of his vague theses); "Periods of Progress in Judaism-10"; "Our Present Needs"; "More Light," (unpublished manuscript), Box 2395 (no pagination). For Weiss, a certified Master Mason (August 15, 1907) of Magnolia Lodge (Ohio) No. 20, the Masonic Order served as a vehicle for reaching these goals. It "levels all men, teaching the noblest virtues and promoting the highest morality"; see *Glints of Masonic Light: Scintillated by Rabbinical*

Sparks, 2nd edition (n.p., 1904), p. 21.

75. "Theology and Religion."

76. "Israel's Conception of God," "The Wise Formation of the Universe," "Is There a God?," "Epitome of Primitive and Modern Christianity" (unpublished manuscript), Box 2395 p. 3; *More Light*, p. 19; "Why We Are Jews-II"; "How Far is the Bible Inspired?"

77. "The Refining Influence of Woman," "Influences of Woman-Home Influence."

78. *CEP*, April 6, 1896; T. I. Minute Books, April 5, 1896.

79. T. I. Minute Books, June 3, June 7, October 18, 1896.

80. See *CEP*, August 14, 1896; *AJYB* 5664 (1903-04), p. 68; *Menorah* 21:2 (August 1896), p. 113; CCAR *Yearbook* 26 (1916): p. 499, 36 (1926): pp. 177-78; Ohio State University Alumni Information Center (Klein received his B.Ph. in 1900 and M.A. in 1903 from The Ohio State University;) Leo M. Jacobson to Marc Lee Raphael, correspondence, August 15, 1975.

81. T. I. Minute Books, September 24, 1896, June 16, 1900, June 2, 1901; January 18 and April 22, 1906; *AI* April 9, 1903.

82. T. I. Minute Books, September 4, 1899, May 13, 1902, December 14, 1904; *AI*, May 15, 1902.

83. T. I. Minute Books, February 6, April 3, May 8, 1898, September 24, 1899, October 14, 1900, June 1, 1902.

84. T. I. Minute Books, November 11, 1901, October 20, 1902; *CED*, July 14, 19, and 23, 1903; *Der Tägliche Westbote*, July 20, 1903.

85. T. I. Minute Books, March 1, 1903, May 31, June 3, 4, and 5, September 15, 1904; *CED*, June 3, 4, and 6, 1904; *CSD*, June 5, 1904; *Der Westbote*, June 7, 1904.

86. T. I. Minute Books, April 12, 1902, April 2, 1904, June 11, July 12, August 6 and 27, September 3 and 10, December 7, 1905, February 18, April 8, May 17, 1906.

87. *OSJ*, September 20, 1906; *AI*, October 11, 1906. The officers consisted of Isaac Topper, owner of a junkyard (president), Jacob Newman, owner of a rail and steamship ticket agency (vice-president), Mrs. Max Sussman (treasurer), Jacob Schlesinger, an attorney (secretary), and Harry Freidenberg, owner of a liquor store (financial secretary). Mr. Topper (1866-1934), who together with his brother Max founded Topper Brothers, emigrated from Russia (Bialystok); *OJC*, March 1, 1934, *Eminent Jews of America*, pp. 304-05, and Reva Goldberg Shaman to Marc Lee Raphael, telephone conversation, September 12, 1975.

88. *AI*, October 11, December 6, 1906; March 7, 1907; *OSJ*, November 18 and 25, 1906, April 28, 1907; *AJYB* 5668 (1907-08), p. 359.

89. *OSJ*, April 28, 1907.

90. *AJYB* 5664 (1930-34), p. 70; *WWAJ*, 1926, Volume 1, p. 334.

91. *WWAJ*, loc. cit.; T. I. Minute Books, October 30, 1910, October 26, 1913; *AI* July 7, 1910; *OSJ*, September 28, 1915, September 6, 1916. Kornfeld was also elected president of the midwestern B'nai B'rith region in 1914; T. I. Minute Books, January 24, 1915. For some insight into his scholarship, see his biography of Ludwig Philippson, in CCAR *Yearbook* 21 (St. Paul, 1911), pp. 149-92. For his strong stand against the introduction of religion into public schools, see *OSJ*, November 27, 1908.

92. T. I. Minute Books, May 13, 1906. May 5, 1907; October 10, 1909.

April 10, 1910, October 8, December 10, 1911, January 7, October 13, 1912, January 24, 1915, April 9, 1916. A study by Joseph Schonthal revealed that an average of sixteen persons attended Saturday services during 1909.

93. T. I. Minute Books, October 11, 1908, October 26, November 30, 1913, April 26, 1914, January 24, 1915, July 25, 1916; *OSJ*, September 23, 1935.

TABLE 40
TEMPLE ISRAEL PRESIDENTS

1890-91	Jacob Goodman	1894- 95	Simon Burgunder
1891-92	A. B. Cohen	1895- 96	Arnold Steinhauser
1892-93	Herman Rieser	1896-1903	Simon Burgunder
1893-94	A. B. Cohen	1903-1929	Joseph Schonthal

94. Persian Jews were not only frightened into wearing special hats, but beatings and lootings culminated in Teheran with a pogrom. Kornfeld's appeal to the Persian government brought out troops which quelled the riots and protected the Jews; *OJC*, May 4, 1923; *NYT*, October 15 and 30, 1921, April 5, 1922, April 28, 1923, October 23, 1924. From Toledo's Collingwood Avenue Temple (1925-34) to his death while serving Toronto's Holy Blossom Temple in 1943, Kornfeld's career, and his sad final years, are detailed in CCAR *Yearbook* 53 (1943), p. 245, and *OJC* July 2, 1943.

11. SOMETHING FOR EVERYONE: ORGANIZATIONAL LIFE

Just as the German Jews of Columbus had established their own organizations and societies, so too did the "new" immigrant Jews. A subculture encompassing education, the home, the neighborhood, institutional facilities, and associations functioned on a communitywide basis. This organizational network provided a comprehensive medium aiding the immigrants in the attainment of their business careers and in the maintenance of social stability in the urban environment.

Unable, or unwilling, to join the German-dominated B'nai B'rith Zion Lodge, "an effort was made [in 1892] to organize a lodge among the Russians." German Jews agreed that the need appeared great; for "there is no class of our people who are more in need than they of the humanizing effects of a society devoted to benevolence and brotherly love." No evidence exists to determine whether or not a new lodge was formed; but by the turn of the century Zion Lodge began admitting east European Jews.[1]

Some fraternal associations did emerge, however, among the immigrant Jews. The Independent Order of the Sons of Benjamin, founded on December 23, 1877, was incorporated in Columbus on January 9, 1901; six years later there were fifty lodges across the nation. Nathan Skuller (1865-1927), an immigrant peddler, became the first president of the Columbus City Lodge No. 156 which met on alternate Sundays at Fourth and Mound streets in Steltzer's Hall. Additionally, the Independent Western Star Order maintained an exclusively east European membership as did both Franklin Lodge 15 and Columbus Lodgc 74 of the Order Knights of Joseph. The Columbus Home Lodge, which was founded in 1912, enjoyed a membership of 150 by 1927. None of these, however, grew as large as the Knights of Israel, another exclusively east European lodge. By 1922, also under the leadership of Nathan Skuller, this lodge had enrolled 600 members. Formed as a mutual benefit society "to protect widows and orphans," the Knights of Israel became the "largest Jewish organization of its kind in the city."[2]

Immigrant women, like the men, formed mutual benefit organizations. The largest, the Columbus Rebecca Home Lodge, claimed 150 members by 1919. Dues of twenty-five cents a month entitled each member to a weekly five dollar benefit when ill; a modest life insurance fund made membership even more attractive.[3]

Status within the immigrant community did not come from membership in a lodge but in the popular Excelsior Club. Prohibited from joining German Jewish social clubs for some time, the immigrants created their own organization on February 21, 1924, patterned after a Cleveland club with the same name. The Excelsior Club provided entertainment and fellowship for immigrant Jewish men and their female companions. Organized at the Chittenden Hotel by seven men, and meeting initially in a carpet warehouse, the membership grew to sixty within two months. A $25 initiation fee, annual dues of $25, and a $100 stock certificate purchase plan, as well as a blackball system, kept the club "exclusive." Parties, dances, and entertainments dominated the group's activities, although cultural symposia occasionally drew a crowd; at the first Open Forum, Rabbi Lee Levinger reviewed *Elmer Gantry*. By 1927 the club operated a "home of our own" on the corner of Rich Street and Parsons Avenue; although dues barely met expenses, this provided a modest equivalent to the German Jewish social and country club. One former Excelsior Club member described it as: "a social club filling the need for some of the younger men who wanted a little bit of social status they couldn't get at the Winding Hollow [Country Club]."[4]

In addition to mutual benefit organizations and social clubs, the immigrant Jews organized at least one fraternal association which was initially limited to men from the same Russian province — Volhynia. The Voliner Society was established between 1915 and 1918, and provided Voliners with an opportunity to find fellowship and culture. The society sponsored annual picnics where hundreds of friends and relatives joined members, presented cantorial concerts which attracted sell-out crowds, and arranged various events to raise funds for Torahs, Hebrew books, and other vital synagogue and educational needs. Voliners also continued the practice, begun early in the century, of sponsoring repertory and stock companies from New York for Yiddish theatrical productions; more than a thousand Columbus Jews attended the Lyceum during the summer of 1929 to see Maurice Schwartz star in "Tevya der Melchicker."[5]

East European Jews, especially in east coast metropolitan centers, played leading roles in the national labor movement and created a rich working class cultural life of their own. Two labor groups, neither with any extant records, emerged in Columbus: the Hebrew Tailors Benevolent Association was founded by Jacob Herman in 1906, and the Jewish Workman's Circle, or Arbeiter Ring, was formed the next year. Affiliated with the national organization of the same name, the Arbeiter Ring not only spread the social gospel to Jewish workers but also provided disability and death benefits. Furthermore, this organization loaned workers small sums of money for a variety of purposes.[6]

In the early years of the Jewish Workman's Circle, men with conflicting ideologies joined together uneasily, for they did not have enough followers to survive independently. Conflicts erupted repeatedly between assimilationists, who detested nationalisms such as Zionism, and Yiddish culturalists, who sought to preserve a secular culture in Columbus.

> They were socialist. The Arbeiter Ring people were socialist. I got news for you, a lot who belonged to that were not extreme leftist. It was because they had no other organization to belong to or their friends belonged. Landsleit from the old country, a *landsman,* so he took them in. They may not have been committed, you know, or understand any kind of the European leftist background.[7]

Religious and non-religious Jews participated actively in both arenas. While the majority attended the synagogue, many behaved like Will Jacob's father:

> He would come by on Yom Kippur with his horse and wagon right down in front of the big *shul* (Agudas Achim), and of course, would get all the curses that ever were given to anybody . . . from everybody. So Willie Jacob's father was the greatest leftist in this town.

The assimilationists, called variously "the left" and "communists," resigned in 1930, and the Arbeiter Ring settled into a quiet cultural phase. Relatively non-political and non-Zionist (but not non-religious), Workman's Circle Branch 154 sponsored lectures and concerts in Yiddish, and offered the immigrants a forum for discussions of issues central to the workingman.[8]

In addition to fraternal and social organizations, many groups were brought together by a desire to help local immigrants. One of these was the Hebrew Educational and Benevolent Society, which made a major effort to facilitate the settlement of newly arrived Russian immigrants. Organized in February 1905 by Dr. Joseph Lipman, a Columbus physician and Russian Jew, the society had its own headquarters at 447 East Mound Street by 1906. Dr. Lipman's attempt to provide assistance to these immigrants began when he discovered twenty or more of them boarding in the same house at 438 East Livingston Avenue; they were unable to speak English, and virtually lost in a strange land. Soon afterward, he formed the society to provide instruction in spoken English as well as American history and government, to "make them good citizens" and "inculcate patriotism." Lipman also wanted to find employment for them in areas other than peddling. Within one year of its founding, the society sponsored classes four nights each week, numerous clubs, and Friday and Sunday evening lectures in Yiddish about history, civics, and other subjects by Dr. Lipman. The officers and directors of the society were exclusively east European Jews, who were anxious to demonstrate that they could take care of their coreligionists. A local reporter noted that "out of the 400 who have attended the school not one has applied to outsiders for charity."[9]

While some local Jews were concerned about the immigrant population, there was also quite a bit of support for the Zionist dream of a Jewish Palestine. The Zionist movement came to America together with the mass immigration. In 1895 Theodor Herzl published his *Der Judenstaat,* and within two years the First Zionist Congress met in Basle. Shortly thereafter immigrant Jews formed the Federation of American Zionists in New York City, later reorganized as the Zionist Organization of America (ZOA). Soon local Zionist societies sprang up in cities all over the country. In 1900 the Zionites first appeared in Columbus as a group dedicated to raising money to fund the resettlement of European Jews in Palestine; two years later they organized the Columbus Zionist District (CZD).[10]

One of many Zionist organizations in Columbus in the early decades of this century, the CZD promoted social, cultural, and educational programs on Zionist themes and conducted campaigns for the Jewish National Fund (JNF) which sought to raise money to purchase land in Palestine. Louis Lipsky, Maurice Samuel, and Rabbis Wolf Gold, Stephen S. Wise, and Abba Hillel Silver were among the distinguished Zionist leaders who lectured in Columbus under CZD aegis. Henry Feinberg presented five community lectures about Zionism in 1918. Other local Zionists also delivered lectures with CZD support, elected delegates to attend Zionist conventions, and upon returning from their infrequent trips to Palestine, shared pictures of the journeys at public meetings.[11]

Fund raising for Palestinian causes became a major function of the CZD. The annual "flower day" project began in 1914. "One of our primary functions was to have a collection of funds from the sale of flowers and we used to have members of the group stationed on downtown corners for that purpose." In 1918, the fifth annual campaign disposed of twenty-five hundred flowers by eight-thirty on a warm morning in May, and in 1925 "flower day" raised $400. To this the CZD added the semi-annual collection of JNF charity boxes from private homes: "*Pushkes* . . . little square boxes . . . and they would nail on your kitchen door and you always put money in it . . . and it was nothing to go into a home and see ten *pushkes*." This enabled the CZD to send hundreds of dollars annually to the national ZOA office.[12]

While the men pursued their dream of a Jewish homeland in Palestine, women dedicated to the Zionist cause rallied to support Palestine through Hadassah. Formed three years after Henrietta Szold organized the national group in 1912, the local chapter grew rapidly in its early years, spurred by the excitement created by the Balfour Declaration in 1917. Hadassah featured study groups, lectures, cultural programs, social events, and raised funds for the Palestinian Milk Fund, as well as Palestinian medical units and hospitals.[13]

Several smaller Zionist organizations operated actively in the community during the second and third decades of this century. These included Poale Zion (Workers of Zion), a socialist or left-wing Zionist group; Mizrachi, the Orthodox or religious Zionist group, organized early in the century; the Geulah Club for "practical Zionism"; Ladies Mizrachi, like its male counterpart, an exclusively Yiddish-speaking group; and several youth organizations: Young Judea, Sinai Club, Kol Zion (Voice of Zion), Blossoms of Israel, Lilies of Zion, and Daughters of Zion.[14]

The Mizrachi Organization was formed in Europe in 1905; nine years later it came to America, enabling traditional Jews to reconcile their faith with their nationalism. Founded in Columbus at Beth Jacob synagogue on May 6, 1915, Mizrachi met in Orthodox synagogues on a monthly basis, and collected annual dues of three dollars. A 1919 membership list reveals eighty-five members who were almost exclusively Russian-born Orthodox members of Beth Jacob or Agudas Achim. Several were university students, many were peddlers, and more than a dozen owners of companies like Livingston Iron & Metal, Columbus Bag & Burlap, or Star Furniture. Two dues-paying members even came from as far away as Logan and Chillicothe, Ohio.[15]

While the men had their card and social clubs, Jewish women were enjoying hitherto unknown leisure due to the advent of prepared foods, innovative household equipment, and their husbands' economic success; finally they had time to organize their own societies. Prominent among them was the Jewish Ladies Aid Society of B'nai Israel which was also known as the Ladies Koffee Klatch, the Hebrew Ladies Aid Society, and by 1915, the Temple Israel Sisterhood. Seeking a "weekly social meeting" and funds to purchase an organ for the temple, this group of

Facing Page: *Columbus Jews joined many non-sectarian local and national organizations which provided services to less fortunate persons. In the center of this World War I Red Cross Canteen photo are Amy Weiler Harmon, Bernice Stern Levy, and Frances L. Gundersheimer.*

Rose E. (Mrs. Fred) Lazarus served as the president of the B'nai Israel Sisterhood from 1898 until her death in 1923. In addition to fund-raising activities for B'nai Israel and a wide variety of cultural programs for members, the sisterhood was involved in community service projects.

middle-class women organized on December 18, 1890, at 392 East Town Street, the home of Rosalie Lazarus (Mrs. A. B. Cohen). Glass caskets (small jewelry boxes), egg cups, dolls, and crumb trays were raffled and dues collected to provide the treasury with as much as $15 each week. As early as January 1891 the trustees of B'nai Israel convinced the society to put its funds into the temple treasury rather than to purchase an organ; by March the group's first fund-raising card party netted $469.55.

Late in 1893 the ladies agreed to use part of their meeting time for "domestic work," making doilies, towels, aprons, and pin cushions, to raise more money — and to assist local charities by distributing secondhand clothing and other items to needy individuals. The treasury expanded continuously; in 1901 the society gave the temple a $600 gift, in 1905 a check for $800, and in 1907 the sizeable sum of $1,400. By the end of 1914 the president, Rose Lazarus, could report that since its inception the sisterhood had donated to the temple $15,000, as well as $3,300 for an organ. In addition to fund-raising and charity efforts, meetings provided intellectual stimulation and entertainment: a paper by Mrs. A. B. Cohen on "Woman's Rights," a biography of William McKinley by Mrs. Frank Nusbaum, a violin concert by members' daughters, a performance by Ted Lewis (née Friedman) of nearby Circleville, or a lecture by Professor Ludwig Lewisohn of The Ohio State University.[16]

While decreasing their meetings from four to two a month, the sisterhood grew particularly active during World War I. In addition to sponsoring Red Cross classes, they dispensed with lunches at meetings to increase their donations to the war effort through the Red Cross. The ladies also donated "eatables," cigars, and cigarettes to the men at nearby Camp Sherman.

By the early 1920s the sisterhood broadened their activities. Now meeting only once each month, the ladies sponsored dances for Jewish students at The Ohio State University; visited sick members of Temple Israel; raised scholarship funds for rabbinical students at the Hebrew Union College; organized Sunday morning Bible classes; endorsed the United States' entrance into the World Court, and met often with neighboring sisterhoods in Newark, Zanesville, and Lancaster. When Mrs. Fred Lazarus died in 1923, the group renamed itself the Rose E. Lazarus Sisterhood in honor of her twenty-five years of service.[17]

Dissatisfied with merely devoting their time and effort to the synagogue, the ladies of B'nai Israel sought "to further the best and highest interests of humanity in fields religious, philanthropic, and educational." The Columbus branch of the National Council of Jewish Women was founded by a group of women meeting at the home of Rosalie Lazarus in December of 1893. Seventy-seven women soon joined, among them women from "some of the best families in Columbus."[18] Dormant by the end of the century, the council regrouped in January or February of 1918, again as the exclusive domain of Reform Jewish ladies. Although hesitant at first that the Jewish community could support another society, the Council claimed 125 members by April and 200 in May.[19]

The reorganized council enthusiastically supported the war effort by making hospital supplies and clothing for victims in devastated countries, and selling thrift stamps as well as Liberty and Victory Bonds. After the Armistice the council raised funds for war relief; one project involved selling postcards in front of F. & R. Lazarus & Company to raise $98 for the Fatherless Children of France.[20]

Throughout the 1920s the council continuously increased the scope of its activities, emphasizing civic, educational, and philanthropic projects. Council members endorsed legislation prohibiting discrimination against women; supported the League of Women Voters as well as several female municipal candidates; aided efforts to reduce juvenile delinquency; and visited prisoners at the Ohio State Penitentiary, patients at Children's Hospital, the Imbecile Hospital, and several other institutions. In conjunction with the Columbus Board of Education, the council sponsored Americanization classes which focused on the English language and American customs. One teacher recalled:

> Jewish women realized that there was a need for Americanization classes; someone to teach English to the foreign born, men and women who were anxious to become citizens . . . The women and the few men that were there learned so well . . . The friendships became so close; I visited the homes and got to know the families . . .[21]

The council's other educational efforts included donating books to Schonthal Community House, translating books into Braille, conducting a Sunday School for deaf children, providing educational loans to local college students, and offering several study and discussion groups for members.

Philanthropic efforts related closely to the council's other projects: donations were sent to special schools and hospitals; on one occasion a "motor unit" to bring X-ray machines to the neighborhood was funded. The council also established a free prenatal clinic at the Schonthal Community House. At holiday times the council often provided food, clothing, and cash for recent immigrants and needy Jewish families in Columbus.[22]

One of the most active charity societies, the Willing Workers, was formed by twenty B'nai Israel single girls in 1895; one year later there were forty-six members. During 1894-95 they began to sew clothing for poor Russian Jewish children, as well as to teach the immigrants how to make their own clothes. Like other women's groups in Columbus,[23] the Willing Workers became particularly active in the autumn months, sewing winter clothing for those without the funds or skills to make them. Occasionally their work extended beyond the Jewish community; during the winter of 1897-98 the press lauded them for rendering "great assistance . . . to recent flood sufferers here." By the end of World War I the group had grown to 225 members, who made large contributions of time and clothing. In 1916 the women distributed 1,050 pieces of underwear and linens and 200 pairs of shoes, while in 1917 they delivered 1,330 new garments, 273 pairs of new shoes, and 1,325 used articles of clothing to immigrant and poor Jews. In addition, the Willing Workers continued to visit the sick and cooperate with the public school officials in looking after the immigrant children's welfare.[24]

The women of two Orthodox synagogues, Agudas Achim and Tifereth Israel, organized in 1908 and 1912 respectively. Fourteen ladies, led by Mrs. S. Weinfeld, formed the Ladies Aid Society of Tifereth Israel on February 14, 1912, at the home of Mrs. Arthur Ginzler. By the end of the first year as a result of several raffles, $255 accumulated in the treasury, and by 1921 the women were able to contribute $800 to the congregation's building fund. During these eight years only dances, suppers, lawn fetes, and raffles fill the organization's minutes.[25]

Around 1900 ten Orthodox Jewish women, under the leadership of Mrs. Abe Goldberg (1860-1954), organized the Ezras Noshim,[26] "to relieve the distress among the sick and needy of Columbus." By 1923, 350 dues-paying members were raising funds through two major annual events: a gigantic summer picnic and a winter ball. Under the guidance of Toba Goldberg, president for more than forty years, Ezras Noshim supplied Ohio Penitentiary inmates with Jewish holiday dinners for many years, assisted needy families in obtaining Pesach supplies, and provided generous and regular aid to needy individuals and families. Sylvia Schecter remembers:

> We had some women here in the city who was very active in those days . . . I would call one of those women and say I got a family in. I put them in such and such a home, on such and such a street, and they would go down and see that they got living quarters and furniture that they had to have . . . I would call Mrs. Goldberg. She was head of . . . the Ezras Noshim, and she would take care of those people.[27]

Numerous social and cultural organizations dotted the immigrant Jewish section of Columbus. The busiest was Schonthal Center at 555 East Rich Street. Originally founded in 1918 as the Hermine Schonthal Community House, the center served the underprivileged primarily; but eventually it evolved into a genuine center serving all of Columbus Jewry. "The Schonthal Center when it opened was the busiest place as far as activity was concerned . . . they had everything there. It was the center of the Jewish community."[28] Joseph Schonthal purchased the old Louis P. Hoster residence — a large sixteen room stone mansion with parquet floors, stained glass windows, and bronze fireplaces — and had it remodeled: the large tiled bathroom was converted into a dental clinic, the conservatory into offices, the bedrooms into club rooms, the third floor ballroom into an auditorium, the drawing room into a kindergarten, and the carriage house behind the residence into a very small gymnasium, even though the ceiling rose only two feet higher than the ten-foot-high baskets!

During the first full year of operation in 1919 clubs formed the heart of the program, but a wide variety of activities filled the community house morning, afternoon, and night, except on the Sabbath: kindergarten, sewing, arts and crafts, dancing, gymnastics, basketball, cooking, printing, music, electric shop, dramatics, Girl Scouts, Boy Scouts, and Sunday School for juveniles; and for their older counterparts, a YMHA, a YWHA, and sewing, reading, debating, singing, football, basketball, and several clubs. Adult activities included English and citizenship classes, as well as meeting places for the National Workers' Alliance, Voliner Society, Workman's Circle, etc. Regular concerts, lectures, dances, parties, and performances drew large crowds,

while dental, hayfever, and "Infant Welfare" as well as ear, eye, nose, and throat disease clinics served hundreds of persons. During December of 1919 alone, 7,494 persons attended the center; the staff could not only boast of an average monthly attendance of six thousand, but of the "remarkable fact that during the past six months not a Jewish boy or girl has been in the Juvenile Court."[29]

The membership lists of the early years of the Schonthal Center's juvenile activities include scores of immigrants and their children, whose subsequent paths included *yeshivot* and crime, business and sports, medicine and scrap iron. One immigrant lad, eventually a nationally known sculptor, recalled:

> When I finished my daily meat delivery for Harry Center the butcher [1920] I went to the Schonthal Center and met with other boys in the basement where we set up science laboratories provided for us by Mr. Schonthal and with the help of Ms. Sugarman, the Executive Director.
>
> Some of the boys I was involved with in the laboratories were Morris Feinstein, later an osteopath, Jake Rosofsky, later became an outstanding cardiologist, Abe Kantrowitz, now Dr. Abe H. Kanter . . .[30]

Schonthal Center served the community for thirty years — a fine tribute to Hermine and her husband, Joseph Schonthal, who gave the building to the Federation of Jewish Charities in his

Facing Page: *The Louis P. Hoster mansion at 555 East Rich Street in the late 1890s before it was sold to Joseph Schonthal.*

Philanthropist Joseph Schonthal is well remembered for his tireless efforts on behalf of Columbus youth of all faiths.

wife's memory.[31] One of the foremost philanthropists in Columbus, and the leading Jewish philanthropist during the first century of Columbus Jewish life, Joseph Schonthal was born in Budapest, Hungary, on August 15, 1854. The son of a middle-class Jewish family, he served in Franz Joseph's army and managed the estates of an Austrian nobleman before leaving Budapest in April 1887 to come to Ohio. After settling in Chillicothe and peddling through Ross, Pike, and Highland counties for a few years, he brought his wife and four children to Columbus in 1891. For the next year he worked for Wolf, Goodman & Company and then formed a partnership with Henry Goodman to begin a scrap iron business on an alley corner of Third Street between Spring and Chestnut streets. By 1897 Schonthal established his own iron and steel scrap company at 450-470 Neil Avenue, and eight years later relocated on the southwest corner of Buttles and Factory streets where the Joseph Schonthal Iron and Steel Company developed into a five-acre plant with branches in Detroit and Buffalo and another plant in Lackawanna, New York.[32]

"Uncle Joe" or "Pop" Schonthal, as he affectionately became known, retired in 1910 upon the death of his wife Hermine in order to devote virtually all his time and money to philanthropy and social service efforts. In addition to the Hermine Schonthal Community House, Schonthal began the Jewish Infants Home of Ohio.

For many years the Cleveland Orphan Asylum was generously supported by the Columbus community; in return the institution cared for Columbus' Jewish orphans.[33] When the asylum directors decided to accept only infants from Cleveland, several Ohio cities initiated discussions about establishing a second home to serve Jewish orphans. By 1919, with commitments of annual support from Dayton, Youngstown, Akron, Toledo, Hamilton, and Cincinnati, Joseph Schonthal purchased and remodeled a building at 571 East Rich. In February 1920 the home was opened; it was dedicated two months later as the Jewish Infants Home of Ohio. Governed by a state board of directors, a local board of directors, and a local administrative board, the infants home had accepted twenty-eight children by early 1922.[34]

Schonthal also established the Schonthal Camp near Magnetic Springs; a school and asylum for indigent children in Riga, Latvia; scholarships to hundreds of students at The Ohio State University; and gave abundant personal attention to juveniles appearing in court. Up to his death on December 15, 1929, Schonthal had been serving as the president of Bryden Road Temple since 1903 and of the Federated Jewish Charities from its inception.

Schonthal's will allotted almost $200,000 to charity, with dozens of generous gifts ($3,000 to the Colored Old Folks Home,

$2,000 to the Godman Guild, etc.) to non-Jewish causes as well as very large bequests to his favorite Jewish charities. More than his gifts of money were Schonthal's gifts of person; hundreds of Columbus Jews remember parties he hosted for numerous children's groups, visits he made to hospitals and clubs, and counsel he provided to groups as diverse as Big Sisters, Girl Scouts, the Hebrew Free Loan Association, and confirmation classes.[35]

Directly across the street from Schonthal Center stood the Columbus Hebrew School, another important institution of the immigrant community. The school, or Talmud Torah, had been founded early in the century to offer Jewish children late afternoon Hebrew classes four days a week; for many years it had "moved frequently from one public school to another and from one basement of a synagogue to another." On November 5, 1922, through the generosity of Hirsh Kobacker, the school dedicated a permanent facility: a remodeled building with six classrooms, a large assembly hall, a principal's room and a library.[36]

Admitting that the "old system of the *cheder* and the antiquated Talmud Torah was a disastrous failure," the new principal, Nathan Savage, adopted an innovative teaching method (*Ivrith B'Ivrith* — Hebrew through Hebrew). After one year in the new building, he boasted that the students in the advanced classes could speak and write Hebrew, knew the Bible and modern Hebrew literature, and conducted their own worship services on Saturday mornings.[37] Not all students, however, were impressed with the academic program. Almost fifty years after he attended the Talmud Torah, Rabbi Eugene Borowitz, one of the most distinguished Jewish theologians of contemporary America, recalled:

> The Columbus Hebrew School was very substantially tied up, in our minds, with riding the bus. The bus would come to pick up the kids. There was always someone riding on the bus who was supposed to keep order. The social experience of riding on a bus after school, the yelling and hitting and screaming at one another, was a major part of Jewish growing up and socialization in Columbus. The classes . . . made no impression on one whatsoever.[38]

Nevertheless, the program grew rapidly. Within two years of the dedication three hundred Hebrew volumes filled the Columbus Hebrew School Library. Two hundred pupils were taught by seven teachers under the guidance of the new principal, Moshe Epstein, a Russian-born composer and scholar. A regular schedule of examinations, including Hebrew dialogues and Talmudic discussions, were conducted by Rabbi Pelkovitz and the officers.

Fund-raising efforts multiplied as well; appeals were made, in one month alone, at Irwin Stein's *brit* where $200 was collected, at private High Holiday services, and at a *pidyon ha-ben* (Redemption of the First Born) ceremony. In these years Columbus Hebrew School's four major sources of income were: memberships, tuition, Ivreeyah (the Women's Auxiliary), and donations. Together these managed to keep expenses lower than income.[39]

Organized at the time of the new building's dedication by the wives of the school's founders, the Ivreeyah actively arranged picnics, dances, and banquets to support the Columbus Hebrew School. Ivreeyah's dances were quite successful: one thousand attended the fourth annual dance in 1927 while the fifth annual dance realized $2,000 for the Columbus Hebrew School. For years the Ivreeyah continued to supply vital moral and financial support to the institution, and provided scholarships to children of needy families: "[We] raised money for the kids to go the *cheder* — they didn't have the money, in those days, to even send their child to Hebrew school. . . . when your child was bar mitzvah, you gave money to the Ivreeyah."[40]

Among the Reform Jewish men, and eventually the east European males as well, Zion Lodge No. 62 of the B'nai B'rith continued to be the most popular organization in Columbus. Retaining its attractive life insurance, unemployment, funeral and sick benefit policies; expanding its social service and philanthropic efforts; and gaining increasing recognition within the larger district, the lodge grew to a membership of more than four hundred by the end of World War I.

Discussions, debates, and even heated confrontations about benefits dominate the lodge's records after 1890. For example, when William J. Goodman's request for sick benefits in 1892 was denied by the lodge on a technicality, he filed an appeal with the District Grand Lodge's Board of Appeals. The children of M. L. Hyneman, who were denied their father's death benefits because his dues payments lagged, carried their appeal to the board as well. Lengthy arguments, preserved in the minutes, were filed by both the plaintiffs and Zion Lodge quite frequently, though the decision of the board rarely appears in the minutes. Few issues generated as much discussion and dispute as the mutual aid features of the lodge.[41]

The major fund-raising activities of the lodge continued to benefit selected institutions including the Cleveland Jewish Orphan Asylum and the National Jewish Hospital for Tuberculosis in Denver. In 1914 when B'nai B'rith established the Leo N. Levi Memorial Hospital in Hot Springs, Arkansas, for the treatment of arthritis and related diseases, Zion Lodge contributed generously. The local lodge also supported Jewish relief in eastern Europe,

Asia, and the Middle East; American Jewish communities and individuals in need of help; as well as special funds established by the District Grand Lodge No. 2.[42]

During the first decade of this century dozens of Russian Jews — peddlers, petty merchants, and other recently arrived immigrants — regularly became initiated; indeed, by 1908 twenty-four of the twenty-six initiates consisted of east Europeans. These new members came not only from Columbus, but from smaller cities and towns throughout central and southern Ohio like Circleville, Chillicothe, Delaware, Marion, and even tiny Murray.[43]

Zion Lodge members' wives conducted regular sewing classes for the immigrants throughout the 1890s, and raised money for immigrant organizations such as the Hebrew Educational Benevolent Society during the first decade of this century. In November of 1911 the B'nai B'rith House at 335 South Washington opened to supply a variety of services to the newcomers. The house sponsored four afternoon classes for youngsters and evening Americanization classes with Yiddish-speaking teachers who discussed American history and government. The house contained a library with eight hundred volumes and many Yiddish dailies as well as weekly and monthly publications. Located in the heart of the immigrant community, the B'nai B'rith House served to "elevate and educate our less fortunate coreligionists who come here from foreign lands."[44]

Zion Lodge also played an active role in gathering information about Jewish "juveniles and defectives" in local institutions — especially the Ohio State Penitentiary — and in providing religious opportunities for their Jewish "residents." By the first decade of the new century several members conducted regular worship services at the penitentiary as well as other places around central Ohio. The lodge also sponsored dinners and holiday celebrations at various institutions.[45]

With the presence of myriad Jewish newcomers from eastern Europe, "nauseating practices" rather than pogroms became common throughout America. Late in 1909, some members of B'nai B'rith Zion Lodge No. 62 noticed "offensive lithographs caricaturing the Jew" on various Columbus theatres' billboards and one year later "obnoxious caricatures and prejudicial misrepresentation" carried by a Columbus daily newspaper. In both cases, the Committee on Publicity, led by Fred Lazarus, Jr., met privately with the non-Jewish president of the Columbus Bill Posting Company and the editor of the *Columbus Citizen*, who offered apologies and discontinued the "nauseating practices." In 1913 the Anti-Defamation League of the B'nai B'rith was founded "to counter the defamation of Jews and assaults on their status and rights."[46]

In 1925 the lodge's local efforts culminated in the establishment of the first Hillel Foundation in District No. 2 and the second in the United States — The Ohio State University B'nai B'rith Hillel Foundation. Until 1934 a tiny house on Eighteenth Avenue near Waldeck was the center of Hillel activities. During its early years, Hillel was guided by an advisory board of lay leaders and the first director, Rabbi Lee Levinger, who served from 1925 to 1935. For more than fifty years it has made significant contributions to American Jewish life by serving the university and the local community.

By the early 1920s Zion Lodge had attained sufficient distinction that one of its past presidents, Edwin J. Schanfarber (1886-1944), was elected head of the District Grand Lodge No. 2 in 1921. "E. J.", as he was popularly known, was born in Coshocton to Jacob and Carrie Weil Schanfarber, who were the only Jews in this small Ohio town. In 1898 or 1899 Jacob brought the family to Columbus so that his children could meet some Jewish youngsters. He opened a small clothing store, Schanfarber Brothers, at State and High streets.

E. J. attended North High and received his law degree from The Ohio State University in 1907; he immediately established a law firm — Schanfarber and Schanfarber — with his older sister, Celia. Schanfarber's leadership abilities were evident before his

Edwin J. Schanfarber

fortieth birthday. In addition to serving as president of Lodge No. 2 and visiting lodges in more than thirty cities, he headed the building campaign for the Infirmary Building in the National Jewish Hospital in Denver, served as an original member of the National Hillel Commission, led the drive to establish The Ohio State University Hillel Foundation, and established the United Jewish Fund. Gaining distinction as an attorney, Schanfarber was perhaps the only Columbus Jew trusted, loved, and even idolized by all Jewish groups in Columbus. He became persona grata everywhere, even among those with differing philosophies, and is remembered affectionately by Orthodox, Conservative, and Reform Jews.[47]

On November 21, 1904, Jewish Charities of Columbus — the earliest centralization of Jewish philanthropies — was formed with Joseph Schonthal as president. Constituents included the Ladies Benevolent Society, the Helping Hand Society, and the Sheltering House. The purposes of Jewish Charities of Columbus were more expansive than those of the Hebrew Relief Association, which primarily assisted transient Jews. Admitting the existence of a permanent immigrant population and fearing that czarist terror would cause the stream of refugees to continue, Jewish Charities sought to relieve the distress, suffering, and poverty of local Jews. Additionally, by organizing its own philanthropies, the Jewish community was able to eliminate Jewish dependency on Associated Charities of Columbus. During 1908-09 Associated Charities served 1,688 Protestants, 218 Roman Catholics, and only 15 Jews; during 1914-15, 3,275 Protestants, 3,894 Catholics, and 16 Hebrews were assisted; while in 1915-16 Associated Charities aided 2,471 Protestants, 406 Catholics, and 15 Hebrews. Noting this impressive self-help effort, Associated Charities remarked that the "policy of the [Jewish Charities] is that no Jews shall be allowed to become a tax on any other organization."[48]

In January 1909 the Jewish Charities reorganized into a formal federation — the Federated Jewish Charities (FJC). As communitywide organizations designed to unify and standardize relief efforts, and to centralize fund raising, federations had been developing in Jewish communities ever since 1895 when the first Federation of Jewish Charities was established in Boston. Within twenty years the movement spread to approximately forty cities.

The Columbus federation included all local and outside Jewish relief agencies; members who annually subscribed at least three dollars elected a twenty-five member board of directors which met monthly. Fifteen of these directors, the Relief Committee, met weekly and reviewed all cases seeking assistance, while an Executive Committee of five officers and two directors allotted the funds to institutions outside of Columbus. These out-of-town recipients of Columbus Jewish philanthropy included the Cleveland Orphan Asylum, Cleveland Old Folks' Home, Denver Juvenile and Infants' Asylum, and Denver Juvenile Hospital for Tuberculosis Patients — institutions strongly supported by German Jewish philanthropic efforts in many midwestern communities.[49]

During the first four months of operation expenditures totaled $1,847, of this $915 were spent on local relief. This involved two parts: the relief work itself and the care of "professional" as well as "temporary dependent" transients. The Relief Committee maintained the Sheltering House, a room in a private residence for anyone needing food and shelter. Several members of the committee had the privilege of signing a card, which entitled the transient to one night's lodging and meals. A secretary, the only paid officer of the federation, and several volunteers had charge of the local relief work.[50]

The cards appeared in the following form:[51]

Columbus, Ohio, ________________, 19_____

To Hachnasos Orchim, of Columbus, Ohio:

Please provide
☐ Supper
☐ Lodging
☐ Breakfast
☐ Dinner

For Mr. ________________, the bearer hereof, and charge to the account of THE JEWISH CHARITIES OF COLUMBUS. The first night's lodging may be provided on request of any member of the Board of Directors. Further service shall require an order from the Relief Committee.

One local resident reminisced about the Sheltering House:

> . . . for people who had nowhere to sleep overnight, eat overnight — they could go to the Salvation Army, these beggars and sleep, but they felt it was a shame to let these people go to places like that, so they opened up this organization and they would make a great big dinner, charge fifty cents a ticket, and the women would go in and do their own cooking . . . Any Jewish person that wanted to stay overnight, have a kosher meal — I think they allowed them two days, something like that to stay there free.[52]

On certain occasions, transients arrived who appeared dangerous to the community. Late in 1902 D. Naaman and S. Leverski, temporary residents at the Sheltering House who spoke only Yiddish, pawned a fake gold chain for a considerable sum at

Wolf Levinson's pawn shop. Before the afternoon ended, they pawned similar chains at other shops owned by Sam Friedlander, Sam Levy, Isaac Cramer, and I. B. Jashenosky. After Sabbath prayers at the synagogue, several of the pawnbrokers realized during their conversation that they had been duped by the same con men, and filed writs for the arrest of the criminals.[53]

The Sheltering House, despite its usefulness, served as a focal point for a philosophical difference in philanthropy between the Reform Jewish leadership of the FJC and the immigrant community. Twenty of the twenty-two directors were long standing members of the community's Reform temple in 1916; they viewed the house as a one-night lodging place for transients approved by the FJC. The east European Jews, however, insisted it be available to anyone from outside Columbus who wished to lodge there. The most explicit attack on the immigrants came in 1916, when FJC's superintendent, H. Joseph Hyman, presented his annual report:

> The transient poor, an endless stream, formed about one-fifth of our applicants . . . the great majority of transients are parasites and will remain so just as long as there are sympathetic persons who will relieve their conscience by assisting without aim other than getting rid of the individual. The Jewish transient is . . . an increasing menace. The Hachnasos Orchim and the Shelter Home are the Schnorrers' [Beggars'] Hotel, and help perpetrate the evil. Just as long as it is known that there is food and shelter awaiting him the transient will continue to travel. The remedy in most cases is work. Should the transient refuse to work, no other aid should be given. And there is the difficulty. After assistance is refused by the Federation there are always sympathetic individuals willing to help. It is needless to say that this sort of aimless assistance is worthless; that it does more harm than good.[54]

The directors appointed a committee to control the situation, and in his next annual report Hyman announced: "The imposter, the schnorrer, the *magid,* the tramp, the self-appointed collector of Palestinian charities has suddenly disappeared . . ." That these persons disappeared is without foundation; that the FJC ceased to serve them is certain.[55]

Nevertheless, the Associated Charities remained impressed with the Federated Jewish Charities' organization and operation. It saw the federation exercising "care and precision," possessing a "pleasant sense of efficiency and lack of waste," and providing deliberation in all its work. Located at 498 East Mound for several years, the federation moved into the old Louis P. Hoster residence at 555 East Rich Street when Joseph Schonthal donated the building to them in 1918.

The FJC raised $6,656 in 1916, $9,550 in 1917, $19,812 in 1919 and used most of the money for local Jewish needs. Relief dominated their efforts; in 1916, for example, there were 906 applications for relief. Sickness, accidents, and the premature deaths of breadwinners were continuous events. Like many charity societies of the period, almsgiving was the main activity of the society. Several organizations assisted FJC in the relief work: the Hebrew Free Loan Association, the Jewish Educational Alliance, the Jewish Infants Home of Ohio, and the Ezras Noshim.

The Hebrew Free Loan Association provided crucial support to the FJC by offering needy immigrants quick loans without interest. Joseph Schonthal noted that the FJC "could not have survived without the HFLA." During 1916 the association made seventy-four loans totalling $3,063, and in the following year gave $2,108 to forty-seven applicants; loans were used to replace a peddler's dead horse, to supply a peddler with his first pack of merchandise, and to provide rent money for those unable to meet their payments. In addition to making interest-free loans, the association required only small weekly payments. Almost half of those who borrowed money in 1916 were peddlers who requested funds to buy merchandise for resale. Whatever the motivation, people threw themselves into the work of fund raising for the association as they did for almost every other Jewish charity in Columbus. An endless round of fairs, picnics, theater productions, and plain schnorring at social gatherings fattened the association's treasury.[56]

Founded in 1911 in a single room, the Jewish Educational Alliance moved to a large assembly hall with eight spacious rooms on the corner of Washington Avenue and Mound Street within six years. As the forerunner of the Schonthal Center and then the Jewish Center, the alliance's programs were primarily for children. Offerings included a five-day kindergarten in the morning; sewing, library, dancing and music classes in the afternoon; classes for adults, teenage clubs and study rooms at night; a Sunday school for children whose parents did not affiliate with a synagogue or whose synagogue had no school, concerts, lectures, debates, dramatics, and much more. Its director, H. Joseph Hyman (b. 1890), was a graduate of the University of Cincinnati and a disciple of Boris Bogen, one of the pioneers of social work. Hyman gained valuable experience in Columbus before assuming more difficult duties with the Joint Distribution Committee after World War I.[57]

With the influx of the new immigrants a wide range of groups emerged in the community and Jewish life teemed. Immigrant lodges, clubs, and *landsmanschaften* swelled with members; Schonthal Center quickly gained a reputation for its wide ranging programs and became the starting place for almost every immigrant Jew who would later achieve success; and Zionist organizations expanded rapidly with the immigrants' arrival and especially after the Balfour Declaration, supplying Columbus Jewish immigrants with a vital program of culture and education.

The children and grandchildren of the German Jewish immigrants continued to develop their web of ethnically exclusive men's and women's organizations. The women, envisaging more than simply emergency care for needy immigrants, undertook a vigorous program of lectures and discussions as well as a far flung program of social work, while the men, greatly expanding the base of their primary organization without any dimunition in its tradition and prestige, multiplied activities and promoted a diversified group of programs. And B'nai B'rith also enabled Columbus Jewry, more so than any other Jewish organization, to maintain contact with larger Jewish centers in Cleveland, Cincinnati, and Chicago while helping to sustain Jewish life in the outpost communities of Ohio. This rich organizational life, when linked with the intensive network of business affiliations and social ties reinforced in the lodge and synagogue, provided economic opportunities and social stability for Columbus Jews.

NOTES FOR CHAPTER 11

1. *AI*, January 21, 1892.
2. "Sons of Benjamin, Independent Order of" in B'nai Zion, Order of (American Jewish Historical Society, Waltham, Massachusetts); *AJYB* 5661 (1900-01), p. 131; *OSJ*, January 8, 1900, January 1, June 18, 1901, February 11, 1927; *AJYB* 5668 (1907-08), p. 89; *OSJ*, June 23, September 15, December 29, 1922.
3. *CJC*, January 3, 1919.
4. *OJC*, March 7, 1924, January 27, 1928; Excelsior Club, Minutes, 1927-32, presented to the Ohio Historical Society by Harry Schwartz; interview with Harry Schwartz.

TABLE 41
EARLY EXCELSIOR CLUB PRESIDENTS

1924	Max Weinberger	1927	Dewey Rosenfeld
1925	Max Weinberger	1928	Martin Rosenthal
1926	Morris Goldberg	1929	Louis Rosenthal

5. *OJC,* November 1, 1906, April 30, 1907, January 21, August 19, 1927, June 7, August 16, November 2 and 9, 1929; October 9, 1931, June 17, 1932; *CJC,* January 3, 1919; interview with Jacob Pass.

6. *OJC,* February 13, 1931; *Columbus City Directory* 1916; Judah Shapiro, *The Friendly Society* (New York, 1970); Morris Weinstock to Marc Lee Raphael, telephone conversation, August 4, 1975.

7. Interview with Harry Schwartz.

8. Ibid.; Henry Goldstein to Marc Lee Raphael, telephone conversation July 10, 1974; interviews with Benjamin W. Abramson and Robert Mellman; *OJC,* January 28, 1927, February 3, 1928, April 7, 1939.

The Jewish National Workers' Alliance (Yidisher Natzionaler Arbeiter Farband), Branch 37, a smaller Yiddish-speaking Labor Zionist group, emerged in Columbus in 1912. A social and cultural group, the alliance sponsored regular cultural programs to raise money for Palestinian causes; *OJC,* July 22, 1927.

The Jewish Labor Committee, organized by Jewish workingmen and women in 1934 to oppose communism and fascism, received support from both the Workman's Circle and the Jewish Welfare Federation; Philip Rabin, "A Study of American Jewish Community Backgrounds: A Description of Jewish Organizations and the Jewish Community Council of Columbus, Ohio," M.A. thesis, The Ohio State University, 1942.

9. *OSJ,* May 27, October 26, and November 5, 1905, March 10 and 11, 1906; *AJYB* 5668 (1907-08), p. 359; *CD,* March 11, 1906. Henry Gumble succeeded Dr. Lipman as president when a criminal investigation and professional developments in Lipman's medical career forced him to flee to Canada; *OSJ,* November 13, 1906, July 4, 1907, and B'nai B'rith Minutes, February 25, August 12, 1907.

10. *OSJ,* April 22, 1900.

11. *OSJ,* December 27, 1918, December 8, 1922, December 16, 1927; *OJC,* May 17, June 28, July 5, August 16, September 27, 1918, November 4 and 18, 1927.

12. Interview with Dora Abrams; *OJC,* June 23, December 22, 1922, April 20, 1923, August 8, 1924, June 12, 1925; *Agudas Achim Sunday School Bulletin* I:3 (June 1918).

13. *OJC,* May 17 and 31, 1918, December 28, 1923, July 3, October 9, 1925, March 14, 1930.

14. *AJYB* 5668 (1907-08), pp. 40, 44; *Maccabean,* July 1916, p. 199; *CJC,* January 20, July 12, 1918; *OJC,* December 8 and 22, 1922, July 27, 1923.

15. *Pinkas shel Agudath Hamizrachim of Columbus.*

16. Ludwig Lewisohn (1893-1955) held a professorship in German language and literature at The Ohio State University from 1911 to 1918, and found the campus a "singular perversion of middle-class values" filled with "cowardice, effeminacy of mind, stupidity and emptiness" (faculty) as well as "football and fudge" (students). His outspoken praise of German culture during the war years shadowed his days in Columbus, and the resulting "silence, conformity and slavish submission," together with personal upheavals, made the Columbus years enormously difficult ones. See William O. Thompson to M. B. Evans, correspondence, in Miscellaneous Correspondence (L), 1918, WOY, 3/e/15, The Ohio State University Archives; "History of the Department of German" in *College of*

Humanities Centennial, The Ohio State University, pp. 13-15; L. Lewisohn, *Upstream: An American Chronicle* (New York, 1922), pp. 160-219; Adolph Gillis, *Ludwig Lewisohn: The Artist and His Message* (New York, 1933).

17. Minutes, Jewish Ladies Aid Society of Temple B'nai Israel, December 18, 1890-February 28, 1894; Minutes, November 11, 1896, to April 25, 1900; The B'nai Israel Sisterhood Journal, May 9, 1905, to June 1, 1909; The Ladies Auxiliary of B'nai Isreal [sic] Temple, October 20, 1909, to January 27, 1915; Minutes, Temple Israel Sisterhood, February 10, 1915, to February 25, 1917; Continuation of 1916-17, March 11, 1917 to February 12, 1924.

18. *AI*, December 24, 1896; *OJC*, January 12, 1923; Edith J. R. Isaacs, "What Jewish Women are Doing for the Jews," *Twentieth Century Magazine*, January 1912, pp. 214-21.

19. *CJC*, April 5, May 10, 1918; *OJC*, January 12, 1923.

20. *OJC*, January 12, 1923; *Handbook of Social Resources* (Columbus, 1922), pp. 52-53.

21. *OSJ*, December 15, 1929; interview with Rabbi Morris Skop.

22. The Papers of the National Council of Jewish Women, OHS, Box 2, Folders 3, 8, 9-10, 12.

23. Non-Jewish ladies' philanthropies active in Columbus at this time included the East Side Workers of Protestant Hospital, Ladies Aid Society of the Universalist Church, the Diet Kitchen, and the Ladies Aid Society of the Fifth Avenue Presbyterian Church.

24. *AI*, October 24, 1895, October 8, 1896, September 23, 1897. March 31, 1898; *AJYB* 5680 (1919-20), pp. 530-31; "Fifteenth Annual Report . . . 1915" in *The Social Servant* (December 1915); "Sixteenth Annual Report . . . 1916" in *The Social Servant* (December 1916); *Nineteenth Annual Report . . . 1919* (Columbus, 1919).

25. *OJC*, March 30, 1928; Regular Minutes, 1912-23, Ladies Aid Society of The H. H. Congregation T. I., Reorganized February 1912 at Tifereth Israel.

26. Various dates are given for its inception; it celebrated its thirtieth anniversary in 1930 and its thirty-fifth anniversary in 1932, while as early as 1907 its beginnings were listed as 1899; see *OJC*, January 10, 1930, December 2, 1932; *AJYB* 5668 (1907-09), p. 359, *Agudas Achim Sunday School Bulletin*, I:2 (April 1918).

27. *OJC*, May 27, 1932, April 21, 1933, April 12, December 6, 1935, April 24, 1936, May 6, 1938, April 21, 1939; interview with Sylvia Schecter.

28. Interview with Robert Mellman.

29. *OJC*, January 3 and 10, February 1, 1919; *Nineteenth Annual Report of the Federated Jewish Charities and Affiliated Societies of Columbus* (Columbus, 1919).

30. "Autobiography of Herman Perlman," typescript.

31. *OSJ*, November 2, 1910.

32. Among Schonthal's other business activities were the West Virginia Rail Company, headquartered in Huntington, West Virginia, which he established in 1907, and local companies such as Kinkade & Liggett, New American Elevator, and Uneedme Tool.

33. Founded in 1868, there were three Columbus Jewish children among the initial group of "inmates"; between 1868 and 1927 thirty-one of four thousand children admitted came from Columbus. See *First Annual Report*

of the Board of Trustees of the Orphan Asylum, District No. 2, I.O.B.B. at Cleveland, Ohio, For Year Ending October 1, 1869 (Cincinnati, 1869), p. 13, and *OSJ,* July 10, 1927.

34. *OJC,* March 3, 1922, August 17, October 12, 1923, January 25, 1931.

35. *OJC,* August 11, September 15, 1922, April 25, October 17, 1924, December 17, 1926, April 15, 1927, December 17 and 20, 1929; *CD,* December 16 and 19, 1929; *CC,* December 16, 1929; *AI,* June 10, 1909. For a description of suits filed against the executors of the will for more than a quarter million dollars, see Columbus daily newspapers on July 24 and November 19, 1931, June 8, 1932, and February 10, 1933.

36. "Jewish Education and the Columbus Talmud Torah," in *OJC,* November 3, 1922; interview with Irving Seff. The new building was necessitated, in part, by the refusal of Agudas Achim, the only Orthodox synagogue sufficiently large, to house the Columbus Hebrew School; see interviews with Abe Yenkin and Fred Yenkin. During at least one summer prior to 1922, the Talmud Torah conducted classes five days a week (9:00-1:00) at the Agudas Achim; *Agudas Achim Sunday School Bulletin* I:3 (June 1918).

37. *OJC,* November 3, 1922. The first graduating class consisted of Rhoda Horowitz, Joseph Metchnick, Nathan and Sophie Pelkovitz, Theodore Savage, Arthur Seff, and Rose Thall.

38. Interview with Rabbi Eugene Borowitz.

39. *OJC,* July 6, September 21, October 12 and 19, 1923, May 23, 1924, March 20, 1925.

40. *OJC,* June 1, 1923, September 26, November 14, 1924, June 11, 1926, January 14, November 11, December 2, 1927, March 23, April 20, May 11, 1928; interview with Dora Abrams. Mrs. Sadye Tushbant (1889-1944) served as the first president of Ivreeyah.

41. B'nai B'rith (B. B.) Minutes, October 13 and 27, November 10, 1895, September 27, 1896, June 11, November 12 and 25, 1899, March 11, 1900, May 8 and 22, 1922.

42. B. B. Minutes, October 9, 1898; January 28, April 22, May 13 and 27, 1907; January 13, March 9 and 23, 1908; February 26, 1912. During the spring of 1907 the lodge collected $58 for the "ghetto poet Morris Rosenfeld." The Cleveland Jewish Orphans Asylum, founded in 1868 by the B'nai B'rith as an orphanage to care for children of Civil War casualties, eventually became an institution for emotionally disturbed children, under the name Bellefaire. The National Jewish Hospital was organized a decade or so before the B'nai B'rith took it over at the 1899 Convention of District Grand Lodge No. 2.

43. B. B. Minutes, November 22, 1891, May 22, 1892, April 13 and 27, 1908.

44. B. B. Minutes, July 26, 1893, March 25, 1894, March 10, 1895, February 28, 1897, February 13, 1898, March 25, May 13, 1907, October 9, 1911, February 12, May 24, June 10, 1912; *CJC* March 29, 1918.

45. B. B. Minutes, November 25, 1909, November 14, 1910.

46. B. B. Minutes, December 24, 1909, November 14, 1910.

47. Nettie Schanfarber Wolf to Marc Lee Raphael, correspondence, July 18, 1975; (Coshocton) *Democrat Standard,* July 19 and 23, 1889; (Coshocton) *Democrat and Standard,* April 14, 1903; *WWAJ,* 1928, 2nd edition, p. 614;

CED, July 2, 1944; *CC*, July 2, 1944; *National Jewish Monthly*, September 1944; *NYT*, July 3, 1944; *OJC*, May 26, June 2 and 9, 1922.

48. *AJYB* 5668 (1907-08), p. 359; Associated Charities of Columbus, Ohio. *Sixth Annual Report*. November 1904 to November 1905, p. 21; *Ninth Annual Report*, p. 27; "Fifteenth Annual Report . . . 1915" in *The Social Servant* (December 1915): 6-12; "Sixteenth Annual Report . . . 1916" in ibid. (December 1916): 25-32.

49. Barbara M. Solomon, *Pioneers in Service* (Boston, 1956), pp. 1-69; Jacob Neusner, "The Impact of Immigration and Philanthropy upon the Boston Jewish Community (1880-1914)," *AJHQ* 46:2 (1956): 71-85; Boris D. Bogen, *Jewish Philanthropy* (New York, 1917); Joseph Jacobs, "The Federation Movement in American Jewish Philanthropy," *AJYB* 5676 (1915-16): 159-98. The fullest discussion of the history, development, and orientation of the Jewish welfare federation movement in America is in Harry L. Lurie, *A Heritage Affirmed: The Jewish Federation Movement in America* (Philadelphia, 1961).

50. *Charities of Columbus: Report of the Committee on Charities and Corrections of the Chamber of Commerce* (Columbus, 1910), pp. 37-38; *Third Annual Report . . . November 1, 1901 to November 1, 1902*, p. 22. The Sheltering House, relatively unused during the 1920s, became a busy way station once again during the depression. An eight-room house was dedicated in 1931 at 485½ Livingston, and replaced by a new home at 525 Livingston in 1934. See *OJC*, May 1, June 5, July 10 and 24, 1931, August 17, 1934, November 1, 1935; Council of Social Agencies of Columbus and Franklin County. *Handbook of Social Resources of Columbus and Franklin County* (1936), p. 38.

51. *Charities of Columbus* . . . (Columbus, 1910), p. 38.

52. Interview with Dora Abrams.

53. *OSJ*, November 20 and 21, 1902.

54. "Fifteenth Annual Report . . . 1915."

55. "Sixteenth Annual Report . . . 1916."

56. Associated Charities. "Fifteenth Annual Report"; "Sixteenth Annual Report"; *Eighth Annual Report; Ninth Annual Report; Eleventh Annual Report;* Chamber of Commerce. *Handbook of Social Resources* (Columbus, 1922), p. 73; The HFLA was incorporated in February 1912; *Annual Statistical Report of the Secretary of State to the Governor . . . November 15, 1912* (Springfield, Ohio, 1913), p. 38.

57. Joseph Hyman's close relationship with Schonthal continued for some years. In 1920 and 1921 he worked in Poland for the Joint Distribution Committee, and from 1921 to 1924 he served as Director of Reconstruction, Medical Work, Child Care of Refugees for the committee in the Baltic States. In the latter capacity he organized the Schonthal Children's Summer Home in Riga during 1923; see *OJC*, April 13, 1923, January 18, 1924. For a more complete biography, see *OJC*, August 17, 1928, and *WWAJ*, 1928, Volume 1, p. 316.

12. THE JEW IS OF SEDENTARY HABITS: SOCIAL AND RECREATIONAL LIFE

The last two decades of the nineteenth century initiated the age of clubs in America; the Jewish upper layer, reflecting its growing wealth and Americanization, created an exclusive social milieu to match the blue book and social registers of the larger society. Exclusively Jewish clubs emerged with typical Victorian names — Harmonia, Excelsior, Progress, and Standard — as German Jews, with newly-acquired money, manners, and homes, preferred social ties with other Jews of the same class. Their programs, like their names, were overwhelmingly secular, featuring cards, billiards, dances, and all night parties.

As the German Jews of Columbus became affluent, acculturated, and secularized, their social life — like that of the wealthy non-Jews they imitated — overflowed with an endless round of fairs, parties, balls, debuts, and amateur performances. This lavishness, however, began long before the Gilded Age when it dominated local as well as out-of-town newspaper accounts of Columbus Jewish life.[1]

On January 3, 1854, Columbus Jewry celebrated its first double wedding. Isaac and Caroline Gundersheimer took part in the double ceremony sanctified by Joseph Goodman: Isaac Gundersheimer, a clerk in his brother Joseph's clothing store, married a Bavarian girl, Louise Hacker, while his sister Caroline married Isaac Hoffman, a salesman at Joseph's shop and later a charter member of B'nai B'rith Zion Lodge No. 62. (Joseph Gundersheimer, who became the first president of Bene Jeshuren, had been married in Columbus' first wedding involving two Jews on July 7, 1848.)

Contemporary accounts of the double ceremony and reception describe it as "one of the most brilliant and notable events of the season," duly mentioning that while the wedding invitations read six p.m., the first guests arrived at the rented hall at six-thirty, and the wedding procession began at seven-fifteen. After the wedding, the Gundersheimers and Hoffmans "went to housekeeping immediately in handsome homes already provided for them."[2]

By the 1870s, the most important social events of the year were lavish weddings. Several receptions set "Jewish circles agog": in 1876, at the temple wedding of Samuel Smit and Flora Frankel, where "an orchestra struck up the grand old Mendelssohn Wedding March, the bride's diamond ornaments were valued at $40,000." A check for $5,000 together with a "pair of very costly diamond earrings," and a grand upright piano were among the presents, "the handsomest . . . our reporter ever gazed upon." The gifts at several other weddings during these years appear almost as "rich and costly," as Columbus Jewry impressed itself, out-of-town guests, and non-Jews with its recent affluence.[3]

In September of 1863 Marcus W. Childs and twenty-four men formed the Harmonia Club. Early in 1881 its new club rooms in the Zettler Building at Fourth and Friend streets were inaugurated with a "brilliant and fashionable ball." The gentlemen "were gallants of the most gallant"; dinner arrived at ten p.m., supper at one a.m., and dancing continued until dawn. According to one Columbus newspaper, the club was composed of "our best and most refined Jewish citizens," whose goals of enjoyment and recreation of a "broad social nature" became realized through "some of the most brilliant occasions of the seasons." By beautifying its quarters, the club "purged" itself of all its "old associations." The new quarters included a stage, frescoed walls, a billiard room, and a "large chandelier surrounded by numerous hanging cages each occupied by a bird."[4]

Fund-raising affairs continued to be the social occasions of the year, and life cycle events — coming-out parties for young ladies, twenty-first birthday spectaculars for young men, and especially silver anniversaries — provided occasions for grand celebrations. In 1885 the Morris Mayers celebrated their twenty-fifth year together at their home with "elegant invitations" and an "elaborate and elegant" dinner for fifty persons. One guest described the party as the "nicest, without doubt, that has been seen in this city for months." The Sol Schwarz' silver anniversary celebration in 1883 brought them twelve dozen bottles of wine from one couple, and equally lavish gifts from others.[5]

By the turn of the century, if not earlier, B'nai Israel congregants enjoyed long summers at popular vacation spots around the midwest and on the east coast. In 1903 they went to Atlantic City and French Lick; in 1908 to Shell Beach at Buckeye Lake, Atlantic City, Asbury Park, Berkshire Hills, Thousand Islands, Magnetic Springs, and French Lick; and in 1911, 1912, and 1913, to Cedar Point, Magnetic Springs, Mackinac Island, Ocean

City, and Atlantic City. Lengthy vacations at comfortable resort areas became commonplace; affluent Jews rarely failed to mention their vacation sites in the local or Anglo-Jewish press.[6]

At the same time the Columbus press regularly featured and generously described large weddings in the Orthodox immigrant community. Apart from the ceremony, there appears little difference between east European and German Jewish weddings. Isaac Baker and Annie Cominsky, "two leaders of Orthodox Jewish society circles," served dinner for five hundred guests at the Buckeye Hall following their wedding in December 1901, while Samuel Fleischman and Rose Bendersky feted three hundred at Schenck's following their Orthodox ceremony in 1907. (Perhaps the expense of this celebration accounted for Sam and Rose making their home with Rose's mother and father immediately following the wedding.) Typical of the larger east European weddings is the following newspaper description:

> Beneath the immaculate white canopy in the center of the room, beautifully decorated with potted palms, and the national colors, in the presence of 500 relatives and friends seated in semi-circles on either side, while pleasing strains of music emanated from a stringed orchestra concealed behind potted plants on the stage, Miss Fannie Noskoff and Heiman Rosen, both prominent in local Hebrew circles, last nite in Schenck's Hall . . .[7]

For many years, numerous expensive celebrations not only followed elaborate weddings among German Jews but preceded them, too. Teas, dinners, and parties, for local friends as well as distant relatives, highlighted the pre-nuptial activities. Prior to their wedding on December 30, 1901, eight women alternated entertaining Minnie Gugenheim and Sol Hirshberg for eight consecutive days; Mrs. Ben Harmon culminated the festivities the night before the wedding with a dinner for more than one hundred at the Southern Hotel.[8]

Throughout their first seventy-five years in Columbus, Jews were virtually absent from the elite social circles. None of the forty-five Jewish stockholders of Winding Hollow Country Club displayed career paths typified by promotion upward through the bureaucratic structures of the large corporations. Rather, they entered the Jewish elite through family-based businesses, organized either by themselves or their fathers. Instead of providing needed organizational or technical skills to Columbus businesses, Jews moved into elite Jewish circles as part of emerging or growing Jewish firms. Their success stories revealed the need for assistance from a fellow Jew who had "made it," or, more often, a member of one's own family.

Grand family parties like Mr. and Mrs. Fred Lazarus' thirty-fifth anniversary celebration were quite common at the turn of the century. Here guests are pictured in the dining room transformed into a garden of the Lazarus' three-story home at 1080 Bryden Road.

Jews remained outside the financial elite of Columbus as well. In 1907 270 individuals served on the boards of directors of nine Columbus national banks, thirteen state banks, and four trust companies. Only two Jews, Fred and Simon Lazarus, were included in the 270. Despite the extraordinary economic success of the Columbus Jews as a group, they could not penetrate the economic elite of the city.[9]

Feeling that "the social lines are being drawn about our people," shortly after World War I concluded, Henry Gumble, Simon Lazarus, Leon Bornheim, Samuel Summer, and several other Columbus Jews began to discuss the idea of a Jewish country club. Largely in response to both the lack of public golf courses and the refusal of at least one Columbus country club to admit Jews, these men were not sure that enough Jews had developed a passion for golf to make such a club feasible. With the opening of a municipal course in 1920, "a great number of our people acquired a genuine love for the game," and one year later, despite a national business depression, Winding Hollow Country Club incorporated on December 14,

> for the purpose of profit and to provide diversion, recreation, amusement and entertainment for, and to promote association, social relations and intercourse and mutual improvements among, the stockholders and members, and to maintain a social club devoted to outdoor sports, rural amusements and country pastimes.[10]

The club received its financing from a $150,000 capital stock offering of 1,500 shares; within one year, more than 670 shares had been sold to more than forty-five members — every one a member of the Bryden Road Temple. The country club was composed exclusively of Reform Jews, but only the most exclusive Reform Jews who could afford a $500 membership fee and annual dues of $200. New members not only needed two members to sponsor them, but the approval of eight of the nine directors as well.[11]

Immediately upon incorporating, the club purchased 178 acres and hired a golf architect. Construction of a course began quickly; upon completion of the $100,000 golf course, the president noted:

> the Jew is of sedentary habits and prone to avoid even necessary exercise; golf . . . is mild, pleasurable and healthful. It prevents illness . . . affords real companionship and friendly rivalry, and even effects a cure after great damage to health has been done.

The Reform Jews now had an enviable country club of their own, and the sustained growth of Winding Hollow had begun.[12]

The best indicator of Columbus' Jewish social elite is still "the club." Even in 1975, when we asked more than four hundred and fifty Columbus Jews "to which organizations do you think the socially prominent Jews of Columbus belong?" the first choice of more than 75 percent was Winding Hollow Country Club. The club, of course, paralleled upper-middle- and upper-class clubs in Columbus. Non-Jewish metropolitan clubs like the Columbus Athletic Club served a dual function: they acted as monitors of entrance into the uppermost stratum of power and prestige, as well as informal loci of important community decision-making. Since the leading metropolitan clubs restricted membership to Anglo-Saxons through World War II, the Jews created their own hierarchy with the German Jewish community at the top.

The overwhelming majority of German Jews and their children in the late nineteenth and early twentieth centuries belonged to the Reform synagogue, B'nai Israel. Reform Judaism had adapted itself to the tastes of prosperous, middle-class Columbus Jews anxious to worship with formality and decorum and to present themselves and their faith in a fashion acceptable to (and little different from) the non-Jewish community. This American Reform, however, had little appeal for the east European immigrants arriving in Columbus in these same years. They huddled close together and sought to recreate in their New World neighborhood — even in the heart of the midwestern United States — as much of the Old World as possible.

NOTES FOR CHAPTER 12

1. *OSJ,* March 22 and 23, 1886, February 25, 1887; *AI,* March 25, 1881; *SMN,* January 30, 1876.
2. *Ohio Statesman,* January 7, 1854; *Ohio State Democrat,* January 7, 1854; *Der Westbote,* January 6, 1854.
3. *OSJ,* February 10, 1876, January 26, 1885; *AI,* March 18, 1881, October 14, 1887; *OSJ,* May 16, 1878, March 10, 1884, October 15, 1886, March 16, 1888, December 5, 1889. See also *OSJ,* March 22, 1886, February 25, 1887; *AI,* March 25, 1881; *SMN,* January 30, 1876.
4. *SMN,* February 6, 1881; *OSJ,* January 26, February 2, 1881, October 25, 1882; *AI,* October 23, 1863.
5. *AI,* August 7, 1885, November 2, 1883. "Debutante" celebrations at either the Progress or Standard clubs also became very common among affluent Jews; typical was the large dancing party (November 9, 1911) at the Progress Club for Beatrice Gumble (*AI,* November 16, 1911, and *OSJ,* November 4, 1902).
6. *AI,* June to August, 1903, 1908, 1911 to 1913.
7. *OSJ,* December 23, 1901, December 31, 1906, November 25, 1907.
8. See the *OSJ* and *CC* during the last week of 1901, and *AI,* January 2 and 16, 1902.
9. Herbert Brooks, "The Financial Interests of Columbus," *The Ohio Magazine* (December 1907): 506-09.
10. Winding Hollow Country Club, Record of Proceedings, p. 1.
11. "Members and Stockholders," October 16, 1923, WHCC Papers.
12. "President's Report to Stockholders," October 16, 1923, WHCC Papers.

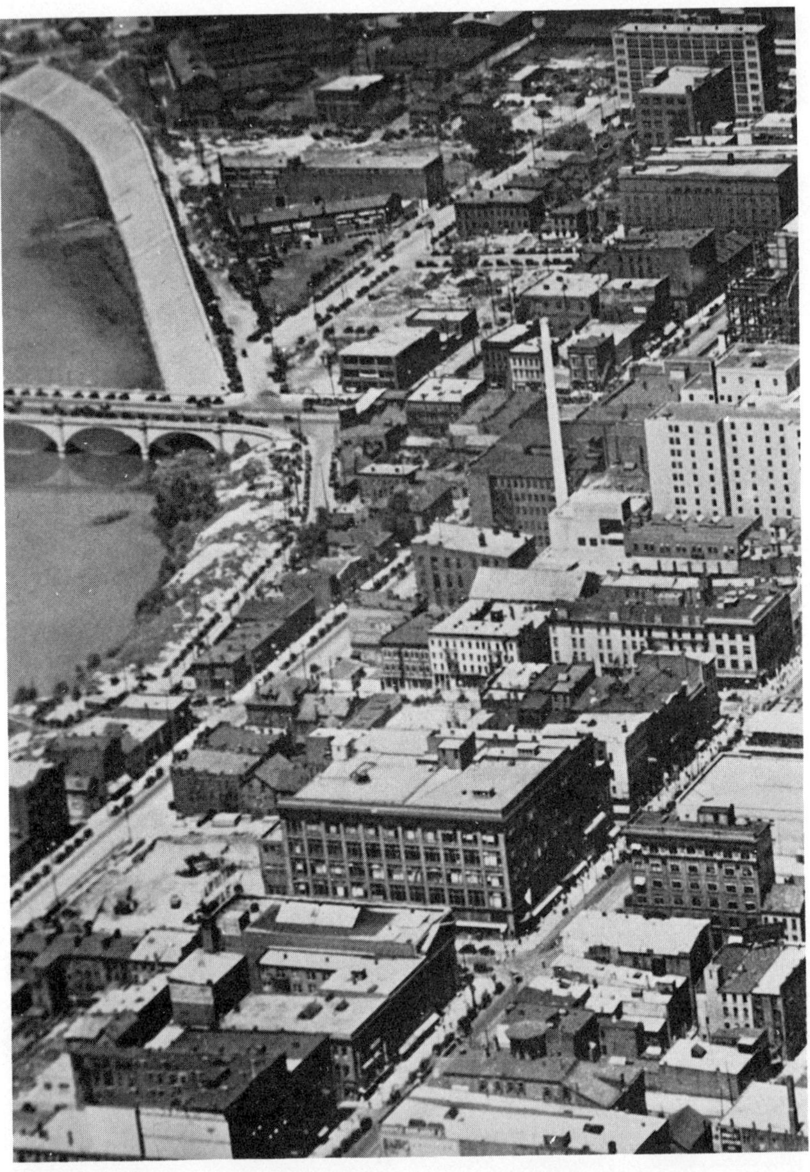

In this aerial view of Columbus taken in the early twenties, note that the steelwork (right edge) was up on the AIU Building (LeVeque-Lincoln Tower), the lot at Town and Front streets had been cleared for construction of the Lazarus building, and the present site of the riverfront Civic Center was a shamble of old structures.

PART III

DEFINING THE COMMUNITY

1926 – 1950

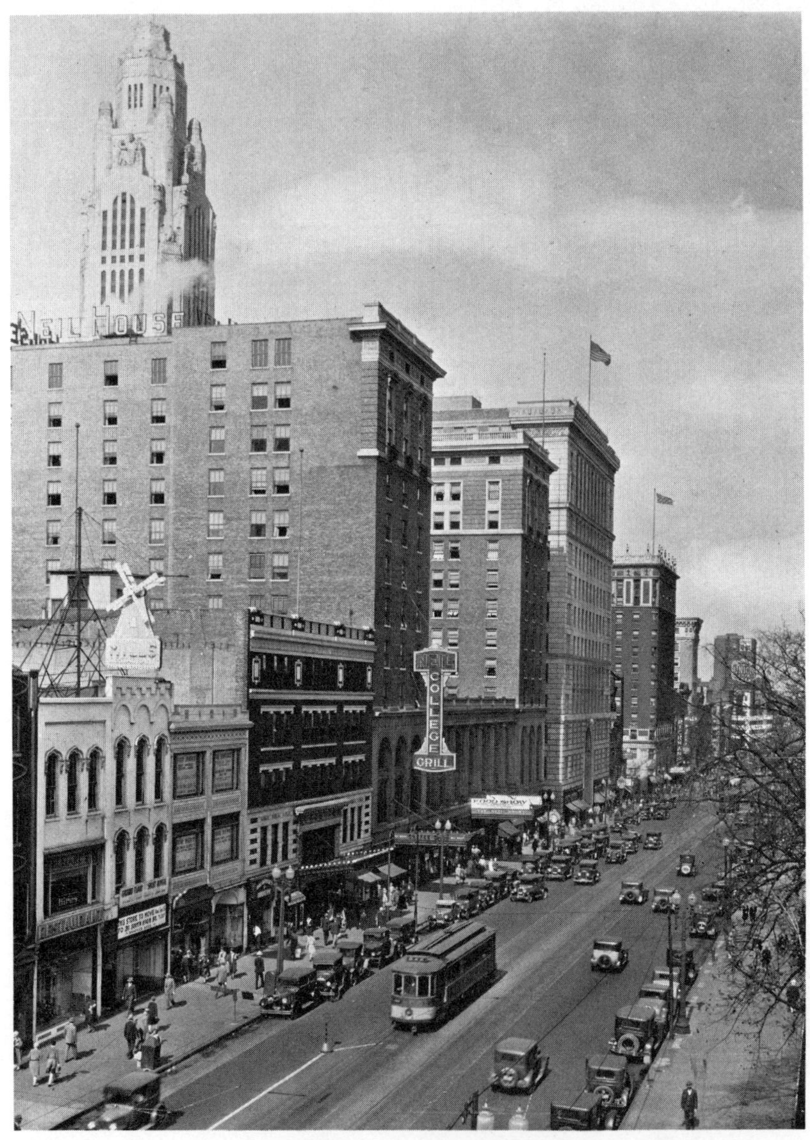

Columbus' South High Street, c. 1928.

Columbus' first major urban renewal project was stimulated by the 1913 flood which devastated the city's west side and riverfront. After the riverfront area had been razed, the first building erected in the new Civic Center area was the City Hall in 1926; three years later the Central Police Station was built. The Federal Building and the U.S. Court House were added later along with the State Office Building. Nearby was the fifth tallest building in the world in 1926 — the fifty-five story American Insurance Union Citadel — later known as LeVeque-Lincoln Tower.

In addition to slowing construction and industrial growth, the beginning of the Great Depression temporarily halted Columbus' civic improvement program; $7 million were spent in 1929 and only $4 million in 1930. City and state governments began to look for ways to reduce deficit spending; one solution employed at the beginning of 1933 was to cut state officials' and employees' salaries for the next two years. City administrators followed suit, looking for ways to offset the escalating cost of meeting relief needs. Thirty-four hundred families were receiving relief assistance at the beginning of 1932; by December the number was slightly under eighty-three hundred families, each of which received $25.40 a month. Throughout Franklin County official relief efforts were supplemented by volunteers; one hundred and fifty organizations assisted the Red Cross in sewing 10,565 garments for the indigent in December of 1932; 24,480 pairs of shoes were also distributed. A typical newspaper of the time gave equal space to the articles about legislative efforts to repeal prohibition; attempts to recover savings from defunct building and loan associations; and stories about organizations which spearheaded relief efforts, sometimes doing very simple things like making mittens from old socks and administering "share your job" programs. A huge Public Works Administration program was initiated in Columbus in 1932 which continued through 1935.

Two years before the Great Depression, Columbus' location continued to insure its predominance as a distribution center; on an average day 19,332 passenger cars and trucks passed through Columbus on eleven major highways. One hundred and sixty passenger trains ran over the four hundred miles of railroad tracks maintained in Columbus by twelve railroads. Industrial exports totaling $75,000 were freighted and flown to forty-eight countries. The completion of the city's fifth airport, Port Columbus, in 1929 inaugurated transcontinental air service. As evidence of the shift in transportation, in the late forties only five railroads served the city; there were, however, seven airports.

During the depression gambling — especially the numbers racket — became one of the city's most successful activities. This business maintained its hold on society to such an extent that in

1938 there were over forty-seven thousand arrests for gambling in Columbus. After years of tacit acceptance, vice and gambling became the major campaign issue in 1939.

World War II brought Columbus a mixed bag: defense contracts with a new airplane factory and related industries. War shortages also resulted, some were felt nationally: in 1943 rationing limited shoe purchases to only three pairs a year; also, Columbus' housing shortage was duplicated across the country. Other shortages occurred only in Columbus: in 1944 a coal crisis closed plants and schools. Unrelated to the war effort was the drought that same year, which was caused by civic lassitude. The following year voters approved a bond issue to remedy the water shortage; this bond issue was the first to be approved for twenty years.

War shortages were replaced by postwar prosperity which was especially noticeable in the construction industry. One evidence of the postwar building boom was Town and Country Shopping Center — the first shopping center in the country — which was built in 1948. Other evidences were the eighty-four places of worship which were erected in the first decade after the war.

Between 1930 and 1950 Columbus added less than two square miles to the city which totaled forty square miles. During this same time, the population increased by 29 percent from 290,564 to 375,901; the Jewish population was estimated to be between seven and nine thousand during this same period.

The face of the Columbus Jewish community changed considerably from the twenties to the forties. Immigrant peddlers steadily disappeared as immigrant merchants and professionals increased. The occupational changes of Beth Jacob's 127 members form a microcosm of the entire community's occupational structure. A working class congregation in 1912, seventeen years later Beth Jacob's membership included 37 percent of the members who worked as proprietors or managers and 25 percent who held skilled jobs. Another 10 percent found work as clerks, salesmen, or semi-professionals.

Most significantly, during the three decades or so following World War I, many American Jewish communities centralized, unified, and defined themselves. Columbus was no exception. As the immigrants moved out of the 1912 neighborhood and into new residential districts along Livingston Avenue and Broad and Main streets, they began a new life within the larger Jewish community, and institutions began to take on long-term identities. The congregations clearly defined themselves along denominational lines, and selected rabbis who devoted long years of service to the synagogues. New laypersons emerged in the twenties to provide several decades of leadership in the community; organizations enlarged their base of support and expanded their programs.

Internalizing American standards and norms, the immigrants embraced American recreational forms and moved eagerly into the general community. Most importantly, philanthropic impulses coalesced into the United Jewish Fund in the mid-twenties and cemented the tightest bond and fittest expression of the common unity. "New" and "old" immigrants had been marrying each other for a full generation in the late forties when they began to give money in unprecedented sums to build the edifices of a postwar community they would share together.

13: TAKING CARE OF OUR OWN: SECTARIAN PHILANTHROPY

According to the Talmud (Sotah 14a): "The Torah begins and ends with deeds of beneficence, of human kindness." Love of fellow Jews, care of the young and old, the sick, the underprivileged, the lonely, the disturbed, the fleeing, and the uprooted — all these modes of *tzedakah* (philanthropy or humanity) stem from the basic message of the Torah. The Halacha, which made of philanthropy a collective project encompassing both the *kupah* (long-term) and the *tamhuy* (short-term) emergency components, institutionalized in the corporate community what otherwise might have remained an individual — and thus potentially capricious — obligation. And the federations represent this public, corporate community in American Jewish philanthropy.

Nationally, federation fund raising has attracted some of the most enterprising and successful men and women whose talents for soliciting funds are now considered the chief asset for Jewish communal leadership. Observing this process, both individuals and organizations in various sectors of the community have reflected upon the leadership, priorities, self-determination, responsiveness to consumer preferences, and especially the fund-raising and allocations procedures of the federations.[1]

Locally, the 1920s marked a new beginning for Jewish philanthropy in Columbus which became increasingly systematic and efficient, both in terms of its expenditures and its fund raising. Because of the ambiguous implications of "charity," the leadership of the Federated Jewish Charities assumed that the populace would erroneously picture someone doling out money, rather than taking into consideration the multiplicity of services — such as preventive casework — provided by the federation's constituents.[2] Therefore, "in accordance with the spirit of the times," the Federated Jewish Charities changed its name in 1923 to the Jewish Welfare Federation (JWF). Fund-raising efforts centered around intensive short-term campaigns with elaborate systematic canvassing machinery, organized "teams" with "captains," and friendly competition chronicled in the Jewish press to assure maximum collection of monies. The pattern of the campaign paralleled the Liberty Bond drives held in fourteen hundred American communities during World War I, and a $14 million nationwide emergency drive conducted in 1922 to raise funds for European Jewish war sufferers. The war and its aftermath elevated to national principles the businessmen's ideals of efficiency and voluntarism, rewarded businessmen with positions of prominence and leadership, and launched philanthropy into the forefront of American Jewish priorities. Reflecting upon the "war chest" drive of 1917, Jewish War Relief Director Jacob Billikopf grasped the immediate results of the campaign:

> I venture to say that there is not a city in America where there is a single Jewish inhabitant in which, at one time or another, we have not made an appeal . . . A large number of individuals with good ratings were approached and asked to become chairmen of the Jewish War Relief Committee in their own towns. No sooner was the War Relief Campaign over, than a great many of the same captains and the same lieutenants . . . threw themselves heart and soul into the Federation campaign.[3]

Columbus Jewry collected $16,500 for Jewish war sufferers in 1917 and more than $57,000 five years later. The 1922 campaign was significant not because of the total raised but because of the method employed. The wealthiest members of the community, invited to a carefully planned program at the Progress Club, heard distinguished out-of-town speakers. Gratifying results followed; in one night pledges totalled $42,000. The drive demonstrated how much more easily funds could be raised for international emergencies than for local needs, and how much war relief drives had enhanced the prestige of philanthropy and created new heroes, while confirming the thesis that centralized fund raising could amass more money with less annoyance to givers than several independent drives.[4]

On June 24, 1926, under the direction of General Campaign Chairman Edwin J. Schanfarber and Treasurer Simon Lazarus, a new centralized philanthropic organization emerged in the Columbus Jewish community. Although the Jewish Welfare Federation utilized its budget to meet local demands, the lay leadership of the community believed that national, international, and local fund raising should be coordinated by a single agency. Capturing the imagination of businessmen by emphasizing American Progressive business ideals, the United Jewish Fund (UJF) promised efficient coordination and organization of the

TABLE 42
1922 COLUMBUS DRIVE FOR JEWISH WAR SUFFERERS
CONTRIBUTIONS OVER $99

Donors	Contribution	Donors	Contribution
1	$5,000	1	$350
7	1,500	8	300
3	1,000	5	250
1	800	19	200
3	750	6	150
13	500	77	100

SOURCE: *Ohio Jewish Chronicle,* March 28, 1922.

communal welfare machinery. The fund had two goals: to collect and distribute money for "human welfare" (i.e., combine appeals for European Jewry, Palestine, and American Jewry), and to "avoid duplication of effort and expense in [cultural, philanthropic, educational] fund-raising programs" within the Jewish community. Promoted by businessmen and large donors who sought an end to the confusion and inefficiency of a multitude of agencies competing for funds, the UJF operated under the authority of a twenty-five member board of directors, elected by persons who had contributed fifty dollars or more to the campaign.[5]

Five days later the board made its first allocations, and by mid-December 1926 the UJF had distributed almost $30,000. With its very first allocations the UJF established a pattern which characterized disbursements for fifty years; the overwhelming majority of its funds — $135,000 of $167,000 — was contributed to national and international causes rather than local charities.[6] For example, from April 1, 1926, to March 31, 1929, $50,000 was allocated to the Jewish Orphans Home of Cleveland, $55,000 to the Joint Distribution Committee, $30,200 to the Columbus Hebrew School, $20,000 to the United Palestine Appeal, and $10,000 to the B'nai B'rith Wider Scope Committee. Table 43 further illustrates the diversity of UJF allocations.

Within one year, the first challenge to the UJF's control over secular fund raising was issued by the Orthodox community, which threatened independent fund raising because allocations distributed to its favorite organizations were insufficient. At a March meeting in 1927 the board of directors reaffirmed its "objection to Jewish fund raising . . . not through the Fund" and appointed a committee to discourage competing fund raising. While this type of conflict surfaced periodically, the board successfully stifled the first challenge.[7]

The Orthodox community's dissatisfaction with the UJF is not

TABLE 43
UNITED JEWISH FUND OF COLUMBUS, OHIO
CASH DISBURSEMENTS: OCTOBER — DECEMBER, 1926

Joint Distribution Committee	$ 4,658.33
Hebrew School of Columbus	2,500.00
United Palestine Appeal	1,666.66
Hebrew Sheltering Home of Columbus	475.00
United Trades Drive (N.Y.)	300.00
Hebrew Immigrant Aid Society	250.00
Intercollegiate Menorah	150.00
Building Fund D.S.H.	150.00
Ex-Patients' Tuberculosis Home	100.00
Ezras Torah	100.00
Joseph Schonthal Home in Riga	100.00
Local Menorah Society	82.00
Chafetz Chayim Yeshiva [of Jerusalem]	60.00
Mokylos Yeshiva	60.00
Kovno Yeshiva	60.00
Kenesseth Israel Yeshiva	60.00
United Aged Home of Jerusalem	60.00
American Pro-Falasha Committee	50.00
Isaac Elchanan Rabbinical College	50.00
Ex-Patients' Aid Society of Los Angeles	50.00
Israel Orphan Girls Home	50.00
Polish Yeshiva	35.00
J.C.R.A of Los Angeles	30.00
Mir Rabbinical College	25.00
Palestine Yeshiva	25.00
Rabbi Fine of Poland	20.00
Or Torah High School of Palestine	20.00
Beth Chazan College	20.00
Ezras Noshim of Palestine	20.00
General Jewish Hospital	20.00
Ohel Moshe Yeshiva	20.00
Grand General College of Jerusalem	20.00
Public Kitchen High School	20.00
Jewish Hospital Misgav [Ladach of Jerusalem]	20.00
General Jewish Institute of Jerusalem	20.00
United Galil Aid of Jerusalem	20.00
Hachnosath Orchim of Jerusalem	20.00
Zion War Orphanage of Jerusalem	20.00
Jerusalem Jewish Orphan Girls Home	20.00
Ezras Orphan Home of Jerusalem	20.00
Lomsa Yeshiva	20.00
Torah Emet Yeshiva [of Jerusalem]	20.00
Total	$11,481.98*

*This amount includes miscellaneous disbursements of $5.01.

hard to understand. Not only did Bryden Road Temple members dominate both the board of directors and the officers, but the UJF held its meetings at the Progress Club, a private social club of the Reform Jewish community. Bryden Road Temple members contributed more than three dollars for every dollar given by non-members — $185,299 compared to $55,045 from 1926 to 1929. Therefore the pet institutions of the Reform movement or established Jewish community received the heaviest funding from the communal treasury. It was no wonder then that the representatives of the immigrant Orthodox Jews argued continuously with the board over allocations, demanding greater support for their favorite organizations.[8]

From its inception, the UJF demonstrated superb fund-raising skills, and utilized many of the techniques characteristic of financial federation campaigns in the 1920s. Effective community organization — leadership continuity, year-round interpretation, and community involvement — all laid the foundation on which the Jews of Columbus built successful campaigns in the future.

Launched with a Big Gifts program at the Progress Club, the first campaign from April 11 to 18, 1926, raised more than half of its $250,000 three-year goal in one evening. Gifts included $36,000 pledged by the family of Fred Lazarus, Sr., $12,000 by Joseph Schonthal, $9,000 by Alfred J. Kobacker, $6,000 by S. M. Levy, and $4,500 by Frank M. Glick. The UJF, however, did not neglect smaller contributors; chairmen were appointed for thirty-three central Ohio counties, and intense efforts were made to place one or more Jewish canvassers in even the smallest towns. At the same time in metropolitan areas, welfare became a product to be marketed; attractive printed literature was sent to every identifiable Jewish businessman in the city, as business advertising provided the only model for an effective public relations campaign. The UJF solicited individual Jews in their offices rather than homes, as the marketplace provided the proper setting for Jewish philanthropy. Thus, many of the techniques which later gained sophistication first appeared in the 1920s, the decade when public relations emerged as a distinct occupation.[9]

The onset of the Great Depression put an end to UJF's initial era of successful fund raising. Early in 1929 E. J. Schanfarber already despaired of raising necessary funds over the next three years: "a campaign cannot be successfully conducted at this time . . ." By the end of 1929 the board could only note that all cash reserves from the 1926-29 campaign had been exhausted; that with "the death of 'Pop' Schonthal we lost our largest giver [whose] contribution would represent 6 or 7 percent of the total"; that "there is a great deal of enthusiasm, but not much money, among the mass of smaller givers in the community" and that "there seems to be a lack of interest and enthusiasm among the medium-sized givers." The board thus recommended a severely shrunken 1930 campaign of fifty to sixty thousand dollars, an amount which Schanfarber felt would neither be subscribed nor collected. The community's reaction showed that these fears were well founded: $42,000 was raised, but the UJF did not receive any contributions larger than $1,800. Federated Jewish philanthropy clearly felt the impact of the Great Depression.[10]

TABLE 44
UNITED JEWISH FUND OF COLUMBUS CONTRIBUTIONS OVER $99

1926				1930	
Donors	Contribution	Donors	Contribution	Donors	Contribution
1	$12,000	22	$600	4	$1,800
5	9,000	24	500	1	1,400
1	6,000	4	450	2	1,000
1	4,500	5	400	1	750
4	3,000	40	300	2	600
3	2,500	4	250	3	500
2	2,400	1	240	2	400
1	2,000	5	225	3	350
8	1,800	10	200	3	300
7	1,500	6	180	5	250
3	1,200	47	150	19	200
17	1,000	1	125	22	150
3	900	8	120	50	100
5	750	4	105		
1	800	1	102		
		123	100		

SOURCE: *Ohio Jewish Chronicle*, May 28, 1926, and February 14, 1930.

Forced to subordinate local needs to critical national and international concerns even more than before, by June of 1930 the Reform-dominated board recommended that the Columbus Hebrew School no longer be funded. Including the school in the budget hindered fund raising among "the larger giving group in the community that is lacking in a Jewish background," as well as among those who "should be tensely interested in this sort of a program." Allocations to small *yeshivot* and other organizations in eastern Europe and Palestine supported by the immigrants also disappeared. Later that year, as it became obvious the depression was not going to end soon, the board received a recommendation from Schanfarber that UJF operations cease at the end of 1930. The proposal gained board approval on November 10, 1930, and shortly thereafter E. J. Schanfarber wrote: "Columbus has completely suspended the operation of its UJF . . ."[11] After the UJF board "disintegrated" a committee of nine wealthy men — all leaders at Bryden Road Temple — allocated funds as they became available.[12]

As a result of this retrenchment, no fund raising occurred during 1931; in the following two years only 210 and 112 persons contributed $9,900 and $8,000 respectively. While the Jews of Columbus could not care for others through the United Jewish Fund, the Jewish Welfare Federation kept enormously busy providing relief, counseling, medical services, and shelter for members of the local Jewish community.

As the depression worsened, the JWF intensified its local relief efforts. In 1931 the federation cared for 745 persons in 136 families, provided 400 free meals to transients and free clinical services to 430, sheltered 7 aged persons, and cared for orphans at the Jewish Infants Home as well as transients at the Sheltering House.[13] During 1932 JWF's services became even broader: 285 persons in 67 families received relief, 271 persons received services which enabled them "to make the proper adjustments in their affairs," 1,010 homeless men utilized the Sheltering House, 825 persons received dental care, and 556 individuals with "problems" ranging from unemployment to desertion accepted moral and financial assistance. The Jewish Welfare Federation, which expended $32,000 in all of its 1932 programs, received $31,000 from the nonsectarian Community Fund.[14]

Another indication of the demands placed upon the local community is reflected in the statistics submitted by all of the Ohio Jewish Family Welfare agencies to the national Council of Jewish Federations and Welfare Funds. (The council was organized as the umbrella organization of local federations in 1935.) Although the demands multiplied rapidly in all of the cities except Dayton, only Columbus and Cleveland continuously increased the money spent on needy Jews between 1929 and 1933. By the end of the depression, Columbus Jews provided almost twice the relief assistance to more than three times the number of families they helped on the eve of the depression.[15]

As the depression receded in 1934, Columbus Jews contributed increasingly larger sums to the UJF each year. The number of contributors, as well as the amounts pledged, rose steadily through the 1930s, increased dramatically with the outbreak of the Second World War, and skyrocketed on the eve of the establishment of the Jewish State. Because of these successful campaigns, the UJF could again share its largess with Jews everywhere. As early as 1934 allocations included $8,000 to the Joint Distribution Committee, $2,700 to the B'nai B'rith, $1,500 to the Cleveland Jewish Orphans Home, $1,000 to the American Jewish Committee, and $800 each to the Hebrew Immigrant Aid

Society and the National Jewish Hospital. With the distribution of funds in 1935, the allocation pattern shifted even further in the direction of national and overseas funding. Local organizations received only $300 of the more than $24,000 allocated, while needs outside of Columbus accounted for $23,000 or 95.1 percent. This was an aberrant pattern in 1935, for 86 of the other 87 federation campaigns across the nation allocated a higher percentage to local needs: Akron, 4.2 percent; Cincinnati, 27.3 percent; Cleveland, 27.3 percent; and Dayton, 20.3 percent. Like Columbus, all of these cities had separate Jewish Family Welfare agencies for relief efforts.[16]

TABLE 45
UNITED JEWISH FUND 1935 DISBURSEMENTS

Local (1.2%)	$ 300	$ 300	Settlements and Center
Regional (6.6%)	1,600	1,400	Cleveland Jewish Orphan Home
		200	Cleveland Jewish Education League
National (33.1%)	8,000		
Overseas (55.4%)	13,400	12,500	United Jewish Appeal
		400	Hadassah University Hospital
		250	Jewish National Fund
		200	American Friends of the Hebrew University
		50	Misc.
Administrative (3.7%)	893		
Total (100%)	$24,193		

Not until 1939 did E. J. Schanfarber, who had been the campaign chairman and UJF president since 1926, receive sufficient pressure to permit "greater participation on the part of the community in raising . . . [and] disbursing the funds." Part of this pressure was external; events in Europe on the eve of the Second World War almost immediately doubled the budget demands made on local federations and welfare funds by national and international organizations. Meeting these goals without broad communal participation was impossible. Part of the pressure was internal; philanthropy drives within the Orthodox community to support organizations not funded by the UJF were accelerating. As a result, the UJF reorganized and enlarged the board to twenty-five members.

In addition to expanding the UJF board, three decisions made in 1939 and 1940 had significant effects in subsequent decades. First, to broaden the fund's appeal, a Women's Division and a Junior Division were established. Second, none of the community's six rabbis was included in UJF's reorganized board, although "each plays an important part in the moulding of public opinion and has an interest in the welfare of human beings which

Success Deserves Recognition!

1940
United Jewish
Fund
Campaign

Ralph Lazarus

I. W. Garek

Robert W. Schiff
Campaign Chairman

Mrs Alfred J. Kobacker
Chairman, Women's Division

Leon Friedman
Chairman, Junior Division

Robert Weiler

Leonard Kohn

Herbert Levy

William Wasserstrom

Albert Schiff

Dr. Don Shusterman

AN APPRECIATION

The officers and Board of Directors of The United Jewish Fund of Columbus desire to take this opportunity to express to Mr. Robert W. Schiff, Chairman of the 1940 campaign, to his Vice-Chairmen, to the women and junior division, and to the remarkable staff of co-workers, their heartfelt appreciation and that of the entire community, as well as the innumerable beneficiaries, of their efforts in concluding the most successful campaign in the history of the Jewish community of Columbus.

The Chairman and his co-workers, as well as the multitude of men and women who have given their time, their energy, their hearts and their minds to the successful conclusion of this remarkable work, will long be remembered for their splendid achievement.

THE BOARD OF DIRECTORS OF THE UNITED JEWISH FUND OF COLUMBUS

Chairman.

BOARD OF DIRECTORS

Dr. B. W. Abramson
Joseph Basch
Harry Beckman
I. A. Glick
Harry Gilbert
Arthur Goldberg
Dr. E. J. Gordon
Allen Gundersheimer
Max L. Herzberg
Walter Katz

Alfred J. Kobacker
Louis Lakin
Ralph Lazarus
Simon Lazarus
Herbert Levy
Sigmund Ornstein
Jack S. Resler
E. J. Schanfarber
Albert Schiff
E. F. Schlezinger

Justin L. Sillman
J. W. Steinhauser
Samuel N. Summer
Robert A. Weiler
Leo Yassenoff

HONORARY
A. Goldberg (Deceased)
S. M. Levy
I. H. Schlezinger

1940 CAMPAIGN COMMITTEE

Richard Abel
Dr. L. R. Basch
Frank Bayer
Harry Beckman
Troy Feibel
M. D. Feinknopf
B. Feitlinger
Ted Finkelstein
B. B. Friedman
I. W. Garek
Louis Gertner
Robert Glick
Arthur Gluck
Arthur Goldberg
Dave Goldsmith
Jos. Goldstein
Jack Goodman
I. M. Harris
Max L. Herzberg
S. M. Isaac
Dr. R. A. Jaffee
Wm. Kahn
Walter Katz

Leonard Kohn
Malcolm Kohn
Harry Krakoff
Dr. M. A. Krakoff
Sanford Lakin
Chas. Lazarus
Ralph Lazarus
Herbert Levy
Herman Lieverman
Samuel D. Luchs
Herman Luckoff
Sam Luper
Ben Lurie
Robert L. Mellman
Moehler Pass
Dr. Henry Piatt
Jack Ratner
Fred Rosenfeld
Louis Ruben
E. F. Schlezinger
Sam Schlonsky
Harry Schwartz
Sam Shinbach

Dr. Don Shusterman
Abe Shustick
Gilbert Siegel
Justin Sillman
Jos. Slaven
Chas. Solomon
Milton Staub
Dr. S. C. Swerdlow
Allan Tarshish
Ben Tolpen
Wm. Wasserstrom
Robert A. Weiler
Abe Weinfeld
Sig Weisskerz
Irwin Wolf
Marcus Wolf
Abe Wolman
Jack Wolstein
Leo Yassenoff
Abe Yenkin
Ben Yenkin
Fred Yenkin

does or should transcend that of all others." The board explained that in light of congregational jealousies, to include one rabbi and not all would cause envy; the best solution would be to not include any rabbis. This decision created a tension between the rabbinate and the fund raisers in the community, a tension which grew as the years passed.[17]

Finally, even though both the Jewish and non-Jewish press delighted in highlighting generous philanthropic gifts, the UJF "unanimously decided that no publicity be given to the nonsectarian or Jewish press concerning donors, amounts of contributions, or the total amount sought or raised in the campaign." Although the UJF ignored the last of these strictures, ever since 1940 it has not publicized individual contributions. While disappointing some who desired positive publicity for themselves and embarrassment for less generous contributors, this obviously satisfied the majority of subscribers.[18]

The results of the reorganization looked impressive: both the number of contributors and amounts collected increased by more than 100 percent between 1938 and 1939.[19] The new board of directors included seven or eight east Europeans who quickly expanded UJF allocations to encompass numerous small Palestinian organizations — ranging from the Palestine Orchestra Fund to the Palestine Hebrew Culture Fund — as well as *yeshivot* and east European cultural groups. While the largest sums still went to the traditional organizations like Cleveland's Jewish Orphans Home, National Jewish Hospital, B'nai B'rith, and the American Jewish Committee and only token amounts were allocated to Palestinian agencies, the precedent had been set. With each succeeding year the UJF became less and less of an exclusive club for the Bryden Road Temple board, and more of a charity network responsive to diverse groups. While communal democracy remained more an ideal than a reality, E. J. Schanfarber's decision to enlarge the board in 1939-40 had lasting import.[20]

Despite the change in the board's makeup, the basic relationship between national, international, and local funding did not change. More than 50 percent of the funds collected between 1939 and 1948 — as much as 63 percent in 1939 — went directly to the United Jewish Appeal: $70,000 in 1939, $110,000 in 1944, and $520,000 in 1947. The vast majority of the remainder funded other national and overseas agencies. Between 1939 and 1944 only $56,162 of the almost $1 million raised — 6 percent of the total — remained in Columbus to benefit local organizations; from 1944 to 1948 the percentage increased only slightly to 7 percent. This continued the pattern begun in the 1920s and never altered — allocating the overwhelming bulk of contributions outside of Columbus.[21]

This ratio — and the increasing demands of the United Jewish Appeal — caused several heated board of directors' meetings during the decade prior to the establishment of the State of Israel. Schanfarber articulated the dilemma clearly at the Jewish Welfare Federation annual meeting in 1941:

> Last year Columbus raised $140,000 for overseas and national causes, defense, refugee work and sustaining life of the depressed people and national institutions. That was at least $125,000 more than we raised for outside causes 15 years ago, and today we are operating our Jewish Welfare Federation, which includes our Center, on $9,000 a year less than we had 15 or 16 years ago.
>
> We have to figure to the penny, we have to figure $.25 a week carfare for a family of five and we have to figure $.30 for recreation and entertainment for a family in which the breadwinner is incapacitated and we have to figure the exact cost of bread and milk and gas consumed and coal purchased and I think that the time is approaching when we must give serious consideration to at least trying to do for our own unfortunates in our own community something that will approach at least that which we are trying to do for newcomers and for those overseas.

The increasing anger culminated in a bitter letter to UJA in 1947 because of Columbus' $600,000 quota which represented 83 percent of the JWF goal. The board narrowly missed rejecting the assigned quota.[22]

Another pattern remained consistent: the bulk of the money came from a tiny minority. During 1941, for example, thirty-five persons or 1.5 percent of the contributors gave $80,000, a full 53 percent of the funds; while in 1945 thirty-five persons or 3 percent of the subscribers contributed $132,000 which represented 57 percent of the total. Each year, despite the hopes of fund raisers to alter the situation, less than 10 percent of the givers accounted for 80 percent of the total campaign. Aware of this, the board concentrated its annual efforts on Big Gifts by continually establishing rating committees "to appraise all prospects whose ability is greater than indicated by their [previous] contribution"; by finding new ways to solicit such gifts at the traditional Winding Hollow Country Club Big Gift Campaign opening; and by asking men who gave the biggest Big Gifts to contact those whose Big Gifts were not quite as large. The results satisfied most leaders, as the campaign kickoff dinner brought in progressively more impressive totals each year from a minority of donors who accounted for a majority of contributions.[23]

One of the major contributors to the UJF, Harry Gilbert, was also the most outspoken member and articulated best some of the issues raised within the UJF. His most incessant demand urged

TABLE 46
UNITED JEWISH FUND BIG GIFTS CAMPAIGN

Year	Kickoff Total	Total Campaign Goal	Source *OJC*
1932	$ 6,000	$ 12,000	May 27, 1932
1936	25,000	34,000	July 3, June 26, 1936
1937	37,000	45,000	June 11, 1937
1938	42,500	52,500	July 1, June 24, 1938
1939	81,500	115,000	June 16, 23, 1939
1941	c. 90,000	c. 150,000	June 13, 1941
.1942	c. 120,000	c. 160,000	June 12, 1942
1943	c. 138,750	c. 185,000	June 18, 1943
1946	c. 277,500	370,000	May 24, 1946
1947	400,000	725,000	May 9, 23, 1947

direct election of the Allocations Committee because this committee was composed almost entirely of old-line Reform Jewish families, and was sharply unrepresentative of the community. As a Tifereth Israel member, Gilbert was particularly piqued at the committee's continuous refusal to support the Columbus Hebrew School and argued correctly that Allocations Committee members revealed little sympathy for Hebrew language instruction. Further, Gilbert urged greater funding of local Jewish organizations and even argued regularly for the right of local groups to initiate their own — and competitive — fund raising. E. J. Schanfarber led the continuous opposition to Harry Gilbert, because "proceeding along democratic lines . . . would entail the hiring of a larger office staff" and might "place too much emphasis upon matters which might be harmful to the campaign." Thus, the consensus remained to "exercise care to take no action which might in any way interfere with the successful prosecution of the fund-raising effort."[24]

The founder of Gilbert's Shoes, Harry Gilbert, was a wealthy and generous member of the Jewish community; his arguments reverberated throughout the postwar era, both inside the federation leadership and within the community. The combatants themselves were as significant as the content of the controversy. By inexorably controlling philanthropy in the Jewish community, the federation brought secular and religious, traditional and non-traditional, Zionist and non-Zionist together around the same table. Although many encounters produced more confrontation than communication, no other significant forum emerged in the community where these persons actually spoke — not to mention listened — to each other. Through the years, despite louder and more frequent criticisms, the federation raised more and more money. Greater than the enormous amounts of money raised, perhaps, were the benefits of interaction within the community. As one former federation youth "captain" reminisced:

> here was an activity that went through all of the social classes and institutional affiliations in the community. I remember people whom I had only seen from a distance before and working with them and that was a very nice thing. One should not forget how this helped to shape and to unify our community.[25]

NOTES FOR CHAPTER 13

TABLE 47
UNITED JEWISH FUND STATISTICAL ANALYSES

Year	Pledges	Pledged	Collected	Campaign Cost	Campaign Percent
1926-28	825	$240,000	$223,800	$8,758	3.5%
1930	790	43,000	42,000	3,039	7.0
1932	210	10,000	9,850		
1933	112	8,000	7,991		
1934	397	23,000	22,922	865	4.0
1935	476	27,400	27,414	978	3.5
1936	515	35,900	35,950	1,356	3.7
1937	601	47,800	47,811	1,541	3.3
1938	724	55,300	57,358	1,853	3.3
1939	1,545	113,900	111,000	2,479	2.1
1940	2,497	143,000	143,000	3,789	2.6
1941	2,459	153,000	153,000	4,700	3.1
1942	2,616	165,000	165,000	4,582	2.7
1943	2,450	196,000	196,000	4,615	2.4
1944	2,771	222,798	222,798	6,398	2.9
1945	2,857	256,793	256,793	7,704	3.0
1946	3,237	370,927	370,851	9,200	2.5
1947	3,376		651,157		
1948	3,403		748,100		

SOURCES: Campaign Analysis, July 16, 1947; *OJC,* December 30, 1948; *Notes and News* (Council of Jewish Federations and Welfare Funds) No. 70 (December 3, 1941), 1:1 (October, 1943), 2:1 (October 11, 1944), 2:6 (October 11, 1945).

1. For an introduction to the abundant literature engaged in commenting on the role of the Jewish federations in America, see E. Ginsberg, "The Agenda Reconsidered," *Journal of Jewish Communal Service* [JJCS], (Fall 1966): 275-82; J. Neusner, "Jewish Education and Culture and the Jewish Welfare Fund," *The Synagogue School* (Winter 1967): 9-40; J.

Shapiro, "The Philistine Philanthropists: The Power and Shame of Jewish Federations," *Jewish Liberation Journal* (October 1969): 1-4; M. Greenberg, "Planning for the Jewish Community — the Process of Establishing Priorities and Goals," *JJCS* (Winter 1971): 151-58; C. Zibbell, "Federations, Synagogues, and Jewish Education in the 70s," *Jewish Education* (Fall 1974): 40-45; D. Polish, "Rabbis and the Federations," *Jewish Spectator* (Fall 1975): 220-22; G. Bubis, "*Brokha* Brokers and Power Brokers," *Jewish Spectator* (Spring 1975): 58-61; S. Dresner, "The Dais and the Pulpit: The Tension Between Federation and Synagogue," *Moment* (December 1975): 24-28; Gary S. Schiff, "American Jews and Israel: A Study in Political Conduct," *Forum* 24:1 (1976): 15-38.

2. *OJC*, February 9, 1923.

3. United War Work Campaign, *Bulletins* I-XV (1918); Jacob Billikopf, "Campaign Methods," *Jewish Charities* IX:11 (March 1919); Morris Engelman, *Four Years of Relief and War Work by the Jews of America 1914-1918* (New York, 1918); *OJC*, March 24, 1923, April 7 and 14, 1922. Valuable experience in fund raising also accrued during World War I when leading Columbus Jews participated in the United War Work Campaign and the Liberty Loan Drive, and Rosh Hashanah worship services served as the primary fund-raising forum. One ad, in the local Jewish newspaper, accused Jews who hadn't purchased Liberty bonds of being "a discredit to your country . . . a blot on the fair name of Judaism . . . and an aid to the Kaiser!" See *CJC*, April 26, September 27, November 1 and 22, 1918; *Bulletin*, Joint Distribution Committee 2:7; and *Jewish Outlook* (Columbus, Ohio) I:7 (October 1918) in the New York Public Library.

4. Agudas Achim Sunday School Bulletin, I:2 (May 1918); *OJC*, March 31 and April 7, 1922; and Robert H. Bremner, *American Philanthropy* (Chicago, 1960), pp. 129-35.

5. "Articles II and IV," Constitution of the United Jewish Fund, June 24, 1926, Columbus Jewish Federation. The first treasurer of the UJF, Simon Lazarus (1882-1947), served in that capacity through 1944 and then as president. On federations in the 1920s, see William J. Norton, *The Cooperative Movement in Social Work* (New York, 1927) and "Federation to Eliminate Campaigns," *American Hebrew*, May 21, 1920, p. 3, and on fund raising see Edward Jenkins, *Philanthropy in America: An Introduction to the Practices and Prospects of Organizations Supported by Gifts and Endowments, 1924-1948* (New York, 1950).

6. UJF Board of Directors Meeting, June 29 and September 21, 1926; Finance and Budget Committee, October 22, 1926, OHS.

7. Regular Meeting, Board of Directors of the United Jewish Fund, March 27, 1927, Columbus Jewish Federation. Everywhere federations emerged they included a self-denying ordinance on the part of the constituent bodies whereby the latter declared that they would not collect money themselves; see Jacobs, op. cit.

8. Grouping Analysis, September 29, 1926; Edwin J. Schanfarber to UJF Board of Directors, December 20, 1929, OHS.

9. *OJC*, April 2, 16 and 23, 1926. See also Charles Stillman, *Social Work Publicity: Its Message and Its Method* (New York, 1927).

10. Schanfarber to UJF Board of Directors, March 28, 1929; Special Meeting of the Board of Directors of the UJF, December 20, 1929; Schanfarber to Board of Directors, April 10, 1930, OHS.

11. First Regular Meeting of the UJF Board of Directors for the Year 1930, June 15, 1930; Schanfarber to UJF Board of Directors, November 8, 1930; Regular Meeting of the UJF Board of Directors, November 10, 1930; Schanfarber to Isaac Werne, n.d., *CJF.* The Columbus Hebrew School was indeed deprived of its funding; see *OJC,* December 12, 1930.

12. The nine men consisted of Allen Gundersheimer, Alfred J. Kobacker, Simon Lazarus, Sol M. Levy, Morris Resler, E. J. Schanfarber, Robert W. Schiff, J. W. Steinhauser and Samuel N. Summer. E. J. Schanfarber affirmed and the records confirmed that a direct relationship existed between "Big Gifts" and inclusion on the board of directors. All nine made "big gifts" — the top fifteen or twenty contributions in the community — while all of the nineteen Bryden Road Temple members serving on the board in 1943 made "big gifts" of $1,000 or more.

13. *OJC,* November 20, 1931.

14. Annual Report, 1932, Jewish Welfare Federation, OHS. On the relationship between Jewish welfare federations and community funds/chests in the 1930s, see Maurice J. Karpf, *Jewish Community Organization in the United States* (New York, 1938), pp. 103-16.

15. Jewish Social Work, 1930, Statistical Report of Volume and Trends in Four Functional Fields and Comparisons with Previous Years (Bureau of Jewish Social Research, New York, July 1931); Jewish Social Work, 1932, Statistics of Service: Relief and Family Welfare, Child Care, Care of Aged, Hospitals and Out-Patient Service; Jewish Social Work, 1933. Council of Jewish Federations and Welfare Funds Collection, American Jewish Historical Society (Waltham, Massachusetts).

16. Yearbook of Jewish Social Work, 1935, CJFWF Collection.

17. General Subscribers Meeting, UJF, Report of the President, April 2, 1940, OHS. The Junior Division, first organized in 1936 under the direction of Jane Schanfarber and Regina Kobacker, reorganized periodically; see *OJC,* July 10, 1936, June 16 and 30, 1939. Mrs. Ida Kobacker (1891-1972) headed the Women's Division launched in 1940; see *OJC,* May 24, 1940.

18. General Subscribers Meeting, UJF, April 2, 1940, OHS.

19. General Subscribers Meeting, United Jewish Fund, Report of the President, April 2, 1940, OHS; *OJC,* October 28 and December 16, 1938.

20. 1940 United Jewish Fund of Columbus Budget, March 15, 1941, OHS.

21. Calculated from Disbursements to Beneficiary Agencies and United Jewish Fund Income, 1939-1948, OHS.

22. Jewish Welfare Fund, Annual Meeting, May 8, 1941, OHS. Board of Directors Meeting, February 18 and May 5, 1947, Jewish Welfare Federation Papers. Only eight abstentions saved the UJA request.

23. Meeting of Vice-Chairmen and Committee Chairmen, May 9, 1940; R. to Schanfarber, correspondence, February 5, 1942; UJF Campaign 1945, October 27, 1945, OHS.

24. R. to Schanfarber, correspondence; Pre-campaign meeting of the allocations committee of the UJF, April 4, 1944; Allocations Committee, April 4, 1944; Minutes of Board of Directors Meeting, October 10, 1944; Budget Committee Meeting, October 24, 1944, OHS.

25. Interview with Eugene Borowitz.

14: PRESERVER OF SEPARATENESS, MODEL OF ACCULTURATION: SYNAGOGUE LIFE

In Columbus, as in eastern Europe at an earlier time, the synagogue represented only one of several institutions within the immigrant community. However, in the New World as well as in the Old, the synagogue remained the primary institution of traditional Jewish life. Membership was a matter of individual choice, for five synagogues existed in Columbus. Wealth and a respected profession like law or a business — especially insurance — bestowed leadership, and synagogue leadership still brought abundant *koved* (glory).

At the Reform temple it was not greatly different. No other institution challenged the Bryden Road congregation as the focus of Jewish identification, and support for other groups did not detract from the special status of Temple Israel. While wealth remained a prerequisite for leadership, a small group of men — related by ties of kinship and business — governed the congregation. As time passed, they utilized business principles in the administration of the temple more and more; the result was a smooth, efficient, and somewhat bland organization.

During the years between the world wars, Columbus synagogues stood within walking distance of each other. This offered several advantages:

> It was quite customary in Columbus, Ohio, for people to move around from synagogue to synagogue; indeed, in the thirties it was a common Yom Kippur Day afternoon activity, while the services were drumming on at the various synagogues, for young people to walk from one Orthodox synagogue to the other, or to the Conservative synagogue, or to the Reform temple and eventually get back to their own synagogue. It was a pleasant day. It was not too long a walk and it made the time pass very nicely. That was, beside the public school system and various other such activities, one way of getting to know

people at other congregations. On the whole, one felt reasonably free at doing that, although the Reform congregation was very much more of another social class.[1]

Later in this period of transition the synagogues moved farther east, away from the Jewish neighborhood. The diverse paths that each of the five congregations followed were shaped by finances, religious emphasis, and the personalities of the various rabbis and lay leadership. Records for four of these congregations abound; however, there are no reliable sources available to use in reconstructing synagogue life at Ahavas Sholom.

Even before the difficult years of the depression, Agudas Achim, the self-styled "leading Orthodox *shul* of the city," was in severe financial difficulty. At the end of 1927 the congregation borrowed $1,500 to meet current expenses. Early in 1928 the trustees negotiated a $5,000 loan; later that year they found generous loans indispensable as temple expenses of $18,000 far outweighed dues payments of $9,000. Disorganized at best, the dues structure appears to be the primary culprit; while the minimum required was $20, almost 90 percent of the members paid less than $25 annual dues, and of more than two hundred contributing members, only three paid more than $50. This small amount was further undermined by the treasurer's fee — ten cents for every dollar he collected from the membership. The result? A strong dependency upon *ad hoc* contributions from the more substantial members, feverish activity to sell seats to non-members for High Holiday worship, and the "selling" of various honors associated with religious services.[2]

At the depth of the depression in 1932, this financially unstable congregation somehow lured Rabbi Mordechai Hirschsprung (1894-1954) from Canton, Ohio, where he had served since 1929. A native of Cracow who was educated in several Polish *yeshivot*, Hirschsprung came to the United States in 1911 and graduated from the City College of New York and Yeshiva College in 1919. After serving in Mobile during 1920, Hirschsprung led congregations in Savannah from 1922 to 1927 and in Syracuse for the next two years before going to Canton.[3]

According to his successor at Agudas Achim, Rabbi Hirschsprung was a "*talmid chacham* [great scholar] and a tremendous orator in Yiddish." He wrote many carefully researched and cogently argued *responsa* (legal decisions) in Hebrew, ranging from discussions of "The International Dateline and the Sabbath" to interpretations of laws regarding ritual purities. In addition to preaching in Yiddish, English, and Hebrew, Hirschsprung devoted many hours of his week to the Columbus Hebrew School, and participated frequently on Jewish communal boards. He also served as president of the Columbus Mizrachi and as a member of its national executive board for several years.[4]

Actively supporting the rabbi was his wife, Margaret Hirschsprung, a graduate of the Teachers Institute at the Jewish Theological Seminary in 1917 and of Hunter College in 1920. Directing the Agudas Achim Sunday School for many years, Mrs. Hirschsprung brought to it years of teaching, as well as group work, experience. She was exceptionally active in many Zionist and women's organizations in Columbus.[5]

With the active support of the synagogue's lay leaders, the rabbi waged a continuous struggle within the Jewish community on behalf of Orthodoxy. This effort concentrated upon the "kosher" butchers of Columbus. Board members and the rabbi continuously announced the names, and demanded the congregational censure of, butchers violating Jewish dietary laws. They urged communal censure of butchers who — although their meat was perfectly kosher — did not personally observe Jewish ritual in an Orthodox fashion, and any *shochtim* who slaughtered chickens too close to the beginning or end of the Jewish Sabbath. Some members even went so far as to propose picketing and boycotting these violators of Orthodox procedure.[6]

This careful supervision of *kashrut* (dietary laws) in the community paralleled an equal concern for the amount of ritual observance among Agudas Achim members. The subject dominated several board meetings, for a dilemma faced the congregation: whether or not to honor, with the presidency and calling to the Torah, men who did not personally observe many of the biblical commandments but who contributed generously to the congregation's support. When Agudas Achim's needs demanded a policy of expediency over principle, as they often did, certain members of the board consistently protested. The argument that the synagogue president, as well as those who ascended the pulpit on the Sabbath and High Holidays, should be observers of Orthodox Sabbath regulations gained widespread sympathy but the usual decision was to take no action, as it "would work a hardship on members."[7]

As early as the late 1920s, the congregation actively sought a new location for the synagogue, because many Jews began to desert the periphery of downtown Columbus and move further east. Also, the synagogue's facilities had become woefully inadequate for the Sunday School. A decade later, with an enlarged membership, the rabbinical salary kept low, and several members willing to make large financial contributions for a new building, the board was able to seriously bid on several lots.[8]

From 1939 through 1942 several offers were made to purchase

existing buildings as auxiliary space; finally in 1942 Harry Gilbert agreed to lease, for one dollar a year, a building he owned at 1021 Bryden Road, not far from Temple Israel. It became Agudas Achim's Educational Institute, and by the fall of 1943 housed the Agudas Achim Self-Development or Pre-School under the direction of Rose Schwartz; this was the forerunner of the Jewish Center Pre-School and Torah Academy Day School. The new building came just in time to avert a potential mass exodus of families because of the congregation's poor educational facilities.[9]

Realizing that the Agudas Achim Educational Institute would serve only as a temporary solution, the congregation began raising money for a new synagogue in an area where "Jews will increase." The deterioration of the old neighborhood forced the board to hire plainclothesmen to keep the sidewalk clear of rowdies during services. As the residential centers of Jews moved farther from the synagogue, walking to Washington Avenue on the Sabbath and festivals became impractical. Nearby congregations made plans either to build further east or to remodel existing facilities in convenient locations. As the Second World War drew to a close, Agudas Achim began searching for property in the Columbus suburbs.[10]

The parting of the Hirschsprungs and Agudas Achim was not pleasant; however, the scenario was familiar. While the rabbinical and traditionally-oriented lay leadership of the congregation favored greater conformity to the traditional mode of synagogue Judaism, many elements within the community strained to remold the synagogue into a community center, to conform more closely with the temper of the times. Although Rabbi Hirschsprung was only fifty years old, the board felt he had lost touch with youth, and brought this to the attention of the congregation several times during the final years of his tenure. By 1948 the board openly sought a younger rabbi, one who could communicate with teenage boys, who could preach well in English, and who could provide "attractive" worship services. In a bitter announcement, Rabbi Hirschsprung quit that same year to accept a rabbinate in Des Moines which he held until 1954.[11]

Several years before Rabbi Hirschsprung accepted a position at Agudas Achim, Rabbi Leopold Greenwald began his tenure at nearby Orthodox Beth Jacob in the spring of 1925. Born in Maramarossziget, Hungary, on September 26, 1889, where his father Rabbi Jacob had a Hebrew book store, Greenwald studied at the Satmar, Hust, Unsdorf, and Pressburg *yeshivot.* Ordained at the Offentlich Rabbinatschule in Bratislava, Czechoslovakia, in 1908, Rabbi Greenwald had a varied career before arriving in New York in August of 1924: assistant professor at the Rabbiner Seminary at Frankfort-am-Main; rabbi in Nagy Szeben, Hungary; journalist for several Hungarian publications; and telegraph operator in the Austro-Hungarian army during World War I. (During his stint in the Army, Greenwald conducted a Passover *seder* over the wires for Jews in seven camps covering two hundred miles.) At the age of eighteen Greenwald wrote a biography of Rabbi Jonathan Eibenshutz — his first of many books. Therefore, Rabbi Greenwald was an internationally known figure even before his arrival in Columbus.[12]

As a result of his stature, six out-of-town rabbis and more than eight hundred guests attended his installation at Beth Jacob in August of 1926. The rabbi's three-year contract stipulated that he be paid forty dollars a week; the congregation got their money's worth. Fluent in more than five languages, Rabbi Greenwald preached twice every Shabbat during his early years at Beth Jacob, once in Yiddish and once in Hebrew. As part of Beth Jacob's Friday evening Forum, his lectures about history, philosophy, and theology received scholarly as well as popular recognition. Greenwald's topics ranged from "The Meaning of the Declaration of Independence" and "George Washington and the Jews" to the "History of Medieval Jewish Philosophy" and "An Evaluation of the Historiography of Flavius Josephus." An active Zionist, Rabbi Greenwald became a member of the executive board of Mizrachi and a leader in Columbus Zionist activities, helping to bring to the community such personalities as Abba Hillel Silver, Louis Lipsky, Gedaliah Bublick, and Goldie Myerowitz (Golda Meir). A constant fund raiser on behalf of desperate Jews and *yeshivot* in Europe during the Holocaust, Rabbi Greenwald also gained respect as a dedicated teacher who rejoiced as much when successfully teaching Hebrew to members of the Ladies Auxiliary in his home as at every *siyyum Torah* (study completion celebration) after finishing a Talmud tractate with his study group.[13]

In Columbus Rabbi Greenwald's name is most associated with uncompromising Orthodoxy. His attention to *kashrut* (dietary laws) became so meticulous that his wife even brought his food from home to synagogue dinners; Greenwald himself acted as a self-appointed "watchdog" over community observance of *kashrut*. Periodically the rabbi denounced from his pulpit all kosher butchers who opened their stores too soon after the end of Sabbath, and promised "oppressive retribution" to any violators of the Sabbath. Greenwald, an unyielding opponent of seating men and women together at worship services, refused to enter the new Orthodox Agudas Achim Synagogue because men and women prayed together there. Upon discovering that one of the listeners to his late Friday evening Forum lectures in the 1920s had driven to the synagogue in violation of Sabbath laws, Greenwald immediately cancelled the entire season's series. When Rabbi

Mordechai M. Kaplan, the founder of the Reconstructionist wing of Judaism, published a new Sabbath prayerbook, Greenwald preached and wrote a message of furious denunciation, contending that the book was atheistic and ought to be burned, that its author should be excommunicated, and that all supporters of the new prayerbook had no right to call themselves rabbis.[14]

Not only rigid Orthodoxy but an overwhelming concern with *gemilut chasadim* (acts of righteousness) preoccupied this leader of the Columbus rabbinate. Year after year Rabbi Greenwald led the synagogue's *moes chitim* (Passover charity) drive, often walking from house to house on Carpenter Street, where he lived, to raise money to purchase Passover supplies for needy Columbus Jews. During World War II Greenwald was especially active: he visited each member's home to collect old clothes for destitute Vilna Jews, led a campaign which collected hundreds of dollars to purchase food and clothing for Jewish scholars and rabbis stranded in Siberia, marched in Washington and petitioned Roosevelt to save European Jews, actively raised money to purchase property in Palestine for refugee Jews, and devoted much time and energy to sensitizing the Columbus Jewish community to the plight of its European brethren.[15]

The members of the synagogue appear to have been as active as the rabbi during the late twenties, adding a wide variety of new activities and developing old ones. Annual Voliner Society concerts with distinguished New York and European cantors attracted hundreds of listeners. Timely, informative, and imaginative Forum debates and symposiums were scheduled weekly. Typical was the tussle in 1933 over the issue "Is the Merchant of Venice Anti-Semitic?" featuring Rabbi Greenwald and Dr. Benjamin W. Abramson. Always in the forefront were Zionist activities, such as celebrations of the poet Chayyim Nacham Bialik's birthday and the anniversary of Theodor Herzl's death, as well as visits by *shlichim* (messengers) from Palestine. The Mishnais Society and Memorial Tablets founded in 1927, the Junior Congregation founded in 1928, as well as a *Chevra Kadisha* (burial society), all began to play active roles in congregational life in the late twenties.[16]

Even during the Great Depression in 1931 and continuously throughout that difficult decade, there was no decrease in *Torah, Avodah,* and *gemilut chasadim* at Beth Jacob. The more than sixty Junior Congregation members who regularly worshipped on Shabbat at their own services raised a significant amount of money for the Palestinian children's milk fund. The local *Histadrut* (Palestine Workers) campaign commenced in April with its headquarters at the synagogue. The ladies' Hachnasos Orchim, which supervised the local Sheltering House, was led by a group of Beth Jacob women who sponsored a successful dance attended by two hundred persons; and the Beth Jacob Sisterhood collected enough money to donate a Torah to the congregation, to send Pesach supplies year after year to impoverished Jews in Europe and especially Columbus, and to provide food to poor Jewish scholars in Europe and Palestine.[17]

After lengthy debate and discussions, as well as a decade of building campaigns, the congregation decided to proceed with the construction of a new synagogue with abundant classroom space and a sanctuary which would seat eight hundred. Construction began in 1951 and by June of 1952 the congregation observed the ceremony of "lifting the holiness" from the forty-year-old Donaldson Street synagogue to the new $125,000 Beth Jacob at 959 Bulen Avenue. Rabbis from all over the east and midwest carried the Torahs from the old house of worship to the new. The celebration and dedication continued through August, as the congregation looked at its past with memorial services for the Beth Jacob pioneers, and to its future with the consecration of the cornerstone and the honoring of members who had been present at the 1909 dedication.[18]

Within three years of the new synagogue's completion, and at the beginning of his thirty-third year at Beth Jacob, Rabbi Greenwald died at age sixty-seven. A distinguished historian of Hungarian Jewry who particularly emphasized the part played by Orthodox Jewry in its one thousand years of life, Greenwald wrote five hundred articles about Jewish law and history. He was also a Talmudic scholar who published learned Talmudic discourses in scholarly journals as well as books "overflowing with erudition in all the chambers of the Torah." Greenwald's forty-fifth book appeared posthumously. Receiving wide recognition as a *halachist* (expert in Jewish law), Greenwald's 414-page Hebrew *Compendium on Mourning* achieved instant and international success because he discussed in realistic terms Jewish practice concerning euthanasia, autopsies, cornea transplants, mourning, burial, etc. All in all he was an uncompromising gentleman who paralleled the biblical phrase, "And Jacob was a plain man, dwelling in tents."

Despite his prodigious scholarship and language facility, Rabbi Greenwald did not speak English very well. Those who knew him best and most admired him agreed with one of his colleagues that when Greenwald spoke in English "most of the time the people didn't understand him." Ineffective as a preacher, for "he spoke a type of Yiddish which most people could not understand" and "he hardly knew English," in his later years Greenwald became "just a fixture in the *shul*." Because he could not communicate with a generation of youngsters who did not understand Yiddish, and was unable to attract new members to the synagogue, Rabbi Greenwald merely watched as Agudas Achim emerged as the self-proclaimed "Big *Shul.*"[19]

While Columbus' Orthodox congregations were still pondering the need to move and conducting building funds, Congregation Tifereth Israel purchased a $20,000 site at 1354 East Broad Street in 1923. The synagogue was dedicated in September of 1927 before more than one thousand persons and consecrated, in the emerging style of Conservative Judaism, to "a spirit of reverence for Judaism and the highest ideals of Americanism." Yielding to the optimistic affluence of the twenties, this two-hundred-family congregation contracted for an enormous mortgage of $175,000. With the collapse of the economy two years later, Tifereth Israel struggled more feverishly for survival than any other synagogue in the community.[20]

As the temple neared completion, the congregation brought Rabbi Solomon Rivlin (1894-1952) from Des Moines, Iowa. A native of Jerusalem, Rivlin was a graduate of the City College of New York in 1917 and the Jewish Theological Seminary in 1921; he also received a law degree at Drake University in 1923. "A great Talmudist, speaker, and organizer," according to his successor, Rabbi Rivlin came to Tifereth Israel early in 1927 and distinguished himself primarily by his intense devotion to Zionism and Zionist work. When the loss of almost half the members immediately after the 1929 crash forced the board of directors to take drastic measures, Rivlin resigned his position early in 1930 to save the synagogue money. After working as a Sun Life Insurance salesman in 1935, Rivlin and his family settled in Palestine. Unable to remain there, Rivlin returned to Columbus in 1937 and spent more than a decade serving the Zionist cause in several cities and in various roles.[21]

During 1930 and 1931 the membership of the congregation steadily declined and the congregation had no regular minister. By January of 1932, when the directors elected twenty-seven-year-old Rabbi Nathan Zelizer to revive the temple, membership had dropped to less than one hundred families and the large mortgage payments could no longer be met. Fresh out of the seminary, Rabbi Zelizer initiated and led an intensive membership drive — "The Rabbi Zelizer Class of '32" — an activity which dominated the efforts of the synagogue for at least a decade as it struggled for life:

> I came here in the depression; we needed money badly. The only conversation which was of interest to us was to increase the membership of the congregation or fold up, and tell the mortgage people to leave us alone for another month and another month, until we were able to pay a little bit of interest. I'll bet you I took in 1,500 people. It was a question of survival.[22]

"Red" teams competed with "Blue" teams for prizes in

membership drives, and not even the team captains recruited more diligently than the rabbi. Walking "door-to-door" for "heart-to-heart sales talks," Rabbi Zelizer convinced persons to "sign on the dotted line" for only fifty cents down and three dollars a month (two dollars for singles). The board expected him to "bring in his quota of new members" each year, and they quite explicitly stated that a renewal of contract depended on successful recruitment.[23]

The congregation consistently renewed Rabbi Zelizer's contract, but they could rarely afford even his small salary. As a result, the rabbi survived on hand-outs during the early years of his rabbinate:

> The sisterhood helped out quite a lot; they had a number of functions and when I wasn't paid for months sometimes, and I had to pay my lodging, my room and board, I remember they had luncheons and collected $.25 a lunch. We took in about $60 and they gave me $35, and I had it in nickels and dimes and pennies; I had money to live on for another week or two.[24]

Zelizer's membership recruitment efforts paid off well; by 1936 one hundred and sixty-eight paid members belonged to Tifereth Israel and in the fall of 1938 alone forty new members joined the synagogue. By the early 1940s the congregation boasted of four to five hundred members. Forced to default on mortgage payments a decade earlier, Tifereth Israel could now envision paying off the mortgage. When members subscribed forty thousand dollars at a kick-off dinner for Defense Bonds in 1942, the board concluded there was money available. An intensive ten-day drive in January of 1943, led by Samuel Melton and Harry Gilbert, collected almost twenty-five thousand dollars and enabled the congregation to stage a mortgage burning celebration.[25] As the congregation's prosperity increased, so too did Rabbi Zelizer's annual salary which rose from $2,400 in 1932 to $5,000 in 1947.

Reflecting the position of the Conservative movement during the thirties and forties, Tifereth Israel's Board, like those of Columbus' Orthodox synagogues, consisted exclusively of men. Important committees were also composed of men. Women's names rarely, if ever, were entered in the congregational minutes. Indeed, during ongoing discussions of poor attendance at Sabbath services, the announced figures included only men. And the numbers, in the early years of Rabbi Zelizer's ministry, seemed small indeed:

> We used to meet on Shabbos morning in the balcony because the temple was too big. Many times we had to get five children, we had only five men. We had to wait until Mr. Schlezinger would get in his

Immediately after World War II Tifereth Israel Synagogue sponsored a day camp under the direction of Rabbi Nathan Zelizer (left) and Mike Schwartz.

> car and pick up a couple of children to make a *minyan* [ten men]. Friday night we had ten people, fifteen people, sometimes no *minyan* at all.[26]

Although the congregation was part of the Conservative movement, Zelizer and others saw little which differentiated them from an Orthodox synagogue. While it is true that men and women sat together, the services started on time and decorum remained important; committees sought to enlarge membership, and worshippers drove their cars to Sabbath and High Holiday services. This situation was repeated at Columbus' Orthodox synagogues. Additionally, the rabbi conducted services virtually identical to the Orthodox liturgy:

> Every Conservative synagogue was a *shul*. There were no changes except I preached in English, not in Yiddish, and I didn't wear my *yarmulka* when I was outside the synagogue . . . so that in my behavior as a rabbi there was really very little difference between the Conservative and the Orthodox.[27]

In contrast to Rabbi Zelizer's unobtrusive door-to-door campaign to keep Tifereth Israel afloat, youthful Rabbi Jacob Tarshish (1892-1960) provided Temple Israel's Reform congregation with a very visible ministry. Lithuanian-born and American-educated, the rabbi graduated from the University of Cincinnati in 1914, Hebrew Union College in 1915, and received a

M.A. from Lehigh University the following year. He served congregations in Allentown, Pennsylvania, from 1915 to 1919 and in Yonkers, New York, from 1919 to 1922 before replacing Rabbi Joseph Kornfeld in July of 1922.[28]

Blessed with exceptional good looks and a magnificent voice, Tarshish instinctively addressed himself to *au courant* themes with a style that captivated his audience. By the fall of 1925 the trustees and the congregation voted to hear this voice on Sunday mornings at brief "interdenominational worship services open to the public" which were followed by an address; this forum allowed Tarshish to develop his message of hope and comfort.[29]

Early in 1926, with the lectures drawing large crowds of Jews and Christians, Tarshish proposed radio broadcasts of the "nonsectarian" morning services. The trustees tabled the proposal for some months, but eventually approved the weekly broadcasts which began on February 20, 1928, over WAIU with a talk about George Washington. By the second week, Tarshish's lecture became front page news in Columbus.[30]

Tarshish offered a popular message of psychological advice that brought "sun to dark places, hope and strength when happiness seemed gone forever." His psychological wisdom was essentially Jamesian: religion means more life, religion means vitality. The business of religion consisted in unlocking inner resources. Like James, Tarshish saw this power of religion as both a source of support in moments of breakdown and as a stimulus to high endeavors. The rabbi delivered his message in several characteristic ways. First, poetic vagueness: "God [is] the genius of music, the rhythm of poetry, the curves of sculpture. He who has religion in his soul sees beauty and goodness in a thousand places." Second, marital advice: "What kind of woman will hold her husband the longest?" — "What makes a woman beautiful?" — "Love, how can we recognize it?" And third, oversimplified religious insights: "I choose to believe that if there be a life after death, it will be a happier one than the life before death" — "Prayer is the instrument by which we come in tune with that which is noblest in ourselves and in the world" — "What others lack let us supply; and, in return, what we do not have, others will give. This is the heart of religion."

Most often, and perhaps most significant for his appeal, Tarshish brought words of comfort and healing to soothe every troubled breast. Like his typical congregants — comfortable people of the middle and upper-middle classes — Tarshish consistently avoided social, political, or economic critiques of modern life. What was the secret of contentment? "It is a state of mind in which we are pleased with what we have, and are not unduly disturbed by what we don't have." The essence of hope? "In life we must all take less than we hoped for and dreamed of . . . when we have failed in one or two things, there are always a hundred others we can do with pleasure." And the meaning of religion? Religion "brings me courage when I am in sorrow, hope when I am in despair and when I am in sickness." And most often he asked, "What gives meaning to our individual existences?"

> Perhaps you will tell me you are not in the same class with these great — that you have no light of genius to give to the world. Maybe not — but it is not for you to say just how valuable you are. We none of us can tell how far-reaching our work can be. Never underestimate yourself. You were born for a purpose — a very worthy purpose. Find it. Believe in it. And do the best you can.[31]

Tarshish became both the most popular — and the most controversial — of Columbus' many rabbis. Scores of letters of approval and vituperation poured into the radio station and newspapers as a result of broadcasts in which he attacked Henry Ford as a Pharaoh, Haman, Torquemada, and "unadulterated ignoramous"; argued that Jews could believe in Christian Science and still be loyal Jews; described Orthodox Judaism as "minutia" and Reform Judaism as "morality"; applauded Reform Jews for "assimilating some of the Christian customs and mingling with the Christians"; attacked prohibition after "ten years of failure"; and urged that "differences between Jewish and Christian beliefs be eliminated."[32]

Wherever Rabbi Tarshish spoke, huge crowds assembled, and the non-Jewish press eagerly awaited his message. After his thrilling "Is Man a Machine?" debate against agnostic Clarence Darrow in 1928, the press enthusiastically applauded him. When Tarshish repeated his strong performance the following year before forty-two hundred at Memorial Hall, one reporter felt that Tarshish had "reached the pinnacle of greatness as a public speaker, and among his people at this time doubtless has no peer." Whether Tarshish was reviewing a book for a Women's Club; addressing a PTA group about "Safety"; debating "Is Civilization Worthwhile?" with Bata Kindai Amgaza Ibn Lobagola, the famous African savage; holding forth at a large table at Mills Buffet after Friday evening services; or talking to the Friendly Sons of St. Patrick, large crowds of non-Jews came to hear him and reporters summarized his talks on the front pages the next day. By 1929 the Sunday morning lectures grew so popular that Tarshish began to speak at the temple on Sunday evenings as well, "to attract Christians and Jews."[33]

Early in 1932, Tarshish's bubble burst.[34] The trustees were angry about the rabbi's refusal to cease his commercial broadcasting on Tuesday and Thursday — a remunerative position

TABLE 48
RABBI JACOB TARSHISH'S SERMON TITLES

Sabbath Eve		Sunday Morning	
10-17-30	Adolph Hilter, Germany's Would Be Mussolini	10-12-30	Does Hate Get Us Anywhere?
11- 7-30	Under the Skin Are We Really Devils or Angels	10-19-30	Play Review
11-14-30	Does It Become the Jew to Be a Missionary?	11- 9-30	What Do the People of the U.S. Really Want?
12-12-30	Christmas and the Jewish Feast of Lights	11-16-30	Is the World 12 Years Behind Us or 12 Years Ahead of Us?
12-26-30	Professor Albert Einstein, The Man and His Work	12-14-30	Story Review: *The Necklace*
1- 2-31	What Resolutions Shall We Make for the New Year?	12-28-30	When Christianity and Judaism Parted
3-27-31	The Hebrew University	1- 4-31	If all Religions Were to Unite, What Kind of a Religion Would We Have?
4- 3-31	The Jew and the American Revolution	3-29-31	Marrying for Money
11- 6-31	What Can the Jew Do to Eliminate Prejudice?	4- 5-31	Passover and Easter
11-20-31	Louis D. Brandeis — The People's Advocate	11- 8-31	Is the Soldier's Duty Done When the Battle is Over?
12- 4-31	Who Were the First to Battle for Religious Liberty?	11-22-31	What Does Japan Want?
12-18-31	Are There No Frankensteins?	12- 6-31	Woodrow Wilson — The Man of Yesterday and Tomorrow
1- 8-32	The Dreyfus Case	12-20-31	Jesus the Man and the Jew
1-22-32	The Man Who Knew How to Be Rich	1-10-32	The Ten Resolutions for the New Year
1-29-32	How Shall We Spend Each Day?	1-24-32	The Happy Hypocrite
2-19-32	Movie Review: *The Man Who Played God*	1-31-32	Benjamin Franklin — Philosopher and Statesman
2-26-32	Who is Benjamin Cardozo?	2-21-32	George Washington — Patriot and Builder
3- 4-32	The Broken Lullaby	2-28-32	The Benefits of the Depression
3-11-32	Is There Need for a God in our Modern World?	3- 6-32	Stalin — The Mystery Man of Russia
3-25-32	My Work is Finished — Why Wait?	3-13-32	The Lindbergh Crime
4- 1-32	The Jewish Religion of Yesterday and Today	3-27-32	Questions and Answers
4- 8-32	Friendship — True and False	4- 3-32	Who Crucified Jesus and Why?
4-15-32	The Very Best We Can Get Out of Life	4-10-32	Shakespeare and Shylock
4-27-32	Passover and Easter — Have They Anything in Common?	4-17-32	Why Marriages Fail
		4-24-32	The End of My Radio Ministry at Temple Israel
		4-29-32	The Life of Moses

which required that he review downtown movies, provide brief news items from Hollywood, and read advertisements. At a special meeting the trustees decided such activities appeared "unbecoming and inconsistent with his duties" and resolved to fire him if the programs did not cease. Tarshish replied that he used the money to finance the Sunday morning broadcasts; that if he yielded to their demands in this area, they would strip him of freedoms elsewhere and that his only decent alternative was to resign.

Having agreed to leave the temple by May 1, Tarshish used his radio time in April to blast the trustees, claiming that they opposed both his "daring to do something different" and his "liberalism," and that they had asked him to take a salary cut because of his outside earnings. Tarshish promised that his radio broadcasts would continue even after his contract with the congregation expired: "I will answer the call of my radio audience." Trustee President Leon J. Goodman rebutted these charges over the air by announcing that the only point of dispute involved Tarshish's commercial broadcasts, for it was "undignified for a rabbi earning $12,000 annually" to receive money from radio commercials.[35]

Radio broadcasting became Jacob Tarshish's full-time profession after he left Temple Israel. Like Protestant and Catholic radio preachers across the country, he tried to use the new medium to win a mass audience. In 1932 he was unsuccessful in establishing a "radio congregation" in Columbus, where he desired "to minister to the educational, spiritual, and moral needs of my large radio audience." After broadcasting from WLW in Cincinnati for two years, Tarshish was heard over WOR in Newark, New Jersey, from 1934 to 1935. During the next four years he broadcast almost daily on national networks. Tarshish published these addresses in three small volumes, and for much of the 1930s, the "Lamplighter" brought "sun to dark places" all over America.[36]

During Tarshish's ministry at Temple Israel, the congregation experienced both the boom of the twenties and the difficulties of the early thirties. In the affluent twenties, the trustees confidently took action: they considered but then rejected selling their Bryden Road site to Tifereth Israel and purchasing the latter's Broad Street lot. Jacob Tarshish was awarded a five-year contract in 1927 totaling $58,000. Several sites for a new temple were inspected during the late 1920s. On the eve of the depression 325 members paid a total of $25,520 in dues, and the trustees, while following a conservative fiscal policy, seemed confident of sustained growth.[37]

By the winter of 1930-31 financial problems became a recurrent theme once again. The brotherhood cancelled dinner meetings because of "the conditions," dues paid to the Union of American Hebrew Congregations decreased substantially, and at every board meeting members petitioned for a reduction in dues. For example, on the night of October 5, 1931, even some of the congregation's most generous contributors acknowledged the impact of the depression. Julius Feibel asked for a reduction from $200 to $150, J. C. Goodman from $200 to $100, Louis Feibel from $110 to $75; the widow of Frank Glick petitioned for her dues to be lowered from $500 to $150. As a final indication of these difficulties, the congregation paid Rabbi Samuel M. Gup only $6,000 in 1932 when he succeeded Rabbi Tarshish. Several years passed before the temple was again solvent.[38]

Born and raised in Mobile, Alabama, Samuel M. Gup (1893-1955) graduated from the University of Cincinnati in 1914 and Hebrew Union College in 1917. He served congregations in Springfield, Ohio, from 1916 to 1918 and in Natchez, Tennessee, the following year before being called to Providence, Rhode Island.[39] During his thirteen-year tenure at Congregation Beth El in Providence, he particularly emphasized interfaith work. After the first appearance of a rabbi at Mathewson Street Methodist Episcopal Church in 1929 Gup noted: "The difference between Jew and non-Jew living in the modern world of free contact with one another must never consist in externalities. The pressure of social conformity compels us all to demean ourselves as merely alike as possible."[40] Often Gup spoke of Judaism as the "religion of democracy" which would unite Jew and non-Jew:

> The Religion of Democracy . . . will usher in the spiritual unity of all people [and] . . . stress those great ethical sentiments of justice, kindliness and service which fasten the links in the chain of human brotherhood . . . promote the highest weal of public fellowship by relying on the capacity of change in the human consciousness through the highest representation of the moral consciousness of all time — the religion of the prophets.[41]

Finally, Gup won nationwide publicity in the 1920s as the rabbi who lauded the virtues of Christianity and the lessons Jews might learn from the life of Christ:

> Praise the Christmas spirit which brought into the world joy and gladness, and which, epitomized in the person of Christ, will some day reign throughout the world . . . We laud the preachings of Christ and exalt Him as an inspiration and guide to moral conduct. The Jews should have no hesitancy in expressing their wholehearted admiration and even reverence for His saintly character.[42]

Gup's interfaith approach and "enthusiasm for justice" impressed the trustees of Temple Israel; his installation sermon,

"The Three-Fold Task of the Ministry," promised more of the same. Not only would Gup "actively engage Jew and non-Jew" and attempt to "embody saintliness," but when asked "what is the religious life?" he would reply that "he is religious whose moral and spiritual reach exceeds his grasp."[43]

All of Rabbi Gup's extant sermons and addresses develop these themes. "Jew and Christian have infinitely more in common than in difference," he declared over the radio in 1937, and they "can meet . . . by renewed dedication to ethical principles and ideals." Exuding optimism throughout the difficult years of the depression and World War II, he urged Jews and Christians "to summon the sentiments of justice and love in such overwhelming volume as to crush prejudice and scatter its ashes to the four winds of heaven."[44]

Gup himself attempted to create a "community of brotherliness with non-Jewish Columbus" and a "sweet and happy world for all" through a continual flurry of interfaith and communal activities which ranged from interfaith dinners, sharing temple facilities with churches recovering from fires or rebuilding, preaching at Protestant and Catholic churches, serving as vice-president of the Franklin County Ministerial Association, and sponsoring annual "Institutes on Judaism for Christian Clergy and Educators," to encouraging the "Templers'" regular participation in the church basketball league. No less active in the city than in the

TABLE 49
RABBI SAMUEL GUP'S SERMON TITLES

10-28-32	The Conquest of Fear
11-11-32	World War for World Peace
11-18-32	The Lens Maker of Holland
11-25-32	Is Suicide Justifiable?
12- 2-32	On Being Ourselves
12- 9-32	The Dimensions of Life
12-16-32	If Jesus Comes
12-23-32	The Conflict of Cultures
12-30-32	At the Turn of the Year
1- 6-33	Josephus
1-13-33	Whither Democracy?
1-20-33	Does Life Begin at Forty?
1-27-33	Atheism — Why Not?
2- 3-33	Albert Einstein
2-10-33	Abraham Lincoln and the National Outlook
2-17-33	George Washington, The Revolutionist
3- 3-33	The Inauguration of FDR
3-10-33	The Eternal Whys
3-17-33	Our Country
3-31-33	The Road to Happiness
4- 7-33	The Progress of Liberalism
4-14-33	Can Jew and Non-Jew Meet?
4-21-33	Why Stand Alone?
4-28-33	Sayings of the Fathers
5- 5-33	Fighting with Giants
5-12-33	How Shall We Meet Anti-Semitism?
5-19-33	Authority and Leadership

churches of Columbus, Gup was regularly appointed by elected officials to local and statewide bodies, including the City Safety Council, the Citizens' Committee to Survey Revenues and Expenditures, the Ohio State Commission on Marriage and Divorce, the City Commission for Jobs and Progress, the Ohio Motion Picture Censorship Board, and a five-member citizens' committee to crystalize public opinion and force a settlement of the lengthy Columbus streetcar strike of 1946[45] Just before he left Columbus in 1946, a local editorial noted that:

> Gup is active in virtually every beneficient endeavor and for years has been sought after to address the church, civic, and educational groups. This attitude on the part of Rabbi Gup reflects the general philosophy of Temple Israel congregation itself.[46]

Within the walls of the temple, educational, social, cultural, and worship programs changed little in substance from the twenties, although Gup made several efforts to attract post-confirmation (high school) students to serious programs of Jewish study. German Jewish refugees came to Columbus in significant numbers during the late 1930s and Temple Israel opened its doors wide to receive them without any fees, but it was another group of outsiders, the Central Conference of American Rabbis (CCAR) which created the most excitement for the congregation during Gup's rabbinate.[47]

An indication of the high acculturation of the temple programs is suggested by the persons and subjects the brotherhood sponsored between 1929 and 1935. More than 80 percent of the guests consisted of non-Jews and an even larger percentage of the lectures dealt with non-Jewish themes. Jewish and non-Jewish brotherhood programs at the temple and several Columbus churches could have been interchanged in the early thirties; this suggests not only a conscious attempt to pattern the Jewish group after the non-Jewish organziations of the community, but a desire to be like the dominant society.

Even though Rabbi Gup's "profound moral earnestness" had gained wide acclaim, he was virtually forced to resign his position by the fall of 1946. When certain members of the board of trustees no longer wished Gup to serve the congregation, he secured an unattractive position in Mobile at $6,600 a year. "I do not want to go to Mobile," he wrote the secretary of the board, but because he was convinced that "members of his flock who are circulating a petition requesting him to retain the local pulpit" would not secure his reelection, he quietly left town, a sad and broken man. After briefly serving congregations in Mobile and Dothan in Alabama, and in Chicago, Gup and his wife returned to Columbus when the rabbi retired in 1952.[48]

TABLE 50
TEMPLE ISRAEL BROTHERHOOD'S PROGRAMS

Date	Speaker	Topic
Jan. 29, 1929	Henry Goddard, Psychology professor	Some Abnormalities of Normal People
Nov. 23, 1930	Ruth Bryan Owen, Daughter of William Jennings Bryan	This Business of Being a Congresswoman
Dec. 8, 1930	Thomas Skeyhill, Author, soldier, poet	Mussolini and the Black Shirts
Jan. 27, 1931	Maurice Hindus, Author	My Recent Impressions of Russia
Mar. 17, 1931	Jehan Warliker, Noted Hindu	The Problems of India
Nov. 21, 1933	Hugh Fullerton, Journalist	Prominent Jews I Have Known
Dec. 12, 1933	Carlton Matson, Editor	What News Today?
Jan. 16, 1934	John W. Bricker, Attorney General of Ohio	Crime in Ohio
Feb. 6, 1934	Theodore Beckman, Economics professor	The New Deal
Apr. 3, 1934	Fred Lazarus, Jr., Local businessman	Taxation in Ohio
Nov. 5, 1934	Charles B. West, Congressman	Where is America Heading?
Jan. 6, 1935	Francis Schmidt, Football coach	OSU Football
Mar. 5, 1935	Vinton McVicker, Jr., John A. Connor, J. G. Collicott, Robert Tucker	Better Understanding Between Jews and Christians
Apr. 26, 1935	Norman Imrie, Editor	What America Needs
Oct. 22, 1935	E. A. Helms, Political science professor	Should America Stay Out of Foreign Affairs?

SOURCE: Temple Israel *Bulletins.*

The second quarter of the twentieth century was a time of building, financial crises, and increased visibility for Columbus' Jewish congregations. Three new synagogues were built to serve an eastward shifting Jewish community; they were no longer within walking — or shouting — distance of each other. Without these focal points, the old east European Jewish neighborhood lost its Jewishness, and the community undoubtedly lost a little of its cohesiveness. Although Rabbis Gup, Zelizer, Greenwald, and Tarshish approached their ministries in radically diverse ways, for the time and situation, each was effective. Yet in the midst of transition, some things remained the same: the consoling familiarity of the traditional ceremonies and holidays, the bitter disagreements between rabbis and lay leadership, and the continuous fund raising for Palestine and the European Jews.

NOTES FOR CHAPTER 14

1. Interview with Rabbi Eugene Borowitz.

TABLE 51
AHAVAS SHOLOM PRESIDENTS

1939-40	Morris Jonas	1945-46	George Goodman
1940-41	Harry Beckman	1946-47	William Givets
1941-42	Harry Beckman	1947-48	William Givets
1942-43	Harry Beckman	1948-49	Barney Ringer
1943-44	Harry Beckman	1949-50	Barney Ringer
1944-45	George Goodman		

2. *OJC*, March 8, 1929, October 4, 1940; Agudas Achim Minutes, December 14, 1927, March 5, August 6, 1928, July 1, 1940, January 29, 1946.

3. *OJC*, August 12 and 19, 1932; *WWAJ*, 1938-39, Volume 3, p. 444; B. G. Rudolph, *From a Minyan to a Community: History of the Jews of Syracuse*, New York (Philadelphia, 1970), p. 208; *OJC*, October 29, 1954. Rabbi Hirschsprung was the grandson of Rabbi Abraham Joseph Jacob

Gelernter, scion of a famous rabbinic dynasty in Poland (*OJC*, October 15, 1937) and, according to his son, valedictorian of the first group of American rabbis graduating from the Rabbi Isaac Elchanon Theological Seminary (Abraham Hirschsprung to Marc Lee Raphael, correspondence, April 13, 1976).

4. Interview with Rabbi Samuel Rubenstein; *HaPardes* 13:6 (September 1939): 13-14, 13:7 (October 1939): 20-29, 23:1 (October 1948): 27-29; *OJC*, September 30, 1932, June 11 and May 21, 1937; Jacob Meskin, *Sulam Ya'akov* (New York, 1940), pp. 81-83.

5. *WWAJ*, 1938-39, Volume 3, p. 444; *OJC*, October 7, 1932.

6. Agudas Achim Minutes, October 1, August 6, 1928, October 9, 1939, June 3, 1940, July 7, August 29, 1942, January 29, October 31, 1946, January 2, 1947.

7. Agudas Achim Minutes, February 13, 1931, October 4, 1937, March 23, 1941.

8. *OJC*, March 8, 1929; Agudas Achim Minutes, April 5, 1928, October 9 and 16, 1939, August 8, 1941. Rabbi Hirschsprung's three-year contract, in 1942, totalled only $4,000 per year; Minutes, February 3, 1942.

9. Agudas Achim Minutes, March 4, May 20, 1940, September 17, 1942, February 28, October 26, 1943, November 7, 1944; *OJC*, July 16, 1943.

10. Agudas Achim Minutes, October 3, 1940, November 28, 1944.

11. Agudas Achim Minutes, June 11, July 22, 1946, January 2, February 25, July 31, 1947; *OJC*, July 2, 1948, September 16, 1949; interviews with Marvin Fox and Samuel Rubenstein; [A. W. Robins], "Let's Think It Over!" [1949], at OHS.

TABLE 52
AGUDAS ACHIM PRESIDENTS

Year	President	Year	President
1927-28	Bert Wolman	1935-36	Morris Gertner
1928-29	Louis Lakin	1936-37	Morris Gertner
1929-30	Louis Lakin	1937-38	Morris Gertner
1930-31	Morris Levison	1938-39	Sam Levy
1931-32	Joseph Zilberman	1939-40	Jacob Krakowitz
1932-33	Joseph Zilberman	1940-41	Jacob Krakowitz
1933-34	?	1941-42	Joseph L. Schwartz
1934-35	Jacob Schottenstein	1942-43	Joseph L. Schwartz
		1943-44	Joseph L. Schwartz

12. *WWAJ*, 1938-39, Volume 3, p. 392; *Universal Jewish Encyclopedia*, Volume 5, p. 99; *Biographical Encyclopedia of American Jews*, Leo M. Glassman, editor (New York, 1935), p. 198; *OJC*, April 11, 1941, August 13, 1943, December 2, 1949, April 15, 1955; Leopold Greenwald, *Sefer Hazichronot* [War Diary], 1916 and idem, *Toledot Gedoley HaDor: Beyt Yonathan* (1907-08); *Montreal Daily Jewish Eagle* (Yiddish), November 10, 1942, p. 5 and July 3, 1946, p. 4; N. Katzburg in *Sinai* 37 (1955): 277-81 and 40 (1957): 313-14.

13. Scrapbook of Leopold Greenwald, in possession of his son, Jack

Greenwald, Denver, Colorado; *OJC,* May 22, November 20, 1925, July 9, August 6, 1926, May 29, 1931, June 3, 1932, December 22, 1939, January 9, 1940.

14. Interviews with Edward Schlezinger, Jacob Pass and Marvin Fox; *OJC,* June 21 and 28, 1940, February 23, June 29, 1945. For details of the nationwide attack against Kaplan and his excommunication by the Orthodox rabbinate, see the *NYT,* June 15, September 6, 1945, and *Time,* June 25, 1945.

15. *OJC,* February 2 and 9, 1940, March 3, July 30, October 8, 1943, March 24, July 28, 1944, March 26, 1948.

16. *OJC,* April 5, July 26, 1929; November 24, December 15, 1933.

17. *OJC,* April 10, December 4 and 11, 1931, March 26, 1937, March 18, 1938, March 26, 1948. Older members of the synagogue recall that dues, during "good times," were twenty-five cents per week, and "G. use to come to collect and get a percentage from the collection . . . he use to come every week, or every other week, to collect."

18. *OJC,* November 10, 1944, May 5, September 8, 1950.

19. Interviews with Rabbi Samuel Rubenstein, Rabbi Julius Baker, and Sylvia Schecter. For a detailed bibliography of more than thirty-five of Greenwald's books covering forty years of scholarship, see Ch. Block's "Afterword" in the last section of Greenwald's *L'Toledot HaReformatsizyan HaDateet B'Germanyah u'Va'ungaryah* (by the author, Columbus, Ohio 5708).

TABLE 53
BETH JACOB PRESIDENTS

1922-23	Charles Furman	1939-40	Morris Beim
1923-24	Charles Furman	1940-41	Charles Furman
1924-25	Charles Furman	1941-42	Morris Beim
1925-26	Charles Furman	1942-43	Morris Beim
1926-27	?	1943-44	Morris Weinstock
1927-28	Morris Beim	1944-45	Morris Weinstock
1928-29	Morris Beim	1945-46	Morris Weinstock
1929-30	George Shustick	1946-47	Louis Levin
1930-31	William Cohen	1947-48	Louis Levin
1931-32	William Cohen	1948-49	Louis Levin
1932-33	Morris Beim	1949-50	William Goodman/ Joseph Swartz
1933-34	Morris Beim		
1934-35	George Shustick	1950-51	Joseph Swartz
1935-36	George Shustick	1951-52	Joseph Swartz
1936-37	Abe Goodman	1952-53	Joseph Swartz
1937-38	Abe Goodman	1953-54	Joseph Swartz
1938-39	Morris Beim	1954-55	Joseph Swartz

20. *OSJ,* September 12, 1927; *OJC,* September 16, 1927.

21. *WWAJ,* 1926, Volume 1, pp. 500-01; Rose L. Rivlin to Marc Lee Raphael, correspondence, October 27, 1974; interview with Rabbi Nathan Zelizer; *OJC,* May 6 and 13, 1927, January 13, 1928, July 12, December 13,

1929, March 21, 1930, February 27, 1932, August 16, 1935, November 10, 1937, March 4, 1938, February 3, May 28, November 24, 1939. For an example of Rivlin's scholarship, see his "Influence of Jewish Tradition on Exegesis of Jerome," M.A. thesis, Drake University Bible College, 1925. Three members of the Tifereth Israel Board interviewed and hired Rabbi Rivlin in Des Moines; *OSJ*, February 16, 1927.

22. Interview with Rabbi Nathan Zelizer; *OJC*, January 29, 1932.

23. Tifereth Israel Minutes, September 3, 1936, November 1 and 11, 1937, January 3, 1938, July 1, 1940; *OJC*, January 29, 1932.

24. Interview with Rabbi Nathan Zelizer.

25. Tifereth Israel Minutes, October 5, 1936, November 7, 1938, January 21, 1943; *OJC*, January 2, 1942.

26. Tifereth Israel Minutes, February 17, 1941, June 5, 1947; interview with Rabbi Nathan Zelizer, August 7, 1975.

27. Conversation with Lawrence Polster, November 9, 1974; Rabbi Hyman Chanover to Marc Lee Raphael, correspondence, August 28, 1974; interview with Rabbi Nathan Zelizer.

TABLE 54
TIFERETH ISRAEL PRESIDENTS

1918-25	Morris Polster	1933-35	Harry Masser
1925-29	Leon Nason	1935-41	I. H. Schlezinger
1929-31	I. H. Schlezinger	1941-45	William Wasserstrom
1931-33	Harry Winter	1945-49	Louis Schlezinger

28. *WWAJ*, 1938-39, Volume 3, p. 1071.

29. *Prelude to Happiness, By the Lamplighter* (Jacob Tarshish), Third Volume (Columbus, Ohio, 1937), p. 5; *OSJ*, September 8, October 5, 1925, November 6, 1931.

30. *OJC*, December 4, 1925; Temple Israel Minute Books, February 1, 1926, January 3, 1928; *OSJ*, February 20 and 27, March 5, 1928.

31. We culled the radio talk and lecture excerpts from the daily press and from his own writings.

32. *OSJ*, February 5 and 19, April 30, 1927, December 17, 1928, January 1, 1929, February 17, 1930.

33. *OSJ*, May 1, 1928; January 1 and 24, February 8, March 13, April 9, 1929, October 21, 1932; *OJC*, April 6, May 4, 1928, December 22, 1929; interview with Mildred Tarshish.

34. For a different explanation of Tarshish's leaving, placing the blame on one influential member, see Manuel B. Tarshish to Marc Lee Raphael, correspondence, September 11 and 19, 1974.

35. Temple Israel Minute Books, January 20, February 1 and 2, 1932; *OSJ*, February 2, April 25 and 29, 1932; *CC*, April 29, 1932; *OJC*, February 5, 1932. Details of Tarshish's contract are in Temple Israel Minute Books, April 12, 1927.

36. *OJC*, May 13, 1932; *CD*, February 2, 1932; *WWAJ*, 1938-39, Volume 3, p. 1071; Harold M. Wagner, Public Affairs Director for Mutual Broadcasting System to Marc Lee Raphael, correspondence, October 9,

1975; *Little Journeys with the Lamplighter* (Jacob Tarshish), Second Volume (Columbus, 1935) and *Half Hours with Rabbi Jacob Tarshish,* First Volume (Columbus, 1933). Rabbi Eugene Borowitz provided an anecdote illustrating Tarshish's appeal as a radio preacher:

> Tarshish was an incredible phenomenon of the early radio days. When many years later I came to Parkersburg, West Virginia, as the biweekly rabbi, they still remembered how they had to write a letter to Columbus, Ohio, to ask Jacob Tarshish to prevent the local radio station from broadcasting his program Sunday mornings at 11:00 a.m. because it interfered with church services and the people weren't coming to church (see interview with Eugene Borowitz).

37. Temple Israel Minute Books, June 2, 1925, April 12, 1927, April 8, 1928, February 4, 1929.

38. Temple Israel Minute Books, January 5, October 5, 1931, and passim.

39. *Springfield* [Ohio] *News,* March 19, September 17, 1917; *Providence Journal,* January 12, 1920; *CED,* June 20, 1932; *CC,* June 20, 1932, March 31, 1955; *OJC,* June 24, 1932, October 25, 1946, April 1, 1955; *OSJ,* April 1, 1955.

40. *Providence Evening Bulletin,* December 28, 1929.

41. *Boston Jewish Advocate,* September 12, 1919, "The Religion of Democracy." For similar thoughts subsequently, see *B'nai B'rith News,* December 1921, "Enemies Within the Camp"; *Providence Journal,* November 8, 1921, November 29, December 1, 1924, April 19, 1926; *Providence Evening Bulletin,* June 25, 1923. Gup's statement that Jesus was "an ethical light which Judaism gave to the world" received national publicity; see *NYT,* December 26, 1925; *New York Evening World,* December 26, 1925; *Mobile Register,* December 27, 1925; *Worcester Daily Telegram,* December 26, 1925.

42. *Providence Journal,* December 25, 1922. Gup later invoked Jesus to explain why he denounced the proposed boycott of German goods; Jesus "taught us to return good for evil." See *OSJ,* December 23, 1933.

43. Samuel Gup to Leon J. Goodman, correspondence, March 2, 1932 and Leon J. Goodman to Samuel Gup, correspondence, March 19, 1932, in Rabbi Samuel Gup, Papers, Box 2; [Providence] *Jewish Herald,* July 8, 1932; *CC,* June 25 and September 17, 1932; "The Three-Fold Task of the Ministry," Gup Papers, Box 2.

44. *American Hebrew,* November 26, 1937, "Common Ground" "If I Only Had One Sermon to Preach," February 21, 1943, Gup Papers, Box 2. See also *Jewish American* [Yiddish], June 24, 1938; *OSJ,* October 16, 1933, August 1934; *CED,* November 28, December 3, 1932, April 7, 1934.

45. "What Men Live By," February 3, 1946, and "The Nature of Priorities," January 28, 1945, in Gup Papers, Box 2; *OSJ,* June 12, 1933, June 12, 1935, November 17, 1937, October 22, 1946; *OJC,* March 3, June 26, 1936, February 4, 1938, January 27, 1939, April 6, 1945; *CED,* November 3, 1939, October 12, 1946; *CC,* June 6 and 15, 1935, October 12 and 14, 1946; *Jewish Post and Opinion,* June 23, 1944; *Ohio Christian News,* June 1940.

46. *OSJ,* January 29, 1946.

47. Temple Israel Minutes, December 5, 1932, May 6, 1935, April 4, September 12, 1938, March 6, 1939. At the 1933 annual congregational

meeting, it was said that during the past year Rabbi Gup had called at the home of every temple member! See Bryden Road Temple Bulletin, May 19, 1933.

48. Interviews with Mildred Tarshish, Ruth Gup, Jerome Folkman (where a different view of Gup's leaving is offered), and Nathan Zelizer; *OJC*, October 25, 1946; *CC*, November 18, 1946; Samuel Brown to Samuel Gup, correspondence, September 20, 1946; Gup to Brown, September 23, 1946; Gup to Arthur Loeb, September 25, 1946; Gup to Temple Israel Trustees, October 18, 1946, in Samuel M. Gup Papers, Box 2. The president of Temple Israel, during the Tarshish and Gup rabbinates from 1929 to 1948 was Leon J. Goodman.

15: TO ESTABLISH GOOD PUBLIC RELATIONS: ORGANIZATIONAL LIFE

A complete picture of Jewish organizational life during the second quarter of the twentieth century would have to include at least forty identifiable agencies and organizations which crisscrossed the community. These encompassed religious, educational, Zionist, social service, cultural, defense, civic, patriotic, fraternal, recreational, and social groups. Several *landsmanschaften* — social organizations which provided mutual aid and which were based on Old World communities or regions — and even "family societies" were also included. This chapter, however, attempts to delineate only the activities of several of the most active and significant Columbus Jewish organizations.

Primary among these organizations was the forerunner of the Jewish Center, Schonthal Center. A major addition to the center's programming during the twenties was Schonthal Camp, twenty acres of land near Magnetic Springs in Delaware, Ohio, donated by Joseph Schonthal. Opening in 1927, and continuing at this location for two decades, the camp featured a four-week session for boys and another for girls. Twelve bungalows housed as many as one hundred campers, more than half from Dayton, Cincinnati, Pittsburgh, Charleston, and Wheeling. Mothers were encouraged to join their children as the camp's primary goal was to "produce strong and healthy mothers, boys, and girls." Kosher meals, Friday evening services, Hebrew songs, and Jewish content were combined with outdoor sports to make the Schonthal Camp a positive experience for hundreds of Jewish youth.[1]

During the second quarter of the century, despite limitations of space and budget, the center continued to feature a wide range of programs for youth and adults. Under the direction of Dr. Louis Mark (1892-1954),[2] a clinic served hundreds of hay fever and asthma sufferers each year. The debating team won high honors year after year in the Jewish Midwestern Debating League. Industrial arts courses and exhibits attracted wide attention throughout the city, as did the center's powerful basketball team. No less important was the small orchestra founded and voluntarily funded by center members; subsequently the orchestra developed into the Columbus Philharmonic.[3]

All of this activity continued despite an aging facility with far too little space, a poor location, and a woefully inadequate budget:

> The Hermine Schonthal Community House and the Jewish Welfare Federation is receiving from the Community Chest and expending for its entire program $9,000 less today (1941) than it expended fifteen or sixteen years ago when we became a part of the Community Chest.[4]

Funded by the Jewish Welfare Federation (JWF), which received its budget from the Community Fund, the center supplemented the JWF allocation with only a few dollars each month. During more than twenty-five years of iron-handed administration, Executive Director Rose Sugarman (1885/6-1961)[5] used extraordinary talents to make the limited funds stretch as far as they did. Her efforts did not, however, always succeed. In the winter of 1944-45 gas, electricity, and water service all ceased because the center could not afford $200 per month for their operation. In the opinion of Dr. E. J. Gordon (1888-1963),[6] Schonthal Center Board president for

Dr. Elijah Joseph Gordon (1888-1963) taught anatomy and medicine at The Ohio State University for almost sixty years and received national recognition for his treatment of aplastic anemia. His wife, Reva Silberstein Gordon (1890?-1963) was very active in Schonthal Center, the Jewish Infants Home, the 571 Shop, the Council of Jewish Women and many other Jewish and non-Jewish welfare activities. Her Americanization efforts were especially famous; for many years newcomers to Columbus stopped first at the Gordon home on Town Street.

sixteen years, "this center is no different now [1941] than when I came here as a kid; we have not improved." Not until the 1950s, with the construction of a new center, was adequate funding even contemplated.[7]

TABLE 55
SCHONTHAL CENTER BUDGETS

1926	$12,275	1932	$9,880
1928	14,700	1933	7,903
1930	11,800	1934	8,175
1931	11,279	1938	9,000

SOURCES: Compiled from reports in Columbus Jewish Center, Schonthal Center (1920-40), Miscellaneous Reports, Box 1.

No less difficult than funding remained the question of philosophy, a particularly tough problem for a Jewish agency supported by public funds and located in a neighborhood virtually without Jews. By the Second World War, the Rich Street area had changed considerably:

> the neighborhood of which we are a part and which we serve had, over a period of years, undergone important changes that must be considered in planning our present and future program. Twenty short years ago the Center was predominately Jewish, with almost half of the Jewish population living in the vicinity. Today, very few Jewish people live in the vicinity. Keeping these facts in mind, the role today that we must play is nevertheless important.

As a result of these changes, the center board began to define its goals in vague, non-parochial, and patriotic words: "to establish good public relations, promote democracy and good will among all social classes, and religious groups." When confronted by activities supported largely by non-Jews, many members of the board wrestled with these questions: Was it a *Jewish* Community Center or a community center? What were the fundamental purposes of a Jewish Center? Can it be Jewish and nonsectarian at the same time? The decision, reaffirmed frequently, was to remain open to all persons in the community, but to emphasize Jewish programs. The center thus provided a place to emphasize Jewish identity while affirming its commitment to American values.[8]

Equally committed to American values was the Council of Jewish Women, one of the most active women's organizations in the Jewish community during the 1930s and 1940s. Drawing largely upon the non-Orthodox population, the council claimed one thousand members in 1939; they engaged in a multitude of activities ranging from working with juvenile delinquents and for prison reform to sponsoring adult Jewish education and holiday celebrations. No other activity, however, received the breadth of commitments as did service for the foreign born.[9]

Adolf Hitler's rise to power in Germany and subsequent Nazi decrees throughout the 1930s created a dire need for overseas relief and resettlement assistance for the thousands of German Jews who fled to the United States. The exodus began in 1933-34; by the late 1930s the arrival of these refugees posed problems for Jewish communities across the land. In Columbus, however, the absorption of the immigrants was handled with relative ease.

Some of the persecuted came to Columbus under a quota set by the National Refugee Service in New York. Most, however, came because they had relatives in Ohio's capital — some who had been in Columbus for years (Otto Stern, Greta Forchheimer) and others for only a short time (Daniel Haas, Ilse Ebstein, Morris Paine). Usually relatives signed affidavits required by United States Immigration Service guaranteeing that the newcomers would not become public charges. Sometimes a compassionate Jew like Robert Levy, president of the Union Company, assumed responsibility for several families who were complete strangers.

Most of the refugees arrived in Columbus in 1938 and 1939, thus they were absorbed into the economy more quickly than those refugees who arrived during the depression. Physicians, such as Walter Boenheim, found the transition easy, while others blessed with vocational education in Germany, found jobs in their adopted land as dressmakers, secretaries, teachers, and merchants. Not all, of course, found such employment immediately; Ilse Ebstein scrubbed floors in New York for more than a year while her husband sought employment.

The catalyst for leaving Hitlerian Germany varied from one refugee to another. Some of the Jews who came to Columbus had lost their jobs by Nazi decrees; one was jailed for treason for a full year, another hid underground for ten months before crossing the border, and a third left after seeing the notice "Dogs and Jews not allowed in any theater or concert." Several escaped from concentration camps during the war, and a few — such as Helga Eisen — were taken out of Germany by their parents after the Nazis expelled them from public schools in 1937-38. One or two had parents who discerned the impending doom immediately:

> we left Germany in 1933. Goering made a speech on a Friday, after Hitler came to power, in which he indicated second-class status that Jews would have. I can remember my mother started to cry like at 10:00 in the morning. I can remember having Shabbos dinner at my grandma's house on Friday night. I can remember boarding a train

> for Paris later that same evening. My mother kept repeating over and over again, "I will not have my children grow up as second-class citizens." And that was that.[10]

These German Jewish refugees were assisted by the Council of Jewish Women in many ways. The council supplied refugees with adequate housing and furniture, helped them find jobs, and raised funds through weekly bingo games at Fort Hayes for scholarships to The Ohio State University and Schonthal Camp. Council women also sought out sponsors for refugees; convinced them to sign affidavits; and then made sure the sponsors assisted in meeting, settling, finding employment for, and periodically visiting, the newcomers. Also, the council sponsored Americanization classes at the Livingston Avenue School during the day and Janet Wasserstrom's night classes at Schonthal Center which prepared the refugees for citizenship. Regular contributions from the Gift and Memorial Scholarship Fund helped German Jews in Europe complete educations, while council members regularly filled coin banks at home to rescue Jewish children from Europe. The National Council of Jewish Women rated Columbus' involvement as "high or higher than any city of similar size in the country."[11]

Americanization classes attracted a large number of non-Jews, for though "few immigrants come to our city, those who do, all need our help." Even during the early thirties when scores of members could not afford dues and unemployment relief drives became common occurrences, Americanization classes continued to meet regularly, serving Jewish as well as non-Jewish immigrants. One observer described a class she visited:

> A beginners' class of twenty-six men and women, most of whom were Germans, Italians and Swiss, were having their first lesson in reading and writing the English language. They were for the most part older people; two of the women brought their children, who sat in the rear of the room while the mothers recited their lessons.[12]

As more refugees arrived in the late thirties, classes increased until, in 1939, five teachers offered classes four nights each week to ninety students. Teachers' interest was high and pupils were eager; one visitor commented that "with such ambitious immigrants and such patient teachers the immigrant problem is being solved."[13]

While the influx of refugees virtually ceased during the Second World War, a very slightly liberalized American immigration policy opened the country to some of the Jewish survivors immediately after the war. Unlike the healthy German Jews of the 1930s, these refugees arrived broken in both mind and body.

The council and the Jewish Welfare Federation accepted twelve families of "New Americans" in 1948; the following year they were asked to accept sixty families. The care of these Jews necessitated housing and employment; while the expansionist economy of the period somewhat eased employment problems, housing for the refugees could be obtained only with some difficulty. Many of the newcomers, for example, were housed at the 571 Shop on Rich Street, a bake and thrift store opened in 1940 by the council and jointly managed by numerous women's organizations. In addition to housing, this shop provided jobs for European refugees "who could not otherwise be absorbed into the economic life of the community."[14]

Another of the council's postwar activities was the "Save Our Survivors" (SOS) program. In addition to gathering food and clothing for the survivors, the SOS sensitized large numbers of Jews to the plight of displaced persons in Europe. Late in 1947 the council shipped 1,069 pounds of food and clothing, toys and games to Chateau de Maubuisson orphanage; by the end of that year Columbus Jews had collected and shipped a total of ten tons of materials.[15]

As displaced German Jewish immigrant families were adjusting to life in Columbus, established Jewish families were disrupted by the deaths of loved ones killed in action. At least twenty-five of the more than one hundred Columbus Jewish men

In addition to its Americanization efforts, the Council of Jewish Women pursued various community service activities. In this 1959 photo, from the left, Mrs. R. Louis Zalk, Mrs. Armand Abel, and Mrs. Saul Kolton are mending clothing for youngsters at the Columbus State School.

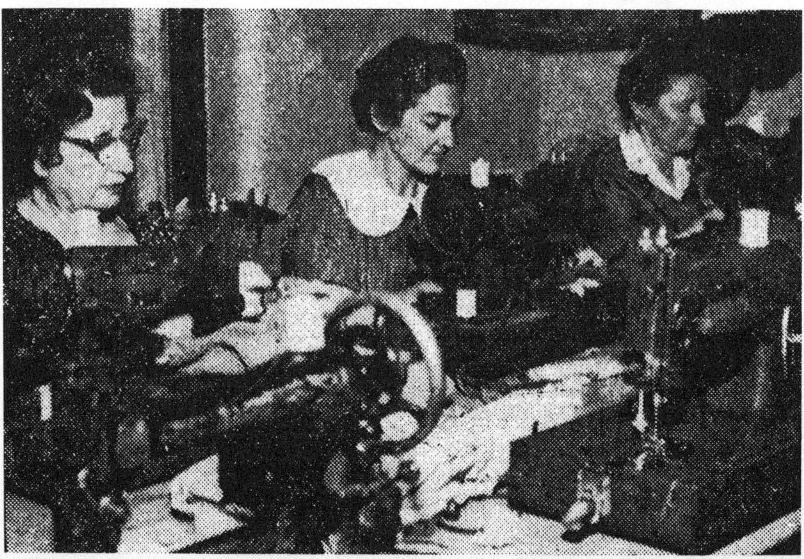

who served in the Armed Forces did not return home alive from World War II, a large number for such a small Jewish community. They included Millard F. Bornstein (B.A., The Ohio State University, 1940), who held the Distinguished Flying Cross; Benny Klayman, a bomber pilot who completed thirty-eight missions; and Maxwell J. Papurt (B.A., The Ohio State University, 1931). Dr. Papurt was captured when the Germans attempted to raid a fuel dump north of Naples. Concealing light and medium antiaircraft guns, Papurt held his fire until the Germans bombed the target. Then he opened up with the light guns, driving the planes up into the cross fire of the heavier guns. Twelve of the eighteen German planes crashed in flames. Major Papurt, a counterintelligence operator, was killed in an Allied air raid during his imprisonment

TABLE 56
WORLD WAR II JEWISH SERVICEMEN KILLED OR MISSING IN ACTION[16]

Name (Decorations)	Date Killed or Missing
Ralph Tarod	August 16, 1942
Sanford Sommsky	September 10, 1942
Sanford I. Lakin (Purple Heart)	September 24, 1942
Nathan Rinkov (Purple Heart)	April 26, 1943
Robert B. Blum	May 12, 1943
Morris Howitz (Purple Heart)	May 30, 1943
John E. David	August 2, 1943
Irvin Godofsky	November 19, 1943
Maurice K. Topson	December 20, 1943
Irvin B. Furman (Air Medal, Purple Heart)	June 4, 1944
Benjamin Klayman (Air Medal, Purple Heart)	June 14, 1944
Bernard Lieberman (Purple Heart)	June 11, 1944
Leon Shkolnik (Purple Heart)	September 12, 1944
Herbert V. Marx (Purple Heart)	November 29, 1944
Maxwell J. Papurt (Bronze Star Medal, Purple Heart)	November 29, 1944
William H. Wolstein (Purple Heart)	April 6, 1945
Louis B. Shiffman	April 20, 1945
Richard L. Greenberg (Purple Heart)	April 24, 1945
Robert P. Gitlin	May 17, 1945
Harold I. Shuman (Purple Heart)	June 2, 1945
Millard F. Bornstein (Distinguished Flying Cross)	December 15, 1945
Maurice Bloom	Not available
Frank Levin (Purple Heart)	Not available
Harold Levinson	Not available
Wolf Zapolan	Not available
Morris Perlis	Not available

by the German government.[17]

Capitol Post No. 122, the local Jewish War Veterans post, welcomed the soldiers returning from World War II. Established by twenty-nine World War I veterans in 1935, the post claimed one hundred and fifty-eight members by the spring of 1946. During its first decade, members of the post were occupied with discovering and reporting "un-American activities" and continuously raising money for the war effort. By 1942, with its first World War II veteran on hand, the post turned its attention to promoting the welfare and rehabilitation of Columbus Jewish soldiers and ex-GIs. The post sent magazines, holiday cards, a newsletter, and copies of the *Ohio Jewish Chronicle* to local men fighting overseas. It also helped returning soldiers make the transition from war to peace. A Women's Auxiliary, established in 1938, supported most of the Jewish War Veterans' activities, but gave more attention to disabled vets than to any other program.[18]

The Jewish community of Columbus took advantage of the respite between world wars to analyze and change its organizational approach. Throughout the 1930s, communities across the United States formed Jewish Community Councils to democratize both the structure as well as the functions of communal activities, to coordinate local activities, and to provide a united voice in defense of Jewish rights. All of these objectives seem to have been present in the formation of Columbus' Jewish Community Council (JCC).[19]

Columbus' council was conceived by Harry Rosen and Nathan Meyer late in 1938; Sig Weisskerz and Harry Bayer joined them during 1939 in bringing one hundred and ten persons to the Neil House to discuss establishing a council. By May of 1940, all but three of Columbus' forty-five Jewish organizations had voiced their approval of a Jewish Community Council, a constitution had been adopted, officers elected, constituent organizations instructed to elect one council delegate for each one hundred members, and the entire budget of the JCC provided by the UJF.[20]

Within its first two years of existence, the council's accomplishments were varied and significant. In the area of Jewish education the council sponsored a survey by Dr. Lee Levinger which demonstrated the strengths and weaknesses in Jewish educational programs, and resulted in the formation of the College of Jewish Studies in 1941. This was Columbus' first attempt at Jewish communal education for adults, and its first semester (January-March) included courses in Jewish history, Jewish ceremonies, contemporary Jewish movements, and a marriage and divorce course taught by six Columbus rabbis as well as Judge Clayton W. Rose. The second season (November 1941-March 1942) began even more ambitiously, as the faculty and courses doubled in size.[21] A second survey by Dr. Azriel Eisenberg of Cleveland evaluated the Columbus Hebrew School, and led directly to the decision to hire a full-time director for the school.

During 1940 and 1941, the council engaged in civil rights and public relations activities as well as the compilation of a community calendar of events. During the next few years, the organization's influence and prestige increased until, during 1944, it successfully challenged the election procedures of the United Jewish Fund. Arguing that neither the board nor the Allocations Committee fully represented the community, the council proposed — with UJF concurrence — election procedures which brought a "democratic process" and "safeguard" to the fund, according to Simon Lazarus. Flushed with success, early in 1946 the JCC announced a Ten Point Plan whereby the "entire community" through its delegates to the council would elect the UJF Board and its Allocation Committee as well as the boards of the JWF and Schonthal Center, and the budget and policy committees of the center. Although opposition prevented the passage of this plan, the council's proposal was not without impact. Only in the postwar period did communal agencies become the clear possession of the community, and not merely the tool of one sector of that community.[22]

Traditionally, while the federation provided a sounding board for both elements of the community, the Orthodox sector usually made minority reports. In the following dispute about care of the aged, Orthodox persistence won the day.

Although there were no serious discussions of how best to care for aged Jews in Jewish Welfare Federation's minutes until the 1940s, the federation provided assistance to the aged throughout the previous decade. Food, clothing, holiday supplies, medical assistance, and especially rent were the primary services provided, but this assistance accounted for a fraction of the federation's small budget.[23] In 1941, however, the concerns of the aged dominated an entire federation board meeting.

Early in the fall of that year, Mrs. Rose Schiff (1900-72) reported to the board that Jewish aged faced "deplorable conditions . . . some are living in homes with two and three in one room, no food . . . and sick as they can possibly be." Urging that the aged be given "medical care and attention because most of them are bed-ridden," Mrs. Schiff then documented her report by providing the names, addresses, and condition of fifteen Jews, aged fifty-five to eighty, cared for by the JWF. She and E. J. Schanfarber urged the board to consider institutional care funded by both individual residents and the community. Some of the affluent Reform members responded swiftly with two arguments. First, why should the community serve as a substitute family? Is it not the responsibility of the children and/or relatives to care for their aged? Second, why didn't Columbus Jews take greater advantage of the "Old Folks Homes" in Cleveland and Cincinnati? (At that time five aged Jews from Columbus resided in the Montefiore Home in Cleveland.) More precisely, the financially comfortable members of the community, who either provided institutional care for their elderly parents or could afford to support them locally, saw no need to subsidize the parents of those in the community unable to do the same. (The Home for the Jewish Aged in Cincinnati charged a $1,000 admission fee and $25 per month.) Further, as one dowager indelicately put it, her mother was not going to live with the "kosher riff-raff of the community." Although he felt that supporting a home would entail a "destructive expense," E. J. Schanfarber nevertheless urged the establishment of a committee to study three alternatives: institution, placement, or subsidy. All thirty-three persons present refused to serve on the committee; so Schanfarber appointed Dr. Elijah Gordon as chairman.[24]

Seven weeks later Dr. Gordon reported to the JWF Board that though the "general outlook of all these cases is much more acute" than indicated in his report, he didn't think a home was necessary. This suggestion received widespread support from the Reform members who proposed that extra funds should be raised and allocated to provide the Jewish aged with "the bare necessities." E. J. Schanfarber agreed, noting a home would be "a silly thing," because they had no means to raise even the extra $1,500 for minimal needs of the elderly. Yet there remained many mental cases that needed attention, and the consensus of the board was to accept Schanfarber's recommendation that the committee investigate the problem further. The sharp reaction of the Orthodox members is summed up best by an interchange between a prominent Orthodox leader and Schanfarber:

> Mr. Goldberg asked how long the Federation had been in existence.
> Mr. Schanfarber replied that the Federation has been in existence about thirty-five or forty years.
> Miss Sugarman remarked that the Federation started in 1903.
> Mr. Goldberg asked how long the Federation has been interested in care for the aged.
> Mr. Schanfarber replied that the Federation has been interested for thirty-eight years.
> Mr. Goldberg remarked that still nothing has been done.[25]

The committee investigated twenty-four cases of the Jewish aged living alone or with other aged persons during November of 1941, and found ten cases in "desperate need" while the fourteen cases in Table 57 were "requiring no assistance."

TABLE 57
PER CAPITA MONTHLY INCOME OF AGED JEWS IN 1941

Name	Persons	Family Asst.	City Relief	Old Age Pension	JWF	Ezras Noshim	Per Capita
Cruce	1	$ 8.67	—	—	—	$ 5.00	$13.67
Elkind	2	34.67	—	—	$51.00	10.00	47.83
Gordon	1	20.00	—	—	—	4.00	24.00
Harmon	3	—	—	$60.00	25.00	—	28.33
Kesselman	1	40.00	—	—	—	—	40.00
Parish	2	—	$12.00	—	36.25	8.00	28.12
Tansky	1	3.00	—	—	23.58	—	26.58
Weiner	2	—	—	—	26.00	—	13.00
Young	1	31.33	—	—	—	12.00	43.33

SOURCE: "Reports of Cases Investigated in Reference to Home for the Aged and Infirm," December 1, 1941.

The federation continued to provide assistance to the aged throughout the 1940s, but serious discussions about a home for the aged did not resume until 1947 and 1948. When the JWF asked Robert Mellman to chair a committee to undertake another survey, non-Orthodox members repeated the same arguments against a home. In the spring of 1948 so little support existed for a home that Mellman could only report, on behalf of the Committee for the Care of the Aged, that the federation would attempt to work out better arrangements with the Montefiore and the Orthodox homes in Cleveland.[26]

Concomitant with this renewed apathy, concerned members of the Orthodox community had established a committee to discuss a home for the aged in 1947. Two years later the Jewish Home for the Aged Society held their first fund-raising dinner, and in July of 1951 they purchased a house at 115 Woodland Avenue for $13,000 in cash and established a fourteen-bed Home for Aged Jews. Opened in the fall of 1952 with three residents, the home had eleven residents with an average age over eighty by the end of 1953 as well as a lengthy waiting list. Although operated according to Orthodox regulations and thus initially shunned by the Reform community, within two years the United Jewish Fund recognized that the home "was performing a needed service for Columbus and agreed to support it." Almost immediately the Woodland Home became inadequate for the community's needs. A 1959 survey enumerated more than eleven hundred Columbus Jews over sixty-five years of age, and, with the completion of the new fifty-bed, $800,000 Heritage House on College Avenue in 1961, care for the aged dominated the consciousness of Columbus Jewry.[27]

Possibly because the Jewish aged were not as visible as the

The Jewish Home for the Aged Society purchased this home at 115 Woodland Avenue in 1951.

Jewish university students, and because of the traditional importance of education, it was not difficult to garner community support for the establishment of a Hillel Foundation at The Ohio State University.[28] E. J. Schanfarber, a member of the original National Hillel Commission and the founder of the Hillel Advisory Board, led the campaign. In 1925 the national B'nai B'rith established the country's third foundation which was directed by Rabbi Lee and Elma Levinger.

Lee Levinger (1890-1966) brought abundant academic training and practical experience to Hillel. After receiving ordination in 1914 at Hebrew Union College and a doctorate at the University of Pennsylvania in 1925, Levinger held rabbinical positions in Paducah, Kentucky, from 1913 to 1918; in Evansville, Indiana, from 1919 to 1920; and in Wilmington, Delaware, from 1922 to 1925. Rabbi Levinger had also served as the executive director of the New York City YMHA from 1920 to 1922, and as an army chaplain during World War I. Out of his war experience came Levinger's book, *A Jewish Chaplain in France;* while his doctoral dissertation

The Hillel Players presented "He Who Gets Slapped" in May of 1927.

appeared as *Anti-Semitism in the United States: Its History and Causes.*[29]

In its initial years, and for several decades, Hillel competed with fraternities and sororities for Jewish students' time. Rabbi Levinger estimated in 1927 that at least one third of seven hundred Jewish students at The Ohio State University were Greeks, and a large reservoir of unaffiliated students still remained. As one active Hillel member recalls from those days:

> At that time the pressure of fraternities and sororities was very great and not all of the students were invited nor were they financially able to be part of the fraternity life which was very active on campus. The students who could not get into the fraternities felt sort of left out hearing about the many campus activities and the many social affairs held at the fraternity houses. [Hillel] became an active Jewish source of activities . . . and gradually became as popular as many of the fraternities.[30]

While social activities dominated the programs as "the life of the foundation" for at least forty years, the Levingers initiated, and often led, a wide variety of educational, cultural, and religious activities. Traditional services on Friday evening and non-traditional worship on Sunday mornings served a sizeable group. The Open Forum brought distinguished musicians, rabbis, and academicians to campus while Rabbi Levinger regularly offered courses in Hebrew, Jewish philosophy, and Jewish history.

Hillel's debating team competed in a midwestern league,[31] many student Zionist groups found a warm welcome at the foundation, and the Hillel Players established themselves as one of the community's outstanding drama groups. Performing everything from Chekhov, Pirandello, Shakespeare, O'Neill, Wilder, Ansky and Odets to Elma Levinger's plays, the players frequently toured campuses and Jewish centers in the midwest.[32]

Rabbi Levinger stated that "Hillel alone has been able to draw the fraternities and sororities and unaffiliated together in any measure or to bridge the gaps which jealousy and competition have [created] between the various fraternities and sororities themselves." There is, however, no evidence to suggest that the program at the Hillel Foundation attracted the Greeks during the forty years or so of fraternity and sorority predominance on campus. Our survey of more than sixty-two alumnae of The Ohio State University's first Jewish sorority, Sigma Delta Tau, revealed almost no interest in Hillel's Jewish programs and even less desire to attend its social functions. As a 1942 female graduate explained, "Hillel was just the wrong thing to do socially," and there is no evidence of much greater enthusiasm among men.[33]

As a member of the Hillel Players in the late 1930s, Paul Lipson acted, directed, and – as president of the Broom and Pan – cleaned up the stage. On Broadway Lipson has gained fame primarily in musical comedies. Here Lipson (left) was pictured with classmate Rabbi Harry Kaplan and Mrs. Kaplan.

While Hillel as an institution might have been unattractive to the Greeks, a wide spectrum of Jewish students were drawn to Lee and Elma Levinger. Elma, particularly, is recalled — indeed, generally romanticized — by Columbus Jews, not as a super-mother who solved Jewish students' problems with bowls of steaming chicken soup, but as a woman who made valuable contributions outside her home, and gained national recognition.

The daughter of a second generation Illinois family, Elma Ehrlich (1887-1958) left high school upon the death of her father in 1905 to teach in rural schools in Illinois and Iowa. Two years later she attended the University of Chicago and subsequently spent one year as director of the Junior Drama League of Chicago. As a result of a play she wrote, Elma received a scholarship to Radcliffe College's prestigious drama workshop, Baker's 47, from 1911 to 1912. After serving as the editor of the *Jewish Child* for one year, Elma became the director of the entertainment department of the New York Bureau of Jewish Education from 1913 to 1915.

Elma first met Lee Levinger at the University of Chicago; in 1916 she married him. Almost all her nationally recognized novels, stories, and dramas concerned Jewish persons and events. Among her many awards were national prizes from the Drama League of America for *Jephtha's Daughter* in 1919 and *Return of the Prodigal* in 1921; a national Jewish book award and a $2,000 prize for her most impressive novel, *Grapes of Canaan,* in 1931; and several more national Jewish literary awards. The honors culminated in 1957 when the Jewish Book Council of America recognized her pioneering work and cumulative contributions to Jewish juvenile literature. The council noted that an entire generation of Jews grew up on her writing, that her biography of Galileo appeared in more than a dozen languages, and that with more than thirty books to her credit she was America's most prolific and versatile Jewish authoress.[34]

A prolific writer of historical fiction, Mrs. Levinger studied the available sources of each period she reconstructed and offered rich history without subordinating imaginative literature.[35] Elma's plays, stories and novels present a broad and detailed portrait of the American Jewish experience in particular, and Jewish social history in general. Her forte was creating Jewish characters who raised issues of some urgency in the American Jewish community: intra-Jewish hostility exhibited by German Jews and Russian Jews, Zionists and non-Zionists, Orthodox and Reform Jews; conflict between generations; influences which made "What would the Gentiles say?" the impetus for Jewish behavior; social anti-Semitism experienced by a Jewish girl at a Thanksgiving fraternity dance; and congregational anonymity exemplified by the rabbi who did not recognize one of the seventy-three persons in his confirmation class when they met on the street after Sabbath School.[36]

More than any other subject, Mrs. Levinger devoted herself to illuminating the role women have played in Jewish history. Her biographies of biblical women such as Deborah and Esther, and modern figures like Sophie Loeb — the former president of the New York State Child Welfare Board and an extraordinarily unselfish champion of the underprivileged in America — provided models of dedicated Jewish women to both juveniles and adults. Textbooks for congregational schools, coauthored with her husband, demonstrated extreme sensitivity to woman's role in the Jewish historical experience.[37]

During the fifteen years she lived in Columbus, Mrs. Levinger left an indelible imprint on the community through her lectures in the (Hadassah) Women's Institute for Jewish Studies and courses sponsored by the Council of Jewish Women; through storytelling to children; through organizing, directing, and writing dramas for the Hillel Players; and through the creative writing classes she taught at the penitentiary. Her Urban League work brought together thirty of Columbus' most illustrious intellectuals in the league's Book Evaluation Group.[38]

Most of those who remember Elma speak of her as a brilliant conversationalist, who loved language, told stories with great skill, and enjoyed being the center of sparkling conversation. No less remembered was her ability to listen, and as a result to draw out shy, taciturn people. Mrs. Levinger became especially well known as a speaker for Hadassah, regularly touring midwestern Jewish communities; also she was constantly sought as a lecturer by Zionist organizations in Columbus. In October of 1931, four hundred persons listened to Elma's description of her five-month trip to Palestine sponsored by Columbus' Hadassah organization.[39]

In addition to delivering lectures with great frequency, writing constantly until late in the evening, running a house with seven people on a very small budget and bringing up children, Mrs. Levinger frequently entertained university students. As her daughter, Leah, recalls:

> . . . suddenly an hour and a half or so before she was to appear at a certain place she would exclaim in horror "Oh my God, I have to be at such a place tonight!" and would then race upstairs and go to her card file where on three by five cards she would neatly type the outline of the speech. While she was doing this I would be asked to lay out the proper clothes for her to wear and my brother would get the car ready. She would then somehow manage to shower, comb her hair (fortunately it was naturally curly and merely wetting it and running the comb through made her look like most women when they come from the beauty parlor) and then have Sam drive her over

> to the meeting five minutes before it was due to start.
>
> In the same way her entertaining for the students of Ohio State University often would start ten minutes after the first guest arrived when she would remember the group was coming and leave her typewriter and put on different clothes and somehow have a meal thrown together.[40]

Tragedy and fulfillment commingled in Elma Levinger's life. Joseph, her second son, died in infancy while Lee served overseas as a chaplain. Samuel, her first born, brought the most joy and sorrow to her life, for Elma was closer to him than to the other children. Emphatic in support of their children's independence, Lee and Elma encouraged them to be political activists. Leah was arrested in Cleveland, because she was one of what the *Cleveland Plain Dealer* described as "radical students illegally congregating on a sidewalk," or picketing, during the film "Red Salute."[41] A poet, singer, avid reader, and radical activist, Sam hitchhiked through the country. He, too, was jailed for a time, once in Kentucky at the Harlan mines and later while trying to organize unemployed coal miners in Cambridge, Ohio. When Sam chose to leave The Ohio State University and fight in the International Brigade for the Loyalist forces of the Spanish Republic, Lee's ardent pacifism and Elma's fondness for him were severely tested. Sam died in Spain in September of 1937, at the age of twenty.[42]

In October of 1934 Hillel moved to 46 East Sixteenth Avenue and the following year Rabbi Harry Kaplan (1901-69) began thirty years of devoted leadership at the foundation. Born and raised in Minneapolis (A.B., 1923, University of Minnesota), Kaplan benefited from both a traditional Talmud Torah education as well as several years of work in settlement houses. When he left Pittsfield, Massachusetts, where he had served for eight years, an editorial noted that he stood as

> the foremost intellectual leader among the clergy of Pittsfield and his efforts to inculcate Pittsfield at large with his own large ideals of collective justice and social problems have been particularly memorable. Motivated by deep social instincts which he freely expressed, he has led a great many people, in and outside his faith and congregation, toward a more realistic and thoughtful attitude on the many issues that beset the world.[43]

From the beginning of his campus career, Kaplan realized the difficulties inherent in attempting to attract college students to a religious institution:

> Young people, particularly in the great coeducational centers of American education, are motivated by a set of interests and drives

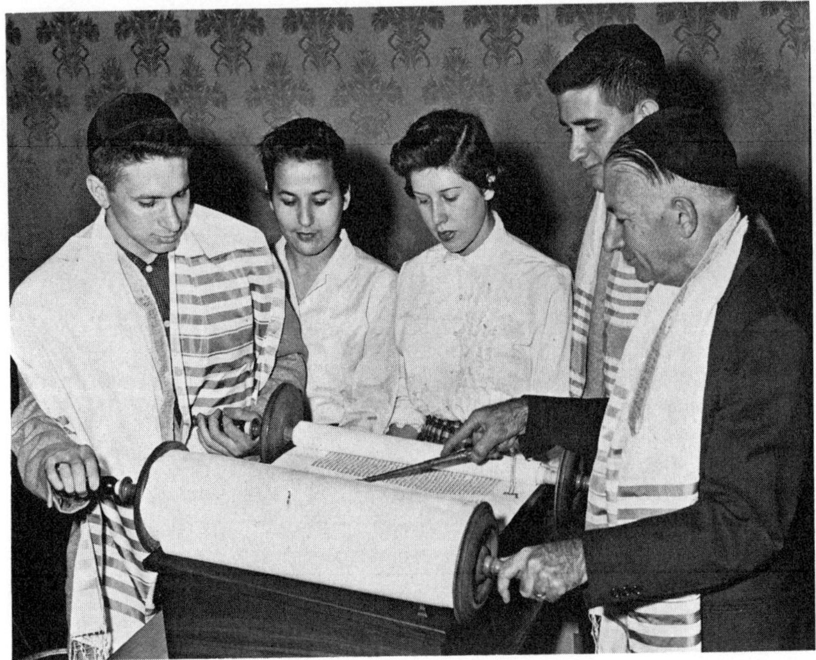

Rabbi Kaplan showing the sefer Torah *(Hebrew Pentateuchal Scrolls) to four Hillel members.*

> which leave little time either for the formal expression of religion or for the spiritual disciplines of meditation, prayer, introspection and reflection.

His response — and that of Hillel Foundations everywhere to those decades — was to "not restrict programs to the purely religious Sabbath services and holiday celebrations" but to "attempt to meet the student on the cultural and social plane as well." Therefore, Rabbi Kaplan could note that:

> Through Hebrew language and Judaica classes, forums, debates, philanthropy drives and interfaith programs, dramatic productions, dances, smokers, personal counseling, lectures and study groups, the Hillel program reaches out as a dynamic force for Jewish living in the midst of a busy campus Jewish life[44]

With the spread of Nazi activity throughout America and a visible increase in anti-Semitism, Rabbi Kaplan was bombarded by requests from the local Advisory Board and the National Anti-Defamation League of the B'nai B'rith to expand Hillel's interfaith programs. "In a world where misrepresentation of the

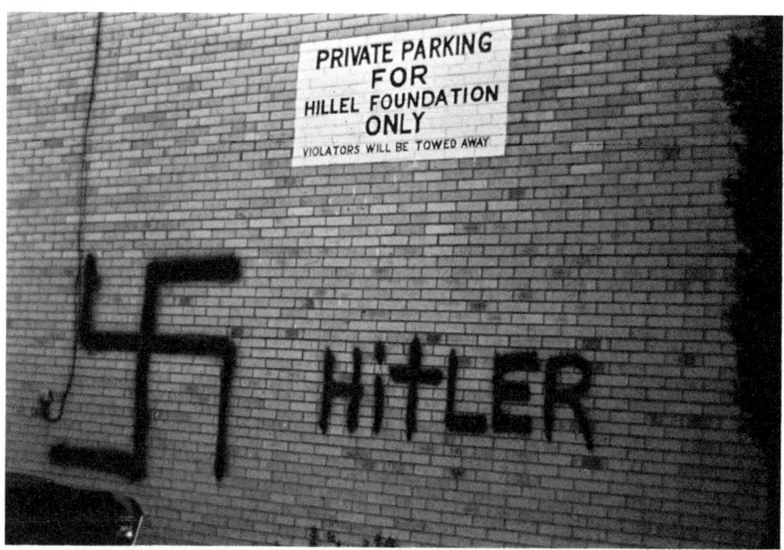

Acts of anti-Semitism against individual Columbus Jews have steadily decreased, although from time to time there have been attacks on Jews and Judaism as a whole like this swastika painted on the Hillel building in October of 1970.

Jew is growing, and where anti-Jewish moves are multiplying, this role cannot be too strongly emphasized," he noted. At the same time the board cautioned Jewish students "Not to be too eager to rush into leadership in undue numbers but rather to work quietly and with dignity in the ranks," for they "represent the Jewish group on campus."[45]

Rabbi Kaplan and the Jewish students responded in various ways: by keeping a careful watch on potential anti-Semitic groups and individuals on campus who distributed a notorious anti-Semitic tract, *The Protocols of the Elders of Zion;* by continuing active involvement with Christian clergymen and organizations initiated by the Levingers; and by communicating with university officials on a variety of levels. The most sensitive situation concerned the 1936 Summer Olympics in Berlin, because the Nazis invited prominent American universities to send selected seniors as guests of the German Reich. The university's athletic department enthusiastically endorsed the project, and Rabbi Kaplan sadly noted that "their ethical sensitivity is not strong enough to offset the personal desire for travel and new experience." In protest he convinced Jewish students on Olympic Games social and athletic committees to boycott the meetings and subsequent events.[46]

In 1937 on one of the few occasions that Jewish fraternities and sororities cooperated with Hillel students, Rabbi Kaplan organized the Refugee Relief Campaign. Student groups raised funds to rescue Jewish students from Europe and then sponsor them at the university. In return for tuition and scholarships, as well as room and board at a fraternity or sorority, the students devoted several hours each week to foreign language tutoring and chores at the Hillel Foundation. As a result of this cooperative effort, "scores of brilliant young men and young women were rescued from Hitler's Europe and brought to Ohio State to

Holding blood drives was only one of many war-related activities conducted by Hillel women.

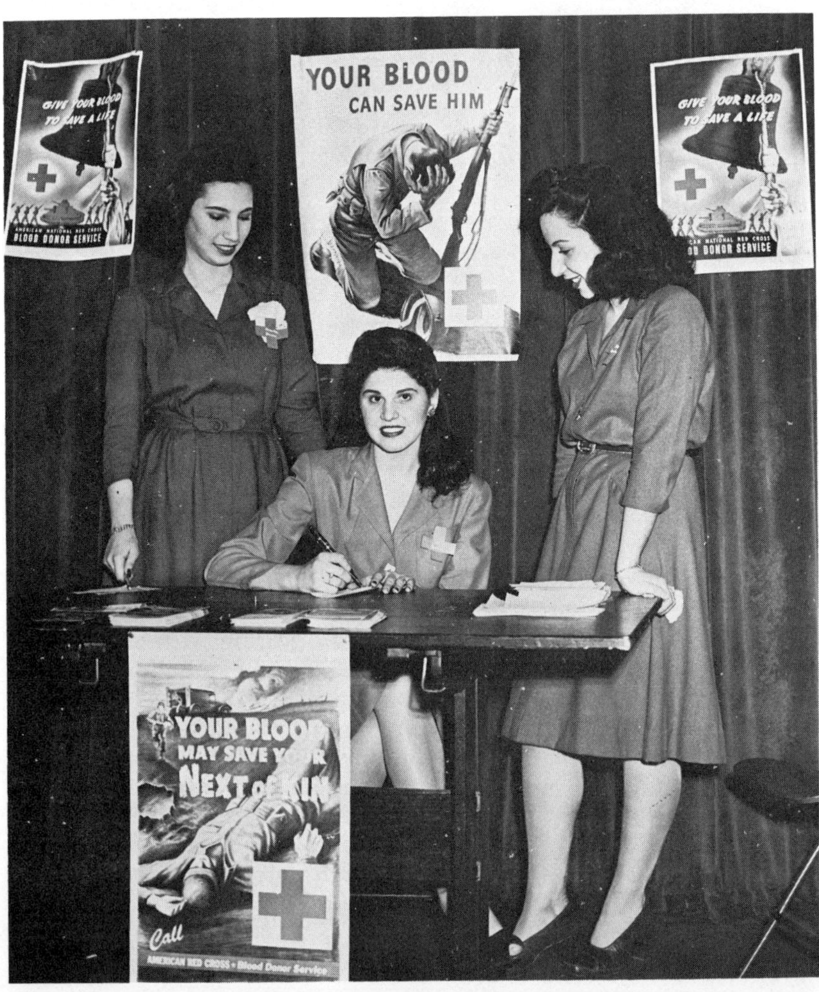

continue and complete their educations."[47]

The forties brought a tremendous surge of war-related activity to the foundation. Hillel was designated as the year-round center for Jewish servicemen from more than six central Ohio colleges and universities. The students not only cooked and baked; held war service carnivals, worship services, Passover *seders* and brunches; and promoted War Stamp and War Bond sales; but they initiated and sustained a program of correspondence with Ohio Jewish servicemen. All of this activity was carried out by women; "our committee members are now all young ladies" and the Hillel Players had "an all woman cast." Rabbi Kaplan himself, during the war years, had even greater responsibilities, as he explained in a letter to the fraternity leaders:

> The present war crisis and the resulting uncertainty have undoubtedly affected many of your boys. There will be problems and I will be eager to be of assistance, constantly on duty, and eager to offer a counseling service to anyone who is interested.[48]

For two decades after the war, Kaplan spoke and wrote regularly about college students. An idealist for the most part, the rabbi expressed concern that religion function as a guarantor of ethical and moral values, and took an uncompromising stand against the sexual revolution. While arguing throughout the postwar years that absolutes existed, Kaplan employed his ideals in activating students and guiding the community through troubled times.[49]

Columbus Jewish organizations, in the second quarter of the twentieth century, passed clearly into a new stage. The activities of several older groups greatly expanded in quality and in quantity in response to the crises of the thirties and forties. Several new organizations also sought to contribute to the cultural, social, and educational life of the community as well as to enhance the dignity of their members. Three of the primary organizations of these years, the Jewish Center, Heritage House, and the Hillel Foundation, made even more significant contributions to Columbus Jewry in the third quarter of the twentieth century.

NOTES FOR CHAPTER 15

1. *OJC*, May 18, June 8, 1928, March 22, April 5, May 3 and 10, 1929, March 21, 1930, April 3, 1931, April 5, 1935, March 22, 1946, March 26, 1948; "Camp Schonthal, 1932" in Ledgers and Photographs (1927-40), Miscellaneous, Box 5, Columbus Jewish Center Papers.

2. Dr. Louis Mark, a practicing physician in Columbus since the early 1920s, not only gained a reputation as an international chest and tuberculosis specialist but one of America's leading contract bridge players. He also became the owner and medical director of the Rocky Glen Sanatorium at McConnelsville, Ohio, the largest privately owned institution of its kind in the United States. See *OJC*, February 26 and March 5, 1954.

3. *OJC*, January 18, March 1, May 24, 1929, November 6, 1931, April 4, December 30, 1932; Annual Meeting, Minutes, Schonthal Center, May 8, 1941; Report of Schonthal Center Activity, May 8, 1941; Dr. Louis Mark to Rose Sugarman, correspondence, August 21, 1924, in Schonthal Center (1920-40), Miscellaneous Reports, Box 1, Columbus Jewish Center Papers.

4. Annual Meeting, Minutes, Schonthal Center, May 8, 1941 (E. J. Schanfarber), ibid.

5. Miss Sugarman, a brilliant executive and administrator born and educated in Atlanta, engendered either strong feelings of love or hate among hundreds of Columbus Jews who worked intimately with her. Her presence was everywhere; she was executive secretary of the JWF for thirty-two years, executive secretary of the Schonthal Center for thirty years, executive director of the JWF for twenty-nine years, director of the Schonthal Camp for twenty-one years, and secretary of the Jewish Infants Home for ten years. See *OJC*, August 8, 1952; interviews with Sylvia Schecter and Morris Skop; Marvin M. Sugarman to Marc Lee Raphael, correspondence, March 10, 1976. Miss Sugarman, at the age of fifty-eight, received her B.S. degree from The Ohio State University; *Atlanta Constitution*, June 7, 1961, and Alumni Information Office, The Ohio State University.

6. Dr. Elijah Joseph Gordon came to the United States from Lithuania at the age of five; after a brief stay in Parkersburg, West Virginia, his family journeyed to Columbus during the panic of '93. A graduate of Capital University (1905) and The Ohio State University College of Medicine (1909), Dr. Gordon taught anatomy and medicine at the university until his retirement, served as a major in the Medical Corps and a surgeon in the 134th Field Artillery, 37th Division, received national attention for his treatment of aplastic anemia, and achieved a distinguished reputation within the Jewish community. He served as the first president of the Jewish Community Council, president of the Schonthal Center Board (1930-46), president of the Hillel Foundation Board (1930-32), a long-time trustee at Temple Israel, and honorary president of the new Jewish Center. See OJC, November 12, 1948, October 13, 1961, September 6, 1963; OSJ, November 27, 1929; *WWAJ*, 1926, Volume 1, pp. 252-53; ibid., Volume 3, 1938-39, pp. 373-74; *Biographical Encyclopedia of American Jews*, p. 190.

7. Annual Meeting, Schonthal Center, October 11, 1945 [Minutes]; Schonthal Center Annual Meeting, Minutes, December 5, 1946; Board Meeting, Schonthal Center, October 16, 1941, in Columbus Jewish Center Papers.

8. Annual Report, January 1 — December 31, 1947 [Schonthal Center]; Annual Report, Schonthal Center, October 1, 1938 — October 1, 1939 in ibid. See also Oscar I. Janowsky, *The JWB Survey* (New York, 1948).

9. National Council of Jewish Women, Columbus Section Papers, Boxes 1-12, OHS.

10. Interview with Terry Gottfried Robinson (Brandeis University National Women's Committee Living History Series; copy of tape at OHS.) The preceding paragraphs are based upon sixteen survey questionnaires, on file at the OHS, returned by Jewish refugees from Central Europe. See also interviews with Bertha Krausz and Aurelia Stern at Brandeis University.

11. *OJC,* December 16, 1938, January 13, March 10, 1939; Box 3, Folders 11, 12, and 14 of CJW Papers. See also Harold Field, *The Refugee in the United States* (New York, 1938).

12. Box 2, Folders 7-10, Box 3, Folders 9 and 11-12 in ibid.; *OJC,* December 4, 1935.

13. *Record Book 1939,* Council of Jewish Women Americanization and Citizenship Classes, Hermine Schonthal Center in Columbus Jewish Center Papers; *OJC,* December 4, 1935.

14. *OJC,* July 19 and September 20, 1940, February 28, 1941.

15. *OJC,* October 3, November 7 and 28, 1947, November 19, 1948, November 10, 1950.

16. Reconstructed from Jewish War Veterans Papers, and *OJC.* For the names of Columbus Jewish soldiers wounded or decorated in World War II, see *American Jews in World War II,* Volume II (New York, 1947) and "List of Jewish servicemen [50] from Columbus wounded in action, cited for bravery, etc. [May 1945]," National Jewish Welfare Board, Item 3083.

17. Grave Registration Cards, OHS; Miscellaneous press releases; "Official statement of the military service and death of Maxwell J. Papurt, Major, Counter-Intelligence Corps, June 18, 1948"; Robert H. Dunlop to Mrs. Maxine C. Papurt, correspondence, December 16 and 22, 1944, and O. C. Doering, Jr. to Mrs. Maxine C. Papurt, correspondence, July 18, 1945, in possession of Maxine Papurt; typescript of Cecil Brown broadcast, Mutual Broadcasting System, December 25, 1944, in Jewish War Veterans Papers; Maxine Papurt to Marc Lee Raphael, telephone conversation, February 6, 1976.

18. Jewish War Veterans Papers, Capitol Post No. 122, OHS. "A List of Jewish people in service from Columbus, August 1, 1945," contains 783 names; see National Jewish Welfare Board, Item 1560.

19. "Community Councils — Their Organization and Objectives." Council of Jewish Federations and Welfare Funds, January 9, 1938, American Jewish Historical Society (Waltham, Massachusetts).

20. *OJC,* February 9 and 16, April 26, May 10, 1940; Quarterly Meeting, Schonthal Center, Minutes, June 11, 1946; "Constitution of the Jewish Community Council of Columbus," Revised, October 24, 1946, Columbus Jewish Center Papers.

21. *OJC,* May 31, November 29, December 6, 1940, July 4, 1941; "College of Adult Jewish Studies" (Brochure) January 15, 1941; "College of Jewish Studies" (Brochure) October 29, 1941, in ibid.

22. *OJC,* June 20, 1941, September 29, 1944, March 22, 1946.

TABLE 58
JEWISH COMMUNITY COUNCIL PRESIDENTS

1940-42	Elijah J. Gordon	1946-47	Justin Sillman
1942-45	Harry Gilbert	1947-49	Fred Yenkin
1945-46	Albert Schiff	1949-50	Robert Mellman

23. *OJC,* November 16, 1934.

24. Jewish Welfare Federation Board Meeting, September 11, 1941, in Jewish Welfare Federation Papers.

25. JWF Board Meeting, October 30, 1941, in ibid.

26. Minutes of the Meeting of the Jewish Welfare Federation, October 28, 1948; Quarterly Meeting of the JWF, May 19, 1949; *OJC,* July 28, 1947, in ibid.

27. *OJC,* November 17, 1950, July 13 and 27, November 30, 1951, March 21, August 29, November 28, 1952, January 16, 1953, February 26, June 25, 1954, July 3, November 13 and 20, December 4 and 25, 1959, January 1, June 17, November 4, 1960, June 30, November 10, 1961; interview with Sylvia Schecter; Mrs. Rachel Finkelstein (1876-1961) served as the first president of the JHA Society, and Louis Mellman (1871-1954) the chairman of the building committee. For a detailed discussion of the origins of the Home for the Aged, see interview with Maurice Bernstein.

28. *OJC,* November 6, 1925. The original Hillel House stood at 96 East 18th Avenue.

29. *WWAJ,* 1928, 2nd edition, p. 412; ibid., Volume 3, p. 627; "The Causes of Anti-Semitism in the United States," Ph.D. thesis, University of Pennsylvania, 1925. Other significant works by Levinger include *Mr. Smith, Meet Mr. Cohen* (coauthor) (New York, 1940), *History of the Jews in the United States* (New York, 1930), and *The Story of the Jew* (coauthor) (New York, 1929).

30. The Ohio State University B'nai B'rith Hillel Foundation Papers, "Report: September 1926 — February 1927," Box 27, Folder 3, OHS; interview with Morris Skop.

31. Even before Rabbi Levinger arrived and the Hillel Foundation was established, campus Jewish organizations sponsored debates. Typical was the Northwestern Menorah Society vs. The Ohio State University Menorah Society Debate at the Seneca Ball Room on Saturday evening May 2, 1925. With attorney Henry Gumble as chairman, Ben Braunstein, Anne Goldman and Roy Stone (all of Columbus) argued in the affirmative: "Resolved, that Zionism offers the best possible solution to the preservation of the Jewish race." Program, Box 4, Folder 13, ibid. See also *OJC,* December 14, 1928, and February 6, 1931.

32. On the Hillel Players, who celebrated their thirty-fourth season in 1959 and whose patrons read like a "Who's Who" of Columbus Jewry, see

OJC, March 5, 1926, May 20, 1927, January 11, 1929, February 22, 1946; Box 17 (Folder 12) Box 57 (Folders 2, 5, 6, 21, 22, 28, 29, and 30) Box 125 (Folder 1) in Hillel Papers; "Hillel Players Present Hotel Universe," Playbill, February 24-25, 1932, in "Student Organizations — Hillel Players," University Archives, The Ohio State University.

The two most distinguished alumni of the Hillel Players are Jerome Lawrence (née Schwartz, B.A., Journalism, 1937), coauthor of *Inherit the Wind* and *Auntie Mame* and the winner of two first prizes in Hillel playwriting contests, and Paul Lipson, a Broadway actor of distinction, who not only directed and acted in several plays but also cleaned up the stage after the performances in his role as Hillel caretaker.

33. "Report: September 1927 — March 1928," and "Report: September 1925 — March 1930," Box 27, Folder 3 in Hillel Papers; *OJC*, December 16, 1927; "Sorority and Fraternity Survey of The Ohio State University Graduates," Columbus Jewish History Project. One striking exception was the first president of the Hillel Foundation, Alex "Shon" Klein, a member of the ZBT fraternity and, as a center on the football team, both a *New York Times* All-American Honorable Mention recipient and a member of the Associated Press All-Western Conference Second Team. See *OJC*, December 18, 1925, May 21, September 24, 1926; Bernard Postal et al., *Encyclopedia of Jews in Sports* (New York, 1965), p. 253; Dr. Alexander W. Klein to Marc Lee Raphael, correspondence, [December 25, 1975] and [May 20, 1976].

34. *Women of Ohio: A Record of Their Achievements in the History of the State*, Ruth Neely, editor in chief, Volume II (S.J. Clarke Publication Company, n.d.), p. 789; *American Jews: Their Lives and Achievements*, Volume II (New York, 1958), p. 757; *WWAJ*, 1938-39, Volume 3, p. 627; *WWAJ*, 1938, 2nd edition, p. 412; *OJC*, September 16, 1927, April 2, 1954; *Jewish Book Annual*, Volume 15 (5718: 1957-58); *AJYB*, Volume 60 (1959), p. 384; *Cumulative Book Index*, 1928-32, p. 1217; *Cumulative Book Index*, 1933-37, p. 1663; interview with Leah Levinger. For an enthusiastic review of *Grapes of Canaan* by a prominent Columbus minister, Rev. M. H. Lichliter of the First Congregational Church, see *OJC*, January 8, 1932. For two mostly negative critiques, see *Saturday Review*, December 19, 1931, p. 40 and *New York Times Book Review*, September 13, 1931, p. 7.

35. At the age of sixty-eight, while seriously ill, Elma complained to an old Columbus friend not only of her "frequent lamentation that not enough books are written to edify and educate Jewish children," but that her short letter is to be excused for "I'm rather busy reading up for a new book's background." Elma Ehrlich Levinger to Mildred Tarshish, correspondence, October 9, 1955, in possession of Mildred Tarshish.

36. In addition to *Grapes of Canaan* (Stratford, 1931) and its sequel, *Bread for Beauty* (London, 1935), a full year's cycle of stories in the *Ohio Jewish Chronicle* would reveal all these themes. See, for example, "A Pot of Honey — A Story for Rosh Hashanah" (September 10, 1926), "The 10th Man — A Folk Tale for Yom Kippur" (September 17, 1926), "A Succah for Two" (October 1, 1926), "Mothballs — A Thanksgiving Story" (November 19, 1926), "A Little Boy from Modin — A Chanukah Story" (November 26, 1926), "Dorothy Dances — A Story for Purim" (March 11, 1927), "Five Flights Up — A Story for Passover" (April 15, 1927), "A Jewish Child — A

Shavuoth Story" (June 10, 1927), "My Country 'Tis of Thee — A Story for the Fourth of July" (July 1, 1927).

37. See especially *Great Jewish Women* (New York, 1940), *Folk and Faith – The Confirmant's Guide Book* (New York, 1942), *The Story of the Jew* (New York, 1929), *Albert Einstein* (New York, 1949), and "The Golden Staff: A Succoth Operetta" (Cincinnati, 1923).

38. *OJC,* January 13, 1927, January 10, 1930, February 1, 1935, July 29, 1938; Mary T. Zimmerman to Marc Lee Raphael, correspondence, June 17, 1974; interview with Leah Levinger.

39. *OJC,* February 6 and October 2, 1931; interview with Leah Levinger; Nimrod B. Allen to Marc Lee Raphael, telephone conversation, December 9, 1975; interviews with Robert Mellman, Bertha Seff, Mildred Tarshish, and Samuel Edelman.

40. Interview with Leah Levinger.

41. For a detailed summary and critique of "Red Salute," an anti-pacifist and anti-student film, see *NYT,* September 30, 1935, p. 3.

42. *OSJ,* April 30, 1932; interview with Leah Levinger; *Cleveland Press,* January 6, 1936; *Cleveland Plain Dealer,* January 5, 1936; Murray Kempton, *Part of Our Time: Some Ruins and Monuments of the Thirties* (New York, 1955), pp. 314-17; *OSJ,* September 17, 1936 ("Letter to the Editor" from Samuel Levinger) and October 5, 1937. Samuel was fatally wounded September 5 when the Abraham Lincoln Battalion captured the village of Belchinte on the Aragon front.

43. *OJC,* October 12, 1934; *WWAJ,* 1938-39, Volume 3, p. 510; Vita [1935], Box 27, Folder 8, Hillel Papers; *Pittsfield Eagle,* July 26, 1935.

44. Harry Kaplan, "The Religion of the College Student," CCAR *Yearbook,* Volume 47 (1937), pp. 367-71. See also idem, "Religion, Democracy, and Social Work — A Study in Origins and Inter-Relationships," M.A.S.A. thesis, The Ohio State University, 1940; *Selected Addresses, published in honor of his 25th anniversary as Hillel Director at The Ohio State University 1935-1960;* "The Hillel Foundation as Educator" in *Religious Education* (March-April 1947).

45. Correspondence, and Miscellanea, Box 27, Folders 8 and 14 in Hillel Papers.

46. "Reports," Box 27, Folder 5; Harry Kaplan to Richard Gutstadt, correspondence, April 29, 1936; Miles Goldberg to Harry Kaplan, correspondence, February 6 and 8, 1939 in ibid.

47. "Reports," Box 41, Folder 46 in ibid.

48. Correspondence, Box 27, Folder 13; "Report: 1936-1942," Box 22, Folder 15; Miscellaneous, Box 27, Folder 10; "Report: 1941-46," Box 17, Folder 5; Correspondence, Box 16, Folder 29 in ibid. For information on the campus life during World War II, when more than thirty thousand trainees used the university for the Army Specialized Training Program, see *The Bevis Administration 1940-1956,* Part I: 1940-45 (Columbus, 1967).

49. On Rabbi Kaplan's views about Jewish students and Jewish life in the two decades after the war, see *Selected Addresses;* "Preaching to College Students," CCAR *Yearbook,* Volume 62 (1952), pp. 515-19; in *Religious Education:* "The Place of Religion in the Counseling Process" (November-December 1956): 411-19, "Changing Religious and Moral Values on a Campus" (January-February 1960): 43-45, "The Sexual

Revolution and Religious Education" (November-December 1966): 424-29.

The faculty member most involved in Hillel during the thirties and forties was Theodore Beckman (1895-1973), a Russian immigrant who came to Columbus at the age of nineteen and received his B.S., M.A., and Ph.D. degrees from The Ohio State University. A faculty member as early as 1920, and professor of marketing from 1932 to 1966, Beckman's *Marketing* (coauthored) went into its ninth edition in 1975. He was a New Deal economist who earlier had directed the wholesale census of distribution for the Bureau of Census during the Hoover Administration and consulted for the federal and state government repeatedly thereafter. But he also became well known as a communal Sunday school and Jewish adult education teacher, as well as a professor who intimately involved himself with Hillel's programs for years. See *OJC,* April 13, 1962; *WWAJ,* 1938-39, Volume 3, p. 68; *Biographical Encyclopedia of American Jews,* Leo Glassman, editor (New York, 1935), p. 38; *Who's Who in America, (WWA)* 37th edition (1972-73) Volume 1, (Chicago, 1973), p. 202.

16: A HAVEN OF REFUGE FOR THE OPPRESSED: ZIONISM

Intense Zionist activity took place within the Columbus Jewish community from the mid-twenties until the establishment of Israel. After the British Mandate over Palestine came to an end, fund raising for the first independent Jewish State in nineteen centuries reached a sacrificial level in Columbus. Before statehood, the Columbus Zionist District (CZD) provided centralized direction by organizing memorial programs on the anniversaries of the deaths of Chayyim Nachman Bialik and Theodor Herzl; by selling more than $150,000 in War Bonds in 1943 and more than $700,000 in 1945; by sponsoring distinguished visitors like Rabbi Abba Hillel Silver, Eleanor Roosevelt, Rabbi James Heller, James McDonald, Rabbi Stephen S. Wise and Maurice Samuel; and by arranging discussions, rallies, and protests. The largest protest occurred in 1939 when Great Britain attempted to strangle Jewish immigration into Palestine in order to ensure Arab support against the Axis powers. Reacting to the White Paper — a plan to create an Arab majority in Palestine — Columbus Jews and non-Jews joined Americans in scores of cities in verbal and printed attacks against the British.[1]

During the war years, CZD membership rolls expanded rapidly; non-Zionists were left with few practical answers other than the acquisition of Palestine when faced with the Nazi onslaught, immigration restrictions, and the problem of Jewish refugees from Europe. As one recruit recalled:

> When Hitler started his campaign against Jews, I was already at Ohio State and I became active in the Zionist organization for the reason that I felt that a Jewish homeland would give dignity and self-respect to Jews which they would never attain without a Jewish homeland.

Fred Yenkin was only one of hundreds of Columbus Jews recruited by the CZD; four hundred new members enrolled in the autumn of 1943, and by the end of the Second World War the CZD claimed eleven hundred paid members. With this large constituency available, it is not surprising that more than twenty local Zionist organizations were active in the community. The women in the Pioneers of Palestine, Ladies Mizrachi, Jewish Mothers Alliance, Junior Hadassah, B'nos Mizrachi, Pioneer Women, and Hadassah staged abundant fund-raising events for Palestinian causes.[2]

Organized about 1912 by Mrs. A. Reed and Mrs. A. Seff, Hadassah became the largest Zionist women's organization and generated support for hospitals, needy children, and vocational education in Palestine. The first Donor Dinner was held in 1929; thereafter these dinners became Hadassah's main source of income. Each year the women collected thousands of dollars and honored guests like Stephen S. Wise, Abba Hillel Silver, Pierre Van Paassen, Eddie Cantor, Dr. Louis Finkelstein, and Eleanor Roosevelt.[3]

A number of Zionist men's organizations appeared on The Ohio State University campus: Avukah was founded in 1926, while

A memorial to Samuel Levinger, son of Rabbi Lee and Elma Levinger.

the Aleph Zadik Aleph (AZA) was organized for boys from sixteen to twenty-one. Other organizations included Young Judea (Bialik and Herzl chapters), Mizrachi, Jr. Mizrachi, Poale Mizrachi, and Young Israel for Orthodox young men; all of these raised money with carnivals, sponsored guest lecturers like Gedaliah Bublick and Rabbi David Polish, and organized Hebrew language discussion/study groups. In addition, many of these groups worked actively within Columbus' Conservative and Orthodox synagogues. For example, Mizrachi led a drive to collect funds for a special Palestine Emergency Fund; other groups, inspired by Rabbi Greenwald, purchased six hundred dunam — 150 acres — in Palestine to establish a Jewish colony in 1943. Zionist organizations of both sexes joined in a "Food for Israel" campaign during 1949 which shipped more than five thousand dollars' worth of goods.[4]

All of these local activities were intimately connected to the international Zionist movement, as local Zionists vied to represent Columbus at Zionist congresses. During the years of the British Mandate, the *shekel* (fifty-cent membership fee) served as a type of poll-tax, required for voting privileges at the World Zionist Congress. Throughout the thirties, among a vigorous minority of *shekel* purchasers, activity centered on the biennial elections for American delegates at the World Zionist Congresses. The most interesting contest occurred on Sunday, June 23, 1935, when in five hundred polling places in forty states and two hundred cities, American Zionists surrendered their *shekolim* to vote for Ticket 1, 2, or 3, to represent them at the Nineteenth World Zionist Congress in Lucerne in August.

Ticket 1, or the General Zionists, included Zionist Organization of America, Senior and Junior Hadassah, and Order Sons of Zion; it controlled about 65 to 70 percent of the 135,000 or so vote-bearing *shekolim* sold in the United States. In theory and practice, General Zionism represented the broad middle-of-the-road approach which placed the needs of the *Yishuv* (Palestine) above separate ideologies. Ticket 2, or the Labor Zionists *(Poale Tsiyon),* held about 25 percent of the vote.[5] Socialists formed the *Poale Tsiyon* party in 1907 and created their own schools, labor organizations, and cultural institutions in the *Yishuv.* Ticket 3, or the Mizrachi, represented Orthodox Jewry; their party was formed in 1902; they also created their own institutions in the *Yishuv.* While Tickets 2 and 3 represented only a minority of the vote-bearing *shekolim,* they got out the vote and captured thirty-eight of the fifty-seven American delegate seats at the upcoming congress.[6]

Although a prominent Columbusite, Mrs. William A. Hersch, became a delegate on Ticket 1, the Mizrachi swamped the other tickets in Columbus. When the votes were counted at Agudas Achim synagogue, Mizrachi emerged with 63 votes to 35 and 39 for Tickets 1 and 2 respectively. Led by Rabbi Greenwald, the local Orthodox community demonstrated its concern with the issue which would dominate the Nineteenth World Zionist Congress: the Mizrachi demand, in the face of so-called "irreligious acts," for Sabbath observance in agricultural settlements financed by Zionist funds. This was to be no idle threat at the August Congress, for only last-minute Labor Zionist pressure and compromise prevented the Mizrachi from joining the "Revisionists" at their first Congress in Vienna in September of 1935. During all the Zionist in-fighting of early 1935, Rabbi Greenwald hammered home for weeks and even months before the election the need for strong Mizrachi representation and the imposition of penalties against Sabbath violations. Unlike some Ohio cities where the Mizrachi captured less than 2 percent of the vote (3 of 256 votes in Akron), the Mizrachi ticket dominated Columbus Zionism.[7]

At the Reform temple, however, it was different. Reform Judaism was still following the logic of early theories of Jewish emancipation by a deliberate negation of Jewish nationhood and anything — such as fund raising for the economic development of Palestine — which might encourage it. Jews were to be Americans of the Jewish faith, with only one national allegiance; support of another land would weaken the Reform Jewish optimism in America as the Promised Land. Not until the late 1930s, when it became obvious to almost everyone that there was no other place for the Jews of Europe to flee, did the temple cease to be a bastion of anti-Zionist sentiment.

As these changes were slowly taking place, the forty-eighth annual convention of the Central Conference of American [Reform] Rabbis, one of the most controversial and significant ever, took place in Columbus. Following nearly a month of daily newspaper publicity placed by Simon Lazarus' committee, the rabbis met at the Deshler Hotel from May 25 to 30, 1937. At the Tuesday evening gala opening, Lazarus delivered a welcoming address on behalf of the congregation. The next morning 194 rabbis, less than half the CCAR membership, got down to work. By Thursday morning, when the sessions shifted to Winding Hollow Country Club for the tumultuous report of the Commission on Guiding Principles of Reform Judaism, attendance had dwindled to 162.[8]

Following a reading of the principles, Rabbi Samuel Schulman, whose statement of principles was rejected by the commission as a long polemical sermon, led a large and vocal opposition to that commission. When the conference was finally charged with revising the 1936 Declaration of Principles — the first affirmed by American Reform rabbis since 1885 — an eighty-one to eighty-one tie vote prevented the conference from thanking the commission and rejecting the declaration. Barely able to complete the count because of the commotion, the chairman adjourned the meeting for lunch.

For their afternoon activity, the rabbis had to choose between the commission report and the golf tourney sponsored by the temple. While more than sixty-five rabbis toured the links, only two votes (48-50) prevented the declaration from being tabled for one year, while several other very close votes almost prevented seriatim consideration of the principles. Late that afternoon, after eight hours of debate and with some men back from the fairways, the Declaration of Principles, or "Columbus Platform," received approval. These principles included this controversial plank, which signalled a shift in rabbinic rhetoric and official position if not yet in heart, and angered non-Zionists sufficiently that many walked out of the conference before dinner that evening:

> We affirm the obligation of all Jewry to aid in its [Palestine's] upbuilding as a Jewish homeland by endeavoring to make it not only a haven of refuge for the oppressed but also a center of Jewish culture and spiritual life.[9]

The single most memorable Zionist event which occurred in Columbus, however, was not the Central Conference of American Rabbis but the forty-sixth national convention of the Zionists of America, held in Columbus from September 11 to 13, 1943. The local CZD and especially Albert Schiff, a member of the national convention committee and honorary convention chairman, worked hard to bring the event to Columbus. An entire galaxy of national Zionist leaders convened at the Deshler-Wallick Hotel. Among them were Rabbis James Heller, Stephen S. Wise, Abba Hillel Silver, Raphael Gold, Israel Goldstein, and Joshua Loth Liebman, as well as Dr. Nahum Goldmann, president of the World Jewish Congress, and Louis Lipsky, a past president of ZOA. The evening before the convention opened national Zionist leaders had spoken at the synagogues: Raphael Gold at Tifereth Israel, Isaac Carmel at Agudas Achim, and James Heller at Temple Israel. The cochairmen of the convention committee, Robert Mellman and Fred Yenkin, opened the first session before more than one thousand delegates on Saturday evening, September 11.

After the delegates sang the "Star Spangled Banner" and "Hatikvah," Governor John Bricker, Mayor Floyd Green, and Albert Schiff brought greetings to the convention, while ZOA president Louis E. Levinthal delivered the presidential message. Judge Levinthal declared that Britain and America had ignored both the contributions Jews in Palestine made to the war effort, and the enormous amount of Jewish persecution and homelessness in Europe. The next afternoon CZD President Roy Stone read a telegram from President Roosevelt, who responded in part by saying that "all feasible measures are being adapted to lessen the sufferings of the persecuted Jews of Europe." The highlight of the convention was the Sunday evening session which attracted so many local visitors it had to be moved to Memorial Hall; Stephen S. Wise, Abba Hillel Silver, and Nahum Goldmann addressed the delegates about "Palestine and the World Scene." Along with subsequent speakers including the newly-elected president, Dr. Israel Goldstein, they pleaded for United Nations assistance to Jewish refugees seeking Palestine, asked for the emergence of a Jewish homeland in the postwar world, and attacked the White Paper of 1939. In addition they affirmed the full cultural and religious rights of the Arab population in Palestine, attempted to describe the seriousness of the European Jewish tragedy, and enthusiastically endorsed the resolutions of the American Jewish Conference which had met the previous month in New York.[10]

The broadly-based American Jewish Conference was organized by Henry Monsky, the national president of B'nai B'rith, in Pittsburgh early in 1943. Representatives of thirty-two national Jewish organizations were concerned about the same problems which agitated the ZOA: Palestine, the European Holocaust, and the postwar world. From August 29 to September 2, 1943, one hundred and twenty-five delegates representing all major national groups, and three hundred and seventy-five delegates from seventy-eight local communities and fifty-eight regions throughout the country assembled at the Waldorf-Astoria Hotel in New York City. They affirmed resolutions demanding commonwealth status for Palestine, the end of the 1939 White Paper, and the creation of a Jewish Army to defend the *Yishuv* (Palestine) from the Axis.

Columbus' delegate to this convention was Albert Schiff (1893-1977). The Columbus District Election Committee, chaired by Dr. Elijah Gordon, arranged procedures for choosing one delegate to represent the thirty Jewish organizations in the community:

> Every local Jewish group which was functioning prior to December 7, 1941, and engaged in Jewish activity, if it has a membership of more than fifty is urged to . . . elect one delegate for its first fifty members and an additional one delegate for each additional seventy-five members or major fraction thereof.
>
> Each such organization may also nominate candidates for election for the American Jewish Conference. Any one hundred Columbus Jews not entitled otherwise separately to representation at the local election conference may also nominate a candidate for the American Jewish Conference by petition to be filed with the C.D.E.C.[11]

On Thursday night, May 27, 1943, at the Schonthal Center, the delegates unanimously chose the distinguished communal leader, Albert Schiff, as their representative to the American Jewish Conference. This election catapulted Schiff from local and regional Zionist activities in Columbus and the Ohio Valley to national leadership of the ZOA.

Born in Lithuania and educated at the famous Telshia *yeshiva* (1911), Schiff came to the United States in 1912 and eventually became vice-president of the Columbus-based SCOA (Schiff Shoes); vice-president of Bryden Road Temple; president of the Jewish Community Council, Hillel Advisory Board, and United Palestine Appeal organization of Ohio; and a member of the executive board of the UJF, Schonthal Center, and CZD. Zionist activities became "the single burning passion of his life"; his vision and spirit were remembered by men like Fred Yenkin:

> Albert Schiff . . . was a man of very deep-rooted Jewish feelings; a man of great dignity; a humble person. He and I would spend hours and hours walking the streets . . . talking about Palestine and he gave me a great deal of insight on the early Zionist movement. He taught me a great deal about the necessity of Jewish identification and the purpose of survival. I would say that on an intimate basis he probably influenced me more than any other single individual over a lengthy period of time. He had a very extensive library, mostly Hebraic. My experience was that he could feel very deeply, but expressed himself with a great deal of calmness. He was a man of high character and deep Jewish learning.[12]

Schiff was one of about twenty American Jews invited to a now famous meeting with David Ben-Gurion on August 1, 1945, at the New York home of Rudolph Sonneborn, secretary-treasurer of a multimillion-dollar corporation and scion of a wealthy German-Jewish family in Baltimore. As a result of this meeting, the "Sonneborn Institute," an informal, nationwide, secret organization was formed. In addition to purchasing guns, tanks, medicines, ambulances, planes, and clothing for the clandestine *Haganah* (Jewish Army), the institute acquired ships to effect the mass exodus of European Jewish survivors into Palestine. The Sonneborn Institute bought more than a dozen ships for *Mossad* (the Committee for Illegal Immigration); the vessels included the *S.S. President Warfield* (renamed the *Exodus.*). Through its discreet purchases the institute virtually created a secret navy for a nonexistent state, as well as supply depots in various parts of the world. Writing about this meeting years later, Ben-Gurion noted that: "Most of the machines and tools which are today at the disposal of the military industry in Israel are the products of this meeting."[13]

As a Sonneborn associate, Albert Schiff held "meetings in basements of prominent Columbus Jewish homes and . . . raised substantial sums of money which were forwarded to what was known as the Zionist Emergency Fund." From this experience Schiff learned enough to form, with influential ZOA businessmen, the Israel Corporation of America (ICA), on September 21, 1948. Later renamed the Palestine Economic Corporation, the ICA was organized for industrial, commercial, and agricultural development in Israel with an authorized capital of 750,000 preferred shares, 3.99 million common shares, and 10 special shares. Offered in a $25 unit of one eighty-cent preferred share and one common share, the shares initially financed a $6 million housing project for Tel Aviv and Haifa.

In 1950 Schiff became the national president of the ZOA; throughout the 1950s and 1960s he continued to hold the highest offices in the Zionist movement and to make important financial and spiritual contributions to Israel. In the words of Rep. Emanuel Celler of New York, Albert Schiff was "a dreamer and an activist, a visionary and a builder — and combined within himself the highest ideals of an American and of a Jew."[14]

Many other Columbus Jews made invaluable contributions to the creation of a Jewish state in these critical decades. Included were gifts of time and money, collections of needed commodities, visits to Israel followed by talks to Columbus groups, and in the following two cases, very special gifts of soul and spirit.

Izler Solomon (b. 1910) had been the American-born music director and conductor of the Columbus Philharmonic Orchestra

Izler Solomon

since its inception at the Schonthal Center in 1941. He accepted an offer from the Palestine Philharmonic of Tel Aviv to be its guest conductor for six weeks, beginning May 19, 1948. Scheduling concerts throughout the land in the midst of warfare and an uncertain truce, the renamed Israel Philharmonic performed as often as three or four times a week to enormous crowds, and brought music back to besieged Jerusalem by riding armored buses along the "Burma Road" in July. Solomon remained in Israel through the summer to complete the season, and returned in 1949 to initiate the summer series with eleven concerts in the first seventeen days of the season.[15]

Sam Melton (b. 1900), a Hungarian-born Columbus industrialist who first visited Palestine in 1938, culminated three years of planning by shipping the first prefabricated manufacturing plant from the United States to Israel in 1949. Duplicating Melton's Columbus-based Capitol Manufacturing Company on a smaller scale by fabricating, tapping, and threading pipe nipples and other plumbing fittings from steel pipe, under Melton's supervision the prefabricated plant was unfolded between April 11 and June 11. In 1955 he donated the plant to several Israeli organizations.[16]

Zionism played an important role in the development of a cohesive Jewish community at the beginning of the twentieth century. Despite the initial hesitancy of the Reform movement within Judaism, by 1948 the community had united to nurture the new-born State of Israel.

NOTES FOR CHAPTER 16

1. *OJC,* July 20, 1934, February 5, March 5, 1943, July 13, 1945, June 2, December 29, 1939, October 24, 1947.

2. Interview with Fred Yenkin; *OJC,* December 7, 1928, February 28, 1930, October 30, December 4, 1931, July 12, 1935, April 1, July 29, 1938, February 3, April 28, 1939, January 4, 1944, December 21, 1945.

3. *OJC,* October 16, 1936, March 26, 1937, November 24, 1939, March 21, 1947, December 10, 1948. For a list of featured guest speakers at the first twenty Donor Dinners, see *OJC,* December 9, 1949.

4. On AZA, see interview with Eugene Borowitz; on Mizrachi, see interview with Julius Baker; *OJC,* March 25, 1927, January 13, 1928, July 6, 1934, April 12, 1935, February 28, April 3, December 25, 1936, July 28, December 22, 1939, April 18, 1941, February 13, 1942, July 30, 1943, December 31, 1948.

5. Only those *shekolim* sold in the year of the congress guaranteed the privilege of voting.

6. *The New Palestine,* May 31, June 21 and 28, September 13, 1935; *The Jewish Forum,* July 1935, p. 152. The Labor Zionists recorded twenty-five thousand votes to the General Zionists' nineteen thousand, although holding only one-third the number of *shekolim.*

7. *Jewish Frontier,* June, July, August, and October 1935; *OJC,* June 21 and 28, 1935. See also Samuel Rosenblatt, *The History of the Mizrachi Movement* (New York, 1951).

8. CCAR *Yearbook,* XLVII (1937); *CC,* May 1, 8, 19, 22, 1937; *OSJ,* May 14, 25, 26, 1937; *CED,* May 9, 14, 18, 23, 25, 26, 1937; "Address of Welcome by Simon Lazarus," May 25, 1937, Gup Papers, Box 2.

9. CCAR *Yearbook,* XLV (1935), pp. 260ff., 309ff.; CCAR *Yearbook* XLVI (1936), pp. 89ff.; CCAR *Yearbook,* XLVII (1937); *OSJ,* May 27 and 28, 1937; *CED,* May 27 and 28, 1937; *CC,* May 27, 1937; edited transcript of interview with Jerome Folkman; Arthur Lelyveld, "The Conference View of the Position of the Jews in the Modern World," in Bertram Korn, ed., *Retrospect and Prospect Essays in Commemoration of the 75th Anniversary of the Founding of the CCAR 1889-1964* (New York, 1965), pp. 159-61.

10. *OJC,* September 3, 10, and 17, 1943; *OSJ,* September 10-14, 1943; *CD,* September 10-14, 1943; interviews with Robert Mellman and Fred Yenkin; Annual Report of the 46th Annual Convention of the ZOA, September 11-13, 1943 (Columbus, Ohio); *The New Palestine* 34:1 (September 24, 1943).

11. Alexander Kohanski, editor, *American Jewish Conference: Its Organization and Proceedings of the First Session, August 29 to September 2, 1943* (New York, 1944); *American Jewish Conference: A Statement of the Organization of the Conference and A Summary of Resolutions Adopted at the First Session Held in New York City, August 29 to September 2, 1943* (New York, n.d.); *NYT,* August 27, 29, and 31, September 3, October 25, 1943; *OJC,* May 21, 1943.

12. *OJC,* June 4 and 11, 1943; *WWA,* 37th edition, 1972-73, Volume 2, p. 2793; Elaine Schiff Milstein to Marc Lee Raphael, correspondence, December 11, 1974, and January 15, 1975; *OJC,* May 4, September 13,

December 11, 1975; interview with Fred Yenkin; Milstein to Raphael, correspondence, December 19, 1975. For the numerous contributions to local and national Jewish life made by Albert's brother, Robert, see *OJC*, October 5, 1962, and *Who Was Who in America*, Volume V, p. 640.

13. Interview with Fred Yenkin; Robert St. John, *Ben-Gurion: A Biography* (New York, 1971), pp. 95-99, 101-02; Jacob A. Rudin, *Partners in State Building: American Jewry and Israel* (New York, 1969), pp. 269-71; Fred Yenkin to Marc Lee Raphael, telephone conversation, April 30, 1976. The most detailed account of the "Institute" and its operations is Leonard Slater, *The Pledge* (New York, 1970).

14. Interviews with Robert Mellman and Fred Yenkin; Milstein to Raphael; *OJC*, February 8, 1952; *New York Herald Tribune*, November 13, 1948; *NYT*, November 15, 1948; *The Israel Corporation of America: Aims and Objectives*, November 1948, 11pp.; *The Jewish American* (Yiddish), July 1, 1960; *Jewish National Fund Bulletin* VIII:10 (August-September 1961); *Land and Life* XX:4 (Passover, 1967), p. 9. In 1960 Schiff was elected president of the Jewish National Fund of America; see *OJC*, May 27, 1960.

15. *WWA*, Volume 27, 1952-53, p. 2272; *OJC*, May 7, July 16, 1948, July 22, 1949; Annual Meeting, Schonthal Center, May 8, 1941, in Jewish Center Papers. Solomon led the Israel Philharmonic during its 1951 American tour.

16. *OJC*, August 19 and 26, September 23, October 7, 1949; interview with Sam Melton. On Melton's later gifts to Israel, see the Samuel Melton Papers, OHS.

17: UNORGANIZED AND SUPERFICIAL: JEWISH EDUCATION

During the thirties and forties Jewish education was professionally scrutinized for the first time; it was found to be lacking the very bedrock of all education: commitment. Secular education retained its high priority within the Jewish family — but the day of a proliferation of Jewish parochial schools appeared relegated to the misty future when acculturation was no longer a survival tactic. Columbus Hebrew School's continual struggle for financial stability illustrated the community's lack of commitment to religious education.

Another educational tool, albeit an informal one, was the *Ohio Jewish Chronicle,* the primary source of information about Jewish life inside and outside of Columbus. The first Anglo-Jewish newspaper in Columbus, the *Columbus Jewish Chronicle* appeared every week from May 29, 1918, through January 10, 1919.[1] A large, informative newspaper filled with details of innumerable Jewish activities, the early *Chronicle* failed to find sufficient advertising.[2] Not until the Neustadt brothers came from Indianapolis in 1921 and established the *Ohio Jewish Chronicle* on March 3, 1922, did Columbus Jewry have a permanent English newspaper of its own.

Enticed to Columbus by the "elite" Jews — who correctly saw the need for a local newspaper to sensitize Jews to the concerns of world Jewry if fund raising were to succeed — the Neustadts established a dignified, comprehensive newspaper.[3] In exchange, many prominent Jews generously aided them in securing advertisements. Ben (b. 1896) and Aaron (1898-1952)[4] Neustadt subscribed to the recently established Jewish Correspondence Bureau, which later became the Jewish Telegraphic Agency. This worldwide clearinghouse of Jewish news made possible quick and accurate coverage of events affecting Jews everywhere. Concomitantly the Neustadts stressed Jewish activities at home, invited prominent local Jews like Lee and Elma Levinger to write regular features, heartily endorsed the rebuilding of Palestine, generously covered Reform and Conservative (less so Orthodox) religious life, and studiously avoided communal controversies.[5] Well-edited and handsomely produced, the *Chronicle* offered generous amounts of ink to social news — especially weddings, vacations, and parties among Columbus Jewry's most notable and wealthy. From detailed accounts of mah-jongg and local Jewish sports to rabbinic commentaries, there was something for everyone in the *Ohio Jewish Chronicle*.

Looking at the more traditional forms of education, the Jews of Columbus sent their children almost exclusively to public elementary and secondary schools, and then to The Ohio State University. Jewish education was much more informal and much less intensive, for no daily Jewish parochial schools existed. The synagogues bore the major responsibility for Jewish education in Columbus, as there was little communal sense of responsibility. Jewish education faced many obstacles, including inadequate funds, limited hours, poor curricula, untrained teachers, and minimal standards. Especially detrimental was the lack of sustained commitment among the majority of Jewish parents and leaders. The seriousness of this situation was documented by Rabbi Lee Levinger.

As the national research director of B'nai B'rith, Rabbi Levinger devoted himself to several extensive surveys of Jewish education. His first, "The Jewish Student in America," obtained statistics from more than thirteen hundred, or 91 percent, of the American and Canadian institutions of higher learning in 1937. According to this survey, there were 105,000 Jewish students; of these 13.5 percent attended college. Levinger realized that this high percentage reflected the great emphasis immigrant families placed on education and that there was no way to measure the effect of discrimination against the admission of Jewish students to colleges in the twenties. Taking these factors into account, he suggested that there was a serious need for a vocational guidance program for college-bound students. The survey also provided extensive information about Jewish students' social organizations and yielded numerous insights for college administrators.[6]

Before Dr. Levinger left Columbus for chaplaincy positions on the west coast, his final survey was requested by the Jewish Community Council in 1940.[7] His study of Jewish education in Columbus enumerated 701 enrollees — but only 575 individuals — registered in Sunday schools, Hebrew programs, and private Hebrew instruction.

TABLE 59
JEWISH EDUCATION IN COLUMBUS: 1940

School	Students	Teachers	Grades	Hours/Week
Temple Israel Sunday School	201	12	K-11	2
Tifereth Israel Sunday School	167	10	1-10	2
Agudas Achim Sunday School	111	6	K-9 (mixed)	2
Columbus Hebrew School	152	4	2-7	8
Tifereth Israel Hebrew School	40	3	4-7	4
Private Teachers	30	3	—	—

Levinger's survey revealed that:

1. Compensation for teachers was very low; the two leading teachers at the Columbus Hebrew School, who made their livelihoods in this work, each received $1,760 for eleven months' work.
2. All three Sunday schools, despite denominational differences, seemed similar in purpose, method, and curriculum. They all followed an English curriculum, with Bible, history, beliefs, and ceremonies forming the core study. Both the Conservative and Orthodox synagogues relied heavily on texts published by the Reform movement or written by rabbis trained at the Reform seminary. Especially popular then (and today) were two books by Lee Levinger: *The Story of the Jew* (with Elma Levinger) and *History of the Jews in the United States*.
3. About 70 percent of the identifiable Jewish youth in Columbus from six to fourteen were enrolled in Sunday or Hebrew schools; however, this rather high percentage left about two hundred youngsters not enrolled in any Jewish school. Of the two hundred and forty teenagers fourteen and over, only fifty — or 21 percent — attended a Jewish school. Hence, minimal formal Jewish education existed in Columbus for teenagers; religious education virtually ceased with either a boy's bar mitzvah at thirteen or confirmation at fifteen.

In surveying adult education, Rabbi Levinger discovered eleven organized classes and twenty-one organizations with occasional Jewish programs. The classes included weekly Talmud classes taught by Rabbis Hirschsprung, Greenwald, and Zelizer; a biweekly class in Hebrew literature with Rabbi Hirschsprung; a ten-lecture series by Rabbi Kaplan for the Council of Jewish

Women; a ten-lecture series by Elma Levinger for Hadassah; and an eighteen-week winter lecture series at Beth Jacob by Rabbi Greenwald. No adult education classes met at Bryden Road Temple, but the other synagogues and organizations with regular courses served perhaps three to four hundred adults in 1940. The result? "Much of the material is unorganized and most of it is superficial," concluded Levinger. "In other words, we are doing a great amount of talking, but little actual education."[8]

Of all the formal programs in Jewish education, the Columbus Hebrew School, opened in 1922 at 558 East Rich Street, struggled hardest merely to survive. The United Jewish Fund cut off its support in 1930 when limited resources gave Hebrew instruction a low priority. Fortunately, women's groups like Ivreeyoh supported the school by holding dinners, raffles, picnics, and collections — managing, month by month, to meet the budget and, literally, "save the school."[9] They collected $12,000 merely to keep it alive in 1931, and a barebones $8,000 in 1933.[9]

Novel approaches to fund raising emerged in the difficult years prior to the Second World War. Appeals from the pulpits of Orthodox synagogues on the most solemn day of the Jewish year, Yom Kippur, annually interrupted services and yielded hundreds of dollars for the Columbus Hebrew School. Annual "Jubilee" festivals — called by the school's president *shnorerei* (begging) — began in 1935, featured Yiddish "talkies" like "Yiddle and His Fiddle," and collected several thousand dollars each year. Community leaders, especially Alfred J. Kobacker of Temple Israel, led annual drives to recruit contributing members and patrons, while several organizations within the Orthodox community donated funds from their treasuries for a new bus and other necessary items.[10]

Despite these intense efforts, by the late thirties the Columbus Hebrew School, with its approximately one hundred and sixty students, neared collapse. At the close of the 1938-39 academic year, the board threatened not to open in the fall unless a budget deficit of over one thousand dollars was eliminated; simultaneously they tried unsuccessfully to persuade Tifereth Israel, which zealously guarded the autonomy of its Hebrew program, to merge with the Columbus Hebrew School. The board's final response was to extend the annual membership effort to a year-round drive.[11]

The board angered the United Jewish Fund which prohibited competitive fund-raising activities in the community. A compromise was hammered out early in 1939: the Columbus Hebrew School agreed to cease its annual jubilee, membership drives, and all fund-raising activities, when the UJF agreed to permit contributors to earmark up to 25 percent of their contributions for the Columbus Hebrew School — with a communal limit of $4,500. Thus the UJF shut off competition, and the Columbus Hebrew School was guaranteed enough funds to run a school.[12]

During the war years, the financial plight of the school remained serious; income remained lower than expenses every year until there was a $2,000 deficit early in 1944. Feeling strong leadership would create stability and solvency, the board convinced the UJF to allocate $3,500 for a principal. The board hired Daniel Harrison (b. 1905), a graduate of Butler University, as director of both the Columbus Hebrew School and the Bureau of Jewish Education. A native of Poland, Harrison was educated in a Kassov *yeshiva*, lived in Palestine from 1920 to 1923, served as principal of the San Antonio Hebrew School and then headed the Indianapolis Jewish Education Association for fifteen years. Harrison began his thirty years of service in Columbus at a time when the school faced problems with finances, morale, and declining enrollment.[13]

Together with an ambitious board of directors led by Dr. Max Kanter, Harrison secured increased enrollments, generated larger and balanced budgets, and even initiated a building fund drive. Early in 1946 the directors purchased property on Livingston Avenue near Bulen Avenue in the Driving Park area, the heart of the Orthodox community of the 1940s. The campaign ceased as soon as it began, when all local organizations agreed not to compete with fund raising for the new Jewish Center.[14]

The respite was chastening, for the board became aware that raising funds for a new building was a dream, yet the size, location, and condition of the present building were most unsuitable. Tifereth Israel rebuffed renewed attempts to merge as well as requests to use the synagogue's facilities. Receiving temporary permission to use Fairwood Avenue School, the board desperately sought a long-term solution to the problem. As the Jewish Center building campaign proceeded full steam ahead, the board approved the only possible compromise solution. In exchange for permanent quarters, the Columbus Hebrew School turned over all of its building funds — including income derived from the sale of the Rich Street school and the Livingston Avenue lots — to the Columbus Jewish Center.[15]

Thus toward the end of the forties and into the fifties, there was an upswing in the valence of religious education. In 1943 Agudas Achim created their Education Institute and in 1948 Tifereth Israel's $180,000 Educational Center was completed. And in the fifties concerned individuals generated enough interest in the Columbus Hebrew School to finally move it out of the old east European neighborhood.

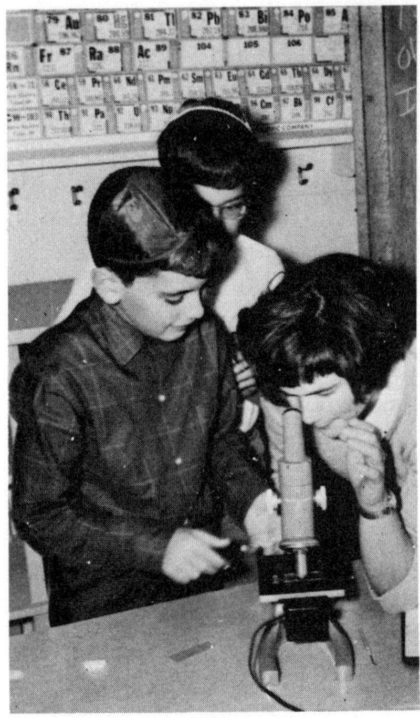

Still in the future of Columbus' Jewish community was the Torah Academy which combined Jewish tradition and secular studies. In the late fifties Steve Rudnick (foreground), Michael Weiss, and Sherry Fox were students at the academy.

NOTES FOR CHAPTER 17

1. The *Columbus Jewish Chronicle* was variously edited and published by E. L. Parker, Andrew Roth, and Louis Rich. As promised in its first issue, it followed "an independent and fearless policy, attacking and defending, criticizing and approving."

2. Lack of local advertising forced the *Chronicle* to search outside Columbus for patronage. Hoping to attract national advertising, the *Columbus Jewish Chronicle* dropped the "Columbus" and, as *The Jewish Chronicle,* appeared in February 1919 as a monthly review. Subsequent issues never appeared.

3. Interview with Ben Neustadt.

4. *OJC,* August 8, 1952. See also *WWAJ,* 1926, Volume 1, p. 456.

5. The most intense controversy never appeared in the pages of the *Chronicle,* but enjoined lively letters and phone calls. During two consecutive UJF Campaigns (1926 and 1930) the newspaper published the names, and pledges, of each contributor; the reaction was so strong that this listing would never appear again. See interview with Ben Neustadt.

6. *The Jewish Student in America* (Cincinnati, Ohio, 1937); *Jewish Social Studies I* (1939): 261-63.

7. In April of 1938 the B'nai B'rith asked Levinger to survey the distribution of Jews in the seven major professions in fifty-six of Ohio's fifty-nine cities of ten thousand or more persons. The purposes included stimulating vocational guidance, responding to charges of "overcrowding the professions," and helping young graduates of professional schools choose a city in which to initiate their careers. For the distribution of Jewish professionals in Columbus, see *Jewish Social Studies II* (1940): 401-34.

8. Lee J. Levinger, "Survey of Jewish Education in Columbus, Ohio" (Jewish Community Council, November 1940). For an interesting comparison, see Isaac B. Berkson and Ben Rosen, "1936 Jewish Education Survey of Cleveland" (mimeographed) in Cleveland Public Library and Abraham Franzblau, "Toward the Reorientation of Jewish Religious Education" in CCAR *Yearbook* 46 (1936), pp. 13-29.

9. *OJC,* January 10, December 12, 1930, January 9, July 10, 1931, November 18, 1932, January 13, November 10, 1933, November 22, 1935.

10. Interview with Robert Mellman; *OJC,* October 13, 1933, March 8, 1935, April 30, 1937; Columbus Hebrew School Minutes, October 18, 1935, October 2, 1936, March 9, 1937, March 17, 1938; *Second Annual United Jubilee Benefit* [Booklet], April 21, 1936, p. 8.

11. *OJC,* May 5, June 2, 1939; CHS Minutes, April 13, May 11, 1937, July 13, November 1, 1938, January 12, February 7, October 14, 1939.

12. CHS Minutes, June 11, 1939.

13. CHS Minutes, January 11, May 9, October 11, 1944, June 21, October 4, 1945; *OJC,* August 4, 1944. Not everyone expressed enthusiasm about the direction in which the CHS was moving. The former chairman of the Board of Education of the CHS viewed the movement "to modernize the school" as an attempt to eliminate "Orthodox teachings, customs, and instructions as practiced in the school for the past thirty years." He urged the board to "make sure the Hebrew School remains a *Hebrew* school, and not a playground and a laboratory for bankrupted schemes and experiments." *OJC,* May 29, 1942, July 6, 1945.

14. CHS Minutes, July 16, October 4, 1945, January 2, February 12, March 7, October 4, 1946; *OJC,* July 1, November 4, 1949.

15. *OJC,* October 11, 1946; CHS Minutes, September 9, 1946, January 7, February 16, April 18, July 15, August 17, 1948, January 17, March 15, 1949; interview with Fred Yenkin; Tifereth Israel Minutes, Board of Directors, January 13, 1948, and June 15, 1950. For both the advantages and disadvantages of being housed in the Jewish Center, see "Excerpts from an Article by Daniel Harrison, Principal of the Columbus Talmud Torah — Published in 'Omer,' a publication of the Midwest Conference of Hebrew Teachers — Translated from the Hebrew" (May 1954), Columbus Hebrew School.

18: ON THE PERIPHERY OF THE COMMUNITY: CRIME AND SPORTS

Criminal activity has long been a business which some ethnic groups — especially the Irish, Italians, and Jews — have used as a ladder of upward mobility. Sports have provided a similar way out of ethnic ghettoes for these very same groups. Because stealing bases has always been more socially acceptable than stealing property, the athlete was a source of pride, frequently showcased during ethnic celebrations as "one of ours who made good." Criminals were not chauvinistically applauded, yet both elements were bona fide segments of any ethnic neighborhood. Therefore, although only a minority of any ethnic group engaged in illegal activity, their criminality nevertheless was reflected in the larger cultural pattern of each community.[1] Dozens of popular writers have commented about criminality and certain ethnic groups; Theodore Bingham, New York's police commissioner, labeled Italians and Russian Jews as the "most dangerous malefactors in the city," in his description of "Foreign Criminals of New York."[2]

Long experienced in trade and merchandising, Jews used their criminal skills primarily in illegal commercial and financial ventures; both as advisers to large criminal organizations and as independent profiteers. Between 1928 and 1939, according to Columbus' daily press, Jewish criminal activity centered on illegal possession of liquor until the repeal of the Eighteenth Amendment in 1933; after this, numbers and gambling occupied Jewish criminals.[3]

Prohibition violations abounded. One Agudas Achim member surrendered when firemen found a still in his bathhouse, while police arrested a local mother and her children for possessing a fifteen-gallon still and forty-eight gallons of liquor in their home as well as transporting fifteen gallons in their car. Other entrepreneurs restricted their business activities to their stores; law officials apprehended several men for possession of beer, liquor, bars, tables, and tanks in backrooms and basements of pharmacies, as well as clothing and confectionary stores. Some Jews were caught engaging in bootleg liquor traffic occasionally of "wholesale proportions," and indicted with dozens of Columbus non-Jews. Most common, however, became the arrest of Columbus Jews, sometimes after federal grand jury indictments, for simple possession of illegal liquor. City and federal officials brought such indictments against both prominent and obscure local Jews, although the latter certainly dominate the newspaper accounts.[4]

After 1933, bookmaking emerged as the major criminal activity of Columbus Jews. This included betting on horses, managing numbers houses, establishing gambling casinos behind respectable store fronts, and conducting illegal betting operations of various kinds. Bookmaking schemes included both occasional synagogue leaders and individuals outside the organized community; the local press gave their activities wide attention.[5]

The organized Jewish community's reaction to these crimes was generally a quiet one. "Being busted for booze," one rabbi noted, "was merely bad luck." Those in gambling were always considered a miniscule, and deviant, segment of the community. During the community's most celebrated case of accidental wrongdoing, all united to quietly solve the problem:

> Rabbi ____ was a young fellow that came here, and before Passover, rabbis, at that time [Prohibition], were given permission to buy wine for Pesach, and he would sign the applications of the committee, or people who said they were members of the committee, to get enough wine for Pesach and, unfortunately, he was made to sign; I'm sure unknowingly, because I talked to him once a little bit about it. Unfortunately, he signed certificates which he didn't read and that was application for more than Passover wine. It so happened that some of this Passover wine was found in grills and bars. In other words he was, unknowingly, made a partner in bootleg wine utilizing the Passover prerequisites as an excuse. There was almost a Watergate scandal in Columbus, but some of the finest leadership, from all congregations, joined hands in covering up and in having that person removed from town — and he left in a hurry. Covering up sometimes is not such a bad thing.[6]

In comparison with the larger Ohio community, the crime rate within the Jewish community does indeed seem low, although not quite "miniscule." While serving as the chaplain at the Ohio Penitentiary in Columbus, Rabbi Lee Levinger gathered information about the Jewish inmates in Ohio's five penal institutions as of December 31, 1938. (Non-Jews who claimed to be Jews in order to be given special treatment by the B'nai B'rith Social Service Committee were eliminated.) The results revealed

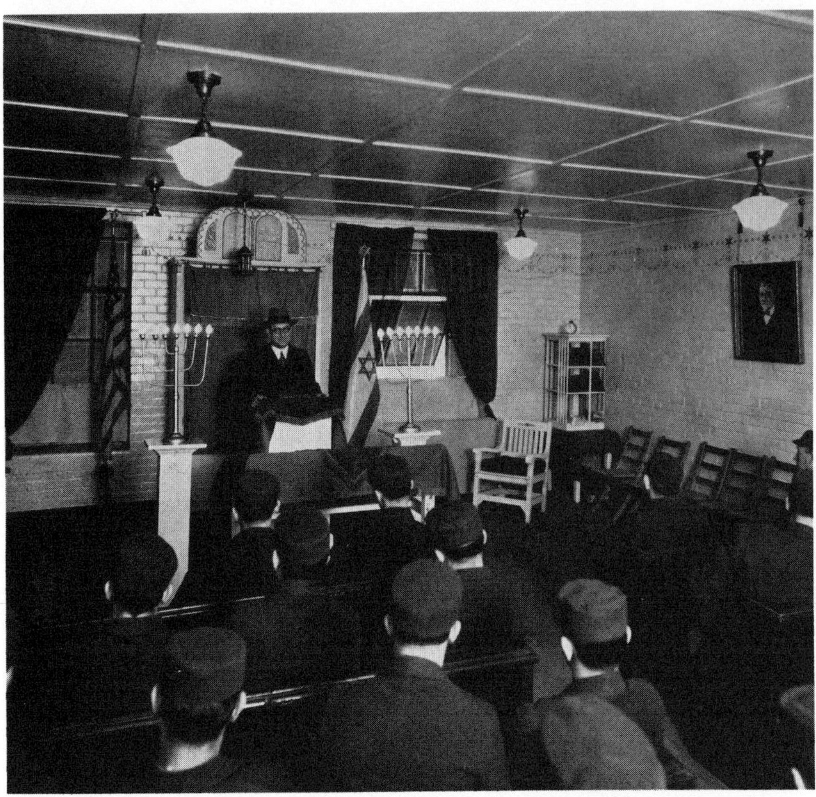

Many Columbus Jewish organizations, including B'nai B'rith, Ezras Noshim, and the Council of Jewish Women, provided support services to Jewish inmates at the Ohio Penitentiary. I. B. Jashenofsky began conducting High Holiday services there early in the century, and Jack Myers, head of the B'nai B'rith Social Service Committee, conducted weekly worship services in the penitentiary by the 1920s. When the permanent Jewish chapel pictured above was established in 1927, it included a picture of Mr. Jashenofsky on the wall.

that the courts more frequently convicted Jewish prisoners for crimes against property than for crimes against the person, that Jews were older and better educated than the general prison population, and that the total percentage of Jewish prisoners stood very low (1.1 percent of the total prisoners, 1.5 percent of the white prisoners).[7]

While local newspaper headlines occasionally touted the criminal activity of Jews, more frequently the sports writers exclaimed over the latest records broken by Jewish athletes. During the twenties and thirties a wide variety of Columbus Jews achieved success in sports, some rising to national and even international prominence. As sports became a big-time business in

America, Columbus Jews, like many others, sought a piece of the pie. Columbus' most distinguished sports celebrities included an auto racer, boxer, two baseball players, and two table tennis stars, as well as dozens of athletes who achieved only local fame.

Race car driver Mauri Rose's father came to Columbus late in the nineteenth century; Harry Rose worked in a circus, jewelry store, and factory during the early 1900s. He and his wife Carrie Goldsmith Rose became the parents of Mauri in 1906; their son spent most of the early 1920s racing cars in Driving Park. By 1934 Mauri gained sufficient skill to finish second in the Memorial Day 500 at Indianapolis, and came in first in 1941, 1947, and 1948.[8]

The most prominent professional Jewish athlete in Columbus, Lou Bloom, was born in Minsk, Russia, in 1905 and was brought to the United States three years later. Although the "flashiest defensive boxer ever turned out in Columbus" lacked a knock-out punch, "the little Heb" became a local and state champion; later he became the national champion of Australia. Bloom generally received acclaim as the "outstanding ring great in Columbus history." Like dozens of other Jewish boxers of the 1920s, Lou learned his art at the Schonthal Center, and practiced in Columbus gyms after school hours. Reaching his peak in 1927, when he went undefeated in more than ten scheduled ten- and twelve-round local fights, Lou defeated Johnnie Carpenter ("who enters with twenty-six consecutive kayoes") for the Ohio lightweight championship before five thousand "wild, howling, jeering" fans in the "Battle of a Decade."[9]

Bloom became an extremely popular boxer, both in Jewish and non-Jewish circles. Mass spectator sports boomed in the twenties due to newly discovered leisure time and higher living standards — fans wagered $20,000 on the Bloom-O'Dowd match in February 1928. The need for both individual expression and heroes in a society where the individual was rapidly being submerged, led Columbusites to support athletic contests of all kinds. Large crowds followed Lou, whether he fought one of the local West Side's Hilltop Irish favorites, Eddie, Phil, or Mike O'Dowd, or an "import."[10] E. J. Schanfarber, Rabbi Jacob Tarshish, Julius Feibel, Morris Levison, and Aaron Neustadt saw Bloom defeat Johnny Datto early in 1928, while crowds of four to five thousand regularly filled theaters and arenas year after year. When Bloom lost his last major fight to Al Gahn in December of 1932, relinquishing the Columbus lightweight title he held for five years, more than fifty-five hundred cheered the man one local sportswriter described as "the cleverest boxer ever turned out in Columbus."[11]

Other prominent Columbus Jewish boxers who trained at the Schonthal Center during the 1920s included Ben Bloom, Abe Goldberg, "Bugs" Goodman, Chuck Izman, Jake Mellman and

Sammy Goldberg.[12] Despite the popularity of boxing, when baseball became the sport of the twenties Columbus Jewry had interesting representatives on the diamond. Two members of the Schonthal Center — star player Mose Solomon and coach Joe Bonowitz — remain the best known of these athletes.

Moses H. Solomon (1900-1966), the son of an immigrant junk dealer, starred as an outstanding athlete at Columbus Commerce High and became an all-city selection in three sports during his career. Winner of fifteen straight games as a pitcher in 1917, and a sensational drop-kicker and quarterback, Mose broke into professional baseball in his hometown in 1920. Dubbed the "Rabbi of Swat" within two years, in 1923 he completed one of the most remarkable minor league seasons ever recorded. His 143 runs scored, 222 hits, 40 doubles, 49 homers, and .421 average led the Southwestern League. John McGraw of the New York Giants paid $50,000 for his contract and announced he had purchased the "Jewish Babe Ruth." Mose, an outfielder/first baseman, promised to be the million-dollar player McGraw had long sought as he stroked three hits in two games for New York at the end of the season. This, however, ended his major league career as McGraw sent him to the minor leagues after learning either that Mose continued to play football during the off-season or that he could not field.[13]

Columbus' Joe Bonowitz was a Jewish player who *could* field as well as hit. Of the nine children born to David P. (1864-1940) and Sarah Ida Bonowitz (1867-1928), Joe was the second to be born in Columbus. A native of Poland, Joe's father left his wife and four children in Poland and came to Circleville, Ohio, at the invitation of a cousin. By 1895 he resided in Columbus with his family; Joe was born in 1899.[14]

One of the founders of Beth Jacob synagogue in 1898, David Bonowitz was struggling to earn a living at the turn of the century. Joe worked at many jobs in his early school years to supplement the family's income. Despite their circumstances, the Bonowitzs gave their eldest son saxophone and violin lessons which enabled him to earn his college tuition by playing at dances. Later he performed on several radio shows in the mid-twenties: introductions usually ran something like, "This is station WBAP, Ft. Worth, Texas; we will now have a saxophone solo from our star left fielder."

While at South High Joe quarterbacked the state champion football team of 1916, lettered in basketball, and led the city baseball league with a .525 average. At Marietta College he lettered in three sports, distinguishing himself especially in football, and by 1926 had graduated from Palmer School of Chiropractic as Dr. Joe Bonowitz. Fluent in four languages, an accomplished musician, and educated, Joe chose professional baseball as his primary occupation and youth work as his secondary interest.

His baseball career was quite significant. Praised widely as the "best defensive outfielder in the minor leagues" during the golden decade of sports, Bonowitz made only one error in 130 games for Shreveport as a center fielder in 1926 and led the Texas League in fielding several years in a row. A fine hitter, Bonowitz's lifetime average in the tough Texas League was .313; five times in his career he hit better than .350; and the seventy-three doubles he hit in one season still stand in 1976 as a Southern League record. Before he left professional baseball in 1936 to begin a successful career in business, Bonowitz had managed a Southern League team; barnstormed with Rogers Hornsby, Babe Ruth, Lou Gehrig, and Ty Cobb; hit safely against Dizzy Dean; and played on more than ten teams.

Joe Bonowitz made his winter home in Columbus after he broke into professional baseball in 1919 as a catcher with the Columbus Senators. Serving as the athletic director of the Schonthal Center during the off-season for most of the twenties, Bonowitz provided instruction in the center's varied sports programs sometimes thought of as "Americanization activities." He supervised boxing, gymnastics, basketball, and exercise. In September of 1929, while at the Schonthal Center, Bonowitz received a telegram from the Cincinnati Reds announcing that they had purchased his contract from Ft. Worth. Although he did not play a single game in the major leagues, Bonowitz had a tremendous impact upon the Jewish youth of Columbus for a full decade. As one of his former pupils recalled:

> Joe was widely cultured and educated . . . In his home he was a gracious host with numerous interests; he possessed a marked intellect and acquired a sophistication that came from extensive travel and from his brief career as a professor of romance languages in college. . . .[15]

Columbus Jewry's two most famous female athletes, the Thall sisters, were Columbus natives who developed extraordinary table tennis skills as teenagers. "Tybie" (Thelma) was a former president of the Junior Jewish Community Council and recipient of the first varsity letter in tennis ever awarded a girl on a boys' team at East High in 1941. Tybie joined her older sister, Leah, in a grueling national and international schedule of table tennis competition. After winning more than twenty major titles, Tybie's career peaked in 1949 when she played on the American team which won the Women's World Team Championship (Corbillon Cup). Leah ("Miss Ping") stayed at the top of the table tennis world for almost two decades. Between 1941 and 1956 Leah won twenty-five United

States national titles (seven in singles, six in mixed doubles, twelve in women's doubles) and eight Canadian national championships. By 1972 Leah had compiled an amazing record: forty-one United States and twenty-nine Canadian national titles. Even after more than thirty years of competitive table tennis Leah received the number-one seed at the Eighth World Maccabiah games in Israel. As a guest of the Canadian team, she visited the People's Republic of China in 1971.[16]

While Columbus Jewry's sports elite held the spotlight, abundant organized athletic opportunities existed for the entire Jewish community. Not only did this include B'nai B'rith men's and women's league bowling and a wide variety of Schonthal Center youth leagues, but the very popular Sunday Morning League. Almost exclusively the domain of the sons of immigrant parents, this fast-pitch softball league "occupied a special niche in the life of the Columbus Jewish community."

Baseball served as one of the many "American" cultural activities which attracted second-generation Jews, helped to define them as Americans, and thus differentiate them from their immigrant parents. In the thirties and forties softball was "in." Not yet liberated sufficiently from their traditional parents to play on

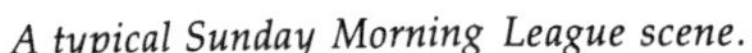
A typical Sunday Morning League scene.

the Jewish Sabbath, and unable to find Sunday morning leagues during church hours, Jews organized their own league. First proposed at The Ohio State Univeristy's Phi Sigma Epsilon fraternity early in 1930, this Jewish league began play that same summer and initiated its first play-offs in 1931. Hundreds of fans witnessed the championship games, while the *Ohio Jewish Chronicle* devoted several columns every week to scores and statistics and even featured a regular column by Lou Berliner titled "Shmoos" describing the highlights, fights, and more colorful personalities which peopled the games. As one ex-player recalled:

> It became a major Jewish community matter. There were personalities involved, as well as the desire for accomplishment and competition. For somebody who's in religious school, like myself, to go out to the park and watch the games, it was really an extraordinary kind of social event. Part of it was not just the playing of the game but the kibitzing going on and the socializing around the sidelines.[17]

And so on the periphery of the community there were two rather divergent paths to glory; some people became famous while a small group became notorious. Frequently, Jewish self-help organizations made the difference; concerned citizens turned delinquents who could have become sly, relentless criminals into clever, determined athletes.

Leon Mendel's "Interurbans" were one of the earliest baseball teams formed by East European Jewish immigrants who used a variety of sports to aid in the process of Americanization.

NOTES FOR CHAPTER 18

1. Daniel Bell, *The End of Ideology* (New York, 1960); Mark Haller, "Organized Crime in Urban Society: Chicago in the Twentieth Century," *Journal of Social History* V (Winter 1971-72): 210-34; idem, "Urban Vice and Civic Reform: Chicago in the Early Twentieth Century," in Jackson and Schultz, editors, *Cities in American Life* (New York, 1972): 290-305.

2. *North American Review* CLXXXVIII (1908): 383-94; W. M. F. Round, "Immigration and Crime," *The Forum* VII (December 1899): 437-38; Arthur Train, "Imported Crime," *McClure's Magazine* XXXIX (May 1912): 83-94.

3. During this period Jews stood out as the least likely group to be labeled "delinquent" because they were handled outside the courts by the many Jewish self-help agencies. See Sophia Robison, *Can Delinquency Be Measured?* (New York, 1936), p. 67.

4. *OSJ*, January 11, February 24, May 1, June 9, 13, 24, August 14, 1928, January 1 and 6, December 15, 1929, December 19, 1930, April 14, December 10, 1932, January 14, 1933. Criminal activities by prominent Columbus Jews appear in the daily press as early as 1901; see *OSJ*, November 2, 5, 6, and 7, December 1, 1901.

5. *OSJ*, March 30, June 16, 1932, November 21, 1934, April 21, 1937, June 7, 1939.

6. Interview with Rabbi Nathan Zelizer.

7. *Jewish Social Studies* II (1940): 209-12. The validity of Levinger's conclusions were challenged, on the grounds of using the religion as the sole variable, by Robert A. Silverman, "Criminality Among Jews: An Overview," *Issues in Criminology* 6:2 (Summer 1971).

8. *Columbus City Directories;* Lillian Rose Warner, Los Angeles, to Marc Lee Raphael, September 24, 1947, correspondence; *NYT,* May 31, 1947, May 31, 1948.

9. *OJC*, March 29, 1929; *OSJ*, June 7, August 1 and 2, November 20, 1927, December 11, 1928, May 20, 1935; interview with Jake Mellman. Lou's father, Morris (1863-1942), worked as a tailor in Columbus at least by 1906, and became quite active at Agudas Achim synagogue; see *OJC*, September 23, 1938.

10. Yiddish writers, in describing the Jewish adjustment to American life, often wrote about boxing in general and Jewish-Irish fights specifically. A story by Aaron Weitzman focuses on the Jewish immigrant parents' reaction to the *pogrom* (fight), their horror over the brutality of the sport, and the *nachas* (joy) resulting from their son's "American Victory." See Abraham Cahan, "New Writers of the Ghetto," *The Bookman* (August 1914): 630-37.

11. *OSJ*, February 21 and 28, 1928, September 8, December 17, 1931, December 22, 1932; *OJC*, November 11, 1927, January 6, August 8, 1928.

12. Sammy Goldberg, the son of the tailor Max Goldberg, fought as a middleweight and once strung together seven consecutive first round knockouts. See *OJC*, March 21, 1930, and interview with Jake Mellman. On Jews and boxing, see S. Kirson Weinberg and Henry Arond, "The

TABLE 60
LOU BLOOM'S BOXING RECORD
PARTIAL LISTING

Date	Opponent	Round Ended	Verdict
May 1926	"Monkey" Roberts	3	Win
June 1926	Phil O'Dowd	8	W
August 1926	Phil O'Dowd	12	W
January 1927	Eddie O'Dowd	12	Loss
April 1927	Dick McDome	12	Draw
June 1927	Dick McDome	12	W
June 1927	Eddie O'Dowd	12	W
July 1927	Frankie Bob	7	W
August 1927	Johnnie Carpenter	12	W
August 1927	Charlie Lupica	12	W
October 1927	Jacinto Valdez	10	W
November 1927	Frankie Susnell	12	W
November 1927	Jacinto Valdez	10	W
January 1928	Johnny Datto	12	W
February 1928	Eddie O'Dowd	12	W
May 1928	Eddie O'Dowd	12	L
June 1928	Lou Janita	6	W
July 1928	Al De Rose	?	W
July 1928	Homer Ronan	?	L
July 1928	Mike O'Dowd	9	W
August 1928	Johnny O'Keefe	12	D
October 1928	Mike O'Dowd	12	L
November 1928	Babe Ruth	?	W
December 1928	Homer Ronan	?	L
March 1929	Eddie Shea	10	L
June 1929	Billy Grime	15*	L
June 1929	Jack Roberts	?*	W
July 1929	Norm Gillespie	15*	W
January 1931	Eddie Anderson	10	W
February 1931	Mike O'Dowd	10	W
September 1931	Johnny Conley	8	L
October 1931	Johnny Conley	12	L
December 1931	Al Gahn	10	L
January 1932	Al Gahn	6	W
February 1932	Jackie Hoster	?	W
June 1932	Press Johnson	10	L
September 1932	Tiger Kid Walker	10	W
December 1932	Al Gahn	10	L
May 1935	Eddie O'Dowd	10	W
February 1943	Al Gahn	5	L

*Australia

SOURCE: Daily newspapers, Columbus, Ohio.

Occupational Culture of the Boxer," *American Journal of Sociology* 57 (March 1952), pp. 460-69.

13. *Encyclopedia of Jews in Sports*, Bernard Postal et al., editors (New York, 1965), p. 54; *The Baseball Encyclopedia* (New York, 1969), p. 1504; Lee Allen, *The Giants and Dodgers: the Fabulous Story of Baseball's Fiercest Feud* (New York, 1965), p. 122; Harold Seymour, *Baseball: The Golden Age* (New York, 1971), p. 83; Stanley B. Frank, *The Jew in Sports* (New York, 1936), p. 88; Frederick C. Lane, "Why Not More Jewish Ball Players?" *Baseball Magazine* 36 (January 1926): 341, 372; Clifford Kachline, National Baseball Library, to Marc Lee Raphael, correspondence, August 26, 1974; *OSJ*, June 2, 1917, March 31, 1922; *Boston Advertiser*, October 2, 1923; *OJC*, July 18, 1947.

TABLE 61
SELECTED SEASON RECORDS OF MOSES SOLOMON AND JOE BONOWITZ

	Year	Games	AB	Runs	Hits	2B	3B	HR	SB	RBI	BB	SO	Avg.
Moses Solomon Hutchinson, KS	1923	134	527	143*	222*	40*	15	49*	12	—	—	—	.421
Joseph Bonowitz Ft. Worth, TX	1927	152	563	61	165	43	5	8	15	92	—	—	.293
Ft. Worth, TX	1928	155	578	87	193	54*	3	3	6	—	26	19	.334
Ft. Worth, TX	1929	150	571	108	205	43	7	16	12	104	24	15	.359
Chattanooga, TN	1932	161	576	73	202	73*	9	9	4	86	—	—	.351

*Led League

14. On Circleville, Ohio, see following note, "The Early Jews of Circleville, Ohio."

15. Mrs. Faye Bonowitz, Atlanta, to Marc Lee Raphael, correspondence, May 30, 1974; Scrapbooks, in possession of Mrs. Faye Bonowitz; South High School, Register and Records, 1916-17; *Chattanooga News*, May 14, 1932; *Palm Beach Post-Times*, November 3, 1968; *OJC*, March 23, 1928; *OSJ*, May 27, 1917; Anonymous questionnaire, Columbus Jewish History Project, 1975.

16. *NYT*, May 28, 1956; *New York Post*, July 18, 1969, and March 12, 1974; *Stockholm Expressen*, April 10, 1967; *Canadian Table Tennis News*, July 1972; *OJC*, April 7 and 28, December 29, 1944, April 27, 1945; Leah Thall Neuberger to Marc Lee Raphael, correspondence, August 15, 1974; Thelma "Tybie" Thall Sommer to Marc Lee Raphael, August 11, 1974, correspondence; Britannica, *Book of the Year*, 1949: p. 682, 1950: p. 656; Lou Thall to Marc Lee Raphael, telephone conversation, January 26, 1976. William Thall (1882-1948), Tybie and Leah's father, came to Columbus early in the century from Berditchev, Russia.

17. Interviews with Eugene Borowitz and Lou Berliner; *OJC*, passim. A large number of players in the league, especially in the 1940s, played in non-Jewish circuits as well; Sammy Gordon, for example, played simultaneously in 1947 for the Nationals of the National League, Kahns of the Buckeye Night Loop, Sully's in the Linden League, and Champo (player-manager) of the Sunday Morning League. See *OJC*, July 18, 1947.

TABLE 62
1947 SUNDAY MORNING LEAGUE'S FINAL BATTING AVERAGES (AT LEAST 12 TIMES AT BAT)

Player-Team	G	AB	R	H	AV
R. Benjamin, Green's	6	24	7	13	.542
K. Kauffman, Sully's	9	35	11	17	.486
S. Gordon, Champo	8	31	8	15	.484
S. Kaufman, AZA	13	43	12	20	.465
G. Zisenwine, Sully's	10	37	11	17	.459
J. Frid'berg, Champo	12	33	11	15	.455
H. Soppel, Sully's	13	46	19	20	.435
R. Feldman, AZA	13	35	11	15	.429
S. Komesar, Capitol	6	14	3	6	.429
S. Harnett, Capitol	10	39	8	16	.410
S. Fink, Cap-Sun	9	32	8	13	.409
H. Landes, Sully's	8	20	6	8	.400
E. Kohn, Sun's	14	43	16	17	.395
H. Eisman, Sully's	13	41	22	16	.390
E. Grayson, Greens	13	41	15	16	.390
P. Cohen, Greens	7	19	5	7	.368
H. Grayson, Greens	6	22	8	8	.363
M. Wolstein, Champo	8	22	4	8	.363
H. Pollock, Sully's	8	31	9	11	.355
C. Young, Champo	11	34	11	12	.354
L. Topy, Capitol	11	34	10	12	.354
R. Katz, Champo	11	34	10	12	.354
J. Fisher, Capitol	10	34	5	12	.354
M. Rising, Pepsi	11	40	4	14	.350
A. Clowson, Sully's	12	54	14	18	.333
B. Meisner, Sully's	11	36	10	12	.333
A. Hackman, Capitol	4	15	0	5	.333
J. Greenberg, Champo	14	49	17	16	.327
H. Munster, Greens	14	46	9	15	.326
R. Goldstein, Pepsi	11	40	9	13	.325
M. Bender, Pepsi	10	31	6	10	.323
Z. Rosenfeld, Sun's	11	25	3	8	.320
I. Licht'nst'n, Sun's	12	41	5	13	.317
B. Robbins, ESAT	5	19	1	6	.316
W. Jonas, Capitol	9	35	6	11	.314
M. Cooper, Greens	9	16	8	5	.312
P. Goldberg, Champo	13	45	13	14	.311
A. Rosen, ESAT	12	36	7	11	.305
S. Wolk, Greens	13	33	12	10	.303
S. Thall, Pepsi	11	33	10	10	.303
S. Seigle, Pepsi	11	33	4	10	.303
M. Weisman, Sully's	12	43	11	13	.302
El Fisher, ESAT	12	40	6	12	.300
S. Handler, Champo	11	30	10	9	.300
M. Koblentz, Greens	6	17	2	5	.295
M. Goodman, Sun's	10	34	6	10	.294
A. Byer, Sully's	12	55	11	16	.291
A. Thall, Champo	13	35	17	10	.286
M. Leiberman, Sun's	12	39	12	11	.282
M. Handler, Champo	12	32	7	9	.281
H. Silverst'n, AZA	11	29	5	8	.276
E. Ableman, ESAT	10	22	4	6	.273
L. Gordon, Greens	14	37	10	10	.270
B. Sully, Capitol	4	15	1	4	.267
S. Stern, Sully's	9	34	9	9	.265
F. Kaplan, Champo	12	34	7	9	.265
B. Bernst'ker, ESAT	13	46	11	12	.261
B. Cohen, AZA	12	23	3	6	.261
H. Fink, Capitol	12	47	9	12	.255
L. Stein, Sun's	14	44	11	11	.250
I. Cohen, Sully's	7	20	1	5	.250
Ed Fisher, Champo	8	16	4	4	.250
J. Zimmerman, Greens	11	37	9	9	.243
R. Thall, Pepsi	12	37	6	9	.243
I. Kerstein, AZA	12	33	7	8	.242
M. Kreske, ESAT	10	25	5	6	.240
M. Freedman, Sun's	14	47	14	11	.234
J. Eisenberg, Greens	14	43	7	10	.233
R. Kriss, ESAT	11	26	6	6	.231
A. Kauffman, Sully's	4	13	1	3	.231
I. Cohen, Sun's	14	44	7	10	.228
T. Green, Capitol	7	22	4	5	.228
D. Erkis, Greens	11	37	6	8	.216
S. Kimm, Capitol	7	19	1	4	.210
K. Solomon, Pepsi	9	29	5	6	.207
M. Maggied, Greens	11	29	3	6	.207
J. Esterkin, Pepsi	10	34	6	7	.206
J. Grotsky, Champo	8	25	5	5	.200
D. Cohen, Greens	12	41	11	8	.195
H. Young, AZA	13	42	10	7	.167
B. Mellman, Sun's	13	42	8	7	.167
E. Borowitz, ESAT	7	26	3	4	.154
J. Gaiser, AZA	13	39	10	5	.128
M. Furman, Capitol	11	34	3	3	.088

SOURCE: *OJC*, September 5, 1947.

TABLE 63
TABLE TENNIS TITLES WON BY THE THALL SISTERS

Year	Contest Won	Thall
1946	U.S. National Women's Singles: Quarters	Tybie
1947	U.S. National Women's Singles: Quarters	T
	U.S. National Women's Doubles	T & Leah
	U.S. National Women's Singles	L
	Canadian International Women's Singles: Semis	T
	Canadian International Mixed Doubles: Semis	T
	World's Women's Doubles (Paris): Semis	L
	World's Women's Singles (Paris)	L
1948	U.S. National Women's Doubles	T & L
	U.S. National Women's Singles: Semis	T
	Canadian International Women's Singles: Semis	T
	Canadian International Mixed Doubles: Semis	T
	Irish Leinster Open Women's Singles (Dublin)	T
	Irish Leinster Open Women's Singles (Dublin) runner-up	L
	World's Women's Singles (London) Quarters	L
	World's Mixed Doubles (London)	T
	World's Women's Doubles (London) Semis	L & T
1949	U.S. National Women's Doubles	T & L
	U.S. National Women's Singles: Quarters	T
	U.S. National Mixed Doubles: Quarters	T
	U.S. Women's Singles	L
	English Open Mixed Doubles	T
	English Open Women's Doubles	T
	English Open Women's Singles: Semis	T
	World's Women's Team Champions Corbillon Cup (Stockholm)	T
	World's Women's Team Champions Corbillon Cup (Stockholm) Semis	T
	World's Women's Team Champions Corbillon Cup (Stockholm) Semis of Women's Singles	?
1951	U.S. Women's Singles	L
	World's Women's Singles (Vienna) Semis	L
	World's Women's Doubles (Vienna) Semis	L
1952	U.S. Women's Singles	L
1953	U.S. Women's Singles	L
1955	U.S. Women's Singles	L
	German Open Women's Singles (Hamburg) runner-up	L
	World's Women's Singles Consolation (Utrecht)	L
1956	World's Mixed Doubles (Tokyo)	L
	U.S. Women's Singles	L

Year	Contest Won	Thall
1957	U.S. Women's Singles	L
	World's Women's Singles Consolation (Stockholm) Semis	L
1959	Belgium Open Women's Singles (Brussels) Semis	L
	English Open Women's Singles Consolation Winner (London)	L
1961	U.S. Women's Singles	L
1969	Gold Medal Women's Team	L
	Gold Medal Women's Doubles	L
	Bronze Medal Women's Singles	L
1973	Maccabian Games (Jewish Olympics) (Tel Aviv)	
	Silver Medal — Women's Doubles	L
	Bronze Medal — Mixed Doubles	L
n.d.	U.S. National Women's Doubles (3 times)	L & T
	Canadian International Women's Doubles (2 times)	L & T

THE EARLY JEWS OF CIRCLEVILLE, OHIO

Central and east European Jewish families began to settle in Circleville, a small community twenty miles south of Columbus, during the 1870s.[1] Almost exclusively peddlers and merchants, their business establishments included Benjamin Friedman's Bazaar,[2] Katz Brothers Clothiers, Henry Levy Dry Goods and Clothing, M. Dulsky Junk, and S. Wasserstrom Wholesale and Retail Dealer in Staple and Fancy Dry Goods, Notions, Hosiery, Gents' Furnishing Goods, Etc.[3] By the first decade of the twentieth century there were enough Jewish families among Circleville's seven thousand residents to form Congregation B'nai Israel, with Moses Polster as president.[4] Circleville served as the principal "feeder" town for Columbus' immigrant Jewish community, especially the Hungarians, and depended upon Columbus for most of its ritual and ceremonial needs.[5]

1. 1880 federal manuscript census schedules, volume 5, enumeration district 228, page 9 (Pickaway County, City of Circleville).
2. Benjamin's son Theodore became, as Ted Lewis, Circleville's most famous native son.
3. A. R. Van Cleaf, *A History of Pickaway County, Ohio and Representative Citizens* (Chicago, 1906), pp. 24-90, 208ff.; *Pickaway County Business Directory and Cook Book* (Circleville, 1899); Petition to Sue, *S. Wasserstrom* v. *Moses Leichtig*, Court of Common Pleas of Pickaway County, June 26, 1882 (brought to my attention by Randall Wasserstrom).
4. *American Jewish Year Book* 5668 (1907-08), p. 354.
5. The Circleville Jewish families that moved to Columbus included the Bonowitzs, Dulskys, Friedmans, Polsters, Topoloskys and Wasserstroms. For more information on Circleville's Jews, see oral interviews with Milton and Max Friedman, and Ben Gordon.

19: A NEW ERA: POSTWAR EDIFICES

By the early forties, many secular and religious Jewish organizations were housed in aging, inadequate buildings in non-Jewish neighborhoods. This situation created communitywide commitments to extensive building campaigns. During World War II, however, both governmental regulations and popular pressure prevented the increasingly affluent Jewish community in Columbus from undertaking building programs. Immediately after the war, flushed with prosperity and energy, Columbus Jews initiated major building programs at Schonthal Center, The Ohio State University Hillel Foundation, Agudas Achim, Beth Jacob, and Tifereth Israel. These projects, which cost more than $1.5 million, created the bulk of the contemporary edifices within the Columbus Jewish community. Such developments were by no means unique to Columbus; by the fall of 1949 more than sixty-nine Jewish communities in twenty-two states had embarked on building programs totaling $18 million during the previous twelve months alone.[1]

As early as 1939, Dr. Elijah J. Gordon, president of the Schonthal Center, initiated a survey conducted by the National Jewish Welfare Board, the parent organization of Jewish Centers. The conclusion was: "Columbus should and could support a Jewish Center." When the center board continued to propose such a program year after year, the United Jewish Fund rebuffed Dr. Gordon, stating that they feared such a project would conflict with the collection of funds to support and rescue European Jewry. As one board member, E. J. Schanfarber, put it:

> to make any reference to a fund that is to be used in the future for a building for a center in connection with the campaign which was to be launched would be a detriment rather than a help in the campaign.

Despite a series of rejections by the UJF, the center board voted to set aside part of its annual allocations for a new building; reluctantly UJF agreed to this. In 1942, $10,000 was invested in government bonds, and by 1946, $50,000 had been reserved from the annual allocations.[2]

As the war drew to an end, communal support for a new center increased, and the UJF initiated its own local survey under the direction of Simon Lazarus. He, and then the UJF itself, quickly became convinced that there "was a crying need for the Jews in Columbus to have a center." In the winter of 1945-46 the Jewish Community Council, the UJF, and the Schonthal Center boards jointly announced that Samuel Summer (1884-1949) would head the $425,000 building fund drive for a new Jewish Center. This figure was not out of reach, for the announcement of the campaign had been preceded by an Advance Gifts dinner in July of 1945 at which "leadership" pledged more than $200,000. Other pledges — $100,000 pledged by the UJF if the campaign achieved $325,000 and two $50,000 special funds — along with an excited community, led Summer to conclude that $425,000 was easily attainable.[3]

TABLE 64
LARGEST ADVANCE GIFTS PLEDGED DURING THE JEWISH CENTER'S BUILDING CAMPAIGN DINNER ON JULY 17, 1945[4]

Schiff Shoe Company	$20,000
Harry Gilbert	10,000
Robert Lazarus	10,000
Simon Lazarus	10,000
The Levy Family	10,000
Jack Resler	10,000
Samuel Summer	10,000
Samuel and I. J. Stone	10,000
Hebrew Free Loan Association	6,600
Sons Bars and Grills	6,600

During the first three years of the campaign, pledges rolled in so rapidly that early in 1949 the center awarded a $643,000 contract to Leo Yassenoff of F & Y Building Service, Inc. to begin building on their $37,000, twenty-five-acre College Avenue site, although less than $500,000 had been collected. The full amount, however, was raised only with great difficulty. Charles Y. Lazarus warned the center board at the time of the contract signing that "one-third of the subscribers to the Jewish Center have not paid their pledges." Correspondence from 1949 reveals continual doubts about whether the building would be completed, for the board could not meet its

While the Columbus Jewish Center organizes programs and activities for persons of all ages, since World War II its preschool programming has received special acclaim. Pictured above is a preschool seder *in the late forties.*

obligations to Yassenoff. Despite the final difficulties, the last $100,000 was raised; by 1951 some 877 persons already had contributed more than $600,000 to the new one-million-cubic-foot, $750,000 Jewish Center.

Dedicated on March 18, 1951, the center had bowling alleys, indoor and outdoor pools, handball courts, a health club, kosher kitchen, gymnasium, auditorium, and meeting rooms. Its builders felt that the center would "usher in a new era in the history of the Columbus Jewish community."[5]

What would this "new era" bring? Although new Jewish centers around the country stressed increased Jewish identity during this period, the publicity releases about the center's dedication expressed the hope that the center would serve the entire Columbus community. As Fred Lazarus, Jr. predicted in his dedicatory address:

> it will show the Jewish and non-Jewish youngsters that they are not necessarily unlike. It will create an increased ease on the part of our Jewish boys and girls with their non-Jewish neighbors; it will eliminate a great deal of aloofness and develop greater understanding and respect; it will show both the Jewish and non-Jewish groups that they are generally alike and that they can get along well with one another if they make up their minds to be smart about it and do so. Rabbis are learning more Christian ideas all the time, and to have more understanding of them. Perhaps other churches are going to exchange ideas. In the use of this Center you will find added incentive to participate in the American way of life.

While the organization's leaders eventually became concerned about the Jewishness of the Jewish Center, their first years in the new building evinced much more concern with being a recognized part of the community. Perhaps the tension of the times created by the Rosenbergs' trial and Senator McCarthy's dominance account for the similarity between the activities sponsored by the Jewish Center and those at the Columbus YMCA. After more than a decade of bidding to "out-American" its competition, uniquely Jewish programming dominated the center.[6]

Hillel did not face the same funding difficulties which dogged the Jewish Center. In July of 1944 the national B'nai B'rith proposed a $100,000 E. J. Schanfarber Memorial Building Fund which would provide the "seed money" for the first new Hillel building in the country, in memory of a devoted friend of B'nai B'rith and a long-time member of the National Hillel Commission. By September the founder of B'nai B'rith Women in Columbus, Sara Schwartz, headed a National Hillel Alumni Committee composed of former members from The Ohio State University. Three months later Simon Lazarus, who took charge of the local campaign, announced that the Columbus community had already contributed $50,000.[7]

The campaign enjoyed sufficient success for ground to be broken on May 23, 1948, at 46 East Sixteenth Avenue. That same year the Hillel board dedicated the E. J. Schanfarber War Memorial Chapel to the fifty Jewish Ohio State University students who died in World War II. Designed and built by Leo Yassenoff's F & Y Building Service, Inc., the two-story, debt-free $200,000 Hillel Center was dedicated on February 6, 1949. Facilities included an auditorium seating 600; a chapel for 100 persons; and several meeting, study, and recreation rooms.[8]

Hillel's rapid fund-raising success was not duplicated by Agudas Achim. Faced with a forty-year-old building in an area rapidly being deserted by the Jewish community in 1945, Congregation Agudas Achim prepared to construct a new synagogue. After considering more than eleven possible lots, the congregation approved a site at Broad and Stanwood in suburban Bexley, a small and rather exclusive municipality three miles east of downtown.[9] Agudas Achim purchased a lot for $16,500 in March of 1946, and in the same month announced a $250,000 building fund campaign. Simultaneously, a mortgage-burning party celebrated complete ownership of the Washington Avenue synagogue.[10]

The board instructed Rabbi Hirschsprung to appeal for funds for the new synagogue on Yom Kippur, 1945; the following April, Ohio State University Professor Marvin Fox stirred a dinner gathering to pledge $100,000 toward the new edifice. Between these two occasions, the board asked members to pledge $200 a

This building served the Hillel Foundation at 46 East Sixteenth Avenue for fourteen years before being demolished to make room for the $200,000 Hillel Center.

year during 1946, 1947, and 1948, in addition to paying their dues. By January of 1946 pledges already totalled $90,000. Unfortunately, a serious deficit in operating funds resulted, and the congregation automatically raised every member's dues by 25 percent.[11]

The building drive abated for about eighteen months in deference to the communitywide campaign for a new center; in 1948 Agudas Achim began again with a $375,000 goal. A $25,000 pledge from the sisterhood in February brought the total to $200,000, and monthly announcements with photos of generous donors followed. By April 23, 1950, Agudas Achim broke ground for the new synagogue, "although moneys on hand are not sufficient." The cornerstone laying on July 15, 1951, found generous contributors to the campaign, Max and Harry Silberstein, setting the stone. By the High Holidays the congregation worshipped in its new $300,000 structure.[12]

Like Agudas Achim, Tifereth Israel's congregation simultaneously burnt their old mortgage and began planning a new building. In 1943, following a successful ten-day drive headed by Harry Gilbert and Sam Melton, one hundred and ten persons gave $24,820 which enabled the congregation to burn its mortgage. In the fall of 1944 Sam Melton's $1,000 donation initiated a campaign for a new educational center on property adjacent to the synagogue. By the summer of 1945 Melton headed the $100,000 campaign; early in 1947, he announced the hiring of architects and a new goal of $135,000. On November 23, 1947, although short of the goal, Max and Harry Silberstein again set the cornerstone. Following continual pleas for funds throughout the summer of 1948, the congregation dedicated the $180,000 Tifereth Israel Educational Center, with thirteen classrooms, on September 17, 1948.[13]

Immediately after the war, like Agudas Achim Congregation Beth Jacob established a building fund which would enable it to move in the midst of the Jewish population. Then the board initiated a creative alternative to an independent building campaign — a merger with Agudas Achim. First proposed in 1947 or 1948, a merger was appealing because the "rabbi [Greenwald] was too old," the Beth Jacob "synagogue too Orthodox," and "there was not enough of a congregation in either one to build a great big synagogue; by merging the two, Orthodoxy would be strengthened"; it seemed to "much of the community that there was no more sensible thing that could be done than to merge the two congregations." During 1948 and 1949, the merger appeared certain to the congregations involved, for joint statements, salutations, and even designs of the proposed Beth Jacob-Agudas Achim Synagogue filled the *Ohio Jewish Chronicle* as late as December 1949.[14]

Early in 1950, however, at an emergency meeting, Beth Jacob Congregation "took a vote, a very close vote, and the merger failed by a very small margin." While passions still are stirred by the subject and each version of the event is colored by personal or synagogue loyalties, most observers agree that several factors convinced Rabbi Greenwald, and then the congregation, to build on its Bulen Avenue property rather than to join Agudas Achim in Bexley. Among the reasons for Beth Jacob's decision were the roles of the rabbis, religious principles, and the fear of loss of identity.

The "big question was what would be the role of Rabbi Greenwald." A scholarly and prolific writer, Rabbi Greenwald presided over a small, close to moribund, and poor congregation. Nevertheless, he had no plans to retire, and when Agudas Achim proposed that he assume the position of rabbi *emeritus* and leave the young, dynamic Agudas Achim rabbi, Samuel Rubenstein, in charge, the fifty-nine-year-old Greenwald "got a core of people and they argued against the merger." Indeed, most agree with one combatant that if Greenwald "had let things alone, we could have all been over at Agudas Achim together."[15]

The issue of *mechitzah* (a physical partition between men and women) also separated the congregations, for Rabbi Greenwald "would never go into a shul with mixed seating," while Agudas Achim not only planned to permit some mixed seating in the new structure but already permitted it at the old Washington Avenue *shul*. Ironically, Greenwald, who used this issue to defeat the merger, later discovered that within his own congregation there existed strong opposition to separate seating. The new Beth Jacob, as a compromise, had no *mechitzah*, only separate pews.[16]

Finally, Beth Jacob had serious reservations about being "swallowed up" by the larger congregation. Not only might Greenwald be subordinated to Rubenstein, but the "small and poorer *shul* might lose its independence." This loss of identity, combined with the potential threat to their rabbi, convinced the congregation to withdraw from the merger and prepare to construct a new building on Bulen Avenue. Ground breaking took place on September 17, 1950, after a building campaign yielded more than $50,000 with promises of another $50,000 to $60,000. Construction began on April 12, 1951, with $92,000 at hand, and the synagogue opened its doors in June of 1952. On September 7, 1952, Max and Harry Silberstein set their third cornerstone.[17]

Described at the cornerstone ceremony as a place where "traditional Orthodox Judaism will be interpreted within the walls," Beth Jacob prominently announced its policy of separate seating in all of its promotional literature. While noting that the "partition between ladies and gentlemen [was] in accordance with traditional Orthodox procedure and law," the members were well aware that the board nearly voted against Rabbi Greenwald and *with* a vocal and sizeable group of members who urged mixed seating in order to compete with Agudas Achim and attract new congregants. For "the man who literally . . . raised the money, it was almost as if he wouldn't be able to go into his own *shul*."[18]

As demonstrated by the debate over *mechitzah*, Columbus Jewry consciously chose a process of acculturation to American customs while defining its philanthropic, religious, organizational, and associational life between 1925 and 1950. This process involved the adoption of the culture of non-Jewish Columbus — the language, clothing, work habits, recreation, forms of organizational activity, style of institutional religious life, and fund raising. Simultaneously, aspects of Jewish cultural, religious, organizational, philanthropic, and associational life were maintained. Both minimally affiliated and religiously observant Jews chose to live near other Jews, to join Jewish organizations, to support Jewish charities, and to worship in Jewish institutions. For their colleagues, co-workers, neighbors, friends, and mates, Jews chose Jews. Thus the acculturation to an American environment emerged concomitantly with a commitment to Jewish identification and group life.

Mediating between Jewish and American cultures and creating an American-Jewish style of life which combined the pluralistic aspects of American society and the richness of Jewish civilization, the process of acculturation continued in the postwar decades. For example, the Jewish Center evolved from a typical community center to an Americanized focal point of Jewish culture. In Part IV the results of a 1975 community survey and exploration of several aspects of Jewish life in Columbus further define the multi-faceted process of acculturation.

Members of the Beth Jacob Synagogue are shown here carrying the Torah Scrolls as the congregation moved from Donaldson Street to Bulen Avenue in 1952.

NOTES FOR CHAPTER 19

1. *Jewish Telegraphic News,* September 4, 1949.

2. *OJC,* December 21, 1945; Board Meeting, Schonthal Center, Minutes, October 16, 1941; Miscellaneous Reports, Columbus Jewish Center Building, The New Center 1940-51; 1942 Budgetary Allocations, United Jewish Fund, July 15, 1943; Allocations Committee Meeting, United Jewish Fund, April 14, 1943; Disbursements, United Jewish Fund, March 31, 1944, and May 8, 1946. Columbus Jewish Center.

3. Board Meeting, Schonthal Center, May 31, 1945; *OJC,* December 21, 1945, January 4 and 25, February 1, June 14, 1946; Board Meeting, Jewish Center, Minutes, June 7, 1949; Miscellaneous Reports, Columbus Jewish Center Building, The New Center 1946-52. Columbus Jewish Center.

4. "List of Subscribers and Amounts Pledged," March 24, 1947. Columbus Jewish Center.

5. Board Meeting, Jewish Center, Minutes, November 17, 1947, February 3, 1949; Miscellaneous Reports, Columbus Jewish Center Building, The New Center 1940-51; Charles Y. Lazarus to I. W. Garek, correspondence, February 15, 1949; Leah Rosenfeld to Sam Stone, correspondence, September 27, 1949; Jack Resler to Robert Mellman, correspondence, September 22, 1949; *OJC,* February 11, 1949, March 23, 1951; *Dedication of Jewish Center of Columbus, Ohio, March 14, 1951.* Columbus Jewish Center.

6. Herbert M. Biskar, "A History of the Jewish Centers Association of Los Angeles, " D.S.W. dissertation, University of Southern California, 1972, p. 25; *OJC,* March 19, 1951; *Dedication Jewish Center, Columbus, Ohio, March 14, 1951.* Subsequent discussions focused on whether the Jewish Center was becoming a "community center" (worrying excessively about physical, cultural, and social activities which were available elsewhere) or a "Jewish center" (introducing a significant Jewish element into the programming to build bridges from the Jewish present back to the past and forward to the future).

7. *OJC,* July 28, September 15, 1944; Hillel Papers, Box 4, Folder 14.

8. *OSJ,* February 5 and 7, 1949, May 24, 1948; *OJC,* May 21 and 28, April 30, 1948, January 21, February 4 and 11, 1949; Hillel Papers, Box 4, Folders 13 and 14, Box 16, Folder 39.

9. Although Jews began to settle in some limited parts of Bexley, even before 1925, covenants restricting the sale of homes were quite common in deeds. See also following note, "The Early Jews of Bexley, Ohio."

10. Agudas Achim Minutes, February 27, July 31, August 5, 1945; *OJC,* March 8, 22, 29, 1946.

11. Agudas Achim Minutes, August 28, 1945, January 29, July 22, August 6, 1946; *OJC,* April 12, 1946.

12. *OJC,* January 16, February 27, 1948, April 14 and 21, 1950, July 13 and 20, September 21 and 28, 1951, January 4, 1952; *OSJ,* April 22, 1950, July 14 and 16, September 22, 1951; *CCJ,* July 15, September 22, 1951.

13. Tifereth Israel Minutes, January 21, 1943, September 7, 1944, January 16 and 30, June 5, 1947, March 18, June 17, 1948; *OJC,* October 10 and 31,

November 21 and 28, 1947, September 17, 1948; *OSJ,* November 22, 1947, September 18, 1948.

14. Interviews with Sylvia Schecter, Marvin Fox and Jacob Pass; *OJC,* November 10, 1944, September 16 and 30, December 23, 1949.

15. Interviews with Sylvia Schecter and Marvin Fox.

16. David Stavsky, "A *Mechitza* for Columbus," *Jewish Life* (Winter 1974): 22-27.

17. *OJC,* September 8 and 15, 1950, April 20, 1951, June 27, September 5, 1952; "Financial Statement, January 1, 1951 to July 1, 1951," Beth Jacob Congregation Building Fund. Beth Jacob Synagogue.

18. "Consecration of a Cornerstone, September 7, 1952," Beth Jacob Congregation; *OJC,* April 11, 1952; *OSJ,* September 8, 1952. Beth Jacob Synagogue.

THE EARLY JEWS OF BEXLEY, OHIO

Bexley, an incorporated city and school district four square miles in area three miles east of downtown Columbus, is one of Columbus' affluent suburbs. For fifty years the wealthiest members of the Columbus Jewish community have chosen to live in Bexley. This village of fifteen thousand in 1970 began as a combination of faculty homes when Capital University moved out to this area in 1876. By the first decade of the twentieth century the Bexley of today began to take shape, for three wealthy Columbus men built palatial mansions. Others followed, and established a pattern of elegance along its western edge.

Prior to 1920 no Jewish family lived in Bexley, and property deeds routinely restricted both Negroes and Jews. The first twelve Jewish families to live in the community purchased dwellings between 1920 and 1923. Three families purchased parcels on the same day in 1920, and the others followed one year later. By 1924 twelve families had dwellings upon which the county levied property taxes.

TABLE 65
BEXLEY'S JEWISH RESIDENTS IN 1924

Name	Parcel	Address	Date of Purchase	Built * Bought † Home	1924 Appraised Value Land	Homes	Total
Levy, R.	2886	78 S. Drexel	4-11-20	*	$ 6,740	$11,500	$18,240
Lazarus, S.	2022	172 S. Columbia	4-11-20	*	25,550	47,150	72,700
Joseph, R.	3048	2180 Bryden	4-11-20	*	3,310	8,050	11,360
Stern, J.	1268	2350 Bryden	3-23-21	†	2,420	8,460	10,880
Meyer, J.	2020	2173 Bryden	5- ?-21	*	4,010	5,470	9,480
Polster, L.	3487	314 S. Drexel	5- 8-21	*	5,050	13,140	18,190
Kobacker, A.	1987	295 S. Parkview	6- 8-21	†	9,800	14,120	23,920
Weinfeld, S.	260	508 S. Parkview	6-29-21	†	3,830	6,750	10,580
Gilbert, H.	2045	419 S. Columbia	10-26-21	*	9,440	11,690	21,130
Gumble, M.	1425	2488 Bryden	8- 1-22	†	2,170	10,080	12,250
Glick, F.	873	381 S. Columbia	3-28-23	*	9,440	13,440	22,880
Levin, L.	3620	2265 Bryden	10- 3-23	*	3,460	9,890	13,350

SOURCE: Map Department Parcel Room, Personal Property Tax Room of Franklin County Auditor's Office; *Columbus City Directories* 1919-24.

PART IV

THE POSTWAR COMMUNITY

1951-1975

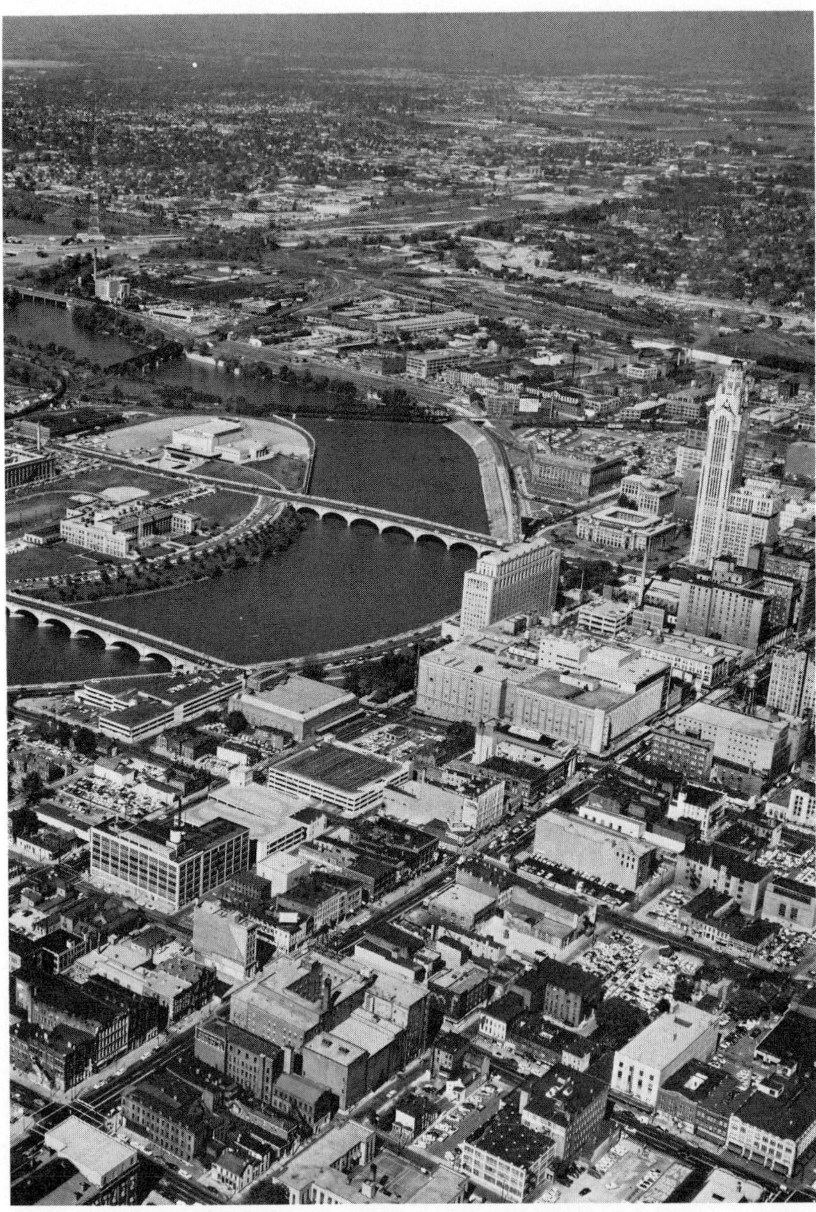

Aerial view of Columbus in 1958, looking northwest. In the background is the LeVeque-Lincoln Tower, to the left the riverfront Civic Center and, across the Scioto River, the Franklin County Veterans Memorial Building.

With fourteen hundred miles of paved streets, no plank sidewalks, and a population over half a million, the capital of Ohio in 1975 bore little resemblance to its 1840 counterpart. Once a swampy, rugged area, the center city has undergone a series of facelifts to obliterate urban decay. In the mid-fifties the city established the Market-Mohawk area rehabilitation program; after the dust settled eight years later the first building in the new Market-Mohawk area, a Holiday Inn, was completed. This razing and rebuilding civic improvement cycle is continuing in the center city.

In the seventies, Columbus is maximizing strengths evident over one hundred and fifty years ago. Girdled and quartered by freeways, Columbus' location in the line of east-west travel, as well as its proximity to prosperous farming areas and sources of iron, gas, and coal, have predetermined its destiny as a commerce and manufacturing center. Slightly under nine hundred diversified industries employed approximately eighty-six hundred workers in 1975. In addition to Columbus' publishing and printing industry, the principal manufactures for national and international consumption included packing, foundry, and machine-shop products; shoes; meat and food; auto parts; glass; aircraft; electrical appliances; electronic and telephone equipment. A healthy mix of federal, state, city, and county government offices; universities and colleges; research facilities; as well as diversified industries and businesses, have created a stable community with a built-in financial resiliency.

Columbus' major annexation program began in 1955; by 1960 the city's size had doubled to 89 square miles, by 1975, city boundaries encompassed 168.8 square miles. As the city enlarged, a corresponding population shift began emptying the center city. In 1950 the Columbus population was 375,901; by 1959, it had increased by over 75 percent to 665,555. During the same period center city population dropped by 11.8 percent. The Jewish population increased from an estimated 9,000 in 1956 to 13,000 in 1971 and 14,000 by 1975.

Columbus Jewry, during the third quarter of the twentieth century, became caught up in the hectic social mobility of urban and suburban America. Middle-class suburban housing developments, as well as new synagogues and communal buildings, appeared throughout the community during these years of growth, prosperity, wealth, and educational achievement. The Jews of Columbus not only entered new homes and buildings, but they selected well-qualified professionals to head their agencies, enlarged some old organizations like the sisterhoods and Hadassah, and created new associations like Brandeis Women. During this period recreational and cultural activities were expanded at the Jewish Center. More concertedly than before, synagogues developed into family institutions where primary relations and long rabbinical careers predominated.

American life, especially in the sixties, produced not only a new generational viewpoint but an upsurge in specifically Jewish expressions as well. There emerged new forms of Jewish consciousness, not the result of any direct experience with overt anti-Semitism but the outcome of a decade or so of Jewish participation in movements to change the society. Some Jews rejected the prevailing Jewish lifestyle and created their own, while others demonstrated a willingness to emphasize their Jewish identity and uniqueness. A small number began to think about what it meant to be Jewish, while a few more felt that America's honeymoon with the Jews was over and that it was necessary to constantly alert the Jewish community and general public to the "new" anti-Semitism. As Israel became more and more ingrained in American Jewish consciousness, others made fund raising into the most important task of the Jewish community. The wide variety of responses to these years of change and excitement can be briefly documented here.

One word of caution, however, is necessary. I have consciously refrained from writing about living persons — especially those in positions of leadership — and from narrating the history of communal agencies, organizations, and religious institutions in the postwar decades. Not only are the sources so overwhelming that the limitations of time and space prevented their adequate study, but the roles of many leaders and resolutions of many issues are so passionately felt in the community that interpreting them would have proven extremely sensitive. Distance aids objectivity, and to describe the part played in Columbus Jewish life by men and women with whom I work and live will be the task of a future historian.

20: A DEMOGRAPHIC SURVEY: COLUMBUS JEWRY 1975

During 1975 a sixty-question survey was sent to six hundred of the more than nine thousand adult members of Columbus' Jewish community. This total adult population figure was compiled from Columbus Jewish Federation lists of contributors and non-contributors, synagogue and organizational membership lists, and with the help of several persons who knew many newcomers and those Jews who had neither philanthropic nor affiliating tendencies. Four hundred and ninety of the recipients in this random probability sample returned the survey — an exceptionally good 82 percent return. Their responses — and those from smaller supplementary surveys — provide a rich source of information about a contemporary middle-sized, suburban Jewish population. Respondents' answers to questions about permanency, social structure, income, voting patterns, divorce, and premarital sex are included in this chapter. Other survey results have been interwoven in the following chapters wherever applicable.

One of the most basic characteristics explored by the 1975 survey was the degree of permanency displayed by the Jewish community. Reflecting Columbus' nativity trends, the respondents were predominantly — 89 percent — American born, with 20 percent born in Columbus.[1] Of the 11 percent foreign born, the two largest groupings consisted of elderly east Europeans who immigrated between 1900 and 1920, and well-educated Germans who immigrated in the 1930s. Roughly ten European countries have provided the bulk of Columbus' foreign-born Jewish immigrants since World War II.

Forty-eight percent of Columbus' Jewish population was American-born, with foreign-born parents and grandparents. Coupled with the 11 percent foreign born, it would appear that 59 percent of the community maintained very close connections with the values and culture of foreign-born Jews. Another 37 percent had foreign-born grandparents, leaving only 4 percent of the adult community untouched by European influences.

Most of Columbus' Jews were not newcomers to the community; 45 percent have lived in the community for twenty-five years or more, and the median length of residence was more than twenty years.[2] Nevertheless, as in the greater metropolitan area, Jews were constantly moving into the community; more than a quarter of the Jewish residents have moved to Columbus during the past ten years.[3] A large majority of these initially moved to Columbus to attend The Ohio State University.

As a rule, such a high percentage of permanency within any community would create a closely-knit, clannish community. Aside from Jews eighteen to twenty-five years of age, three out of five stated that all — or almost all — of their closest friends were Jews; for more than half of the remainder, Jewish friends comprised half of their close friendships. Although Jews represented less than 3 percent of the Columbus community, more than half of those surveyed claimed they had no close Protestant or Catholic friends. Interestingly, there was a positive correlation between the length of residence in Columbus and the number of close Jewish friends, suggesting that a sense of clannishness develops with integration into the Jewish community.

TABLE 66
1975 COLUMBUS JEWISH COMMUNITY SURVEY: CLOSEST FRIENDS

	Age Brackets						
Jewish Friends	18-25	26-35	36-45	46-55	56-65	66+	All
All or Almost All	25%	51.5%	57.1%	75.0%	61.5%	57.7%	56.1%
At Least Half	60	33.3	28.6	18.7	23.1	26.9	30.1
A Few	15	12.1	12.5	6.3	15.4	15.4	12.5
None	—	3.0	1.8	—	—	—	1.3
Total	**40**	**132**	**112**	**64**	**78**	**52**	**478**

Young native Columbus Jews used the term "townies" to set themselves off from Jewish newcomers to the community, and to describe clans, cliques, or interlocking friendship networks. The common denominator of all townies was life-long familiarity with the traditions and characteristics of Columbus Jewry. While townies served as models for what many Columbus Jews wanted to become, there were, of course, disadvantages to growing up Jewish in Columbus:

> Jews were very, very class conscious, very status conscious — you had to live on this street or you had to drive this particular car. It was

> all based on your pocket . . . because of the closeness of the Jewish community and the cliquishness of it, it was very hard for a person that didn't fit in, perhaps in high school, to fit in later on in life. This guy, for example, was really a nothing in high school; now he is in his early thirties and he's still a nothing, for people that have lived in this community their entire life still judge people on the way they were in their adolescent years. It's very, very hard if you've lived there and maintained your same set of friends, to advance. You're labeled, so to speak.[4]

The abundance of native-born Jews — or at least their prominence in the community — created the impression of excessive familism within Columbus Jewry. Indeed, Columbus Jewish natives prided themselves on their close relationships with kin — especially parents and siblings. In suburban Bexley, where residential turnover was minimal, it was not unusual to find three generations of a Jewish family living within a short walk of each other. This closeness was also obvious in nearby Eastmoor:

> My parents lived on a street in Eastmoor. My mother lived at 756, my grandfather lived at 750, my mother's brother lived at 745, and my mother's sister lived at 740. They all lived together on that one street.[5]

Friday evening dinners together, Sabbath afternoon visits by grandchildren, shopping, recreation, and holiday celebrations were most common. Generally a source of financial and moral support, especially with the growing number of single-parent Jewish families in the community, the tri-generation family was abundant in Columbus' Jewish areas.

After growing up in an extended family environment, many townies moved into the Greek "family" on campus. In addition to giving some insight into sorority life, the responses of our Sigma Delta Tau (SDT) alumnae indicate that being Greek was as important in the twenties as it was in the fifties. During the 1920s, SDT consisted of a homogeneous group: seventeen of the eighteen received all of their dues as well as tuition, living expenses, and spending money from their parents. Sixteen defined their families as "middle class"; no east European girls lived in the sorority. Fifteen of the girls could not recall any specifically Jewish sorority activities. Additionally, widespread agreement existed that the "town girls" were both the "leaders of the sorority" and the "socially desirable group."

During the fifties and sixties "You weren't much if you weren't Greek" at The Ohio State University. To choose not to join Sigma Delta Tau meant cutting oneself off socially; to join SDT, within the rigid hierarchy of status, was to enter the elite of Jewish sororities and be well on the way to being pinned to a Jewish pre-law, pre-med, accounting or business major. The sorority clearly remained segregated not only by religion but also by social class; twenty of the twenty-two respondents of the 1950s claimed they came from upper middle-class families. The "best" Jewish girls still joined SDT exclusively, and the results of its rush were "heartbreak, humiliation, resentment and tragedy for many."

The Greek system began even before college for Columbus Jewish youth. Divided off into clubs, fraternities, and sororities, Bexley High School was so intensely social that it appeared to be a mini-university. Of two hundred and thirteen Jewish high school students surveyed in 1956-57, only twenty-nine did not belong to social clubs, fraternities, or sororities — and two-thirds of these were in their first year of high school. The investigator concluded:

> The social clubs play a dominant role in the lives of these teenagers; there are very few unaffiliated boys and girls. There is a caste system, following much the same stratification as the adult population. There is very little socializing between groups and individuals in different status categories.[6]

The social value of being Greek has declined on high school and college campuses in the seventies. And those who were — or wanted to be — Greek in the earlier decades of this century now look for other benchmarks in evaluating their fellow Jews. In 1975, survey respondents indicated that those in the uppermost strata of economic, philanthropic, religious, academic, and residential hierarchies were considered to be what the sociologists term the "elite."[7] Included in this umbrella term were federation officers, rabbis of the largest and most prestigious synagogues, top corporate and financial leaders, owners of the community's most ostentatious homes, and teachers of Judaica.

With the exception of Orthodox respondents, Columbus Jews of all ages admired economic leaders the most — individuals who headed the dominant Jewish corporate and financial enterprises in Columbus. Listed most often, without any special ranking, were these establishments and individuals:

Manufacturing Concerns

Capitol Manufacturing Company	Sam Melton
N. Wasserstrom & Sons	Wasserstroms
Yenkin-Majestic Paint Corp.	Abe, Ben, and Fred Yenkin
R. G. Barry Company	Gordon Zacks
Thurman Manufacturing Company	Millard Cummins
Hercules Trousers	Jack Resler

Department Stores	
F. & R. Lazarus & Company	Charles Lazarus
Schottenstein Stores Corp.	Alvin Schottenstein
Retail Stores	
Glick's Furniture Company	William and Robert Glick
White's Fine Furniture and Sleep Shops	Gordon Schiffman
B. Goodman Fashions	Ben Goodman
Madison's, Inc.	
The Union Company	Robert Levy
The Limited	Leslie Wexner
Sun TV and Appliances	Herb and Macy Block
Rite Rug Company	Stanley Goldberg
Gilbert Shoes	Gilberts
Wholesale Concerns	
SCOA Industries	Herbert Schiff
Continental Office Supply	Ernest Stern
Miscellaneous	
Columbus Outdoor Advertising Company	Thomas Kaplin, Jr.
Yellow Cab Company	Marvin Glassman
Wyandotte Communities	Irving Schottenstein
Ellman Financial Corporation	Ed Ellman
Burger Chef	Elliott Grayson

Campaign leaders of the Columbus Jewish Federation were chosen as the second most admired group in the community, and as the most admired by half of the Orthodox respondents. The general chairman and the federation president were especially favored; many persons used the term more broadly to include the highest-ranking officers of the organization. This image of fund raisers as the elite confirms the central role which this activity plays in the Jewish community.

Rabbis and Judaica professors emerged as the choices of about a quarter of the community; amazingly they outranked those in prestigious neighborhoods. Equally surprising was the fact that rabbis were designated at all. For many reasons, during the past two centuries the position of the rabbi has been undergoing a transformation. The basic function of the traditional rabbi was that of religio-legal authority; the sole patent of the authority was his learning. Scholarship bestowed a position of dignity. Today scholarship has a low priority; other functions like membership recruitment and organizational maintenance have become central.

TABLE 67
1975 COLUMBUS JEWISH COMMUNITY SURVEY: THE ELITE

	Percentage Admiring Each Elite Characteristic				
	Corporate/ Financial	CJF Campaign	Rabbis	Judaica Teachers	Neighborhood/ Country Club
Denominations (N)					
Reform (136)	46%	25%	13%	12%	4%
Conservative (166)	44	27	12	11	6
Orthodox (126)	24	48	16	8	4
All (428)	39	33	14	10	4
Income Levels (N)					
Under $ 7,000 (20)	50%	40%	—	10%	—
$ 7/12,000 (30)	53	20	20%	7	—
12/15,000 (40)	45	15	20	15	5%
15/20,000 (54)	52	19	7	11	11
20/35,000 (130)	38	31	14	14	3
35/50,000 (52)	54	31	8	4	4
50/75,000 (38)	47	37	11	—	5
75/100,000 (16)	50	50	—	—	—
Over $100,000 (12)	33	50	17	—	—

As a result, Columbus rabbis were involved in a vast complex of activities which were once peripheral.

The rabbi's role as a literate and learned teacher, preacher, minister (officiant at public ceremonial events) or pastor was not cited as often by our respondents as his role as "messenger to the gentiles" or enthusiastic supporter of interfaith activities. Despite the ease with which Jewish lay leaders met their counterparts in the general community, there was still a sense of awe — so common a generation or two ago — reserved for those few rabbis who have been most prominent in keeping the bridges of communication open between Jews and non-Jews.

According to recent studies after World War II, Jewish income levels have consistently been higher than those of the general population, a fact which correlates with the Jewish community's high regard for corporate and financial leaders. As early as 1957, United States Government census surveys revealed that 17 percent of the Jewish males — in contrast to 3.6 percent of all males — had incomes of $10,000 and over; while 41 percent of the total male population earned under $3,000, only 25 percent of the Jewish males earned this amount. And two decades later, no measurable group had higher income figures than Jewish males.[8]

No matter how the evidence was arranged, the Columbus Jews surveyed were a very affluent group:[9] 77.5 percent of those

TABLE 68
1975 COLUMBUS JEWISH COMMUNITY SURVEY:
INCOME LEVELS

Income Levels	Age Brackets						Cumulative Percent
	18-25	26-35	36-45	46-55	56-65	All	
Under $ 7,000	27.8%	1.5%	2.0%	**	6.3%	4.6%	4.6%
$ 7/12,000	33.3	10.8	3.9	**	6.3	8.7	13.3
12/15,000	27.8	9.2	7.8	**	9.3	9.2	22.5
15/20,000	11.1	13.8	11.8	**	18.8	11.7	34.2
20/35,000	**	38.6	35.4	60.0%	31.2	36.2	70.4
35/50,000	**	15.4	23.5	16.7	12.5	15.8	86.2
50/75,000	**	7.7	7.8	16.7	12.5	9.2	95.4
75/100,000	**	1.5	3.9	3.3	3.1	2.6	98.0
Over $100,000	**	1.5	3.9	3.3	**	2.0	100.0
Total	**36**	**130**	**102**	**60**	**64**	**392***	

*Not all of the 490 respondents answered each question.

**Our failure to discover any persons in these categories does not mean that they do not exist — but suggests that the number is very, very small.

responding had incomes above $15,000; 65.8 percent earned more than $20,000; and nearly three of every ten respondents reported an income of more than $35,000. Few had to wait for economic success; of those under thirty-six years of age, 78 percent earned more than $15,000 and 61 percent reported incomes over $20,000. Not one respondent between forty-six and fifty-five reported a family income of less than $20,000.[10]

In addition to supporting multimillion dollar fund drives for Jewish philanthropies, the substantial incomes in the Jewish community enabled hundreds of families to enjoy the luxury of a very expensive Jewish country club. While the majority of country club members were middle-aged, Winding Hollow Country Club's membership list included quite a few Columbus Jews between twenty-five and thirty-five, some of whom were the children of members. Whether young or old, the club served as a leisure time retreat; many members invested substantial portions of their earnings to provide family members with the good life — fashionable, elaborate entertainment and recreation.

The country club style paid only minimal homage to culture or to the quest for personal intellectual development. Rather, fresh air, sun, and fun were emphasized. Included were sports of all kinds — particularly tennis — outdoor parties, extensive travel, snow and water skiing, and trips to warmer climates in the winter. This style attracted both the young nouveau riche and those with inherited wealth who have become the club's aristocracy.

Like the rest of mankind, Columbus Jews tended to join organizations whose constituents reflected their own status, thus perpetuating the exclusiveness of these groups. This process of self-selection may be seen in the many Jewish women's organizations which form one of the fundamental bases of the community. Included were the synagogue sisterhoods, the Council of Jewish Women, Brandeis Women, the Women's Division of the CJF, and Hadassah. Generally, the higher the family income, the more Jewish organizations the adults joined; more than half of those families with incomes between thirty-five thousand and one hundred thousand dollars belonged to three or more Jewish organizations. Conversely, the lower the income level, the fewer the organizational affiliations; only two of thirty-eight persons with incomes between seven and twelve thousand dollars joined three or more organizations.

TABLE 69
1975 COLUMBUS JEWISH COMMUNITY SURVEY: AFFILIATIONS WITH JEWISH ORGANIZATIONS

Income	Jewish Organization Memberships				
Levels (N)	0	1	2	3	Over 4
Under $7,000 (26)	23%	31%	31%	8%	8%
$ 7/12,000 (38)	21	37	37	5	—
12/15,000 (42)	19	29	24	14	14
15/20,000 (54)	19	30	37	7	7
20/35,000 (132)	17	23	29	12	20
35/50,000 (52)	8	23	15	19	35
50/75,000 (40)	20	10	5	20	45
75/100,000 (14)	—	—	29	29	43
Over $100,000 (8)	25	25	25	—	25
All (406)	17	24	26	13	20

Given a median income level of over $20,000, Columbus Jews have paid less than adequate attention to the poor Jews in their midst in the past two decades. At best, attention centered around physical hardships resulting from inadequate food, housing, health care, and recreation. Virtually no concern has been expressed for the ways in which a lack of money prevented participation in religious and secular Jewish institutions.

One of the results of the community's overall affluence was the very high cost of services in the Jewish community, for fee schedules everywhere reflected the dominant clientele. In the last several years, single-parent families particularly have been hurt. Increased demands for service, as well as rising costs, have caused many Jewish institutions in Columbus to increase their service fees as a way of financing programs. While scholarships were provided by most of the agencies and institutions, some eligible people did not apply for scholarships or reduced fees because they believed the fee was absolute or the cost of admitting their need was too great.[11] As a consequence, many aspects of Jewish life were closed to them: synagogue facilities, Jewish Center activities, religious education, and membership in Jewish fraternal organizations.

Despite the Jewish community's affluence and its high regard for wealth, Columbus Jewry has resisted the change in political preference which usually follows movement into the middle and upper-middle classes. Our survey revealed that, like Jews everywhere in America, who consistently were described as Democratic and liberal,[12] more than 69 percent of Columbus Jewish adults surveyed were registered Democrats, and almost 80 percent of Jews who voted regularly, voted for Democrats. Columbus Jews of all ages, in the words of one elected official, "generally avoided the Republican party."

This voting pattern emerged even in 1972, an election year which "revealed more torment and indecision among Jews than in any other voting group in the nation,"[13] for the Democratic candidate's liberalism seemed inconsistent with Jewish self-interest. George McGovern received about 60 percent of the Jewish vote nationwide, which was "disappointing" when compared to traditional Jewish support for a Democrat. When compared to the percentage of all other white voters, however, McGovern did exceptionally well.[14] George Gallup's preelection survey accurately predicted McGovern would not obtain a majority in traditional Democratic strongholds except among Jews and blacks.[15] Democratic loyalty was maintained among Columbus Jews despite the Nixon landslide. More than half the Jews sampled — 51.7 percent — voted for McGovern, while less than 40 percent voted for Richard M. Nixon.

These election results confirm the importance of liberalism among Jewish voters as a whole. With the exception of senior citizens, Jews of every age and income level, as well as both sexes, showed a preference for McGovern and other Democrats.[16] None of McGovern's apparent detriments — his weakness as a candidate, his advocacy of social change, Republican suggestions that McGovern had questionable commitments to Israel's security, or the other controversies surrounding him — neutralized McGovern's normal advantages: he was a Democrat and a liberal.

Despite the support Columbus Jews gave McGovern — and Carter four years later — it has been difficult to convince local Jews of this pattern for two reasons. First, some of the more visible lay leaders of the Columbus Jewish Federation — along with many national Jewish leaders — participated vigorously in the Nixon and

Ford campaigns, expressed public appreciation for both presidents' outspoken support of Israel, and sent out signals which suggested McGovern was an isolationist dove who would compromise Israel's security. Second, some leading Columbus Jewish lay leaders and at least one rabbi actively supported the reelection of the Twelfth Congressional District Representative Samuel L. Devine, who had voted conservatively on every issue upon which Jews desired a liberal vote. For example, Devine voted against the Foreign Assistance Appropriations Act for fiscal years 1974 ($2.2 billion for Israel), 1975 ($664.5 million for Israel), 1976 ($2.2 billion for Israel) and 1977 ($1.7 billion for Israel) as well as against the International Security Assistance Act for fiscal year 1976-77 ($4.4 billion for Israel).[17]

Israel was to Columbus Jewry as civil rights were to American blacks. No other single issue seemed to arouse and unite Columbus Jews more, and hence motivate them to mobilize their political resources to their maximum potential. The more involved people were in Jewish life, the more salient the issue became. But the choices here surfaced more subtly; Samuel Devine's opponent in 1974 was Fran Ryan, a liberal Democrat, and in 1976 his opponents consisted of Mrs. Ryan and William Moss, a black Independent candidate. Although both candidates enjoyed great popularity in parts of the Twelfth District, they seemed certain to lose the election. Jewish leadership pragmatically recognized that it would have to continue to work with the incumbent in Congress. Thus while openly supporting Nixon and Ford, Jewish leadership remained much more neutral in the congressional race despite the challengers' pro-Israel positions. And though Samuel Devine gained reelection, he either barely carried, or did not carry, precincts with heavy concentrations of Jews. Further, 57 percent of the voters in our sample voted against him.

Even though the Jewish community has been politically liberal, historically its attitudes toward moral issues like premarital sex and divorce have not been liberal. Like other Americans, Columbus Jews have been caught up by the twentieth century shift in moral values. Traditionally beginning after the staid middle-class Victorian stereotype[18] yielded to the "flapper" image of the 1920s, American sexual mores[19] remained rather stable from the twenties through the early sixties. During these four decades therefore, apparently no marked increase in sexual activity occurred although there was a liberalization of attitudes about, and reports of increased sexual foreplay.[20] Sociologists have observed that in the late 1960s a new cycle of the sexual revolution began when the level of premarital intercourse jumped. A sizeable body of information about Columbus Jewry's sexual activity since World War II has been accumulated, although little such information exists prior to 1914. The data support the traditional view: signs of changing sexual mores appear in the 1920s, level off for several decades, and accelerate again in the late 1960s and early 1970s.

Our knowledge of sexual behavior comes from a variety of sources: anonymous questionnaires from Columbus Jews who graduated from high school in 1918, 1928, 1938, 1948, or 1958; Columbus Jewish students attending The Ohio State University during 1974 and 1975; and anonymous solicited letters from Columbus alumnae of Sigma Delta Tau (SDT) sorority at The Ohio State University, one of the largest and most active Greek campuses in America between 1921 and 1965. Eighteen SDT alumnae who graduated in the twenties responded, six from the forties, twenty-two from the fifties, and sixteen from the sixties.

No SDT respondent challenged the statement that the 1920s saw a sexual shift. But by the middle twenties petting and necking "became more prevalent," although the "fear was that the boys would 'kiss and tell' and thus a girl could get a bad reputation." Most agreed that Clevelanders introduced this "revolution." However, coitus before marriage apparently was not experienced by a single SDT respondent, nor by other SDTs known to the respondents, or by any of the female high school graduates of 1918 or 1928. Only two of the men who graduated from high school in 1918 or 1928 claimed premarital intercourse, and neither involved a Jewish girl.

All but one of the forty-four respondents who joined SDT between 1940 and 1965 apparently remained virgins through their years at the university. Almost all agreed that chastity ranked as a high value in their homes, and that "parents drilled virginity into us to such an extent that under the most tempting circumstances we knew we could never 'go all the way.'" There is much evidence, therefore, from sixty-two SDT alumnae, that between 1920 and 1965 attitudes were changing but actions were not.

Our final survey, conducted in the seventies, sought to determine whether the great amount of verbalization everywhere was paralleled by changes in sexual behavior.[21] Our sample consisted of Jewish students confirmed in Columbus synagogues, who attended The Ohio State University during 1974 and 1975.[22] Each of the anonymous one hundred and sixteen respondents was unmarried, more than half affiliated with Hillel — far out of proportion to campuswide Jewish student affiliation — and more than three-fourths estimated their families' annual incomes at more than $18,000.

This study of sexual intercourse within the year preceding the survey correlated each respondent's age and sex. In sum, 66 percent of the men and 52 percent of the women had had intercourse during the twelve months under study. Further, Table

70 illustrates that, as the students became older, they were more likely to be sexually active. Major changes in sexual mores, at least as measured by premarital intercourse, had certainly encompassed Columbus Jewish youth fairly recently.

TABLE 70
PREMARITAL SEXUAL ACTIVITY OF 116 JEWISH COLLEGE STUDENTS

	Intercourse During One Year									
	Every Week		Every Two/ Four Weeks		Every Two Months		Every Six Months		Never	
	No.	Percent	No.	Percent	No.	Percent	No.	Percent	No.	Percent
All respondents	25	21.5%	27	23.0%	9	8.0%	7	6.0%	48	41.5%
Men	14	25	13	23	5	9	5	9	19	34
Women	11	18	14	23	4	7	2	3.5	29	48.5
Men										
18 and 19	4	15	6	23	2	8	2	8	12	46
20 and 21	6	30	5	25	1	5	2	10	6	30
22 to 25	4	40	2	20	2	20	1	10	1	10
Women										
18 and 19	4	10	10	25	2	5	1	2.5	23	57.5
20 and 21	3	25	3	25	1	8.3	1	8.3	4	33.3
22 to 25	4	50	1	12.5	1	12.5	0	0	2	25

In Table 70 the activities of 116 college students reflect the shifting values pattern of America in the seventies. Another indication of changing values has been the dramatic rise in divorce. As recently as a decade ago in Columbus, divorce was met with widespread disapproval and punitive attitudes toward those who dissolved their marriages. By 1975 divorce was commonplace[23] and casually accepted; most Columbus Jews could name dozens of Columbus Jews who were divorced, and it was no exaggeration to say that every month several prominent names were added to the daily newspaper listings of dissolutions or of divorces granted. As one former Ohio State University student and divorced person saw it: "Only one Columbus girl from my Jewish sorority is still married, and her marriage is more punishing than divorce." Although this observation in 1975 by a "townie" does not allow room for meaningful and happy marital relationships, it was echoed over and over within the community:

> The divorce rate is unreal. I would say, just an uneducated guess, that of the people in my age group [mid-30s], that over 50 percent are divorced. The other 50 are unhappily married, and stick together in quiet desperation. How many happy marriages do you know? It's a simple case of having too much too soon and not knowing how to handle it.

Divorce was so common that there was no longer any need for social pretense. Until recently, during the process of alienation leading toward divorce, couples would make deliberate attempts to deceive others — giving what Erving Goffman called "a performance — trying to control how others saw their situation."[24] This acting has diminished greatly; there was little surprise when separations were announced because the signs had been obvious for months.

Who were the divorced persons of Columbus Jewry in 1975? And why the large increases in dissolved marriages? It was difficult to discuss divorce among Columbus Jews in isolation from the larger trend toward the alienation of families in the community, and the broader human relations network of society. Nevertheless, using as our sample all of those Jews listed in the divorces granted and dissolutions granted newspaper columns during 1975, as well as dozens of previously divorced persons in the Jewish community, the following generalizations can be made.[25]

Naturally there were as many reasons for marital disharmony as there were reasons for getting married; not only were individuals unique but each combination of individuals was unique. Undoubtedly though, the most common of all cliches was true: the older the couple at the time of their marriage, the less chance of a divorce.[26] Over and over the same pattern emerged. Couples dated during high school and married during college; couples were "pinned" during college and married upon graduation. More than four-fifths of the divorced persons married before the age of twenty-five; most commented that they were immature or "unready for closeness and responsibility" at the time of the wedding.

Another widely held cliche, that "the greater the social status, the greater the marital stability,"[27] has been negated by Columbus Jewry. Divorce was unusually high among Jewish dentists, physicians, lawyers, and psychiatrists.[28] In part, this was a general function of early marriages, as professionals in Columbus have not married much later than non-professionals; in part this was a function of the high percentage of professionals in the community. But it was also much more; repeatedly the professionals explained their divorces in words quite similar to those of this divorced dentist:

> Columbus Jewish dentists, you know, have a divorce rate second only to psychiatrists. The knowledge of divorce among other Jewish dentists promoted admiration toward dentists who were able to withdraw from unhappy marriages. We all had a similar problem, and it was not primarily our hygenists. Our financial success was achieved early, and relatively easily, and with that security the question was "what more is there?"

And from another dentist, the same reflections: "Money came quickly and easily and my whole life was before me. What do I do with it?"

A generation ago this problem would have arisen with success at forty, the so-called middle-age crisis, but affluent Columbus Jewry reached unprecedented professional heights by the early and middle thirties. And then the rush began to "re-live an adolescence I felt I missed." Concomitant with husbands questioning what does it all mean came a similar self-reflection by Jewish wives. Divorced women told repeatedly of emptiness, meaninglessness, loneliness and despair, of missed opportunities for personal growth, and of searching outside of marriage for deeper and more enriching relationships: "My second income was a threat to his male provider role and . . . my absence from the home — and the resulting demands upon him — a threat and a nuisance."

To be Jewish and divorced in Columbus was very difficult for the women we interviewed; moderately difficult for the men. When they complained, men spoke primarily of loneliness, and this generally meant more an emptiness caused by a lack of children in the home than by the absence of a woman. Most, however, claimed greater happiness divorced than when married; even those who retained custody of children found a struggling one-parent family much better than an unhappy two-parent family.

Among the women, the most serious of their complaints was the trauma of financial dependency upon their husbands, for most frequently mothers received custody of their children.[29] At every income level, women were expected to depend on the incomes of their husbands for the major part of their own and their children's support; economic opportunities for women without husbands were limited. Further, since housework was viewed as a female responsibility, family and relatives provided more help to men than to women. Home maintenance work once done by a husband, even if limited, had to be purchased or remain undone.

Few of the women we interviewed spoke of any difficulty in meeting men, as accessible networks of Jewish divorced men and women exist, and there seems to be little evidence to support the final cliche that divorced men re-marry very quickly while the women, burdened with children, struggle for many years to find a mate because "men want younger women." Among Columbus Jewish divorced persons in 1975 there were two divorced men for every three divorced women, allowing for out-migration of the former.

Finally, there can be no doubt that the religious involvement of Columbus divorced persons was virtually minimal. Weekend visitations — "Sunday is my only day with the girls; I will not have them spend half of it in [religious] school" — and finances offered serious obstacles. Divorced parents perceived synagogue membership to be totally beyond their financial capabilities, rarely considered requesting special financial arrangements. Also, Columbus Jewish life, especially synagogue life, centered around couples and families. Along with other formal institutions and agencies in the community, synagogues offered little emotional support for singles. Most synagogues promoted a wide range of social, cultural, and religious activities designed to appeal to different age, sex, and interest groups, but not until 1976 did the first synagogue-sponsored activity exclusively for singles and single-parent families take place. No doubt a growing number of both Columbus Jewish singles and divorced persons viewed the synagogue as a place for married people and felt out of place at regular synagogue functions.[30] In 1975 Columbus Jewry had not even begun to wrestle with the problem of the relationship between divorced persons and the organized Jewish community or with the persistent notion that the single life was an impaired life: thus compounding the isolation and loneliness of divorced persons, who were also Jews.[31]

In summarizing the survey results, words like clannish, permanency, wealth, and liberal Democrats most easily come to mind. Naturally, a multitude of questions also arise, but our purpose has been simply to use our survey data to describe Columbus Jewry in 1975. Therefore, these five words should not be understood to be either conclusive or exclusive, as much of the following information about the community's growth from 1950 to 1975 and the community's reaction to the survey show.

NOTES FOR CHAPTER 20

1. The national average of foreign-born Jews still remains high; as of the early 1970s it stood at 23 percent. See F. Massarik and A. Chenkin, "United States Jewish Population Study: A First Report," *AJYB* 74 (1973): 275.

2. A 1957 study of 110 Columbus Jewish families found 62 percent having resided in the city for twenty or more years; Walter Bernstein, "A Study of Factors Affecting Affiliation of Jewish Non-Member Families with the Columbus Jewish Center." M.S.W. thesis, The Ohio State University, 1957.

3. For some reflections on comparing Jews born in a community with migrants to the same community, see Barry D. Lebowitz, "Immigration and the Structure of the Contemporary Jewish Community," *Jewish Sociology and Social Research* 2:1 (Fall/Winter 75): 3-9.

4. Interview with Stan Robins.

5. Ibid.

6. Ronald T. Cahn, "A Study of the Leisure Time Patterns of the Jewish Teen-Age Population of Columbus, Ohio, with Reference to Their Attitudes Toward and Relationships with the Jewish Center of Columbus," M.S.W. thesis, The Ohio State University, 1957, pp. 58 and 61. Cahn also noted that large numbers of youths belonged to a variety of Jewish-sponsored youth groups.

7. On elites, especially those which are "social," see S. F. Nadel, "The Concept of Social Elites," in *International Social Science Bulletin* 8 (1956): 413-24; G. W. Domhoff, *The Higher Circles* (New York, 1970) and T. B. Bottomore, *Elites and Society* (Harmondsworth, England, 1964).

8. Sidney Goldstein, "American Jewry, 1970: A Demographic Profile," *AJYB* 72 (1971): 81; Andrew M. Greeley, *Ethnicity, Denomination, and Inequality*. Sage Research Papers in the Social Sciences, Series Number 90-029 (Beverly Hills, 1976).

9. In 1968 the median income of Columbus Jewry reached $18,050, the highest of any Jewish community ever studied. By 1975 the median income stood somewhere between $20,000 and $35,000, and more earned over $50,000 than received less than $12,000. See Albert Mayer, op. cit., p. 32.

10. When Columbus Jewry as a whole (excluding those over sixty-five) was compared with Jews thirty to fifty-nine years of age nationwide, the differences were large. Of those in the latter group, 44.4 percent had incomes over $20,000 (vs. 66 percent in Columbus) and 24 percent had incomes below $12,000 (vs. 12 percent of Columbus Jews). See F. Massarik and A. Chenkin, op. cit.: 288.

11. A member of the Jewish Center Board of Directors already recognized this in 1967 when he noted that the fee policies were "disenfranchising a substantial segment of the Jewish community." Columbus Jewish Center Minutes, March 7, 1967.

12. The Democratic proportion of the Jewish presidential vote through 1968 had never fallen below 60 percent; see M. R. Levy and M. S. Kramer, *The Ethnic Factor* (New York, 1973), p. 103.

TABLE 71
1975 COLUMBUS JEWISH COMMUNITY SURVEY:
POLITICAL PARTY REGISTRATION

Party Registration	Age Brackets						
	18-25	26-35	36-45	46-55	56-65	66+	All
Republican	15.8%	10.2%	13.7%	21.9%	25.0%	33.3%	18.1%
Democrat	73.7	62.7	74.5	75.0	69.4	62.5	69.2
Other and None	10.5	27.1	11.8	3.1	5.6	4.2	12.7
Total	**38**	**118**	**102**	**64**	**72**	**48**	**442**

TABLE 72
1975 COLUMBUS JEWISH COMMUNITY SURVEY:
1972 ELECTION RESULTS

Voting Preference	Age Brackets						
	18-25	26-35	36-45	46-55	56-65	66+	All
Nixon	11.1%	30.8%	44.6%	42.0%	45.0%	61.5%	39.8%
McGovern	72.2	58.4	46.4	54.8	50.0	30.8	51.7
Neither	16.7	10.8	9.0	3.2	5.0	7.7	8.5
Total	**36**	**130**	**112**	**62**	**80**	**52**	**472**

13. Samuel Lubell, *The Future While It Happened* (New York, 1973), pp. 59-60.

14. A representative sample of precincts from Detroit suggests the gains Nixon made between 1968 and 1972 in predominately Jewish areas:

	1968		1972	
	R	D	R	D
Oak Park	12%	86%	39%	60%
Royal Oak	12%	87%	34%	66%
Southfield	18%	81%	49%	50%
Huntington Woods	32%	67%	47%	53%

15. *Gallup Opinion Index,* Report No. 90 (December 1972), p. 10.

16. This also apparently held true for the Democratic presidential candidate in 1976. While Ford defeated Carter by a margin of almost three to one in all of Bexley (73 percent to 27 percent), the closest races (55 percent to 45 percent) were in the most heavily Jewish precincts.

17. *OJC,* October 2, 1976.

18. For an impressive challenge of traditional Victorian attitudes toward sexuality which argues that the so-called Victorian conception of women's sexuality was more that of an ideology seeking to be established than the prevalent view or practice of even middle-class women, see Carl Degler, "What Ought To Be and What Was: Women's Sexuality in the Nineteenth Century," *American Historical Review* 79:5 (December 1974): 1467-90.

TABLE 73
COMPARISON OF VOTING PATTERNS IN THE TWELFTH AND TWENTY-EIGHTH DISTRICTS WITH THE MOST HEAVILY JEWISH PRECINCTS IN THESE DISTRICTS

Precincts	Congressional Contests	
	1974	
Twelfth District	Devine (R)	Ryan (D)
R*	129 (53.5%)	112 (46.5%)
H	209 (78.6%)	57 (21.4%)
T	138 (73.0%)	51 (27.0%)
All	3,829 (62.6%)	2,286 (37.4%)
Twenty-Eighth District		
J	111 (33.1%)	225 (66.9%)
All	1,480 (45.1%)	1,804 (54.9%)
	1976	
Twelfth District	Devine (R)	Ryan (D) + Moss (I)
R*	140 (53.0%)	124 (47.0%)
H	269 (80.5%)	65 (19.5%)
T	142 (72.1%)	55 (27.9%)
All	4,300 (61.2%)	2,720 (48.8%)
Twenty-Eighth District		
J	101 (25.1%)	301 (74.9%)
All	1,525 (38.6%)	2,428 (61.4%)

*This Bexley precinct is bordered by Broad (north), Gould (east), Powell (south), and Stanwood (west) and 57 percent of the heads of households (105/184) in 1976 were Jewish.

SOURCE: Abstract of Votes Cast at the General Election Held on Tuesday, November 5, 1974, and Tuesday, November 2, 1976, in Franklin County, Ohio.

19. On the image of women in the 1920s, see Eleanor Flexner, *Century of Struggle: The Women's Rights Movement in the United States* (Cambridge, Massachusetts, 1959) and William O'Neill, *Everyone Was Brave: The Rise and Fall of Feminism in America* (Chicago, 1969).

20. Mervin B. Freedman, "The Sexual Behavior of American College Women: An Empirical Study and a Historical Survey," *Merrill-Palmer Quarterly of Behavior and Development* 11 (January 1965): 33-39.

21. While all commentators accept the fact that the late sixties saw a change in sexual attitudes, they disagree on whether a change occurred in actual practice, i.e., whether or not pre-marital sexual intercourse increased. Affirming a change were V. Packard, *The Sexual Wilderness* (New York, 1968); G. R. Kaats and K. E. Davis, "The Dynamics of Sexual

Behavior of College Students," *Journal of Marriage and the Family* [*JMF*], August 1970: 390-99; R. Bell and J. B. Chaskes, "Premarital Sexual Experience among Coeds, 1958 and 1968," *JMF*, February 1970: 81-84; K. Davis, "Sex on the Campus: Is There a Revolution?" *Medical Aspects of Human Sexuality* [*MAHS*], January 1971: 128-42; I. E. Robinson et al., "The Premarital Sexual Revolution among College Females," *The Family Coordinator*, April 1972: 189-94; and D. Yankelovich, Inc., *The Changing Values on Campus* (New York, 1972). Denying a "revolution" were I. L. Reiss, "Premarital Sexual Standards" in C. B. Broderick and J. Bernard, *The Individual, Sex and Society* (Baltimore, 1969) and J. Gagnon and W. Simon, "Prospects for Change in American Sexual Patterns," *MAHS*, January 1970: 100-17. See also Mary E. Heltsley and Carlfred B. Broderick, "Religiosity and Premarital Sexual Permissiveness: Reexamination of Reiss' Traditionalism Proposition," *JMF*, August 1969: 441-43; Gary Hampe and Howard Ruppel, Jr., "The Measurement of Premarital Sexual Permissiveness: A Comparison of Two Guttman Scales," *JMF*, August 1974: 451-63; and John Edwards and Alan Booth, "Sexual Behavior In and Out of Marriage: An Assessment of Correlates," *JMF*, February 1976: 73-81.

22. Approximately 35 percent of the sample was confirmed in the Conservative synagogue, 35 percent in a Reform synagogue, and 30 percent in two of Columbus' Orthodox synagogues. Among the basic facts that seem to have persisted for some time about sexual relationships among Americans was that religiousness was an inhibiting influence on sexual permissiveness — thus our restricting the sample to confirmands.

23. Divorce rates have jumped rapidly on a national level as well: in 1963 9.6 divorces occurred per 1,000 married women, a decade later the rate was 18.2 per 1,000, and in 1976 the divorce statistics rose to unprecedented heights. See *Monthly Vital Statistics Report* 24:4 (1975), 26:1 (1977), and Bernard Weinberger, "The Growing Rate of Divorce in Orthodox Jewish Life," *Jewish Life* (Spring 1976): 9-14.

24. *The Presentation of Self in Everyday Life* (New York, 1959).

25. See especially the anonymous interviews conducted by Marc Lee Raphael on September 2 and 15, 1974.

26. "Persons who marry when they are relatively young are about twice as likely to obtain a divorce as persons who marry when they are older"; *Current Population Reports* (1971), P-20, No. 223, p. 1.

27. Phillips Cutright, "Income and family events: marital stability," *JMF* 33 (1971): 291-306. For a brief introduction to the "stratification" theory, see Richard J. Udry, "Marital Instability by Race and Income," *American Journal of Sociology* 72 (May 1967): 673-74.

28. This conclusion is in contrast to the pattern of California professionals; see Paul C. Glick and Arthur J. Norton, "Frequency, Duration and Probability of Marriage and Divorce," *JMF* 33 (1971): 307-17.

29. Other consistently repeated complaints included visitation arrangements, reaction of friends and family (i.e., social isolation), regaining a sense of individuality, and insecure, rivalrous, and withdrawn children. I note the latter hesitantly, for the prevalent stereotype of the community that children from broken homes will be undisciplined and confused appeared confirmed repeatedly.

30. There are of course, divorced persons who reject

compartmentalization as "singles" or "single parent families" as an arbitrary separation based on marital status.

31. See "Living through Divorce — a Search for Self" and "My Divorce and My Community," *Sh'ma* 6:112 (April 16, 1976); Marcie Jane Schoenberg, "The Relationship Between Jewish Singles and the Organized Jewish Community." M.A. thesis, Hebrew Union College (Los Angeles), 1974.

21: TWO OUT OF THREE ARE AFFILIATED: SYNAGOGUE LIFE

Synagogue growth and expansion, like the development of Jewish agencies and institutions, continued throughout the three decades after World War II. Temple Israel, which erected a large, architecturally stunning building on the Far East Side in 1959-60, reached a membership of nine hundred family units, supported a religious school for more than four hundred children, and a sisterhood of five hundred women. Tifereth Israel and Agudas Achim, both of which expanded their buildings in these decades, each achieved an eight hundred family unit membership by 1975, religious schools with two hundred and seventy-five and one hundred and fifty children respectively, and sisterhoods of four to five hundred members. Beth Jacob moved from Bulen Avenue to a new, striking house of worship adjacent to the Columbus Jewish Federation, Heritage House, and the Jewish Center in 1968, and claimed two hundred and eighty member units in 1975. Ahavas Sholom erected a new synagogue in 1963 for a membership of about one hundred families.

The Jewish community's most recently organized congregation in 1975 was Beth Tikvah — the North Side Temple — which served about one hundred and twenty families. Less than 10 percent of Columbus' Jewish population of fourteen thousand* lived on the North Side in 1975. Despite its small base of potential members, Beth Tikvah has grown steadily since its consecration on November 1, 1961.[1]

In 1975 the North Side had primarily three types of Jews: those who belonged to the temple and perhaps other Jewish organizations; those who belonged to a secular Jewish organization but not the temple, and those who were Jewish in the privacy of

*This figure did not include Ohio State University graduate or professional students whose families do not live in Columbus.

their intellects. In this the North Siders were no different than the East Siders. Also, inter-faith programs on both sides of town involved Jews as *or lagoyim* (ambassadors to the non-Jewish community) who interpreted Hanukkah in public schools, arranged Passover *seders* in area churches, and taught basic Judaism to non-Jews.

But Beth Tikvah's Reform congregation was literally and figuratively miles apart from Columbus' other congregations. The North Side Temple initiated a different, informal approach to the celebration of the liturgy by emphasizing more active involvement by the congregation, and by working to establish a communal spirit. Congregants were encouraged to give of self as well as of substance.

Working together to maintain the temple gave Jews on the North Side a sense of community. Unlike the East Side Jews, they have been unable to proclaim a territory; North Side Jews have had to find their identity within the framework of the temple and in their quest for preserving Jewish literature, thought, and life.[2] Their temple was known for its informality: the majority of worshippers were attired casually, the services were frequently interrupted by questions about the liturgy or sermon, and Torah discussions involving the worshippers and the rabbi were a regular feature of Sabbath worship. Movable chairs and a guitar-playing *hazzan* created a special environment, and made the temple a popular place for members of all ages. Contrasting to larger, more elaborate bar and bat mitzvahs on the East Side, the six or seven ceremonies held at the North Side Temple each year were usually simple in their form and content for small gatherings of friends and relatives.

Maintaining a North Side center of Judaism was quite simple; everyone who joined the Indianola Avenue temple — a converted house with one large sanctuary and five very small rooms — shared the work. Members mowed the lawn, painted the rooms, fixed the roof, and made the food which was served on paper plates after all Sabbath services. In strong contrast to the large East Side temples and synagogues with hundred-thousand-dollar operating budgets, the North Siders had a budget of approximately forty thousand dollars and paid their full-time rabbi eighteen thousand dollars — just above minimum "union" scale.

Lacking a strong desire for religious involvement, many North Side Jews did not join the temple, but affiliated instead with the North Side Jewish Cultural Association founded by Professors Louis Nemzer, Milton Lessler, Leo Lipetz, Manuel Barkan and several others on April 5, 1956.[3] Initially serving both religious and cultural needs, after the establishment of Beth Tikvah the association began to draw almost exclusively upon Jews not affiliated formally with other Jewish organizations in Columbus. For two decades its activities provided fellowship for Jews who have little interest in religious or institutional life, and included a small educational program for children.

Turning from the non-affiliated to the affiliated, our survey indicated that two-thirds of the Jewish community were members of Columbus' three Orthodox, two Reform, and one Conservative synagogues; about 35 percent of the affiliated was Reform, 35 percent Orthodox, and 30 percent Conservative.[4] This was a very high percentage of Orthodox affiliates, for nationwide there were 1.5 Reform and 2.5 Conservative affiliations for every Orthodox membership.[5] Their relative strength, however, may soon diminish; nationally almost three-fifths of Orthodox affiliates were over fifty-five years of age, while Reform and Conservative Jews in Columbus each outnumber Orthodox Jews by two-to-one margins in the twenty-six to forty-five age group.

TABLE 74
1975 COLUMBUS JEWISH COMMUNITY SURVEY: AGES OF SYNAGOGUE AFFILIATES

Age	Reform	Conservative	Orthodox
18-25	7%	9%	11%
26-35	30	28	14
36-45	21	28	7
46-55	12	15	11
56-65	19	10	32
Over 65	10	10	25
Total	**159**	**163**	**136**

Overall, involvement in religious institutions was closely associated with the family life cycle: abundant in childhood and early adolescence, dropping off markedly in late adolescence and early adulthood, and increasing markedly after the birth of children. Therefore, the parents of preteen children were disproportionately involved in the majority of activities in Columbus synagogues. One implication of this pattern was clearly evident to synagogue leaders: the number of those under thirteen years of age had been decreasing for almost a decade; as this age group contracts, the number of participants necessarily will decline.

Those who did affiliate created a shorthand identification for the three largest religious institutions of the community: "the *shul*" was Agudas Achim, "the Temple" was Temple Israel, and "T.I." was Tifereth Israel. In both informal conversation and at formal meetings, these terms not only identified the institutions but proclaimed distinctions in ideology or religious doctrine. Since World War II, these three synagogues had accounted for about 80 percent of the affiliated Jews of the city; they have largely determined the image of Orthodox, Conservative, and Reform Judaism in Columbus.

Agudas Achim, the *shul*, was the oldest and largest traditional congregation in Columbus. Serving about eight hundred families, the *shul* was representative of what observers of American Orthodoxy have called "modern" Orthodoxy. On the one hand, it attempted to perpetuate a viable mode of Jewish living based on *halacha* (Jewish law). On the other hand, it emphasized what it has in common with other Jews — mixed seating, driving to services on the Sabbath, elaborate facility, and salaried administrators — and with non-Jews — entering a float in a bicentennial parade and participation in ecumenical services. As almost all Columbus Jews do, Agudas Achim members view themselves first as Americans and second as Jews.

According to our survey data, Agudas Achim's membership included the largest number of nominal or nonobservant Orthodox Jews of the three Orthodox synagogues in the community. Less than one-quarter of its members observed the dietary laws outside their homes, only one out of ten fully observed the Sabbath, and an even smaller percentage utilized the communal *mikveh* (ritual bath). Why then affiliate with the *shul*?

Parental affiliation was an extremely important indicator of Orthodox affiliation, for 92 percent of those affiliated with an Orthodox synagogue in 1975 grew up in a home where the parents belonged to an Orthodox congregation. This familial loyalty has amazed many observers of Columbus Jewry. While no one was able to fully explain it, one Orthodox affiliate suggested:

> The Agudas Achim Synagogue has the loyalty — always has had — the loyalty of its people to the institution in a way which is utterly beyond imagination. They have treated the institution as if it has its own special sanctity, and no matter what they may think of its personnel, Agudas Achim comes above all else. I've never been able to understand this; I've never known any synagogue that had anything comparable to it and that was able to sustain that. People who by their own admission are not Orthodox in practice would never think of leaving Agudas Achim because you know there's something special about Agudas Achim. Very, very strange.[6]

Or, as one member, a native in his thirties, reasoned:

> We're very Jewish; Jewishness has been put in us and instilled in us, for being Jewish and being religious is two different things. You can

> be very Jewish and be very close to your faith, yet not be religious, not practice the Orthodox customs.[7]

Yet another member, also a native man in his thirties, stated:

> The familial role is a strong psychological one. My father was part of the institution and so there is a strong familial identification for me. It's an identification with the familiar, although I disagree with its formal identification. I am not Orthodox, though psychologically there are a lot of ties.[8]

The community's Reform Jews, however, offer a striking contrast to the Orthodox affiliates — more than half of them were from families which belonged to Conservative or Orthodox synagogues. Among Conservative Jews, nine of ten claimed either Conservative or Orthodox affiliations in their youth. Broadly speaking then, Orthodox Jewish youths later affiliated with all three denominations, although Orthodox synagogues in Columbus drew their constituency almost exclusively from Orthodox-affiliated families. Reform Jews affiliated with only Reform temples although the temple membership came from all denominations; and Conservative Jewish youth affiliated with either Reform or Conservative synagogues.

Synagogue attendance varied from the national norm as much as synagogue affiliation. As a National Opinion Research Center survey of church and synagogue attendance in March of 1974 indicated, our 1975 survey found that Jews were irregular attenders when compared to Protestants and Catholics.

TABLE 75
1975 COLUMBUS JEWISH COMMUNITY SURVEY: WORSHIP ATTENDANCE

Denominations (N)	Monthly Attendance			
	Never	Once/Less	One/Three	Four/More
Reform Jews (160)	8.1%	73.8%	5.0%	13.1%
Conservative Jews (165)	4.8	84.9	5.5	4.8
Orthodox Jews (131)	1.5	83.2	6.1	9.2
All Columbus Jews (456)	5	81	5	9
*National Jews (43)	9	67	19	5
*National Catholics (361)	6	26	21	47
*National Protestants (807)	10	36	25	29

*SOURCE: Roper Opinion Research Center Survey No. 9003 in Jon Alston, "Review of the Polls," *Journal for the Scientific Study of Religion* 14 (1975): 165-68.

The worship pattern of the Columbus Jewish community was even more irregular than the national pattern. More than 80 percent of the community attended synagogue services less than once a month; when those who never attend were included, the total was 86 percent. Only 9 percent was present at least once each week, and of these individuals 55 percent were over sixty-five years of age. Synagogue attendance in Columbus was very low except for the very old, and those at the bottom rungs of the income ladder.[9]

Our 1975 survey also revealed diverse observance of traditional ceremonies and rituals among Columbus' Jewish community. Few religions have more clearly recognized the role of ceremonial than Judaism, and opportunities to consecrate days, objects, and activities abound. "Not learning but doing is the chief thing" an ancient Jewish teacher wrote, and the favored *mitzvot* (commandments) in Jewish tradition were those pertaining not to human relations but to ritual observances. Rabbis consistently noticed that the Bible hallowed the lowliest acts by elevating them into the service of God; thus the daily life of the Jew was thickly sown with rituals and ceremonies.[10]

To what extent were traditional rituals and ceremonies observed among Columbus Jewry? While it was quite possible to disagree over how to interpret ritual practice and religious observance within the community, there can be no doubt that wide variations existed among denominations. Similarities end with participation in *seder* (the ritual meal) of Passover by nine of every ten Columbus Jews.

Among the three denominations Columbus' Reform Jews retained the fewest traditional rituals: 99 percent did not observe the dietary laws outside their homes nor cease work on the Sabbath, 86 percent did not observe *kashrut* (dietary laws) at all, only 63 percent had *mezuzoth* (house blessings) on their doorways, less than half kindle Sabbath candles, and only about half of those with a deceased parent observed the death ritually. Encouraging, however, was the observation that not only did three-fourths of the Reform Jews stay home from work or school on the High Holidays (more than the Orthodox) but that one-third ceased work "somewhat" on the Sabbath.

The Orthodox affiliated Jews of Columbus were, comparatively at least, quite observant. This was in part, perhaps, a function of age, for more than half the Orthodox Jews of Columbus were over fifty-six in comparison with 20 percent of the Conservatives and 30 percent of the Reform Jews. In addition to heavy observance of the *mitzvot* (commandments) of the *mezuzah*, fasting, and *Yizkor* (memorial), more than one-third sanctified eating with a blessing, almost one-half observed *kashrut* outside the home and 86 percent in the home, and a full one-quarter did not work on the Sabbath.

Marring this impressive record, however, was the highest percentage among all denominations of those who worked on Rosh Hashanah or Yom Kippur.

Conservative Jews in Columbus, however, were more difficult to categorize in terms of observance levels than this pessimistic description:

> in advancing observance of the *mitzvot* . . . Conservatism has been an abysmal failure: there has been a steady erosion of observance among Conservative Jews . . . Conservatism's defeat on the ritual front can be demonstrated in almost every area of Jewish observance.[11]

While Conservative Jews rivalled the most highly observant Orthodox in lighting Sabbath candles, affixing *mezuzoth* and fasting on Yom Kippur, in other areas basic to the Conservative movement, like sanctifying the meal, observing *kashrut* (dietary

TABLE 76
1975 COLUMBUS JEWISH COMMUNITY SURVEY: CEREMONIAL OBSERVANCE

	Reform	Conservative	Orthodox	All
A blessing before or after eating	8.8%	6.6%	35.5%	15.9%
Lighting Sabbath candles	41.9	71.7	71.7	61.2
Reciting any other Sabbath blessings	28.8	50.0	60.9	45.9
Making or attending a *seder*	86.9	93.4	96.4	92.0
Observing Kosher dietary laws	13.8	50.0	85.5	48.1
Annual memorial observance for deceased parent	51.9	76.0	89.1	71.6
Practice *Kashrut* outside the home	1.3	8.4	42.8	16.2
Have a *mezuzah* at dwelling entrance	63.1	86.5	92.8	80.4
High Holidays				
Services in morning, work in afternoon	11.3	11.4	14.5	12.3
Stay home from work or school on Yom Kippur	73.8	85.5	71.7	77.3
Fast some or all of Yom Kippur	61.9	81.9	89.1	77.2
Do not observe at all	11.9	4.8	3.6	6.9
Cease work on Sabbath				
Yes, fully	1.3	3.6	24.6	9.1
Yes, somewhat	33.1	37.3	31.9	34.3
No, hardly	20.0	35.5	28.3	28.0
No, not at all	46.3	22.9	14.5	28.4
Total	**160**	**166**	**138**	**464**

laws) outside the home, or completely ceasing work on the Sabbath, their levels of observance were as low as the Reform Jews of Columbus. While *kashrut* has survived in a mangled form and the vestiges of Sabbath observance were few, the ritual observance of Conservative Jews generally fell somewhere between the Orthodox and Reform, as befits their ideology.

By correlating ceremonial observances as a function of age rather than affiliation, an interesting relationship readily was observed. There was much evidence to suggest that a large amount of the measurable ceremonial activity was part of the lives of young adult Jews. Members from eighteen to thirty-five matched or exceeded every other age cohort in most areas of ritual observance, falling way behind only in *Yahrzeit* observance (memorializing a deceased parent) and slightly behind in Sabbath blessings other than kindling candles. The high observance rate of adults under twenty-five revealed that this was not merely a function of having young children in programs of religious education. There was, then, reason for optimism for those who desire higher levels of ritual observance in the coming years, for among both Reform and Conservative Jews, members between twenty-six and thirty-five form the largest grouping.

Although Passover *seder* was by far the most popular ritual, sanctifying a meal with a blessing was the least popular among all groups. Surprising to many was the realization that the *seder* was more widely observed than the High Holidays. Whereas nine-tenths of Columbus Jews had a Passover meal, slightly more than two-tenths worked or studied all or part of Yom Kippur. Generally, those *mitzvot* (commandments) which demanded infrequent observance — *Pesach, mezuzah, Yahrzeit,* High Holidays — were most favored, and those which demanded daily or weekly observance were the least practiced.

Interestingly, the overall meaning which affiliated Columbus Jews attached to Judaism most clearly paralleled observance levels and was related to both income and age levels. Judaism means "very much" to nearly 80 percent of Orthodox Jews, more than 70 percent of the college-age Jews, and sizeable numbers of those with lower incomes. Only 43 percent of the community's Reform Jews, slightly more than half of the Conservative Jews, less than half of those between twenty-six and sixty-five, and a minority of upper-income Jews echoed this affirmation.

A similar attitude toward marrying non-Jews differentiates the denominations and the age groups. For most Reform Jews, love was the main criterion for marriage, as 70 percent approved of a Jew and non-Jew marrying. Only 30 percent of Orthodox and 40 percent of Conservative Jews offer such approval. There was also a relationship between age and attitude toward intermarriage: with

TABLE 77
1975 COLUMBUS JEWISH COMMUNITY SURVEY: PERSONAL SIGNIFICANCE OF JUDAISM

	Does Judaism mean anything to you?			
	Very Much	Yes Somewhat	Very Little	No Not really
Denominations (N)				
Reform (155)	43%	36%	11%	10%
Conservative (162)	56	31	9	4
Orthodox (131)	77	19	0	4
Income Levels (N)				
Under $7,000 (26)	69%	23%	8%	—
$ 7/12,000 (36)	56	39	5	—
12/15,000 (42)	62	14	10	14%
15/20,000 (56)	54	39	3	4
20/35,000 (148)	49	30	10	11
35/50,000 (54)	33	48	12	7
50/75,000 (40)	35	50	10	5
75/100,000 (14)	14	72	—	14
Over $100,000 (8)	75	25	—	—
Age Brackets (N)				
18-25 (41)	71%	24%	5%	—
26-35 (133)	44	46	5	5%
36-45 (109)	49	25	19	7
46-55 (67)	46	24	12	18
56-65 (75)	47	35	5	13
Over 66 (53)	69	19	4	8

each succeeding cohort the preference for love over religion diminishes.

Although Judaism has traditionally placed a greater emphasis on observance than belief, the two religious elements have always been inseparable. From the commandments flow several fundamental beliefs: in one God, Who not only created but takes an active interest in His creation; in the centrality of the Torah (Pentateuch), which was divinely revealed; and in the uniqueness of the Jewish people, recipients of a divine revelation who were chosen by the deity to carry His message of ethical monotheism to the world.

Survey data were of necessity rather crude, and they had the tendency to neatly delineate into compartments the variety of beliefs held by various individuals. Nevertheless, all of these fundamental beliefs were still very much alive in the Orthodox community of Columbus Jewry. Guided by liturgies, educational programs, and rabbis that not only affirmed but inculcated these articles of faith, more than eight of every ten Orthodox Jews in Columbus believed them.

Among Reform Jews, there was enormous doubt, possibly caused by Reform liturgy and school curriculum which did not affirm divine revelation of scriptures or chosenness. Also, their rabbinate stressed human values and paid little attention to matters of faith, belief, and religious tradition. More than half of the community's Reform Jews affirmed divine revelation and God's choosing the Jewish people. But in spite of a liturgy and religious school program that affirmed a creating and caring (though not revealing) God, from 40 to 50 percent of Reform Jewish congregants denied that God was either a Creator or a Provider. Some religious Jews were encouraged by the fact that half of the highly secular Reform Jews living in secular America still believed in an active God. Others, who felt that religious faith was fundamental to full participation in synagogue life, were disconcerted that so many denied the traditional beliefs.

Conservative Jews reflected the ambivalence of the official doctrine of the denomination and the local conveyors of that doctrine. There was very strong support for a creating God, strong affirmation of a guiding God, and moderately strong support of divine revelation and chosenness. This support, however, was substantially lower than Orthodox affiliates' undoubtedly because much less support was given these concepts in the liturgy, curriculum, and sermons of the local Conservative synagogue.

TABLE 78
1975 COLUMBUS JEWISH COMMUNITY SURVEY: TRADITIONAL BELIEFS

	Reform	Conservative	Orthodox
I believe in a God who created the universe	58%	84%	97%
I believe in a God who guides the universe continuously	51	68	90
I believe that the Torah was given by God	41	58	83
I believe that the Jews are a chosen people	48	58	83
Total	**160**	**166**	**136**

Despite the conclusion drawn by students of American Jewish life that the beliefs of the community were converging into a pattern of nearly uniform observance, such was not the case in Columbus. The range in religious beliefs was quite wide and the strength of traditional beliefs quite impressive, in spite of the middle-class homogeneity of the group as a whole.

The three dominant synagogues of Columbus Jewry had confirmation ceremonies or graduations for fifteen year-olds who successfully completed their educational programs. To measure the impact these synagogues have had on their membership, we surveyed confirmation classes listed in the *Ohio Jewish Chronicle* from 1945 through 1969. After current addresses were obtained, about one thousand questionnaires were mailed throughout the nation during 1975, and 721 were returned.

TABLE 79
CONFIRMANDS RETURNING QUESTIONNAIRES

	Orthodox	Conservative	Reform	All
1945-50	9	36	56	101
1951-55	29	41	53	123
1956-60	47	86	75	208
1961-65	29	52	92	173
1966-69	46	18	52	116
Total	160	233	328	721

The largest confirmation classes were generally at "the temple" although during several periods Tifereth Israel classes were nearly as large. Subordinating confirmation to bar mitzvah, "the *shul*" had very small classes, as did Tifereth Israel during years when boys generally ceased their religious education at bar mitzvah age.

Without respect to denomination, confirmation class size reflected the general religious revival of the middle and late fifties when religion became a sine qua non for respectability, synagogues and churches flourished, and the number of Jews receiving Jewish education suddenly increased greatly. Few doubted the enduring value of religious education, and each Columbus synagogue described its program as unique. Rabbinic continuity added to this sense of distinctiveness for Rabbis Samuel Rubenstein,[12] Nathan Zelizer,[13] and Jerome Folkman[14] served these three congregations for more than 85 percent of the years under study. Each rabbi worked hard to develop a program of ideological perspective which would be unique to each institution but still part of the larger denominational ideology.

Broadly speaking then, how did a Jewish education within a

particular synagogue affect the ways in which adult Jews responded to various aspects of Judaism? How did the responses of those educated in one denomination compare with those of another? A very brief summary of the most significant conclusions regarding affiliation, worship attendance, ceremonial observances, beliefs, and a multi-measure of Jewish identification follows.

Men and women confirmed in the Orthodox denomination between 1945 and 1969 had higher rates of synagogue affiliation in 1975 than either Conservative or Reform Jews, and this generally held true among every confirmation cohort — only the 1945-50 Orthodox confirmands were surpassed. Further, in four of the five cohorts (1945-50, 1951-55, 1956-60, and 1961-65) more than 70 percent of the Orthodox confirmands affiliated. The other confirmands did not lag far behind however; more than 60 percent of the Conservative and 58 percent of the Reform graduates in the same four cohorts were affiliated in 1975.

Among graduates of all three denominations worship attendance in 1975 was consistently poor. Reform Jews had the best overall record of worship attendance, but only in the 1945-50 and 1951-55 cohorts did more than three of ten persons attend worship services at least once a month. Among Conservative and Orthodox Jews the attendance was even less, and of all former confirmands ages twenty-one to thirty-four, more than 85 percent worshipped less than once each month.

Our respondents neglected both individual and family ceremonial and ritual observances in the home about as widely as worship. High observance levels existed for Hanukkah; for Passover *seder* the observance was moderate to high; but more often than not the survey yielded low observance generally and few differences emerged between denominations. While more Reform and Conservative confirmands observed none of the eight rituals, they also appeared much more likely than the Orthodox to observe five or six of the ceremonial activities. But overall observance levels measured far from high among any denomination's graduates.

Whether from Reform, Conservative, or Orthodox backgrounds, these confirmands held very traditional Jewish concepts: widespread agreement existed that a creating, working, revealing, protecting, and personal God had a special relationship to the Jewish people.

All of these dimensions of Jewish involvement, plus a great many others, were combined to measure Jewish identity. Seven broad categories resulted: the ritual (ceremonies and observances), marital (extent of in-group dating and marriage), credal (beliefs), intellectual (pursuit of Jewish studies, reading Jewish literature, collecting Jewish art objects), worship (synagogue prayer attendance), communal (participation in Jewish organizations and support for Jews outside the United States), and ethical (interpersonal behavior, especially charity) dimensions.[15]

Only two, ethical and credal, ranked equally among all three denominations; in all the others one or another sector had an advantage. Reform confirmands scored highest in worship and communal dimensions, Orthodox Jews in ritual and marital areas, and Conservative graduates in intellectual spheres. But the differences were generally so small that they were never statistically significant, and the homogeneity was most striking. There seems, in short, little evidence that the specific denomination of confirmation makes a difference in the measurable dimension of Jewish identification among adults now scattered throughout the land.[16]

NOTES FOR CHAPTER 21

1. *OJC,* October 27, 1961, September 28, 1962, April 26, October 25, 1963.

2. Amitai Etzioni, reviewing a new edition of Louis Wirth's *The Ghetto,* argued that "a group can maintain its cultural and social integration and identity" without having a neighborhood basis. He suggested that in the emerging suburbs American Jews constituted a reference group based upon a "common identity, tradition, values and consciousness" which is "maintained by communication and activated in limited social situations and core institutions." "The Ghetto — A Re-Evaluation," *Social Forces* 37 (1959): 258.

Among sociologists, Talcott Parsons has emphasized the perception of territory as fundamental to community. According to Parsons, a community is "that collectivity the members of which share a common territorial area as their base of operations for daily activities." *The Social System* (Glencoe, 1951), p. 91. We use the term community to describe the North Side Jews' sense of common relationship or friendship as well as a common sacred institution. For this suggestion we are indebted to Ferdinand Tonnies' *Gemeinschaft und Gesselschaft.*

3. *OJC,* April 27, 1956, September 25, 1959, January 8, 1960.

4. We calculated this from membership lists of each synagogue supplied to the author during 1975. The percentages represent a relative loss for Conservative affiliates, who outnumbered both Reform and Orthodox in 1968. See A. Mayer, op. cit., p. 107.

5. F. Massarik and A. Chenkin, op. cit., p. 282.

6. Interview with Marvin Fox.

7. Interview with Stan Robins.

8. Anonymous correspondence, May 8, 1975.

TABLE 80
1975 COLUMBUS JEWISH COMMUNITY SURVEY: COMPARISON OF PARENTAL AND FILIAL AFFILIATIONS

Parental Home	Current Filial Denomination		
	Reform	Conservative	Orthodox
Orthodox affiliation	28.5%	39.9%	91.7%
Conservative affiliation	29.2	53.6	8.3
Reform affiliation	42.3	6.5	—
Total	**130**	**138**	**120**
Orthodox practice	17.1%	29.6%	64.6%
Conservative practice	27.9	51.3	25.0
Reform practice	55.0	19.1	10.4
Total	**111**	**115**	**96**

9. Almost a quarter of those with incomes under $7,000, attend synagogue worship services once a week or more, in contrast to 4 percent and 6 percent of those with $35,000-50,000 and $50,000-75,000 incomes respectively.

10. *Avot* 1:17; *D'varim Rabbah* X to Numbers 6:1.

11. Marshall Sklare, *Conservative Judaism: An American Religious Movement* (New York, 1972), pp. 270-71.

12. Interview with Samuel Rubenstein.

13. "Sketch of Rabbi Nathan Zelizer — 1964," in Rabbi Nathan Zelizer Papers, OHS.

14. Jerome Folkman, "Autobiography," September 3, 1969, typescript, OHS.

15. These dimensions owe much of their conceptualization to four articles: "The Relationship Between Jewish Education and Jewish Identification," *Jewish Education* 35:1 (Fall 1964): 37-50; Bernard Lazerwitz, "Religious Identification and Its Ethnic Correlates: a Multivariate Model," *Social Forces* 52 (December 1973): 204-20; Steven M. Cohen, "The Impact of Jewish Education on Religious Identification and Practice," *Jewish Social Studies* 36 (July-October 1974): 316-26; and especially Harold S. Himmelfarb, "Measuring Religious Involvement," *Social Forces* 53 (June 1975): 606-18.

16. I don't think it is necessary to justify a case study by pointing to its representativeness. It seems to me that such studies are valuable for the insights they offer into particular historical processes, for the information they offer indirectly about a society, and for the questions they raise about other similar cases.

22: MORE ORGANIZED AND LESS SUPERFICIAL: JEWISH EDUCATION

Traditionally, immigrant Jews from Germany and eastern Europe had a great reverence for education; this faith in learning lives on in their descendants. Religious education has not received the same acclaim as secular studies, but seems to be gaining some ground, for the value of religious instruction has been acknowledged intellectually and financially by Columbus Jewry. Our 1975 survey indicated that the educationel level of Columbus Jewry was extraordinarily high by any comparative standards. Excluding immigrants over sixty-five, more than 90 percent of the men had completed at least one year of college, and more than 40 percent had completed graduate or professional training. Perhaps as unique was the fact that more than one quarter of all Columbus Jewish men held medical, legal, dental or doctoral degrees, and that 85 percent of all employed men worked in white collar occupations. More than 83 percent of Columbus' Jewish women finished at least one year of college, and more than 60 percent had bachelor's degrees. Further, in comparison with those thirty-six to forty-five, twice as many women between twenty-six and thirty-five had received master's or doctoral degrees; this possibly suggests a growing trend among Columbus Jewish women toward postgraduate education.

In spite of the concern of the Jewish community about the education of its youth, and the very high value placed on education, our survey indicated that the level of formal religious education among all age groups was much lower than the level of secular education. More than half the community's Reform Jews had only a Sunday School background, while more than one-third of the Conservative Jews and one-quarter of the Orthodox Jews had similar minimal Judaic training. Like American Jews everywhere, more than eight of ten adult members were the products of either an afternoon Hebrew School, Sunday School, or

TABLE 81
1975 COLUMBUS JEWISH COMMUNITY SURVEY:
SECULAR EDUCATION

Highest Educational Level	Percentage Men	Percentage Women
Grade school	1.4%	1.0%
Some high school	2.2	1.0
High school graduate	10.9	14.6
Some college	21.7	22.3
College graduate	23.2	48.5
Master's degree	8.0	9.7
Doctoral degree	5.8	2.9
M.D.	8.0	—
D.P.M	1.4	—
D.V.M.	0.7	—
O.D.	5.1	—
L.L.B. or J.D.	11.6	—
D.D.S.	0.7	—
Total	**276**	**206**

TABLE 82
1975 COLUMBUS JEWISH COMMUNITY SURVEY:
BASIC RELIGIOUS EDUCATION

	Reform	Conservative	Orthodox	All
European *Cheder*	1%	8%	15%	8%
Some Sunday School — No Hebrew School	54	36	28	40
Afternoon Hebrew School and Sunday School	37	46	50	44
Day School and/or Yeshiva	2	8	7	6
Other	6	2	0	3
Total	**160**	**166**	**138**	**464**

both. This educational pattern left many Jews without the basic linguistic and conceptual tools which would enable them to understand the Bible, the *siddur* (prayer book) or a modern Jewish poem.

Despite the minimal religious education of the adult community, and the widespread but superficial programs of afternoon and/or weekend study, 65 percent of Reform Jews, 82 percent of Orthodox Jews, and 90 percent of Conservative Jews felt that a two- or three-hour session on Sunday or two afternoons a week was not sufficient; more Jewish education was necessary.

The study of Hebrew was regarded as essential by some Jews

because the language was a vital link to Israel. The Jewish community's actual commitment to the study of Hebrew followed denominational lines. Differences reflected the use of Hebrew within the liturgies of the three denominations. According to our 1975 survey, 60 percent of the Reform Jews agreed that only enough Hebrew to follow the worship service was necessary. In one Reform temple, where Hebrew was not emphasized, it was possible to conduct a bar mitzvah entirely in English. Among Conservative and Orthodox Jews, however, where Hebrew studies were stressed throughout the synagogue programs, 75 to 80 percent agreed that it was necessary to learn more Hebrew than was required to participate in worship.

If budget allocations represent increased interest, the 1975-76 funding levels were encouraging. The Columbus Hebrew School, whose 1975-76 budget reached about $85,000, offered afternoon classes at both a central facility as well as North Side and East Side branches. With a $25,000 budget during 1975-76, the Jewish Education Committee coordinated, enhanced, strengthened, and assisted in financing programs of Jewish education in cooperation with Jewish schools in Columbus. The Columbus Torah Academy, with a $300,000 budget and a new school facility in 1975, offered an intensive day school program of secular and Orthodox education.

Officially, a few Orthodox rabbis and laymen founded the Columbus Torah Academy in the summer of 1958, but the story begins several years earlier. In the summer of 1952 four prominent members of the traditional community[1] — each with a record of commitment to Jewish education — petitioned the Jewish Center Executive Committee for "space to rent a classroom for the first grade of a Jewish All-Day School."[2]

The center's negative reaction was swift and strong, for the suggestion had polarized the community. Threats to cut off twenty-six thousand dollars of the Community Chest funding for the Jewish Center came from one board member and accusations of making an "un-American and subversive proposal" came from another. One member of the board, an officer at Temple Israel, summed up the position of the Reform-dominated board of directors:

> It is quite true that I am entirely uninformed on the subject and have not heard the viewpoints of the proponents of the establishment of a Jewish parochial school, but we must not permit our children to become isolated from their non-Jewish friends.
>
> This letter is not intended to be a threat of any sort but I assure you, in all sincerity, that I would certainly re-examine my intentions as to giving to the United Jewish Fund of Columbus if one cent of the

> money were to be expended in any way toward the establishment or maintenance of a Jewish parochial school of any sort.[3]

Two years later Rabbi Greenwald tried to start a day school, initially for only first graders, at the Beth Jacob Synagogue. Despite a lengthy appeal in the *Ohio Jewish Chronicle* and personal solicitation, the effort quickly died.[4]

What is today the Torah Academy or Hebrew Day School was at last assembled in a series of meetings during the spring and summer of 1958. Despite intense jealousy over the role of each Orthodox congregation in relation to the school, a small group of dedicated laymen and rabbis founded a school incorporating an intensive program of Hebraic and Judaic studies along with a program of general elementary studies.[5]

Only eleven students enrolled in the first grade class for the 1958-59 school year at Agudas Achim; Harry Gilbert was chosen as the first president and Rabbi Harry Frank was hired as the first teacher. By 1962 the academy had grown to include eighty-three students in five grades, who paid tuition fees of $250 each.[6]

What accounted for this rapid and quite unexpected growth? According to the parents of some of the earliest enrollees, the dominant reasons were dissatisfaction with the local synagogue educational programs, the desire for an intensive Hebrew education, the prestige associated with a private school education,[7] the active public support of Orthodox rabbis and their personal commitments to the school, and the "parochial" nature of the program.[8]

Although parochialism was initially a positive attribute, later it became both the strength and the weakness of the Torah Academy. Despite some leniency in their application, Orthodox practices and interpretations set the standard for the school; indeed, in its early years, and again in the mid-1970s, modern Orthodox teachings were unacceptable. For many members of the Orthodox community the fact that the "religious orientation of the Torah Academy is traditional Orthodox — daily practice and biblical interpretations reflect this" was as important as Judaic studies. For almost all of the non-Orthodox Jewish community the primary goal of the school, "to assist our children in acquiring knowledge, understanding and love for Orthodox Jewish tradition," became the major obstacle to participation in the program. Thus, without much appeal to the non-Orthodox, the enrollment of the school grew little during the past decade.

Jewish institutions hardly get started before other Jews begin to study them, and Torah Academy proved no exception. Several studies investigated the relationship between Jewish education and Jewish identification, a burning issue in Jewish educational circles in the early 1960s. When G. Pollak questioned day school students eight years after graduation, he found that they were poor synagogue attenders, ignored *kashrut* (dietary laws) outside the home, and revealed little interest in Jewish books or periodicals. C. Schwartz found that day schools had little impact on the level of Jewish culture, philanthropy, ethnocentricity, and attitudes toward Israel, although they did encourage ritual observance.[9]

In 1962 Harry Frank, Torah Academy's first Hebrew teacher, questioned whether Columbus Torah Academy "has made any religious or cultural impact on the daily lives of the children and their parents in and away from home." By impact, Frank meant not content but "measurable religious observance"; he was interested in discerning "any amount whatsoever" of such observance. The answer to his query was largely no — only three religious practices of the many dozens taught in the school made more than a 50 percent impact among the sixty-three children in grades one through four. The results of Rabbi Frank's survey distressed him, for one of the Torah Academy's goals was religious training.[10]

Our own 1975 survey involved thirty Torah Academy graduates and Orthodox, Conservative, and Reform confirmands more than five years after their graduation or confirmation. There was little evidence of a greater commitment to a Jewish lifestyle by Torah Academy graduates than those not exposed to this educational experience. When compared with Orthodox and Conservative confirmands, academy graduates were no more regular in worship attendance, no more observant of *kashrut* outside the home, and no more likely to observe the Sabbath as a complete day of rest. The Reform confirmands, on the other hand, were more likely to be readers of Jewish periodicals and High Holiday worshippers. The only distinct difference appeared to be that Torah Academy graduates were more strongly attached to traditional Jewish doctrines of faith. More than 90 percent of the graduates affirmed a belief in a creating God who sustains the universe and who chose the Jewish people.[11]

Like the almost five hundred Hebrew day schools in the United States, Torah Academy continuously emphasized its commitment to American values concomitantly with its emphasis upon Jewish beliefs. Supporters argued that a Jewish day school was the best preparation for being a good Jew and a good American, and that it produced "a generation of children well grounded in the learning and culture of both their Jewish and their American heritage."

The only area of conflict between Jewish and American heritages involved federal or state aid to non-public schools. In the Columbus Jewish community, 95 percent were opposed to such aid in 1975. Although almost all the local Jewish organizations shared this view, the Torah Academy strongly favored such aid because finances, not surprisingly, were its greatest problem. In fact, at one legislative session while two prominent members of the Columbus Jewish community testified against such aid, Torah Academy leaders joined other parochial school representatives in supporting this assistance.

Torah Academy's financial plight touched off the most intensely argued question in Jewish day school education: should the Torah Academy relinquish some control over its program and philosophy in exchange for badly needed Columbus Jewish Federation financial support? As the Torah Academy's requests for financial help from the federation increased in dollar amounts, there was pressure to change the religious philosophy on which the school was founded; for example, hiring only strictly observant Judaica teachers. After all, communal funding suggested the right of communal input; the federation desired to make the day school a "community" school in exchange for large subventions. To the day school leadership the uncertain implications of a community — rather than a parochial — school were a serious threat. The school was fearful of the fund raisers, despite their increasing involvement in Jewish education. School lay leadership saw this interest as self-serving and the vision as myopic; they were convinced that those who raised money should not decide questions of educational philosophy. How this issue will resolve itself, given the serious financial problems inherent in private education, is one of the crucial questions on the coming decade's Jewish communal agenda.

Another hopeful sign for religious education was the establishment in 1966 of a program of Jewish Studies at The Ohio State University. Eight years later ten full-time faculty members offered nearly seventy-five formal courses in Judaica. Another Jewish organization on campus, the Hillel Foundation, offered a full range of student activities including worship services, holiday celebrations, Judaica courses, personal counseling, diverse cultural programs, and an active community service program of student volunteers. Their 1975-76 budget totalled about $100,000.

Taking into consideration the community's newly discovered appreciation for religious education, as well as Torah Academy and serious high school religious programs, in 1975 Jewish education seemed well on its way to playing a more significant role in Jewish communal priorities.

NOTES FOR CHAPTER 22

TABLE 83
1975 COLUMBUS JEWISH COMMUNITY SURVEY:
IMPORTANCE OF ONGOING RELIGIOUS EDUCATION

Today's Jew only needs enough religious education to prepare for bar/bat mitzvah or confirmation.	Denominations		
	Reform	Conservative	Orthodox
Strongly Agree	6%	—	3%
Agree	29	10%	15
Disagree	51	56	33
Strongly Disagree	14	34	49
Total	**157**	**162**	**121**

1. The men were Abe Wolman, Marvin Fox, B. W. Abramson, and Harry Gilbert.

2. Columbus Jewish Center Minutes, July 30, 1952.

3. Ibid.; interviews with Marvin Fox and Maurice Bernstein; Abe Wolman to Marc Lee Raphael, telephone conversation, October, 1973; Leon S. Friedman to Ed Schlezinger, correspondence, August 4, 1952.

4. *OJC*, March 19, 1954.

5. Interviews with Sylvia Schecter, Marvin Fox, David Stavsky, and Samuel Rubenstein.

6. *OJC*, August 1, 1958, January 2, 1959, September 27, 1963.

7. Milton Himmelfarb noted this about the same time as Torah Academy was founded: "to send Jewish children to day schools is a way of showing that they have arrived in America." See "Reflection on the Jewish Day School," *Commentary* 30:1 (July 1960): 29-36, and Marvin Fox, "The Jewish Day School Comes of Age" [1953] in Lloyd P. Gartner, editor, *Jewish Education in the United States: A Documentary History* (New York, 1969): 198-206.

8. On parental motivations for Hebrew Day School education, see Louis Nulman, "The Reaction of Parents to a Jewish All-Day School," Ph.D. dissertation, University of Pittsburgh, 1955.

9. G. Pollak, "The Graduates of the Jewish Day School: A Follow-Up Study," Ph.D. dissertation, Western Reserve University, 1961; C. Schwartz, "A Study to Determine the Effects of Religious Education Upon Jewish Identification," M.S.W. thesis, Yeshiva University, 1961. See also D. Raylesberg, "The Jewish Adolescent and His Jewish Identification." Paper presented at the National Staff Conference of the B'nai B'rith Organization, Starlight, Pennsylvania, 1960, Columbus Jewish Federation.

10. Harry Frank, "A Study of the Impact of a Hebrew Program on Children and Their Parents," M.A. thesis, The Ohio State University, 1962.

11. Confirmation and Torah Academy graduates survey, Columbus Jewish History Project.

23: A SUBSTANTIAL PUBLIC SERVICE: ORGANIZATIONAL LIFE

An enclave of organizations serving both the Jewish and the non-Jewish community fell under the long shadow of the Jewish Center's giant menorah on College Avenue in 1975. The tallest of this group was the Heritage House, a retirement center, nursing home, and extended care facility which provided multi-faceted religious, recreational, medical, therapeutic, and social programs to residents as well as out-reach services for the ill or house-bound elderly. The Eleanor and Jack Resler Wing added fifty rooms to Heritage House in the early seventies. By 1975 a staff of nearly one hundred cared for approximately ninety residents; an auxiliary of over fifteen hundred provided spirited volunteers to supplement Heritage House's nearly $1 million budget.

Down the street, the Jewish Center offered programs to meet the leisure time, cultural, recreational, and informal educational needs of the community — from a preschool for the younger children to a Golden Age Club for the elderly. In 1975 the center served as a meeting place for over seventy Jewish and non-Jewish clubs and organizations. Other program areas included classes and special interest groups, as well as the Gallery Players, a drama group which annually presented four major productions. With generous support from the United Way as well as the Jewish community, the center's 1975-76 budget totalled about $800,000 and it served more than five thousand individual members.

The preceding summary of center activities for 1975 is deceivingly simplistic; it leaves out the day to day — sometimes year to year — disagreements such organizations must endure and resolve if they are to survive. One example from this time period was the continuing discussion about the Jewish Center and Sabbath observance. In 1958 the following recommendation was approved by the executive committee and the board of directors as the result of a Jewish Center Self-Study and guidance from the

Sabbath Policy Committee of the National Jewish Welfare Board:

> In view of the fact that Saturday represents an important leisure time period for the center members, particularly children, it is recommended that the center develop a Saturday afternoon program. This program should emphasize small group activities, informal recreational programs, and special activities which will help instill within the participants a feeling of the spirit of Sabbath. A committee should be appointed to actively explore the matter and develop a plan to put this recommendation into effect. Careful attention should be given to process so as to achieve broad community acceptance.[1]

The "broad community acceptance" however, was not easily achieved, as the Columbus Board of Rabbis (CBR) opposed Sabbath afternoon activities at the Jewish Center. Four years later the Sabbath Policy Committee made the same recommendation to the board of directors. An aggressive attempt to win the approval of the CBR in the spring of 1963 was of no avail, however, as the Orthodox and Conservative rabbis termed the proposal "a grave mistake [which] would weaken our efforts to preserve Jewish life in Columbus." Reacting specifically to the suggestion that the Jewish Center outdoor pool be opened on the Sabbath, the CBR president urged the center "not to secularize the little holiness that is left in our Jewish Community by transferring Jewish religious authority to those who are not qualified to pass judgment on what is good for the Jewish soul and what is harmful."[2]

Despite the use of the Jewish Center facilities for a Sabbath teen conclave in August 1964 — which the board carefully noted did not establish a precedent — no action was taken to implement the 1958 decision for a full decade.[3] By 1968 public pressure had intensified, as vocal parents complained that closing the center pool on the Sabbath kept them from joining the center and that the Orthodox members should not be permitted to impose their will on the community. Responding to growing internal and external pressure, the board recommended that the Sabbath Study Committee Report be reconsidered at the spring board meeting in 1969.[4]

Obviously, only rabbinical opposition prevented complete implementation of the 1958 report. On March 24, 1969, the executive committee unanimously resolved to request that the board of directors approve the report, with the accumulated guidelines retaining the "spirit, if not the letter, of the Sabbath." If approved, the outdoor pool would be opened, on a trial basis, on summer Sabbath afternoons following morning synagogue services.[5]

The rabbinical response was immediate. The president of the board of rabbis spoke to the Jewish Center president about CBR's "righteous indignation" at not being asked "their approval or permission" before "implementing a program which would violate the sacredness of the Sabbath." Since only "those qualified by Jewish law" were to render judgment affecting the spiritual life of the total community," the rabbis stated they would "use any means at [their] disposal to combat the effort . . . to secularize our Jewish community."[6]

At the April 14, 1969, board meeting forty-nine laypersons and seven staff members listened to CBR representatives proclaim their "unequivocal opposition to the opening on the Sabbath." After "much heat was generated" the board tabled the executive committee's motion by a narrow four-vote margin.[7]

More than one year later, on May 28, 1970, the board again faced the issue, this time with fifty-four members, fourteen guests, and seven staff members present. Again, the rabbis argued that opening the pool would "constitute a public desecration of the Sabbath by a Jewish Communal Institution" while the proponents urged that the pool would provide an "opportunity for Jewish people to come together in leisure time activities under Jewish auspices." Following almost three hours of ferocious debate, the board approved opening the Jewish Center outdoor pool on Sabbath afternoons by a twenty-five to fifteen vote. The pool opened on Saturday, June 13, 1970; the use of money was forbidden and the snack bar remained closed. In a last bit of opposition, CBR members on the Jewish Center Board of Directors resigned. This was, however, a futile gesture, and the Sabbath pool became a regular feature of Columbus Jewish life.[8]

Sandwiched between the Jewish Center and Heritage House was the Esther C. Melton Community Services Building which was dedicated in May of 1970. Housed within this building were the Columbus Jewish Federation, the Community Relations Committee, and the Jewish Family Service.

Expanding in the years after World War II, the Jewish Family Service became a multiple-function counseling agency. Services included marital, personal, and parent-child counseling; vocational guidance and career counseling; services to the elderly; adoptions; out-reach; emergency financial assistance; and resettlement of "New Americans." A United Way agency, the Jewish Family Service operated on a $170,000 budget in 1975-76.

With the reorganization of the Jewish Family Service in 1953, one of the agency's major responsibilities was to become the provider of services for Jewish refugees or "New Americans." (During the thirties, and then again immediately after the Second World War, the Council of Jewish Women undertook major resettlement work for Jewish refugees in Columbus.) Over a period of two decades or so, a fairly continuous stream of Jewish refugee families moved into the community; through the federation, Columbus Jews contributed tens of thousands of dollars for their maintenance.

TABLE 84
NEW AMERICANS ASSISTED BY THE JEWISH FAMILY SERVICE

Year	Individuals	Families	Cost of Direct Relief
1954-55	42	8	Unavailable
1955-56	52	8	Unavailable
1956-57	31	8	Unavailable
1957-58	24	6	$ 4,838
1958-59	35	6	6,288
1959-60	29	5	6,000
1960-61	22	3	5,662
1961-62	21	5	8,879
1962-63	29	5	8,816
1963-64	28	3	7,658
1964-65	36	4	10,245
1965-66	22	2	4,254
1966-67	23	5	6,961
1967-68	26	5	6,036
1968-69	26	5	4,782
1969-70	24	7	7,297
1970-71	25	5	2,626
1971-72	26	3	4,376
1972-73	36	3	Unavailable

Upon the immigrant family's arrival, the Jewish Family Service assumed responsibility for all of the tasks of settlement, from finding housing, furniture and jobs, to arranging English classes. Such sponsorship was a prerequisite to the issuance of a visa by the United States State Department as well as a guarantee that "the Jewish Family Service would provide financial assistance for such families until they are eligible for citizenship at the end of the five years, thus preventing them from becoming public charges and subject to deportation." At times this meant an overwhelming percentage of the agency's caseload involved New Americans; in 1952, for example, 84 percent of the agency's caseload involved resettlement. At other times, especially during periods when the job market was very tight, refugee programs encountered difficult trials, and sometimes failures.[9]

Who were the refugee Jews that settled in Columbus in the sixties? Not Jews from Latin America, the largest constituency of Jewish refugees to the United States during this period, but primarily East European and North African Jews. From mid-1962 through mid-1964, for example, four families came from Egypt, three from Poland, and one from Rumania, while in 1967-68 families came from the same lands and Morocco. Although several Hungarian Jewish refugees came after the unsuccessful 1956 revolution, and one or two Cuban families arrived in the early 1960s at the peak of Cuban immigration, Polish, Rumanian, Russian, Egyptian, and Moroccan immigrants predominate.[10]

Typical were two Egyptian Jewish families, headed by an accountant and a foundry manager, which arrived in Columbus in 1963 and 1964 "with no clear understanding of what they would be facing in the resettlement process." These families waited for several months in Paris until the Hebrew Immigrant Aid Society obtained American visas after Columbus agreed to sponsor them. Upon their arrival, the Jewish Family Service staff gave the Egyptian families abundant assistance: a monthly allowance (loan) for one year, assistance in securing employment, a furnished apartment, medical care, adult English classes and school arrangements, Jewish Center membership with a center day camp scholarship, and continuous hospitality. A decade later one man was an accountant in a national firm's Columbus office, and his wife was an assistant librarian at The Ohio State University. The second immigrant was an office manager at the pipe manufacturing plant which first employed him in Columbus.[11]

The Jewish Family Service's commitments expanded after the Immigration Act of October 3, 1965. This act abolished national origin quotas, established numerical ceilings for immigrant visas on a first come/first served basis, and instituted new preferences in granting visas. As a result, three-fourths of the American visas went to persons with American relatives; for those without close relatives who possessed college degrees, or vocational skills, the United States Department of Labor demanded job assurance approval. Between 1966 and 1968 the Jewish Family Service responded to this demand by obtaining jobs for immigrants as automobile and typewriter repairmen, bookkeepers, and clerks; other immigrants were employed as a furrier, factory worker, seamstress, shipping clerk, and lab technician.[12]

During the most recent decade, these jobs and many like them have gone predominately to Jewish refugees from one specific land — Russia. Unlike the millions of Russian Jews who came to America early in the century, however, these Soviet families had not lived actively as Jews in the Soviet Union and were relatively well-integrated into Soviet society. Although their reasons for leaving the Soviet Union and coming to Columbus vary, almost all have had enormous difficulty in adjusting to American life.

All Soviet Jews who received permission to leave Russia were given visas to Israel; once in Vienna, many opted for resettlement in America. Jewish organizations helped them obtain American visas once an American Jewish community agreed to include them in its quota, and Columbus generously has been willing to sponsor Soviet Jewish families.

The Jewish Family Service assisted these Soviet Jews by meeting the families at the airport, supporting the families for the initial period of resettlement, providing an orientation to Columbus and Columbus Jewry, and attempting to sustain continual communication. But providing satisfaction has been extraordinarily difficult.

Soviet Jewish immigrants have come to Columbus primarily in pursuit of a better life in America, rather than because they desired to live freely as Jews. Neither impoverished nor degraded in the society they left, these Russians found that their lives here did not measure up to their visions of wealthy Americans, abundant skilled jobs, friendly people who love immigrants, and an easy linguistic adjustment. Finding only menial employment in Columbus, the majority were disappointed if not angry, and eager to vent their hostility either at affluent Jewish businessmen who did not give them good jobs or, more familiar to them, the Jewish Family Service.[13]

The organized Jewish community responded that it had done everything possible for these refugees, and that their lot was not unlike that of their predecessors early in the century. Although they had gotten off to a rough start, perhaps, it was nevertheless still too early to despair, for the acquisition of job and language skills was a slow process.

Soviet Jews responded that while they had a degree of personal freedom not possible in the Soviet Union, they were not optimistic about reaching a position in America even equivalent to that which they enjoyed in Russia. Despairing of any upward mobility, they felt trapped at low socioeconomic levels of existence, and would not encourage friends to emigrate. While an occasional family made a rapid adjustment to Columbus by transferring scientific skills learned in a Russian university to The Ohio State University, disappointment was the response for almost all of the families.[14]

At the same time that the Jewish Family Service was trying to fulfill Soviet immigrants' dreams, the Community Relations Committee (CRC) attempted to tell the story of Soviet Jewry to the community. Other 1975 priorities for the CRC included disseminating information about Israel, strengthening Christian-Jewish relations, and lobbying for equal employment opportunities. Since its inception in 1948, the committee has worked with the Anti-Defamation League in inter-group, inter-racial, and inter-religious activities; defense efforts against real and potential anti-Semitism; and the interpretation of local, national, and international Jewish concerns to non-Jews. While the league received its funding from the national office, the CRC budget of $32,500 in 1975-76 came entirely from the local Jewish community.

Operating with a $7 million budget and twenty-six regional offices in 1975, the Anti-Defamation League (ADL) of the B'nai B'rith was the most prominent organization designed to protect American Jews from anti-Semitism. ADL's prime objective was, and remains, "to counter the defamation of Jews and assaults on their status and rights."

Relating this objective to Columbus, our 1975 survey revealed that Columbus Jews' relationships with non-Jews were generally ambivalent. On the one hand, about 60 percent of Columbus Jewry as a whole had experienced either very little or no anti-Semitism in their lifetimes, while among native-born Jews the figure was 70 percent. On the other hand, 35 to 40 percent of the Jews in Columbus had experienced either a "moderate amount" or a "great deal" of anti-Semitism, and a sizeable proportion of the latter had experienced (not just heard about) some anti-Semitism personally during the past year.

Persistently combating anti-Semitism afforded ADL with a recognized expertise in the field of "fact finding" or intelligence, directed at a wide range of extremist, anti-Semitic, and anti-Israel groups. An example of its local vigilance work took place in the seventies.

TABLE 85
1975 COLUMBUS JEWISH COMMUNITY SURVEY: ANTI-SEMITISM

	Age Brackets						
	18-25	26-35	36-45	46-55	56-65	66+	All
Have you experienced any anti-Semitism in the past twelve months?							
Yes	33%	44%	30%	30%	39%	4%	33%
No	62	42	59	52	40	80	53
Not Sure	5	14	11	18	21	16	14
Total	**42**	**133**	**112**	**66**	**77**	**50**	**480**
Other than the above, how much anti-Semitism have you experienced in your life?							
None	5%	3%	5%	6%	3%	15%	5%
Very Little	62	64	59	36	43	37	55
Moderate Amount	33	27	21	45	42	33	32
Great Deal	—	6	14	12	13	15	8
Total	**42**	**133**	**112**	**66**	**77**	**54**	**484**

Early in the summer of 1971 the Blackman's Development Center (BDC), a narcotics rehabilitation agency headquartered in Washington, D.C., established an office in Columbus. The local director, "Major" Danyil Sulieman (born Overton Daniel Buckner), immediately sought ADL endorsement of the center and its work. The ADL refused, on the grounds that the Columbus BDC was tied to the Washington BDC, which was directed by an "infamous, professional" anti-Semite, "Colonel" Hassan Jeru-Ahmed.[15]

The national director of the para-military BDC and the commander of Blackman's Volunteer Army of Liberation, Hassan Jeru-Ahmed was exposed as a professional anti-Semite as early as 1966 in an article appearing in the *New Republic*. During a Washington D.C. radio interview in 1971, Hassan refused to disavow anti-Semitic tracts published in 1966 and 1967. In the intervening years Hassan's continued anti-Semitic activities had led the ADL to initiate a nationwide letter-writing campaign to strongly condemn a half-million dollar Health, Education and Welfare (HEW) grant to the center in March 1971 on the grounds that taxpayers' money supported a bigot.[16]

In June 1971 HEW Secretary Elliot Richardson announced BDC's funding would be withheld pending an audit; Hassan blamed ADL for Richardson's directive and responded in July with a $4 million libel and conspiracy suit against ADL. The suit was eventually dismissed, as the federal judge noted that the "statements by Defendants [ADL] were made after careful and diligent research and . . . are in fact true as is evident from Plaintiff Hassan Jeru-Ahmed's own utterances."[17]

Although Sulieman was anxious to gain ADL approval of the Columbus center before requesting funds from local business leaders and the government, his refusal to sever ties with the national Blackman's Development Center ultimately made funding impossible. When the BDC received a $25,000 grant from the Ohio Bureau of Community Services and $8,334 in local money from the Franklin County Mental Health and Retardation Board, the Columbus ADL realized that apparently taxpayers' money was supporting bigotry. During December of 1971, Hassan visited Columbus to launch a week-long campaign against drug abuse and announced both that Columbus would replace Washington as the national headquarters of BDC and that Sulieman would replace him as the national director.[18]

On January 6, 1971, HEW announced the results of a General Accounting Office-HEW audit which revealed that BDC had spent the major portion of the first installment of the grant for non-grant purposes between March 15 and June 30, 1971. The auditors recommended that subsequent grant money be withheld. Three days later the local Mental Health and Retardation Board announced an intention to "review its relationship with BDC." Washington's audit had panicked the local board, for the BDC was part of a $2.4 million request by Columbus for an HEW grant to fund a nationwide drug rehabilitation program.[19]

Confident that the federal government would not fund a program with a BDC affiliate included, the ADL was alarmed at the state's support for the center. The chairman of ADL's Ohio-Kentucky Regional Board sent a letter to Governor John Gilligan opposing state funding of the BDC because of Hassan's intimate ties. Five days later, on January 25, 1972, Governor Gilligan replied that the "State's concern is limited to the support of BDC's drug treatment efforts" [which were enjoying wide community support] and the funding would continue. Again ADL's regional board chairmen urged the governor to at least delay funding during an investigation of the local BDC's relationship to Hassan — but there was no reply.[20]

The BDC, however, reorganized as an independent non-profit drug treatment and rehabilitation corporation and was rewarded with a $50,000 grant from the state and continued support by the local mental health board late in January 1971. With these developments the ADL intensified its attack.[21]

In February the local agency hired an investigator, reprimanded the Jewish president of the Columbus Civil Rights Council for its support of BDC, and discussed Hassan's involvement with BDC and anti-Semitism with the Jewish president of Columbus City Council. Meanwhile ADL's Washington-Maryland office convinced Representative Robert Giaimo (D-Connecticut), who had earlier opposed HEW grants to Hassan, to write Secretary Elliot Richardson and question possible federal funding of the BDC through the local mental health board.[22]

All this seemed wasted when, on February 10, the government announced that Columbus' BDC would receive $94,000 in federal and local funds, channeled through the county mental health board as part of a $6.7 million drug control plan for the county — if approved by the National Institute of Mental Health. HEW Secretary Richardson wrote Representative Giaimo that there was a good chance the institute would approve the grant.[23]

ADL knew that federal funding could be stopped only by proving that the BDC in Columbus was closely linked with Hassan in Washington. In Los Angeles the ADL retained a new agent to serve as a contact and do research, while the local office informed Ohio congressmen about the history of the situation, and urged BDC leaders to divorce themselves from the Washington operation.[24]

The results were very gratifying for the ADL, although neither federal nor state officials would at any point state that Hassan's anti-Semitism influenced their decisions. The National Institute of Mental Health delayed funding, then announced their approval although "no funds are available." Finally, the institute refused funding to the Franklin County Mental Health and Retardation Board unless it excluded BDC. Thanks in part to pressure from several prominent Jewish laymen, the state refused to pick up BDC funding. The denouement: the Ohio Board of Pharmacy revoked Sulieman's license to purchase and distribute dangerous drugs because he had not admitted a federal narcotics conviction discovered by the Los Angeles ADL agent. Sulieman had been arrested by the FBI and indicted by a federal grand jury for kidnapping charges that were dismissed six months later.[25]

Once again Hassan proclaimed himself national BDC director in July of 1972, and blamed the fine hand of the ADL for the Columbus center's collapse: "There's no doubt in my mind they're behind it." The Columbus ADL office denied all responsibility for the grant rejection publicly, although a national officer boasted to the regional offices:

> I am certain you recognize that the above outcome — albeit for the wrong reason — would never have come to pass without the persistent efforts of the ADL . . . we performed a substantial public service in helping to expose a fiscally irresponsible program.[26]

In desperation, one year after the grants were denied Sulieman asked to sign an ADL-prepared statement promising disassociation from both Hassan and anti-Semitism which he had never been accused of by anybody. Promising not to use this statement publicly, the ADL offered to share it with anyone who inquired, and noted somewhat sadly that "if Danyil had done this two years ago he would probably not have lost the support he was getting."[27]

Several conclusions seem legitimate from this example of ADL activity: First, there exists a very close relationship between national and regional offices. The New York and Washington offices often prepared statements issued in Columbus, and drafted letters sent from the Columbus office. Generally, the Columbus office fed the eastern offices local newspaper articles and other materials it gathered, but the national office made policy decisions and decided implementation strategies, which were transmitted to the local ADL and Community Relations Committee.

Second, the ADL acted with great courage and zeal. The BDC operation in Columbus received strong support from both black and white communal leaders, had a board of distinguished citizens, received impressive professional evaluations from independent evaluators, and helped to solve a serious communal problem. Its local leader, Danyil Sulieman, was not anti-Semitic nor was there any evidence that any other individuals in the local BDC were. Nevertheless, the ADL pursued Sulieman because he refused to sever his Washington contacts and refused to denounce his friend Hassan, the man who brought Sulieman — a heroin addict — off the streets and placed him in a position of prominence.

Third, the issues under consideration, like all other issues in the community relations field, were the concern of the entire Jewish community. Some community leaders felt the situation should not have been unilaterally handled by individuals or individual organizations but should have involved a large sector of Columbus Jewry. The ADL, however, acted as the defender of the entire Jewish community. Its position, as expressed to the governor ("no community is so bankrupt in human resources that it needs to turn to a paramilitary anti-Semitic organization"), did not necessarily flow out of the community. Indeed, there was no evidence in the ADL files of any attempt among Community Relations Committee and ADL members to involve the community. The link to Hassan and the resulting potential dangers subordinated the highly visible accomplishments of the drug rehabilitation program, which received support from a wide variety of local Jews.[28]

Five years earlier, ample communication existed between the Community Relations Council and the public it represented, as the council organized the entire community to gather political support for Israel during the Six Day War. Concomitant with local fund-raising efforts was a widespread effort by the CRC to gain the support of key political figures and non-Jewish organizations for opening the Gulf of Aqaba and the Suez Canal as international waterways, maintaining the "territorial integrity" of Israel, and creating peace. Well aware that Israel depended on American support of all kinds, the CRC used its unique communication skills to sustain a favorable attitude toward Israel within special interest groups, and Americans at large. Columbus' CRC sent telegrams and press releases to newspapers, radio and television stations; called many prominent organizational leaders; and sent a delegation of local leaders to Washington on June 7 and 8 to accomplish the goal. Senators Frank Lausche and Stephen Young as well as central Ohio congressmen, Ohio state legislators, the mayor of Columbus, the governor of Ohio, the Columbus Area Council of Churches,[29] and major Ohio labor organizations issued favorable statements and even resolutions of support. For example, after a delegation of Columbus Jews met with congressmen Samuel Devine and Chalmers Wylie, they issued a very forceful statement and cosponsored a resolution to recognize the Gulf of Aqaba as international waters, to grant Israel access to the Suez Canal, to demand Arab recognition of Israel's existence, and to support Israel's extension of its old boundaries to include at least Old Jerusalem.[30] Thus the CRC could point with pride to the fact that "Columbus led the way nationally in many of the projects and programs undertaken."[31]

During the third quarter of the twentieth century, the effects of these organizations which cluster together on College Avenue resemble concentric circles beginning in the immediate community and evolving out to touch lives in this country and the world. Professional in their approach and diverse in their offerings, these institutions personify continuing growth — and at times controversy.

NOTES FOR CHAPTER 23

1. National Jewish Welfare Board, Jewish Community Center Division, Digest of the Report of the Committee on the Sabbath Policy of the Jewish Community Centers, June 1957; Sabbath Programming Committee Minutes, Columbus Jewish Center, October 31, 1962, at the Columbus Jewish Center.

2. Sabbath Programming Committee Minutes, November 19, 1962; The Jewish Center Study Committee on Sabbath Programming Progress Report, December 1, 1963; Mayer Rosenfeld to Nathan Zelizer, correspondence, June 21, 1963; Nathan Zelizer to Howard Schoenbaum, correspondence, June 25, 1963; Mayer Rosenfeld to Nathan Zelizer, correspondence, July 2, 1963; Nathan Zelizer to Howard Schoenbaum, correspondence, July 5, 1963; Board of Directors Meeting, The Jewish Center, March 26, 1964, at ibid.

3. Two years later the center's board rejected a request by the center's swim team to participate in a Sabbath meet; Columbus Jewish Center Minutes, November 28, 1966, ibid.

4. Board of Directors Meeting, The Jewish Center, September 30, 1968; Ad Hoc Committee on Sabbath Programming Meeting, March 20, 1969, ibid.

5. Executive Committee Meeting, March 24, 1969, ibid.

6. David Stavsky to Myer Mellman, correspondence, April 11, 1969, ibid.

7. Board of Directors Meeting, The Jewish Center, April 14, 1969, ibid.

8. Board of Directors Meeting, The Jewish Center, May 28, 1970, ibid.; *OJC*, June 4, 11, and 25, 1970; Nathan Zelizer to David Roth, correspondence, June 13, 1970, ibid. For lengthy discussion of a motion to withhold $10,000 of the Jewish Center's allocation, and its eventual

withdrawal, see United Jewish Fund and Council Minutes, Board of Trustees Meeting, June 16, 1970, at the Columbus Jewish Federation.

9. Box 31, Folder 2, Box 5, Folders 60-61, Box 1 (Board of Directors Meeting, April 16, 1953, and President's Report, January 14, 1954), Box 11, Folders 1 and 4, in Jewish Family Service Papers, OHS.

10. Jack J. Diamond, "Jewish Immigration to the United States," *AJYB* 70 (1969): 289-94 and Ilya Dijour, "Jewish Immigration to the United States," *AJYB* 63 (1962): 146-49: Box 19, Folders 2 and 25, especially Board of Trustees Meeting, June 15, 1962, in ibid.

11. Murray I. Daninhirsch to Marc Lee Raphael, correspondence, August 25, 1976; *OJC,* April 5, 1963, July 24, 1964; Andre Douek to Linda E. Kalette, telephone conversation, August 18, 1976. Herman Katz, then president of the Capital Manufacturing Company and a member of the Jewish Family Service Board, employed one of the men. Herbert Schiff, the president of Shoe Corporation of America and a past president of the Jewish Family Service, employed the other head of household. The language barrier, and differences in work expectations between America and Egypt, made the adjustment of these two men as arduous as that of most other New Americans.

12. Sidney Liskofsky, "United States Immigration Policy," *AJYB* 67 (1966): 164-75; Box 11, Folder 4 and Box 7, Folder 18, in Jewish Family Service Papers.

13. Soviet Jewish immigrants to Columbus seem very much like Soviet Jewish immigrants everywhere in America in terms of their motivations for emigration. See George Johnson, "Which Promised Land? The Realities of American Absorption of Soviet Jews," *Analysis,* No. 47 (November 1, 1974), p. 2.

14. Interview with Dr. and Mrs. Julius Goldberg. A list of recent Soviet Jewish immigrants was supplied by the Jewish Family Service during 1975.

15. Justin Finger to Anti-Defamation League Regional Offices, Memorandum, April 13, 1971, at ADL office, Columbus, Ohio, "The Colonel is a Bigot," *ADL Bulletin* (May 1971); Jason R. Silverman to Sidney Sayles, correspondence, June 1, 1971 (ADL office); *CCP,* June 5, 1971; *CD,* July 18, 1971; Dan Pope to Hersh Adlerstein, correspondence, July 7, 1971 (ADL office).

16. James Ridgeway, "Black Mischief," *New Republic,* December 24, 1966; Transcript of Radio Interview: Fred Fiske and Colonel Hassan, WWDC (Washington, D.C.), August 9, 1971 (ADL office); *Washington Post,* April 14 and 15, August 8, 1971; Justin Finger to ADL Regional Offices, Memorandum, June 28, 1971 (ADL office).

17. *Jewish Telegraphic Agency News Bulletin,* June 28, 1971; Justin Finger to ADL Regional Offices, Memorandum, July 16, 1971 (ADL office); U.S. District Court for the District of Columbus, *Hassan Jeru-Ahmed and BDC, Inc.* v. *ADL and Seymour Graubard and Jason Silverman, Order for Summary Judgment and Judgment,* Civil Action 1330-71, November 9, 1971; *JTA News Bulletin,* November 18, 1971.

18. *CCJ,* December 6, 1971; *CD,* December 5 and 23, 1971; *CCP,* December 18, 1971; *Washington Post,* December 31, 1971.

19. U.S. Department of Health, Education, and Welfare, Office of

Education, *HEW News,* January 6, 1972; Report of Review of Costs Claimed on Department of HEW Manpower Development Training Grant No. OEG, O, 71, 1926 (337), BDC, Washington, D.C., For the Period 3-15-71 through 6-30-71 (ADL office); *CD,* January 9, 1972.

20. Jack Resler to John J. Gilligan, January 20, 1972; John J. Gilligan to Jack Resler, January 25, 1972; Jack Resler to John J. Gilligan, February 9, 1972 (Correspondence in ADL office).

21. *CCJ,* January 26, 28, and 29, 1972; *CCP,* February 5, 1972.

22. Sidney Sayles to Justin Finger, correspondence, February 1, 1972; Hersh Adlerstein to BDC File, Memorandum, February 3, 1972; Sidney Sayles to Justin Finger, correspondence, February 7, 1972; Jason Silverman to Jack Resler, correspondence, February 10, 1972; Robert Giaimo to Elliot Richardson, correspondence, January 21, February 22, 1972 (ADL office).

23. *CD,* February 10, 1972; Elliot Richardson to Robert Giaimo, correspondence, February 16, 1972 (ADL office).

24. Justin Finger to Hersh Adlerstein, Memorandum, February 16, 1972; Sidney Sayles to Justin Finger, correspondence, March 1, 1972; Jason Silverman to Justin Finger, correspondence, March 7, 1972; Sidney Sayles to Hersh Adlerstein, correspondence, March 29, 1972; Carol Lister to Hersh Adlerstein, correspondence, May 9, 1972 (ADL office).

25. Hersh Adlerstein to BDC File, Memorandum, February 14, 1972 (ADL office); *CCJ,* June 1, 2, 5, 9, and 16, July 13, December 9 and 13, 1972; *CD,* June 15, 24, 27, 28, and 30, July 4, 11, and 30, August 21 and 23, 1972; Harvey Schecter to Sidney Sayles, correspondence, January 11, 1972; Hersh Adlerstein to Justin Finger, correspondence, June 21, 1972 (ADL office).

26. *CCJ,* July 25 and 28, 1972; *Washington Post,* July 18 and August 3, 1972; Justin Finger to ADL Regional Offices, Memorandum, June 29, 1972 (ADL office).

27. Hersh Adlerstein to BDC File, Memorandum, June 12, 1973, Hersh Adlerstein to Justin Finger, correspondence, June 15, 1973 (ADL office).

28. This summary conclusion was confirmed by several telephone conversations with Columbus Jewish leaders during the autumn of 1976. Unfortunately, CRC minutes from this period seem to be missing.

29. Although the formal establishments of both Protestant and Catholic churches remained, at best, largely silent or even hostile (especially the National Council of Churches) — even withholding an affirmation of Israel's right to exist — Columbus Jewry reaped the dividends of years of Jewish-Christian dialogue and increasing contact between the two faiths through the responses of individual clergymen.

30. Senator Frank J. Lausche's remarks are in *Congressional Record* 113:90 (June 8, 1967); see also Congressman Samuel Devine to Rabbi Samuel Rubenstein, correspondence, June 14, 1967 (CJF).

31. "Columbus and the Middle East Crisis: Report of Community Relations Committee," Columbus Jewish Federation.

24: NEARLY THIRTY MILLION DOLLARS IN TWENTY-FIVE YEARS: SECTARIAN PHILANTHROPY

During the past quarter century or so, volunteering for Jewish philanthropy has become the primary expression of Jewishness for a sizeable portion of the community. As a result, an increasing number of religious leaders in Columbus began to bemoan the fact that "activity has become religion" among Columbus Jews. While the extent to which the philanthropic activity may be considered "religious" is still in doubt, the extent of the activity is widely agreed upon. All agree as well that a love for Israel played a dominant role in this fund raising.

The response to our 1975 survey indicated that, regardless of affiliation or income, there was a deep feeling of attachment and sense of obligation to Israel, except in the area of *aliyah* (immigration). More than nine of ten Columbus Jews enthusiastically gave money to Israel, approved of raising money for Israel, and supported efforts to influence United States' foreign policy on behalf of Israel. Sixty percent of the Reform community and 80 percent of the Orthodox belonged to at least one organization which centers its activities around Israel. Support for Israel has become a measure of Jewish identity.

Paradoxically, almost everywhere in the United States rabbis, educators, and communal lay and professional leaders all revealed reluctance to promote and encourage *aliyah*. In part they reflected their constituents' desires — American Jews would not care for their children to move to Australia either. In addition, full-page fund-raising ads of impoverished *olim* (newcomers), terrorist tragedies, and other catastrophies have convinced them that Israel was highly unstable, insecure, and barely surviving; *aliyah* was a *verboten* topic in most Jewish communities.

The attitude of the Columbus Jewish community toward *aliyah* was strikingly different from American Jewry as a whole. Although Jews do not undergo *aliyah* with any statistical significance, there

TABLE 86
1975 COLUMBUS JEWISH COMMUNITY SURVEY: DESIRE TO VISIT ISRAEL

	Visitation		Have Visited	
	Would Like	Would Not	Would Return	Would Not
Denominations (N)				
Reform (155)	57%	27%	14%	2%
Conservative (160)	57	8	35	—
Orthodox (131)	34	23	43	—
Income Levels (N)				
Under $7,000 (22)	55	18	18	9
$ 7/12,000 (36)	61	17	22	—
12/15,000 (42)	57	19	24	—
15/20,000 (58)	55	17	24	3
20/35,000 (148)	64	16	20	—
35/50,000 (54)	44	22	33	—
50/75,000 (40)	35	25	40	—
75/100,000 (14)	57	—	43	—
Over $100,000 (8)	75	—	25	—

TABLE 87
1975 COLUMBUS JEWISH COMMUNITY SURVEY: DESIRE TO SETTLE IN ISRAEL

	Resettlement			Children's *Aliyah*		
	Would	Would Not	Not Sure	Would Discourage	Would Encourage	Not Sure
Denominations (N)						
Reform (154)	4%	81%	15%	50%	50%	
Conservative (160)	8	65	27	60	38	2%
Orthodox (130)	8	58	34	45	50	5
Income Levels (N)						
Under $7,000 (28)	14	57	29			
$ 7/12,000 (36)	11	44	44			
12/15,000 (42)	5	57	38			
15/20,000 (58)	10	66	24			
20/35,000 (148)	7	70	23			
35/50,000 (54)	—	81	19			
50/75,000 (40)	10	80	10			
75/100,000 (14)	—	100	—			
Over $100,000 (8)	—	100	—			

is a relatively positive attitude toward the concept. The adults, especially the Reform affiliates, have a strong desire not to live in Israel themselves; aside from a sizeable number of wealthy Jews and Orthodox congregants, generally they had not set foot on Israeli soil. Amazingly, however, for such a prosperous Americanized community, 50 percent of all Orthodox and Reform Jews would encourage their children to settle in Israel!

When Israel's very survival in 1967 depended upon victory in the Six Day War, and subsequently in the Yom Kippur War, organized Jewish philanthropy reached new heights. Midway between the two crises, local 1970 totals doubled the highest level achieved in the pre-1967 years, while the national total of $174 million during this same year was the highest since 1948. But the $1 million plus campaigns of 1968 through 1973, and especially the fantastic $3.6 million campaign following the 1973 war, resulted from investing enormous amounts of community organizational skill into the tempest-like days of June 1967 and October 1973.

With the outbreak of the Six Day War, American Jews assumed financial responsibility for vast and unprecedented health, education, welfare, and resettlement needs of immigrants and residents in Israel which the Israeli economy could not absorb. At 4:00 p.m. on June 5, 1967, the UJF representatiaves had just returned from a national United Jewish Appeal-Council of Jewish Federations and Welfare Funds emergency meeting; they were already explaining to the executive committee:

> Israel is totally mobilized for defense as the Arabs have threatened open conflict. As a result of total mobilization of manpower, resources and finances for its security, the health and welfare needs of refugees and much of the civilian population required financial assistance from sources other than the government. A major source of Jewish Agency funds, the government, has been eliminated. The UJA requires immediately millions of dollars.[1]

This so deeply stirred the executive committee that they voted unanimously to begin an Israel Emergency Fund Campaign and to sponsor emergency communal meetings. The UJF Board of Trustees, which met at 8:00 p.m. that same night, heard a report on the progress of the war which had begun that morning; the board approved the executive committee's recommendation.[2] Once an emergency fund was launched, the reaction of Columbus Jewry was far more intense and widespread than anyone could have predicted. All over America Israel's crisis dominated Jewish thoughts and emotions to the exclusion of all else. This held true not only for affiliated Jews, but for many seemingly untouched by such commitments.

American Jews, committed and indifferent, have usually responded to external danger by giving money — but on this occasion the fountains overflowed. Men, women, and children began contributing to the emergency fund and Israel Bonds in amounts no one imagined possible. The Israel Emergency Fund, a cooperative effort of the United Jewish Appeal and the Council of Jewish Federations and Welfare Funds, replaced the "grass roots" emergency committee, which had already sponsored a "special crisis meeting" in Columbus on May 28 where $300,000 was either paid on pledges made to the regular campaign or promised should an emergency fund campaign be launched.[3]

The two to three hundred persons who gathered on that rainy Sunday evening at the end of May needed little incentive, and clearly did not have to await the start of the war. On May 16 Egypt demanded the withdrawal of all United Nations troops from two strategic points, one of which was Sharm-el-Sheikh, the fortress controlling the entrance into the Gulf of Aqaba, and on May 22 announced the closure of the Straits of Tiran to Israel and the blockade of the port of Eilat. On May 26, federation leadership sent two hundred and sixty-two telegrams to the homes of selected Columbus Jews urging attendance at Tifereth Israel on May 28. The UJF prepared and completed this activity even before the United Jewish Appeal Board met in special session in New York.

A week later the Israel Emergency Fund came into existence, and two major events dominated the frenzied week. First, the emergency fund sponsored a "large gifts" meeting on June 8 at the Winding Hollow Country Club for four hundred persons who were exhilerated by the Israelis' overwhelming victory. Later that week on Saturday night, a communal rally was held at Temple Israel for five hundred. With the Six Day War over, the emergency fund raised as much on June 8 as had been raised in the entire 1967 regular campaign which concluded two months earlier. By June 29 more than $611,000 had been collected, and by August 11 the fund had received $727,000 in cash.[4]

In almost every Jewish community, the brief emergency campaign surpassed the regular campaigns although, as in Columbus, 1967 regular campaign totals had achieved their highest levels in twenty years. Men and women pledged unprecedented amounts to the Israel Emergency Fund; these were the same Jews who had recently given substantial contributions to the regular campaign and redeemed those pledges far in advance of planned payments. This became the pattern nationally as well, for the Israel Emergency Fund's $173 million total surpassed the regular campaign total of $145 million by almost 20 percent. By the end of July, Columbus had impressive emergency fund statistics; although outdone by several smaller Jewish communities — Dayton,

Louisville, Memphis, New Orleans, and St. Paul — its community contributed more money than the larger cities of New Haven, Kansas City, Houston, and Buffalo.[5]

Varied activities highlighted the frantic week following June 5 in Columbus. Full-page ads in the two Columbus dailies solicited support for the Israel Emergency Fund; a briefing was held at the Columbus Country Club for top non-Jewish business officials; a TWX machine tied the UJF into the national United Jewish Appeals network extending from coast to coast, bringing messages of support from communities around the country. Hundreds of volunteers sent out mailings, bills, and letters; made calls; sorted envelopes; typed lists; and made contributions of time wherever possible.[6]

The whirlwind month of June concluded with a statewide Israel Bonds dinner ($500 minimum) on June 25 at the executive mansion hosted by Governor and Mrs. James Rhodes for the third consecutive year. The bond organization had postponed the start of its summer and fall campaign in deference to the priorities of war; yet members appeared undismayed by the challenge of raising $500 apiece from "pledged out" Columbus Jews.[7]

One final indication of the impact of the Six Day War and the Israel Emergency Fund upon Columbus Jewry is shown by comparing the gifts of individual contributors to the UJF and Israel Emergency Fund campaigns, before and after 1967. As demonstrated by Table 88 listing the gifts of two representative Jewish leaders, while the events of those six days had some impact upon regular campaign contributions in subsequent years, they strikingly influenced emergency fund donations.

Hundreds, even a thousand, Columbus Jews suddenly found funds previously untapped to contribute to Israel's survival and

TABLE 88
CAMPAIGN CONTRIBUTIONS OF TWO COLUMBUS JEWS

	Jewish Leader 1			Jewish Leader 2		
Year	Regular	Emergency	Total	Regular	Emergency	Total
1961	$ 600	—	$ 600	$ 400	—	$ 400
1962	1,000	$ 250	1,250	500	$ 100	600
1964	1,650	350	2,000	500	—	500
1965	2,000	700	2,700	600	—	600
1966	3,200	—	3,200	750	—	750
1967	3,800	11,000	14,800	1,200	2,000	3,200
1968	4,300	8,200	12,500	975	1,850	2,825
1969	4,700	8,300	13,000	1,200	1,900	3,100
1970	5,000	9,000	14,000	1,310	2,100	3,410
1971	5,500	13,000	18,500	1,600	—	1,600

well-being. Although about a quarter of the Jews in Columbus donated more money to non-Jewish than to Jewish causes, from this time forth Israel acted as a focus of worldwide Jewish emotional loyalty and as a preserver of a sense of Jewish identity for Columbus Jews.

Utilizing Israel's potential to the utmost, the UJF kept interest in Israel alive by continually dispensing information all year long, even though the campaign formally lasted for less than a season. Israel programming became a top priority, as reflected in budgets, staffs, projects, and concerns. By the beginning of the Yom Kippur War, Israel was the number-one item on the UJF agenda.[8] Israel permeated UJF programs and publicity; Israeli generals were brought to appeal for more overseas support at board of trustees' meetings; and continual full-page ads ran in the *Ohio Jewish Chronicle*. This had been done so successfully that support for Israel almost became a sine qua non for leadership in the community — nonsupport was sometimes cause for communal censure.[9] Rewards for the leadership, and the large contributors, included lunch in Jerusalem with the prime minister, a tour of a battlefield with a general, or dinner with an ambassador.

Despite the continued precariousness of Israel's survival and the enormous needs of the American Jewish community, the enthusiasm generated by the events of 1967 and 1973 was not self-sustaining. People had to be "sold," for saving and consumption are much more natural than giving; in order to sell them on Jewish philanthropies a vast organization of volunteer "salesmen" was formed and convinced of the campaign's importance before going out to convince the community's potential givers. Volunteers had to be continuously recruited, trained, motivated, utilized, rewarded, and retained. As one Columbus Jewish Federation leader noted, "involvement and commitment of

TABLE 89
1975 COLUMBUS JEWISH COMMUNITY SURVEY: CONTRIBUTIONS TO CHARITY — 1974-75

Donations	Age Brackets							1969 results*
	18-25	26-35	36-45	46-55	56-65	66+	All	
Non-Jewish	28.6%	28.6%	22.6%	21.9%	18.0%	11.5%	22.8%	5%
Jewish	57.1	70.0	71.6	75.0	76.9	88.5	73.0	59
Same to both	4.8	—	5.7	3.1	5.1	—	2.9	32
None	9.5	1.4	—	—	—	—	1.2	**
Total	**42**	**140**	**106**	**64**	**78**	**52**	**482**	

*A. Mayer, *Columbus Jewish Population Study*, Table 46, p. 60.

**Four percent responded "don't know."

top, qualified, and experienced persons to assume leadership roles is a serious dilemma."[10] Continuity, or "maintenance," was very difficult in a voluntary organization, and required a multifaceted approach. New adherents had to be found each year and previous volunteers evaluated. Members had to be encouraged to learn more about the organization and the Jewish causes it served, and essential contributions of effort and resources had to be secured from them. Sometimes a sense of guilt was instilled — "If I were born in Europe rather than America I too would have been exterminated" — deep enough to impel volunteers to work toward goals. Further, the leadership vigilantly reduced conflict, whether in the form of membership withdrawal or disputes over purpose, challenges by persons outside the organization, or excessive demands of time and energy on key leaders.

The reward system depended on the maintenance of this construct. For some, fund raising served as a sufficient reward itself, a kind of heroism, capitalism's current equivalent of the entrepreneur of an earlier age. For others, campaign participation as solicitors and contributors became an expression of Jewishness — sometimes their only identification with the Jewish community. For campaigns became the secular foci of Jewish life, as Israel became the authority-giving source of Jewish life. Involvement in fund raising was an expression of identification with the Jewish community, a fundamental religious response which takes overwhelming events seriously. The meetings and conferences consisted of secular rituals designed to provide inspiration and stimulus for Jews who, by and large, had few other rituals.[11]

For others, there were incentives or rewards to sustain participation in the organization. In the UJF these consisted of intangible rewards of various kinds, for example, individual incentives, such as offices, publicity and honors, available only to leaders. One unplanned reward was Senator John Glenn's announcement to the United States Senate in 1976:

> May I also take this opportunity, Mr. President, to note . . . the transition of the Columbus Jewish Federation presidency and that Mr. . . . will be guiding the organization for the next two years, succeeding Mr. . . .[12]

Another intangible reward consisted of the fellowship, fun, and sense of exclusiveness, provided regularly for those who participated in federated philanthropy, especially at the executive committee and Advance Gifts Division levels. The most important intangible reward was the knowledge that they were contributing to both the group's specific goal of raising $3 million and to its larger purpose of helping Jews everywhere.

Others were rewarded by a fulfilling experience during campaign time; the federation attracted and retained otherwise busy men by conveying a sense of personal worth and pride in the accomplishment of the goals which, after all, constituted the purpose of the organization. And these goals were expressed through a set of symbols felt to transcend limited individual purpose. If all this came together correctly, a volunteer would move up the ladder of promotion and become an "elder statesman":

> I've always felt very strongly Jewish and I was ready to do something, "to do my share." I hesitated because of my own feelings of not knowing whether I could do the job that was required. And they let me know each year that I could do the job. For twenty years I have been active, moving up from worker to vice-chairman of trades and professions, twice, and chairman of trades and professions and advance gifts chairman, general campaign chairman, and so forth. And then I was put to pasture [laughter] by becoming an administrative officer.[13]

Such a process of continuity kept many of Columbus Jewry's "best men," who would have been synagogue leaders exclusively, in the federation leadership. The constant use of influence, prestige, esteem, newspaper publicity, "hubbas" at the annual meeting, fellowship, incentives, and public acclaim made volunteering for many much more fulfilling than tedious. And ultimately, as a member of the 1976 executive committee put it: ". . . the federation is where the action is, and fund raising is the quintessence of Jewish tradition and values."

Events in Israel orchestrated the levels of giving from the late 1940s through the early 1970s, as the United Jewish Fund* totals paralleled national federated fund-raising totals. Nationally, the peak years were 1947 through 1949; more than $200 million came in during 1948. Contributions declined for the next six years as the events of the forties lost their impact; the national total hovered at $110 million in 1954 and 1955. The level of giving stabilized between 1956 and 1964, as only $23,000 separated the 1956 and 1964 totals in Columbus, while the national campaigns netted $123 million in 1959 and $129 million in 1964. A steady upward climb began in 1965-66 as national totals rose to their highest since 1957. Although campaign totals in Columbus and the nation flattened out just before the Yom Kippur War, the years after 1973 represented new levels of generosity.[14]

In each of these years, regardless of a campaign's degree of success, the Advance Gifts Division was the pivotal unit in the

*The United Jewish Fund became the United Jewish Fund and Council in 1959 and the Columbus Jewish Federation in 1973.

campaign. Henry L. Zucker, executive director of the Jewish Community Federation of Cleveland, noted in 1958:

> The strategy of a welfare fund campaign must take into account the fact that a relatively small number of gifts produces the bulk of the money. Two-thirds of the money is contributed by 3 percent of the givers; three-fourths of the money by 5 percent or 6 percent of the contributors.[15]

Almost twenty years later, Irving Warner echoed this fact in *The Art of Fundraising:*

> Usually, 90 percent of the money in a campaign comes from about 10 to 15 percent of the donors. So spend 90 percent of your time and effort on the few, as undemocratic as it may appear to be. Always try to get as many smaller gifts as you can for balance but don't spend more than 10 percent of your energies getting them.

This pattern remained identical in Columbus and throughout the nation as exemplified in four different Jewish communities in 1970 where 3 percent gave 63 percent — $7 million; 4.5 percent gave 70 percent — $3 million; 5 percent provided 75 percent — $3 million; and 7 percent delivered 76 percent — $13 million of the total campaign.[16] In Columbus one year earlier, 10 percent of the pledges yielded 82.5 percent of the campaign total. As the CFJ executive vice-president, Ben Mandelkorn, noted in 1974 "in all candor it must also be pointed out that approximately 80 percent of the funds are received from approximately 10 percent of the givers."[17] Thus the key to a successful campaign became enticing the biggest givers to make pledges early to set a good pace. The selection of leaders and workers in the Advance Gifts Division received abundant care and attention, including high-prestige "missions" to Israel which culminated in larger contributions.[18] Chosen primarily for their willingness to work, prestige, status, and giving potential, the individuals in this division determined the hierarchy of voluntary leadership and the reputation of the professionals in federated Jewish philanthropy.

The federation reserved its most elaborate preparations for Advance Gifts Dinners at Winding Hollow Country Club. During the fifties alone the amount of the minimum gift which enabled donors to attend these events increased from one hundred to one thousand dollars. Internationally-known speakers, including Rabbi Abba Hillel Silver and General Moshe Dayan, addressed the gatherings; quite frequently, these dinners raised large percentages — as much as 80 percent in 1964 — of the campaign total.[19]

Who were these "big givers?" An analysis of the forty largest contributors from the Advance Gifts Division during the 1971

TABLE 90
UNITED JEWISH FUND AND COUNCIL ADVANCE GIFTS PLEDGES

Years	Pledges	Percent of Total Campaign	Dinner Guests Present
1950	$190,000	36%	—
1952	328,534	61	200
1953	368,950	66	200
1954	341,136	63	—
1955	366,000	70	250
1956	477,692	72	250
1957	531,000	72	300
1958	310,000	45	—
1959	501,320	68	—
1960	460,000	65	126
1961	441,805	66	136
1962	415,610	59	116
1963	310,485	46	—
1964	512,000	80	140

SOURCE: *Ohio Jewish Chronicle.*

TABLE 91
UNITED JEWISH FUND
ADVANCE GIFTS PLEDGES BY TWENTY-FOUR ANONYMOUS DONORS FOR 1948/49 AND 1953

1953	1948/49	1953	1948/49
$80,000	$85,000	$5,000	$ 9,000
18,000	22,000	5,000	6,000
16,300	20,500	5,000	Not Available
15,500	22,500	5,000	Not Available
10,000	12,000	4,200	Not Available
10,000	11,000	4,000	6,000
8,500	22,000	4,000	4,500
7,250	18,000	4,000	Not Available
6,800	11,950	4,000	10,000
6,600	11,000	4,000	6,000
6,000	12,350	4,000	8,000
6,000	10,000	3,600	Not Available

campaign revealed that only one of the forty was a professional; that thirty-eight were presidents, owners, or the highest executives and/or major shareholders in local, regional, or national businesses; and that nineteen inherited the businesses from their fathers or in-laws.

In addition to the Advance Gifts Kickoff Dinner and the very important face-to-face solicitation, the necessities of time and space demanded a variety of fund-raising events. The federation used a series of carefully organized measures, beginning with the selection of a volunteer general chairman, preferably a citizen with widespread community influence. Closely following was the appointment of various division chairmen — Advance Gifts, Trades and Professions, Young Men, Women, Young Matrons, College Youth, Juniors — men and women with compatible interests or the same occupations who could best assess each other's ability to contribute. After the establishment of general policy by a campaign cabinet and a campaign advisory committee, at last the campaign began. The chain of command which harnessed volunteers to the professionally designed machinery descended from the top leaders to division chairmen, captains, and teamworkers. An elaborate organization thus emerged, supplemented by publicity, rallies, quotas, careful preparation, and allotment of prospect cards. And behind everything — the professionals.

A wide range of functions, from small parlor meetings to citywide mass rallies, was carefully organized. Usually contributors were grouped by sex, occupation, or minimum gift — $7,500 minimum — "kick-off" gatherings. Smaller functions also took place with technical precision because the professionals were aware that each detail was important. These details included evaluating a prospect's capacity to make a pledge, assigning each key prospect to the right worker, selecting a speaker who has been "on the scene," arranging the guest list, making certain the guests arrived, and preparing the agenda's feature: card calling. Each guest's card contained the past year's gift as well as the about-to-be-announced current gift. The chairman announced his own pledge, the percentage increase it represented, and then called upon the leadership one by one to do the same. None gave less than the past year; the opening increases were usually very generous and hopefully inspired the one or two guests who had not committed themselves in advance. Although 95 percent of the pledges had already been solicited, card after card was solemnly announced, and polite applause followed even the most modest increases. Periodic outbreaks of planned spontaneity also occurred: an individual who already had given his pledge declared that he had been so moved by the speaker's address that he wished to pledge an additional sum. An annual and almost sacred ritual in its dramatic unfolding, card calling became an anxiously awaited event.

To be sure, a vocal minority wished to eliminate ratings and announcements of gifts, but a majority of the "pacesetters" approved of this method of fund raising. And why not, for many men make charitable donations not to earn the gratitude of the recipients whom they never see, but to earn the approval of their peers who participate in the philanthropic campaign. The ability to distribute valuable possessions has become a socially defined mark of superiority. Federated Jewish philanthropy combined the display of wealth with the worthy purpose of helping a good cause. By offering public *koved* (honor) to a few big givers, federations make the size of a pledge the measure of a man's status.[20]

Despite the care in planning, with the exception of the Advance Gifts Dinners, events usually succeeded in inverse proportion to their size. That is, personal solicitation enjoyed the most success, parlor meetings rated next, and larger gatherings usually resulted in contributions at a lower level. But a variety of gatherings seemed desirable; and the various fund-raising functions held during any winter campaign made an impressive listing indeed.

TABLE 92
UNITED JEWISH FUND AND COUNCIL FUND-RAISING SCHEDULE

Date	Time	Place	Division	Speaker
Jan 5	8:00 p.m.	A home	Young Men's Division	Israeli Ambassador
Jan 12	10:00 a.m.	Jewish Center	Traveling Salesmen	Out of Town Man
Jan 14	8:00 p.m.	A home	Young Matrons	Executive Committee Members
Jan 16	6:00 p.m.	A home	Advance Gifts $5,000 Dinner	National Jewish Leader
Jan 19	10:00 a.m.	Jewish Center	Trade & Professional Leadership	Executive Committee Members
Jan 21	10:00 a.m.	A home	Women's Division Golden Circle	Out of Town Lady
Jan 23	8:00 p.m.	A home	Special Advance Gifts Unit	Executive Committee Members
Jan 30	6:00 p.m.	A home	Advance Gifts $2,500 Minimum	Israeli General
Feb 9	9:30 a.m.	A bank	Trade & Professional Telethon	
Feb 12	10:00 a.m.	A restaurant	Women's Division Trendsetters	
Feb 12	5:30 p.m.	Hillel Foundation	The OSU Division	Executive Committee Members
Feb 14/15		Synagogues	UJFC Sabbath Services	
Feb 16	10:00 a.m.	Jewish Center	Engineers	Local Jewish Leader
Feb 19	12:00 noon	Battelle	Battelle	National Jewish Leader
Feb 19	6:00 p.m.	A restaurant	Dentists	National Jewish Leader
Feb 20	8:00 p.m.	A home	Retail Merchants	National Jewish Leader
Feb 23	1:30 p.m.	Jewish Center	Jr. Division Citywide Rally	
Feb 24	8:00 p.m.	A home	Building & Real Estate	National Jewish Leader
Feb 25	8:00 p.m.	A home	Scrap & Steel Manufacturers	National Jewish Leader
Feb 26	6:00 p.m.	A hotel	Physicians	Non-Jewish Local Physician
Feb 27	6:00 p.m.	Winding Hollow	Advance Gifts $500 Minimum	National Jewish Leader

The crucial role the board of trustees and the executive committee have played in the regular and emergency campaigns cannot be overemphasized. The image of the roughly seventy-five member board which sponsored the campaign in the community became an essential part of the campaign. Many members of the 1975 board felt a direct correlation existed between the board's prestige and status, and the success of a campaign. Thus, while the federation chose board members for many reasons, a primary consideration was the need to project status and influence, and to select men, and occasionally women, who would contribute as generously as their means permitted.

These criteria were even more stringently applied to the executive committee — elected officers, some committee chairmen in key positions, and special appointees and/or invitees. The federation called upon these men to provide a major share of the overall campaign goal; as prestigious businessmen in the community, they represented a key group for any campaign. UJF's executive committee in 1969, for example, consisted of fifteen business men who contributed 25 percent of the total campaign achievement. The smallest executive committee pledge was $3,000 and the median gift was $8,500 (the median rose by $1,000 in 1970, one year later it was $12,500, and in 1973; $10,000). Such beneficence launched a very successful campaign — $1.3 million in a community of approximately thirteen thousand Jews.

This committee of relatively stable and very affluent men had an enormous influence on certain community processes, including fund raising and allocation. This stood, of course, well within the American tradition of one family, or group, controlling "Main Street."[21] Americans have a long and strong history of community political coordination or centralized concentration of power by dominant businessmen. The sheer magnitude of the need compelled the Jewish leadership to organize itself in the pattern of the large American industrial enterprises. Parallel to the coordination of the society by leaders who headed America's key institutions, emerged the control of multimillion dollar federation budgets by a score of wealthy men. Unlike the interwar years however, when Schanfarber and Lazarus ruled the Jewish community, no single power pocket existed in the three decades after World War II. The rulers and demirulers were Advance Gifts, general campaign, and budget committee chairmen and the federation officers, as power was spread out among ten to twenty men who by close social relationships, ideological alignments, financial successes, and support for Israel, dominated the organized community.

It should come as no surprise that oligarchy was (and is) the persistent form of American Jewish philanthropy. Inherent in the voluntary nature of financial contributions and participation was the pervasive influence wielded by an individual contributor or group of contributors who had a favorite cause or agency. Community decisions affecting that cause or agency were under their control. This may not be exactly inevitable, but the federation not so structured has yet to be identified. Democratic decision-making — where large and small contributors represent a basis of participation — generally remains what could be, not what is.

TABLE 93
1975 COLUMBUS JEWISH FEDERATION ORGANIZATION CHART

Campaign Contributors[1]

Executive Committee[3] — **Board of Trustees**[2]

Campaign *(9 committees)*	Advance Gifts, Trades & Professions, Young Men, Women, Young Matrons, College Youth, Juniors, Out of Town, Study Missions to Israel
Budgeting/ Planning *(16 committees)*	Capital Needs, Community Relations, Education & Culture, Social Services, Budget Steering, Aging Services, Development — Land and Facilities, Social Legislation, Apartment House for Elderly, College Youth and Faculty, Demographic Studies, Manpower, Priorities, Salary & Benefits, Coordination — Agency Services, Large Cities Budgeting Conference
Council of Organizations *(5 committees)*	Multiple Appeals, Calendaring, Soviet Jewry, Education, Council on Jewish Culture
Jewish Education *(5 committees)*	Budgeting Local Services, Council of Jewish Educators, Special Projects, Planning — Coordination, Enrollment Promotion
Administration *(8 committees)*	Office Operation, Cash Collections, Finance, Building and Grounds Maintenance, Insurance — Property & Personnel, Staff Development, Personnel, Central Services (Bookkeeping, Payroll, Mailing, Printing, Purchasing, Group Benefits)
Education Communication *(7 committees)*	Women's Divisions, Young Men's Executive Board, Young Leadership Development Program, Retreats, Annual Meeting, Public Relations (Press, TV, Radio, Publicity, Newsletters, Campaign Materials), Advance Leadership Programs
Other *(12 committees)*	Nominating, Constitution, Young Leadership Award, Rabbinical Award, Leadership Recruitment, United Way, National & Overseas Agencies, Council of Jewish Federations and Welfare Funds, Inter-Agency Staff Meetings, Community Scholarship, Israel Relations (Shaliach), Legal Services
Community Relations *(3 committees)*	Israel, Domestic, Soviet Jewry
Endowment and Foundation Program *(2 committees)*	Endowment Funds, Philanthropic Funds

1. All adult Jews in Franklin County over ten years of age who contribute $10 a year to the CJF are eligible to vote for officers and trustees.
2. The seventy-five to eighty-member board is the chief decision-making and policy-setting body in the CJF. At ten meetings a year it ratifies decisions made by the officers and leadership.
3. This committee works closely with the professional staff on federation operations, policies, programs, and finances and then makes recommendations to the board.

Federation leadership picked and groomed affluent givers who exercised power in the community. Dozens, with emerging economic and social power, aspired to the positions which governed the UJF, but only a few were selected to fill the slots after careful screening of the professionals. Many came up through the Young Leadership Development Program, begun in 1955, where "young couples and individuals with demonstrated leadership qualities and community interests [were] invited to participate" and then, selectively, placed on UJF committees.[22] Thus the leadership had freedom of choice; although by making the position seem attractive to the aspirants it could not help but guarantee some rejected and discontented persons.[23] Many of the most successful — those who rose to the top most easily and quickly — carried the prestige associated with inherited wealth and family position which was a potent combination in a Jewish community whose *median* length of residence was more than twenty years. The identification of these old-line families with the central mythos of the leadership — Israel's survival — gave a position of high status to both the mythos and the leadership.

One of the most complex and vital parts of federation operation became allocations or "budget politics"; the pattern changed rather strikingly during the 1950s. Between 1946 and 1950, at least eighty cents of every dollar was allocated overseas to bring hundreds of thousands of Jews out of the displaced persons camps and ruined cities of Europe and other tens of thousands from North Africa and the Middle East. Distributing these funds was the United Jewish Appeal, the fund-raising organization for three constituent agencies: the United Palestine Appeal, which furnished aid to hundreds of thousands of newcomers to Israel and made it possible for Israel to absorb and settle more than a million people in less than eighteen months of nationhood; the Joint Distribution Commiteee, which directed the rescue operation of postwar Jewry; and the United Service for New Americans, which cared for tens of thousands of Jewish refugees who entered the United States.[24]

As the first decade after Israel's creation unfolded, a steady pattern emerged: overseas allocations, which consumed eighty-five cents of every dollar in 1948 and 1949, were slowly but steadily decreased until in 1959 they accounted for only sixty-five cents of the communal dollar. This did not, however, drastically affect the money sent overseas. On the contrary — the funding increased between 1950 and 1959 several times, and only once fell below $395,000. The explanation was found in the Special Survivor Fund (later the Israel Emergency Fund, where all funds went directly to Israel), initiated after the Suez Crisis of 1956. Contributors bypassed the allocations procedure and sent funds — with some

TABLE 94
COMPARISON OF COLUMBUS JEWS' ALLOCATIONS WITH FOUR MIDWESTERN JEWISH COMMUNITIES' ALLOCATIONS

		Overseas	National	Local	Total Dollars Regular	Total Dollars Special
1949	Columbus	85.2%	5.5%	9.3%	$662,463	
	Akron	81.8	4.1	14.2		
	Indianapolis	78.1	7.3	14.6		
	Louisville	77.1	8.1	14.8		
	U.S. Jewry	63.3	5.5	31.2		
1951	Columbus	77.9	5.3	16.8	562,477	
	Akron	78.1	4.8	17.0		
	Indianapolis	73.3	9.7	17.0		
	Louisville	73.9	9.0	17.0		
	U.S. Jewry	62.8	4.5	32.7		
1953	Columbus	73.0	9.7	17.3	556,411	
	Akron	71.8	5.0	23.2		
	Indianapolis	62.9	10.1	27.0		
	Louisville	73.7	9.6	16.7		
	U.S. Jewry	61.5	4.9	33.6		
1955	Columbus	70.5	9.6	19.9	525,701	
	Akron	73.3	5.9	20.8		
	Indianapolis	59.3	11.0	29.7		
	Louisville	69.3	9.2	21.5		
	U.S. Jewry	60.0	5.0	35.0		
1957	Columbus	77.7	7.4	14.8	561,972	$171,810
	Akron	82.5	4.7	12.8		
	Indianapolis	76.2	8.4	15.4		
	Louisville	75.6	8.1	16.3		
	U.S. Jewry	66.6	4.0	28.6		
1959	Columbus	64.6	6.0	29.4	577,311	158,310
	Akron	78.2	5.8	16.0		
	Indianapolis	69.1	9.1	21.8		
	Louisville	73.7	8.8	17.5		

SOURCE: Calculated from "Budget Control Sheets" in The Papers of the Council of Jewish Federations and Welfare Funds, American Jewish Historical Society (Waltham, Mass.). Columbus, Ohio (Box 210), Akron, Ohio (Box 201), Indianapolis (Box 220), Louisville (Box 225), U.S.A. (Box 227).

qualifications — directly to Israel. In its four years of existence, the Special Survivor Fund collected almost $600,000.

As the funds allocated overseas dropped during the fifties and sixties, the funds available for local agencies increased slightly. Remaining below almost every city in the country in local allocations meant that UJF's constituent agencies struggled hard to provide a high level of quantity and quality of services. Nevertheless, the total campaign dollars distributed to the Columbus Hebrew School,[25] The Ohio State University Hillel Foundation,[26] Home for the Aged,[27] Jewish Center,[28] Jewish Education Committee,[29] Jewish Family Service,[30] and Anti-Defamation League/Community Relations Committee[31] moved slowly upward. Actual dollar figures for allocations, however, could be quite misleading. Jewish education, for example, received $29,231 in 1965 and $125,265 in 1974. But concomitant with this four-fold increase was a six-fold increase in total funds allocated; the percentage of local funds allocated to Jewish education increased by only 5 percent; and the percentage of the total allocations which went to Jewish education actually decreased from 5 percent in 1965 to less than 4 percent in 1974. Most budget items were fixed by prior commitments evolved over long periods of time and reflected a balance of interests within each allocating body.

The decision to sponsor a special or emergency campaign together with the regular campaign became the most crucial part of the allocation or pre-campaign budget formula during the 1960s

TABLE 95
COLUMBUS JEWISH FEDERATION'S LOCAL ALLOCATIONS

Year	CHS/Jewish Education Committee	Hillel Foundation	Home for Aged	Jewish Center	Jewish Family Service	ADL/ CRC
1948	$ 15,000	$ 5,000	—	$ 30,000	—	—
1950	16,500	5,000	—	41,000	—	—
1952	20,000	6,000	$ 3,000	41,000	$ 3,000	$ 3,500
1956	23,900	8,000	3,000	49,000	9,300	3,500
1958	25,900	8,000	4,140	49,000	6,700	3,500
1959	30,658	8,000	8,965	51,593	6,000	3,500
1961	23,495	8,000	20,894	49,000		8,800
1963	28,293	8,000	20,535	49,000	9,000	15,000
1965	29,231	8,000	25,537	49,000	12,500	15,000
1967	40,159	8,000	39,280	60,900	10,000	15,000
1969	57,981	10,000	47,699	67,100	13,000	15,000
1971	77,997	17,500	37,201	93,165	8,500	18,000
1973	92,162	22,500	65,268	135,000	32,289	18,000
1974	125,265	26,500	92,500	135,000	40,561	20,000

and early 1970s. This formula, instituted in 1961, consistently guaranteed that a large percentage of the campaign (more than 40 percent every year since 1967) would bypass the local allocation process and go directly to Israel, thus allocating three or even four times as much money to overseas needs as to local agencies year after year.[32]

This decision represented the wishes of part of UJF's leadership who felt that no local need could be as prominent and pressing as the survival of Israel. As one local officer put it, "the success or failure of the campaign hinged largely on the dramatic needs of Israel." These leaders were very excited, intense, dedicated, and wealthy men who provided the opportunity for people to use the "second line" of their card and contribute generous amounts to the Israel Emergency Fund.

Concomitant with the UJF campaigns, Israel Bond Drives solicited funds year-round. The first national and local sales campaign was launched in May of 1951; Americans purchased bonds worth more than $52 million in 1951 alone; and in the initial eighteen months Columbus residents bought a total of $400,000 in bonds. One rally in November featuring Vice-President Alben Barkley sold $300,000 in bonds which paid 3.5 percent interest. While Jews purchased small denomination bonds for everything from bar mitzvah, wedding, and birthday gifts to investments, bond leaders most eagerly sought big sales. Using the successful UJF technique, a select group of one hundred persons purchased more than 80 percent of the year's total at a dinner meeting before the 1951 rally. Synagogues served as the primary forum for bond

TABLE 96
COLUMBUS JEWISH FEDERATION ALLOCATIONS

	OVERSEAS				NATIONAL	LOCAL
Year	Regular Total	% of Total Campaign	Special or Emergency Fund Total	% of Total Campaign	% of Total Campaign	% of Total Campaign
1962	$ 431,556	70.2%	$ 53,117	8.6%	5.4%	24.4%
1963	388,931	66.8	77,136	13.4	6.0	27.2
1964	341,069	62.6	42,815	7.9	6.5	30.9
1965	362,369	63.8	53,504	9.4	5.9	30.3
1966	395,674	63.7			5.5	30.1
1967	1,318,460	84.6	919,000	59.2	2.2	13.2
1968	806,270	75.8	431,452	40.5	3.3	20.9
1969	881,560	75.2	477,108	40.7	3.2	21.6
1970	1,019,680	77.0	568,821	43.0	2.9	20.1
1971	1,242,052	78.2	773,901	48.7	2.5	19.2
1972	1,363,634	76.8	865,956	48.8	2.5	20.6
1973	1,277,578	73.0	770,046	43.7	2.6	24.4
1974	2,657,465	81.5	2,103,724	64.5	1.6	16.9
1975	1,725,876	72.6	1,150,940	48.4	2.2	25.2

sales, as every congregation but Temple Israel regularly interrupted Rosh Hashanah or Yom Kippur worship to appeal for the purchase of bonds. In 1954 Agudas Achim, Tifereth Israel, Beth Jacob, and Ahavas Sholom sold $55,000, $35,000, $17,000 and $7,000 respectively, while in 1956 High Holiday appeals alone yielded $135,550 from four hundred and five purchasers. The next year, six hundred and thirty Jews invested $190,200 in Israel Bonds, and successive drives easily topped the $200,000 mark. The year 1970 recorded more than $600,000 in sales; while bond support peaked in 1973 when purchases totalled $1,473,000 in Columbus.[33]

After considerable competition for the philanthropy dollar in the early years, Israel Bonds and the United Jewish Fund worked out a compromise whereby each organization's solicitations would be conducted in different months. But the increasing centralization of fund raising by the fund provided the background to a problem which surfaced throughout subsequent years — competitive fund raising. By the early 1960s the UJF was challenged by communitywide appeals by non-member Jewish organizations inside and outside of Columbus. After almost two years of discussion, hoping to "restore the harmony and cooperation which has always been the hallmark of the Columbus Jewish community," the Multiple Appeals Study Committee found a solution in 1964. The committee recommended that the UJF campaign period be extended to include February, March, and April, that "non-beneficiaries of [the UJF] respect the primacy of the [UJF] campaign," and that such agencies "confine their fund raising among their own members." Approval of this recommendation placed the UJF in a position to dominate fund raising, and much else in Columbus Jewry, during the subsequent decade, although as late as 1976 a formal committee met to discuss continued problems in this area.[34]

The early Jews of Columbus, Ohio, helped shape the city's growth through their concentration in retail trade, especially the clothing industry. They participated in a complex national manufacturing and distributing network, and purveyed a diverse assortment of ready-made clothing, accessories, and dry goods items. Scores of clothing, jewelry, dry goods, and grocery stores provided employment for several hundred Jewish men and women and helped the nineteenth century German Jews of Columbus achieve economic security.

The organizational network which the German and east European Jews created also contributed to Columbus' development and their own enrichment. Membership in the B'nai B'rith and similar associations imbued Jews with a sense of civic responsibility, brought aspects of the American cultural experience into ethnic neighborhoods, and aided the Americanization process. At the same time, membership reinforced loyalties established through business and residential networks while creating a deeper sense of ethnic identity.

Prejudice and discrimination are, to a large extent, initiated by differences between groups; the intensity of such prejudice against newcomers usually depends on the size of the incoming group and the rate at which its members enter the host society. The virtual absence of anti-Semitism in Columbus Jewish history can be explained, perhaps, by the fact that Jews came to Columbus in very small numbers and, in part, by the speed and ease with which Jews moved into the mainstream of American society. Any immigrant group's adjustment to a new country is certainly facilitated by an absence of attacks against their ethnic traditions.

A sense of territory has helped to maintain Jewish ethnic identity for the majority of Columbus Jews. During the twentieth century, Columbus Jewry has created a neighborhood with enough Jews to support synagogues, clubs, markets, organizations, and other necessities of community and ethnic identification. Going about their mundane activities in the neighborhood, men, women, and children could feel equally Jewish and American — all this against a background which provided abundant security. The neighborhood synagogue, for example, served the religious, educational, and even social needs of Columbus Jewry, as well as perpetuated Jewish identity, served as a bulwark against assimilation, and provided the primary group contacts so necessary for Jewish group survival. The philanthropic organization expressed traditional Jewish charitable impulses — giving to a Jewish charity demonstrated a Jewish identity based on Jewish values — and reformulated them in terms of emerging American charitable practices so successfully that the legitimacy of sectarian charity went unchallenged.

All through the Columbus Jewish experience, close social relations with other Jews have been developed to a far greater degree than relations with non-Jews. Participating primarily in Jewish familial, residential, philanthropic, and religious institutions, Jews have constituted a communal social system — a social unit with its own identity — as well as a community which has shared friendships, neighborhood, and "sacred" places.

Jews tend to confine their participation in primary groups and primary relationships to their own social class within their own groups — what Milton Gordon once called their "ethclass." And this has been especially true of Columbus Jewry, from its early years to the 1970s. Within this ethclass particularly Jewish concerns have been mixed with American urban values. In the neighborhoods which they created, or to which they moved, Columbus Jews shaped their community to reflect Jewish acculturation to America even as they built and pursued Jewish ethnicity. Blending middle-class American activities, forms, and styles with traditional functions of the synagogue, philanthropy, and various associations, the large majority of Columbus Jewry found itself belonging to the Jewish community. Growing up Jewish and American in hospitable Columbus, Ohio, was a pleasant experience.

This compromise has been the story of much of Columbus Jewish history. In their neighborhoods, organizations, and institutions Jews have maintained Jewish identification and group life while feeling comfortable with American customs and values. The friendly environment permitted maximum acculturation, while this acculturation encouraged a vital ethnic identity.

NOTES FOR CHAPTER 24

TABLE 97
COLUMBUS JEWISH FEDERATION CAMPAIGN AND ALLOCATION TOTALS

Year	Contributors	Regular	Emergency	Total	Allocated	Campaign Chairman
1960	4,060	$ 557,266	$ 149,234	$ 706,500	?	Charles Goldsmith
1961	4,151	666,317	—	666,317	$ 594,612	Ben Yenkin
1962	3,889	655,470	53,117	708,587	615,376	Morris Skilken
1963	3,668	599,778	77,136	676,914	582,731	Herman Katz
1964	3,503	595,267	42,815	638,082	544,596	Harold Schottenstein
1965	3,593	631,755	53,504	685,259	567,943	Edward Schlezinger
1966	3,718	730,043	—	730,043	621,650	William Glick
1967	3,700	748,000	919,000	1,667,000	1,559,165	Marvin Glassman
1968	3,918	745,000	431,452	1,176,452	1,063,370	Sidney Blatt
1969	4,152	839,973	477,108	1,317,081	1,172,577	Norman Meizlish
1970	4,237	922,140	568,821	1,490,961	1,324,337	Sol Zell
1971	4,391	1,002,956	773,901	1,776,857	1,586,125	Ben Goodman
1972	4,243	1,098,874	865,956	1,964,830	1,770,865	Gordon Zacks
1973	4,227	1,195,274	770,046	1,965,320	1,745,313	Ernest Stern
1974	4,420	1,515,326	2,103,724	3,619,050	3,263,762	Millard Cummins
1975	4,186	1,587,312	1,150,940	2,738,252	2,739,318	Millard Cummins

SOURCE: United Jewish Appeal, New York City.

1. Minutes, UJF Executive Committee, June 5, 1967. Columbus Jewish Federation.
2. Minutes, Special Meeting of the UJFC Board of Trustees, June 5, 1967. Columbus Jewish Federation.
3. *OJC*, June 1, 1967; Minutes, UJF Executive Committee, June 5, 1967 (Columbus Jewish Federation); interview with Edward Schlezinger.
4. *OJC*, June 1, 8, 15 and 22, 1967; Joint Meeting of the Board of Trustees of UJFC and Columbus Jewish Welfare Federation, June 29, 1967. Columbus Jewish Federation.
5. "Amounts Pledged to 1967 Regular and Israel Emergency Fund Campaigns, and Accounts Receivable as of End of July 1967," Columbus Jewish Federation.
6. Interview with Sylvia Schecter; "Report on the Israel Emergency Fund," September 14, 1967. Columbus Jewish Federation.
7. *OJC*, June 22 and 29, 1967. Communitywide financial institutions often contributed to the bonds campaign; in 1964 both City National Bank and Huntington National Bank purchased $25,000 worth of bonds.
8. See, for example, Evaluation 9-1-75 to 8-31-76, Joint Evaluation Committee of the Community Relations Council and Community Relations Council Budget Committee, September 29, 1976.
9. Interview with Chaim Feller.
10. Interview with Myer Mellman.
11. Advance Gifts Training Session, December 1, 1976, Heritage House.
12. *Congressional Record* 122:138 (September 14, 1976).

13. Interview with Ernest Stern.

14. *Annual Reports,* Council of Jewish Federations and Welfare Funds.

15. Henry L. Zucker, "Organizing and Planning the Campaign," in *Building the Successful Campaign,* Council of Jewish Federations and Welfare Funds (New York, 1958), p. 14.

16. *Giving and Givers,* Council of Jewish Federations and Welfare Funds (New York, 1970).

17. An Analysis of the 1969 Campaign Pledges 9-69, Columbus Jewish Federation; The Annual Report, Columbus Jewish Federation, October 20, 1974. Conversely, in the 1970 Campaign, 70 percent of the contributors yielded only 2.5 percent of the total funds. On "big givers" see Marshall Sklare, "The Future of Jewish Giving," *Commentary* (November 1962): 416-26.

18. There is, however, evidence to suggest that the greater the dependency on a few large givers, the more "disappointing is a campaign performance — in relation to opportunity — likely to be." See John R. Seeley et al., *Community Chest: A Case Study in Philanthropy* (Toronto, 1957), pp. 149-50.

19. "Notes for Herman Katz," in Minutes, UJFC Board of Trustees from November 1952 to December 1958, Columbus Jewish Federation; *OJC,* April 17, 1953, March 21, 1958, March 17, 1961.

20. During an evening of card calling in Columbus on November 23, 1976, twenty-five men pledged over $1 million to the 1977 Campaign. For an interesting parallel of this process of winning prestige by a show of expanding wealth — the potlatch among the Kwakiutl and other Indian tribes — see Marcel Mauss, *The Gift: Forms and Functions of Exchange in Archaic Societies* (Glencoe, 1954), pp. 6-16, 31-45. Joseph Willen, the developer of card-calling, discussed this phenomenon (which he called "conspicuous giving") some years ago; see *NYT,* May 5, 1974, and *Newsweek,* December 13, 1965. This paragraph is the result of conversations during 1975-76 with dozens of persons involved in federated Jewish philanthrophy and my own observations throughout the two years.

21. See Robert S. and Helen M. Lynd, *Middletown in Transition* (New York, 1937); Floyd Hunter, *Community Power Structure: A Study of Decision Makers* (Chapel Hill, 1953); W. L. Warner and P. S. Lunt, *The Social Life of a Modern Community* (New Haven, 1941); *The Status System of a Modern Community* (New Haven, 1942); Robert A. Dahl, *Who Governs? Democracy and Power in an American City* (New Haven, 1961). On the monist, or elitist, interpretation of leadership, see T. B. Bottomore, *Elites and Society* (Harmondsworth, England, 1964).

22. *The Annual Report,* Columbus Jewish Federation, October 20, 1974.

23. In my volume on federated Jewish philanthropy, *Understanding American Jewish Philanthropy,* I ask not only who governs Columbus Jewry but reverse this basic question and ask what persons or groups in the community are especially disfavored under the existing distribution of benefits and privileges. Further, to what extent does the utilization of power, authority, and influence shape and maintain a system that tends to perpetuate the status quo? And how, if at all, are new sources of power, authority, and influence generated and brought to bear in an effort to alter

the process? While in theory the membership of a federation manages the organization's affairs at an annual meeting, in practice those who do show up ratify actions already approved by a nominating committee and the board.

24. Columbus Jews played important roles in these national philanthropic organizations throughout the period. In 1960, for example, the Joint Distribution Committee reelected Herbert and Robert Schiff to the board of directors while the committee listed twenty-five Columbus Jews on its national council; *OJC*, January 1, 1960. See also *OJC*, January 18, 1963, January 10, 1964.

25. On the Columbus Hebrew School, see Part III.

26. On the Hillel Foundation, see Part III.

27. On the Home for the Aged (Heritage House), see Part III.

28. On the Jewish Center and its programs, see Parts II and III.

29. The Jewish Education Committee was established in 1967.

30. The Jewish Family Service took this name in 1953 and began to build a professionally educated staff of social workers. Family service assistance previously had centered in the Jewish Center and Jewish Welfare Federation.

31. Rising anti-Semitism served as the chief precipitating agent for the creation, beginning in the 1930s, of community relations councils in American Jewish communities. The common threats of anti-Jewish agitation called for common defense, and these councils began to serve as a policy-making and local action body for the entire Jewish community. The Columbus CRC was established in 1948 and underwent a major reorganization in 1961; see *OJC*, November 17, 1961.

32. For the actual "path" of an UJA dollar, see Milton Goldin, *Why They Give: American Jews and Their Philanthropies* (New York, 1976), p. 202.

33. See especially *OJC*, October 19 and 26, November 9, 1951, October 10, 1952, September 18 and 25, 1953, October 22, 1954, May 25, September 21, 1956, January 4, October 11, 1957, January 3, 1958.

34. For details of Brandeis University's decision to launch a fund-raising drive in Columbus, and the ensuing anger of "several large contributors," see Minutes, Officers and Past Presidents of UJF, July 25, 1957, pp. 2-3; Minutes, Board of Directors, UJF, July 8, 1957, p. 3 (CFJ); *OJC*, February 21, March 6, 1964; Sidney Levant to Benjamin Epstein, correspondence, December 12, 1974, in Community Relations Budget Committee [Workbook], May 12, 1975.

APPENDIX

ORAL HISTORY IN AN ETHNIC COMMUNITY: THE PROBLEMS AND THE PROMISE

Oral history, whether viewed by proponents or detractors, is rarely taken lightly. Barbara Tuchman, for example, has charged that "with the appearance of a tape recorder, a monster with the appetite of a tapeworm, we now have, through its creature, oral history, an artificial survival of trivia of appalling proportions."[1] In contrast, Saul Benison, among the ablest practitioners of the art of oral history, asserts that

> The memoir that emerges as a result of this process [interviewing] is a new kind of historical document. Although it has been created by a participant in past events, it is also the creation of the historian-interviewer who has in fact determined the historical problems and relationships to be examined.[2]

Benison, well aware of charges like Tuchman's, knows too that "this mutual creation contributes to both the strength and weakness inherent in oral history memoirs."[3]

Oral history involves much more than tape recording reminiscences and observations. Initially, the historian must identify those topics where eyewitness accounts can contribute to an understanding of the subject area, and then identify those persons with intimate relationships to the topics, who have sharp memories, and are willing to discuss their experiences. For example, Columbus Jewish History Project topics included the founding of an ethnic institution, the visit of a controversial personality, the relationship of various subgroups to the total community (divorced persons, faculty, organizations), crime

(Prohibition violations, gangsters, petty thievery), the development of an ethnic business, day to day living (suburban housewives), the immigration experience, controversial actions in the community, changing premarital sexual relationships, and decision-making within small groups (families).[4] Especially useful are oral histories of persons, trends, and events that have not received the benefit of conventional documentation. Such a program of topics offers the historian an opportunity to interview those "who made history" as well as those who watched the making of history, the leaders of communal organizations and institutions as well as those generally considered not worth interviewing because they "do not know anything important."[5]

Neither "anonymous" persons nor unique topics, however, can compensate for a well-prepared interviewer. Skillful preliminary work enables the interviewer to spur respondents' memories, to probe sensitive areas with precision, to resolve accidental inconsistencies, and to recognize relevant historical relationships. Possessing a definite and vivid conception of the problems that concern researchers, the interviewer attempts to so fascinate the respondents that they are induced to recall experiences. Preparation should include extensive primary and secondary source study; abundant interviewing experience (both in quantity and in the subjects to be discussed during the interview); and a preliminary or exploratory interview to inform the respondent of the procedure, evaluate the range and depth of the respondent's knowledge, and determine the person's willingness to record.

Preparation is the key to a successful interview. The hours spent by the interviewer studying written documents differentiate a valuable oral history memoir from uncritically recorded reminiscences. While it is not always possible to imitate Professor A. M. Schlesinger's interviewer, who utilized over twenty thousand letters as preparation,[6] it is necessary to acquire a respondent's papers and digest them prior to the interview, to talk with corroborating witnesses who might provide checks on what the respondent says, and in general to learn as much as possible about the subject area and the respondent.[7]

Background research takes many forms. Prior to interviewing the owner of the only surviving kosher meat market in Columbus, we spoke with the former proprietors of three kosher meat markets who had once competed strongly with the only operative market. This enabled us to probe more deeply than otherwise would have been possible and to explore what actions had dictated the survival of only one kosher market. In another case, following a preliminary interview with several immigrants who came from eastern Europe before World War I, we obtained the complete passenger lists of their ships from the National Archives before conducting full-length interviews.

Preparation for another interview session involved ascertaining from the city directories the respondent's annual addresses over the past sixty-seven years. Armed with this information, we were able to question the respondent about rents, mortgages, boarders, mobility, and neighborhoods in some detail. Yet another interview demanded the compilation of a list of a pugilist's professional fights, a task requiring the use of the local sports pages over a twelve-year period. Such research, of course, does not guarantee that interviews will not be disappointing, wasteful, or occasionally frustrating. Adequate preparation does, however, maximize the potential inherent in the oral history technique, and minimize the large number of reminiscences recorded merely on the assumption that something preserved is equivalent to something of value. In short, there are no substitutes for interviewers who have done their homework.

The art of conducting the interview itself is no less tediously developed. One study of President Kennedy's press conferences concluded that a lengthy question called forth a lengthy answer, while a short question evoked a short response.[8] This suggests that the length of the question is a relevant concern during preparation. The danger, however, is not that the interviewer will ask a long question, but that either a double question or an imprecise question will be asked. When one is listening to the answer to a double question, it is difficult to ascertain whether the answer applies to the whole question or to one part of it; when the respondent hears an imprecise question, the confusion is even greater. A good rule is to try limiting the question to a maximum of two sentences: one sentence which states why one is asking the question and a second sentence, ending in a question mark, which asks the question.

This is easily said; but listening attentively is not so easily done. First, one must become accustomed to long periods of silence. Then, one has to endure often lengthy reflections on subjects of no interest to the interviewer (but perhaps of interest to other historians). Both to pay attention (so as not to ask about the same subject again) and to keep from dozing can be grueling tasks. Third, sometimes even the most evocative questions can elicit one sentence answers. Here, an occasional turning off of the recorder, chatting informally, and then attempting again to record the discussion usually relaxes the respondent. Finally, if the interviewer has not established rapport before asking the tough questions, the silence may be endless. Good rapport will encourage candor, minimize reticence, and even provide enjoyment for the respondent.

Generally, the longer the interview lasts, the more easily the respondent will communicate. By beginning with the least sensitive topics and gradually escalating to the central subject, the careful questioner will profit greatly. Early in one of our interviews, we asked a respondent directly about Mr. X, the president of a local synagogue during World War I. The interviewee refused to say anything about the subject because "his family is still here." More than an hour later, however, the word "bathhouse" triggered a comment about the same gentleman:

> Bathhouse. [Pause] The president of the synagogue next door to the bath was at that time a man who was a complete ignoramous. He didn't know any language whatever. He had a mixture of half Russian, half English words, half Yiddish words, but he couldn't read or write. Complete illiterate but he was apparently a rich man and therefore he became the president. Rabbi G. taught me in order to become a teacher over here you've got to write your application in three languages. I wrote the application in these three languages and handed them to the president and the president took it and turned it upside down, couldn't read it. It was a wilderness, no question about it — the cultural wilderness over here.[9]

Even with a carefully constructed questionnaire and solid rapport, an interviewer's biases can cause problems. The successful questioner recognizes such biases and endeavors to overcome or at least conceal them, for respondents in turn will tend to size up the questioner before responding. Age, appearance, sex, vocabulary, actions, and credentials are all important stimuli projected by interviewers. For example, an awareness that a respondent supported Governor Wallace for president in the 1972 campaign led us to form a stereotype of the person in our minds, so that we tailored our inquiries to our assumptions and failed to ask significant questions. Excessive admiration for the interviewee also may have its drawbacks, for the interviewer often becomes lured into the respondent's frame of reference, precluding dialogue, disagreement, and gentle confrontation. Another difficulty is a tendency for questioners to provide the respondents with subtle cues which keep the answers within the frame of reference the interviewer has established, and thus respondents fail to consider alternative answers. An interviewer may minimize this danger by using the language of the respondent whenever possible and by creating an environment which is neither highly structured nor chaotic. The interviewer needs to develop a self-consciousness about what is affecting the respondent — including the impact verbal and physical biases have upon the interview session. The respondent's perception of the interviewer will, in a large measure, determine the style, content, length, and quality of the responses.[10]

One might be tempted at this point to ask at least two questions: Is not interviewing a remarkably expensive method of doing research, and is it reasonable to expect the amount of skill and training discussed above? While there can be no complete substitute for an interviewer who has done the requisite homework and prepared well, interviewers are made, not born. As our use of community volunteers in recording multi-generational family histories has demonstrated, any reasonably intelligent person can become an adequate interviewer with only moderate amounts of time and practice. At worst the neophyte will play the role of a recorder rather than an interviewer, for many respondents know what they want to relate and what they do not. If this is the case, as it inevitably will be at some point, the novice interviewer-recorder should sit forward, keep the conversation moving, and avoid dozing off, for respondents chosen to fill in gaps in written records have much to tell even without a dialogue. Finally, the cost of transcribing ought not to be allowed to loom too large. The tape itself has tremendous value and can be adequately utilized even without transcripts. Neither the unavailability of transcripts, nor the impossibility of the ideal interview, should deter a serious oral history project.

Of course, in any serious oral history program, interviewees' responses are transcribed and edited, a process which can produce additional problems. The goal of transcribing should be a faithful reproduction of the oral record; any deviation from this record is an error. Yet even good transcribers find it difficult not to "improve" the record while transcribing; they are, for example, eager to insert periods in the midst of run-on sentences (few respondents pause at the end of a sentence), change verbs that do not agree with their subjects, and omit "meaningless" words and phrases (such as "you know"). Stylistic attractiveness in a transcript, however, should always be subordinated to accuracy, even when the transcript almost cries out to be "improved."

The best protection against over-anxious transcribers, of course, is the preservation of the oral history tapes in public archives. Not only are the original words thus preserved, but the historian can utilize the voice, age, articulateness, style, and speed of response of the respondent as additional clues to the value of the interview. One warning: voices eventually disappear even from tapes. Voices recorded at the slowest speed (1⅞) and then stored in a file drawer or cabinet sometimes disappear completely in a few years. The best antidotes are a fast speed (thus more tape and greater expense), storage at a proper temperature, and the aid of a professional oral historian or historical society.

How does the historian weigh the veracity of this new kind of historical document jointly created by the participant and the historian-interviewer? Forrest C. Pogue anticipated this question in his study of General George C. Marshall.[11] When Marshall asked how Pogue could be sure that what he told Pogue in 1957 was not something he had invented, Pogue replied, "about every tenth question I give you is on something to which I already know the answer from your testimony in the 1940s or letters you wrote at this particular time."[12] Still other interviewers provide internal checks and clues for historians by including questions which test a person's memory, asking whether the account being given is from eyewitness or indirect evidence, and returning to the same subject, from different angles, repeatedly.

Additionally, almost every answer by a respondent provides at least one piece of specific information which can be verified, so that the entire response can be judged in terms of the correct or incorrect facts. The existence of Judge Black's court on Scioto Street more than seventy years ago lends credence to the following response:

> Q: What was your first job in America?
>
> A: Selling newspapers. I had a stand on the corner of State and High streets. I couldn't speak a word of English, you know, and I was yelling, I had a pretty good voice, and I hollered so loud, in those days you weren't allowed to holler like that, of course, I didn't know anything about it, so all of a sudden there was a whole circle around me, trying to listen to me and all of a sudden I see a big, beautiful wagon come over, and that was the patrol wagon, a horse wagon in those days, and they came over and tried to tell me something and there was somebody right next to me trying to explain it to me what it was, that they want you to sing the way you sang before, so I tried to sing it in loud voice, you know, and they put me on the wagon and took me to the police station. I didn't know anything about it, what it meant, I said, "Gosh, what wonderful country the United States is, you sing and then they give you a buggy ride." The police station was on Scioto Street, I remember distinctly, and the judge was Judge Black and they took me before the judge and they asked me the same thing, that I should perform the singing, the same that I did over there, and I did that and I'm telling you I'll never forget that, Dr. Raphael, and that Judge laughed and laughed and told the police, "Tell him to go back and peddle his papers."[13]

The historian who makes use of oral histories must be aware not only that people do forget, but also that they lie. Sometimes a respondent is more anxious to say what he thinks the interviewer wants to hear than to report what actually happened. At other times a respondent may deny behavior which received social acceptance then but would not now, or claim actions honorable now but of no consequence then. Occasionally a respondent seems to perform for an invisible, future audience as well as to magnify, distort, and exaggerate his own role in an event; for example, one respondent took credit for founding the Columbus Torah Academy two years before he had arrived in Columbus! Frequently a respondent presents a seemingly coherent picture which, however, does not correspond to reality because the individual has fabricated a plethora of incidents to fit into what is remembered.[14]

How can the historian sort out coherence from correspondence, reconstruction from remembrance, fact from fiction?[15] To a large degree, this is the task of the interviewer, who must have the historian in mind while preparing the interview. The questioner must attempt to test the validity of the interviewee's responses through preliminary research, internal clues, open-ended questions which permit both praise and blame, and the querying of several individuals about the same subject. Moreover, the historian must treat the oral history transcripts as raw material or sources which need to be examined with the same care as any other source. The historian particularly must seek to discover the report's reliability, correlating and cross-checking with more conventional sources, and remaining continuously aware that this report is merely the perception of the informant. Under no circumstances should the historian suspend any of the normal critical canons of historical research.

Furthermore, the folklorists have reminded us that more than the "facts" from an interview are of use, especially since most respondents have less interest in what the interviewer is seeking than in relating and amplifying what is relevant to them. Legends, romantic memories, exaggerations, anecdotes, family sagas, jokes, and folklore of all kinds are rich sources of information in and of themselves. After they are enjoyed and utilized, the chaff can be peeled away to expose underlying truth, to provide a self-portrait of the respondent, or to compare with more "factual" data.[16] The following excerpts exemplify responses which might provide information for the folklorist-historian as well as the traditional historian:

> My brother arrived in Columbus and, not being used to toilets, started to use the fences. It didn't work out as he was always chased away. So he went to a house and knocked on the door to ask where he should do it. The woman, hardly awake, thought he was the milkman and handed him a bottle. He took it and filled it; she took the bottle and gave him a dime. He ran home and wrote to me in Russia, "Come here fast, Jacob, a fortune is being pissed here. It's a golden land."[17]

> Sam [Levinger] went to Spain in January of 1937 and the news of his death, which actually occurred in September, reached the family in

> October 1937. Something probably went out of mom and dad's life with the death of this oldest son. Elma kept close touch with many of our high school friends as a way of still trying to recreate the days when Sam had been his most exuberant, and the house was always full of noisy, articulate, politically minded groups of high school students. One of the hardest things for her was when Sam's dog became so old and feeble he had to be killed. The dog had sensed Sam's going away and death as different than many other absences. He had become quite senile and yet would wander back to the high school and wait there until the children came out to see if Sam was still there.[18]

Those who attempt to write local ethnic history cannot overstate how fragmentary the written records might be and how useful interviews can be in both supplementing what does exist and supplying what does not exist. Saul Benison's thoughts provide a final reminder not of the problems, but of the promise which resides in this very new and fragile source:

> As a result of new sound and visual communication, much of the detail of human experience, which was previously put to paper because of the exclusive nature of print and writing communication, has today been sapped from the record and become fleeting and ephemeral. Such experience, if preserved at all, is only to be found in the memory of living men. It is this paradox of simultaneous plenty and scarcity in contemporary records that in large measure defines the tasks of those who work in oral history.[19]

NOTES FOR THE APPENDIX

1. Quoted in Larry Van Dyne, "Oral History: Sharecroppers and Presidents, Jazz and Texas Oil," *Chronicle of Higher Education Review* (December 24, 1973), p. 10.

2. Saul Benison, "Reflections on Oral History," *American Archivist* XXVIII (January 1965): 73.

3. *Tom Rivers: Reflections on a Life in Medicine and Science, an Oral History Memoir Prepared by Saul Benison* (Cambridge, Massachusetts, 1967), p. ix.

4. For an analysis of a group project to document, with oral history, a controversial event, see Irene E. Cortinovis, "Documenting an Event with Manuscripts and Oral History: The St. Louis Teachers' Strike, 1973," *Oral History Review* (1974): 59-63. On the application of oral history interviews to the study of decision-making within small groups, see *Bulletin of*

Cornell Program in Oral History, Cornell University Libraries I:3 (July 1967), II:2 (December 1968), II:3 (July 1969), and II:4 (December 1969).

5. Thoughtful comments on the history of anonymous persons are in Henry Glassie, "A Folklorist Thought on the Promise of Oral History," Peter D. Olch and and Forrest C. Pogue, editors, *Selections From the Fifth and Sixth National Colloquia on Oral History* (New York, 1972), pp. 54-57.

6. Saul Benison, op. cit., p. 73.

7. On the relationship between records and recollections, see Charles T. Morrissey, "Truman and the Presidency — Records and Oral Recollections," *American Archivist* XXVIII (January 1965): 53-61.

8. "The Art of Interviewing," in Gould P. Colman, editor, *The Third National Colloquium on Oral History* (New York, 1969), p. 23.

9. Interview with Dr. Benjamin W. Abramson.

10. On stimuli projected by the interviewer, see James E. Sargent, "Oral History, Franklin D. Roosevelt, and the New Deal: Some Recollections of Adolf A. Berle, Jr., Lewis W. Douglas, and Raymond Moley," *Oral History Review* (1973): 92-109.

11. *George Marshall: Education of a General* (New York, 1963).

12. "Keynote Address of James MacGregor Burns," *Selections from the Fifth and Sixth National Colloquia on Oral History,* p. 37.

13. Interview with Jacob Pass.

14. On remembering and reconstructing, see F. C. Bartlett, *Remembering* (London, 1932), and U. Neisser, *Cognitive Psychology* (New York, 1967).

15. On separating fact from fiction, see David F. Musto and Saul Benison, "Studies on the Accuracy of Oral Interviews," in Colman, *Fourth National Colloquium on Oral History* (New York, 1970), pp. 167-81.

16. See Richard M. Dorson, "The Oral Historian and the Folklorist," *Selections from the Fifth and Sixth National Colloquia,* pp. 40-49, and William Lynwood Montell, "The Oral Historian as Folklorist," *Selections from the Fifth and Sixth National Colloquia,* pp. 50-53. On the general ethnography of communication, see Dell Hymes, "Models of the Interaction of Language and Social Setting," *Journal of Social Issues* XXIII (1967): 8-28.

17. Interview with Jacob Pass.

18. Tape recording from Leah Levinger, New York, 1974.

19. Tom Rivers, op. cit., p. ix.

BIBLIOGRAPHY

Although there are several typical late nineteenth and early twentieth century compendia of reminiscences, topical history and laudatory biographies of the most successful — and mostly Protestant — Columbusites, an interpretive history of Columbus does not exist. Therefore, our study began with the abundant German and English language daily press and, for the years after World War I, the weekly Anglo-Jewish press. Cincinnati's *American Israelite,* a weekly journal, did provide some coverage of Columbus Jewry in the second half of the nineteenth century.

From the press we moved to the federal census schedules and the rich storehouses of state, county, city, institutional and personal documents delineated below. Especially valuable was the generous demographic information about each household member provided in the census schedules, for this made possible the statistical reconstruction of Columbus' immigrant Jewish community in the mid-nineteenth century, while a mixture of the non-federal sources enabled us to piece together the early twentieth century neighborhood that is no more. The Columbus *City Directories,* with their alphabetical listings of city residents and firms, provided home and occasionally business addresses and occupations, while the national papers of the Industrial Removal Office at the American Jewish Historical Society in Waltham, Massachusetts, offered insight into east European Jewish immigration to Columbus. Finally, information from nearly a hundred meetings and nearly sixty oral history interviews added insight and color, fleshed out the human story behind dry organizational records, and enabled us to reconstruct the origin and development of much about which written records were silent.

The bibliography which follows is confined exclusively to cited materials about Columbus and Columbus Jewry.

PRIMARY SOURCES

Manuscripts

Public Documents

Ohio, Division of Soldiers' Claims. Grave Registration Cards. OHS
Ohio, Franklin County, Auditor. Tax Duplicates, 1865-1912.
____________. Board of Deputy State Supervisors and Inspectors of Elections. List of Electors Registered in the City of Columbus, Ohio . . . 1912. OHS
____________. Board of Elections. Abstract of Votes, 1912, Primary and Presidential, OHS
____________. Common Pleas Court. General Index to Declarations of Naturalization, A to Z. 1859-1906. OHS
____________. Probate Court. Birth Records, 1867-1899.
____________. Administrative Records. Inventory and Sale Bills, 1881-1888. OHS
____________. Marriage Records, [1803-1865].
____________. Marriage Licenses, 1866-1975.
____________. Records of Ministers' Licenses, Vol. 2, 1864-1890.
____________. Wills, 1865-1900.
____________. Recorder. Deeds, 1840-1912.
____________. Grantee and Grantor Indices
Ohio, Secretary of State. Articles of Incorporation.
United States, Bureau of the Census. Descriptions of the Enumeration Districts of the 11th Supervisor's Districts of Ohio.
____________. Census Schedules, 1850 through 1880. Franklin County, Ohio. Population.
____________. Census Schedules, 1870. Franklin County, Ohio. Non-population — Products of Industry — Schedule 4.
Works Progress Administration. Survey of State and Local Historical Records, 1936. OHS

Institutional Records

The records of these institutions remain in their possession unless otherwise specified.

Agudas Achim Synagogue. Minutes, 1927-1947.
____________. *Sunday School Bulletin*, Vol. I, 1918. New York City Public Library.
*Agudath Hamizrachim. Pinkas [Records], n.d. OHS
Anti-Defamation League. Blackman File, n.d.

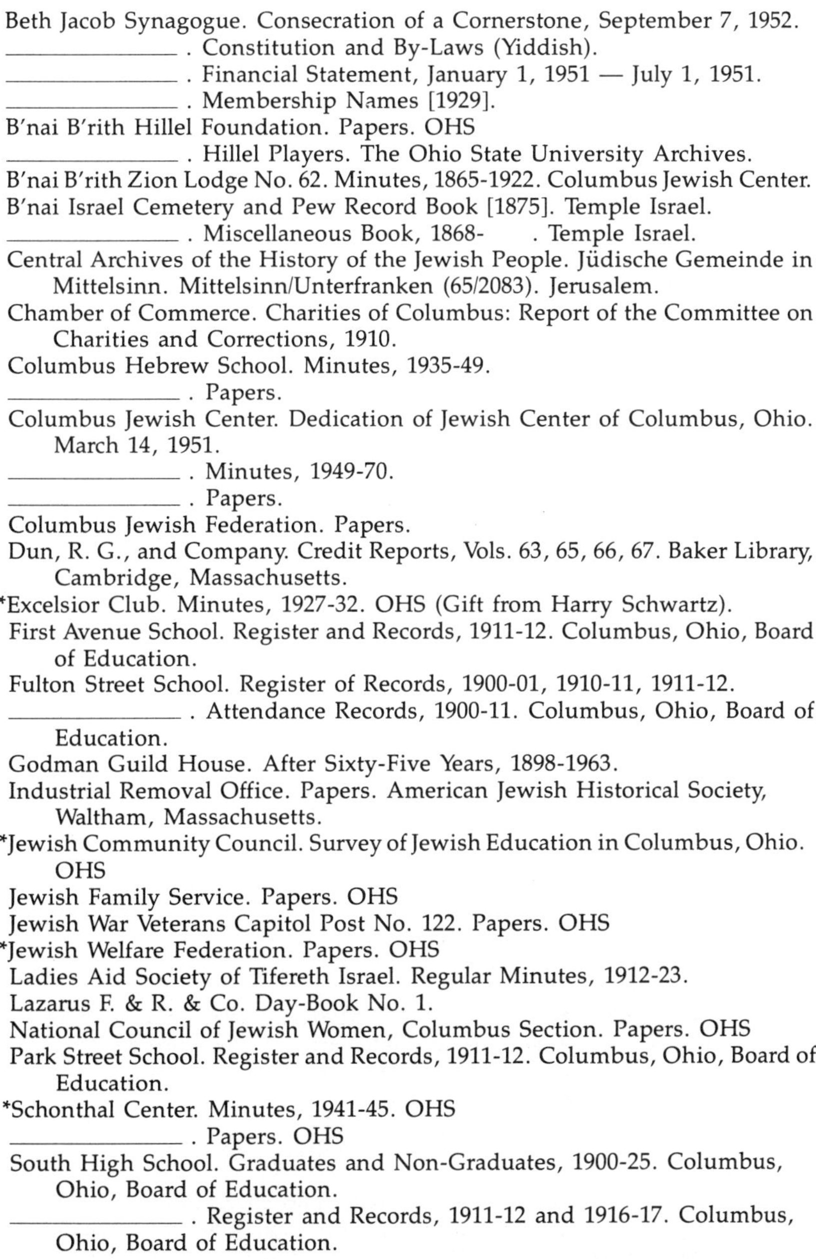

Beth Jacob Synagogue. Consecration of a Cornerstone, September 7, 1952.

_______________. Constitution and By-Laws (Yiddish).

_______________. Financial Statement, January 1, 1951 — July 1, 1951.

_______________. Membership Names [1929].

B'nai B'rith Hillel Foundation. Papers. OHS

_______________. Hillel Players. The Ohio State University Archives.

B'nai B'rith Zion Lodge No. 62. Minutes, 1865-1922. Columbus Jewish Center.

B'nai Israel Cemetery and Pew Record Book [1875]. Temple Israel.

_______________. Miscellaneous Book, 1868- . Temple Israel.

Central Archives of the History of the Jewish People. Jüdische Gemeinde in Mittelsinn. Mittelsinn/Unterfranken (65/2083). Jerusalem.

Chamber of Commerce. Charities of Columbus: Report of the Committee on Charities and Corrections, 1910.

Columbus Hebrew School. Minutes, 1935-49.

_______________. Papers.

Columbus Jewish Center. Dedication of Jewish Center of Columbus, Ohio. March 14, 1951.

_______________. Minutes, 1949-70.

_______________. Papers.

Columbus Jewish Federation. Papers.

Dun, R. G., and Company. Credit Reports, Vols. 63, 65, 66, 67. Baker Library, Cambridge, Massachusetts.

*Excelsior Club. Minutes, 1927-32. OHS (Gift from Harry Schwartz).

First Avenue School. Register and Records, 1911-12. Columbus, Ohio, Board of Education.

Fulton Street School. Register of Records, 1900-01, 1910-11, 1911-12.

_______________. Attendance Records, 1900-11. Columbus, Ohio, Board of Education.

Godman Guild House. After Sixty-Five Years, 1898-1963.

Industrial Removal Office. Papers. American Jewish Historical Society, Waltham, Massachusetts.

*Jewish Community Council. Survey of Jewish Education in Columbus, Ohio. OHS

Jewish Family Service. Papers. OHS

Jewish War Veterans Capitol Post No. 122. Papers. OHS

*Jewish Welfare Federation. Papers. OHS

Ladies Aid Society of Tifereth Israel. Regular Minutes, 1912-23.

Lazarus F. & R. & Co. Day-Book No. 1.

National Council of Jewish Women, Columbus Section. Papers. OHS

Park Street School. Register and Records, 1911-12. Columbus, Ohio, Board of Education.

*Schonthal Center. Minutes, 1941-45. OHS

_______________. Papers. OHS

South High School. Graduates and Non-Graduates, 1900-25. Columbus, Ohio, Board of Education.

_______________. Register and Records, 1911-12 and 1916-17. Columbus, Ohio, Board of Education.

*These papers are part of the Ohio Historical Society's Jews and Judaism in a Midwestern Community: Columbus, Ohio, 1840-1975 Collection.

Temple Israel Bulletin, May 19, 1933.
Temple Israel. Minute Books, 1868-1939. OHS
Tifereth Israel Congregation. Minute Book, April 7, 1907-January 2, 1919.
*United Jewish Fund. Papers. OHS and Columbus Jewish Federation.
United Jewish Fund and Council. Papers. Columbus Jewish Federation.
______________. Minutes. Columbus Jewish Federation.
Winding Hollow Country Club. Papers. Record of Proceedings.

Family and Personal Papers, Memoirs, Diaries, Scrapbooks, Surveys

Bonowitz, Joseph. Scrapbook. In possession of Mrs. Faye Bonowitz in Palm Beach, Florida.
Columbus Jewish History Project. Confirmands and Torah Academy Graduates Survey, 1975, OHS
______________. German Jewish Refugees Survey, 1975, OHS
______________. Sorority and Fraternity Survey of Ohio State University Graduates, 1975, OHS
Feibel Family Scrapbook. In possession of Ron Robins in Columbus, Ohio.
Gilbert, Harry. Scrapbook. In possession of Mrs. Jacob Gilbert of Columbus, Ohio.
Greenwald, Leopold (Rabbi). Papers. In possession of Jack Greenwald in Denver, Colorado.
Gup, Samuel (Rabbi). Papers. OHS
Hart, William. Discharge Papers, 1865. In possession of Edwin Levin in Newark, Ohio.
Horkin, Burnet. Diary [January 1-December 31, 1910]. In possession of Marvin Horkin, in Columbus, Ohio.
Kobacker, Alfred. Scrapbook. In possession of Arthur J. Kobacker, Brilliant, Ohio.
Lazarus Family. Papers. OHS
Lazarus, Fred Jr. Autobiography. OHS
*Melton, Samuel. Papers. OHS
Papurt, Maxwell. Official Statement of the Military Service and Death of Maxwell J. Papurt, Major, Counter-Intelligence Corps, June 18, 1948. In possession of Maxine Papurt in Columbus, Ohio.
*Perlman, Herman. Autobiography. OHS
*Robins, A. W. Let's Think It Over! [1949]. OHS
Taxon, Morris (Rabbi). Papers. In possession of Rabbi Jordan Taxon in Canton, Ohio.
Troy, Ernst. My Biography. In possession of Ron Robins in Columbus, Ohio.
Weiss, Louis (Rabbi). Sermons and Essays. American Jewish Archives in Cincinnati, Ohio.
Werne, Isaac (Rabbi). Vita. In possession of Benjamin Werne, Jamaica, New York.
Zelizer, Nathan (Rabbi). Papers. OHS

Published Sources

Newspapers

Unless otherwise indicated, these newspapers were published in Columbus, Ohio, and are available at the OHS.

American Israelite, (Cincinnati). 1855-1913.
Archives Israélites, (Paris). 1870.
Columbus Citizen, 1929-39, 1944, 1946, 1950-51, 1955-57, 1959.
Columbus Citizen-Journal, 1962, 1969, 1974.
Columbus Daily Press, 1894.
Columbus Daily Times, 1886, 1888.
Columbus Evening Dispatch, 1871, 1883, 1886, 1890, 1903, 1907-10, 1914, 1932-39, 1942-46, 1950-52, 1955, 1961, 1966.
Columbus Evening Post, 1896.
Columbus Jewish Chronicle, 1918-19.
Columbus Jewish Outlook, 1918. In New York City Public Library.
Columbus Post, 1892.
Columbus Press-Post, 1907-08.
Columbus Socialist, 1911-12.
Columbus Sunday Dispatch, Centennial Library Edition, August 26, 1912.
Columbus Sunday Dispatch, 1904.
Columbus Sunday Morning News, 1872-73, 1876, 1881-83.
Columbus Sunday Star, 1932.
Der Westbote, 1849, 1854, 1870, 1872, 1879, 1882, 1888, 1891, 1896, 1903-04.
Die Deborah, (Cincinnati). 1855-56, 1860-61, 1865-66.
Jewish Chronicle, February 1919.
Occident and American Jewish Advocate, (Philadelphia). 1852, 1854, 1859, 1867.
Ohio Jewish Chronicle, 1922-76.
Ohio State Democrat, 1854.
Ohio State Journal, 1851, 1865, 1868, 1870-1918, 1922-37, 1943, 1946-49, 1950-53, 1955.
Ohio Statesman, 1854, 1867, 1870-71.
Tägliche Columbus Express, 1898.

Public Documents

City of Columbus, Ohio. *General Ordinances of the City of Columbus, Ohio In Force January 1, 1882 . . .* Collated by H. E. Bryan, City Clerk (Columbus, 1882).

________________. *Population Characteristics by Census Tracts* (Columbus, 1930).

United States, Bureau of the Census. *Tenth Census of the United States, 1880. Report on the Social Statistics of Cities, Part II, Southern and Western States* (Washington, D.C., 1887).

________________. *Thirteenth Census of the United States Taken in the Year 1910. Population.* Volume 1 (Washington, D.C., 1913).

________________. *Fourteenth Census of the United States Taken in the Year 1920. Population,* Volume 2 (Washington, D.C., 1922).

________________. *Fourteenth Census of the United States . . . 1920. State Compendium, Ohio.* (Washington, D.C., 1924).

Annual Reports and Proceedings

American Jewish Historical Society. *Yearbook of Jewish Social Work, 1935.* (Waltham, Massachusetts).

Associated Charities of Columbus. *First Annual Report of the Federated Jewish Charities and Affiliated Societies of Columbus Ending November 1, 1900.* (Columbus, 1900).

________________. *Sixth Annual Report . . . 1905.* (Columbus, 1906).

________________. *Eighth Annual Report . . . 1908.* (Columbus, 1908).

________________. *Ninth Annual Report . . . 1909.* (Columbus, 1909).

________________. "Fifteenth Annual Report . . . 1915" in *The Social Servant,* December 1915.

________________. "Sixteenth Annual Report . . . 1916" in *The Social Servant,* December 1916.

________________. *Nineteenth Annual Report . . . 1919.* (Columbus, 1919).

B'nai Israel. Annual Report, 1912. Temple Israel.

Columbus, Ohio, Board of Education. *Annual Report of the Board of Education of the Columbus Public Schools for the School Year Ending August 31, 1879.* (Columbus, 1879).

________________. *Annual Report . . . 1880.* 2 Volumes. (Columbus, 1880).

________________. *Annual Report . . . 1905.* (Columbus, 1905).

________________. *Annual Report . . . 1906.* (Columbus, 1906).

________________. *Annual Report . . . 1908.* (Columbus, 1908).

________________. *Annual Report . . . 1911.* (Columbus, 1911).

________________. *Annual Report . . . 1912.* (Columbus, 1912).

Columbus, Ohio, City Council. *Journal of Council Proceedings – Book No. 42, June 8, 1903.*

Columbus Hebrew School. *Second Annual United Jubilee Benefit,* April 21, 1936. CHS.

Jewish Welfare Federation. *Annual Report, 1932.* OHS

Ohio, Secretary of State. *Annual Statistical Report to the Governor . . . For the Year Ending November 15, 1912.* (Springfield, 1913).

SCOA Industries, Inc. *Annual Report, 1972.*

Zionist Organization of America. *Annual Report of the 46th Annual Convention of the ZOA, September 11-13, 1943, in Columbus, Ohio.* (New York, 1943).

Directories, Atlases, and Maps

Baist's Real Estate Atlas of Surveys of Columbus, Ohio, 1910 (Philadelphia, 1910).
Columbus, Ohio, Board of Elections. Ward Boundaries Map. January 1911.
G. Wm. Baist's Property Atlas of the City of Columbus. (Philadelphia, 1899).

The number of city directories in this study is so large as to warrant omission of individual listings. All pre-1860 directories cited are in the microfiche publication, *City and Business Directories of the United States Through 1860* (New Haven, 1967), and are listed in Dorothea Spear, *Bibliography of American Directories Through 1860* (Worcester, Massachusetts, 1961). The post-1860 directories are on file at The Ohio State University Main Library.

Other Sources

Benjamin, I. J. *Three Years in America 1859-1862.* Volume II. Philadelphia, 1956.
B'nai Israel. *Cornerstone Laying of Temple B'nai Israel Programme.* Columbus, 1903.
Chamber of Commerce. *Handbook of Social Resources.* Columbus, 1922.
________________ . *Handbook of Social Resources of Columbus and Franklin County.* Columbus, 1936.
Free and Accepted Masons. *Masonic Directory.* Columbus, 1975.
Gup, Samuel. "Common Ground" in *American Hebrew,* November 26, 1937.
________________ . "Co-Workers in the Vineyard." *Presbyterian Tribune,* June 24, 1937.
Kaplan, Harry. *Selected Addresses, Published in Honor of his 25th Anniversary as Hillel Director at The Ohio State University 1935-60.* Columbus, [1960].
Lazarus, Fred. "The Development of the Delivery System." *Enthusiast,* November 1915.
Lewisohn, Ludwig. *Upstream: An American Chronicle.* New York, 1922.
Mayor, Albert J. *Columbus Jewish Population Study: 1969.* Columbus, 1969.
A Message to the Intelligent Voter. Campaign pamphlet. Columbus, 1935. OHS
Philipson, David. *My Life as an American Jew.* Cincinnati, 1941.
Schwartz, David. *My Townlet – Fachenbrod.* Israel, 1956.
Silber, Saul. *Selected Essays of Rabbi Saul Silber.* Chicago, 1950.
Stavsky, David. "A Mechitza for Columbus." *Jewish Life,* Winter 1974.
Tarshish, Jacob. *Half Hours with Rabbi Jacob Tarshish.* First Volume. Columbus, 1933.
Thurber, James. "The Day The Dam Broke." In *My Life and Hard Times.* New York, 1933.

Interviews

Tapes and transcripts are on file at OHS.

Interviewee	*Interviewer*	*Date*
Abrams, Dora	Linda Elise Kalette (LEK)	5-16-74
Abramson, B. W.	Marc Lee Raphael (MLR)	3-04-74
Baker, Julius	MLR	7-17-74
Bender, Harry	LEK	1-14-75
Berliner, Louis	MLR	6-20-74
Bernstein, Maurice	Lawrence W. Raphael (LWR)	11-13-75
Bornheim, Jerome	MLR	4-28-74
Borowitz, Eugene	LWR	1-21-75
Brandt, Etta	Randall Wasserstrom	1-04-75
Brief, Jenny Goldberg	LEK	5-16-74
Callif, Paul	LEK	4-30-75
Divorced Persons,		
Anonymous	MLR	9-2-74
Anonymous	MLR	9-15-74
Edelman, Samuel	MLR	8-19-74
Feller, Chaim	LEK	7-21-75
Folkman, Jerome	MLR	12-06-74
Fox, Marvin	MLR	6-13-74
**Friedman, Max	Rick Lapine	8-01-74
Friedman, Milton	MLR	7-09-74
Goldberg, Julius	LEK	12-17-74
Gordon, Ben	MLR	8-15-74
**Gup, Ruth	MLR	9-19-74
Kohn, A. S.	LEK	11-10-74
Krausz, Bertha	Ilse Ebstein (IE)	1974
Levinger, Leah	MLR	6-21-74
Mandelkorn, Ben	MLR	4-28-77
Mellman, Jake	David Rosenblatt	12-17-75
Mellman, Myer	LEK	11-13-75
Mellman, Robert	MLR	4-30-74
Melton, Samuel	MLR	7-11-74
Neustadt, Ben	LEK	5-04-76
Pass, Jacob	MLR	5-06-74
Polster, Tobias	LEK	6-23-75
Robins, Stan	LEK	12-04-74
Robinson, Terry	IE	1974
Rubenstein, Samuel	MLR	5-10-74
Schecter, Sylvia	MLR	9-22-74
Schlezinger, Edward	MLR	12-13-74
Schottenstein, Sadie	Mildred Tarshish	5-01-75
Schwartz, Harry	MLR	3-17-74

**Topical index and tape available at OHS.

Interviewee	*Interviewer*	*Date*
Seff, Bertha Josephson	LEK	1-15-75
Seff, Irving	MLR	5-17-74
Skop, Morris	MLR	6-22-74
Sonenstein, Earl	Rosalind Sonenstein	7-74
Stavsky, David	MLR	6-05-74
Stern, Aurelia	IE	1974
Stern, Ernest	LEK	11-17-75
Tarshish, Mildred	LEK	2-25-75
Yenkin, Abe	Eleanor Block (EB)	5-19-75
Yenkin, Ben	EB	5-05-75
Yenkin, Eleanor	EB	7-30-75
Yenkin, Fred	EB	6-08-75
Zelizer, Nathan	MLR	8-18-74
Zisenwine, Gabriel	LEK	11-19-74

SECONDARY SOURCES

Published

Alston, John C. *Cost of a Slum Area.* Wilberforce, Ohio, 1948.

American Jewish Literary Foundation. *American Jews: Their Lives and Achievements.* Volume II. New York, 1958.

Bell, Florence Louise. "The Social Settlement: Columbus, Ohio." *Annals of the American Academy of Political and Social Science* (May 1902).

Brooks, Herbert. "The Financial Interests of Columbus," *The Ohio Magazine* 3:6 (December 1907).

Chanis, M. M. *Robert W. Schiff: A Talmudic Scholar in American Business: A Biographical Portrait and Tribute.* n.p., 1966.

Diehl, William Jr. "Lazarus." *Cincinnati* I:3 (December 1967).

Eminent Jews of America. Toledo, 1918.

Food Store Review 5:8 (September 1946).

Forman, Jonathan. "Ohio Medical History — Pre-Civil War Period — The First Year of the Second Epidemic of Asiatic Cholera in Columbus, Ohio — 1849." *Ohio State Archaeological and Historical Quarterly* (October-December 1944).

Glassman, Leo, editor. *Biographical Encyclopedia of American Jews*. New York, 1935.

History – Columbus High School 1847-1910. Columbus, 1925 [Columbus High School became Central High School in 1893].

"History of the Department of German." *Ohio State University College of Humanities Centennial*, n.d.

History of Franklin and Pickaway Counties. Columbus, 1880.

Hooper, Osman C. *History of the City of Columbus* [1797-1920]. Columbus and Cleveland, n.d.

"Jews of Columbus: Brief History of Their Coming and Progress." Undated newspaper clipping [1897 or 1898?]. Temple Israel.

Kempton, Murray. *Part of Our Time: Some Ruins and Monuments of the Thirties*. New York, 1955.

Lee, Alfred E. *History of the City of Columbus*. 2 Volumes. Chicago and New York, 1892.

Levinger, Lee J. "Jews in the Liberal Professions in Ohio." *Jewish Social Studies* II (1940).

Lieberson, Stanley. *Ethnic Patterns in American Cities*. New York, 1963.

Mahoney, Tom. *The Great Merchants*. New York, 1947.

Mark, Mary Louise. *Negroes in Columbus*. Columbus, 1928.

Martin, William T. *History of Franklin County: A Collection of Reminiscences of the Early Settlement of the County*. Columbus, 1858.

McKenzie, Roderick Duncan. *The Neighborhood: A Study of Local Life in the City of Columbus, Ohio*. Chicago, 1923.

Meyer, Harry, compiler and editor. *History of Humboldt Lodge, No. 476, F. and A. M. of Columbus, Ohio [1873-1948]*. [(Columbus, 1948)].

National Jewish Welfare Board. *American Jews in World War II*. Volume II. New York, 1947.

Peterson, Jon A. "From Social Settlement to Social Agency: Settlement Work in Columbus, Ohio 1898-1958." *The Social Science Review* 39:2 (June 1965).

Pitts, Leonore. "The Italians of Columbus — A Study in Population." *Annals of the American Academy of Political and Social Science* (January 1902).

Rippley, LaVern J. "The Columbus Germans." *The Report: A Journal of German-American History* 33 (1968).

Rosenberg, Charles E. *The Cholera Years: The United States in 1832, 1849, and 1866* (Chicago, 1962).

Studer, Jacob. *Columbus, Ohio: Its History, Resources, and Progress*. n.p., 1873.

Tavenner, Robert L., et al. *Columbus Manufacturers: A Statistical Paper on the City of Columbus, Ohio*. Columbus, 1906-07.

Taylor, William Alexander. *Centennial History of Columbus and Franklin County, Ohio*. 2 Volumes. Chicago and Columbus, 1909.

Welch, Deshler. "The City of Columbus, Ohio." *Harper's Weekly* 76 (1887).

Who's Who in American Jewry 1926. Volume 1. New York, 1927.

Who's Who in American Jewry 1928. 2nd edition. New York, 1928.

Who's Who in American Jewery, 1938-39. Volume 3. New York, 1938.

Williams, Daniel J. *The Welsh of Columbus, Ohio: A Study in Adaptation and Assimilation*. Oshkosh, Wisconsin, 1913.

ABBREVIATIONS

The following abbreviations are used in the footnotes:

AJA	*American Jewish Archives*
AJYB	*American Jewish Year Book*
CC	*Columbus Citizen*
CCAR	*Central Conference of American Rabbis*
CCJ	*Columbus Citizen Journal*
CCP	*Columbus Call & Post*
CD	*Columbus Dispatch*
CDP	*Columbus Daily Press*
CDPP	*Columbus Daily Press-Post*
CDT	*Columbus Daily Times*
CED	*Columbus Evening Dispatch*
CEP	*Columbus Evening Post*
CJC	*Columbus Jewish Chronicle*
CP	*Columbus Post*
CPP	*Columbus Press-Post*
CSD	*Columbus Sunday Dispatch*
CT	*Columbus Times*
JMF	*Journal of Marriage and the Family*
LBIYB	*Leo Baeck Institute Year Book*
MAHS	*Medical Aspects of Human Sexuality*
NYT	*New York Times*
OHS	*Ohio Historical Society*
OJC	*Ohio Jewish Chronicle*
OSJ	*Ohio State Journal*
PAJHS	*Publications of the American Jewish Historical Society*
SMN	*Sunday Morning News*
WWA	*Who's Who in America*
WWAJ	*Who's Who in American Jewry*

Unpublished Theses and Dissertations

Bernstein, Walter. "A Study of Factors Affecting Affiliation of Je Non-Member Families with the Columbus Jewish Center." thesis, The Ohio State University, 1957.

Cahn, Ronald T. "A Study of the Leisure Time Patterns of the Jewis Population of Columbus, Ohio, with Reference to Their Attitu and Relationships with the Jewish Center of Columbus." M.S The Ohio State University, 1957.

Frank, Harry. "A Study of the Impact of a Hebrew Program on Ch Their Parents." M.A. thesis, The Ohio State University, 196

Kaplan, Harry. "Religion, Democracy and Social Work — A Study and Inter-Relationships." M.A.S.A. thesis, The Ohio State U 1940.

Lentz, Andrea. "The Question of Community: The 1910 Street C Columbus, Ohio." M.A. thesis, The Ohio State University,

Marvin, Walter R. "Columbus and the Railroads of Central Ohio Civil War." Ph.D. dissertation, The Ohio State University, 1

Peterson, Jon A. "The Godman Guild." M.A. thesis, The Ohio S University, 1959.

Rabin, Philip. "A Study of American Jewish Community Backgr Description of Jewish Organizations and the Jewish Commun in Columbus." M.A. thesis, The Ohio State University, 194

Snorf, Sue. "A Sociological Study of the Hungarian Settlement in C M.A. thesis, The Ohio State University, 1925.

Speer, Michael. "Urbanization and Reform: Columbus, Ohio 18 Ph.D. dissertation, The Ohio State University, 1972.

TABLES

PHOTO ACKNOWLEDGEMENTS

Members of Columbus' Jewish community who graciously provided photographs for inclusion in this book are: Ann Covel, page 184; Mrs. Benjamin Kahn, pages 149 and 288; Laurie Zofan, Columbus Jewish Federation, pages 163 (Trope), 179, and 252; Mrs. Harry Hofheimer, pages 29, 36, 43, 165, 213; Mrs. Mildred Tarshish, archivist for Temple Israel, pages 59, 61, 65, 71, 84, 151 (Edelman), 178, 188, 212, 217, 222, and 284. In addition, these community members facilitated photo research: Barton R. Schachter, Irving Fried, Donna Zelcowitz, and Phyllis Greene. All other photographs are part of the Ohio Historical Society's collection.

INDEX